MW01273662

E-Government Success around the World:

Cases, Empirical Studies, and Practical Recommendations

J. Ramon Gil-Garcia
Centro de Investigación y Docencia Económicas, Mexico

A volume in the Advances in Electronic Government, Digital Divide, and Regional Development (AEGDDRD) Book Series

Managing Director: Lindsay Johnston
Editorial Director: Joel Gamon
Book Production Manager: Jennifer Yoder
Publishing Systems Analyst: Adrienne Freeland
Development Editor: Myla Merkel
Assistant Acquisitions Editor: Kayla Wolfe
Typesetter: Erin O'Dea
Cover Design: Jason Mull

Published in the United States of America by
Information Science Reference (an imprint of IGI Global)
701 E. Chocolate Avenue
Hershey PA 17033
Tel: 717-533-8845
Fax: 717-533-8661
E-mail: cust@igi-global.com
Web site: http://www.igi-global.com

Copyright © 2013 by IGI Global. All rights reserved. No part of this publication may be reproduced, stored or distributed in any form or by any means, electronic or mechanical, including photocopying, without written permission from the publisher. Product or company names used in this set are for identification purposes only. Inclusion of the names of the products or companies does not indicate a claim of ownership by IGI Global of the trademark or registered trademark.

Library of Congress Cataloging-in-Publication Data

E-government success around the world : cases, empirical studies, and practical recommendations / J. Ramon Gil-Garcia, editor.
pages cm
Includes bibliographical references and index.
Summary: "This book presents the latest findings in the area of e-government success, with the intent to improve the understanding of e-government success factors and cultural contexts in the field of government information technologies in various disciplines such as political science, public administration, information and communication sciences, and sociology"--Provided by publisher.
ISBN 978-1-4666-4173-0 (hardcover) -- ISBN 978-1-4666-4174-7 (ebook) -- ISBN 978-1-4666-4175-4 (print & perpetual access) 1. Internet in public administration--Case studies. I. Gil Garcia, Jose Ramon.
JF1525.A8E23858 2013
352.3'802854678--dc23

2013009737

This book is published in the IGI Global book series Advances in Electronic Government, Digital Divide, and Regional Development (AEGDDRD) Book Series (ISSN: 2326-9103; eISSN: 2326-9111)

British Cataloguing in Publication Data
A Cataloguing in Publication record for this book is available from the British Library.

All work contributed to this book is new, previously-unpublished material. The views expressed in this book are those of the authors, but not necessarily of the publisher.

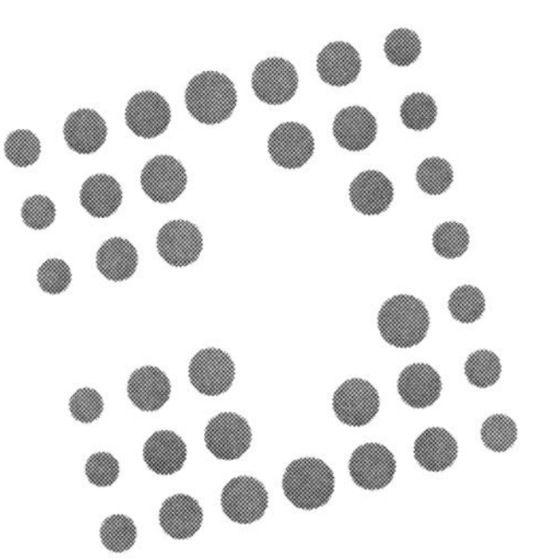

Advances in Electronic Government, Digital Divide, and Regional Development (AEGDDRD) Book Series

ISSN: 2326-9103
EISSN: 2326-9111

Mission

The successful use of digital technology to provide public services and foster economic development has become an objective for governments around the world. The development towards electronic government not only affects the efficiency and effectiveness of public services, but also has the potential to transform the nature of government interactions with citizens. Current research on the adoption of electronic/digital government in organizations around the world aims to emphasize the extensiveness of this growing field.

The **Advances in Electronic Government, Digital Divide & Regional Development (AEGDDRD) Book Series** presents all areas of research involved in these fields, including new applications and methodologies.

Coverage

- Digital Democracy
- E-Citizenship
- Electronic & Digital Government
- ICT Adoption in Developing Countries
- ICT within Government & Public Sectors
- Knowledge Divide
- Public Information Management
- Regional Planning
- Urban & Rural Development
- Web 2.0 in Government

IGI Global is currently accepting manuscripts for publication within this series. To submit a proposal for a volume in this series, please contact our Acquisition Editors at Acquisitions@igi-global.com or visit: http://www.igi-global.com/publish/.

The Advances in Electronic Government, Digital Divide, and Regional Development (AEGDDRD) Book Series (ISSN 2326-9103) is published by IGI Global, 701 E. Chocolate Avenue, Hershey, PA 17033-1240, USA, www.igi-global.com. This series is composed of titles available for purchase individually; each title is edited to be contextually exclusive from any other title within the series. For pricing and ordering information please visit http://www.igi-global.com/book-series/advances-electronic-government-digital-divide/37153. Postmaster: Send all address changes to above address. Copyright © 2013 IGI Global. All rights, including translation in other languages reserved by the publisher. No part of this series may be reproduced or used in any form or by any means – graphics, electronic, or mechanical, including photocopying, recording, taping, or information and retrieval systems – without written permission from the publisher, except for non commercial, educational use, including classroom teaching purposes. The views expressed in this series are those of the authors, but not necessarily of IGI Global.

Titles in this Series

For a list of additional titles in this series, please visit: www.igi-global.com

Developing E-Government Projects Frameworks and Methodologies
Zaigham Mahmood (University of Derby, UK)
Information Science Reference • copyright 2013 • 346pp • H/C (ISBN: 9781466642454) • US $180.00 (our price)

Citizen E-Participation in Urban Governance Crowdsourcing and Collaborative Creativity
Carlos Nunes Silva (University of Lisbon, Portugal)
Information Science Reference • copyright 2013 • 353pp • H/C (ISBN: 9781466641693) • US $180.00 (our price)

E-Government Success around the World Cases, Empirical Studies, and Practical Recommendations
J. Ramon Gil-Garcia (Centro de Investigación y Docencia Económicas, Mexico)
Information Science Reference • copyright 2013 • 358pp • H/C (ISBN: 9781466641730) • US $180.00 (our price)

E-Government Success Factors and Measure Theories, Concepts, and Methodologies
J. Ramon Gil-Garcia (Centro de Investigación y Docencia Económicas, Mexico)
Information Science Reference • copyright 2013 • 352pp • H/C (ISBN: 9781466640580) • US $180.00 (our price)

E-Government Implementation and Practice in Developing Countries
Zaigham Mahmood (University of Derby, UK)
Information Science Reference • copyright 2013 • 348pp • H/C (ISBN: 9781466640900) • US $180.00 (our price)

Global Sustainable Development and Renewable Energy Systems
Phillip Olla (Madonna University, USA)
Information Science Reference • copyright 2012 • 354pp • H/C (ISBN: 9781466616257) • US $180.00 (our price)

City Competitiveness and Improving Urban Subsystems Technologies and Applications
Melih Bulu (Istanbul Sehir University, Turkey)
Information Science Reference • copyright 2012 • 322pp • H/C (ISBN: 9781613501740) • US $180.00 (our price)

International Exploration of Technology Equity and the Digital Divide Critical, Historical and Social Perspectives
Patricia Randolph Leigh (Iowa State University, USA)
Information Science Reference • copyright 2011 • 254pp • H/C (ISBN: 9781615207930) • US $180.00 (our price)

Regional Innovation Systems and Sustainable Development Emerging Technologies
Patricia Ordóñez de Pablos (Universidad de Oviedo, Spain) W.B. Lee (Polytechnic University of Hong Kong) and Jingyuan Zhao (Harbin Institute of Technology, China)
Information Science Reference • copyright 2011 • 276pp • H/C (ISBN: 9781616928469) • US $180.00 (our price)

www.igi-global.com

701 E. Chocolate Ave., Hershey, PA 17033
Order online at www.igi-global.com or call 717-533-8845 x100
To place a standing order for titles released in this series, contact: cust@igi-global.com
Mon-Fri 8:00 am - 5:00 pm (est) or fax 24 hours a day 717-533-8661

Editorial Advisory Board

J. Ignacio Criado, *Universidad Autónoma de Madrid, Spain*
Sharon S. Dawes, *University at Albany, USA & State University of New York, USA*
Enrico Ferro, *Istituto Superiore Mario Boella, Italy*
Jane Fountain, *University of Massachusetts Amherst, USA*
Mila Gasco, *Instituto de Dirección y Gestion Publica, Spain*
Natalia Helbig, *University at Albany, USA & State University of New York, USA*
Marijn Janssen, *Delft University of Technology, The Netherlands*
Luis F. Luna Reyes, *Universidad de las America Puebla, Escuela de Negocios, Mexico*
Sehl Mellouli, *Université Laval, Canada*
M. Jae Moon, *Yonsei University, Korea*
Bjoern Niehaves, *Hertie School of Governance GmbH, Germany*
Theresa A. Pardo, *University at Albany, USA & State University of New York, USA*
Christopher G. Reddick, *The University of Texas at San Antonio, USA*
Hans Jochen Scholl, *University of Washington, USA*
Maria A. Wimmer, *University of Koblenz-Landau, Institute for IS Research, Germany*

List of Reviewers

Alexandru V. Roman, *Florida Atlantic University, USA*
Ann Macintosh, *The University of Leeds, UK*
Anshu Jain, *IBM, India*
Antonio Cordella, *London School of Economics and Political Science, UK*
Cesar Rentería, *Centro de Investigación y Docencia Economicas (CIDE), Mexico*
Cheong Kah Shin, *Institute of Policy Studies, Singapore*
Christophe Premat, *Centre Emile Durkheim, France*
David F. Andersen, *University of Albany, SUNY, USA*
Djoko Sigit Sayogo, *University at Albany, SUNY, USA*
Dušan Munđar, *University of Zagreb, Croatia*
Efpraxia Dalakiouridou, *University of Macedonia, Greece*
Efthimios Tambouris, *University of Macedonia, Greece*
Eleni Panopoulou, *University of Macedonia, Greece*
Fatma Bouaziz, *University of Sfax, Tunisia*
Francisco Rojas-Martín, *Universidad Autónoma de Madrid, Spain*
G.R. Gangadharan, *IBM, India*

Gabriel Puron Cid, *Centro de Investigación y Docencia Economicas (CIDE), Mexico*
Georgousopoulos Christos, *INTRASOFT International S.A., Greece*
Huong Ha, *University of Newcastle, Singapore*
Hyung Min Lee, *Sungshin Women's University, South Korea*
Ilona Biernacka-Ligieza, *University of Opole, Poland*
Jamil Chaabouni, *University of Sfax, Tunisia*
Jeremy Millard, *Danish Technological Institute, Denmark*
John Carlo Bertot, *University of Maryland, USA*
John McNutt, *University of Delaware, USA*
Judith Mariscal, *Centro de Investigación y Docencia Economicas (CIDE), Mexico*
Julie Freeman, *University of Canberra, Australia*
Kate Boland, *Rowan University, USA*
Kevin Y. Wang, *Butler University, USA*
Klaus Lenk, *University of Oldenburg, Germany*
Kokkinakos Panagiotis, *National Technical University of Athens, Greece*
Konstantinos Tarabanis, *University of Macedonia, Greece*
Lei Zheng, *Fudan University, China*
Manish Kumar, *MS Ramaiah Institute of Technology, India*
Marc K. Hébert, *University of South Florida, USA*
Mark Borman, *The University of Sydney, Australia*
Mary Griffiths, *University of Adelaide, Australia*
Mary Schmeida, *Kent State University, USA*
Melanie Bicking, *Bundesverwaltungsam, Germany*
Mohd Azul Mohamad Salleh, *The National University of Malaysia, Malaysia*
Natalie Greene Taylor, *University of Maryland, USA*
Neven Vrček, *University of Zagreb, Croatia*
Paul T. Jaeger, *University of Maryland, USA*
Petra Peharda, *University of Zagreb, Croatia*
Qianli Yuan, *Fudan University, China*
Ramfos Antonis, *INTRASOFT International S.A., Greece*
Ramona McNeal, *University of Northern Iowa, USA*
Ritesh Chugh, *Central Queensland University Melbourne, Australia*
Rodrigo Sandoval-Almazán, *Universidad Autónoma del Estado de México, Mexico*
Shuhua Monica Liu, *Fudan University, China*
Srimannarayana Grandhi, *Central Queensland University Melbourne, Australia*
Sukumar Ganapati, *Florida International University, USA*
Taewoo Nam, *University of Albany, SUNY, USA*
Taher Yehia, *Tilburg University, The Netherlands*
Teresa Harrison, *University at Albany, SUNY, USA*
Ursula Gorham, *University of Maryland, USA*
Walter Castelnovo, *University of Insubria, Italy*
Yejin Hong, *University of Minnesota, USA*
Ziouvelou Xenia, *Athens Information Technology, Greece*

Table of Contents

Detailed Table of Contents

What are e-government success factors for using public-private partnerships to enhance learning and capacity development? To examine this question, the authors developed a comparative case analysis of the development of the Business Reference Model (BRM), a national-level e-government initiative to promote shared information services, in the U.S. federal government and the Korean central government. The results indicate institutional arrangements deeply affect the outcomes of knowledge transfer. The study shows that private sector partners in both countries played various roles as "brokers" of information technology (IT) knowledge between government and the private sector by: raising awareness of the necessity of the BRM; providing best practices; developing pilot projects; and developing implementation strategies. However, the study finds that the two countries took entirely different approaches to working with non-governmental organizations in BRM development with implications for project success and lessons for e-government success. The study is meant to deepen understanding of the embeddedness of public-private partnerships in institutional contexts and the implications of such institutional arrangements for knowledge sharing on e-government success. The study examines knowledge transfer in the context of similarities and differences in partnership structures across two advanced industrialized countries with leading roles in e-governance.

For much of their history in the United States, public libraries made services for immigrants a key part of their mission by offering them many long-term services, such as developing job searching skills and learning English as a second language. Internet-enabled services, such as navigating the citizenship process, establishing residency, and delivering other key functions through e-government, are a recent addition. This chapter reports the findings of a multi-method study that provides insight into the development of e-government partnerships in various realms (including immigration), highlighting the extent to which these partnerships enhance the ability of libraries to overcome the various challenges that arise in connection with providing e-government services to different populations.

Historic inequalities in U.S. Internet usage associated with demographic factors have left the underserved, primarily the poor and rural, with fewer information and options to public health insurance online. Government initiatives to overcome the Internet infrastructure barriers are opening access to Medicare and Medicaid websites for these vulnerable groups. Using multivariate regression analysis and individual level data from the Internet and American Life Project, we explore demographic factors asking: "how successful have government efforts been to bring underserved Americans online to Medicare and Medicaid public health insurance information?" We find some historic inequalities are narrowing as individuals with lower income are more likely to search for insurance information online, with geographic differences not playing a major role. Our findings also suggest that age and gender are important factors in determining which individuals search for insurance information online.

Trust is a critical factor for e-government adoption that has been extensively studied from the citizen's perspective. This study explores the multiple dimensions of trust, but from the perspective of those inside of government responsible to implement and adopt it. As in previous studies of citizen trust, the nature of trust of those inside of government is also complex and multi-dimensional. A confirmatory factor analysis was conducted to uncover the multiple dimensions of trust inside of government. The data come from a questionnaire applied over government officials who participated in a contemporary case of e-government. The questionnaire includes inquiries about different dimensions of trust found in the literature. The main motivation of this study is to extend our understanding of multiple dimensions of trust as possible enablers and inhibitors during e-government adoption inside of government. Derived from the analysis, five practical advises are suggested as trust-building mechanisms during e-government adoption.

Implementation of ICT in policies targeted to alleviate poverty, specifically in conditional transfer programs (CTP), offers two opportunities. On one side, it contributes to improve delivery efficiency to beneficiaries, diminishing transfer costs with better control over beneficiaries' registry. On the other side, ICT incorporation on CTP helps to reduce costs of receiving funds and, from a broader scope, it contributes to social and digital inclusion of poor; this is especially relevant with the emergence of mobile banking. Almost every country in Latin America employs CTP programs as a social policy. Approximately 100 million of people are beneficiaries of CTP in Latin America, which accounts for about half of the people living in poverty in the region. Hence, improving administration of this kind of policy implies for the Latin-American countries, not only savings based on efficiency, but the opportunity of broaden the benefits. The main objective of this chapter is to analyze innovative ICT implementation on CTP in three countries in the region: Bolsa Familia (Brazil), Oportunidades (Mexico) and Familias en Acción (Colombia). These three countries are implementing pilot programs that include ITC. These experiences may important insights for future successful implementation of ICT for CTP in other countries.

E-government readiness is critical and fundamental to e-government success. This paper reviews and differentiates the definitions of e-readiness, e-government readiness and e-government maturity, and examines the literatures on current assessment practices to identify issues, controversies and problems. The chapter then proposes a bottom-up approach to develop a field-based E-government readiness assessment method and factors that could be usable and applicable for a specific local government with its own unique e-government priorities and goals, and then tests the approach in a city government in

systems. Based on in-depth interviews with officers and academics at four research universities, the study found that employees were most concerned with three issues that determined success or failure in this scenario: technological features of the systems; social and human factors; and organizational initiatives. Organizations such as universities and senior management may improve employees' satisfaction with Internet-based systems as e-government applications by implementing several recommendations arising from this study's analysis.

The adoption of e-government signifies a positive way to move ahead in the 21st century with enhanced quality, cost effective government services and a superior relationship between different stakeholders. E-government provides new opportunities to both government and its citizens. The wider acceptance of new communication technologies are helping governments and their agencies worldwide to serve citizens, businesses and other governments with greater efficiency. Yet some of the city councils in Australia are slow in optimally utilising the Internet and Information and Communication Technology (ICT) to serve their stakeholders and offer improved services. This chapter looks at e-government development statistics globally before narrowing down to Internet usage and e-government adoption in Australia. Opportunities and challenges of e-government adoption are presented. The chapter then focuses on the current state of e-government in Australian city councils and seeks to evaluate council websites to understand their usability characteristics. Seven Australian capital city council websites have been chosen and evaluated based on factors such as navigation, searchability, layout and visual clarity, information content, communication methods and transactional services. The research indicates that e-government in Australia is in its early stages and there is scope for further improvement and growth. The high incidence of web presence indicates that government entities, such as city councils are pursuing cyber strategies. Although the majority of government entities utilise websites to disseminate information to the public, optimal use of ICT in the public sector is ad hoc and in infancy albeit growing rapidly. This chapter provides a concise and holistic understanding of issues that can be encountered when exploiting the Internet and ICT for providing e-government services.

This chapter explores local e-government and the provision of online spaces for citizen participation. It highlights how different approaches to e-government development and implementation contribute to the likely success of participatory practices in informing decision-making and enhancing civic engagement with government. A comparative examination is drawn from the experiences of two local governments – the City of Casey in Australia and the Italian City of Bologna. The City of Casey's e-government prioritises service delivery, with opportunities for participation largely restricted. In contrast, the City of Bologna facilitates two-way online citizen discourse and deliberation, which is used to enhance public policy. This chapter highlights that institutional contexts, including insufficient policies and the understandings and motives of political actors, affect the development of participatory e-government and the use of citizen contributions in decision-making. It suggests that successfully facilitating civic participation and engagement through e-government requires strong policy frameworks guiding online content and applications, and a broader change in governmental culture so that representatives are receptive to civic views.

Despite considerable investments made worldwide in e-government initiatives in the past years, whether e-government succeeded in achieving the expected benefits in terms of increased efficiency, effectiveness and quality in the delivery of services is still under discussion. This chapter proposes an evaluation of the outcomes of the National Action Plan (NAP) for the diffusion of e-government at the local level in Italy. The evaluation considers whether the implementation of the projects funded under the action plan determined positive effects at the country level in terms of an increase in the value generated for different stakeholders. The discussion of data from both national and international secondary sources shows that during the period in which the benefits of the NAP should have become apparent no positive effects have emerged with evidence. The chapter argues that this depends on some of the principles the NAP has been based on that limited its capability of achieving the expected results.

The chapter updates a former study on digital communication at local level in France in 2006. The goal is to analyse the explanatory factors which influence the digital communication of municipalities on participatory democracy. Why are there municipalities which communicate more on these resources than others? It is important to compare the situation of these municipalities in 2006 and in 2012 because there was a power shift after the last municipal election in 2008. The focus will be on municipalities of more than 30.000 inhabitants as they have the possible resources to support a digital strategy. A quantitative method was used to select the variables which affect the communication on participatory tools. In other words, the article deals with the way politicians promote citizen engagement at local level through updated websites.

During the past few years, information and communication technologies and especially the internet are increasingly used in a vast range of human activities, including citizens' interaction with government. In this context, advanced technologies are also being used to more actively engage citizens in democratic processes, which is termed electronic participation (eParticipation). eParticipation has attracted considerable attention worldwide. In Europe, a large number of initiatives have been funded providing valuable lessons. The aim of this chapter is to map the current state of eParticipation in Europe and provide practical recommendations. More specifically, we first present the results of a review of policy documents in the European Union in order to understand how eParticipation fits into European policies. We then present an analytical framework to aid theoretical understanding of eParticipation, followed by the results of a European study on eParticipation initiatives. Based on all these, we propose a number of recommendations on eParticipation for policy makers, practitioners, evaluators and research funders.

Foreword

The book, which you are looking at, presents an impressive account and a great collection of recent electronic government case studies, research reports, and practice examples from around the world, which nicely confirm that electronic government has grown out of its infancy and into a pervasive phenomenon in governmental practice around the world. This tendency is echoed in a growing number of studies in academic research on the subject: In 2012 the number of peer-reviewed academic publications in the English language alone has grown by almost 20 percent. So, the field of practice and the academic study domain both appear to be blossoming. However, does that necessarily mean that electronic government is a success story? And what is electronic government about in the first place?

I have always held that the combination of the two terms "electronic" and "government" is a misnomer with no academic merit or precision, but rather an embarrassing label created by the trade press that breathes the air of the 1990s. So, why do we still care? The crux with the unscientific term of "electronic government" is that it has been enshrined into legal language and into law, for example, in the federal Electronic Government Act of 2002 in the US. With such sanctioning, the term has morphed from a misnomer into an official term of legal authority. Moreover, it became a widely accepted label for both certain government practices and for a diverse and multidisciplinary domain of academic research, which brings us back to the question, what is it all about?

Almost a decade ago, my colleagues at the Center for Technology in Government (Albany, NY) and I tried to find a concise although complete definition of what we believed that "electronic government" might stand for. Later the Digital Government Society adopted our definition in its 2005 mission statement, and I still consider it the best I know. In this definition, electronic government is about "the use of information and technology to support and improve public policies and government operations, engage citizens, and provide comprehensive and timely government services."

This definition has the handsome capacity of pointing at areas, for which metrics could conveniently be established to measure success, for example, "improve public policies and government operations." While the area of public policy may present a more difficult proposition for establishing measurable progress, it appears much more straightforward to measure the improvement of internal government operations by means of information technology. Just like in the private sector the elapsed time for completing a transaction can be monitored and measured. In fact, many improvements hidden from public view have occurred in internal government operations since the advent of electronic government. In one of my research projects on the introduction of new methods in government field operations incorporating mobile information and communication technologies (ICTs), we were able to measure field crew productivity increases of up to 400 percent. These gains, albeit invisible to the public, had a great impact on the effectiveness of internal government operations. If productivity increases had been the only measure, this e-government project would have been highly successful. And, of course, similar measures could be established and metered for effectiveness, efficiency, cost savings, time savings, or return on investment, which numerous government agencies actually do.

In a similar vein, the comprehensive and timely provision of government services to businesses and services can be measured, for example, by the number of transactions completed, the number of citizens served online, average start-to-finish times, or the average wait times, if any. Some municipalities, like the City of Bellevue in Washington State, conduct annual citizen satisfaction surveys, by which they measure citizens and businesses' degrees of satisfaction with the City's online services. In the case of Bellevue, service satisfaction rates consistently range in the upper 80 percentage points, which can be seen as a remarkable accomplishment and an electronic government success story given that online transaction now represent over 60 percent of total transactions. In both cases, internal government operations and external service provisions, straightforward metrics could be and were established and recorded to establish e-government success rates. From this perspective it would be easy to declare victory and electronic government a great success.

However, like with public policy improvements, engaging citizens is seemingly a more difficult task to measure. Although ICTs have demonstrated their utility in reaching out to and engaging citizens, for example, via social media, it is not clear what a meaningful measure would be and how to constitute success: the number of "likes" or "dislikes" to government Facebook postings, the number of retweets of government tweets, the number of "views" of Youtube videos, the number of datasets in ~data.gov, or, the number of citizen comments or petitions, for example? In fact, during extreme events such as the recent Christchurch, New Zealand earthquakes or superstorm Sandy that hit the US East Coast, government responders and social-media savvy citizens actively engaged in ad-hoc collaborations by exchanging and co-producing information services, which benefitted responders and affected communities alike. Such collaborations would not have been possible only a decade ago, and besides capable ICTs they required the mindsets and capacities for effective engagement and collaboration on both sides, which in many cases they did.

The true potential of electronic government with regard to more direct participation in governing and public decision-making on part of citizens is not yet completely understood in my view. So, the determination of meaningful measures of e-government success or failure with regard to citizen engagement needs some more consideration. This may lead to a wider debate on the role of the citizenry and its model of democratic self-governance in cybertimes. While in the 18th century the geographical and temporal distance of constituencies to the locus of public decision making necessitated a model of representation (which we proudly call the Western model of representative democracy), we can now bridge these geographies and time zones in nanoseconds. Yet, the representative democracy model also embraced the idea of electing experts capable in advancing and orchestrating public decision making. The wonderful new element that electronic government has brought us is the potential of transparency via open data and open government for scrutinizing public decisions and for assessing the decisions of elected representatives in an informed fashion.

More than half a decade ago my honorable colleague Don Norris and I engaged in a public debate about the transformational capacity of electronic government. While Don was of the opinion that technology would not make any difference in the business of government, and maybe not even add to productivity and efficiency, I was not that pessimistic. I agreed with Don (and still do) that ICTs per se would, of course, not make much of a difference; however, I argued that once a critical mass of incremental steps had been taken, one would see a major impact more clearly and more directly. I believe that now a critical mass has been reached with electronic government, at least in the United States, and maybe in some other leading countries such as South Korea, Denmark, Sweden, Singapore, and the United Kingdom to name a few. Back then I asked Don, what would happen today if government communications were reduced to the telegraph like during the Civil War, that is, to pre-telephone times. Yes, we would still enjoy the same representative model of democracy, as we will I believe in the times to come. But without the telephone, the business of government would have come to a standstill already in the first half of the 20th century. I claim that if we today removed at once all ICT-related (e-government)-dependent modes, the business of government would come to a crushing halt with no easy recovery. I call this the elimination test. Imagine also, for example, the trade of securities without computer networks. Did this ICT-based advance transform the nature of the business? Undoubtedly, yes. Did it change the principles of security trading? Not necessarily, and in most cases probably not. Economists refer to costs that you have to incur in order to stay in business as opportunity costs. At the very least, the cost of electronic government have to be seen as the opportunity cost for running the business of government in the 21st century. So, without hesitation, I believe, we can declare electronic government a success.

Bill Schrier, the former CTO of the City of Seattle, an acclaimed world leader in local electronic government, told me in a personal conversation a while ago that it was by means of smart ICT use in government, that is, electronic government, that the City was able to stem several budget crises, contain cost, and at the same time offer novel services, and to do more with less. Again, this is not a bad way of describing the practical success of electronic government.

However, electronic government is successful also in other ways, which need our attention as academics, albeit these are side effects or undesired outcomes. In my studies of interoperability and interoperation in government, I observed the connecting of data and information sources, which under the principle of division of powers and built-in checks and balances, should not be joined, at least not without the explicit consent of the various constituencies. So, the success of electronic government might have some consequences, which we did not intend or foresee. As academics we need to turn our attention also toward these effects, not only the bright side.

That notwithstanding, as the contributions in this book impressively demonstrate, the positive effects of electronic government are enormous, very tangible, visible, and irreversible. This volume is one of the few that take a worldwide approach and not just the perspective of a single region or country for that matter. The contributions encompass empirical as well as conceptual work; they also balance quantitative, qualitative, and mixed-method approaches. The regional breakdown of contribution with almost equal representation of Asia/Africa, the Americas, and Europe showcase that electronic government and its impacts are truly worldwide phenomena.

Besides its global coverage and balanced approach in representing the various scholarly approaches in the study domain of electronic government, the editor and publisher succeeded in attracting contributions from quite a number of highly prolific and influential scholars in the domain.

In this way, the book represents a milestone in current electronic government research. It greatly complements and updates previous textbooks, monographs, and edited books in the study domain. I am sure that readers interested in recent insights in electronic government research will as much appreciate the material presented in this volume as I do.

Hans Jochen Scholl
University of Washington, USA

Hans Jochen Scholl, *Ph.D. (Information Science) is an Associate Professor in the Information School at the University of Washington. His research expertise includes information management, electronic government, complex systems, systems dynamics, process engineering, and emergency and disaster management using novel information technologies. Jochen has published many quality research articles and seminal books on various issues of e-government, such as "smart government," the uses and challenges of mobile systems in City field operations, or cross-agency integration and interoperability. He has demonstrated effective and energetic leadership in e-government research across the globe. He chairs or co-chairs e-government conferences, such as the International Federation for Information Processing (IFIP) E-Government Conference, as well as the leading E-government Track and E-Government Symposium at the Hawaii International Conference on System Sciences (HICSS). Jochen serves as the Chair of the IFIP TC3 WG 8.5 (Information Systems and Public Administration) and is the past president of the Digital Government Society of North America (2010-2011).*

Preface

Countries around the world have increasingly used electronic government as a strategy for administrative reform. Government officials and public managers invest a great amount of time and financial resources in an attempt to achieve myriad potential benefits. Nevertheless, electronic government initiatives and projects very frequently fail to deliver the expected benefits due to numerous technical, organizational, institutional, and contextual factors. It is important to understand that government information technologies are not only, not even mainly, about using computers or developing information systems; they are truly about dealing with social issues and crafting public policies that could help to solve the most difficult problems in modern society. Therefore, the use of technology in government should not be considered an end in itself, it should be understood as the means to attain crucial public goals in several policy domains (J. R. Gil-Garcia, 2012).

E-GOVERNMENT SUCCESS: SOME FUNDAMENTAL CONCEPTS

Practitioners and scholars agree that government information technologies have not yet delivered their promise of a more democratic, transparent, and efficient public administration (Ashurst, Doherty, & Peppard, 2008; T. Chen, Zhang, & Lai, 2009; Cook, LaVigne, Pagano, Dawes, & Pardo, 2002; G. D. Garson, 2004; Joseph, 2010; Wu, Wu, & Wen, 2010). For instance, the United Nations estimates that approximately 60 percent of all e-government initiatives in developing countries fail (Stevenson, 2003). Given some characteristics of developing countries, such as the lack of adequate infrastructure, there is reason to believe that the success rate of e-government projects could be even lower than this estimate. Adding complexity, the continuous emergence of new technologies brings new opportunities to innovate, but also new and more complex challenges. In contrast, regardless of the disappointing results, governments continue to increase spending for projects involving information technologies, while research and studies of electronic government success also increase. It has become imperative to understand the relationships between e-government success and different institutional, organizational, and environmental variables.

The overall success of electronic government should be connected with the achievement of goals and objectives regarding the provision of services, the enhancement of managerial effectiveness (including efficiency), the advancement of participation and other democratic mechanisms, and the creation of an appropriate legal and regulatory framework (Gil-García & Luna-Reyes, 2007). Again, the achievement of goals should be understood in terms of activities, but also (and mostly) in relationship to processes, outputs, and outcomes. E-government success measures could be conceptualized as ways to measure and evaluate e-government's expected benefits, results, or characteristics. In contrast, e-government success factors could be thought of as different variables, conditions, or factors that affect e-government initiatives. Hence, it is necessary first to understand what e-government is and what its success measures and success factors are to truly comprehend e-government success in theory and practice.

In order to help researchers, managers and public officials know if an IT initiative has accomplished their stated goals and objectives it is fundamental to have success measures. Success measures should go well beyond the efficiency value proposition, resulting in a series of measures for outcomes, outputs, features, benefits and characteristics of government IT projects. Particularly in the public sector, success measures should go beyond efficiency and cost savings. They should include transparency, openness, policy effectiveness, service quality, and citizen participation, among others.

A basic way to understand the results of an IT initiative is by assessing its final outcomes. From this perspective, positive effects such as transparency, efficiency, effectiveness, or service quality appear to derive directly and almost automatically from the use of IT in organizations (Bandyopadhyay & Sattarzadeh, 2010; Baqir & Iyer, 2010; J. Ramon Gil-Garcia & Helbig, 2006; L. F. Luna-Reyes et al., 2010; Lux Wigand, 2010; Nour, AbdelRahman, & Fadlalla, 2008; Rahman, 2010; Sancak & Güleç, 2010; Smith, 2010). E-government initiatives are seen as promoting public participation, transparency, and accountability (Gulati, Yates, & Tawileh, 2010; Margetts, 2009; Rahman, 2010; Reddick, 2010) by creating new communication channels, a place to access and exchange information, and enabling the engagement of citizens in the policy process. Public participation, transparency, openness, and accountability require the development of easy to use and efficient communication channels between citizens and public officials (Noveck, 2009; Yao, Lee, Hong, & Weng, 2010; Zissis, Lekkas, & Papadopoulou, 2009) and should be studied and accounted for as relevant aspects of success in e-government initiatives (Alshawi & Alalwany, 2009; Bertot, Jaeger, & McClure, 2008; Chircu, 2008; Pina, Torres, & Royo, 2009, 2010).

One of the original premises for the use and reliance on IT in government was the persistent need to reduce the draw on resources for day-to-day government operations (Bandyopadhyay & Sattarzadeh, 2010; Baqir & Iyer, 2010; Chwelos, Ramirez, Kraemer, & Melville, 2010; Markaki, Charilas, & Askounis, 2010; OECD, 2003; Rahman, 2010). Although using efficiency and cost savings as a principal or even the sole goal of e-government initiatives presents several problems (OECD, 2003), they should still be considered fundamental e-government success measures. However, IT as a tool for policy effectiveness, where government IT initiatives help to attain critical results in areas such as security, education, and health, has gained visibility (L. F. Luna-Reyes et al., 2010; Markaki et al., 2010; OECD, 2003, p. 37; Olbrich, 2010; Sancak & Güleç, 2010). Another outcome would be the improvement of service quality. E-government projects can help to deliver enhanced services; nonetheless, it is imperative to acknowledge how this potential is diminished because of problems of access (G. D. Garson, 2004). Nevertheless, improving the quality of government services should continue to be an essential success measure for e-government initiatives around the world.

Academics and practitioners contend that the potential results from the use of IT are more than just final outcomes; they also include a significant alteration in organizational structures and the interactions among individuals inside those organizations (Åkesson & Edvardsson, 2008; Bandyopadhyay & Sattarzadeh, 2010; Baqir & Iyer, 2010; J. Ramon Gil-Garcia, Helbig, & Ferro, 2006; Meneklis & Douligeris, 2008; Rose & Grant, 2010; van Veenstra, Klievink, & Janssen, 2011). Hence, benefits extend beyond final outcomes to include a combination of transformations to the current organizational and social structures, which can be sorted into three categories: technical, political, and organizational (1996). Therefore we define success measures as political, organizational and technical benefits, such as data processing, information management, enriched decision making, decentralization, high quality services, integrated services, empowerment, increased revenues, and better productivity, among other (Bandyopadhyay & Sattarzadeh, 2010; Baqir & Iyer, 2010; Choudhury & Kumar, 2009; Cordella & Iannacci, 2010; J.R. Gil-Garcia, Chengalur-Smith, & Duchessi, 2003; Kim, Kim, & Lee, 2009; Peled, 2001; Rowley, 2011; Schuppan, 2009). Technical benefits are enhancing technical standards, helping organizations to share technical resources (Bozeman & Bretschneider, 1986; S. S. Dawes, 1996, 2008; Millerand & Baker, 2010), and attaining usability, reliability and system accessibility (Danziger & Kraemer, 1985; Gant, 2004; Jose Ramon Gil-Garcia, Chun, & Janssen, 2009; Marijn Janssen, 2008; Kling, 1993; T. A. Pardo, Gil-Garcia, & Burke, 2008). In addition, the use of IT may decrease processing time, storage, and duplicate data collection (Ambite et al., 2002; Barrett & Greene, 2000; Caffrey, 1998; S. S. Dawes, 2008; Golubchik, 2002; Maumbe, Owei, & Alexander, 2008). Since technical benefits are the basis for other more substantive results, they should be considered success measures.

Political benefits entail areas of broader public interest, such as comprehensive public information, integrated service delivery and planning, greater public accountability and better understanding for government-wide policy goals (Andersen & Dawes, 1991; Bandyopadhyay & Sattarzadeh, 2010; Bissessar, 2010; Chircu, 2008; J. Ramon Gil-Garcia & Helbig, 2006; Langford & Roy, 2009; Macintosh, Malina, & Farrell, 2002; Panagopoulos, 2004; Pina et al., 2010; Roy, 2009; Ubaldi & Roy, 2010). Finally, organizational benefits refer to the augmentation of inter-organizational capabilities and a solution for organization-wide problems (Ashurst et al., 2008; Baqir & Iyer, 2010; S. S. Dawes & Pardo, 2002; Gant, 2004; Klievink & Janssen, 2009; J.-N. Lee, 2001; Ubaldi & Roy, 2010). Some well-known examples of organizational benefits are cost reductions, improving the decision making process, better coordination, customer satisfaction, and broadened professional networks (Andersen & Dawes, 1991; Bandyopadhyay & Sattarzadeh, 2010; Jose Ramon Gil-Garcia et al., 2009; Gorla, Somers, & Wong, 2010; Kuan & Chau, 2001; Petter, DeLone, & McLean, 2008; Roldán & Leal, 2003; Walton, 1989). In order to obtain certain positive outcomes, most organizations require transformations of their internal rules, channels of communications, hierarchical structures, and business processes.

Benefits are not necessarily or frequently an immediate and direct consequence of information and communication technologies (ICTs). Therefore, understanding the potential results of e-government initiatives is only part of the research endeavor. Identifying e-government success measures helps to assess if the initiative has accomplished its initial objectives and goals, but it says very little about the reasons behind its success or how to improve its performance (J. R. Gil-Garcia, 2012). For this type of analysis, we need to understand e-government success factors; aspects and conditions that have an impact on the selection, design, implementation, use, and overall success of IT in the context of e-government initiatives.

A strong stream of literature concentrates on studying the relationships among the selection, design and implementation of ICTs and several factors embedded in the organization, institution, and environment where they are deployed (Azad & Faraj, 2008; Bandyopadhyay & Sattarzadeh, 2010; Bozeman & Bretschneider, 1986; Caffrey, 1998; Cresswell & Pardo, 2001; S. S. Dawes & Pardo, 2002; S. S. Dawes, Pardo, & Cresswell, 2004; Detlor, Hupfer, & Ruhi, 2010; Eynon & Margetts, 2007; D. G. Garson, 2003-b; Gulati et al., 2010; Herrera & Gil-Garcia, 2010; Khan, Moon, Park, Swar, & Rho, 2010; Landsbergen & Wolken, 2001; Laudon, 1985; Theresa A. Pardo & Scholl, 2002; Rocheleau, 1999; Smith, 2010; Southon, Sauer, & Dampney, 1999). A debate among scholars continues, as there is still a lack of consensus about which factors are crucial in explaining IT success. Nevertheless, serious theoretical work has identified five principal categories(Bandyopadhyay & Sattarzadeh, 2010{Gulati, 2010 #1166; Council, 2008; J. Ramon Gil-Garcia & Pardo, 2005; Gulati et al., 2010; M. L. Markus, 2005; M. Lynne Markus & Silver, 2008; Remus & Wiener, 2010; Rorissa, Potnis, & Demissie, 2010; Rosacker & Olson,

2008a, 2008b; Thomas & Fernández, 2008). First, there are technology-related factors, which connect to the unique characteristics of the technology used. Some challenges are the newness and complexity of technology, technical skills, staff skills, and the issue of incompatibility (Baqir & Iyer, 2010; Barki, Rivard, & Talbot, 1993; Caffrey, 1998; Chang, Gable, Smythe, & Timbrell, 2001; Chengalur-Smith & Duchessi, 1999; Eynon & Margetts, 2007; Ghapanchi, Albadvi, & Zarei, 2008; J. Ramon Gil-Garcia & Helbig, 2006; Joseph, 2010; Theresa A. Pardo, Nam, & Burke, forthcoming; Rahman, 2010; Sancak & Güleç, 2010; Tsai, Choi, & Perry, 2009; Ubaldi & Roy, 2010). Also, a project to design a totally new system differs greatly from the improvement of an existing system. These "legacy" systems carry additional challenges. More recently, government adoption of Web 2.0 technologies has raised new issues in technical and semantic interoperability with the existing legacy systems (Charalabidis, Lampathaki, & Askounis, 2010; Drogkaris, Gritzalis, & Lambrinoudakis, 2010; Ojo, Estevez, & Janowski, 2010). All of these represent restrictions that can possibly impact the results of IT projects.

Secondly, data and information factors, such as data definitions, compatibility, and structures, refer to the quality and management of data. Since one principal purpose of an IT initiative is to integrate, share, improve, or disseminate information, the quality of such information is essential and surprisingly it is often taken for granted (Brown, 2000; Gonzalez, Adenso-Diaz, & Gemoets, 2010; Klischewski & Scholl, 2008). Inconsistencies, inaccuracies, lack of timeliness, and incompleteness of data can all cause problems in information quality (Chutimaskul, Funilkul, & Chongsuphajaisiddhi, 2008; S. Dawes & Pardo, 2008; S. S. Dawes & Helbig, 2010; Madnick, Wang, Lee, & Zhu, 2009; Redman, 1998). Another issue regarding data and information factors is collaboration and information sharing. In this process, complications arise given incompatible database designs, mismatched data structures, incongruous data, and information distribution (Ambite et al., 2002; Barrett & Greene, 2000; Eynon & Margetts, 2007; M. Janssen, Kuk, & Wagenaar, 2008; Umble, Haft, & Umble, 2003). All these factors affect the overall results of information technology initiatives (J. Ramon Gil-Garcia & Helbig, 2006).

Thirdly, there are contextual factors, with examples of political, economic, demographic, and social variables. Some environmental factors identified in the literature are political, demographic, technological, legal, economic, cultural, and ecological (Clegg & Dunkerley, 1980; Hall, 2002; Hatch, 1997). Other authors argue that external pressures or contextual variables like politics, competition, and personnel markets may affect the results of IT initiatives (Bandyopadhyay & Sattarzadeh, 2010; Bellamy, 2000; Bozeman & Bretschneider, 1986; Chengalur-Smith & Duchessi, 1999; Detlor et al., 2010; Laudon, 1986; C.-p. Lee, Chang, & Berry, 2011; K.-S. Lee, 2009; Nour et al., 2008; Pina et al., 2009). The context of organizations is without a doubt a relevant element for the success of IT projects (Detlor et al., 2010; Hassan, Shehab, & Peppard, 2011; Nour et al., 2008; Sancak & Güleç, 2010).

Fourthly, there are the institutional factors, which apply to any set of rules, formal and informal, regulations, legislation, and more. Institutional arrangements are central elements in understanding how information technologies are selected, designed, implemented, and used in public organizations (Cordella & Iannacci, 2010; J.E. Fountain, 2008; Heeks & Bailur, 2007; L. Luna-Reyes, Gil-García, & Estrada-Marroquín, 2008; Luis Felipe Luna-Reyes & Gil-Garcia, 2011). Political factors seem to be unique to the environment of public organizations, and apply to e-government initiatives, since they refer to political realities and challenges present in all government systems (Ahn & Bretschneider, 2011; Baqir & Iyer, 2010; Eynon & Margetts, 2007; J. W. Lee, Rainey, & Chun, 2009; Rorissa et al., 2010; Sancak & Güleç, 2010). Some examples of these institutional factors are (1996, p. 381): the power of agency discretion; external pressures over the decision-making process, such as interest groups, lobbyists, legislative committees, civil servants, and local governments; privacy and security concerns(Baqir & Iyer, 2010; Carter

& McBride, 2010; Duncan & Roehrig, 2003; Joshi, Ghafoor, Aref, & Spafford, 2002; Luis F. Luna-Reyes & Gil-Garcia, 2003; Milner, 2000; Rorissa et al., 2010; Rose & Grant, 2010; Sancak & Güleç, 2010; Zhao, Zhao, & Zhao, 2010); and legislation and regulations (Bandyopadhyay & Sattarzadeh, 2010; S. S. Dawes & Nelson, 1995; Fletcher, 2004; J. Ramon Gil-Garcia & Helbig, 2006; Gulati et al., 2010; Landsbergen & Wolken, 2001; Rose & Grant, 2010; Ubaldi & Roy, 2010), like the budget cycle (Ahn, 2011; Bandyopadhyay & Sattarzadeh, 2010; Y.-C. Chen & Thurmaier, 2008; S. S. Dawes & Nelson, 1995; S. S. Dawes & Pardo, 2002; Jane E. Fountain, 2001; L. F. Luna-Reyes et al., 2010; Rorissa et al., 2010; Wyld, 2009), the existence of a federal system, intergovernmental relationships(Criado, 2009; Eynon & Margetts, 2007; J. Ramon Gil-Garcia & Helbig, 2006; Jaeger, 2002), complexity from checks and balances (Bellamy, 2000; dos Santos & Reinhard, forthcoming; Gottschalk, 2009; Gulati et al., 2010; Harris, 2000; Rocheleau, 2003; Ubaldi & Roy, 2010), and more.

Finally, there are organizational factors and the relationship between aspects such as formalization, size, communication channels, centralization, and IT success. Organizational factors refer to characteristics, processes, structures, and relationships that take place within an organizational setting, including the project and the organizational and individual levels. Two of the most important factors in IT projects are the diversity of the users involved and the size of the initiative itself (Barki et al., 1993; Davis, 1982; S. S. Dawes & Pardo, 2002; J. Ramon Gil-Garcia & Helbig, 2006; McFarlan, 1981). Another aspect to consider is personal interests that drive behaviors and conducts that can translate in resistance to change, conflict, and turf issues (Bandyopadhyay & Sattarzadeh, 2010; Barki et al., 1993; Barrett & Greene, 2000; Bellamy, 2000; Best, 1997; Bwalya & Healy, 2010; Y.-C. Chen, 2010; Ebbers & van Dijk, 2007; Eynon & Margetts, 2007; Gaudino & Moro, 2010; J. Ramon Gil-Garcia & Helbig, 2006; Hossain, Moon, Kim, & Choe, forthcoming; Jiang & Klein, 2000; Joseph, 2010; Leung & Adams, 2009; Nasim & Sushil, 2010; Rocheleau, 2003). Other examples are understanding strategic goals, a project management approach, the need for alignment between the IT project and organizational goals (S. S. Dawes & Nelson, 1995; Marijn Janssen, forthcoming; Meijer & Thaens, 2010; Ubaldi & Roy, 2010; Valdés et al., 2011), the existence of multiple, and sometimes conflicting, goals, the timeframe of the project, the magnitude of change in processes, and the absence of implementation guidelines, (Angelopoulos, Kitsios, Kofakis, & Papadopoulos, 2010; Baqir & Iyer, 2010; Chang et al., 2001; Davenport, 1993; J. Ramon Gil-Garcia & Helbig, 2006; Hossain et al., forthcoming; Joseph, 2010; Rorissa et al., 2010; Seneviratne, 1999; Umble et al., 2003; Yang & Maxwell, 2011). Hence, the politics of the organization can become a difficult hurdle to jump over.

E-government means several things to different social actors and in different contexts (Cordella & Iannacci, 2010; J. Ramon Gil-Garcia & Luna-Reyes, 2003, 2006; Hardy & Williams, 2008; Luis Felipe Luna-Reyes & Gil-Garcia, 2011; Schelin, 2003; Scholl, Mai, & Fidel, 2006), from back office systems and intranets to services provided online, from personal computers in any public office to sophisticated programs and inter-organizational software, or from Web 2.0 and social media to information management and policy. Furthermore, there is no practical nor academic agreement about what IT success and e-government success mean and how to measure them (Alshawi & Alalwany, 2009; Carbo & Williams, 2004; DeLone & Mclean, 1992, 2003; Fasanghari & Habibipour, 2009; J. Ramon Gil-Garcia & Pardo, 2005; Gonzalez et al., 2010; Jun & Weare, forthcoming; Morgeson III & Mithas, 2009). One way to think about e-government success is in terms of certain success measures. New models should propose relationships among factors and, therefore, direct and indirect effects between success factors and the characteristics of an e-government initiative (in terms of success measures). This will allow for disentangling the different causal paths and assessing the actual effects of individual success factors. They could be included from the outset in the goals and objectives that e-government initiatives attempt to accomplish. Following this logic, an e-government initiative is successful to the extent it achieves its goals and objectives, defined as specific success measures, given certain organizational, institutional, and environmental conditions.

AUDIENCE AND CONTENT OF THE BOOK

The target audience of this book is composed of professionals, public managers, scholars, and researchers working in the field of government information technologies. The book provides insights and support to government executives concerned with the development, management, and evaluation of complex e-government initiatives. The chapters provide a wide spectrum of cases, geographic regions, technologies and methodologies that can translate into concrete and practical recommendations.

The first section, the Americas, entails subject matters that are crucial for the region: outlying regions and inequality, service enhancement through public-private partnerships, IT success regarding services for migrants, Medicare and Medicaid, alleviation of poverty programs, and measures of trust in government. In the opening chapter, "Government Services in Outlying Regions," Mellouli and colleagues argue how e-government offers the potential to provide easy and flexible access to a vast array of government services, particularly in outlying regions where traditional service centers are scarce and costly. The chapter identifies factors that influence the use of e-government services in rural regions. They conduct the study from two points of view: the citizens and government managers. Their results show that citizen attitudes significantly affect intention to use e-government services.

Also concentrating on success factors, Eom and Fountain developed a comparative case analysis of the development of the Business Reference Model (BRM), a national-level e-government initiative to promote shared information services in the U.S. federal government and the Korean central government. The chapter "Enhancing Information Services through Public-Private Partnerships: Information Technology Knowledge Transfer Underlying Structures to Develop Shared Services in the US and Korea" examines the success factors for using public-private partnerships to enhance learning and capacity development. The results indicate institutional arrangements deeply affect the outcomes of knowledge transfer. The study examines similarities and differences in partnership structures for knowledge transfer across two advanced industrialized countries with leading roles in e-governance.

Gorham and colleagues contributed the chapter "E-Government Success in Public Libraries: Library and Government Agency Partnerships Delivering Services to New Immigrants." They explain how public libraries made services for immigrants a key part of their mission by offering them many long-term services, such as developing job search skills and learning English as a second language. Internet-enabled services, such as navigating the citizenship process or establishing residency, are a recent addition. This chapter reports the findings of a multi-method study that provides insight into the development of e-government partnerships in various realms (including immigration), highlighting the extent to which these partnerships enhance the ability of libraries to overcome the challenges that arise when providing e-government services to different populations.

Also focusing in the US, Schmeida and McNeal describe how historic inequalities in Internet use associated with demographic factors have left the underserved, primarily the poor and rural, with less information and fewer options for online access to public health insurance. Government initiatives to overcome the Internet infrastructure barriers are opening access to Medicare and Medicaid websites for these vulnerable groups. In "Bridging the Inequality Gap to Accessing Medicare and Medicaid Information Online: An Empirical Analysis of E-government Success 2002 through 2010," the authors use multivariate regression analysis and individual-level data from the Internet and American Life Project to explore demographic factors. Their findings suggest that historic inequalities are narrowing as individuals with lower income are more likely to search for insurance information online.

Puron Cid explores multiple dimensions of trust from the perspective of government managers who collaboratively adopt and implement IT. The chapter "Trust Measures for Implementers of e-Government Adoption: A Confirmatory Factor Analysis" uncovers the multiple dimensions of trust inside government. The data come from a questionnaire sent to government officials who participated in a contemporary e-government initiative; questions covered different dimensions of trust, drawn from past research. This study extends our understanding of multiple dimensions of trust as possible enablers and inhibitors during e-government adoption. Derived from the analysis are five practical suggestions for trust-building mechanisms in e-government.

Closing this section, Mariscal and Rentería explain the two opportunities available when ICTs are incorporated into policies targeted to alleviate poverty, specifically in conditional transfer programs (CTP). On one side, ICTs contribute to improve the efficiency of benefits delivery, diminishing transfer costs with better control over the beneficiaries' registry. On the other side, ICT incorporation on CTP helps to reduce the costs of receiving funds and, from a broader scope, it contributes to social and digital inclusion of poor; this aspect is especially relevant with the emergence of mobile banking. The chapter then analyzes innovative ICT implementation on CTP in three Latin American countries: Bolsa Familia (Brazil), Oportunidades (Mexico), and Familias en Acción (Colombia). The chapter "Implementation of Information and Communication Technologies for Financial Inclusion in Programs to Alleviate Poverty in Brazil, Colombia and Mexico" includes important insights for future successful implementation of ICT for CTP in other countries.

The following section entails six experiences from Asia and Australia. In "Developing E-government Readiness Factors: A Bottom-up Approach," Zheng argues that e-government readiness is critical and fundamental to e-government success. The chapter first reviews and differentiates the definitions of e-readiness, e-government readiness, and e-government maturity; He then examines the literature on current assessment practices to identify issues, controversies and problems. The chapter proposes a bottom-up approach to develop a field-based e-government readiness assessment method, with factors that could be usable and applicable for a specific local government with its own unique e-government priorities and goals. Next, Zheng tests the approach in a city government in China, which received positive feedbacks. In contrast, Liu's and Yuan's study, "Urban Community Grids Management in Metropolitan China: A Case Study on Factors Contributing to Mobile Governance Success," explores the utility and feasibility of Urban Community Grids Management (UCGM) featuring mobile interaction. It is believed to provide not only innovative means for local public operations, but new channels for government-citizen communication and public service delivery. Based on empirical data collected from Beijing, Shanghai, and Wuhan, the authors evaluate and compare the impact of UCGM on local government operations.

Ha describes in "E-Government in Singapore-Critical Success Factors" how e-government developed more than 10 years ago, concurrently with the re-invention of public administration. The chapter discusses the current e-government framework in Singapore, which is internationally recognized for its success, and examines factors affecting that success. Ha makes policy recommendations to improve the efficiency and effectiveness of e-government. Also identifying success factors, Mohamad Salleh explores employees' experiences in Malaysian research universities, and particularly strives to understand successes and problems in the implementation of Internet-based systems. His chapter, "Users' Experiences of Internet-based Systems in Malaysian Research Universities: Success Factors and Barriers as Starting Points to Best Practices in a Developing Country," is based on in-depth interviews with officers and academics at four research universities. The study found that employees were most concerned with three issues that determined success or failure of these systems: technological features; social and human factors; and organizational initiatives.

The next two chapters focus on e-government at the local level in Australia. In "E-Government in Australia: A Usability Study of Australian City Council Websites," Chugh and Grandhi describe how some of the city councils in Australia are slow in optimally utilizing the Internet and ICTs to serve their stakeholders and offer improved services. This chapter looks at e-government development statistics globally before narrowing down to Internet usage and e-government adoption in Australia. Seven Australian capital city council websites have been chosen and evaluated based on factors such as navigation, searchability, layout and visual clarity, information content, communication methods, and transactional services. The research indicates that e-government in Australia is in its early stages and there is scope for further improvement and growth. Freeman also explores local e-government and the provision of online spaces for citizen participation. "Local E-Government and Citizen Participation: Case Studies from Australia and Italy" provides a comparative analysis of the experiences in two local governments – the City of Casey in Australia and the Italian City of Bologna. This chapter highlights that institutional contexts, including insufficient policies and the understandings and motives of political actors, affect the development of participatory e-government and the use of citizen contributions in decision-making.

The last section focuses on Europe, encompassing themes like infrastructure, social media, evaluation, citizen involvement, and e-participation. First, Janssen and Borman describe how effective digital government infrastructures are necessary to support the policies and strategies of governments. ICT infrastructures provide generic functionalities that a large numbers of users share. Typically many stakeholders are involved in the implementation of the infrastructure and the infrastructure is shaped by the interactions among stakeholders. The management of the development of such infrastructures is complicated. The research from the chapter "Critical Success Factors for E-Government Infrastructure Implementation" is conducted by identifying critical success factors for Surfnet, a public organization providing a digital infrastructure for researchers, teachers and students.

The chapter "Social Media and Public Administration in Spain: A Comparative Analysis of the Regional Level of Government" investigates how Spanish regional administrations employ digital social media, including their presence, the factors that determine that presence, and self-perceptions of those responsible for its management. The study is based on a questionnaire sent to those responsible for the management of digital social media in the Spanish regional administrations. Criado and Rojas-Martin's results show that Web 2.0 tools are more likely to spur potential changes in the relations between the public administrations and citizens, rather than to innovate the functioning of public sector organizations.

Castelnovo proposes an evaluation of the outcomes of Italy's National Action Plan (NAP) for the diffusion of e-government at the local level in the chapter "A Country-Level Evaluation of the Impact of E-government: The Case of Italy." The evaluation considers whether the funded projects yielded positive effects at the country level by generating value for different stakeholders. The discussion of data from both national and international secondary sources shows that during the period in which the benefits of the NAP should have become apparent no positive effects have emerged with evidence. For the country of France, Premat updates a former study on digital communication at the local level in 2006. The goal of the chapter, "How do French Municipalities Communicate on Citizen Involvement?

The Success of Participatory Democracy in France," is to analyze the explanatory factors that influence the digital communication of municipalities for participatory democracy. Why are there municipalities that communicate more about these resources than others? The chapter focuses on the way politicians promote citizen engagement at the local level through updated websites.

The chapter "eParticipation in Europe: Current State and Practical Recommendations" closes this section and the book. Tambouris and colleagues describe how the European Union has funded a large number of initiatives in Europe, which provide valuable lessons regarding citizen involvement. The aim of this chapter is to map the current state of eParticipation in Europe and provide practical recommendations. The authors first present the results of a review of policy documents in the European Union in order to understand how eParticipation fits into European policies. They then present an analytical framework to aid theoretical understanding of eParticipation, followed by the results of a European study on eParticipation initiatives. Finally, the authors propose a number of recommendations on eParticipation for policy makers, practitioners, evaluators, and research funders.

FINAL COMMENTS

Researchers have gained a great deal of knowledge about the selection, design, implementation, and use of information technologies in government. However, obtaining the potential benefits of IT-related initiatives is still a difficult challenge that involves high risk (Abdel-Hamid & Madnick, 1990; Ashurst et al., 2008; Baqir & Iyer, 2010; Bissessar, 2010; T. Chen et al., 2009; Joseph, 2010; Wu et al., 2010). For example, a 1998 study found that 30 percent of the IT projects surveyed were canceled and 45 percent were late or over-budget (Cunningham, 1999). Many other studies focus on the difficulties and problems of IT projects, such as cost overruns, project cancellations, limited features, and unintended consequences (Ashurst et al., 2008; Berlin, Raz, Glezer, & Zviran, 2009; Deephouse, Mukhopadhyay, Goldenson, & Kellner, 1995; Gulati et al., 2010; Keil, Cule, Lyytinen, & Schmidt, 1998; Norris, 1999; Rahman, 2010; Rosacker & Olson, 2008b; Weinstein & Jaques, 2010). Most of this literature comes from research in the private sector, but government IT initiatives are similarly complex; therefore, public managers need practical tools to make better IT decisions (Bandyopadhyay & Sattarzadeh, 2010; Carr, 2010; S. S. Dawes, Pardo, & DiCaterino, 1999; S. S. Dawes & Préfontaine, 2003; J. Ramon Gil-Garcia & Pardo, 2005; Hoque, Walsh, Mirakaj, & Bruckner, 2011). These tools should be developed from well-grounded research and consequentially from good theoretical understanding. This book provides examples of the latest empirical research findings in the area of e-government success. Cases from different parts of the world show that not only is e-government success a worldwide concern, but also that it is a reality. Therefore, this book is a compilation of selected high quality chapters covering cases, empirical studies, and practical recommendations on e-government success around the world. It is written for academics and professionals who want to improve their understanding of e-government success factors and success measures, considering very different political, economic, and cultural contexts.

J. Ramon Gil-Garcia
Centro de Investigación y Docencia Económicas, Mexico

REFERENCES

Abdel-Hamid, T. K., & Madnick, S. E. (1990). The Elusive Silver Lining: How we fail to Learn from Software Development Failures. *Sloan Management Review*, 39–48.

Ahn, M. J. (2011). Adoption of E-Communication Applications in U.S. Municipalities: The Role of Political Environment, Bureaucratic Structure, and the Nature of Applications. *American Review of Public Administration*. doi:10.1177/0275074010377654.

Ahn, M. J., & Bretschneider, S. (2011). Politics of e-government: E-government and the political control of bureaucracy. *Public Administration Review*, *71*(3), 414–424. doi:10.1111/j.1540-6210.2011.02225.x.

Åkesson, M., & Edvardsson, B. (2008). Effects of e-government on service design as perceived by employees. *Managing Service Quality*, *18*(5), 457–478. doi:10.1108/09604520810898839.

Alshawi, S., & Alalwany, H. (2009). E-government evaluation: Citizen's perspective in developing countries. *Information Technology for Development*, *15*(3), 193–208. doi:10.1002/itdj.20125.

Ambite, J. L., Arens, Y., Bourne, W., Feiner, S., Gravano, L., Hatzivassiloglou, V., & Zaman, K. (2002). Data Integration and Access. In McIver, W. J., & Elmagarmid, A. K. (Eds.), *Advances in Digital Government. Technology, Human Factors, and Policy* (pp. 85–106). Norwell, MA: Kluwer Academic Publishers. doi:10.1007/0-306-47374-7_5.

Andersen, D. F., & Dawes, S. S. (1991). *Government Information Management. A primer and Casebook*. Englewood Cliffs, NJ: Prentice Hall.

Angelopoulos, S., Kitsios, F., Kofakis, P., & Papadopoulos, T. (2010). Emerging barriers in e-government implementation. In M. A. Wimmer, J.-L. Chappelet, M. Janssen & H. J. Scholl (Eds.), *Electronic Government (Proceedings of the 9th IFIP WG 8.5 International Conference, EGOV 2010)*. Berlin: Springer.

Ashurst, C., Doherty, N. F., & Peppard, J. (2008). Improving the impact of IT development projects: The benefits realization capability model. *European Journal of Information Systems*, *17*, 352–370. doi:10.1057/ejis.2008.33.

Azad, B., & Faraj, S. (2008). Making e-Government systems workable: Exploring the evolution of frames. *The Journal of Strategic Information Systems*, *17*(2), 75–98. doi:10.1016/j.jsis.2007.12.001.

Bandyopadhyay, A., & Sattarzadeh, S. D. (2010). A Challenging E-Journey Along the Silk Road: Lessons learnes from e-governments in China and India. In Reddick, C. G. (Ed.), *Comparative E-Government* (pp. 116–138). New York: Springer. doi:10.1007/978-1-4419-6536-3_6.

Baqir, M. N., & Iyer, L. (2010). E-government maturity over 10 Years: A comparative analysis of e-government maturity in select countries around the world. In Reddick, C. G. (Ed.), *Comparative E-Government* (pp. 3–22). New York: Springer. doi:10.1007/978-1-4419-6536-3_1.

Barki, H., Rivard, S., & Talbot, J. (1993). Toward an assessment of software development risk. *Journal of Management Information Systems*, *10*, 203–223.

Barrett, K., & Greene, R. (2000). *Powering Up: How Public Managers Can Take Control of Information Technology*. Washington, DC: Congressional Quarterly Press.

Bellamy, C. (2000). The Politics of Public Information Systems. In Garson, G. D. (Ed.), *Handbook of Public Information Systems* (pp. 85–98). New York: Marcel Dekker.

Berlin, S., Raz, T., Glezer, C., & Zviran, M. (2009). Comparison of estimation methods of cost and duration in IT projects. *Information and Software Technology*, *51*(4), 738–748. doi:10.1016/j.infsof.2008.09.007.

Bertot, J. C., Jaeger, P. T., & McClure, C. R. (2008). *Citizen-centered e-government services: Benefits, costs, and research needs.* Paper presented at the International Conference on Digital Government Research (dg.o).

Best, J. D. (1997). *The Ditigal Organization*. New York: John Wiley and Sons.

Bissessar, A. M. (2010). The challenge of E-governance in a Small, Developing Society: The case of Trinidad and Tobago. In Reddick, C. G. (Ed.), *Comparative E-Government* (pp. 313–329). New York: Springer. doi:10.1007/978-1-4419-6536-3_16.

Bozeman, B., & Bretschneider, S. (1986). Public Management Information Systems: Theory and Prescriptions. *Public Administration Review*, *46*(Special Issue), 475–487. doi:10.2307/975569.

Brown, M. M. (2000). Mitigating the Risk of Information Technology Initiatives: Best Practices and Points of Failure for the Public Sector. In Garson, G. D. (Ed.), *Handbook of Public Information Systems* (pp. 153–163). New York: Marcel Dekker.

Bwalya, K. J., & Healy, M. (2010). Harnessing e-government adoption in the SADC region: A conceptual underpinning. *Electronic. Journal of E-Government*, *8*(1), 23–32.

Caffrey, L. (1998). *Information Sharing Between & Within Governments*. London: Commonwealth Secretariat.

Carbo, T., & Williams, J. G. (2004). Models and Metrics for Evaluating Local Electronic Government Systems and Services. *Electronic. Journal of E-Government*, *2*(2), 95–104.

Carr, D. (2010). Time and technology: Addressing changing demands. In Shea, C. M., & Garson, G. D. (Eds.), *Handbook of public information systems* (pp. 261–272). Boca Ranton, FL: CRC Press. doi:10.1201/EBK1439807569-c16.

Carter, L., & McBride, A. (2010). Information privacy concerns and e-government: A research agenda. *Transforming Government: People. Process and Policy*, *4*(1), 10–13.

Chang, S., Gable, G., Smythe, E., & Timbrell, G. (2001). *A Delphi Examination of Public Sector ERP Implementation Issues.* Paper presented at the International Computer Information Systems Conference, Brisbane, Australia.

Charalabidis, Y., Lampathaki, F., & Askounis, D. (2010). Emerging interoperability directions in electronic government. In Popplewell, K., Harding, J., Poler, R., & Chalmeta, R. (Eds.), *Enterprise Interoperability IV: Making the Internet of the Future for the Future of Enterprise* (pp. 419–428). London: Springer. doi:10.1007/978-1-84996-257-5_39.

Chen, T., Zhang, J., & Lai, K.-K. (2009). An integrated real options evaluating model for information technology projects under multiple risks. *International Journal of Project Management, 27*(8), 776–786. doi:10.1016/j.ijproman.2009.01.001.

Chen, Y.-C. (2010). Citizen-centric e-government services: Understanding integrated citizen service information systems. *Social Science Computer Review, 28*(4), 427–442. doi:10.1177/0894439309359050.

Chen, Y.-C., & Thurmaier, K. (2008). Advancing e-government: Financing challenges and opportunities. *Public Administration Review, 68*(3), 537–548. doi:10.1111/j.1540-6210.2008.00889.x.

Chengalur-Smith, I., & Duchessi, P. (1999). The Initiation and Adoption of Client-Server Technology in Organizations. *Information & Management, 35*, 77–88. doi:10.1016/S0378-7206(98)00077-9.

Chircu, A. M. (2008). E-government evaluation: towards a multidimensional framework. *Electronic Government, an International Journal, 5*(4), 345-363.

Choudhury, S., & Kumar, S. (2009). E-governance: Tool for e-democracy and citizen empowerment in the horizon of information technology era in developing society in India, Nepal and Bangladesh. In Sahu, G. P., Dwivedi, Y. K., & Weerakkody, V. (Eds.), *E-Government Development and Diffusion: Inhibitors and Facilitators of Digital Democracy*. Hershey, PA: IGI Global. doi:10.4018/978-1-60566-713-3.ch007.

Chutimaskul, W., Funilkul, S., & Chongsuphajaisiddhi, V. (2008). *The quality framework of e-government development.* Paper presented at the 2nd international conference on Theory and practice of electronic governance.

Chwelos, P., Ramirez, R., Kraemer, K. L., & Melville, N. P. (2010). Does Technological Progress Alter the Nature of Information Technology as a production Input? New Evidence and New Results, Research Note. *Information Systems Research, 21*(2), 392–408. doi:10.1287/isre.1090.0229.

Clegg, S., & Dunkerley, D. (1980). *Organization, Class, and Control.* London: Routledge.

Cook, M. E., LaVigne, M. F., Pagano, C. M., Dawes, S. S., & Pardo, T. A. (2002). *Making a Case for Local E-Government* (p. 16). Albany, New York: Center for Technology in Government.

Cordella, A., & Iannacci, F. (2010). Information systems in the public sector: The e-Government enactment framework. *The Journal of Strategic Information Systems, 19*(1), 52–66. doi:10.1016/j.jsis.2010.01.001.

Council, A. C. (2008). Audti Report 2008: City of Austin's e-government iniative. Austin, Texas: Office od the City Auditor.

Cresswell, A. M., & Pardo, T. A. (2001). Implications of Legal and Organizational Issues for Urban Digital Government Development. *Government Information Quarterly, 18*, 269–278. doi:10.1016/S0740-624X(01)00086-7.

Criado, J. I. (2009). Gobierno Electrónico en Latinoamerica. Aproximación desde una Perspectiva Intergubernamental. *Estado, Gobierno y Gestión Pública. Revista Chilena de Administración Pública, 14.*

Cunningham, M. (1999). It's all about Business Needs. *Document World, 4*(5), 34.

Danziger, J. N., & Kraemer, K. L. (1985). Computarized Data-Based Systems and Productivity Among Professional Workers: The Case of Detectives. *Public Administration Review*, *45*(1), 196–209. doi:10.2307/3110149.

Davenport, T. (1993). *Process Innovation: Reengineering Work Through Information Technology*. Boston, MA: Harvard Business School Press.

Davis, G. B. (1982). Strategies for Information Requirements Determination. *IBM Systems Journal*, *21*, 4–30. doi:10.1147/sj.211.0004.

Dawes, S., & Pardo, T. A. (2008). *Critical Issues and Practical Challenges of IT Tools for Policy Analysis and Program Evaluation*. Albany: Center for Technology in Government.

Dawes, S. S. (1996). Interagency information sharing: Expected benefits, manageable risks. *Journal of Policy Analysis and Management*, *15*(3), 377–394. doi:10.1002/(SICI)1520-6688(199622)15:3<377::AID-PAM3>3.0.CO;2-F.

Dawes, S. S. (2008). The evolution and continuing challenges of e-governance. *Public Administration Review*, *68*(S1), S86–S102. doi:10.1111/j.1540-6210.2008.00981.x.

Dawes, S. S., & Helbig, N. (2010). Information strategies for open government: Challenges and prospects for deriving public value from government transparency. In M. A. Wimmer, J.-L. Chappelet, M. Janssen & H. J. Scholl (Eds.), *Electronic Government (Proceeding of the 9th IFIP WG 8.5 International Conference, EGOV 2010)* (pp. 50-60). Berlin: Springer.

Dawes, S. S., & Nelson, M. R. (1995). Pool the risks, share the benefits: Partnership in IT innovation. In Keyes, J. (Ed.), *Technology trendlines. Technology success stories from today's visionaries* (pp. 125–135). New York: Van Nostrand Reinhold.

Dawes, S. S., Pardo, T., & DiCaterino, A. (1999). Crossing the Threshold: Practical Foundations for Government Services on the World Wide Web. *Journal of the American Society for Information Science American Society for Information Science*, *50*(4), 346–353. doi:10.1002/(SICI)1097-4571(1999)50:4<346::AID-ASI12>3.0.CO;2-I.

Dawes, S. S., & Pardo, T. A. (2002). Building Collaborative Digital Government Systems. Systematic Constraints and Effective Practices. In McIver, W. J., & Elmagarmid, A. K. (Eds.), *Advances in Digital Government. Technology, Human Factors, and Policy* (pp. 259–273). Norwell, MA: Kluwer Academic Publishers. doi:10.1007/0-306-47374-7_16.

Dawes, S. S., Pardo, T. A., & Cresswell, A. M. (2004). Designing Electronic Government Information Access Programs: A Holistic Approach. *Government Information Quarterly*, *21*(1), 3–23. doi:10.1016/j.giq.2003.11.001.

Dawes, S. S., & Préfontaine, L. (2003). Understanding New Models of Collaboration for Delivering Government Services. *Communications of the ACM*, *46*(1), 40–42. doi:10.1145/602421.602444.

Deephouse, C., Mukhopadhyay, T., Goldenson, D., & Kellner, M. (1995). Software Processes and Project Performance. *Journal of Management Information Systems*, *12*(3), 187–205.

DeLone, W., & Mclean, E. (1992). Information Systems Success: The Quest for the Dependent Variable. *Information Systems Research, 3*(1), 60–95. doi:10.1287/isre.3.1.60.

DeLone, W., & Mclean, E. (2003). The DeLone and McLean Model of Information Systems Success: A Ten Year Update. *Journal of Management Information Systems, 19*(4), 9–30.

Detlor, B., Hupfer, M. E., & Ruhi, U. (2010). Internal factors affecting the adoption and use of government websites. *Electronic Government, an International Journal* 7(2), 120-136.

dos Santos, E. M., & Reinhard, N. (forthcoming). Electronic government interoperability: Identifying the barriers for frameworks adoption. *Social Science Computer Review*. doi:doi:10.1177/0894439310392196.

Drogkaris, P., Gritzalis, S., & Lambrinoudakis, C. (2010). Transforming the Greek e-government environment towards the e-Gov 2.0 era. In K. N. Andersen, E. Francesconi, Å. Grönlund & T. M. van Engers (Eds.), *Electronic Government and the Information Systems Perspective (Proceedings of the First International Conference, EGOVIS 2010)* (pp. 142-149). Berlin: Springer.

Duncan, G. T., & Roehrig, S. T. (2003). Mediating the Tension between Information Privacy and Information Access: The Role of Digital Government. In Garson, G. D. (Ed.), *Public Information Technology: Policy and Management Issues* (pp. 94–119). Hershey, PA: Idea Group Publishing.

Ebbers, W. E., & van Dijk, J. A. G. M. (2007). Resistance and support to electronic government, building a model of innovation. *Government Information Quarterly, 24*, 554–575. doi:10.1016/j.giq.2006.09.008.

Eynon, R., & Margetts, H. (2007). Organizational Solutions for Overcoming Barriers to eGovernment. *European Journal of ePractice 1*, 73-86.

Fasanghari, M., & Habibipour, F. (2009). *E-government performance evaluation with fuzzy numbers.* Paper presented at the International Association of Computer Science and Information Technology - Spring Conference (IACSIT-SC).

Fletcher, P. D. (2004). Portals and Policy: Implications of Electronic Access to U.S. Federal Government Information and Services. In Pavlichev, A., & Garson, G. D. (Eds.), *Digital Government: Principles and Best Practices* (pp. 52–62). Hershey, PA: Idea Group Publishing.

Fountain, J. E. (2001). Public Sector: Early Stage of a Deep Transformation. In Litan, R., & Rivlin, A. (Eds.), *The Economic Payoff from the Internet Revolution*. Washington, D.C.: Brookings Institution Press.

Fountain, J. E. (2008). *Bureaucratic Reform and E-Government in the United States: An Institutional Perspective*. National Center for Digital Government.

Gant, J. P. (2004). Digital Government and Geographic Information Systems. In Pavlichev, A., & Garson, G. D. (Eds.), *Digital Government: Principles and Best Practices*. Hershey, PA: Idea Group Publishing.

Garson, D. G. (2003-b). Symposium on the theory of technology enactment in Jane Fountain's (2001) Building the Virtual State: an introduction. *Social Science Computer Review, 21*(4), 409-410.

Garson, G. D. (2004). The Promise of Digital Government. In Pavlichev, A., & Garson, G. D. (Eds.), *Digital Government: Principles and Best Practices* (pp. 2–15). Hershey, PA: Idea Group Publishing.

Gaudino, S., & Moro, G. (2010). Evaluation of an e-government project: which are the barriers to e-government integration? *International Journal of Technology. Policy and Management, 10*(1/2), 53–72.

Ghapanchi, A., Albadvi, A., & Zarei, B. (2008). A framework for e-government planning and implementation. *Electronic Government, an International Journal, 5*(1), 71-90.

Gil-Garcia, J. R. (2012). *Enacting Electronic Government Success: An Integrative Study of Government-wide Websites, Organizational Capabilities, and Institutions*. New York, NY: Springer. doi:10.1007/978-1-4614-2015-6.

Gil-Garcia, J. R., Chengalur-Smith, I., & Duchessi, P. (2003). Perceived Impediments and Benefits to Information Sharing Projects: Multiple Perspectives. Albany, NY.

Gil-Garcia, J. R., Chun, S. A., & Janssen, M. (2009). Government information sharing and integration: Combining the social and the technical. *Information Polity, 14*(1/2), 1–10.

Gil-Garcia, J. R., & Helbig, N. (2006). Exploring E-Government Benefits and Success Factors. In Anttiroiko, A.-V., & Malkia, M. (Eds.), *Encyclopedia of Digital Government* (pp. 803–811). Hershey, PA: Idea Group Inc. doi:10.4018/978-1-59140-789-8.ch122.

Gil-Garcia, J. R., Helbig, N., & Ferro, E. (2006, September 4-8). *Is it only about Internet Access? An Empirical Test of a Multi-Dimensional Digital Divide.* Paper presented at the Fifth International Conference on Electronic Government, Krakow, Poland.

Gil-García, J. R., & Luna-Reyes, L. (2007). *Modelo Multidimensional de Medición del Gobierno Electrónico para América Latina y el Caribe*. Santiago de Chile, Chile: Naciones Unidas, CEPAL, Unión Europea.

Gil-Garcia, J. R., & Luna-Reyes, L. F. (2003). Towards a Definition of Electronic Government: A Comparative Review. In Mendez-Vilas, A., Mesa Gonzalez, J. A., Mesa Gonzalez, J., Guerrero Bote, V., & Zapico Alonso, F. (Eds.), *Techno-legal Aspects of the Information Society and New Economy: An Overview*. Badajoz, Spain: Formatex.

Gil-Garcia, J. R., & Luna-Reyes, L. F. (2006). Integrating Conceptual Approaches to E-Government. In Khosrow-Pour, M. (Ed.), *Encyclopedia of E-Commerce, E-Government and Mobile Commerce*. Hershey, PA: Idea Group Inc. doi:10.4018/978-1-59140-799-7.ch102.

Gil-Garcia, J. R., & Pardo, T. A. (2005). E-Government Success Factors: Mapping Practical Tools to Theoretical Foundations. *Government Information Quarterly, 22*(2), 187–216. doi:10.1016/j.giq.2005.02.001.

Golubchik, L. (2002). Scalable Data Collection for Internet-based Digital Government Applications. In McIver, W. J., & Elmagarmid, A. K. (Eds.), *Advances in Digital Government. Technology, Human Factors, and Policy*. Norwell, MA: Kluwer Academic Publishers. doi:10.1007/0-306-47374-7_6.

Gonzalez, P., Adenso-Diaz, B., & Gemoets, L. A. (2010). *A cross-national comparison e-government success measures: A theory-based empirical research.* Paper presented at the Americas Conference on Information Systems, Lima, Peru.

Gorla, N., Somers, T. M., & Wong, B. (2010). Organizational impact of system quality, information quality, and service quality. *The Journal of Strategic Information Systems*, *19*(3), 207–228. doi:10.1016/j.jsis.2010.05.001.

Gottschalk, P. (2009). Maturity levels for interoperability in digital government. *Government Information Quarterly*, *26*(1), 75–81. doi:10.1016/j.giq.2008.03.003.

Gulati, G. J., Yates, D. J., & Tawileh, A. (2010). Towards E-Participation in the Middle East and Northern Europe. In Reddick, C. G. (Ed.), *Comparative E-Government* (pp. 71–91). New York: Springer. doi:10.1007/978-1-4419-6536-3_4.

Hall, R. H. (2002). *Organizations. Structures, Processes, and Outcomes*. Upper Saddle River, NJ: Prentice Hall.

Hardy, C. A., & Williams, S. P. (2008). E-government policy and practice: A theoretical and empirical exploration of public e-procurement. *Government Information Quarterly*, *25*(2), 155–180. doi:10.1016/j.giq.2007.02.003.

Harris, N. D. (2000). Intergovernmental Cooperation in the Development and Use of Information Systems. In Garson, G. D. (Ed.), *Handbook of Public Information Systems* (pp. 165–177). New York: Marcel Dekker.

Hassan, H. S., Shehab, E., & Peppard, J. (2011). Recent advances in e-service in the public sector: State-of-the-art and future trends. *Business Process Management Journal*, *17*(3), 526–545. doi:10.1108/14637151111136405.

Hatch, M. J. (1997). *Organization Theory. Modern, Symbolic, and Posmodern Perpectives*. Oxford: Oxford University Press.

Heeks, R., & Bailur, S. (2007). Analyzing e-government research: Perspectives, philosophies, theories, methods, and practice. *Government Information Quarterly*, *24*(2), 243–265. doi:10.1016/j.giq.2006.06.005.

Herrera, L., & Gil-Garcia, J. R. (2010). Implementation of e-government in Mexico: The case of Infonavit. In Assar, S., Boughzala, I., & Boydens, I. (Eds.), *Practical Studies in E-Government: Best Practices from Around the World* (pp. 29–48). New York: Springer. doi:10.1007/978-1-4419-7533-1_3.

Hoque, F., Walsh, L. M., Mirakaj, D. L., & Bruckner, J. (2011). *The Power of Convergence: Linking Business Strategies and Technology Decisions to Create Sustainable Success*. New York: AMACOM.

Hossain, M. D., Moon, J., Kim, J. K., & Choe, Y. C. (forthcoming). Impacts of organizational assimilation of e-government systems on business value creation: A structuration theory approach. *Electronic Commerce Research and Applications*. doi: doi:10.1016/j.elerap.2010.1012.1003.

Jaeger, P. T. (2002). Constitutional principles and e-government: An opinion about possible effects of Federalism and separation of powers on e-government policies. *Government Information Quarterly*, *19*, 357–368. doi:10.1016/S0740-624X(02)00119-3.

Janssen, M. (2008). *Exploring the service-oriented enterprise: Drawing lessons from a case study*. Paper presented at the 41st Hawaii International Conference on System Sciences (HICSS).

Janssen, M. (forthcoming). Sociopolitical aspects of interoperability and enterprise architecture in e-government. *Social Science Computer Review*. doi: doi:10.1177/0894439310392187.

Janssen, M., Kuk, G., & Wagenaar, R. W. (2008). A Survey of Web-based business models for e-government in the Netherlands. *Government Information Quarterly*, *25*, 202–220. doi:10.1016/j.giq.2007.06.005.

Jiang, J., & Klein, G. (2000). Software development risks to project effectiveness. *Journal of Systems and Software*, *52*, 3–10. doi:10.1016/S0164-1212(99)00128-4.

Joseph, B. K. (2010). E-Government Adoption Landscape Zambia: Context, issues and challenges. In Reddick, C. G. (Ed.), *Comparative E-Government* (pp. 241–258). Springer. doi:10.1007/978-1-4419-6536-3_12.

Joshi, J. B. D., Ghafoor, A., Aref, W. G., & Spafford, E. H. (2002). Security and Privacy Challenges of a Digital Government. In McIver, W. J. Jr, & Elmagarmid, A. K. (Eds.), *Advances in Digital Government. Technology, Human Factors, and Policy* (pp. 121–136). Norwell, MA: Kluwer Academic Publishers. doi:10.1007/0-306-47374-7_7.

Jun, K.-N., & Weare, C. (forthcoming). Institutional motivations in the adoption of innovations: The case of e-government. *Journal of Public Administration: Research and Theory*.

Keil, M., Cule, P. E., Lyytinen, K., & Schmidt, R. (1998). A Framework for Identifying Software Project Risks. *Communications of the ACM*, *41*(11), 76–82. doi:10.1145/287831.287843.

Khan, G. F., Moon, J., Park, H. W., Swar, B., & Rho, J. J. (2010). A socio-technical perspective on e-government issues in developing countries: A scientometrics approach. *Scientometrics*, *87*(2), 267–286. doi:10.1007/s11192-010-0322-5.

Kim, S., Kim, H. J., & Lee, H. (2009). An institutional analysis of an e-government system for anti-corruption: The case of OPEN. *Government Information Quarterly*, *26*(1), 42–50. doi:10.1016/j.giq.2008.09.002.

Klievink, B., & Janssen, M. (2009). Realizing joined-up government: Dynamic capabilities and stage models for transformation. *Government Information Quarterly*, *26*(2), 275–284. doi:10.1016/j.giq.2008.12.007.

Kling, R. (1993). Organizational Analysis in Computer Science. *The Information Society*, *9*(2), 71–87. doi:10.1080/01972243.1993.9960134.

Klischewski, R., & Scholl, H. J. (2008). Information quality as capstone in negotiating e-government integration, interoperation and information sharing. *Electronic Government, an International Journal*, *5*(2), 203-225.

Kuan, K. K. Y., & Chau, P. Y. K. (2001). A perception-based model for EDI adoption in small businesses using a technology-organization-environment framework. *Information & Management*, *38*, 507–521. doi:10.1016/S0378-7206(01)00073-8.

Landsbergen, D. Jr, & Wolken, G. Jr. (2001). Realizing the Promise: Government Information Systems and the Fourth Generation of Information Technology. *Public Administration Review*, *61*(2), 206–220. doi:10.1111/0033-3352.00023.

Langford, J., & Roy, J. (2009). Building shared accountability into service transformation partnerships. *International Journal of Public Policy*, *4*(3/4), 232–250. doi:10.1504/IJPP.2009.023490.

Laudon, K. C. (1985). Environmental and Institutional Models of System Development: A National Criminal History System. *Communications of the ACM*, *28*(7), 728–740. doi:10.1145/3894.3899.

Laudon, K. C. (1986). *Dossier Society. Value Choices in the Design of National Information Systems*. New York: Columbia University Press.

Lee, C.-p., Chang, K., & Berry, F. S. (2011). Testing the development and diffusion of e-government and e-democracy: A global perspective. *Public Administration Review*, *71*(3), 444–454. doi:10.1111/j.1540-6210.2011.02228.x.

Lee, J.-N. (2001). The impact of knowledge sharing, organizational capability and partnership quality on IS outsourcing success. *Information & Management*, *38*, 323–335. doi:10.1016/S0378-7206(00)00074-4.

Lee, J. W., Rainey, H. G., & Chun, Y. H. (2009). OF POLITICS AND PURPOSE: POLITICAL SALIENCE AND GOAL AMBIGUITY OF US FEDERAL AGENCIES. *Public Administration*, *87*(3), 457–484. doi:10.1111/j.1467-9299.2009.01772.x.

Lee, K.-S. (2009). A final flowering of the developmental state: The IT policy experiment of the Korean Information Infrastructure, 1995–2005. *Government Information Quarterly*, *26*(4), 567–576. doi:10.1016/j.giq.2009.05.003.

Leung, T. K. P., & Adams, J. (2009). Explaining IT usage in government through “resistance to change”. *Journal of Chinese Entrepreneurship*, *1*(3), 176–192. doi:10.1108/17561390910999489.

Luna-Reyes, L., Gil-García, J. R., & Estrada-Marroquín, M. (2008). The Impact of Institutions on Interorganizational IT projects in the Mexican Federal Government. *International Journal of Electronic Government Research*, *4*(2), 27–42. doi:10.4018/jegr.2008040103.

Luna-Reyes, L. F., & Gil-Garcia, J. R. (2003, May 18-21). *eGovernment & Internet Security: Some Technical and Policy Considerations*. Paper presented at the National Conference on Digital Government Research, Boston, MA.

Luna-Reyes, L. F., & Gil-Garcia, J. R. (2011). Using institutional theory and dynamic simulation to understand complex e-Government phenomena. *Government Information Quarterly*, *28*(3), 329–345. doi:10.1016/j.giq.2010.08.007.

Luna-Reyes, L. F., Pardo, T. A., Gil-Garcia, J. R., Navarrete, C., Zhang, J., & Mellouli, S. (2010). Digital Government in North America: A comparative Analysis of Policy and Program Priorities in Canada, Mexico and the United States. In Reddick, C. G. (Ed.), *Comparative E-Government* (pp. 139–160). New York: Springer. doi:10.1007/978-1-4419-6536-3_7.

Lux Wigand, D. F. (2010). Adoption of Web 2.0 by Canadian and US governments. In Reddick, C. G. (Ed.), *Comparative E-Government* (pp. 161–181). New York: Springer. doi:10.1007/978-1-4419-6536-3_8.

Macintosh, A., Malina, A., & Farrell, S. (2002). Digital Democracy through Electronic Petitioning. In McIver, W. J., & Elmagarmid, A. K. (Eds.), *Advances in Digital Government. Technology, Human Factors, and Policy*. Norwell, MA: Kluwer Academic Publishers. doi:10.1007/0-306-47374-7_8.

Madnick, S. E., Wang, R. Y., Lee, Y. W., & Zhu, H. (2009). Overview and framework for data and information quality research. *Journal of Data and Information Quality*, *1*(1). doi:10.1145/1515693.1516680.

Margetts, H. (2009). The Internet and Public Policy. *Policy & Internet*, *1*, 1–21. doi:10.2202/1944-2866.1029.

Markaki, O. I., Charilas, D. E., & Askounis, D. (2010). Evaluation of the Impact and Adoption of E-government Services in the Balkans. In Reddick, C. G. (Ed.), *Comparative E-Government* (pp. 91–114). New York: Springer. doi:10.1007/978-1-4419-6536-3_5.

Markus, M. L. (2005). Technology shaping effects of e-collaboration technologies: Bugs and features. *International Journal of e-Collaboration*, *1*(1), 1–23. doi:10.4018/jec.2005010101.

Markus, M. L., & Silver, M. S. (2008). A foundation for the study of IT effects: A new look at DeSanctis and Poole's concepts of structural features and spirit. *Journal of the Association for Information Systems*, *9*(10/11), 609–632.

Maumbe, B. M., Owei, V., & Alexander, H. (2008). Questioning the pace and pathway of e-government development in Africa: A case study of South Africa's Cape Gateway project. *Government Information Quarterly*, *25*(4), 757–777. doi:10.1016/j.giq.2007.08.007.

McFarlan, F. W. (1981). Portfolio Approach to Information Systems. *Harvard Business Review*, *59*, 142–150.

Meijer, A., & Thaens, M. (2010). Alignment 2.0: Strategic use of new internet technologies in government. *Government Information Quarterly*, *27*(2), 113–121. doi:10.1016/j.giq.2009.12.001.

Meneklis, V., & Douligeris, C. (2008, December 1-4). *Technological integration: Evidence of processes of structuring in governmental organizations.* Paper presented at the 2nd international conference on Theory and practice of electronic governance, Cairo, Egypt.

Millerand, F., & Baker, K. S. (2010). Who are the users? Who are the developers? Webs of users and developers in the development process of a technical standard. *Information Systems Journal*, *20*(2), 137–161. doi:10.1111/j.1365-2575.2009.00338.x.

Milner, E. M. (2000). *Managing Information and Knowledge in the Public Sector*. New York: Routledge. doi:10.4324/9780203458631.

Morgeson, F. V. III, & Mithas, S. (2009). Does e-government measure up to e-business? Comparing end user perceptions of U.S. federal government and e-business web sites. *Public Administration Review*, *69*(4), 740–752. doi:10.1111/j.1540-6210.2009.02021.x.

Nasim, S., & Sushil. (2010). Managing continuity and change: a new approach for strategizing in e-government. *Transforming Government: People. Process and Policy*, *4*(4), 338–364.

Norris, D. F. (1999). Leading Edge Information Technologies and their Adoption: Lessons from US Cities. In Garson, G. D. (Ed.), *Information Technology and Computer Applications in Public Administration: Issues and Trends* (pp. 137–156). Hershey, PA: Idea Group.

Nour, M. A., AbdelRahman, A. A., & Fadlalla, A. (2008). A context-based integrative framework for e-government initiatives. *Government Information Quarterly*, *25*(3), 448–461. doi:10.1016/j.giq.2007.02.004.

Noveck, B. S. (2009). *Wiki government: how technology can make government better, democracy stronger, and citizens more powerful*. Washington, D.C.: Brookings Institution Press.

OECD. (2003). *The e-Government Imperative*. Paris, France: Organisation for Economic Co-operation and Development.

Ojo, A., Estevez, E., & Janowski, T. (2010). Semantic interoperability architecture for Governance 2.0 *Information Polity, 15*(1/2), 105-123.

Olbrich, S. (2010). Implementing E-Government Locally - An Empirical Survey from the European Metropolitan Area Rhine-Nechar. In Reddick, C. G. (Ed.), *Comparative E-Government* (pp. 221–237). New York: Springer. doi:10.1007/978-1-4419-6536-3_11.

Panagopoulos, C. (2004). Consequences of the Cyberstate: The Political Implications of Digital Government in International Context. In Pavlichev, A., & Garson, G. D. (Eds.), *Digital Government: Principles and Best Practices*. Hershey, PA: Idea Group Publishing.

Pardo, T. A., Gil-Garcia, J. R., & Burke, G. B. (2008). *Building Response Capacity through Cross-boundary Information Sharing: The critical role of trust*. CTG Working Paper. Suny. Albany.

Pardo, T. A., Nam, T., & Burke, G. B. (forthcoming). E-government interoperability: Interaction of policy, management, and technology dimensions. *Social Science Computer Review*. doi: doi:10.1177/0894439310392184.

Pardo, T. A., & Scholl, H. J. (2002). *Walking Atop the Cliffs: Avoiding Failure and Reducing Risk in Large Scale E-Government Projects*. Paper presented at the 35th Annual Hawaii International Conference on System Sciences, Hawaii.

Peled, A. (2001). Centralization or Diffusion? Two Tales of Online Government. *Administration & Society*, *32*(6), 686–709. doi:10.1177/00953990122019622.

Petter, S., DeLone, W., & McLean, E. (2008). Measuring information systems success: Models, dimensions, measures, and interrelationships. *European Journal of Information Systems*, *17*, 236–263. doi:10.1057/ejis.2008.15.

Pina, V., Torres, L., & Royo, S. (2009). E-government evolution in EU local governments: a comparative perspective. *Online Information Review*, *33*(6), 1137–1168. doi:10.1108/14684520911011052.

Pina, V., Torres, L., & Royo, S. (2010). Is e-government leading to more accountable and transparent local governments? An overall view. *Financial Accountability & Management*, *26*(1), 3–20. doi:10.1111/j.1468-0408.2009.00488.x.

Rahman, H. (2010). Framework of E-Governance at the local government level. In Reddick, C. G. (Ed.), *Comparative E-Government* (pp. 23–47). doi:10.1007/978-1-4419-6536-3_2.

Reddick, C. G. (2010). Preface. In Reddick, C. G. (Ed.), *Comparative E-Government*. New York: Springer. doi:10.1007/978-1-4419-6536-3.

Redman, T. C. (1998). The Impact of Poor Data Quality on the Typical Enterprise. *Communications of the ACM*, *41*(2), 79–82. doi:10.1145/269012.269025.

Remus, U., & Wiener, M. (2010). A multi-method, holistic strategy for researching critical success factors in IT projects. *Information Systems Journal*, *20*(1), 25–52. doi:10.1111/j.1365-2575.2008.00324.x.

Rocheleau, B. (1999). *Building Successful Public Management Information Systems: Critical Stages and Success Factors.* Paper presented at the American Society for Public Administration's 60th National Conference, Orlando, FL.

Rocheleau, B. (2003). Politics, Accountability, and Governmental Information Systems. In Garson, G. D. (Ed.), *Public Information Technology: Policy and Management Issues* (pp. 20–52). Hershey, PA: Idea Group Publishing.

Roldán, J. L., & Leal, A. (2003). A Validation Test of an Adaptation of the DeLone and McLean's Model in the Spanish EIS Field. In Cano, J. J. (Ed.), *Critical Reflections on Information Systems: A Systemic Approach*. Hershey, PA: Idea Group Publishing. doi:10.4018/978-1-59140-040-0.ch004.

Rorissa, A., Potnis, D. D., & Demissie, D. (2010). A comparative study of contents of e-government service websites of Middle East and North African (MENA) Countries. In Reddick, C. G. (Ed.), *Comparative E-Government* (pp. 49–69). New York: Springer. doi:10.1007/978-1-4419-6536-3_3.

Rosacker, K. M., & Olson, D. L. (2008a). An empirical assessment of IT project selection and evaluation methods in state government. *Project Management Journal*, *39*(1), 49–58. doi:10.1002/pmj.20036.

Rosacker, K. M., & Olson, D. L. (2008b). Public sector information system critical success factors. *Transforming Government: People. Process and Policy*, *2*(1), 60–70.

Rose, W. R., & Grant, G. G. (2010). Critical issues pertaining to the planning and implementation of E-Government initiatives. *Government Information Quarterly*, *27*(1), 26–33. doi:10.1016/j.giq.2009.06.002.

Rowley, J. (2011). e-Government stakeholders—Who are they and what do they want? *International Journal of Information Management*, *31*(1), 53–62. doi:10.1016/j.ijinfomgt.2010.05.005.

Roy, J. (2009). E-government and integrated service delivery in Canada: The Province of Nova Scotia as a case study. *International Journal of Electronic Governance*, *2*(2/3), 223–238. doi:10.1504/IJEG.2009.029131.

Sancak, H. Ó., & Güleç, S. (2010). Towards E-Government transformation in Turkey: Policy and Implementation. In Reddick, C. G. (Ed.), *Comparative E-Government* (pp. 331–352). New York: Springer. doi:10.1007/978-1-4419-6536-3_17.

Schelin, S. H. (2003). E-Government: An Overview. In Garson, G. D. (Ed.), *Public Information Technology: Policy and Management Issues* (pp. 120–137). Hershey, PA: Idea Group Publishing.

Scholl, H. J., Mai, J. E., & Fidel, R. (2006). *Interdisciplinary Analysis of Digital Government Work (Birds-of-a-Feather Session).* Paper presented at the 7th International Conference on Digital Government Research, San Diego, CA.

Schuppan, T. (2009). E-Government in developing countries: Experiences from sub-Saharan Africa. *Government Information Quarterly*, *26*(1), 118–127. doi:10.1016/j.giq.2008.01.006.

Seneviratne, S. J. (1999). Information Technology and Organizational Change in the Public Sector. In Garson, G. D. (Ed.), *Information Technology and Computer Applications in Public Administration: Issues and Trends*. Hershey, PA: Idea Group Publishing.

Smith, M. L. (2010). Building institutional trust through e-government trustworthiness cues. *Information Technology & People*, *23*(3), 222–246. doi:10.1108/09593841011069149.

Southon, G., Sauer, C., & Dampney, K. (1999). Lessons from a failed information systems initiative: issues for complex organizations. *International Journal of Medical Informatics*, *55*(1), 33–46. doi:10.1016/S1386-5056(99)00018-0 PMID:10471239.

Stevenson, M. (2003, November 5). Internet Democracy Elusive: Report, *Associated Press*.

Thomas, G., & Fernández, W. (2008). Success in IT projects: A matter of definition? *International Journal of Project Management*, *26*(7), 733–742. doi:10.1016/j.ijproman.2008.06.003.

Tsai, N., Choi, B., & Perry, M. (2009). Improving the process of E-Government initiative: An in-depth case study of web-based GIS implementation. *Government Information Quarterly*, *26*(2), 368–376. doi:10.1016/j.giq.2008.11.007.

Ubaldi, B.-C., & Roy, J. (2010). E-government and federalism in Italy and Canada—A comparative assessment. In Reddick, C. G. (Ed.), *Comparative E-Government* (*Vol. 25*, pp. 183–199). Berlin: Springer. doi:10.1007/978-1-4419-6536-3_9.

Umble, E. J., Haft, R. R., & Umble, M. M. (2003). Enterprise resource planning: Implementation procedures and critical success factors. *European Journal of Operational Research*, *146*, 241–257. doi:10.1016/S0377-2217(02)00547-7.

Valdés, G., Solar, M., Astudillo, H., Iribarren, M., Concha, G., & Visconti, M. (2011). Conception, development and implementation of an e-Government maturity model in public agencies. *Government Information Quarterly*, *28*(2), 176–187. doi:10.1016/j.giq.2010.04.007.

van Veenstra, A. F., Klievink, B., & Janssen, M. (2011). Barriers and impediments to transformational government: Insights from literature and practice. *Electronic Government, an International Journal, 8*(2/3), 226-241.

Walton, R. E. (1989). *Up and Running. Integrating Information Technology and the Organization*. Boston, MA: Harvard Business School Press.

Weinstein, J., & Jaques, T. (2010). *Achieving Project Management Success in the Federal Government*. Vienna, VA: Management Concepts.

Wu, L.-C., Wu, L.-H., & Wen, Y.-F. (2010). Interdisciplinary research of options theory and management information systems: Review, research issues, and suggestions for future research. *Industrial Management & Data Systems*, *110*(3), 433–452. doi:10.1108/02635571011030060.

Wyld, D. C. (2009). *Moving to the Cloud: An Introduction to Cloud Computing in Government*. Washington, DC: IBM Center for the Business of Government.

Yang, T.-M., & Maxwell, T. A. (2011). Information-sharing in public organizations: A literature review of interpersonal, intra-organizational and inter-organizational success factors. *Government Information Quarterly*, *28*(2), 164–175. doi:10.1016/j.giq.2010.06.008.

Yao, Y., Lee, Y. W., Hong, P., & Weng, Z. (2010). *Power of information channels: Participation in e-government discourse*. Paper presented at the Americas Conference on Information Systems (AMCIS).

Zhao, J. J., Zhao, S. Y., & Zhao, S. Y. (2010). Opportunities and threats: A security assessment of state e-government websites. *Government Information Quarterly*, *27*(1), 49–56. doi:10.1016/j.giq.2009.07.004.

Zissis, D., Lekkas, D., & Papadopoulou, A.-E. (2009). Competent electronic participation channels in electronic democracy. *Electronic. Journal of E-Government*, *7*(2), 195–208.

Acknowledgment

This book is the result of great teamwork and the individual dedicated time of many wonderful people. I take this opportunity to convey my regards and thank to some of those who have helped and supported me in the conception and completion of this work. This volume would not have been possible without the contribution and assistance of the authors, reviewers, editorial advisory board, colleagues around the world, and the staff at IGI Global. I am grateful for the guidance of the members of the Editorial Advisory Board, who regardless great distances and time differences were always willing to provide their opinions and general feedback for the book. A special word of thank you to all the reviewers who not only gave their time and effort, but also very constructive and accurate comments that have been incorporated in the final versions of the chapters, enhancing the book's overall quality and contribution to the field. Thank you to all the authors for sharing your knowledge through this editorial project and your interest in electronic government success. From the staff at IGI Global, I would like to mention the dedication and commitment of Myla Merkel during the entire process. I have always received support and useful guidance from her. I want also to thank Ana Catarrivas, my research assistant, whose dedication and tireless effort have been instrumental for the completion of this book. I am very grateful to *Centro de Investigación y Docencia Económicas (CIDE)*, from which I have received strong institutional support and great encouragement and motivation from my colleagues and friends. Finally, I bestow my great love and gratitude to my family, my wife, Nadia, my son, Dante, and my daughter, Julieta. They have always encouraged my efforts and supported wholeheartedly my academic endeavors. I love them with all my heart and I am truly thankful to them.

J. Ramon Gil-Garcia
Mexico City, Mexico

Section 1
Americas

Chapter 1
Government Services in Outlying Regions

Sehl Mellouli
Université Laval, Canada

Marie-Christine Roy
Université Laval, Canada

Anne Chartier
Université Laval, Canada

Diane Poulin
Université Laval, Canada

ABSTRACT

E-government offers the potential to provide easy and flexible access to a vast array of government services, particularly in outlying regions where traditional service centers are scarce and costly. However, past research shows that online services use decreases in non-urban areas. The objective of this chapter is to identify factors that influence the use of e-government services in outlying regions. In the delivery of any government services, there are two parties: citizens and the government. Hence, in order to better identify these factors, we conducted our study from two points of view: the citizens' and the government's managers. These results show that attitude positively affects intention to use e-government services. From the citizens' perspective, attitude is in turn influenced by perceived usefulness, perceived ease of use, perceived risk, and trust. From the managers' perspective, several social, economic, demographic, and psychological factors should be considered for the development of online services.

1. INTRODUCTION

The objective of e-government is to provide better and more accessible services to citizens while reducing service costs. Since these services are used by a variety of citizen profiles such as students or workers, young persons or seniors, and for different needs (Bertot & Jager, 2008), governments must take a segmented approach to study and understand these needs in order to maximize the adoption potential. Past studies show that there is a difference in behavior between urban and outlying citizens in using electronic government services, with a marked decrease in online services adoption in rural areas (Goldfinch et al., 2009; Previtali & Bof, 2009). Consequently, governments must address the specific needs for online services in outlying regions in order to

DOI: 10.4018/978-1-4666-4173-0.ch001

Copyright © 2013, IGI Global. Copying or distributing in print or electronic forms without written permission of IGI Global is prohibited.

deploy better strategies to encourage use (Nam & Sayogo, 2011). However, little is known about what factors affect citizens' from outlying regions intention to use e-government services or behavior.

In this chapter, we describe a large scale study that was performed in the province of Quebec in order to shed some light onto the factors that predispose citizens in outlying regions to use online government services. In any delivered government service, there are at least two parties involved: citizens and government employees. Hence, in order to better understand the adoption of electronic government services in outlying regions, the study was designed to address both the perspective of citizens as well as the perspective of government's officials (Fagan, 2006; Huang, 2007; Moon, 2002; Reddick & Frank, 2007).

Electronic government services adoption was widely studied in the literature (Horst et al., 2007). However, these studies focused on the adoption of people living in central cities. In our knowledge, there are no studies on electronic government services adoption in outlying regions. The difference between an outlying region and a central region is that an outlying region, generally, does not have a decision making power; it mainly depends on the government agencies located in central cities. Furthermore, the technological infrastructure is not the same in outlying regions and central cities; that is called the digital divide. Consequently, it becomes interesting to study electronic government adoption in outlying regions and identify the main barriers that hinder e-government adoption in these regions.

In addition, most of e-government adoption studies conducted interviews with citizens to identify the barriers and the incentives of the adoption of electronic services. However, it is the government who is delivering electronic services to the citizens. Hence, if the citizens perceive barriers that hinder them from using electronic services, it is necessary that government's managers perceive the same barriers than citizens so that they can improve the Quality of Services of the provided electronic government services. Otherwise, and since government's managers do not perceive the same barriers than citizens, actions may be taken on things that do not lead to a better adoption of electronic services from citizens. The aim is to see if managers and citizens perceive the same barriers and incentives for adoption of e-government services.

This chapter is organized as follows. Section 2 presents related work on the digital divide and appropriation of e-government. Section 3 details the conceptual frameworks adopted to study the citizens' and government's point of view. Section 4 presents the results from the field studies. Finally, the last section concludes and argues for future research avenues.

2. RELATED WORK

Our study focuses on the use of e-services by citizens living in outlying regions. To this end, two questions may arise: what are the technological differences between outlying regions and urban areas? And what does it mean to use or adopt e-services in outlying regions? Based on the literature, these two questions are discussed in the following two sections.

Digital Divide and Outlying Regions

The "digital divide" is the difference in use of information and communication technologies between two or more groups: those who have access to the digital technologies and those who do not (Rallet & Rochelandet, 2004). The digital divide can impact economic, demographic, or social divisions between groups and consequently between cities (Edmiston, 2003). Several studies have been conducted to understand the causes of the digital divide between cities (Huang, 2007; Canada, 2012). In Huang (2007), it is stated that the digital divide is rooted in demography, ethnicity, education, property, income, and geography. In Canada, these socio-economic factors are the main cause of the digital divide (Canada, 2012).

In addition, city size positively correlates with adoption of e-government (Moon, 2002). The larger the city, the more it is a pioneer in adopting e-government. Consequently, there may be a risk of fragmentation and unequal treatment of citizens based on their place of residence. To narrow this gap, it is necessary to strengthen the powers of local authorities and seek means of coordination without losing sight of the need to develop vertical and horizontal relationships between various levels of government in order to create a more cooperative structure of authority (Ullmann, 2006).

Appropriation of E-Government

Although several studies have examined how technology is adopted and disseminated (Rogers, 2003), or accepted and used (Venkatesh et al., 2003), more recent schools of thought and research propose the concept of technology appropriation as more relevant to understand the mechanisms underlying use (Erwin, 2004). Technology appropriation can be assimilated into a society's existing values by adjusting some attributes of the culture to the technology's intrinsic requirements. Hence, technological change stimulates social reorganization (Hard, 1998). This social reorganization requires an increase in the supply of online services by local authorities (Leaning, 2005). However, the development of e-government is now being challenged (Erwin, 2004) by social barriers to citizen use. In fact, such development should be "socially appropriated," i.e., incorporated into the social processes of citizens (Erwin, 2004). E-government should not be designed as an external technology imposed on a community, but rather as a phenomenon built and owned by citizens (Leaning, 2005).

The literature has provided several theoretical frameworks to explain the cognitive determinants of e-government use: the Technology Acceptance Model (TAM), the Unified Theory of Acceptance and Use of Technology (UTAUT), the Diffusion of Innovation model (DOI), and the Theory of Planned Behaviour (TPB).

In the Technology Acceptance Model (TAM), two factors influence one's intention to use a technology: perceived usefulness and perceived ease of use (Carter & Bélanger, 2004). TAM ignores one's emotional choices and attitudes, and focuses on technology acceptance rather than on technology use. The Unified Theory of Acceptance and Use of Technology (UTAUT) model, a modified version of TAM, differentiates the intention to use from actual use (van Dijk et al., 2008).

The Diffusion of Innovation (DOI) model also attempts to explain one's intention to adopt new technologies (Carter & Bélanger, 2005). A technology diffuses at a speed determined by (a) its relative advantage, which is perceived in relation to preceding technologies, (b) its perceived complexity, (c) its compatibility with the potential user's values, beliefs, and needs, and (d) its perceived image (Carter & Bélanger, 2005; Lean et al., 2009).

The Theory of Planned Behaviour (TPB) incorporates the concept of intention. A person's decision to use a technology can thus be assessed in contexts where use is mandatory (Lean et al., 2009). In this framework, intention to use e-government depends on three groups of factors: attitude towards the technology, subjective norms, and perceived control of one's behaviour. These factors are in turn influenced by other factors (Hung et al., 2006; Hung et al., 2009). The factors influencing the attitude are perceived usefulness, perceived ease of use, perceived risk, training provided, trust, personal innovativeness, and compatibility (in relation to one's experience with preceding technologies, one's values, and one's current needs). The factors influencing the subjective norm are external influence (influence from information), and interpersonal influence (normative influence). Finally, the factors influencing the perceived control of one's behaviour are one's self-efficacy, and facilitating conditions (time and money).

3. CONCEPTUAL FRAMEWORK

This study tries to understand the issue of e-government services in outlying regions from two different points of view: the citizens' and the government's managers. To this end, two different conceptual frameworks are used: one for citizens and one for government managers.

Views of Citizens

UTAUT model emphasizes four constructs that would affect one's intention to use, i.e., effort estimation, performance expectation, social influence (the degree to which a person believes that other people think he or she should use a new technology), and the conditions that facilitate use (Carter & Weerakkody, 2008). The TPB conceptual framework is used here with its five attitude-related variables: perceived usefulness, perceived ease of use, perceived risk, personal innovativeness, and trust. In addition, the TPB considers only beliefs that are specific to a given system and consequently provides more accurate information (Chuttur, 2009). The TPB takes into account the influence of the attitude variable, which could greatly affect system use (Yang & Yoo, 2003). Moreover, the proposed research model includes moderating socio-demographic variables as in the UTAUT model. In fact, some studies have shown that e-government users are generally men from urban areas with higher educational levels and higher incomes (Goldfinch et al., 2009). We expect that the effect of attitude on intention to use online government services outside the large urban centres is likely to be higher among citizens who are male, richer, more educated, employed, and younger. The joint use of UTAUT and TPB should provide explanatory factors for the user's intention to use a technological application as well as for subsequent behavior.

Our research model (see Figure 1) integrates the assumptions of those two theoretical models, namely the TPB and the UTAUT. Hence, based on the TPB model, an individual's attitude toward a new technology greatly impacts the intention to use this technology. The TPB also assumes that an individual's attitude is enhanced by a group of perceptual variables (Hung et al., 2006; 2009). If the usefulness of a new technology is reinforced in the mindset of potential users, they should then adopt a more positive attitude towards this technology. Usefulness is assessed in terms of expected performance, productivity, effectiveness, and effort and time savings. In addition to its usefulness, a technology must be easy to use. Hence, the ease of use variable is included in our model. If potential users perceive easiness in the use, the handling, and the mastery of the different features of a new technology, they should then develop a more favourable attitude towards this technology. Nevertheless, the adoption of any new technology should not be risky, and the technology should be trusted. Hence, our model stresses that higher levels of perceived risk could produce a more negative attitude towards e-government. Risk

Figure 1. Conceptual framework

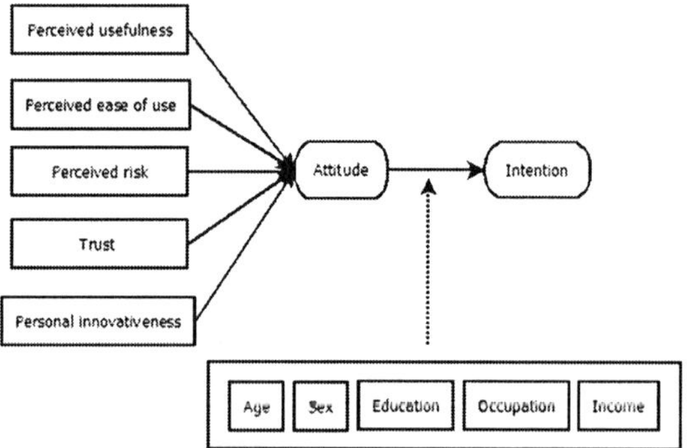

is associated with any perceived loss or mistake due to the use of a new technology.

Trust is the perceived degree of reliability of the technology. If trust in a technology increases, the attitude toward adoption of this technology is more positive. Finally, we assume that any increase in personal innovativeness would result in more positive attitudes toward e-government. Innovativeness is related to a person's willingness to try new things and be challenged by ambiguities and unsolved problems and to preference for originality in thoughts and behaviour (Hung et al., 2006).

The identified assumptions led us to propose six research hypotheses:

H1: *Perceived usefulness* increases positive *attitude.*
H2: *Perceived ease of use* increases positive *attitude.*
H3: *Perceived risk* increases negative *attitude.*
H4: *Trust* increases positive *attitude.*
H5: *Personal innovativeness* increases positive *attitude.*
H6: Positive *attitude* increases *intention.*

In addition to the six research hypotheses, we identified five socio-demographic variables for moderating the interactive effects between attitudinal variables and adoption of e-government services. Compared to the model of While Lean et al. (2009) that included gender and age in their conceptualization, we added three dimensions related to educational level, occupation (or not), and income:

- The influence of positive *attitude* on *intention* decreases when *age* increases.
- The influence of positive *attitude* on *intention* is higher among men.
- The influence of positive *attitude* on *intention* is higher among university degree holders.
- The influence of positive *attitude* on *intention* is higher among job holders.
- The influence of positive *attitude* on *intention* decreases when *income* increases.

The data collection was based on a survey using codified questionnaires filled out by 1,587 citizens in four regions of the province of Quebec (Canada): Côte-Nord, Saguenay-Lac-Saint-Jean, Abitibi-Témiscamingue, and Bas-St-Laurent. Participants were Quebecers over 18 years old. Respondents were questioned via web and phone surveys and were randomly picked from a nationwide database. The period of the field research lasted from January through May 2011. To stimulate responses, a reminder was sent out 2 weeks later by e-mail or by a phone call. The response rate was 40%. Table 1 summarizes the sample profile by region.

View of Government Managers

In this part of the research, we focused on the study of para-public agencies such as municipalities, local libraries, local health care agencies, transportation, and environmental protection. This focus had two main aspects. The first one was that government services were not limited to central government services but to all other agencies that provided services to citizens. The second was that the government of the province of Quebec had already collected data on the use of central government services in outlying regions.

This part of the study was designed to capture the perception of government's managers on use and adoption of electronic government services by citizens (Ramlah et al., 2010). A qualitative approach was adopted to understand the existing processes, relationships, and practices that might hinder adoption of online services in outlying regions.

A questionnaire was used to conduct 37 interviews in four remote areas of Quebec: Bas St. Laurent, Saguenay-Lac-Saint-Jean, Côte-Nord, and Abitibi-Témiscamingue. The Government of Quebec has made the choice of the four regions

Table 1. Sample profile by region

Usage	Region				
Frequency Row percentage	Bas St-Laurent	Saguenay	Abitibi	Côte Nord	Total
Non-users	234 30.12	293 37.71	149 19.18	101 13.00	777
Users	237 29.26	291 35.93	172 21.23	110 13.58	810
Total	471	584	321	211	1587

to be studied. It considers that these regions are representative of the outlying regions in Quebec. In addition, the research team has the choice to determine the managers to be interviewed in each region. To this end, the research team studied over 400 regional websites. These websites were categorized by the domain activities of their agencies. The research team contacted the IT government leaders of each region. The research team and the IT leaders, based on the 400 identified websites, decided on the agencies to be interviewed. The IT leaders adviced the choice based on the experience of each agency to develop electronic services for citizens.

The interviews were face-to-face and conducted individually. The managers who had been interviewed were those who were in contact with citizens for the development of e-government services. Confidentiality of the respondent's identity and remarks was guaranteed. The questionnaire had three parts. In the first part, we tried to understand the current online services provided to citizens and the factors that made citizens use, rarely use, or not use each service. In the second part, we tried to understand the services that citizens would like to have, but were not provided. In the third part, we tried to understand the barriers that hindered local organizations in providing these expected services to citizens. These barriers were addressed at different levels: organizational, financial, technological, social, and psychological. Finally, real-life cases from the experience of the managers were documented. Figure 2 illustrates the barriers investigated by this study.

4. RESULTS

As shown in Table 2, users of electronic government in outlying regions are educated, men aged between 35-54 years, attending or graduated from universities. Moreover, the proportion of users of electronic government services increases as income rises. Finally, there are more users among job holders than jobless respondents. These results show a strong effect of socio-demographic variables on e-government use, and this effect may in and of itself account for the lower adoption rates in rural areas.

Citizens' Views

Data analysis was conducted in three stages. The first stage was a multinomial regression to validate our hypothesis regarding determinants of attitude. In the second stage, a Student t test was conducted in order to assess the influence of attitude on intention to use e-government services. This test

Figure 2. Barriers in outlying regions e-government services in outlying regions

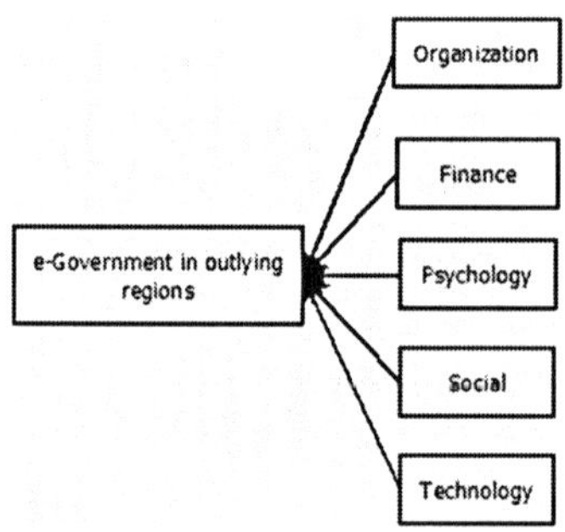

Table 2. Socio demographic variables of users of e-government services

Users of E-Government Services – Gender	
Men	43,16%
Women	56,84%
Users of E-Government Services – Education Level	
People attending or graduated from universities	26%
College level	32%
Primary/secondary level	42%
Users of E-Government Services –Age Group	
Under 34	25,66%
35-54 years	40,76%
Over 55 years	33,58%
Users of E-Government Services – Annual Income	
Less than $39,000CAD	27,85%
Between $40,000 and $79,000CAD	35,16%
Over $80,000CAD	20,54%
Not declared	16,45
Users of E-Government Services – Job Holding or Not	
Job holders	55,16%
Jobless respondents	44,84%

was a uni-variate exploratory analysis that aimed to construct a causal model that would be adapted to outlying regions. The third stage involved using a structural equation model (SEM) to conduct a multivariate analysis to confirm the effects of attitudinal factors on intention to use e-government services and to determine whether the theoretical model would fit our data.

Validation of the Determinants of Attitude

In order to study the relationship between continuous variables, the Pearson correlation (*r*) was calculated. Correlation analysis would allow us to measure the linear link between attitude and other independent variables, i.e., perceived usefulness, perceived ease of use, perceived risk, and trust. The independent variable personal innovativeness was dropped from the basic model because of its limited Cronbach alpha that scored under the 0.6 threshold. As stated in Table 3, all variables were significant at the .01 threshold. Attitude positively correlated with perceived usefulness, perceived ease of use, and trust. Attitude negatively correlated with perceived risk. Perceived risk is the most influent variable on attitude of citizens towards e-government.

Afterwards, a multivariate analysis of concurrent effects exerted by multiple independent variables on attitude was conducted as follows:

$$\text{Attitude} = \beta 0 + \beta 1 \text{ (usefulness)} + \beta 2 \text{ (ease of use)} + \beta 3 \text{ (Risk)} + \beta 4 \text{ (trust)} + \epsilon$$

The variation of attitude was predicted by computing the correlations between independent variables. Table 4 provides the estimates of β parameters for each independent variable. The results show that all these variables were significant. Therefore the research hypotheses were supported by these results. While perceived usefulness, perceived ease of use and trust in government services stimulate the use of e-government services, perceived risk hinders its use by citizens in outlying regions.

Validation Procedure of the Determinants of Intention

The second stage of our research model involved using a student t test to study the effect of Attitude on Intention. The results showed that Attitude had a significant influence on intention to use e-government services. In Table 5, the mean score of Attitude among citizens who intended to use e-government was significantly higher than the mean score for citizens with no intention to use this technology (2.81 vs 3.89).

However, with regard to the moderating effects exerted by socio-demographic variables, the analysis showed that none of these variables had a significant influence on the causal relationships between intention and independent variables.

Table 3. Pearson coefficients

	Attitude
Perceived usefulness	**0.59609**
Perceived ease of use	**0.58361**
Perceived risk	**-0.58570**
Trust	**0.61823**

Table 4. Estimates of parameters

Variable	Estimate of parameters	*t* value	Threshold
β0	1.84912	15.43	<.0001
Perceived usefulness (β_1)	0.25871	10.87	<.0001
Perceived ease of use (β_2)	0.22656	10.46	<.0001
Perceived risk (β_3)	-0.31300	-14.91	<.0001
Trust (β_4)	0.17987	7.16	<.0001

Table 5. Attitude and intention

Intention	N	Mean	Standard deviation
NO	708	2.8145	0.8889
YES	820	3.8880	0.8259
Diff (1-2)		-1.0735	0.8557
Method	Variances	t value	Pr > |t|
Pooled	Equal	-24.45	<.0001

Consequently, there was no support for our hypotheses on socio-demographic effects.

Finally, a SEM analysis was conducted in order to confirm the subsequent causal effects between attitude-related variables and intention as represented in Figure 3. The results of SEM analysis showed that the model did not fit our data. The *p-value* of the test was under 0.5.

Structural Equation Modeling

See Figure 3 for a theoretical model.

Government's Managers' View

The study was conducted in the same regions as for the citizens' views. The objective was to understand the adoption of government electronic services by citizens. We present in what follows a preliminary findings of these interviews. The detailed analysis of these interviews will be presented in future works.

From a first analysis of the interviews, four major categories of concern for the development of e-government services were identified: organizational, financial, technological, and digital divide. For each category, a set of problems were exposed by the interviewees (see Table 6). They are presented hereafter.

At the organizational level, six main problems were identified: cooperation, graphical user interface management, reluctance to change, communication tools, online tracking changes, and availability of IT human resources. Cooperation refers to the cooperation that takes place between service providers. The managers state that citizens are not always served in the same way by the same organization. Sometimes, they are satisfied with the service they receive electronically and in other times they are not. For the managers, this problem is due to a lack of cooperation inside the same organization. The second problem was related to the graphical user interface management. Several interviewees pointed to the complexity of the graphical user interfaces and the frequent changes to the online portals. These changes are not always to manage within the organization since they sometimes require skills that are not available in the organization. In addition, these complex graphical interfaces do not encourage citizens to navigate on the agency website and consequently prevent citizens from using electronic services. The third problem was reluctance to change. Some online initiatives led to increased stress levels within the organization. This stress make employees reluctant to any change because they will be generally added new tasks (e.g.,

Figure 3. Theoretical model

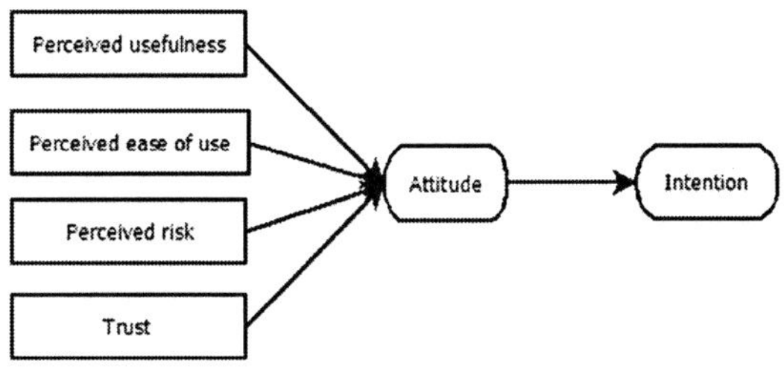

Table 6. Overview of barriers to adoption of e-government services in outlying regions

Digital Divide	Demographic
	Social
	Psychology
Technology	Internet Access
	Ignorance of the computer tools
Finance	Public organism
	Para-public organism
Organization	Cooperation
	Interface management
	Change reluctance
	Communication tools
	Services modification
	Human resources

server administration, web site updating). The fourth problem is related to communication tools. The communication tools refer to the use of social media as a new mean of communication between government agencies and citizens. Public organizations think that these new communication means will make citizens closer to government's agencies. However, government's employees think that they are not well formed to use these new means to exchange with citizens. The fifth problem is related to the tracking of online requests. Government managers expressed the difficulties they have when trying to track an online request. In general, they seem to be tossed back and forth between different services because there was not enough information sharing between the different authorities. The last problem area was the availability of IT human resources. The lack of such specialized staff in rural regions made e-government services more costly.

Financially, the barrier was at two levels. First, the GSEs (government-sponsored enterprises) lacked funding to acquire technical and human resources. These organizations had a role to help citizens become familiar with the use of online services. Second, public organizations had trouble securing additional funding for new online services even though the new services met an expressed need. Thus, very few jobs were created only for the development of online services. These services were instead combined with or added to existing administrative duties.

The third major barrier was technology. Many citizens did not have access to technology or equipment. In all regions, the lack of computer knowledge and of high-speed Internet access in remote areas made it even harder to adopt and use online services. Internet access was more expensive in outlying regions, particularly in rural areas where high-speed Internet was still often unavailable. Moreover, given the vast geographical distances between rural and urban centres, Internet access was not possible for everyone. In some villages, the Internet was only available in libraries. All of these technological barriers excluded a significant portion of the rural population to use electronic services.

The last identified barrier was the digital divide. This barrier had three sub-barriers: demographic, social, and psychological. Demographically, outlying regions suffered from an aging population and youth migration to urban centres. Some managers specifically pointed out that the mean age was older in their local area than in the rest of Quebec. Older people sometimes lacked the skills and technology for access to online services. Socially, outlying regions suffered from a high rate of functional illiteracy. This handicap limited one's ability to understand and use of online services, both the elderly and the young being affected. The school dropout rate was another significant barrier to use of e-government. Expansion of online government services was likely to increase exclusion of this demographic range, thus contributing to further marginalization. Without training in the use of computer technology, there would be a growing number of people with low literacy. Most managers stressed the need to assist this population because of the above-mentioned exogenous factors. Finally, on a psychological level, there was reluctance to use online services because of ignorance of the Internet and how to use it. According to the interviews, the perceived insecurity of Internet access was a barrier to appropriation of ICTs.

In addition to these main barriers, that were shared by quasi all interviewees, other issues were raised by government managers. The first issue was security. People did not believe in the security of Internet transactions. The security risks included identity theft, viruses, hacking of financial accounts, invasion of privacy, and loss of confidentiality. In addition, online services were seen as a potential loss of human contact. Indeed, people feared losing their local services and seeing them replaced with dehumanizing online services. They equated online services with closure of regional offices where they could see and meet government managers, talk about their problems in person, discuss face-to-face, feel listened to and, therefore, receive an appropriate service that met their needs.

Even if the citizens' view has showed that the attitude has an important influence on the adoption of online services, we found that the managers' view confirms what the citizens' think. Consequently, we can conclude that if government's officials consider the common points between citizen's view and managers' view, the adoption of online services should improve. In addition, the managers' view provided elements that are specific to the outlying regions. They mainly pointed to the lack of skilled human resources in outlying regions, the lack of financial resources to the development of online services, and finally the digital divide between outlying regions and central cities. Even if these barriers may be found in central cities but they are not as important as the outlying regions.

CONCLUSION

This chapter presented two field studies that aimed to understand the barriers that discourage citizens in outlying regions from adopting government electronic services. The first study focused on citizens' views and the second study focused on the views of government managers on the adoption of government's electronic services. The novelty of this study is that it examined adoption not only from the point of view of citizens but also from the perception of the government managers.

From the point of view of citizens, four predictors were shown to be significant in this study: perceived usefulness, perceived ease of use, perceived risk, and trust. The usefulness of public online services was perceived in terms of commodity, flexibility, rapidity, mobility, learning and better follow-up of communications and transactions with government bodies. The ease of use was expressed as the comprehensibility and readability of the content as well as proper organization of the information. The perceived risk concerned the security of online transactions with public administration along with the imperfections of the technology (bugs, viruses, and break). Finally, trust in e-government services increased with reliability of information to users. These results indicate that if governments wish to develop strategies to increase e-services use in outlying regions, they must focus on changing the citizens' perceptions along these four variables. These strategies could be, for instance, communication plans to explain the safety of online services, or interface redesign to improve ease of use.

In the second part of our study, government managers provided their perception of the factors that may hinder citizens in outlying regions from using government's electronic services. Four factors were identified: organizational, financial, technological, and the digital divide. The organizational category encompassed six problem areas: cooperation, graphical user interface management, reluctance to change, communication tools, online tracking changes, and availability of IT human resources. Financially, there were two major problems. First, government-sponsored enterprises lacked funding to acquire technical and human resources, and second, public organizations had trouble securing additional funding for new online services even though the new services met an expressed need. From the point of view of technology, many citizens did not have access to technology or equipment. Finally, the digital divide raised three issues that are demographic, social, and psychological in nature.

Several issues remain to be investigated in future research. First, this study did not include other factors than those related to attitudes that may impact on citizen's adoption of e-government services. It is possible, for instance, that variables related to social and cultural particularities in non-urban areas would also have an influence on online service use. Second, the results have to be deepened by including other factors from the TPB model, for example those related to subjective norms and perceived control of behavior. Third, this research studied adoption of e-government services by current users of e-government. This study can be extended to study the limits and problems of appropriation in non-users. Fourth, with regard to the limitations identified from the government officials' point of view, the government has to identify the best approach to communicate with citizens and to structure delivery of regional online services. Finally, more research is required to identify appropriate or effective government strategies to encourage use in outlying regions, for instance the deployment of social media technologies to promote and inform citizens on available online services.

REFERENCES

Bertot, J. C., & Jaeger, P. T. (2008). The E-Government paradox: Better customer service doesn't necessarily cost less. *Government Information Quarterly*, *25*(2), 149–154. doi:10.1016/j.giq.2007.10.002.

Canada, S. (2010). Enquête canadienne sur l'utilisation d'Internet 2010. Retrieved May 29, 2012, from www.statcan.gc.ca/daily-quotidien/110525/dq110525b-fra.htm

Carter, L., & Bélanger, F. (2005). The utilization of e-government services: Citizen trust, innovation and acceptance factors. *Information Systems Journal*, *15*(1), 5–25. doi:10.1111/j.1365-2575.2005.00183.x.

Carter, L., & Weerakkody, V. (2008). E-government adoption: A cultural comparison. *Information Systems Frontiers*, *10*(4), 473–482. doi:10.1007/s10796-008-9103-6.

Chuttur, M. Y. (2009). Overview of the technology acceptance model: Origins, developments, and future directions. *Working papers on Information Systems*, *9*(37), 1-21.

Edmiston, K. D. (2003). State and local e-government: Prospects and challenges. *American Review of Public Administration*, *33*(1), 20–45. doi:10.1177/0275074002250255.

Erwin, G. J., & Taylor, W. J. (2004). Social appropriation of internet technology: A South African platform. *The Journal of Community Informatics*, *1*(1), 21–29.

Fagan, M. H. (2006). Exploring city, county and state e-government initiatives: An East Texas perspective. *Business Process Management Journal*, *12*(1), 101–112. doi:10.1108/14637150610643797.

Goldfinch, S., Gauld, R., & Herbison, P. (2009). The participation divide? Political participation, trust in government, and e-government in Australia and New Zealand. *Australian Journal of Public Administration*, *68*(3), 333–350. doi:10.1111/j.1467-8500.2009.00643.x.

Hard, M. (1998). German regulation: The integration of modern technology into national culture. In Hard, M., & Jamison, A. (Eds.), *In Intellectual appropriation of technology, discourse on modernity* (pp. 33–68). M.I.T press.

Horst, M., Kuttschreuter, M., & Gutteling, J. M. (2007). Perceived usefulness, personal experiences, risk perception and trust as determinants of adoption of e-government services. *Computers in Human Behavior*, *23*(4), 1838–1852. doi:10.1016/j.chb.2005.11.003.

Huang, Z. (2007). A comprehensive analysis of U.S. counties' e-Government portals: Development status and functionalities. *European Journal of Information Systems*, *16*(2), 149–164. doi:10.1057/palgrave.ejis.3000675.

Hung, S.-Y., Chang, C.-M., & Yu, T. (2006). Determinants of user acceptance of the e-Government services: The case of online tax filing and payment system. *Government Information Quarterly*, *23*(1), 97–122. doi:10.1016/j.giq.2005.11.005.

Hung, S.-Y., Tang, K.-Z., Chang, C.-M., & Ke, C.-D. (2009). User acceptance of intergovernmental services: An example of electronic document management system. *Government Information Quarterly*, *26*(2), 387–397. doi:10.1016/j.giq.2008.07.003.

Lean, O., Zailani, S., Ramayah, T., & Fernando, Y. (2009). Factors influencing intention to use e-government services among citizens in Malaysia. *International Journal of Information Management*, *29*(6), 458–475. doi:10.1016/j.ijinfomgt.2009.03.012.

Leaning, M. (2005). The modal nature of ICT: Challenging historical interpretation of the social understanding and appropriation of ICT. *The Journal of Community Informatics*, *2*(1), 35–42.

Moon, M. J. (2002). The evolution of E-government among municipalities: Rhetoric or reality? *Public Administration Review*, *62*(4), 424–433. doi:10.1111/0033-3352.00196.

Nam, T., & Sayogo, D. S. (2011). Who uses e-government?: Examining the digital divide in e-government use. In E. Estevez & M. Jansen (Ed.), *Proceedings of the 5th International Conference on Theory and Practice of Electronic Governance*. Tallinn, Estonia.

Previtali, P., & Bof, F. (2009). E-government adoption in small Italian municipalities. *International Journal of Public Sector Management*, *22*(4), 338–348. doi:10.1108/09513550910961619.

Rallet, A., & Rochelandet, F. (2004). La fracture numérique: Une faille sans fondement? *Réseaux*, 2004/5, *127*(128), 19-54.

Ramlah, H., Norshidah, M., Ahlan, A. R., & Mahmud, M. (2010). E-government application: An integrated model on G2C adoption of online tax. *Transforming Government: People. Process and Policy*, *5*(3), 225–248.

Reddick, C., & Frank, H. (2007). The perceived impacts of e-government on U.S. cities: A survey of Florida and Texas City managers. *Government Information Quarterly*, *24*(3), 576–594. doi:10.1016/j.giq.2006.09.004.

Rogers, E. M. (2003). *Diffusion of Innovations* (5th ed.). New York: The Free Press.

Ullmann, C. (2006). *Les politiques regionales a l'epreuve du developpement numérique: Enjeux, strategie et impacts*. (Doctoral dissertation). In Institut de Géographie, Université Paris 1 Panthéon Sorbonne: Paris.

van Dijk, J., Peters, O., & Ebbers, W. (2008). Explaining the acceptance and use of government Internet services: A multivariate analysis of 2006 survey data in the Netherlands. *Government Information Quarterly*, *25*(3), 379–399. doi:10.1016/j.giq.2007.09.006.

Venkatesh, V., Morris, G. M., Davis, G. B., & Davis, F. D. (2003). User acceptance of information technology: Toward a unified view. *Management Information Systems Quarterly*, *27*(3), 425–478.

Yang, H. D., & Yoo, Y. (2003). It's all about attitude: Revisiting the technology acceptance model. *Decision Support Systems*, *38*(1), 19–31. doi:10.1016/S0167-9236(03)00062-9.

ADDITIONAL READING

Bagozzi, R. P. (2007). The legacy of the technology acceptance model and a proposal for a paradigm shift. *Journal of the Association for Information Systems*, *8*(4), 244–254.

Bélanger, F., Hiller, J., & Smith, W. (2002). Trustworthiness in electronic commerce: The role of privacy, security, and sites attributes. *The Journal of Strategic Information Systems*, *11*(3-4), 245–270. doi:10.1016/S0963-8687(02)00018-5.

Chourabi, H., & Mellouli, S. (2011). E-government: Integrated services framework. In S. Ae Chun, L. Luna-Reyes, & V. Atluri (Eds.), *12th Annual conference on Digital Government Research (dg.o 2011)* (pp. 36-44). University of Maryland.

Dadashzadeh, M. (2010). Social media in government: From egovernment to egovernance. *Journal of Business & Economics Research*, *8*(11).

Davis, F. (1989). Perceived usefulness, perceived ease of use, and user acceptance of information technology. *Management Information Systems*, *13*(3), 319–340. doi:10.2307/249008.

Ebbers, W. E., Pieterson, W. J., & Noordman, H. N. (2008). Electronic government: Rethinking channel management strategies. *Government Information Quarterly*, *25*(2), 181–201. doi:10.1016/j.giq.2006.11.003.

Evans, D., & Yen, D. C. (2006). E-government: Evolving relationship of citizens and government, domestic, and international development. *Government Information Quarterly*, *23*(2), 207–235. doi:10.1016/j.giq.2005.11.004.

Kaylor, C., Deshazo, R., & Van Eck, D. (2001). Gauging e-government: A report on implementating services among American cities. *Government Information Quarterly*, *18*(4), 293–307. doi:10.1016/S0740-624X(01)00089-2.

Layne, K., & Lee, J. (2001). Developing fully functional e-government: A four stage model. *Government Information Quarterly*, *18*(4), 122–136. doi:10.1016/S0740-624X(01)00066-1.

Norris, D., & Moon, J. (2005). Advancing e-government at the grassroots: Tortoise or hare? *Public Administration Review*, *65*(1), 64–75. doi:10.1111/j.1540-6210.2005.00431.x.

Reddick, C. (2004). A two-stage model of e-government growth: Theories and empirical evidence for U.S. Cities. *Government Information Quarterly*, *21*(1), 51–64. doi:10.1016/j.giq.2003.11.004.

Tassabehji, R., Elliman, T., & Mellor, J. (2007). Generating citizen trust in e-government security: Challenging perceptions. *Complete Collection of IGP Information Technology Case Collection Depository*, *3*(3), 1–17.

Tat-Kei, H. A. (2002). Reinventing local governments and the e-government initiative. *Public Administration Review*, *62*(4), 433–444.

Thomas, J. C., & Streib, G. (2003). The new face of government: Citizen-initiated contacts in the era of e-government. *Journal of Public Administration: Research and Theory*, *13*(1), 83–102. doi:10.1093/jpart/mug010.

Verdegem, P., & Verleye, G. (2009). User-centered e-government in practice: A comprehensive model for measuring user satisfaction. *Government Information Quarterly*, *26*(3), 487–497. doi:10.1016/j.giq.2009.03.005.

KEY TERMS AND DEFINITIONS

Canada: The current study is conducted in Canada.

Citizens' View: The study presents the citizens' point of view with regard to the adoption of electronic services.

E-Government: This study is related to e-government in general.

Electronic Services: The paper is about the adoption of electronic services by citizens living in outlying regions.

Managers' View: The study presents the government's managers point of view with regard to electronic services adoption by citizens.

Outlying Regions: This study is specific to the outlying regions.

Theoretical Models: Two theoretical models proposed in the study, which are extended to outlying regions.

Chapter 2
Enhancing Information Services through Public–Private Partnerships:
Information Technology Knowledge Transfer Underlying Structures to Develop Shared Services in the U.S. and Korea

Seok-Jin Eom
Seoul National University, Korea

Jane E. Fountain
National Center for Digital Government, USA & University of Massachusetts Amherst, USA

ABSTRACT

What are e-government success factors for using public-private partnerships to enhance learning and capacity development? To examine this question, the authors developed a comparative case analysis of the development of the Business Reference Model (BRM), a national-level e-government initiative to promote shared information services, in the U.S. federal government and the Korean central government. The results indicate institutional arrangements deeply affect the outcomes of knowledge transfer. The study shows that private sector partners in both countries played various roles as "brokers" of information technology (IT) knowledge between government and the private sector by: raising awareness of the necessity of the BRM; providing best practices; developing pilot projects; and developing implementation strategies. However, the study finds that the two countries took entirely different approaches to working with non-governmental organizations in BRM development with implications for project success and lessons for e-government success. The study is meant to deepen understanding of the embeddedness of public-private partnerships in institutional contexts and the implications of such institutional arrangements for knowledge sharing on e-government success. The study examines knowledge transfer in the context of similarities and differences in partnership structures across two advanced industrialized countries with leading roles in e-governance.

DOI: 10.4018/978-1-4666-4173-0.ch002

Copyright © 2013, IGI Global. Copying or distributing in print or electronic forms without written permission of IGI Global is prohibited.

INTRODUCTION

Public-private partnerships (PPPs) are a vital driver of e-government success. Practitioners require knowledge concerning how to develop and sustain successful PPPs to develop e-government. Researchers require knowledge about the underlying characteristics that lead to success or failure of PPPs in e-government development. Thus, this chapter examines the following types of questions: How do government agencies learn from non-governmental organizations in their quest for e-government success?[1] More specifically, how do governments adopt and adapt policies, practices and knowledge from non-governmental sectors? How do federal governments develop inter-organizational relationships across sectors (public, private and non-profit) to enhance and speed learning and development of new e-government capacity? How do countries differ in their approaches to these challenges?

As an effective way of developing government IT capacity with relationship to private actors, public-private partnerships (PPPs) have been paid attention to not only by government practitioners but also by academic researchers. In e-government developments, PPPs have become an accepted management practice as a large percentage of IS/IT projects have been outsourced (Swar et al., 2012; Currie, 1996). Therefore, various PPP measures of effectiveness such as active communication with e-government users, strategic IS/IT partnerships with various IS/IT experts, and effective outsourcing management have been recommended as key success factors for e-government building by IS/IT project management tools for public agencies (Gil-Garcia & Pardo, 2005). With these trends in practice, recent research has enhanced our understanding of the activities of private firms in providing information services and building e-government (Fountain, 2007; 2001; Dunleavy et al., 2006; Yildiz, 2004; Margetts, 1999). More specifically, a stream of research has developed on the key dimensions of IS/IT outsourcing and the determinants of effective relationships for IS/IT outsourcing success in the public sector (Swar et al., 2012; Moon et al., 2007; Van Der Wal et al., 2006).

However, we argue that research on PPPs in public sector, and specifically for e-government, remains under produced. It is difficult to find prescriptive recommendations for e-government practitioners on IS/IT outsourcing (Lin et al., 2007; Moon et al., 2007). Moreover, close analysis of the concrete activities of private partners and their interactions with government organizations over time remains insufficiently examined. In spite of the prevalence of such practices across governments, little cross-national comparative research on these questions has been undertaken in spite of the fact that different central governments have institutionalized different types of public-private partnerships.

In order to shed light on these issues and to overcome some of the limitations of previous research, the authors developed two detailed case studies to examine inter-organizational developments across sectors, including and moving beyond PPPs. The empirical setting for the two case studies includes the agencies and other organizations central to the development of the Business Reference Model (BRM) in the federal government of the U.S. and the central government of Korea. The BRM, one of the national e-government initiatives in both countries, is a means to develop shared definitions of data across government programs and agencies. A "dictionary" of sorts is created that can then serve the needs of different agencies thereby making shared data and shared, interactive services for civic engagement possible. Private firms spent about a decade developing BRMs for use in the private sector. The U.S. and Korean governments sought to learn from these firms in order to move quickly to develop core capacity to support new shared services for civil society. The BRM is "invisible" to most citizens and clients of e-government, but its influence on the cost and effectiveness of shared services for civil society is a critical e-government success factor.

Primary data sources for this study include the results of face-to-face interviews with key managers and stakeholders from the core organizations involved in the development of the BRM in Washington, D.C. and Seoul. Moreover, the authors gathered and analyzed a wealth of archival information, including white papers, congressional testimony, policy reports, and other internal documents, to build a rich understanding of the network of public, private and non-profit organizations involved in each country and to examine the nature of the interactions among organizations in building the BRMs in each government. The case studies are illustrative and have not been selected to develop or test predictive theory.

The organization of this chapter is as follows. In the next section we briefly review theoretical concepts and previous research on PPPs in the areas of information services and e-government. In the third section, we sketch the development of the BRM initiatives in each government. In the fourth section, we analyze the PPPs that developed during the course of building BRMs centering on the identification and roles of private partners. Based on these analyses, in the final section we identify key similarities and differences between the two governments and discuss the implications of these findings for e-government success.

BACKGROUND

Public-private partnerships may be defined in various ways. By definition, they are organizational arrangements with a sector-crossing or sector-blurring character (Schuppert, 2011). They have been defined as combinations of government resources with those of private agents developed to achieve societal goals with an emphasis on resource mobilization (Skelcher, 2008). In this chapter, we define PPPs not only in terms of collaborative public service provision in the narrow sense, but also in terms of the range of cooperation among actors from public and private actors that can be brought to bear to increase the probability of success in e-government.

Public-Private Partnerships for Information Services and E-Government

According to Borzel and Risse (2005), the functions or the content of PPPs may be distinguished as follows: (1) consultation with and cooptation of private actors; (2) co-regulation of public and private actors; (3) delegation to private actors; and (4) private self-regulation in the shadow of hierarchy. The forms taken by PPPs also vary and include, for example, contracting-out of services, business management of public utilities, and the design of hybrid organizations for risk sharing and co-production between government and private agents. In general, PPP forms may be categorized into: (1) public leverage[2]; (2) contracting-out; (3) franchising; (4) joint ventures; and (5) strategic partnering (Skelcher, 2008).

For more than the past decade, PPPs have been popular as a 'new model of governance' and a key form of 'collaborative governance' (Peters & Pierre, 2000). Public administrators all over the world have sought to adopt PPPs in their government practice; using them has been considered a sign of a modernizing government (Schuppert, 2011). The major rationale for adopting PPPs rests on the benefits that are expected to arise from the combination of public and private resources deployed in pursuit of achieving public goals including improvements in efficiency, promotion of public participation, increasing competition for supplying public services, and enhancement of policymaking capacity. Notions of complementarity, synergy, and positive-sum outcomes between public and private sectors are key drivers

(Pierre & Peters, 2005; Salamon, 2002). In brief, the "theory" of PPPs is that capture of expertise and effective practices from multiple sectors will lead to improvements in governance. The theory has particular weight in e-government because of the rapidity of technological change and the presumed benefits of cross-sectoral knowledge transfer. The justification for examining PPPs in light of e-government success stems from the widespread adoption of this theory and from the ubiquity of PPPs in contemporary governments.

Public-private partnerships have been important as dependent and independent variables in research on information services and e-government. Researchers have tried to identify key participants in e-government policy not only from the public sector but also from the private sector. For example, Fountain (2007; 2001) examined bureaucratic politics in the course of building cross-agency government capacity and analyzed public participants and their interactions under a range of institutional and procedural constraints. A key project examined was Grants.gov, one of the major e-government initiatives of the Bush administration. Yildiz found that a variety of civic groups such as information technology (IT) companies, academia, and non-profit organizations (NPOs) play diverse and critical roles in building Turkish e-government (2004). Similarly, researchers have observed that public enterprises, quasi-governmental research institutes and university professors have participated in the development of Korean e-government policy alongside government agencies, IT firms, and NPOs (Song & Cho, 2007; Phang, 2002).

Some researchers have focused on the significance and influence of specific actors in the e-government development process. It has been argued that IT firms and business consultants have played critical roles in government IT adoption based on their IT knowledge and experiences which have been accumulated with diverse IT/IS projects in several countries including the U.S. and U.K. (Saint-Martin, 2005; 2004; Snellen, 2005; Dunleavy et al., 2006; Fountain, 2001; Margetts, 1999). In addition, a line of research notes that professional associations have played critical roles in the diffusion of IT systems in government. Professional associations have intermediated and coordinated the activities of a group of would-be adopters, have provided best practices, and have set the trends for IT adoption in government (Damsgaard & Lyytinen, 2001; Swan et al., 2000; 1999).

Other lines of research have focused on the status, rationales for and characteristics of government IS/IT outsourcing, a specific type of PPP. For example, Ni and Bretschneider (2007) found that the important factors affecting state-level contracting decisions on IT outsourcing are population size, market size, the competitiveness of the bidding process, the professional management of contracts, the partisan composition of legislatures, and political competition. Lacity and Willcocks (2000) surveyed 600 U.K. and U.S. CIOs to examine the proportion of outsourcing projects, satisfaction level with contractors' performance, and the types of IT outsourcing projects most frequently engaged in. Some scholars stress differences in the characteristics of IT outsourcing between the private and public sectors (Lin et al., 2007; Khalfan, 2004). It is argued that public IT managers should have a good understanding of these sectoral differences because public sector IT outsourcing projects differ systematically from those in the private sector (Swar et al., 2012).

Another important line of research on PPPs in e-government has focused on practical issues. Some studies have articulated key success factors for PPPs when used to improve information services (Institute for Public-Private Partnerships, 2009; Sharma, 2007; Langford & Roy, 2006; Chen & Perry, 2003; Langford & Harrison, 2001). It is argued that the major challenges of PPPs in this field are core partnering tasks including establishing a management framework for partnering; finding appropriate partners and making productive, feasible partnering arrangements; the management of relationships with partners in a network setting; and performance measurement of e-government partnerships (Institute for Public-Private Partnerships, 2009).

Previous research has increased understanding of the structure and behavior of PPPs in information services and e-government building. Nevertheless, some weaknesses can be pointed out as follows. First, several studies note that analysis of the concrete activities of private partners and their interactions with government actors remains insufficiently examined. For example, researchers lack detailed understanding of the specific knowledge on e-government and information services that has been delivered through PPPs and how the division of labor among various private partners has been organized. In particular, issues related to IT knowledge transfer from private to public sector through PPPs have not been fully examined although many government IT studies have noted the asymmetry of IT knowledge levels between public and private partners in building e-government (Dunleavy et al., 2006; Saint-Martin, 2005; Fountain, 2001).

Second, most previous research has focused on PPPs as instruments of implementation. Thus, the authors of this chapter argue that research should be expanded to the planning and policy formulation stages of e-government and IT policy because partnerships in these stages more strongly influence public information services than do partnerships during implementation. The PPPs in the planning and policy formulation stages affect overall orientations of IT projects and important issues such as who participates in policymaking and the contractual terms adopted for initiatives.

Lastly, a cross-national comparative perspective contributes to research because different countries have institutionalized different systems of PPPs (Borins, 2007; Skelcher, 2005; Fountain, 2003). For example, Dunleavy and colleagues (2006) showed that government-IT industry relations in seven developed countries differ based in part on the competition level in government IT contracting and the influence of large IT firms. Considering the importance of these differences for central governments, the authors argue that adopting a comparative perspective can contribute to a more generalized understanding of PPPs in shared information services and IT policy.

In order to fill these gaps, the authors compare the activities of private partners involved in the building of BRMs in the U.S. and Korean central governments. We seek to shed light on the following questions: Who were the private partners for the BRM initiatives in both countries? What activities were carried out by the private partners? What kinds of knowledge and information were transferred through the PPPs? What are the principal similarities and dissimilarities between the two cases, and what accounts for the differences? What lessons might be offered concerning e-government success from an examination of these experiences?

Knowledge Transfer between the Public and Private Sector

A critical argument for the use of PPPs in e-government is that multi-sectoral partnerships enhance effective transmission of knowledge to government from the private sector. Such transmission is critical to e-government success. The roles of knowledge for policy making are important and varied. To make policy, decision makers, including politicians and high-ranking public officials, rely heavily on ideas and knowledge (Rueschemeyer, 2006; Hall, 1989). In other words, ideas and knowledge matter because actors in the political arena act and play their roles based on their ideas and knowledge. It follows that new ideas and knowledge can cause a shift in the decision-making orientation of policy makers and political elites. And once institutionalized, their influence can be reinforced and strengthened over time (Fountain, 2011; Campbell, 2004).

More specifically, ideas and knowledge serve as a road map for actors in uncertain policy environments (Goldstein & Keohane, 1993). They help policy makers to define new policy problems and to determine which of many means will be used to reach desired goals. Moreover, they provide actors with strategies with which to achieve their policy objectives. In sum, ideas and knowledge guide behavior under conditions of uncertainty by delineating causal patterns or by providing compelling ethical or moral motivations for action (Sikkink, 1991).

Ideas and knowledge also matter because they influence formation of institutions and are embedded in institutional arrangements (Hall, 1993). Ideas and knowledge can serve as blueprints for designing organizations and institutions, the core elements for policy implementation. Furthermore, once they are institutionalized, ideas attract constituents who defend them if alternatives are suggested later (Thelen, 2004; Pierson, 2004; 2000; 1994). In other words, the implementation of policy based on specific ideas and knowledge may lead to long-lasting decision-making and institutional legacies that have more subtle, indirect, and self-reinforcing or path-dependent effects that constrain change later on (Campbell, 2004).

Thus, policy ideas and knowledge strongly influence development and implementation of public policy and building government policy capacity – and they play a distinct role in policy in digitally mediated environments. They can change policy orientations and provide new perspectives on social phenomena. In addition, organizations and institutions for policy implementation will be designed differently in different central governments in accordance with systematically different ideas and knowledge. Consequently, modern states have tried to promote increased use of social knowledge for government policy making (Rueschemeyer & Skocpol, 1996). On the one hand, modern states have tried to build strong government institutions concerned with producing their own policy knowledge, but on the other hand, modern states have vastly increased efforts to build institutions for importing social knowledge and have expanded their interactions with knowledge institutions in society including universities, think tanks, and professional groups.

Brokers play a key role in knowledge transfer. Ideas and knowledge for policy cannot be diffused and transferred to different sectors and policy areas automatically and smoothly (Meyer, 2010; Pawlowski & Robey, 2004). Contextual factors may prevent them from being diffused and transferred to other sectors. For example, knowledge produced in the private sector tends to be non-political, but the contexts of decision-making in the public sector, by definition, possess political characteristics. Thus, knowledge produced in the private sector is sometimes ill-suited for decision-making in the public sector. In addition, decentralization of decision-making and the biases produced through the professionalization of decision makers within organizations comprise other obstacles for knowledge transfer and diffusion. The more highly professionalized and decentralized organizations become, the more idiosyncratic the knowledge each organization requires for carrying out its functions (Hargadon, 2002).

These impediments to knowledge transfer mean that actors who carry or mediate policy knowledge are required for knowledge transfer from one realm or sector to another. Actors who play such a role are called "knowledge brokers" and are defined as "individuals or organizations who provide connections between communities of practice, transfer elements of knowledge and practice from one community to another, enable coordination, and through these activities can create new opportunities for learning"(Wenger, 1998, p. 109). In addition, these actors bridge different sectors and broker between different actors and organizations with respect to knowledge transfer. Through their brokering activities, different kinds of knowledge and ideas are linked and through various means transported from one ideational realm to another (Campbell, 2004; Brown & Duguid, 1998).

Restated, knowledge brokers perform the following activities (Meyer, 2010; Feldman & Khademian, 2007; Pawlowski & Robey, 2004): First, they are carriers of knowledge. They participate in multiple communities and transfer knowledge and practices from one community to another. Second, they are translators of knowledge. Language is embedded in situated action, thus the meanings of particular words and forms of speech emerge continuously within, but not necessarily between, communities of practice (Wenger, 1998). The process of translation involves framing the elements of one community's worldview in terms of that of another community. Third, they are synthesizers of the knowledge. Brokers combine and synthesize various kinds of knowledge produced and adopted in diverse communities and create new knowledge and new alternatives for their own organizations.

Scholars have found various knowledge brokers in their research fields. Campbell (2004) names expert advisors, MBAs, consultants, think tanks, business and trade associations, and epistemic communities as examples of brokers. Sheingate (2003) argues that the U.S. President and Congressmen have played the roles of knowledge brokers in the U.S. political system. Cox (2001) pointed out that the members of welfare policy committees played the role of knowledge brokers in the welfare policy process in European countries. More broadly, knowledge brokering has been identified as one of the essential elements of leadership for promoting participation and economic development in local governments (Gibney, 2011; Feldman & Khademian, 2007).

Institutions are critical as mediators of knowledge transfer. The diffusion and transfer of knowledge are constrained by institutional arrangements. The extent of diffusion, its speed and the probability of adoption of new knowledge are affected by institutional arrangements (Skocpol & Rueschmeyer, 1996). Moreover, the formal and informal institutional channels through which knowledge brokers gain access to decision makers mediate the effect that new programs have in influencing decision making and institutions (Hall, 1989). In sum, the degree to which ideas and knowledge affect the policy depends upon how they are embedded in surrounding institutions in the first place.

One example is the difference in the adoption of New Public Management (NPM) ideas in the U.K., Canada, and France. The core NPM ideas were adopted most widely and radically in the U.K because the prime minister at the time, who possessed strong institutionalized power, took the initiative to promote NPM reform in the U.K. By contrast, NPM proposals were initiated by congressional actors in Canada and by the central bureaucracy in France. In these countries, NPM proposals were not supported by institutionalized sources of power in the course of their adoption and spread (Saint-Martin, 2004).

Institutions facilitate or constrain the activities of knowledge brokers. Pawlowski and Robey (2004) argue that decentralization promotes knowledge brokering because it requires organizations to conduct more activities for coordination. This demands more information and knowledge about different organizations and their activities. Moreover, decentralized institutions allow knowledge brokers to behave more actively because institutional constraints on action are weaker in these contexts.

Finally, the question of who takes the role of knowledge broker is affected by institutional arrangements (Campbell, 2004). In some states, for example, policy relevant knowledge comes primarily from an echelon of permanent civil servants who have a virtual monopoly on access both to official information and to the ultimate decision makers. In others, a new administration can bring in its own advisers and consult widely with outside experts (Saint-Martin, 2005).

THE BUSINESS REFERENCE MODEL IN THE UNITED STATES AND KOREA[3]

Definitions and Purpose

The BRM is one of the reference models of the Federal Enterprise Architecture (FEA)[4] framework, one of the e-government initiatives of the George W. Bush administration in February 2002. The development of the BRM in the U.S. and Korea relied on extensive development and use of PPPs, thus the BRM provides an important case for understanding the role of PPPs in e-government success.

The EA approach seeks to build coherence and strategic connections across people, business processes, organizational complexity and technology, in short, across the "enterprise." According to the Institute for Enterprise Architecture Development, "Enterprise architecture frameworks consist of models intended to communicate, at a high level, the complexity and interdependencies of EA to a broad audience, while, at a low level, conveying requirements for complex system design" (quoted in Fountain, 2004). The EA approach is viewed in many central governments as a key underlying factor for success in e-government because it provides a foundation for coherent investment, effective communication of innovations across agencies and ministries, and forms the foundation for architectures to support robust shared services.

The EA approach began in the 1980s with a comprehensive framework developed at IBM by John Zachman. Since its inception, the EA has been used by large companies including General Motors, Volkswagen AG, and Barclays Bank (Fountain, 2004). This rapid adoption brought with it a rapidly growing consulting service market for EA in North America. Kennedy Information Inc. (2007), a market research firm focused on consulting services, found an acceleration in the number of projects to clean up – that is, to make more consistent -- IT architecture and infrastructure and predicted that enterprise architecture would be the fastest growing market in North America increasing from $.6 billion in 2005 to $1.1 billion in 2009 in the IT strategy and planning consulting marketplace.

What is the BRM as developed in U.S. federal e-government? It is part of a flexible architecture across the entire federal government meant to simplify service delivery by making it easier for agencies to collaborate across boundaries. Nested within enterprise architecture, it is defined as a "function-driven framework for describing the business operations of the federal government independent of the agencies that perform them and it provides an organized, hierarchical construct for describing the functions and day-to-day business operations of the federal government" (FEAPMO, 2002). The BRM describes the U.S. federal government's "lines of business," including operations and services for citizens independent of the agencies, bureaus and offices that perform them as illustrated in Figure 1. The first version of the BRM was made available by the Federal Enterprise Architecture Office in July 2002, and was subsequently revised and re-published in June 2003.

The U.S. Office of Management and Budget noted in 2002 that the BRM is beneficial as a means for agencies to identify opportunities to simplify processes. Key areas for collaboration across agencies include financial management, human resources management, public health monitoring, and data and statistics. Moreover, by following the BRM, performance measures, government initiatives, and government agencies can

Figure 1.

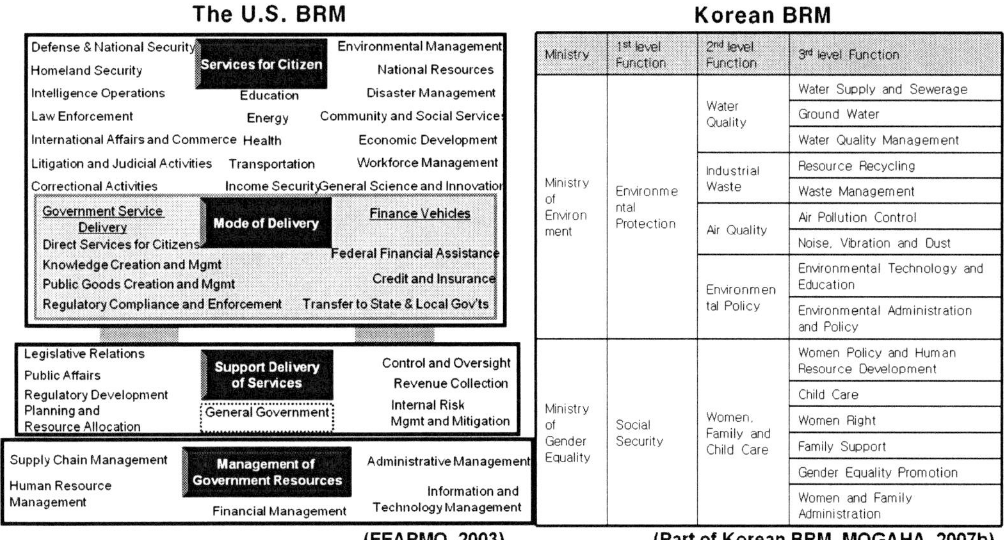

Ministry	1st level Function	2nd level Function	3rd level Function
Ministry of Environment	Environmental Protection	Water Quality	Water Supply and Sewerage
			Ground Water
			Water Quality Management
		Industrial Waste	Resource Recycling
			Waste Management
		Air Quality	Air Pollution Control
			Noise, Vibration and Dust
		Environmental Policy	Environmental Technology and Education
			Environmental Administration and Policy
Ministry of Gender Equality	Social Security	Women, Family and Child Care	Women Policy and Human Resource Development
			Child Care
			Women Right
			Family Support
			Gender Equality Promotion
			Women and Family Administration

(Part of Korean BRM, MOGAHA, 2007b)

be integrated as a single cross-agency initiative.[5] For example, the U.S. federal government launched major cross-agency initiatives in grant processes, benefits processing, surplus sales, e-rulemaking, and other major administrative processes. These benefits of the BRM make it possible for government agencies to provide citizens and public officials with enhanced shared information services across agencies by reducing redundancies and streamlining processes. By describing the federal government in terms of common business areas instead of taking a stove-piped, agency-by-agency view, the BRM promotes agency collaboration, data sharing and integrative services for citizens.

The conceptual example, illustrated in Figure 2, shows how a number of agencies related to the Border Control Initiative can categorize their data and collaborate in providing shared services and data sharing. The business reference model allows the agencies related to the initiative to easily identify by business process the "right" other agencies with whom to collaborate. Moreover, because the BRM is linked with the data reference model, a dictionary of sorts describing the data and information that support program and business line operations, agencies can easily find the data that they need to carry out their programs in other agencies. Consequently, the development of shared models of business processes and shared data dictionaries across agencies is meant to promote data sharing and shared information services among government agencies.

The Federal Enterprise Architecture approach, including the BRM, developed during the George W. Bush administration was benchmarked by the members of the administration of South Korean President Roh Moo-hyun as a template to develop a Korean BRM and 'Governmental Information Technology Architecture (GITA),' a Korean version of the FEA framework. The Korean BRM was officially selected as one of the 'core' e-government initiatives of the Roh administration in August 2003. Like the U.S. model, developers surveyed, categorized, and linked the functions of government agencies and collected feedback from agencies from August 2004 to November 2005. By October 2005, the BRM was used as a reference model for the government's IT architecture and was integrated into govern-

Figure 2.

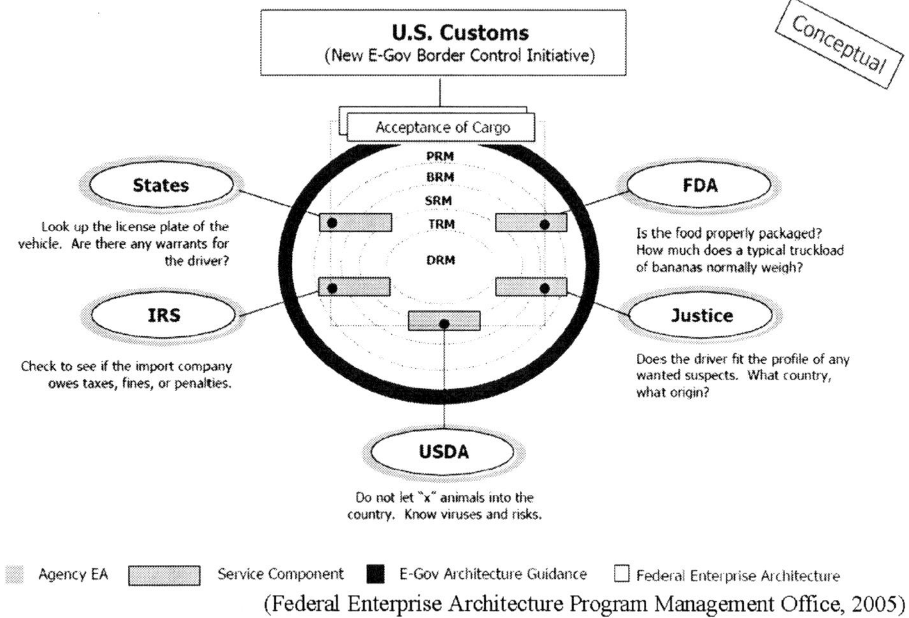

(Federal Enterprise Architecture Program Management Office, 2005)

ment-wide shared applications as the government's common categorization of administrative functions (PCGID, 2005, p. 205-211).

Early in the Roh administration, there were criticisms and concerns about redundancies in IT investments and the low efficacy of e-government systems in providing citizen-centric services and enhancing government performance. E-government systems built in a stove-piped manner with a low level of information sharing between e-government agencies were viewed as major causes of these problems. In seeking a way to redress these deficiencies, the Korean government viewed the U.S. enterprise architecture approach as a useful model, and the BRM was selected as one of the core e-government projects of the Roh administration (PCGID, 2005, p. 205-211).

For these reasons, the definition and purpose of the Korean BRM were similar to its U.S. counterpart. The Korean BRM was defined as "a government-wide functional map independent of government agencies for providing citizen-centric public services, driving government innovation and enhancing the effectiveness and efficiency of e-government" (PCGID, 2005, p. 205-211). The purpose of the Korean BRM was: (1) to promote government reform by identifying opportunities to simplify processes and to enhance the level of collaboration across agencies; (2) to reduce the redundancy of IT investments; and (3) to promote information-sharing and integrative information services for citizens with information systems linkage across agencies (MoGAHA, 2007a).

Differences between the U.S. and Korean Business Reference Models

Although both initiatives began with similar goals, and Korean policy makers followed the U.S. BRM model, project outcomes differed between the two governments. In terms of structure, the U.S. business reference model has a function-oriented structure, independent of federal agencies, as illustrated in Figure 1. The current U.S. BRM has a three-tiered hierarchical structure, consisting of four business areas, 39 lines of business, and 153 sub-functions (FEAPMO, 2003).

The Korean model, however, has an organization-oriented structure because the root category of the Korean BRM is the 'Ministry'. Furthermore, the levels of functions follow the organizational structure of the ministry. That is, the second-level of the Korean BRM consists of functions carried out by bureaus and offices, the higher-level organizations within a ministry. The third-level pertains to the functions of divisions, which represent lower-level organizations in a ministry (MoGAHA, 2007b).[6] Thus, when the initial organization in Korea was completed in August 2008, under these principles of functional categorization, the Korean BRM has a three-level hierarchical structure, containing 15 first-level functions, 67 second-level functions, and 491 third-level functions. The primary purpose of an enterprise approach, that is, to bring consistency and to reduce redundancy across ministries and programs was explicitly omitted from the Korean business reference model.

These differences between the core organizational structure in the U.S. and Korean BRMs led to a divergence in results and evaluations in the two governments. In the U.S. federal government, redundant IT initiatives could be identified and the level of information sharing among federal agencies was enhanced by using the BRM. For example, the U.S. Office of Management and Budget found that information systems which the Department of Education had tried to build provided services similar to those of the Grant.gov system, a government-wide IT system developed during the Bush administration following adoption of the BRM. As a result, OMB refused to allocate resources for the Department of Education system (OMB, 2002). Similarly, the Departments of Labor, Housing and Urban Development, and Education discovered through their use of the BRM that they provided similar job training programs for the unemployed. As a consequence, the three departments began to share information among themselves and coordinated the programs of each agency (Rocheleau, 2006, p. 148-155).

By contrast, the Korean design of the BRM limited the potential to develop government-wide management systems and thus did not provide the expected benefits. According to research conducted by the Korean Institute of Public Administration (KIPA) (2007, p. 123), a national think tank in public administration and policy, agency administrators were prevented from finding similar programs to collaborate with and from linking together government-wide programs and functions because the BRM had an organization-centric structure. In addition, the BRM was of little use in enhancing levels of information sharing due to its organization-centric structure. In brief, it was difficult for users to identify the functions and organizations in which information sharing was required for better performance and higher efficiency from use of the BRM.[7] For these reasons, public officials in e-government doubted the usefulness of the BRM. As a consequence, the Korean BRM has seldom been used in the Korean government.[8]

PUBLIC-PRIVATE PARTNERSHIPS AND THE BRM

Developments in the United States Federal Government

The Office of E-Government and IT (OEG), located within the U.S. Office of Management and Budget, assumed a leadership role for e-government building during the Bush administration as mandated by the E-Government Act of 2002 (EGA, Public Law 107-347) which prescribes the formal roles of federal agencies, resources, and their accountability for e-government building. The Act states that the OEG shall assist the Director of the OMB:

in carrying out (1) all functions of management and promotion of e-government services; (2) all of the functions assigned to the Director under federal management and promotion of electronic government services; and (3) other electronic government initiatives, consistent with other statutes.[9]

The E-Government Office institutionalized the following linkages with private partners. Inside OMB, contractors, consultants from major consulting firms, were hired to support e-government decision makers.[10] The consultants were all professionals with extensive expertise in IT, and many had MBA degrees. They supported "everything in the Office" directly and constantly with offices in neighboring rooms in order to maintain "symbiotic relations" with the government staff.[11] Some contractor groups carried out specific projects related to e-government programs, others supported high-ranking public officials with carrying out relatively general tasks such as gathering perspectives on e-government policy from diverse stakeholders, making and analyzing policy alternatives, providing statistics related to e-government initiatives and joining decision-making meetings.

For example, Tim Wang worked for the Office as a supporting contractor. He won an award as one of the '2007 Federal 100 Winners' from *Federal Computer Week*, a business newspaper, for his contributions to e-government development. The award focused on his critical role in the Office: "Tim Wang, principal consultant at SRA Touchstone Consulting Group, provided exceptional contractor support and continuity to the Office of Management and Budget's Office of E-Government and Information Technology during a time of high turnover among key portfolio managers. Wang has worked at OMB since 2003, when the e-government initiatives were new, and he has gathered a wide range of perspectives. Although the [portfolio] manager positions were empty, Wang attended all portfolio meetings so that he could relay important issues to senior OMB officials to keep the office running smoothly. Wang also volunteered his expertise to OMB officials who were updating OMB Circular A-11 to improve the federal budgeting process. (Circular A-11 is the primary guidance to federal agencies on the preparation, submission and execution of the U.S. federal budget.) Wang's efforts helped organize an annual flood of information from departments and agencies. Although contractors do as they are told, "consultants do that and then some," said Tim Young, associate administrator for e-government and IT at OMB." From the above, we get hints about the concrete activities of supporting contractors and the organizational mood of the Office.[12]

Outside the U.S. government, the Industry Advisory Council (IAC) has supported the E-Government Office. The IAC is a non-profit organization of about 400 IT companies. Its goal is to share professional experiences and information in order to promote communication, and increase the degree of trust in IT among public officials and entrepreneurs in the IT field.[13] The IAC provides its perspectives on "best practice" for IT adoption and IT governance in the private sector and research results, often business research, on e-government initiatives. Through its formation of Shared Interest Groups (SIGs), it has encouraged the consultants and researchers of private IT companies to draft working papers on e-government policy on topics of short- and long-term importance such as modification of IT adoption in the private sector, strategy and governance structures for e-government policy, and stakeholder and constituent reactions to current issues of e-government policy. These working papers are delivered to decision-makers in the Office of E-Government and IT and often referred to in the policy process.[14]

These two groups, supporting contractors and the IAC, were networked during the Bush Administration. For example, the consulting firms of the supporting contractors joined the IAC and actively participated in the Enterprise Architecture (EA) SIG, a research group focused on federal enterprise architecture formed by the IAC. In this group, supporting contractors and IAC member researchers had opportunities to discuss e-government initiatives and the FEA.[15] Furthermore, some of the U.S. Office of E-Government professional staff had previously worked for IT companies. For example, Mark Forman, the first Office of E-Government administrator, had previously worked for IBM, and Tim Young, an associate administrator, had previously worked for the Office of E-Government as a supporting contractor.

From the planning stage to adoption, supporting contractors were actively engaged in each stage of the development process.[16] First, they raised awareness of the necessity of the BRM. While they supported the OMB task force team whose main job was to make e-government strategy, supporting contractors argued that building "cross-agency" enterprise architecture would be one solution for the problems that U.S. e-government was facing at that time.

Second, supporting contractors contributed to development of a pilot BRM named 'An Integrated Government-wide Business Architecture' (OMB, 2002). This model was used by the task force to find linkages between agencies' functions and redundant IT investments in the federal government. For building the pilot BRM and making e-government strategy, supporting contractors adopted a modern e-strategy approach, a commercial practice.[17] In addition, they carried out an analysis of functions and of the status of IT in federal agencies, conducted surveys on the opinions of interested parties, developed a performance index of e-government initiatives, and provided policy alternatives, among other activities.

Third, private sector experts were involved in implementing the BRM projects and developed implementation strategies and feedback systems to enhance feasibility and institutionalization. They aided decision makers in OMB's E-Government Office by surveying public managers for their various perspectives on the BRM, finding solutions to problems, and monitoring the status of BRM development and implementation. They also supported establishment of guidelines for using the business reference model and federal enterprise architecture and provided federal agencies with case studies on BRM and FEA usage. In addition, they carried out projects for calculating the return on investment of the FEA initiatives.

They also joined in the development of the BRM and the FEA projects in other ways. For example, Booz Allen Hamilton carried out the projects for producing the following guidance documents: "Five Interrelated Reference Models to Facilitate Collaboration and Communication;" "Detailed guidance to help federal agencies comply with FEA requirements included in OMB Circular A-11;" and "The FEA Management System (FEAMS), an Internet-based EA tool to aid FEA analysis, maintenance, planning, and architecture development."[18]

The Industry Advisory Council was asked to research the FEA and the BRM by the OMB because large U.S. IT firms had accumulated knowledge over several years about the EA, in part through their experience in solving IT management challenges such as those that stemmed from Y2K.[19] To conduct the requested research the IAC formed the enterprise architecture special interest group in which more than 100 IT companies participated. Its ultimate goal was "to help government leaders develop approaches to address the challenges they face in delivering quality products and services to citizens." The EA SIG was meant to provide an objective, vendor-neutral and ethical forum to address enterprise architecture issues of common interest to government and industry.[20] As previously noted, the working papers produced by the EA SIG which contained their research findings were delivered to the OMB and referred to in building the government's business reference model and its federal enterprise architecture. The Industry Advisory Council also conducted research about implementing the BRM projects and developed implementation strategies and feedback systems. For example, the E-Government Office was provided with working papers outlining solutions to technical problems such as the linkage between the BRM and the budget process following the revision of OMB Circular A-11. The Industry Council's enterprise architecture group also created prototypes for the 'Enterprise Architecture Assessment Framework' for the E-Government Office.[21]

Developments in the Government of Korea

Since the Korean government started building e-government systems in earnest in the early 1990s, several laws have been enacted regarding the construction of e-government systems, with different rules giving authority for e-government promotion to different ministries (Yoo & Yoon, 2005; Phang, 2002). To resolve the conflicts that ensued from multiple jurisdictions exercising authority over e-government, the Korean government amended the Government Organization Act in 2004, adjusting government agency functions and authorities over e-government promotion. As a result of the amendments, the Korean Ministry of Government Administration and Home Affairs (MoGAHA) was put in charge of e-government promotion. Consequently, the MoGAHA was able to wield primary power for managing the development of the business reference model for the Korean government.

Many IT vendors and consulting firms joined in the process of e-government system implementation in Korea. The Korean government outsourced IT system implementation and maintenance projects to IT vendors and gave consulting firms opportunities to be involved in projects for developing government-wide information strategies and business process reengineering projects for public agencies. Similar to the U.S cases, IT vendors were involved in the IT/IS projects through contracts with public agencies which begin with a request for proposals and rigorously monitored bidding and selection processes.

However, IT vendor roles were limited to system implementation so they did not develop ongoing working relations with IT policymakers in government. Instead, the National Computerization Agency (NCA),[22] a major quasi-autonomous non-governmental organization (quango, hereafter) played this role. The NCA researchers and IT professionals supported the decision-makers in government and mediated between the government and the private sector. The NCA supported policy-makers by providing them with related knowledge and by suggesting policy options (NIA 2007). The NCA was established in 1987 as statutory agency founded through the enactment of the Act on Expansion of Dissemination and Promotion of Utilization of Information System. Under its legal framework, the NCA was controlled by the government authorities concerned, but its employees were not public officials.

At the initial stage, the NCA was established as a technology-oriented agency. Its primary mission was developing auditing guidelines and performing audits for the National Administrative Information System, promoting standardization of IT/IS, and providing technological supports for public agencies. However, as demands for promoting informatization increased, its mission expanded to include provision of expertise in promoting informatization in Korea by developing and implementing the National Framework Plans on Informatization Promotion and the e-Government Promotion Plans, managing and operating information networks of public organizations, supporting information resource management in the public sector, and managing e-government and IT initiatives, and related activities.[23]

For carrying out these complex tasks, well-educated professionals have worked for the Agency. As of 2003, about 14 percent of total employees of the NCA had a Ph.D degree and about 51 percent held a masters degree as shown in Table 1. In addition, the NCA maintained an IT professional pooling system for getting advice and IT knowledge. About 300 professionals were registered in the pooling system as of 2005 (Yoo & Yoon, 2005).

From the planning to the adoption stage of the Korean BRM, the NCA was actively engaged in the process. First, the agency proposed that the business reference model and the GITA, the Korean version of the federal enterprise architecture, should be adopted to overcome a variety of problems which had stemmed from the stove-piped structure of early Korean e-government efforts, including IT investment redundancy and low levels of IT system effectiveness. Against this backdrop, the BRM and the FEA were proposed as tools for building cross-agency e-government and upgrading information services for citizens by the NCA.[24]

Second, the NCA tried to produce and share knowledge of the business reference model with government agencies. Specifically, an NCA research department translated U.S. government reports on the BRM and the FEA. They delivered those translations to their public partners to be referred to for development of related policies (NIA, 2003a; 2003b). In addition, the NCA held several conferences about the BRM and the EA and created "the ITA/EA Forum" where government officials, IT vendors and enterprise architecture experts from the NCA could discuss how to build the business reference model and enterprise architecture for Korean government. In these conferences and forums, private firms presented their best practices and the experiences of IT vendors and consulting firms were shared among participants.

Third, the National Computer Agency developed a pilot BRM, again referring to its U.S. counterpart as a model. The goals of the pilot project were to surface expected problems and the unanticipated effects of adopting the U.S. BRM in advance and to examine what dimensions of the U.S. BRM should be modified to enhance its feasibility for Korean government (NIA, 2003a; 2003b). These NCA activities were conducted in cooperation with specialists in IT firms.[25] In fact,

Table 1. Education level of NCA employees as of 2003

Degree	Ph.D.		Master		B.A.		Non-Degree	Total
Field	Humanities & Social Science	Natural Science & Engineering	Humanities & Social Science	Natural Science & Engineering	Humanities & Social Science	Natural Science & Engineering	13	230
Number of Employees	19	13	50	67	35	33		
	32		117		68			
Percentage (%)	13.9		50.9		29.6		5.6	100.0

(Source: NCA)

the pilot project's task force team was composed of NCA researchers and IT company consultants.

Fourth, NCA researchers were involved in implementing the BRM projects and developed implementation strategies and feedback systems. They made mid- and long-term plans for developing and adopting the EA, established guidelines for adopting the ITA in public agencies, and set standards for enterprise architecture frameworks. In addition, they contributed to opening ITA training programs for public officials. The NCA also was involved in managing business reference model projects such as writing and disseminating requests for proposals for the projects, developing contracts with companies, and managing the procedures for the projects.

The U.S. and Korean Cases Compared

Several similarities between the two cases can be identified. From the macro perspective, case analysis results show that both governments had a structure for IT knowledge transfer that included extensive use of PPPs. Through the PPPs, both governments learned from non-governmental organizations about the business reference model. Key actors in both governments adopted and adapted policies, practices and knowledge from non-governmental sectors. Both cases provide support for research on the extensiveness and importance of PPPs for knowledge transfer and policymaking in modern governments.

From the micro perspective, the case studies indicate that private sector actors were involved in actually building the BRM and carried out similar activities in terms of knowledge transfer in both governments. Specifically, private partners performed the following tasks: (1) raising awareness of the necessity of the BRM in order to develop shared services for the public good; (2) providing best practices from private firms and methods for adopting these practices to government; (3) developing pilot BRM projects for the governments and evaluating their effectiveness; and (4) developing implementation strategies and feedback systems to enhance feasibility and institutionalization.

Private partners in both countries played roles as "knowledge brokers" in the BRM building process. They carried knowledge about business reference models from the private to the public sector in the form of best practices, implementation strategies for BRM adoption and design of feedback mechanisms. Moreover, they provided their own tacit knowledge, which they had gained from working on similar projects in the private sector.

However, they did not transfer knowledge across sectors without revisions. Private partners in both countries translated knowledge in the course of transferring it from one realm to another. In the U.S., for example, private partners tried to embed the BRM into the budget process by revising OMB's Circular A-11, its primary guidance to agencies on budget preparation, because they understood that the budget is the most powerful method for requiring new activities in the public sector. In Korea, NCA researchers paid close attention to the differences between the U.S. federal government and the Korean government. They were careful to examine whether the U.S. business reference model could be successfully adopted in the Korean government. Lastly, private partners in their knowledge brokerage role were synthesizers. Combining several kinds of knowledge and information, they produced the BRM and measures for implementing it. In turn, these activities became sources for other knowledge concerning the BRM and government IT.

Our case analysis also finds that the two countries took entirely different approaches to working with non-governmental organizations in building the BRM. The U.S. federal government embedded private and non-profit actors deeply within the central e-government decision-making structures of federal agencies and OMB to enable rapid knowledge transfer. But in Korea, the roles of IT vendors and consultants were limited to system implementation. Instead, the NCA, one of Korea's quangos in IT policy, was deeply engaged in building the BRM.

What accounts for this difference between the two cases? One explanation stems from differences in the historical development of IT policy in the two governments. In the U.S., after the 1970s the federal government began to fall rapidly behind the private sector in using computing and managing information resources although it had been regarded as a leader and innovator in computer usage in earlier stages of computing (Head, 1982; OTA, 1981, quoted in Margetts (1999)). This widening gap between public and private use of IT caused political concern, and federal agencies were criticized for not using more contemporary IT. These concerns and criticisms led to expanding IT expenditures in federal agencies and brought IT companies and consulting firms to government IT projects (Margetts, 1999).

By contrast, in Korea informatization started in a different context in the early 1980s. National informatization was led by the central government because political elites at that time believed that the IT industry should be grown to promote economic growth. Therefore, government started early to establish a governance structure for IT policy, to make major investments in IT research and development, and to strongly subsidize IT companies in order to promote the Korean IT industry. Government began to expand government IT systems not only to make government more efficient but also to increase demand for Korean IT products and services.

In the course of this government-led informatization strategy, many quangos were established and were delegated authority for IT development and regulations over business and civil society. The quangos provided the Korean government with the ability to implement public policy effectively and efficiently. The quangos participated in program implementation with the delegated authorities for IT promotion and regulation. For business, they played the role of mediators by aggregating opinions about IT policy from business and delivering them to the appropriate authorities in government. In the IT policy field alone, 72 quangos had been established as of 1994, the NCA being one of them (Jung, 1997).

Another difference between the U.S and Korean cases relates to project outcomes, specifically related to the structure of the BRM in each country. As previously noted, the U.S. business reference model has a function-oriented structure, but the Korean model has an organization-oriented structure. This fundamental and highly consequential difference in structures came about although the knowledge brokers in both countries provided virtually the same ideas and knowledge, namely a BRM model with a function-oriented structure. What accounts for this difference between the two models? The answer may be traced to key differences in the institutional contexts in which the knowledge was diffused and in which adoption took place. Specifically, the Office of E-Government in the U.S. exerted strong and broad authority for e-government building through the mandate of the E-Government Act and had at its disposal several vehicles and tools for coordination.

For example, the E-Government Office, located within the U.S. Office of Management and Budget which is the largest entity in the Executive Office of the President, used budgetary power, working in collaboration with the budgetary units of OMB and its authority to administer the e-Government Fund. In addition, the Office of E-Government used evaluation frameworks and persuasion through government-wide bodies such as the CIO Council, a decision-making body comprised of agency chief information officers. This varied institutional structure for e-government promotion empowered the U.S. Office of E-Government to adopt and implement the idea of the function-oriented BRM and to overcome conflicts and criticisms of the BRM from federal agency decision makers. Although implementation was by no means rapid, easy or simple, the institutional mechanisms and authorities developed within

OMB through the Office of E-Government made possible far-reaching changes in the course of e-government, specifically in shared services, in the U.S. federal government.

By contrast, the implementation of the Korean BRM suffered from fragmented authority, ineffective managerial tools, and conflict among agencies. There was a "turf war" among the public authorities with jurisdiction over e-government promotion. In the course of resolving the conflict, the Special Committee, the initial adopter of the idea of "a cross-agency BRM," lost the power and authority for promoting e-government. In addition, the leaders of the MoGAHA, a public partner that came to power in a later stage of the BRM initiative, did not understand the cross-agency concept or its benefits and did not have the authority or vehicles to control and coordinate implementation of a function-oriented BRM. Consequently, the Korean government had no choice but to abandon its original plan for a function-oriented system, and produced a much weaker, less effective organization-oriented form of BRM.

Thus, this study shows that the ideas and activities of knowledge brokers and private partners working through PPPs are insufficient to ensure the realization of even well-established business model ideas in government. Building appropriate institutional arrangements to support realization of ideas and knowledge across sectoral boundaries must accompany knowledge brokering (Eom, 2012). The study demonstrates the not only the importance but also the limitations of knowledge brokering and knowledge transfer in PPPs when government institutions are not structured to absorb and implement new models. The comparative case study suggests that when agency or ministry autonomy is threatened by integrative IT systems that governments must use powerful institutional means, including the budget process, to effect change. These findings, although suggestive, offer important lessons for research and practice concerning e-government success.

Solutions and Recommendations

How do governments develop public-private partnerships to enhance and accelerate learning about and development of new capacity? How do governments adopt and adapt policies, practices and knowledge from non-governmental sectors to enhance e-government success? To shed light on these questions, the authors analyzed the concrete activities of private partners in the development of the business reference model, a key component of enterprise architecture and shared services, in the central governments of the U.S. and Korea.

The results indicate that private sector partners in both nations played roles as "brokers" of IT knowledge between the government and private sector, primarily performing the following tasks: (1) raising awareness of the necessity of the BRM; (2) providing best practices from private firms and the best methods for adopting the practices to government; (3) developing pilot BRM projects and evaluating their effectiveness; and (4) developing implementation strategies and feedback systems to enhance feasibility. More broadly, both governments learned from non-governmental organizations about the BRM. That is, PPPs have been institutionalized as a channel for knowledge transfer between government, civil society and business in both nations.

However, we also find important dissimilarities between the two cases. Two countries took entirely different approaches to working with non-governmental organizations in building the BRM. In the U.S., IT consulting firms and a non-profit organization of IT companies, the ICA, played the roles of knowledge brokers. In Korea, by contrast, the NCA, one of several quasi-governmental organizations in IT policy, was deeply engaged in building the BRM and acted as an intermediary between the government and private sectors. The study finds that the institutional arrangements in which PPPs are embedded strongly influence the outcome of e-government projects when the projects pose a perceived conflict between the interests of agencies or ministries and the government as a whole. Institutional arrangements influence the outcomes of knowledge transfer.

This study indicates that the roles of private experts are markedly greater when and where they serve the knowledge needs of other powerful actors and policy decision makers in modern governments, especially in the IT policy field. We recommend that governments analyze the level and type of relationships involved in their knowledge transfer strategies. Yet another important finding of this study is that history and institutions matter. We recommend that government decision makers examine the institutional arrangements for e-government to identify sources and limitations of power and authority to successfully transfer appropriate knowledge from the private sector and to implement e-government projects. This study shows that differences of institutional context where the same knowledge was transferred had an influence on producing different outcomes of the BRM projects. And the different historical backgrounds of IT policy and informatization in the two governments offer partial explanations for the different institutions of the PPPs.

FUTURE RESEARCH DIRECTIONS

This study suggests the importance of studying PPPs and knowledge transfer in their institutional context. With respect to e-government success, the institutional arrangements and mechanisms that government decision makers develop have important consequences for the ability of decision makers to adopt and adapt new ideas and knowledge across sectors. The wide variation in project success in e-government invites a closer examination of the institutional arrangements by which governments incorporate new ideas and implement e-government projects. The results of the present study should be considered suggestive. In this study predictive theory was not tested. Rather, a more exploratory approach drawing from rich veins of theory and research on PPPs and knowledge transfer was used to inform comparison of two case studies that examined factors that influence e-government success. There is a great disparity between the two political economies compared in this study in terms of the institutional characteristics of the governments in which the BRMs are embedded. Future research might include development of case studies based in a variety of political economies selected on variables that would allow for continued and refined comparative analysis. Second, statistical testing or large-N case study design should be considered for future research to test the external validity of some of the claims introduced here. Future research directions might include construction of variables that might be operationalized for quantitative study. Finally, the business reference model, our empirical referent, tends to be examined statically. Future research might consider the dynamic nature and needs of such reference models over time.

Research directly related to practitioners might also useful extend and further develop some of the insights drawn from the present study. In this regard, close examination of key actors and their relationships across sectors in the course of formulation and implementation of complex e-government projects would generate recommendations for practice.

CONCLUSION

This comparative study extends the typical views of public-private partnerships beyond a focus on contractual relationships to examine knowledge sharing and the transmission of practices and policies from the private to the public sector. It deepens our understanding of public-private partnerships, a key element of e-government success, by examining at close range knowledge transfer across the nodes of multi-sectoral networks. From a comparative perspective, the cases describe and explain different structures for public-private partnership and their embeddedness in distinct institutional contexts holding constant the policy area. The results have important implications for development of shared services in e-government..

REFERENCES

Boozallen.com. (2013). Website. Retrieved August 15, 2008, from http://www.boozallen.com/consulting

Borins, S. (2007). Introduction. In Borins, S. et al. (Eds.), *Digital state at the leading edge*. Toronto: University of Toronto Press.

Borzel, T., & Risse, T. (2008). Public-private partnership: Effective and legitimate tools of transnational governance? In E. Grande & L.W. Pauly, L. W. (Eds.), Complex sovereignty: Reconstituting political authority in the twenty first century. Toronto: University of Toronto Press.

Brown, J. S., & Duguid, P. (1998). Organizing knowledge. *California Management Review*, *40*(3), 90–111. doi:10.2307/41165945.

Burnes, B., & Anastasiadis, A. (2003). Outsourcing: A public-private sector comparison. *Supply Chain Management: An International Journal*, *8*(4), 355–366. doi:10.1108/13598540310490116.

Campbell, J. L. (2004). *Institutional change and globalization*. Princeton: Princeton University Press.

Chen, Y., & Perry, T. (2003). Outsourcing for e-government: Managing for success. *Public Performance & Management Review, 26*(4).

Cox, R. H. (2001). The social construction of an imperative: Why welfare reform happened in Denmark and the Netherlands but not in Germany. *World Politics*, *53*(April). PMID:17595731.

Currie, W. L. (1996). Outsourcing in the private and public sectors: an unpredictable IT strategy. *European Journal of Information Systems*, *4*, 226–236. doi:10.1057/ejis.1996.4.

Damsgaard, J., & Lyytinen, K. (2001). The role of intermediating institutions in the diffusion of electronic data interchange (EDI): How industry associations intervened in Denmark, Finland, and Hong Kong. *The Information Society*, *17*(3), 195–210. doi:10.1080/01972240152493056.

Dertz, W., Moe, C., & Hu, Q. (2003). Influential factors in IT sourcing decisions of Norwegian public sector: An exploratory study. Tampa: *Proceeding of Ninth Americas Conference on Information Systems*.

Dunleavy, P., Margetts, H., Bastow, S., & Tinkler, J. (2006). *Digital era governance: IT corporations, the state, and e-government*. Oxford: Oxford University Press. doi:10.1093/acprof:oso/9780199296194.001.0001.

Eom, S. J. (2012). 'Institutional dimensions of e-government development: Implementing the business reference model in the United States and Korea. *Administration & Society*. doi:10.1177/0095399712445870.

Fcw.com. (2013). Website. Retrieved June 15, 2007, from http://fcw.com/Articles/2007/03/26/2007-Federal-100-winners--From-Q--Z.aspx?Page=7

Feldman, M. S., & Khademian, A. M. (2007). The role of the public manager in inclusion: Creating communities of participation. *Governance: An International Journal of Policy, Administration and Institutions*, *20*(2), 305–324. doi:10.1111/j.1468-0491.2007.00358.x.

Fountain, J. E. (2001). *Building the virtual state: Information technology and institutional change*. Washington, DC: Brookings Institution Press.

Fountain, J. E. (2003). *Information, institutions and governance: Advancing a basic social science research program for digital government*. Kennedy School of Government Faculty Research Working Paper, RWP03-004.

Fountain, J. E. (2004). *Prospects for the virtual state*. Center of Excellence Program on Invention of Policy Systems in Advanced Countries, Graduate School of Law and Politics, University of Tokyo. Working paper.

Fountain, J. E. (2007). Challenges to organizational change: Multi-level integrated information structure. In Mayer-Schöenberger, V., & Lazer, D. (Eds.), *Governance and information technology: Form electronic government to information government*. Cambridge, MA: MIT Press.

Fountain, J. E. (2011, June). Bringing institutions back in to strategic management: The politics of digitally mediated institutional change. Unpublished paper presented at the Public Management Research Conference. Syracuse, NY.

Gibney, J. (2011). Knowledge in a shared and interdependent world: Implications for a progressive leadership of cities and regions. *European Planning Studies*, *19*(4), 613–627. doi:10.1080/09654313.2011.548474.

Gil-Garcia, J. R., & Pardo, T. A. (2005). E-government success factors: Mapping practical tools to theoretical foundation. *Government Information Quarterly*, *22*, 187–216. doi:10.1016/j.giq.2005.02.001.

Goldstein, J., & Keohane, R. O. (1993). Ideas and foreign policy: An analytical framework. In Goldstein, J., & Keohane, R. O. (Eds.), *Ideas and foreign policy: Beliefs, institutions, and political change*. Ithaca, NY: Cornell University Press.

Gordon, M. L., & Walsh, T. P. (1997). Outsourcing technology in government: Owned, controlled, or regulated institutions. *Journal of Government Information*, *24*(4), 267–283. doi:10.1016/S1352-0237(97)00026-9.

Hall, P. A. (1983). Policy innovation and the structure of the state: The politics-administrative nexus in France and Britain. [Implementing Government Change]. *The Annals of the American Academy of Political and Social Science*, 466.

Hall, P. A. (1989). Conclusion: The politics of Keynesian Ideas. In Hall, P. A. (Ed.), *The political power of economic ideas: Keynesianism across nations*. Princeton, NJ: Princeton University Press.

Hall, P. A. (1993). Policy paradigms, social learning, and the state: The case of economic policymaking in Britain. *Comparative Politics*. doi:10.2307/422246.

Han, H.-S., Lee, J.-N., & Seo, Y.-W. (2008). Analyzing the impact of a firm's capability on outsourcing success: A process perspective. *Information & Management*, *45*(1), 31–42. doi:10.1016/j.im.2007.09.004.

Hargadon, A. B. (2002). Brokering knowledge: Linking learning and innovation. *Research in Organizational Behavior*, *24*, 41–85. doi:10.1016/S0191-3085(02)24003-4.

Head, R. (1982). *Federal information systems management: Issues and new directions. Staff Paper*. Washington, DC: Brookings Institution.

Iaconline.org. (2013). Website. Retrieved March 5, 2008, from http://www.iaconline.org/portal

Jung, Y. (1997). Administrative reorganization in the strong state: The case of the Kim Young-Sam Regime. In Cho, Y. H., & Frederickson, H. G. (Eds.), *The white house and the blue house: Government reform in the United States and Korea*. New York: University Press of America, Inc..

Kennedy Information Inc. (2007). IT strategy and planning consulting marketplace 2006-2009: Key data, trends and forecasts. Peterborough, NH.

Khalfan, A., & Gough, T. G. (2002). Comparative analysis between the public and private sectors on the IS/IT outsourcing practices in a developing country: A field study. *Logistics Information Management*, *15*(3), 212–222. doi:10.1108/09576050210426760.

Khalfan, A. M. (2004). Information security considerations in IS/IT outsourcing projects: A descriptive case study of two sectors. *International Journal of Information Management*, *24*, 29–42. doi:10.1016/j.ijinfomgt.2003.12.001.

Korean Institute of Public Administration (KIPA). (2007). *The impact of PMIS on the effectiveness of public organizations: Centering on 'ON-Nara' system*. KIPA Policy Report 2007-06. Seoul: Korean Institute of Public Administration.

Lacity, M. C., & Willcocks, L. (2000). Survey of IT outsourcing experiences in US and UK organizations. *Journal of Global Information Management*. April-June.

Langford, J., & Harrison, Y. (2001). Partnering for e-government: Challenges for public administrators. *Canadian Public Administration*, *44*(4). doi:10.1111/j.1754-7121.2001.tb00898.x.

Langford, J., & Roy, J. (2006). E-government and public-private partnerships in Canada: When failure is no longer an option. *International Journal of Electronic Business*, *4*(2).

Lin, C., Pervan, G., & McDermid, D. (2007). Issues and recommendations in evaluating and managing the benefits of public sector IS/IT outsourcing. *Information Technology & People*, *20*(2), 161–183. doi:10.1108/09593840710758068.

Margetts, H. (1999). *Information technology in government: Britain and America*. London: Routledge. doi:10.4324/9780203267127.

Meyer, M. (2010). The rise of the knowledge broker. *Science Communication*, *32*(1), 118–127. doi:10.1177/1075547009359797.

MoGAHA. (2007a). *Annual Report of e- Government 2006*. Seoul: MoGAHA.

MoGAHA. (2007b). *Request for Proposal: On-Nara system*. Internal Document.

Moon, J., Jung, G.-H., Chung, M., & Choe, Y. C. (2007). IT outsourcing for E-government: Lesson from IT outsourcing projects initiated by agricultural organizations of the Korean government. *Proceeding of the 40th Hawaii International Conference on System Sciences*, Hawaii, USA.

National Information Society Agency (NIA). (2003a). *Policy Implications of the U.S. FEA. NCA Policy Report*. Seoul: NIA.

National Information Society Agency (NIA). (2003b). *A Study of the Development and the Usage of BRM. NCA Policy Report*. Seoul: NIA.

National Information Society Agency (NIA). (2007). *20th Anniversary National Information Society Agency*. Seoul: NIA.

Ni, A. Y., & Bretschneider, S. (2007). *The decision to contract out: A study of contracting for e-government services in state governments. Public Administration Review*. May/June.

O'Looney, J. (1998). *Outsourcing the city: State and local government outsourcing*. New York: Quorum Books.

Office of Management and Budget (OMB). (2002). *E-government strategy 2002*. Washington, DC: Author.

Office of Technology Assessment (OTA). (1981). Computer-based national information systems: Technology and public policy issues (Washington DC: OTA).

Pawlowski, S. D., & Robey, D. (2004). Bridging user organizations: Knowledge brokering and the work of information technology professionals. *Management Information Systems Quarterly*, *28*(4), 645–672.

PCGID. (2005). *E-government of participatory government*. Seoul: Author.

Peters, B. G., & Pierre, J. (2000). *Governance, politics, and the state*. New York: St. Martin's Press.

Phang, M. (2002). *A study on policy network in the e-government building*. (Unpublished doctoral dissertation). Sungkyunkwan University, Korea.

Pierre, J., & Peters, B. G. (2005). *Governing complex societies: Trajectories and scenarios*. New York: Palgrave Macmillan. doi:10.1057/9780230512641.

Pierson, P. (1994). *Dismantling the welfare state? Reagan, thatcher, and the politics of retrenchment*. Cambridge, UK: Cambridge University Press. doi:10.1017/CBO9780511805288.

Pierson, P. (2000). Increasing returns, path dependence, and the study of politics. *The American Political Science Review*, *94*(2), 251–267. doi:10.2307/2586011.

Pierson, P. (2004). *Politics in time: History, institutions, and political analysis*. Princeton: Princeton University Press.

Rocheleau, B. (2006). *Public management information systems*. Hershey, PA: Idea Group Publishing.

Rueschemeyer, D. (2006). Why and how ideas matter. In Goodin, R. E., & Tilly, C. (Eds.), *The Oxford handbook of contextual political analysis*. Oxford: Oxford University Press. doi:10.1093/oxfordhb/9780199270439.003.0012.

Saint-Martin, D. (2004). *Building the new managerialist state* (2nd ed.). Oxford: Oxford University Press. doi:10.1093/acprof:oso/9780199269068.001.0001.

Saint-Martin, D. (2005). Management consultancy. In Ferlie, E., Lynn, L. E., & Pollitt, C. (Eds.), *The Oxford handbook of public management*. Oxford: Oxford University Press.

Salamon, L. (2002). The new governance and the tools of public action: An introduction. In Salamon, L. M. (Ed.), *The tools of government: A guide to the new governance*. New York: Oxford University Press.

Schuppert, G. F. (2011). Partnership. In Bevir, M. (Ed.), *The Sage handbook of governance*. London: Sage Publication Inc. doi:10.4135/9781446200964.n18.

Seifert, J. W. (2006). *Federal enterprise architecture and e-government: Issues for information technology management. Congressional Research Service, Report for Congress*. Washington, DC: The Library of Congress.

Seo, S. (2004). *The prospect of e-government promotion in participatory government*. A presentation in the Korea IT Leaders Forum.

Sharma, S. (2007). Exploring best practices in public-private partnership (PPP) in e-government through select Asian case studies. *The International Information & Library Review*, 39.

Sheingate, A. D. (2003). Political entrepreneurship, institutional change, and american political development. *Studies in American Political Development*, *17*(2), 185–203. doi:10.1017/S0898588X03000129.

Sikkink, K. (1991). *Ideas and institutions*. Ithaca, London: Cornell Univ. Press.

Skelcher, C. (2005). Public-private partnerships and hybridity. In Ferlie, E., Lynn, L. E., & Pollitt, C. (Eds.), *The Oxford handbook of public management*. Oxford: Oxford University Press.

Skocpol, T., & Rueschemeyer, D. (1996). Introduction. In Rueschemeyer, D., & Skocpol, T. (Eds.), *States, social knowledge, and the origins of modern social policies*. Princeton: Princeton University Press.

Snellen, I. (2005). E-government: A challenge for public management. In Ferlie, E., Lynn, J. L. E., & Pollitt, C. (Eds.), *The Oxford handbook of public management*. Oxford: Oxford University Press.

Song, H., & Tak, C. (2007). E-government in Korea: Performance and tasks. *Informatization Policy*, *14*, 20–37.

Swan, J., Newell, S., & Robertson, M. (1999). Central agencies in the diffusion & design of technology: A comparison of the UK & Sweden. *Organization Studies*, *20*(6), 905–931. doi:10.1177/0170840699206001.

Swan, J., Newell, S., & Robertson, M. (2000). The diffusion, design & social shaping of production management information systems in Europe. *Information Technology & People*, *13*(1), 27–46. doi:10.1108/09593840010312744.

Swar, B., Moon, J., Oh, J., & Rhee, C. (2012)... *Information Systems Frontiers*, *14*, 457–475. doi:10.1007/s10796-010-9292-7.

The Institute for Public-Private Partnerships. (2009). Public-private partnerships in e-government: Handbook. Washington, DC: infoDev/World Bank.

Thelen, K. (2004). *How institutions evolve: The political economy of skills in Germany, Britain, the United States and Japan*. New York: Cambridge University Press. doi:10.1017/CBO9780511790997.

U.S. Government. (2002). The Business Reference Model Version 1.0. Washington, DC.

U.S. Government. (2003). The Business Reference Model Version 2.0. Washington, DC.

U.S. Government. (2005). Enabling citizen-centered electronic government 2005-2006: Federal enterprise architecture program management office action plan. Washington, DC.

Van Der Wal, Z., Huberts, L., Van Den Heuvel, H., & Kolthoff, E. (2006). Central values of government and business: Differences, similarities and conflicts. *Public Administration Quarterly*, *30*(3), 314–364.

Vilvovsky, S. (2008). Difference between public and private IT outsourcing: common themes in the literature. The *Proceedings of the 9th Annual International Digital Government Research Conference* (289, pp. 337–346).

Wenger, E. (1998). *Communities of practice: Learning, meaning and identity*. Cambridge: Cambridge University Press.

Whitehouse.gov. (2013). Website. Retrieved March 12, 2008, from http://www.whitehouse.gov/omb/egov

Yildiz, M. (2004). *Peeking into the black-box of e-government: Evidence from Turkey*. (Unpublished doctoral dissertation). Indiana University, Indiana.

Yoo, H., & Yoon, S. (2005, Winter). *A study of the conflict between the MoGAHA and the MIC in the course of e-government building*. Paper presented at the Annual Conference of the Korean Association of Public Administration. Seoul, Korea.

KEY TERMS AND DEFINITIONS

Business Reference Model: A functionally driven framework to describe federal government business operations independent of the agencies that perform the operations providing an organized, hierarchical construct to describe the functions and business operations of the government.

Enterprise Architecture: An approach to architecture meant to convey requirements for complex system design highlighting interdependencies across entities and connections among people, business processes, organizational complexity and technology.

Federal Enterprise Architecture: Encompasses five reference models including performance, business, service component, data and technology and designed as a planning and management tool to guide federal information technology investments and focused on identification of common applications across government that can be used to reduce duplication and overlap and thereby improve efficiency.

Knowledge Brokers: Individuals or organizations that connect communities of practice, transfer knowledge and facilitate coordination.

Non-Governmental Organization: Includes private and nonprofit sector organizations.

Public-Private Partnerships: Organizational arrangements with a sector-crossing or sector-blurring character. Combinations of government resources with those of private agents encompassing the range of cooperation among actors from public and private sectors.

ENDNOTES

1. We define "non-governmental organizations" to include private and nonprofit sector organizations.
2. The public leverage is a kind of PPP where governments use their legal and financial resources to create conditions that they believe will be conducive to economic activity and business growth when government wishes business or not-for-profits to be the means of realizing a goal that might otherwise be achieved through public bureaucracies (Skelcher, 2008).
3. This section is based on Eom (2012).
4. The FEA, which has five reference models, performance, business, service component, data, and technical, is a planning and management tool used to guide federal information technology investments, with a specific focus on improving efficiency and identifying common applications that can be used government-wide (Seifert, 2006). Retrieved from http:www.feapmo.gov/feahistory.asp, last accessed March 10, 2008.
5. The FEA reference models can be easily integrated along business lines, providing a foundation for the Component-Based Architecture design. Therefore, "The BRM serves as the foundation for the FEA" (FEAPMO, 2003).
6. Ministries of the Korean government consist of several 'bureaus' or 'offices'. In turn, there are several 'divisions' in a bureau or office. Thus, ministries, bureaus or offices, and divisions are hierarchically aligned in the organizational system of the Korean government.
7. From an interview with the consultant who participated in the government-wide information sharing project of the Roh administration on September 15, 2009.

8. From an interview with current civil servant who engaged in e-government policy formulation of current Lee administration on June 11, 2010.
9. Title I. § 3602 Office of E-Government of the E-Government Act of 2002.
10. Major supporting contractors in the field of e-government were Booz Allen Hamilton and SRA International. From the interview with the consultants supporting the OMB on July 12, 2007.
11. From the interview with the consultant supporting the OMB on July 10 and 12, 2007 and the interview with then Federal Chief Architect of the OMB on July 10, 2007.
12. See fcw.com (2013).
13. See whitehouse.gov (2013).
14. Interview with the chairman of the IAC, July 13, 2007.
15. Interview with the chairman of the IAC, July 13, 2007.
16. Interviews with a supporting consultant to OMB, July 10 and 12, 2007.
17. Interview with Mark Forman conducted by IBM Center for Business of Government, May 30, 2002.
18. See boozallen.com (2013).
19. Interview with the Chairman of IAC on July 13, 2007.
20. See iaconline.org (2013).
21. Interviews with a consultant for OMB, July12, 2007, and the Chairman of IAC, July 13, 2007.
22. The name of the NCA was changed to the National Information Society Agency (NIA) in 2006.
23. More specifically, the NCA was designated as the exclusive organization for: (1) constructing the Korea Information Infrastructure (KII) in 1994; (2) supporting specialized technologies for national informatization in 1996; (3) supporting e-government technology in 2001; and (4) supporting e-government projects in 2004. In addition, the NCA launched e-approval certification services in the public sector in 2001 and constructed the backup center for National Backbone information System in 2002 (NIA, 2007).
24. For example, the former president of the NCA, Dr. Sam-Young Seo, maintained that the BRM and the GITA should be built for the reasons in his speeches in many IT forums (Seo, 2004).
25. Interviews with consultants on December 13, 2007 and the NCA researchers who participated in the pilot project on February 20, 2008.

Chapter 3
E-Government Success in Public Libraries:
Library and Government Agency Partnerships Delivering Services to New Immigrants

Ursula Gorham
University of Maryland, USA

Paul T. Jaeger
University of Maryland, USA

John Carlo Bertot
University of Maryland, USA

Natalie Greene Taylor
University of Maryland, USA

ABSTRACT

For much of their history in the United States, public libraries made services for immigrants a key part of their mission by offering them many long-term services, such as developing job searching skills and learning English as a second language. Internet-enabled services, such as navigating the citizenship process, establishing residency, and delivering other key functions through e-government, are a recent addition. This chapter reports the findings of a multi-method study that provides insight into the development of e-government partnerships in various realms (including immigration), highlighting the extent to which these partnerships enhance the ability of libraries to overcome the various challenges that arise in connection with providing e-government services to different populations.

INTRODUCTION

Following the advent of the World Wide Web (the Web), the use of e-government by national, state/provincial, and local governments to deliver information, communication, and services to citizens has grown dramatically around the globe. E-government has since matured into a dynamic socio-technical system encompassing issues of governance, societal trends, technological change, information management, interaction, and human factors (Dawes, 2009).

DOI: 10.4018/978-1-4666-4173-0.ch003

Copyright © 2013, IGI Global. Copying or distributing in print or electronic forms without written permission of IGI Global is prohibited.

E-government development primarily focused on interactions between the government and members of the public, with many government agencies viewing e-government as their primary method for public engagement (Bertot & Jaeger, 2006; 2008; Ebbers, Pieterson, & Noordman, 2008; Streib & Navarro, 2006). The promise of e-government is often presented as being either to engage citizenry in government in a user-centered manner or to develop quality government services and delivery systems that are efficient and effective (Bertot & Jaeger, 2008). In practice, however, agencies typically focused on making the interactions easier for themselves, rather than for citizens (Jaeger & Bertot, 2010). Increasingly, government content and services are available only online, and even when a physical version is still available, many governments strongly encourage citizens to use e-government. As a result, the average individual now uses e-government to fulfill important needs – paying taxes, seeking unemployment benefits and other social services, registering to vote, completing license applications and renewals, enrolling children in school, navigating the immigration process, establishing water rights, finding court proceedings, submitting local zoning board information, searching property and assessor databases, and innumerable other important federal, state, and local government functions (Bertot, McClure, & Jaeger, 2008; Gibson, Bertot, & McClure, 2009; Holt & Holt, 2010).

In many locations in the United States, however, the lack of availability of computers, Internet access, or even basic telecommunications infrastructure, is a barrier to successful e-government interactions. Many households lack Internet access and many with Internet access lack broadband capacity, which is necessary for many online activities, including many types of social media (Bertot, Jaeger, & Hansen, 2012).

Lack of access to technology is far from the only barrier to universal usage of e-government. Members of the public seek assistance with e-government from public libraries because they lack the technical skills to use the online functions or simply are uncomfortable engaging in online interactions without guidance (Bertot, Jaeger, Langa, & McClure, 2006a; 2006b) Moreover, as awareness of political information and how to use it depends heavily on the awareness of the people with whom an individual interacts (Lake & Huckfeldt, 1998), it is likely that e-government awareness and usage functions in a similar social manner. Notwithstanding an ability to ultimately locate the e-government information or service they need, individuals may still not be able to fully interact with e-government services due to issues of government literacy, terminology, transparency, understandability, and timeliness, among other factors (Fenster, 2006).

The public library has become established as the primary place to which members of the public turn when seeking help with e-government, creating considerable new responsibilities for libraries in ensuring access to e-government (Jaeger & Bertot, 2011; Heanue, 2001). Paradoxically, the ongoing economic downturn has resulted in even more people coming to the public library for assistance with completing applications for employment or social services online at a time when public libraries are facing significant budget cuts (Bertot, Lincoln, McDermott, Real, & Peterson, 2012). In order to rise above the challenge of having to provide more services with fewer resources (namely, computer workstations, broadband capacity, and staff members with expertise in these areas), public libraries are increasingly seeking opportunities to collaborate with government agencies and community groups to provide enhanced or entirely new services to members of the public.

Drawing upon findings from a multi-method study conducted by the authors during the summer and fall of 2011, as described in greater detail in the methodology section, this chapter focuses on the development of successful e-government partnerships in the immigration realm. In recent years, public libraries have assumed a central role in helping recent immigrants[1] (i.e., individuals who have entered the country within the last ten years) navigate the citizenship and residency processes handled by the United States Citizenship and Immigration Services (USCIS). As USCIS continues to shift an increasing number of forms and services online, immigrants are finding themselves in need of assistance more than ever. Due to the complexity of immigration processes, public libraries often hesitate to move beyond serving as an access point to information (e.g., providing the forms/applications) to answering questions about the processes and otherwise providing assistance. Rather than shying away from providing services in this area, however, innovative public libraries are partnering with government agencies and community organizations to connect immigrants with the information, resources, and services that they need.

After exploring the e-government service context in which public libraries are currently operating, this chapter highlights several noteworthy partnerships that demonstrate how collaboration between public libraries, government agencies, and community organizations can enhance the ability of each of these institutions to better serve immigrants, as well as offer immigrants new ways to become engaged in government activities. The authors provide insights into what factors contribute to the success of these partnerships, emphasizing how other community organizations interested in creating e-government partnerships can adapt the practices developed in connection with these collaborations.

BACKGROUND

History of Libraries and Immigrants

Services to immigrant populations have long been a core function of public libraries in the United States, with new immigrants turning to public libraries for information on citizenship, employment, education, social services, health, safety, housing, and learning English, as well as materials in their native languages, programs, services, and referrals (Cuban, 2007; McCook, 2011). In some communities, the public library is the most important institution available to immigrants in adapting to their new lives and new communities, while also helping to preserve identities and connections to original cultures (Cuban, 2007; Lukenbill, 2006). Public library outreach and services for immigrants date back to the early years of the public library movement in the late 1800s and early 1900s (Burke, 2008b; Jones, 1999). Before World War I, public libraries focused on providing services to immigrant children and first generation Americans (Larson, 2001; McDowell, 2010; 2011). Libraries provided a range of materials and services for young patrons individually and in reading and social groups focusing on a range of subject matters – literature, arts, economics, politics, and employment – with a heavy emphasis on enculturation and acclimation to the United States (Larson, 2001). Libraries also viewed these services for children as a way to reach and help Americanize their parents (McDowell, 2011).

By the time America entered World War I, public libraries in urban areas widely accepted immigrant services as a key function, as the country absorbed many more immigrants from a wider range of places then previously (Wiegand, 1986; 1989). The American Library Association (ALA) developed programs seeking to promote the socialization of these new waves of immigrants and to provide assistance in the transition from new immigrant to citizen through public library services (Burke, 2008b; Jones, 1999; Wiegand, 1986). The increasing focus on the needs of immigrants led to increased attention to the needs of other disadvantaged groups, playing a significant part in the maturation of the public library into a progressive community institution (Jones, 1999).

As such, public libraries have a long history of helping immigrants with personal needs, such as employment, housing, and with community engagement through social connections and civic participation (Caidi & Allard, 2005). Public libraries regularly provide immigrant communities in their service areas with information about life in the new country and other materials in native languages, English as a second language (ESL) courses, computer training, civics education, job seeking help, and other resources for acclimating (Varheim, 2010). As a result of these targeted programs and services, immigrant populations typically perceive the public library as a place of building social networks, learning about their place of residence, meeting new people in the community, staying connected to their native cultures, and learning to trust social institutions, in addition to the information resources and language services available (Audunson, Essmat, & Aabo, 2011; Chu, 1999; Varheim, 2010). The advent of the Web offered new opportunities for public libraries to provide innovative services to immigrants. For example, in the Chicago area, the SkokieNet (http://skokienet.org) library system provides resources on their website in the native languages of new immigrant populations that have moved to the area, including Indian, Korean, and Assyrian, among others, with new languages being added to meet the changing demographics of a multicultural city.

E-Government, Immigrants and Public Libraries

With state and federal agencies increasingly viewing e-government as their primary method for delivering government services, members of the public are increasingly encouraged to engage in transactions. As the USCIS shifts a growing number of its services online[2], recent immigrants have been acutely affected by this transition. Hailed as a "digital leader" among government agencies, USCIS began to deliver services online in 2003, with the creation of InfoPass, a service that allows individuals to schedule appointments with USCIS Immigration Officers through the Internet. From its inception, InfoPass has been lauded as a vast improvement over the previous process, which often required individuals to go to a USCIS office early in the morning with only the hope of receiving an appointment that day (Naficy, 2011). In addition to expanding InfoPass to all district offices and sub-offices, USCIS has begun to offer an increasing number of services online over the past decade, including e-filing for a number of frequently used forms and case status checking.

Notwithstanding an emerging mandate for the public to engage in e-government transactions, or the brisk adoption of e-government practices by USCIS, many immigrants lack the means to access, understand, and use e-government. A report by the Center for Immigration Studies (Camarota, 2007) found that 31 percent of immigrants have not completed high school, that 33 percent of immigrant-headed households use at least one major welfare program, and that the poverty rate for immigrants is 17 percent (Naficy, 2011). Therefore, as USCIS has focused on building a robust online presence purportedly to increase the effectiveness and efficiency of its customer service, their primary customary base – immigrants – have found it increasingly difficult to access the range of information and services provided by the USCIS online.

In an effort to overcome existing barriers to access, immigrants turn to libraries for assistance with their e-government needs. The reason for this reliance upon libraries is multifold. Recent immigrants turning to public libraries for assistance with meeting their basic day-to-day needs is not a new phenomenon. In addition to immigration forms and applications, their information needs often include citizenship test study materials; healthcare information; financial assistance information; transportation information; and information about finding housing or employment (Tetteh, 2011; Zhang, 2001; Su & Conaway, 1995). In a review of library services provided to immigrants over the past century, Burke (2008a) noted that the libraries studied provided various forms of language and literacy training (e.g., ESL classes, conversation programs, and literacy tutoring) and computer services (e.g., availability of computer interfaces in different languages, computer skills training, and Internet/e-mail access).

Further, many federal, state, and local government agencies explicitly direct residents to the nearest public library for access and assistance with e-government (Jaeger & Bertot, 2009; Bertot, Jaeger, Langa, & McClure, 2006b). Even people who have other means of Internet access often still use e-government in public libraries because libraries and librarians have exceptionally high levels of social trust, making their guidance in accessing and using e-government uniquely trusted by residents (Fisher, Becker, & Crandall, 2010; Heanue, 2001).

STUDY METHODOLOGY

The findings presented in this chapter rely principally on three interrelated data collection efforts:

- Data collected through The Public Library Funding and Technology Access Survey (PLFTAS) between September 2011 and November 2011;
- Site visits to U.S. public libraries between April 2011 and October 2011; and
- Interviews with state library staff, government officials, and community organization leaders between April 2011 and October 2011.

Funded by the American Library Association and the Bill & Melinda Gates Foundation, PLFTAS drew a proportionate-to-size stratified random sample that considered the metropolitan status of the library (*i.e.*, urban, suburban, and rural) and state in order to generate, through weighted analysis, both national and state-level generalizable estimates of public library Internet connectivity and service provision. This Internet-based survey produced 7,260 responses, for a response rate of 83.1%. More specific information regarding the survey's methodology is available at http://www.plinternetsurvey.org.

After conducting an extensive literature review focused on the identification of existing e-government partnerships, the authors conducted site visits to seven geographically dispersed public libraries in five states, each of which serves a diverse set of communities. Using a selective and purposive sample, however, enabled the selection of libraries that reflect diversity in terms of geography, library size, and communities served by the libraries (e.g., rural, suburban, and urban communities with high immigrant concentrations, underserved populations, and/or high poverty rates), and known e-government library-agency partnerships. Selected site visits included interviews with 1) state library agency staff who oversee library services across their states, 2) library e-government partnership staff, 3) locally-based government agency (e.g., USCIS field office) staff, and/or 4) relevant non-profit organization staff.

The combined national survey, interview, and site visit approach provided aggregate and generalizable data regarding public library e-government service provision and challenges, while simultaneously allowing for on-the-ground assessments of library and government collaborative efforts. Moreover, the site visits allowed for an expansion and better understanding of the service context of library-provided e-government services, as the visits occurred during the libraries' hours of operations, thus enabling the researchers to observe staff members' interactions with users and the time of service delivery.

CURRENT E-GOVERNMENT SERVICE CONTEXT

Through the above-described interrelated data collection efforts, the authors were able to explore the public libraries' steadily expanding e-government role. Key findings from the 2011-2012 PLFTAS Survey reveal the many facets of this role, ranging from assistance with access, to help with forms, to training classes and translation services (see Figure 1).

As this role has developed and evolved, libraries have identified a number of issues that impact their ability to effectively provider e-government services, and these issues are amplified when one considers the needs of, as well as the challenges that arise in connection with providing service to, foreign-born users. In this particular context, it appears that e-government has at least two dimensions to it: 1) those dealing with user issues (i.e., what a user needs in order to access e-government), and 2) those dealing with library issues (i.e., what a library needs in order to provide e-government services). The ability of libraries to address both groups of issues is critical to the successful delivery of e-government services in this realm.

User Issues

At the most basic level, the presentation of government information online may present multiple challenges for users who lack digital, basic, or civics literacy. In the case of digital literacy (defined in the National Broadband Plan [Federal Communications Commission, 2010, p.174] as "the sum of the technical skills and cognitive skills people employ to use computers to retrieve information, interpret what they find and judge the quality of that information"), although access to technology is critical, the ability to use the technologies for e-government purposes is equally important. Many users lack these skills, thus requiring substantial training and assistance in order to effectively utilize e-government services and resources. This is especially relevant for a foreign-born population because of the significant gap between the technology use of U.S.-born citizens and foreign-born immigrants (Livingston, 2010).

The Federal government has launched a variety of initiatives, such as the instructional website DigitalLiteracy.gov, in support of its overarching goal to create a more digitally inclusive infrastructure and, more recently, issued a Digital Government plan (White House, 2012), which provides a blueprint for furthering digital government innovation and services. This plan, in part, creates a push for mobile digital government services. Interacting with government services via mobile devices is quite different than through more traditional computer-based services, which will introduce additional complexity, as well as opportunities, for users. Notwithstanding the government's current focus on digital literacy, however, challenges remain in this area.

In addition to these digital challenges, users who lack basic literacy skills will require varied forms of assistance. The National Center for

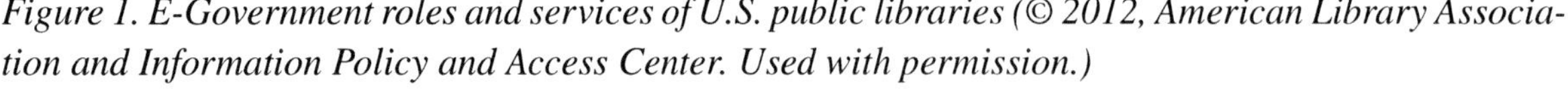
Figure 1. E-Government roles and services of U.S. public libraries (© 2012, American Library Association and Information Policy and Access Center. Used with permission.)

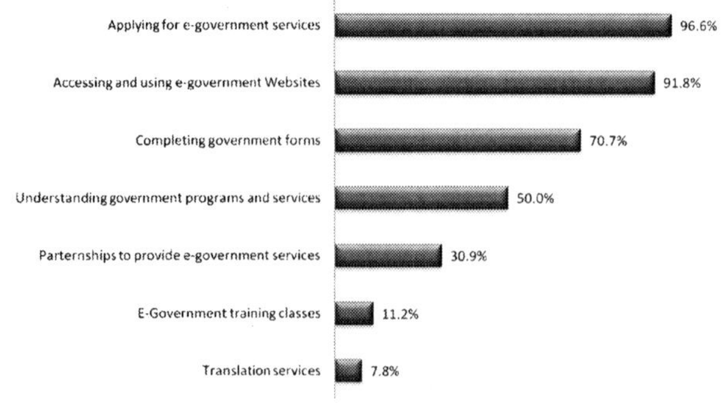

Education Statistics reports that, as compared to U.S. born individuals, foreign-born adults obtained overall lower average scores on all three literacy (prose, document, and quantitative) scales (Warkentien, Clark, & Jacinto, 2009). This finding presents librarians with the challenge of addressing key literacy skills while simultaneously attempting to explain sometimes complicated e-government content. Though the government has attempted to adapt their resources to "plain language" (http://www.plainlanguage.gov/), 64% of government websites are written at the 12th grade reading level or higher (West, 2008), which is far higher than even the reading level of Americans who speak English as their first language.

For users of e-government, civics literacy, or the understanding of government processes, is almost as important as basic literacy. Users with e-government needs struggle to understand the structure of government or how to engage with those government agencies. The situation is particularly complicated for immigrants, who must first discern which government processes are applicable to their particular situation and then attempt to navigate these processes.

In addition, users may not be proficient in English or any of the other languages through which agencies might make their e-government services available. Government standards are not clear regarding the extent to which agencies must provide translations. There are guidelines for providing services to users with limited English proficiency (LEP), including Executive Order 13166 (Department of Justice, Civil Rights Division, 2012), as well as various agency guidelines, available for review at the Limited English Proficiency Federal Interagency Website.[3] The enforcement of these provisions is weak, however, and the complaint process is complex, leaving public librarians struggling to serve users who cannot read the very information they need to carry out e-government tasks.

Library Issues

Compounding user challenges are issues affecting libraries. One particularly acute challenge for public librarians is a lack of sufficient technology. In some cases, libraries simply do not have adequate public access technology (Figure 2) or connectivity (Figure 3) to accommodate the full spectrum of users' e-government needs (Bertot et al., 2012). Although some libraries have started offering special purpose computers for e-government and employment needs, time limits can pose a problem for e-government users.

Staffing issues also present challenges. E-government skills, time and resources, and an understanding of the users' needs are all factors that complicate service. Indeed, 41.1% of public libraries reported that they did not have sufficient staff to provide e-government services, while 51.4% indicated that they did not have staff with e-government expertise (Bertot et al., 2012). This is an urgent need in the realm of immigration, where the multi-step process for becoming either a permanent resident or a citizen is rather complex. In order for librarians to assist users throughout these lengthy processes, librarians must understand – and be able to explain - what actions are required of the applicant at each step. The problem

Figure 2. Sufficiency of public library public access workstations (© 2012, American Library Association and Information Policy and Access Center. Used with permission.)

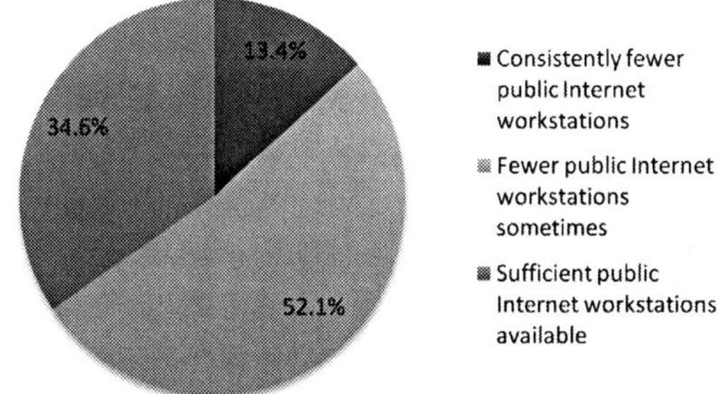

Figure 3. Sufficiency of public library connection speed (© 2012, American Library Association and Information Policy and Access Center. Used with permission.)

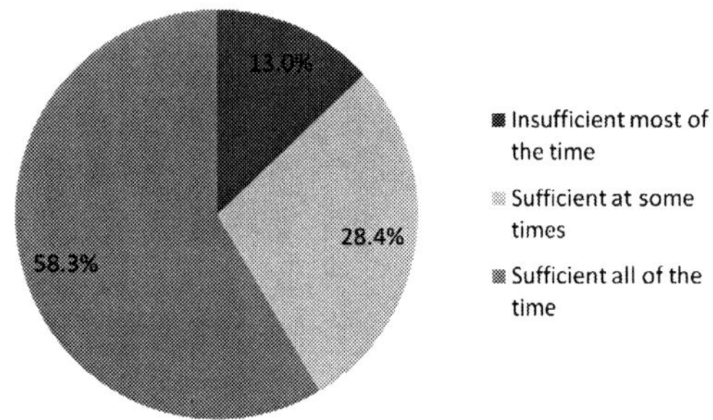

is amplified by the fact that government agencies have yet to adopt a uniform e-government approach, leading librarians to feel as though they must familiarize themselves with the many different systems, technologies, and forms used by various local, state or federal agencies.

Recession-induced shortages of staff and reductions in operating hours make time and resources scarce commodities in many public libraries (American Library Association, 2010; Jaeger & Bertot, 2011). In this era of budget and staffing constraints, it can be challenging to assist users with more complex needs. Within the immigration realm, while some libraries are able to accommodate these complexities (*e.g.*, Hartford Public Library in Connecticut hosts swearing-in ceremonies for new citizens, in addition to offering a multitude of resources to immigrants in the early stages of the citizenship process), others simply lack the resources to provide such a full range of services.

Librarians also face the challenge of fully understanding the diversity of user needs. Users have different e-government requirements, and the breadth of a given user's need is not always apparent at first glance. As mentioned, some users lack rudimentary skills required for interacting with government, such as knowledge of how to create an e-mail account or complete required documentation, or adequate levels of language literacy, whereas other users understand the technology and already possess the necessary documentation, minimizing the need for guidance. As an example, librarians working at the New Immigrant Project (NIP) housed in Austin Public Library in Texas observed that one of the biggest challenges they face is dealing with the inconsistency of user skills and needs. With respect to users at one end of the spectrum (*e.g.*, users who have no experience with computers), there are a number of skills that must be developed as a prerequisite to these users having the capacity to effectively utilize the resources offered by the NIP.

Library management can sometimes help staff members deal with these problems, but, at the present time, many libraries have yet to implement procedures that provide adequate guidance. One missing element of many public libraries' e-government service operations is a clearly articulated policy on the extent of service to be provided to users. The librarians interviewed consistently mentioned the need for the development and dissemination of e-government service policies that focus on what the library will and will not help with, due to liability, privacy, and other concerns that surface in relation to e-government transactions and services.

Challenges Created by User and Library Issues

These user and library issues, when taken together, present a formidable challenge in terms of providing a more comprehensive approach to e-government service provision. As librarians' understanding of short-term and long-term user needs continues to evolve, they have started to look across the entire span of library services (and perhaps even outside the library) to meet these needs. For example, a user may come to the library needing to complete a particular government form or to access a specific service and, increasingly, may come to the library with his or her own mobile device looking for device-specific assistance. To fully meet this need, the user may have to first establish an e-mail account or PIN number, go through a quick "how to" lesson, or address any number of short-term needs in order to successfully engage in that e-government transaction. However, as part of addressing this immediate need, the user may also require, for instance, literacy instruction (digital and/or traditional), language instruction, child care, and/or citizenship classes. Librarians need to consider how best to meet both types of user needs and to adopt an integrated approach across services.

Other challenges arise with respect to defining the role to be played by the government agency in the library's e-government service operation. From discussions with librarians that occurred during the various site visits, the development and maintenance of relationships between librarians and the agencies creating the e-government content was viewed as helpful, and perhaps even necessary. For example, the librarians interviewed lamented that they were often positioned at the end of a long march towards e-government, during which time government agencies gave little thought as to how users were actually going to use the services and information provided online. They also indicated that they would benefit tremendously from being kept up to date about changes to e-government services, mandates, and other aspects that would impact the public's interaction with the agency's e-government services.

To summarize:

- Users may have a range of needs that extend beyond basic e-government services.
- Users and librarians may not understand the larger policy/governance/jurisdictional context of e-government.
- Libraries do not necessarily have the budgetary, space, equipment, and technological (e.g., bandwidth) resources for users to access and successfully participate in e-government services.
- Library e-government roles, which can vary from library to library, have yet to be clearly defined and differentiated in light of local service context.
- Libraries and critical e-government service agencies with which users most frequently interact lack wide-scale coordination.

These issues have a significant impact upon the ability of public libraries to provide immigration-related e-government services.

Solutions

As libraries have taken on an increasing number of e-government service responsibilities while confronting the challenges discussed above, they recognize that creating partnerships with government agencies and/or other community organizations is an essential factor in e-government success (Bertot & Jaeger, 2012; Jaeger, Bertot, Shuler, & McGilvray, in press; Sigler, Jaeger, Bertot, DeCoster, McDermott, & Langa, 2012). The PLFTAS data (see Figures 1-3) documents the existence of these partnerships and, through an extensive literature review, site visits and interviews, the authors were able to acquire a more nuanced understanding of how these partnerships operate in practice. The creation of these formal partnerships is driven by community needs and economic realities, as the partnerships are better able to deliver existing services or can pool resources to provide new services in response to rapidly changing community needs. Whether viewed as an unfunded mandate or as an opportunity to extend e-government services through community-based institutions such as the public library, the end result is that public libraries and government agencies are de facto collaborators in the provision of e-government services.

In the realm of immigration services, partners can serve as a point of access to a particular immigrant community that the library is trying to reach (Sundell, 2000). These organizations, particularly those who are already working closely with particular ethnic groups or certain segments of immigrant populations (e.g., students), can often offer invaluable insight into the needs of these groups. A 2010 report co-authored by USCIS and the Institute of Museum and Library Services (IMLS) encouraged libraries to form partnerships with government agencies as well as a wide variety of community organizations (e.g., local public schools, business associations, and faith-based organizations) to "bridg[e] the resource gap" (p. 1). In connection with their ongoing research, the authors identified several innovative partnerships that are enhancing the quality of e-government services provided to immigrants. Each of these partnerships and programs demonstrates how libraries serve as key intermediaries between those in need of e-government services and agencies implementing those services. For each partnership presented in this section, we list the success factors that enabled those involved to overcome the challenges discussed in the previous section.

Queens Borough Public Library

Success Factors:

- Addresses language diversity of users;
- Situates services within the community by providing referrals to local organizations; and
- Maintains dedicated e-government staff.

Historically, Queens has been the most ethnically diverse of New York City's five boroughs (Carnesi & Fiol, 2000). According to the most recent American Community Survey published by the U.S. Census Bureau (2005-2009 American Community Survey 5-Year Estimates), 47.1% of Queens residents are foreign born and 54.4% speak a language other than English at home. Established in 1977, the New Americans Project (NAP) run by the Queens Borough Public Library (QBPL) was a pioneering effort to provide better services to immigrants through ESL classes, cultural arts programs, coping skills programs, and collection development in a variety of other languages (Carnesi & Fiol, 2000). Due to the linguistic diversity of its staff (Winkel, 2007), QBPL is able to provide programming in a wide variety of languages and on a wide range of topics, often in conjunction with one of the many community organizations that are part of its extensive network of partners.

In addition to reaching out to immigrants through programming, QBPL has also compiled a number of citizenship and immigration resources on its website,[4] including referral lists for both citizenship and ESL classes offered by various community organizations (*e.g.*, the Turkish Cultural Center, Catholic Charities), as well as the New York City Department of Education. Also available through the QBPL is a Community Resources database of agencies offering low cost or free social and human services, searchable by services offered, locations, target groups, languages, and ethnic groups.

A partnership with the Mayor's Office of Immigrant Affairs, focused on assisting immigrants with the application process for the Diversity Visa Lottery, is a prime example of successful e-government collaboration. Shortly after the U.S. Department of State mandated that the application process be completed online, a partnership between QBPL and the Office of Immigrant Affairs was conceived following city officials' recognition that the electronic application system "created another hurdle for some low-income immigrants who lack computer access" (Yaniv, 2005). Detailed guidance prepared by the Office of Immigrant Affairs is published on QBPL's website, thereby ensuring that immigrants are receiving accurate information from the actual provider of the e-government service. In addition to encouraging applicants to use the library's computers to complete the application, QBPL has also set up designated times at different branches during which immigrants can receive assistance with scanning photographs to be submitted with their applications.

Austin Public Library

Success Factors:

- Addresses language diversity of users;
- Employs dedicated technology for e-government services; and
- Promotes a clearly developed e-government mission for librarians to follow.

Austin Public Library (APL) created the New Immigrants Program (NIP) in 2000 as a result of recommendations made in 1998 by a task force charged with investigating the effects of then recent changes to immigration laws on local residents. A committee of APL staff from libraries in neighborhoods with large immigrant populations generated the idea of English and citizenship study centers, leading to the establishment of such centers at three APL locations.

In the years since its inception, the NIP expanded to eight locations, the study centers were renamed New Immigrants Centers (NICs) to better reflect the broader mission of the NIP, and the City of Austin increased the number of bilingual employees based upon the composition of the surrounding communities (Miranda-Murillo, 2006). Currently, the NICs provide a number of face-to-face services, including an English conversation practice program and computer classes in English and Spanish, and offer immigrants access to materials and equipment for English language study and the U.S. citizenship test (Miranda-Murillo, 2006). Moreover, the NIP developed a website that, in addition to providing information about the aforementioned face-to-face services, links to USCIS information, international news, and online tools to help immigrants with their English language skills.

Demographic trends in the APL's service area demonstrate the persistent need for the NICs. According to the most recent statistics available from the U.S. Census Bureau (2005-2009 American Community Survey 5-Year Estimates), 18% of the population of Travis County is foreign born and 31.9% speak a language other than English at home. Notwithstanding the burgeoning immigrant population in the library's service area, the librarians interviewed at APL identified a number of challenges that impede the delivery of services by the NICs:

- Key library resources do not effectively meet immigrant needs. By way of example, websites and web resources have yet to be translated into appropriate languages, due to constraints on staff time.
- The services available through the NICs have not been effectively promoted to immigrants.
- Usage of NIP computers has decreased over time. Suggested reasons for this decline include the separation of NIP workstations from other workstations in the library, the ability of other community organizations to provide more comprehensive help, and the political climate toward immigrants.

In addition to these specific challenges, librarians staffing the NICs have struggled with serving users with a wide range of skills and needs. In some cases, the deficiencies in language and/or computer skills must be addressed before the NICs can assist users with their e-government needs. Some of these needs (e.g., family services, health services, and employment) are outside the scope of the NIC's mission.

Librarians at APL, however, understand the importance of "connecting the dots" between services provided by the NICs and those provided by other government agencies and community organizations, advocating for increased integration of these services. The opportunity for a more comprehensive approach to service provision is now presenting itself through a newly formed partnership between public libraries, the Texas State Library and Archives Commission, and the Texas Workforce Center. Funded through a Broadband Technology Opportunity Program (BTOP) grant, the Technology Expertise, Access and Learning for All Texans (TEAL) project seeks to enable participating libraries to better serve the most vulnerable members of their communities, including foreign born residents. Of particular relevance to immigrants are the ESL, citizenship, General Education Development (GED) test training and support funded through this project. The project also offers training through a series of webinars to the staff of participating libraries with the goal of enabling librarians to more effectively meet the needs of the targeted groups. By enhancing immigrants' e-government experiences through broadband access and by helping immigrants to improve their basic, digital, and civics literacy skills, this project is providing participating libraries with the resources needed to overcome existing barriers to effective e-government service delivery.

Hartford Public Library

Success Factors:

- Designed services to meet a wide diversity of user needs;
- Dedicated funding for e-government; and
- Designed services specifically to address users' lack of digital, basic, and civics literacy skills.

In 2000, the Hartford Public Library (HPL) in Connecticut created the American Place (TAP), a program with the principal goals of helping an increasingly diverse group of immigrants secure citizenship and achieve language literacy (Naficy, 2009). According to the most recent data available from the U.S Census Bureau (State & County QuickFacts), 13.5% of the population of Hartford County is foreign-born and 22.7% speak a language other than English at home. In an effort to make immigration information more easily accessible to those individuals who most need it, HPL created an electronic information center that provides links to the most frequently requested items on the USCIS website (e.g., forms, online case status check), as well as to legal and support service providers (Naficy, 2009). One of the most interesting aspects of TAP's web site is the way in which the information is presented. As described by Naficy, the homepage "is minimalist in approach, using small graphics, simple, broad topic headings, and a minimum of other text" so as to "mirror[] the puzzled state in which TAP's customers come to the site with their unanswered questions" (p. 166). In so doing, they hoped to make the process of locating needed information more intuitive to users who lack familiarity with e-government.

TAP, through a partnership with a local USCIS office that makes effective use of HPL's in-house resources, serves nearly 2,500 immigrants and refugees through ESL classes, life skills workshops, instruction on the use of the Internet and various software, and assistance with applying for the annual U.S. State Department visa lottery. TAP hosts an annual Naturalization Ceremony and, furthermore, provides assistance to newly naturalized citizens through passport services and voter registration support. TAP's success lies not only in the way it provides immigrants with the tools they need to access e-government by enhancing their basic, digital and civics literacy skills and by presenting USCIS's online resources in an understandable manner but also in the way it ushers immigrants through various e-government processes – a feat made possible only through collaboration with the government agencies mandating those processes.

Recommendations

Through this study of innovative e-government partnerships thriving in libraries across the country, the authors have been able to identify a number of considerations that should guide the development of e-government partnership, including:

- Both the library and the agency see mutual benefit to entering into a partnership designed to provide collaborative e-government services;

- Agencies view the partnerships as a way through which to extend e-government services to the intended service recipients through libraries, rather than as a means to shift service provision costs to libraries;
- Agencies regard the library as a true partner and consider librarian feedback regarding e-government service design and delivery;
- Agencies are willing to help librarians better understand the e-government services, resources, and technologies;
- Agencies provide library-specific support (via dedicated e-mail or phone line) through which librarians can obtain assistance;
- The library considers providing e-government services to be part of its mission to serve the public; and
- The library has built a support infrastructure (e.g., information resources, technology training, staff assistance) around the e-government services.

These guidelines apply not only to e-government partnerships in other areas (e.g., taxation, employment assistance), but also to collaborations undertaken by other community-based organizations willing and able to serve as e-government intermediaries.

Further, as public libraries start to formalize collaborations with government agencies and community organizations, they should also conceive of these new partnerships as a vehicle for advocacy. Such partnerships enable libraries to demonstrate to partnering government agencies the e-government roles that libraries are capable of playing, which may prompt partnering organizations to vocalize their support for increased funding for libraries. At a broader level, libraries need to use the unique services being made available as a result of partnerships to directly advocate for greater financial support – not just to stem budget cuts, but to generate budget increases. It has been the case for nearly a decade that e-government services present a significant opportunity for libraries to engage in advocacy at local, state, and national levels (Bertot, Jaeger, McClure, & Langa, 2006a) and e-government partnerships – and their potential to enhance service delivery - can bolster a library's case for additional funding.

FUTURE RESEARCH DIRECTIONS

This chapter highlights the authors' work in identifying the range of issues impacting both users and libraries, as well as a collection of "best practices" adopted by libraries across the country that have recognized the potential for e-government partnerships to transform the way in which they serve recent immigrants in their communities. Further research, however, is needed to address a larger set of policy issues that have emerged from the findings made to date:

1. Libraries need to engage in a range of pre-e-government activities. Users come to e-government with a broad set of needs (e.g., assistance with basic, language, and/or digital literacy) that libraries strive to meet. Libraries need more guidance on how to identify – and ultimately meet – these user needs.
2. E-government is bigger than libraries and government agencies. There are critical non-governmental entities that often play significant roles in the e-government space. It is not uncommon for these entities to work with a particular constituency – e.g., seniors, households with certain income levels, persons from a particular country, or persons with disabilities. The wide array of organizations, from bar associations to local businesses, can be difficult to navigate, thus obscuring the potential for partnerships. Libraries need assistance with identifying and connecting with other potential partners.
3. Different community needs mandate different levels of e-government services. Depending on a community's particular need or set of

needs, a library may offer differing levels of e-government services simultaneously. Libraries need assistance with determining, based upon the specific communities they serve, which e-government services are vital and therefore should be a priority.

CONCLUSION

The e-government partnerships discussed in this chapter demonstrate the extent to which collaborations between libraries and government agencies can address the challenges created by government agencies' increasing reliance on e-government to interact with members of the public. For certain groups, such as immigrants, these partnerships provide assistance in navigating the e-government maze that is difficult to find elsewhere. If the goals of e-government are to provide enhanced services to the public and to generate more public engagement, there is a need to ensure that these goals extend to all e-government users. If we recognize the capability of e-government partnerships to bridge the gap between the agencies providing these services and the individuals who need these services, we must place greater emphasis on devising strategies for developing e-government partnerships that involve community organizations as well as libraries. The success factors and recommendations set forth in this chapter can serve as the backbone for such strategies, and future research in this area will reveal other elements that contribute to the creation of successful e-government partnerships.

REFERENCES

American Library Association. (2010). *A perfect storm brewing: Budget cuts threaten public library services at time of increased demand*. Chicago, IL: American Library Association. Retrieved from http://www.ala.org/ala/research/initiatives/plftas/issuesbriefs/issuebrief_perfectstorm.pdf

Audunson, R., Essmat, S., & Aabo, S. (2011). Public libraries: A meeting place for immigrant women? *Library & Information Science Research*, *33*, 220–227. doi:10.1016/j.lisr.2011.01.003.

Bertot, J. C., & Jaeger, P. T. (2006). User-centered e-government: Challenges and benefits for government Web sites. *Government Information Quarterly*, *23*, 163–168. doi:10.1016/j.giq.2006.02.001.

Bertot, J. C., & Jaeger, P. T. (2008). The e-government paradox: Better customer service doesn't necessarily cost less. *Government Information Quarterly*, *25*, 149–154. doi:10.1016/j.giq.2007.10.002.

Bertot, J. C., & Jaeger, P. T. (2012). Implementing and managing public library networks, connectivity, and partnerships to promote e-government access and education. In Aikins, S. (Ed.), *Managing e-government projects: Concepts, issues and best practices* (pp. 183–199). Hershey, PA: IGI Global. doi:10.4018/978-1-4666-0086-7.ch007.

Bertot, J. C., Jaeger, P. T., & Hansen, D. (2012). The impact of polices on government social media usage: Issues, challenges, and recommendations. *Government Information Quarterly*, *29*, 30–40. doi:10.1016/j.giq.2011.04.004.

Bertot, J. C., Jaeger, P. T., Langa, L. A., & McClure, C. R. (2006a). Public access computing and Internet access in public libraries: The role of public libraries in e-government and emergency situations. *First Monday*, *11*(9). Retrieved from http://www.firstmonday.org/issues/issue11_9/bertot/index.html.

Bertot, J. C., Jaeger, P. T., Langa, L. A., & McClure, C. R. (2006b). Drafted: I want you to deliver e-government. *Library Journal*, *131*(13), 34–39.

Bertot, J. C., Lincoln, R., McDermott, A. M., Real, B., & Peterson, K. J. (2012). *Public libraries and the Internet 2012: Study results and findings*. Information Policy & Access Center, University of Maryland, College of Information Studies. Retrieved from http://www.plinternetsurvey.org

Bertot, J. C., McClure, C. R., & Jaeger, P. T. (2008). The impacts of free public Internet access on public library patrons and communities. *The Library Quarterly*, *78*, 285–301. doi:10.1086/588445.

Burke, S. K. (2008a). Public library resources used by immigrant households. *Public Libraries*, *47*(4), 32–41.

Burke, S. K. (2008b). Use of public libraries by immigrants. *Reference and User Services Quarterly*, *48*, 164–174.

Caidi, N., & Allard, D. (2005). Social inclusion of newcomers to Canada: An information problem? *Library & Information Science Research*, *27*, 302–324. doi:10.1016/j.lisr.2005.04.003.

Camarota, S. A. (2010). *Immigration and economic stagnation: An examination of trends, 2000 to 2010*. Washington, DC: Center for Immigration Studies. Retrieved from http://www.cis.org/articles/2010/highest-decade.pdf

Carnesi, M. S., & Fiol, M. A. (2000). Queens Library's New Americans Program: 23 years of services to immigrants. In Guerena, S. (Ed.), *Library Services to Latinos: An Anthology* (pp. 133–142). Jefferson, NC: McFarland & Company, Inc., Publishers.

Chu, C. M. (1999). Literacy practices of linguistic minorities: Sociolingusitic issues and implications for literacy services. *The Library Quarterly*, *69*, 339–359. doi:10.1086/603093.

Cuban, S. (2007). *Serving new immigrant communities in the library*. Westport, CT: Greenwood.

Dawes, S. S. (2009). Governance in the digital age: A research and action framework for an uncertain future. *Government Information Quarterly*, *26*, 257–264. doi:10.1016/j.giq.2008.12.003.

Department of Justice, Civil Rights Division. (2012). Executive Order 13166. Retrieved from http://www.lep.gov/13166/eo13166.html

Ebbers, W. E., Pieterson, W. J., & Noordman, H. N. (2008). Electronic government: Rethinking channel management strategies. *Government Information Quarterly*, *25*, 181–201. doi:10.1016/j.giq.2006.11.003.

Federal Communications Commission. (2012). *National Broadband Plan*. Washington, DC: Federal Communications Commission. Retrieved from http://www.broadband.gov/plan/

Fenster, M. (2006). The opacity of transparency. *Iowa Law Review*, *91*, 885–949.

Fisher, K. E., Becker, S., & Crandall, M. (2010). E-government service use and impact through public libraries: Preliminary findings from a national study of public access computing in public libraries. In *Proceedings of the 43rd Hawaii International Conference on System Sciences* (pp. 1-10).

Gibson, A. N., Bertot, J. C., & McClure, C. R. (2009). Emerging role of public librarians as E-government providers. In R. H. Sprague, Jr. (Ed.), *Proceedings of the 42nd Hawaii International Conference on System Sciences* (pp. 1-10). doi: 10.1109/HICSS.2009.183

Heanue, A. (2001). In support of democracy: The library role in public access to government information. In Kranich, N. (Ed.), *Libraries & democracy: The cornerstones of liberty* (pp. 121–128). Chicago: American Library Association.

Holt, L. E., & Holt, G. E. (2010). *Public library services for the poor: Doing all we can*. Chicago: ALA Editions.

Jaeger, P. T., & Bertot, J. C. (2009). E-government education in public libraries: New service roles and expanding social responsibilities. *Journal of Education for Library and Information Science*, *50*, 40–50.

Jaeger, P. T., & Bertot, J. C. (2010). Designing, implementing, and evaluating user-centered and citizen-centered e-government. *International Journal of Electronic Government Research, 6*(2), 1–17. doi:10.4018/jegr.2010040101.

Jaeger, P. T., & Bertot, J. C. (2011). Responsibility rolls down: Public libraries and the social and policy obligations of ensuring access to e-government and government information. *Public Library Quarterly, 30*(2), 1–25. doi:10.1080/01616846.2011.575699.

Jaeger, P. T., Bertot, J. C., Shuler, J. A., & McGilvray, J. (in press). A new frontier for LIS programs: E-government education, library/government partnerships, and the preparation of future information professionals. *Education for Information*.

Jones, P. A. Jr. (1999). *Libraries, immigrants, and the American experience*. Westport, CT: Greenwood.

Lake, R. L. D., & Huckfeldt, R. (1998). Social capital, social networks, and political participation. *Political Psychology, 19*, 567–584. doi:10.1111/0162-895X.00118.

Larson, K. C. (2001). The Saturday evening girls: A progressive era library club and the intellectual life of working class and immigrant girls in turn-of-the century Boston. *The Library Quarterly, 71*, 195–230. doi:10.1086/603261.

Lukenbill, W. B. (2006). Helping youth at risk: An overview of reformist movements in public libraries to youth. *New Review of Children's Literature and Librarianship, 12*, 197–213. doi:10.1080/13614540600982991.

McCook, K. D. P. (2011). *Introduction to public librarianship* (2nd ed.). New York: Neal Schuman.

McDowell, K. (2010). Which truth, what fiction? Librarians' book recommendations for children, 1877-1890. In Nelson, A. R., & Rudolph, J. L. (Eds.), *Education and the culture of print in modern America* (pp. 15–35). Madison, WI: University of Wisconsin.

McDowell, K. (2011). Children's voices in librarians' words, 1890-1930. *Libraries & the Cultural Record, 46*, 73–100. doi:10.1353/lac.2011.0005.

Miranda-Murillo, D. (2006). New immigrants centers at the Austin Public Library. *Texas Library Journal, 82*(4), 144–147.

Naficy, H. (2009). Centering essential immigrant help on the library Web site: The American Place (TAP) at Hartford Public Library. *Public Library Quarterly, 28*(2), 162–175. doi:10.1080/01616840902892440.

Office of Citizenship, U.S. Citizenship and Immigration Services. (2010, September 15). *Library services for immigrants: A report on current practices*. Retrieved from http://www.uscis.gov/USCIS/Office%20of%20Citizenship/Citizenship%20Resource%20Center%20Site/Publications/PDFs/G-1112.pdf

queenslibrary.org. (2013). Website. Retrieved from http://www.queenslibrary.org/services/citizenship-immigration

Sigler, K. I., Jaeger, P. T., Bertot, J. C., DeCoster, E. J., McDermott, A. J., & Langa, L. A. (2012). Public libraries, the Internet, and economic uncertainty. In A. Woodsworth (Ed.), Advances in librarianship, vol. 34: Librarianship in times of crisis (pp. 19-35). London: Emerald.

Streib, G., & Navarro, I. (2006). Citizen demand for interactive e-government: The case of Georgia consumer services. *American Review of Public Administration, 36*, 288–300. doi:10.1177/0275074005283371.

Su, S. S., & Conaway, C. W. (1995). Information and a forgotten minority: Elderly Chinese immigrants. *Library & Information Science Research*, *17*(1), 69–86. doi:10.1016/0740-8188(95)90006-3.

Sundell, J. (2000). Library service to Hispanic immigrants of Forsyth County, North Carolina: A community collaboration. In Guerena, S. (Ed.), *Library Services to Latinos: An Anthology* (pp. 143–168). Jefferson, NC: McFarland & Company, Inc,Publishers.

Tetteh, B. (2011). Serving African immigrants in Colorado Public Libraries. *Colorado Libraries*, *35*(4). Retrieved from http://coloradolibrariesjournal.org/?q=content/serving-african-immigrants-colorado-public-libraries

Uscis.gov. (2013). Website. Retrieved from http://www.uscis.gov/portal/site/uscis

Varheim, A. (2010). Gracious space: Library programming strategies towards immigrants as tools in the creation of social capital. *Library & Information Science Research*, *33*, 12–18. doi:10.1016/j.lisr.2010.04.005.

Warkentien, S., Clark, M., & Jacinto, B. (2009). *English literacy of foreign-born adults in the United States: 2003*. National Center for Education Statistics. Retrieved from http://nces.ed.gov/pubs2009/2009034.pdf

West, D. M. (2008). State and federal electronic government in the United States, 2008. Washington, DC: Brookings Institution. Retrieved from http://www.brookings.edu/~/media/Files/rc/reports/2008/0826_egovernment_west/0826_egovernment_west.pdf

White House. (2012). *Digital government: Building a 21st century platform to better serve the American people*. Washington, DC: The White House. Retrieved from http://www.whitehouse.gov/sites/default/files/omb/egov/digital-government/digital-government.html

Wiegand, W. A. (1986). *The politics of an emerging profession: The American Library Association, 1876-1917*. New York: Greenwood.

Wiegand, W. A. (1989). *An active instrument for propaganda: The American public library during World War I*. Westport, CT: Greenwood.

Winkel, J. (2007). Lessons on evaluating programs and collections for immigrant communities at the Queens Borough Public Library. *Colorado Libraries*, *33*(1), 43–46.

www.lep.gov. (2013). Website. Retrieved from www.lep.gov

Yaniv, O. (2005, Oct. 19). Immigrants warned on green card cons. *New York Daily News*. Retrieved from http://articles.nydailynews.com/2005-10-19/local/18313877_1_immigrants-application-eligible-countries

Zhang, X. (2001). The practice and politics of public library services to Asian immigrants. In Lueveno-Molina, S. (Ed.), *Immigrant politics and the public library* (pp. 141–150). Westport, CT: Greenwood Press.

ADDITIONAL READING

Al-Qallaf, C. L., & Mika, J. J. (2009). Library and information services to the Arabic-speaking community: A survey of Michigan public libraries. *Public Library Quarterly*, *28*(2), 127–161. doi:10.1080/01616840902892390.

Allen, M., Matthew, S., & Boland, M. J. (2004). Working with immigrant and refugee populations: Issues and Hmong case study. *Library Trends*, *53*(2), 301–328.

American Library Association. (2007). Guidelines for the development and promotion of multilingual collections and services. Retrieved from http://www.ala.org/rusa/resources/guidelines/guidemultilingual

Bertot, J. C., & Jaeger, P. T. (in press). Public library and government partnerships: Transformative e-government and public service in times of economic hardship. In Weerakkody, V., & Reddick, C. G. (Eds.), *Public sector transformation through e-government: Experiences from Europe and North America*. New York: Routledge.

Doln, J., & Kahn, A. (2011). The more they change, the more they stay the same: Public libraries and social inclusion. In Baker, D., & Evans, W. (Eds.), *Libraries and society: Role, responsibility and future in an age of change* (pp. 81–100). Oxford, UK: Chandos.

Fisher, K. E., Durrance, J. C., & Hinton, M. B. (2004). Information grounds and the use of need-based services by immigrants in Queens, New York: A context-based, outcome evaluation approach. *Journal of the American Society for Information Science and Technology*, *55*(8), 754–766. doi:10.1002/asi.20019.

Fisher, K. E., Marcoux, E., Miller, L. S., Sánchez, A., & Cunningham, E. R. (2004). Information behaviour of migrant Hispanic farm workers and their families in the Pacific Northwest. *Information Research, 10*(1).

Fong, Rowena, & Furuto, S. B. C. L. (2001). *Culturally competent practice: Skills, intervention, and evaluation*. Needham Heights, MA: Allyn & Bacon.

Gibson, A.N., McClure, C.R., Bertot, J.C., McGilvray, J.A., & Andrade, J.C. (2008). Community leadership through public library e-government services. *Florida Libraries*, 4-7.

Gonzalez, L. (2001). Public libraries step up to the plate: Knowing and responding to the needs of our rapidly changing communities. *North Carolina Libraries*, *59*(2), 68–71.

Guerna, S. (Ed.). (2000). *Library services to Latinos: An anthology*. Jefferson, NC: McFarland & Company, Inc., Publishers.

Hoffert, B. (2008, September 1). Immigrant nation. *Library Journal*, 34–36.

Jaeger, P. T., Bertot, J. C., Kodama, C. M., Katz, S. M., & DeCoster, E. (2011). Describing and measuring the value of public libraries: The growth of the Internet and the evolution of library value. *First Monday*, *16*(11). Retrieved from http://firstmonday.org/htbin/cgiwrap/bin/ojs/index.php/fm/article/viewArticle/3765.

Jaeger, P. T., & Fleischmann, K. R. (2007). Public libraries, values, trust, and e-government. *Information Technology and Libraries*, *26*(4), 35–43.

Jaeger, P. T., & Thompson, K. M. (2004). Social information behavior and the democratic process: Information poverty, normative behavior, and electronic government in the United States. *Library & Information Science Research*, *26*(1), 94–107. doi:10.1016/j.lisr.2003.11.006.

Jenson, B. (2002). Service to day laborers: A job libraries have left undone. *Reference and User Services Quarterly*, *41*(3), 228–233.

Kranich, N. (2005). Civic partnerships: The role of libraries in promoting civic engagement. *Resource Sharing & Information Networks*, *18*(112), 89–103. doi:10.1300/J121v18n01_08.

Luevano-Molina, S. (Ed.). (2001). *Immigrant politics and the public library*. Westport, CT: Greenwood Press.

MacDonald, S. L. (2010, June). *The library settlement partnerships: A case study*. Paper presented at the 38th Annual Canadian Association for Information Science, Concordia University, Montreal, Quebec, Canada.

Michel, T. A., Sabino, E. E., Stevenson, A. J., Weiss, E., Carpenter, A., & Rapkin, B. (2011). Queens Library HealthLink: Fighting health disparities through community engagement. *Urban Library Journal*, *17*(1), 1–15.

Najera, D. (2007, June 4). U.S. public library services to Latin American immigrants: A survey of information needs, barriers to access, best practices and guidelines for developing library services at a local level. Retrieved from http://www.webjunction.org/155/articles/ content/445210

Oder, N. (2010). Permanent shift? *Library Journal*, *135*(1), 44–46.

Overall, P. M. (2009). Cultural competence: A conceptual framework for library and information science professionals. *The Library Quarterly*, *79*(2), 175–204. doi:10.1086/597080.

Sin, S. C.-J., & Kim, K.-S. (2008). Use and non-use of public libraries in the information age: A logistic regression analysis of household characteristics and library services variables. *Library & Information Science Research*, *30*(3), 207–215. doi:10.1016/j.lisr.2007.11.008.

Thwaites, M. B. (1993). Barriers to library use for ethnic minorities. *Library Management*, *14*(2), 32–34. doi:10.1108/01435129310026166.

ENDNOTES

1. Throughout this chapter, the term "foreign-born," defined by Camarata (2010) as "persons living in the United States who were not U.S. citizens at birth" - is used interchangeably with the term "immigrant." The term "foreign-born" includes naturalized U.S. citizens, lawful permanent residents, temporary migrants, humanitarian migrants, and people illegally present in the U.S.
2. See uscis.gov (2013).
3. See lep.gov (2013).
4. See queenslibrary.org (2013).

Chapter 4
Bridging the Inequality Gap to Accessing Medicare and Medicaid Information Online:
An Empirical Analysis of E-Government Success 2002 through 2010

Mary Schmeida
Kent State University, USA

Ramona McNeal
University of Northern Iowa, USA

ABSTRACT

Historic inequalities in U.S. Internet usage associated with demographic factors have left the underserved, primarily the poor and rural, with fewer information and options to public health insurance online. Government initiatives to overcome the Internet infrastructure barriers are opening access to Medicare and Medicaid websites for these vulnerable groups. Using multivariate regression analysis and individual level data from the Internet and American Life Project, we explore demographic factors asking: "how successful have government efforts been to bring underserved Americans online to Medicare and Medicaid public health insurance information?" The authors find some historic inequalities are narrowing as individuals with lower income are more likely to search for insurance information online with geographic differences not playing a major role. The authors' findings also suggest that age and gender are important factors in determining which individuals search for insurance information online.

DOI: 10.4018/978-1-4666-4173-0.ch004

Copyright © 2013, IGI Global. Copying or distributing in print or electronic forms without written permission of IGI Global is prohibited.

INTRODUCTION

Studies show that historic inequality in U.S. Internet usage is narrowing, improving citizen access to e-government information and services online. Past differences in Internet access are found to be based on demographic factors, such as age, education, income and race/ethnicity, creating an inequality gap on accessing valuable online public health insurance information, such as Medicare and Medicaid (Schmeida & McNeal, 2009; Schmeida & McNeal, 2007). The variation in Internet practices attributed to these demographic factors has been linked to underlying inequalities not only in Internet access, but also in technological skills and psychological barriers (Mossberger, Tolbert, & McNeal, 2007). Overtime, the narrowing of these inequality gaps suggest that federal and state policies and programs aimed at providing equitable Internet access may be working, bringing public health insurance information into the homes of needy Americans. The objective of this chapter is to explore "how successful have government efforts been to bringing underserved Americans online to Medicare and Medicaid insurance information?" To examine this question, this chapter will provide an empirical analysis of demographic factors influencing access to Medicare and Medicaid websites for years 2002 through 2010 using survey data from the Internet and American Life Project.

BACKGROUND

Over the past decade, U.S. federal, state and municipal governments have adopted some form of electronic government (e-government) practice, referring to "the delivery of information and services via the Internet or other digital means" (West, 2004, p. 2). The rise of e-government has brought high expectation that government information and service delivery would be more effective and efficient (Schmeida & McNeal, 2007), bringing transparency to the public, cost-cutting promises (McNeal & Schmeida, 2007; McNeal, Tolbert, Mossberger, & Dotterweich, 2003), reshaping government to be catalytic and enterprising (Schmeida, 2004), and improving the access to delivery of government information and services to citizens and other government stakeholders (Layne & Lee, 2001, p. 123). E-government promises to not only benefit the citizen, but the public organization implementing electronic delivery of services to citizens (Al-Sobhi, Weerakkody, & El-Haddadeh, 2012, p. 94).

As healthcare consumers are becoming more sophisticated and demanding better quality of care, advanced communication technology has potential to provide this quality of service. To government, Internet technology can make product and service delivery more convenient (Schmeida, 2004). The predicted benefits may improve the chance that Internet usage for U.S. government goods and services will continue to increase (Schmeida, McNeal, & Mossberger, 2007). One such service is the distribution of government Medicare and Medicaid public health insurance information and services to Americans online. To improve access to these public health insurance programs, the federal government has established Web-based information on Medicare eligibility criteria, enrollment guidelines, public health service centers, among other information. This is important since the influx of retired baby boomers has increased the demand for Medicare insurance, and the economic climate has increased demand for Medicaid and food stamps. States have also made considerable progress in Website technical development (West, 2005) with each of the 50 states providing residents with Medicaid online service information. Medicaid demand is highest in rural regions due to a smaller share of employers offering health insurance, and because of a greater share of lower income jobs (Gamm, Hutchinson, Dabney, & Dorsey, 2003). It is believed that making public health information available online will minimize historic disparities in health insurance distribution (Schmeida & McNeal, 2007), reaching more underserved populations.

Although e-government practices come with the prediction of many benefits including transparency, efficiency, and delivery of government services to underserved populations, the adoption of these strategies does not guarantee successful outcomes. Regardless of the goal, success is contingent on other factors, in particular, that the clients of a government program have both access to and use the Internet. This is evident from research exploring the impact of e-government practices established to help those most in need of Medicare and Medicaid services to receive them. Early studies show that Medicare and Medicaid websites had not been accessible to vulnerable groups. Those in most need of Internet access to these sites, the poor and underserved, were not accessing the Internet at home (Schmeida, 2005). Although earlier studies on Internet access were discouraging, later studies show some disparities narrowing for vulnerable population groups. In exploring differences across socioeconomic groups, Schmeida and McNeal (2007) found that disparities in searching Medicare and Medicaid information online are narrowing as the elderly and poor, among those in greatest need for publicly subsidized health insurance, began accessing program information online. These changes mirror the spread of Internet access in the U.S. Although individuals who are elderly or less affluent got online later than other groups, once they did, they were more likely than their counterparts to take part in online searches for Medicare and Medicaid information. This finding suggests that online Medicare and Medicaid outreach strategies have the potential for increasing enrollment, but success is contingent on increasing Internet usage. This conclusion is bolstered by Schmeida and McNeal (2009) who found those least likely to use the Internet (the poor, less educated, African-American, and Latino) were most likely to take steps toward improving their health if they do access healthcare information online.

In the past decade, the Internet has influenced information behavior and various mediums to accessing information (Jaeger & Bertot, 2010, p. 373). The use of advanced communication technology to improve government transparency, efficiency, and citizen trust in government has successfully improved citizen access to online public health insurance information for some while disenfranchising those without Internet access. Many early studies show an inequality or "digital divide" to Internet access in the U.S. (limiting the success of programs aimed at meeting the medical insurance needs for underserved populations), while some more recent studies and reports show mixed results and the inequality gap to be narrowing. Newer studies provide us with some expectation for a future equality or successful e-government to citizen information sharing. This narrowing of gaps in accessing the Internet for public information is a critical step toward meeting e-government goals for disseminating information to all groups. In the next section, this study will begin looking at the relationship between e-government success in expanding Medicare and Medicaid services to vulnerable groups, and how demographic factors influence Internet access and usage in the U.S.

Internet Access and Usage

Earlier researchers exploring variation in Internet use (Neu, Anderson, & Bikson, 1999; Putnam, 2000; National Telecommunications and Information Administration [NTIA], 2000; Compaine, 2001) focused solely on differences in Internet access based on demographic variables or the "digital divide." Taken together, the studies found enduring disparity based on gender, age, income, education, race, ethnicity, dual/single parent households, urban/rural areas, and mental or physical disabilities. Individuals with Internet access were more likely to be male, younger, more educated, affluent, Asian American or white, and to live in urban/suburban areas. Those least likely to have Internet access (especially at home) were poorer, older, uneducated, African American or Latino, and resided in rural areas. By 2002, research (NTIA, 2002) found that while other barriers remained, gender based differences had disappeared. This early group of researchers treated the differences in Internet use as a problem of access. The focus was on a binary dependent variable where individuals where classified as either having Internet access or not. Under this scenario, there is little call for government intervention. It was argued (for example, Compaine, 2001) that similar to radio and television; technical innovation will eventually result in lower prices for computers and Internet service. The Internet will spread just as radio and television had done previously. The one exception to this argument was the barrier to Internet access resulting from geography. Stover (1999) found those living in rural areas with Internet access had fewer choices for service providers and higher connection fees in comparison to urban/suburban areas. These differences were unlikely to change since telephone and other telecommunication service providers had little incentive to invest in telecommunication infrastructure in sparsely populated rural areas.

While early studies focused on differences in Internet access or the "digital divide," later research argued that variation in Internet usage is based on a more complicated set of factors. These latter studies (e.g., Norris, 2001; Hargittai, 2002) say that differences in Internet use need to be thought of in terms of a "second-level" digital divide, with significant variation in how individuals access the Internet and how they use it. These differences are the result of a divergent set of factors. Access alone cannot account for why some individuals do not go online.

Technical skills are among the factors found to influence whether an individual goes online and benefits from using the Internet. As described by Mossberger, Tolbert, and Stansbury (2003), technology skills can be thought of in terms of two broad categories. The first (technical competencies) include the necessary skills to use hardware and software such as typing and using a mouse. The second category (information literacy) concerns the ability to determine which information to obtain from the Internet for specific tasks, and is related to basic literacy (Mossberger, Tolbert, & Stansbury, 2003, p. 38). The deficiencies they found in both forms of skill mirrored the digital divide. Individuals lacking these technology skills were older, less educated, Latino, African American and less affluent.

Some researchers add psychosocial variables to the list of barriers to developing these skills. For example, Van Dijk and Hacker (2003) examined the variables influencing technology skills acquirement. Their study revealed age, gender and literacy as the strongest predictors of digital skills. With regard to age and gender, they conclude that motivation may be more relevant to attaining computer skills than formal levels of education (Van Dijk & Hacker, 2003, p. 319). Stanley (2003) and Adams, Stubbs, and Woods (2005) have added support to the argument that psychological factors including motivation were a significant element of digital skill development and Internet use. Other researchers (Mossberger, Tolbert, & McNeal, 2007; Selwyn, 2004) find the quality of accessing the Internet including Internet speed to be important for influencing the development of these skills. Individuals having convenient (at home) and quick (broadband) access were more likely to make greater use of the Internet that can lead to the development of technology skills.

The literature points to three barriers to Internet use: lack of motivation, limited access and deficiencies in technical and information literacy skills. These factors seem to reinforce each other for certain demographic variables. Socioeconomic variables such as age, education, income and ethnicity were identified as predictors of motivation, access and skill. While these barriers existed during the initial spread of the Internet, federal and state-local governments have worked to eliminate them, encouraging citizen use of the Internet.

Federal and State Policies Increasing Internet Access for Public Health Information and Services for All Americans

Starting in the 1990s and continuing throughout the 2000s, state and federal governments passed legislation designed to improve access to online government information and services. Federal Internet policy began with the Clinton Administration during which providing public access was the primary strategy used by the federal government to bring the public online. Policies implemented to address disparities in information technology usage were expressly designed to increase Internet access by providing access to the Internet in public places such as schools, libraries and Community Technical Centers (CTCs).

A major focus of the Clinton Administration was to expand Internet access to rural areas. By 1995, there were 28 programs administered by 15 different federal agencies providing funds that were expressly designated for rural telecommunication projects. They included such projects as the Health and Human Service's Rural Telemedicine Grant Program that provided grants for using telecommunications to improve medical care in rural areas (GAO, 1996, p. 2-6). Additional rural telecommunication programs were developed under the Bush Administration including the Health Technology to Enhance Quality Act, advancing health information technology infrastructure development (House of Representatives Bill 2762, 2005).

The passage of the Telecommunications Act of 1996 further added to the list of programs providing the expansion of telecommunication services. The Telecommunications Act made major changes to the 1934 Communication Act that was primarily directed toward increasing competition. Regulations were put into place to break up local telephone and cable monopolies, promote greater competition in long-distance telephone service, and encourage growth of the Internet. While increased competition was a major theme of the Act, so was providing telecommunication services to all areas of the country. A key section of the Telecommunications Act is the *Universal Service Provision*. This section gave the Federal Communication Commission until May 8, 1997 to develop plans for making affordable telephone service available to all Americans. It requires all competing telecommunication companies in the market to share in the cost of providing this service. The *Universal Service Provision* also makes available discounts to schools, libraries and rural healthcare facilities for more advanced technologies, such as the Internet and videoconferencing (Austin, 1996, p. 3-45).

To improve Internet access, several programs were developed, such as the 1994 Technology Opportunities Program (TOP) under the direction of the U.S. Department of Commerce and the 1999 Community Technology Center (CTC) program created under the direction of the Department of Education. These programs made monies available for creating and maintaining community centers for public computer access and training. The TOP program also provided matching grants for projects using technology in effort to solve community problems. During their existence, the TOP provided approximately 600 different community programs with a total of $230 million and roughly $160 million in grants (Jayakar & Park, 2012). Both programs were eliminated in 2004 under the Bush Administration. A much larger program, the E-rate (with a budget of $2.25 billion), administered under the Universal Service Administration Company (USAC) was also created to increase public Internet access, but through a different strategy. Instead of providing funds for the creation of community technical centers, it provided discounts to schools, school districts and libraries to cover the costs associated with connecting to the Internet (Jayakar & Park, 2012). In addition, the Library Service and Construction Act was updated and restructured in 1996 as the Library Service and Technology Act (LSTA). The LSTA stresses providing public access to technology and is administered through the Institute of Museum and Library Services (IMLS), which distributes federal funds to the states for local libraries (McClure & Bertot, 2002). The federal government was not alone in providing CTC. States such as Texas (Stover, Chapman, & Walters, 2004) and private non-profit groups including the Bill and Melinda Gates Foundation provided funding to create and maintain CTCs.

Under the Bush Administration, the direction of federal policy to increase Internet usage changed strategy. Believing, as argued by some (e.g., Compaine, 2001), that market forces would eventually correct the "digital divide," federal policy moved away from providing Internet access in public places and instead concentrated on increasing technology skills among American youth. During the 2000 presidential campaign, U.S. President George W. Bush promoted the No Child Left Behind (NCLB) Act as the "cornerstone" of his administration. One feature of this new federal education program was the goal of increasing technology skills, ensuring that all students become technologically literate no later than the eighth grade (Dickard, 2003).

The direction of federal policy aimed at increasing Internet use again changed course under the Obama Administration. It returned to a strategy that more closely resembles policy implemented under the Clinton Administration. However, the solution was no longer entirely seen as providing access in public places, but also includes provisions for increasing access to broadband services in the home. In order to increase the availability of broadband in underserved areas, a number of programs were implemented fostering necessary infrastructure construction for broadband services in residential areas. Through the American Recovery and Reinvestment Act of 2009, $7.2 billion in grants and loans were provided to state and local communities to improve telecommunication infrastructure in underserved residential areas. Included among the projects eligible for funding under these programs are those that support the creation and maintenance of CTCs. In addition, $100 million dollars was awarded to four satellite companies to help increase broadband service in rural areas (Recovery Accountability and Transparency Board, 2010).

At the federal level, increasing Internet use has been a consistent goal across the last three presidential administrations, even though the strategies used for solving this problem have changed with each new administration. The response at the state level is not as easy to summarize because of the telecommunication service providers influence in state capitals. Some states have taken a number of creative approaches to increasing Internet access, including reducing infrastructure costs to service providers by allowing them to patch into existing infrastructure initially created for government needs. This process is referred to as "backhaul capacity." In other states, some local and regional governments have begun providing communication services themselves. This strategy has been met with resistance by existing telecommunication service providers, who in a number of states have successfully lobbied state legislatures to ban municipal owned broadband service (Federal Communication Commission, 2010).

While U.S. government action at all levels (federal, state and municipal) play an important role in solving the problem of uneven Internet use, decisions made at the individual level also influence whether online health insurance information will be sought. An April 2012 Pew Internet and American Life Project survey found that roughly half of the adult respondents who do not go online cited their main reason as not feeling it has relevance to them. Most of these individuals were found to have never gone online and not having anyone in their household who does. The belief that the Internet held little relevance in an individual's life not only influences the likelihood that they will go online, but also unfavorably impacts opinion regarding government policy to increase Internet access. A Pew Internet and American Life Project (2010a) survey found that only about 53% of adults did not believe that making affordable high-speed Internet access to all citizens should be a top government priority. Which of these factors (governmental or individual) are more important in determining whether underserved Americans will conduct online searches for Medicare and Medicaid insurance information?

EMPIRICAL MODEL: DATA AND METHODS

Data

To examine our research question, this chapter will rely on secondary data analysis or data collected by another entity. More specifically, the study utilizes the *Internet and American Life Daily Tracking Survey 2002, 2004, 2006, 2008, and 2010* conducted for the Pew Internet & American Life Project, by the Princeton Survey Research Associates. The Pew Internet & American Life Project is part of the Pew Research Center, a nonpartisan, nonprofit group that conducts studies and provides information regarding factors that shape American society. Pew surveys are random digit dial national telephone surveys limited to individuals 18 years or older and live in the continental United States. This study is based on five surveys conducted for the Internet and American Life Project with a sample size (n) of 2,500+ for 2002; 2004 (n = 1,000+); 2006 (n = 3,000); 2008 (n = 3,030); 2010 (n= 3,000). There are advantages and disadvantages associated with all forms of data analysis. One disadvantage associated with secondary data analysis is that the data was collected for a specific purpose and may not be ideally suited for other research. In general, these datasets have been well suited for this study with two exceptions. In 2008, the categories for income were altered and the wording for the question utilized for the dependent variable was changed. These differences make it difficult, in some instances, to explain changes in findings over time.

Methods

Demographic and geographical factors associated with citizen online searches for Medicare or Medicaid public health insurance information are analyzed for each of these years using logistic regression analysis, and explore the trends for 2002 through 2010. Logistic regression analysis is used because the dependent variable is binary. Independent variables were selected based on findings from prior research on barriers to Internet usage. For the years 2002-2006, the dependent variable was constructed as a dummy variable using the question: "Have you ever searched for online information about Medicaid or Medicare?" For the years 2008-2010, the question underwent a change in wording. The dependent variable for these latter two years was constructed as a dummy variable using the question: "Have you ever searched for online information related to insurance, including private insurance, Medicare or Medicaid?" The variables are coded 1 for someone looking for health insurance information online and 0 otherwise.

Explanatory or independent variables include an *Income* measure for the years 2002 to 2006 based on an 8-point scale where 1 indicates that family income ranges from $0 to $10,000 and 8 signifies a family income of $100,000 or more. Starting in 2008, the income measure was expanded to a 9-point scale where 1 indicates that family incomes range from $0 to $10,000 and 9 signifies a family income of $150,000 or more. For all years, *Education* is measured using a 7-point scale, ranging from eighth-grade education or less to post-graduate training/professional training, which includes Masters/Ph.D., law and medical school. Based on both the literature on Internet access and technology skills it is expected that both income and education would be positively associated with Internet searches. There is conflicting research (Schmeida & McNeal, 2007) that finds those with lower income levels are more likely to conduct online searches for Medicare and Medicaid information. Efforts to account for differences in their findings for income and those based on Internet access and skills was found in the literature on citizen-initiated government contact (Sharp, 1986), which argues that citizens are more likely to contact government when they have a need or a perceived need.

Age is measured in years, and *Gender* is measured using a binary variable coded 1 for male and 0 for female. The literature on Internet access and skills provides little help in predicting the impact of gender for online searches and suggests that age will be negatively associated with online information searches. Other research (Schmeida & McNeal, 2007; Chen & Dimitrova, 2006) has found gender and age to be associated with citizen willingness to search public information using government Web portals. As with income, the conflicting predictions regarding age can be, in part, moderated by findings from research on citizen-initiated government contact (Sharp, 1986). The role that gender plays in online healthcare searches can be understood through the role that women play as caregivers in the United States. Part of the healthcare burden in the United States is "relieved" through family members caring for aging and ill loved ones at home. Women have dominated the caregiver role at approximately 73% (Tong, 2007). It is not surprising that women are more likely to conduct online searches for healthcare information, including searches on Medicare and Medicaid.

To control for race and ethnicity, dummy variables were included for *African Americans*, *Asian Americans*, and *Latinos* with *non-Hispanic Whites* as the reference group. Based on the literature on Internet access and technology skills, it is assumed that Asian Americans would be most likely to conduct Internet searches, followed by non-Hispanic Whites. Dummy variables were included for *No Home Internet Connection* and *Home Dialup Connection*, with broadband access at home as the reference group. Controls were included for the type of home Internet access, because research (Selwyn, 2004; Mossberger, Tolbert, & McNeal, 2007) argues that access to home broadband encourages greater use of the Internet and develops Internet skills. Following these studies, it is predicted that individuals with broadband at home would be most likely to conduct Internet searches and those without home Internet connection would be least likely to search for information online.

Since research on Internet access (NTIA, 2011) found a persistent gap in urban/rural areas, two dummy variables were included for the respondent's geographic area (*Suburban* and *Urban*) with rural as the reference group. Residents living in suburban and urban areas are expected to be more likely to conduct Internet searches compared to those living in rural areas. Dummy variables for the *Midwest, Northeast and West* regions were included to control for regional differences. The South was designated as the reference group because West and Miller (2006) found this region to have the lowest levels of Internet connectivity. Table 1 summarizes the expected relationships between variables.

FINDINGS AND DISCUSSION

In Tables 2 and 3, both dependent variables are coded with higher scores associated with increased likelihood of searching for information online. Since the dependent variables are binary,

Table 1. Expected relationship between independent variables and dependent variable

Variable	Expected Relationship
Suburban	Positive
Urban	Positive
Midwest	Positive
Northeast	Positive
West	Positive
Age	Conflicting Literature
Male	Negative
Latino	Negative
African American	Negative
Asian American	Positive
Education	Positive
Income	Conflicting Literature
Dial-Up Connection	Negative
No Home Connection	Negative

models are estimated using logistic regression. Table 2 presents the findings for 2002, 2004 and 2006 using the dependent variable: "Have you ever searched for online information about Medicaid or Medicare?" Table 3 presents the findings for 2008 and 2010 using the dependent variable: "Have you ever searched for online information related to insurance, including private insurance, Medicare or Medicaid?" Taken together, these tables suggest that individual-level variables play a larger role than geographic factors in determining who searches for Medicare and Medicaid public health insurance information online.

There were only two variables found related to online Medicare and Medicaid information searches in the year 2002. This is not entirely surprising, since very few adults were online at this point in time and it is not expected that many would have searched for health insurance information. One variable found to be significant in 2002 was income. In the years 2002, 2006 and 2008, individuals with lower income levels were found to be more likely to search for health insurance information online. Although this finding is inconsistent with the literature on Internet access and use, it is supported by Schmeida and McNeal (2007) who found that individuals with lower income levels were more likely to search for online information about Medicare and Medicaid. It is also consistent with the literature on citizen-initiated government contact (Sharp, 1986), which argues that citizens are more likely to contact government when they have a need or a perceived need. The finding that a group (those with lower income levels) predicted by the literature on both Internet usage and access to be less likely to conduct Internet searches was more likely to search for information online provides some evidence of government success in using e-government practices to expanding Medicare and Medicaid services to vulnerable groups.

The only other variable found to be significant in the year 2002 was no home Internet access. Across all five years of study, individuals without home Internet access were less likely to search for Medicare and Medicaid information online. This finding supports Mossberger, Tolbert, and McNeal (2007) and Selwyn (2004) who argue that access to home broadband encourages greater use of the Internet and leads to the development of Internet skills. While this finding is not surprising, the fact that the only year where individuals with dialup were less likely to look for health insurance online was 2010 was unexpected. It is assumed that those individuals with dialup access at home would use the Internet less often and have more limited Internet skills. One possible explanation for this finding is that there has been slow adoption of broadband access in the home. According to the Pew Internet and American Life Project (2012) only about 4% of U.S. citizens had broadband access in the home in 2001, and by 2011 this number grew to 62%. This suggests that it took until 2010 for the development of a sufficiently large number of individuals with home broadband to allow for

Table 2. Medicare and Medicaid internet searches, 2002-2006

	Year 2002		Year 2004		Year 2006	
Variables	β (se)	p>lzl	β (se)	p>lzl	β (se)	p>lzl
			Environmental Variables			
Suburban	.154(.287)	.593	-.151(.423)	.721	-.213(.194)	.272
Urban	.087(.317)	.782	.093(.454)	.837	.157(.214)	.728
Midwest	-.277(.200)	.347	-.423(.433)	.329	**-.372(.186)**	**.045**
Northeast	-.233(.331)	.483	-.279(.539)	.702	**-.378(.222)**	**.089**
West	-.282(249)	.256	.221(.391)	.572	-.249(.205)	.224
			Individual Level Variables			
Age	.006(.007)	.364	**.029(.010)**	**.006**	**.019(.005)**	**.000**
Male	-.085(.197)	.666	**-.720(.322)**	**.026**	-.049(.147)	.742
Latino	-.425(.327)	.192	.318(.666)	.623	-.337(.318)	.288
Black	.107(.404)	.791	.717(.488)	.142	-.358(.293)	.222
Asian	.560(.500)	.184	-.025(1.11)	.982	-.692(.582)	.234
Education	.261(.054)	.326	**.326(.118)**	**.006**	**.146(.058)**	**.012**
Income	**-.115(.052)**	**.026**	-.067(.086)	.434	**-.081(.042)**	**.054**
Dial-up Connection	-.325(.224)	.146	.251(.346)	.469	-.225(.241)	.349
No Home Internet Connection	**-2.89(.433)**	**.000**	**-1.97(.541)**	**.000**	**-2.35(.326)**	**.000**
Constant **Pseudo R2**	**-1.89(.589)** .1119	**.001**	**-4.36(.914)** .1460	**.000**	.063(.414) .0903	.879
LR Chi² (14)	98.91	.000	53.53	.000	130.52	.000
N	1895		676		2151	

Source: *The Pew Internet & American Life Project Daily Tracking Survey December 2002, Activity Tracking Survey November 2004, and August 2006 Daily Tracking Survey.* Logistic regression estimates with standard errors in parentheses. Reported probabilities are based on two-tailed tests. Statistically significant coefficients at .10 or less in bold. "Have you ever searched for online information about Medicaid or Medicare?"

a difference to become statistically significant. The finding also provides some evidence that the Obama Administration is achieving some success in its goal of encouraging the spread of broadband to underserved areas.

Internet searches for online health insurance information have been found more likely done by individuals with higher education levels, with the exception of the year 2002. This finding is expected, since these individuals are not only more likely to have Internet access but both greater technical and information literacy skills. Consistent across all five years of study was that race/ethnicity factors are not associated with Internet health insurance searches. These findings conflicts with trends (both past and recent) that indicate racial/ethnic minorities are less likely to have Internet access. Research findings by Mossberger, Tolbert, and Gilbert (2006) provide a possible explanation; the appearance of variations in Internet usage by race/ethnicity is actually the result of concentrated poverty and racial segregation and not differences among racial groups. When variables such as education attainment and median family income are controlled for, differences in Internet usage based on race disappear.

Table 3. Public and private health insurance internet searches, 2008-2010

	Year 2008		Year 2010	
Variables	β (se)	p>lzl	β (se)	p>lzl
Environmental Variables				
Suburban	- .107(.216)	.619	.154(.155)	.320
Urban	**.532(.234)**	**.023**	.168(.161)	.295
Midwest	.139(.201)	.489	-.058(.142)	.683
Northeast	-.002 (.227)	.993	.024(.539)	.878
West	.095 (.212)	.652	-.176(.142)	.217
Individual Level Variables				
Age	**-.020(.005)**	**.000**	**- .006(.003)**	**.066**
Male	**-.963(.161)**	**.000**	**-.720(.322)**	**.026**
Latino	-.337(.318)	.288	-.007(.163)	.974
Black	-.358(.293)	.222	-.035(.144)	.807
Asian	- .693(.582)	.234	-.125(.299)	.676
Education	**.146(.058)**	**.012**	**.253(.039)**	**.000**
Income	**-.081(.042)**	**.054**	.013(.026)	.621
Dial-up Connection	-.225(.241)	.349	**-.476(.230)**	**.038**
No Home Internet Connection	**-2.35(.326)**	**.000**	**-2.31(.219)**	**.000**
Constant **Pseudo R2**	.063(.414) .1678	.879	**-1.68(.271)** .1652	**.000**
LR Chi² (14)	214.50	.000	435.27	.000
N	1280		2330	

Source: *The Pew Internet & American Life Project Fall Tracking 2008*, and *August Change Assessment 2010*. Logistic regression estimates with standard errors in parentheses. Reported probabilities are based on two-tailed tests. Statistically significant coefficients at .10 or less in bold. "Have you ever searched for online information related to insurance, including private insurance, Medicare or Medicaid?"

Women were found more likely to search for healthcare information in three of the study years (2004, 2008, & 2010), as expected based on gender and caregiver literature (Tong, 2007). Geographic differences including region and community type (urban, suburban and rural) were not found to play a major role in Internet searches for health insurance information, despite trend studies showing that residents in rural areas and the South have less access to the broadband service. There are two possible reasons for this finding. First, broadband access at home has been slow to spread regardless of region or community type. Second, searching for information online is one of the less technical online activities. Broadband may not prove to be greatly superior to dialup in this circumstance.

The impact of age was found to change over time. It was not found to be significant in 2002, while in 2004 and 2006 older individuals were more likely to search for Medicare and Medicaid information online. Older individuals, while most in need of services such as Medicare and Medicaid, have historical been less likely to go online. These findings provide some evidence of government success to use e-government practices to expand public health insurance services to vulnerable groups. Starting in 2008, younger individuals were more likely to search for medical insurance information online. Schmeida & McNeal (2007) found that older individuals were more likely to search for Medicare and Medicaid information online and attributed this to the literature on citizen-initiated government contacts. They argued that older individuals were more likely to search for this information because of a greater need. However, because of the current economic climate, that may no longer be true. The number of individuals relying on Medicaid continues to rise. In 2010, for the first time Medicaid overtook K-12 education as the most expensive item on state budgets (Vestal, 2012). The other possibility is that the change may simply reflect the change in question wording from 2006 to 2008. From 2002 through 2006, the dependent variable read: "Have you ever searched for online information about Medicaid or Medicare?" In 2008, the question changed to: "Have you ever searched for online information related to insurance, including private insurance, Medicare or Medicaid?"

As a final mechanism for examining the success of government policy to use e-government strategies for providing Medicare and Medicaid information to vulnerable populations, the percentage of individuals who obtained such information is presented in Table 4, by year. Since the dependent variable changed starting in 2008, the percentages are only calculated through 2006. To further aid in examining the impact of government policy, individuals were grouped by age using generational categories with Millennial denoted to those between age 18 and 34 in 2010, Generation X as between 35 and 46, Young Boomer between 47 and 56, Old Boomer between 57 and 65, Silent Generation between 66 and 74 and G.I. Generation age 75 or older in 2010 (The Pew Internet & American Life Project 2002; 2004; 2006). Table 4 provides evidence of e-government success. The percentage of individuals searching for Medicare and Medicaid information online increased over time for each generation. The two generations having the greatest jump in percentage for searching online information were Older Boomers and the Silent Generation. This is expected since these two groups would have been at retirement age or approaching retirement, and in greatest need of this insurance information.

Table 4. Online search for Medicare and Medicaid information by year and generation showing e-government success

Generation/Year	1992	1994	1996
Millennials	7.6%	3.9%	8.6%
Generation X	6.0%	8.2%	9.2%
Younger Boomers	5.0%	7.2%	7.9%
Older Boomers	3.8%	9.9%	11.0%
Silent Generation	6.7%	7.4%	10.7%
G.I. Generation	3.1%	5.4%	5.7%

Source: *The Pew Internet & American Life Project Daily Tracking Survey December 2002, Activity Tracking Survey November 2004, and August 2006 Daily Tracking Survey.* Percentages were calculated for the question: "Have you ever searched for online information about Medicaid or Medicare?"

FUTURE RESEARCH DIRECTIONS

Taken as a whole, the findings from this study are mixed. They confirm some of the expectations of research on Internet access and usage while contradicting other. Trend studies starting in the early 2000's have shown disparities in Internet use based on age, income, education, race, ethnicity, dual/single parent households, urban/rural areas, primary language spoken at home, and mental or physical disabilities. Initially, gender was also a factor but was found to disappear by 2002. Of these factors, the rural/urban divide appears to have one of the more difficult gaps to close. A number of studies using statistical methods point to three individual-level factors that account for differences in use: lack of motivation, limited access, and deficiencies in technical competency and information literacy skills. In addition, there has been research pointing to government policy (particularly in rural areas) that has been at least, in part, responsible for differences in access based on geographical factors.

The first two U.S. presidents to assume the challenge of disparities in Internet use (Bill Clinton and George W. Bush) mostly targeted the individual-level barriers to Internet use. Recently, President Obama has taken a new approach with a strategy that combines elements of the Clinton Administration (providing monies for the maintenance and creation of Community Technology Centers) plus providing financial incentives to state and local governments to establish the necessary infrastructure to bring broadband services to previously underserved areas of the nation. The implementation of policies under the Obama Administration depends on the cooperation of state government. However, programs are relatively new and yet to have full effect. Future research is needed to examine not only how the outcome of Obama policy differs from previous administrations, but to explore factors that determine levels of cooperation from the individual states.

CONCLUSION

This chapter began with the premise that no matter how technically sophisticated an e-government program, its success hinges on a number of factors, most importantly, whether the clients of the program have access to the Internet and use it. To examine the efforts of the U.S. government to overcome gaps in Internet usage and improve the likelihood of success in all e-government, this chapter looked at changes in use of one e-government program. This research examined the question, "how successful have government efforts been to bringing underserved Americans online to Medicare and Medicaid insurance information?" This is an ideal program to examine since the clients of Medicare and Medicaid (elderly and poor) are among those least likely to have Internet access or the skills necessary to use the Internet effectively.

This study examined the years 2002 through 2010 in an attempt to capture the impact of a variety of strategies undertaken to increase Internet usage through three Executive Administrations (Bill Clinton, George W. Bush, and Barack Obama). Although this study does not use data from the Clinton Administration, it begins with the year 2002; findings for the earlier years of this study (2002 and 2004) do suggest that this policy may have had some initial success. Those individuals least likely to have Internet access at home (older and less affluent) were among those most likely to seek out Medicare and Medicaid information online. This suggests that citizens were using public Internet access, such as the library. This provides some evidence that Clinton's strategy of providing monies to public facilities such as schools and libraries to support free public Internet access and training to increase Internet skills was having the intended effect.

While this study finds some support that government strategies are bringing citizens online and increasing the likelihood of e-government success, it also found evidence that the government has more to do in this area. For example, having Internet access at home (either dialup or broadband) was found to be a consistent predictor of online health insurance information searches. For 2010, the finding changed with those individuals with broadband (at home) being more likely to search for insurance information online, than either those with no home access or dialup access. In part, this is consistent with Mossberger, Tolbert, and McNeal (2007) and Selwyn (2004) who argue that access to home broadband encourages greater use of the Internet and develops Internet skills. This outcome suggests that providing free Internet access in public facilities can be limited to insuring that citizens will make use of government services and information provided online. Efforts are also needed to provide needed infrastructure, important to extending broadband to underserved residential areas. Such efforts are currently underway as part of the Obama Administration's effort to bring more citizens online. However, these policies depend on the cooperation of state governments that have not been consistent in their response to these programs. These varying state responses may lead to regional differences in Internet access and usage. The implementation of these programs is in the beginning stages and this study cannot adequately predict their impact. Future research will be necessary to determine if policy under the current administration further increases Internet usage and the likelihood of increased e-government success.

REFERENCES

Adams, N., Stubbs, V., & Woods, V. (2005). Psychological barriers to Internet usage among older adults in the U.K. *Medical Informatics and the Internet in Medicine*, *30*(1), 3–17. doi:10.1080/14639230500066876 PMID:16036626.

Al-Sobhi, F., Weerakkody, V., & El-Haddadeh, R. (2012). Building trust in e-government adoption through an intermediary channel. *International Journal of Electronic Government Research*, *8*(2), 91–106. doi:10.4018/jegr.2012040105.

Austin, J. (Ed.). (1996). *Praise, protest greet telecom bill. 1996 CQ almanac* (*Vol. LII*, pp. 3–46). Washington, DC: CQ Inc..

Chen, Y., & Dimitrova, D. (2006). Electronic government and online engagement: Citizen interaction with government via Web portals. *International Journal of Electronic Government Research*, *2*(1), 54–76. doi:10.4018/jegr.2006010104.

Compaine, B. (2001). Epilogue. In Compaine, B. (Ed.), *The digital divide: Facing a crisis or creating a myth?* (pp. 337–339). Cambridge, MA: MIT Press.

Dickard, N. (2003). Edtech 2002: Budget challenges, policy shifts and digital opportunity. In N. Dickard Benton (Ed.), *The sustainability challenge: Taking edtech to the next level.* The Foundation and the Education Development Center's for Children and Technology. Retrieved December 19, 2003, from http://www.benton.org/publibrary/sustainability/sus_challenge.html

Federal Communication Commission. (2010). *National broadband plan: Connecting America.* Retrieved April 11, 2011, from http://www.broadband.gov/

Gamm, L. D., Hutchinson, L. L., Dabney, B. J., & Dorsey, A. (Eds.). (2003). *Rural healthy people 2010: A companion document to healthy people 2010* (Vol. 1). College Station, TX: The Texas A & M University System Health Science Center, School of Rural Public Health, Southwest Rural Health Research Center. Retrieved February 19, 2003, from http://www.srph.tamhsc.edu/centers/rhp2010/publications.htm

Government Accounting Office. (1996). *Rural development: Steps toward realizing the potential of telecommunications technologies (GAO/RCED-96-155).* Washington, DC: U.S. Government Printing Office.

House of Representatives Bill 2762. (2005). *Health Technology To Enhance Quality Act of 2005.* 109th U.S. Congress.

Jaeger, P., & Bertot, J. (2010). Transparency and technological change: Ensuring equal and sustained public access to government information. *Government Information Quarterly*, *27*(4), 371–376. doi:10.1016/j.giq.2010.05.003.

Jayakar, K., & Park, E. (2012). Funding public computing centers: Balancing broadband availability and expected demand. *Government Information Quarterly*, *29*(1), 50–59. doi:10.1016/j.giq.2011.02.005.

Layne, K., & Lee, J. (2001). Developing fully functional e-government: A four stage model. *Government Information Quarterly*, *18*(2), 122–136. doi:10.1016/S0740-624X(01)00066-1.

McClure, C. R., & Bertot, C. J. (2002). *Public library internet services: Impact of the digital divide*. Retrieved March 12, 2003 from http://slis-two.lis.fsu.edu/~jcbertot/DDFinal03_01_02.pdf

McNeal, R., & Schmeida, M. (2007). Electronic campaign finance reform in the American states. In Anttiroiko, A.-V., & Malkia, M. (Eds.), *The encyclopedia of digital government* (*Vol. III*, pp. 624–628). Idea Group Publishing.

McNeal, R., Tolbert, C., Mossberger, K., & Dotterweich, L. (2003). Innovating in digital government in the American states. *Social Science Quarterly*, *84*(1), 52–70. doi:10.1111/1540-6237.00140.

Mossberger, K., Tolbert, C., & McNeal, R. (2007). *Digital citizenship: The internet, society and participation*. Cambridge, MA: MIT Press.

Mossberger, K., Tolbert, C., & Stansbury, M. (2003). *Virtual inequality: Beyond the digital divide*. Washington, DC: Georgetown Press.

National Telecommunications and Information Administration. (2000). *Falling through the net: Toward digital inclusion. A report on Americans access to technology tools*. Retrieved October 14, 2005, from http://www.ntia.doc.gov/files/ntia/publications/fttn00.pdf

National Telecommunications and Information Administration. (2002). *A nation online: How Americans are expanding their use of the internet*. Retrieved October 14, 2005, from http://www.ntia.doc.gov/report/2002/nation-online-internet-use-america

National Telecommunications and Information Administration. (2011). *Digital nation: Expanding internet usage*. Retrieved March 15, 2012, from http://www.ntia.doc.gov/files/ntia/publications/ntia_internet_use_report_february_2011.pdf

Neu, C., Anderson, R., & Bikson, T. (1999). *Sending your government a message: E-mail communication between citizens and government*. Santa Monica, CA: Rand Corp..

Norris, P. (2001). *Digital divide: Civic engagement, information, poverty, and the internet worldwide*. New York, NY: Cambridge University Press. doi:10.1017/CBO9781139164887.

Pew Internet & American Life Project. (2002). *Health information online. Daily tracking survey December 2002*. Retrieved February 20, 2012, from http://www.pewinternet.org

Pew Internet & American Life Project. (2004). *Health information online. Activity tracking survey November 2004*. Retrieved February 20, 2012, from http://www.pewinternet.org

Pew Internet & American Life Project. (2006). *Health information online. August 2006 daily tracking survey*. Retrieved February 20, 2012, from http://www.pewinternet.org

Pew Internet & American Life Project. (2007). *Information searches that solve problems*. Retrieved February 20, 2012, from http://www.pewinternet.org/reports/

Pew Internet & American Life Project. (2008). *Health information online. Fall tracking 2008*. Retrieved September 15, 2010, from http://www.pewinternet.org

Pew Internet & American Life Project. (2010a). *Home broadband*. Retrieved February 20, 2012, from http://pewinternet.org/Reports/2010/Home-Broadband-2010.aspx

Pew Internet & American Life Project. (2010b). *Health information online. August change assessment 2010.* Retrieved February 20, 2012, from http://www.pewinternet.org

Pew Internet & American Life Project. (2012). *Digital Differences*. Retrieved February 20, 2012, from http://pewinternet.org/Reports/2012/Digital-differences/Overview.aspx

Putnam, R. (2000). *Bowling alone: The collapse and revival of American community*. New York, NY: Simon & Schuster. doi:10.1145/358916.361990.

Recovery Accountability and Transparency Board. (2010). *Recovery funds satellite broadband to rural America.* Retrieved March 15, 2011, from http://www.Recovery.gov

Schmeida, M. (2004). *Telehealth and state government policy. Book Chapter. Encyclopedia of Public Administration and Public Policy*. New York, NY: Marcel Dekker, Inc..

Schmeida, M. (2005). *Telehealth innovation in the American states*. Ann Arbor, MI: ProQuest.

Schmeida, M. (2006). *State government policy initiatives: Improving access for the medically underserved. Encyclopedia of Public Administration and Public Policy*. New York, NY: Marcel Dekker, Inc..

Schmeida, M., & McNeal, R. (2007). The telehealth divide: Disparities in searching public health information online. *Journal of Health Care for the Poor and Underserved, 18*, 637–647. doi:10.1353/hpu.2007.0068 PMID:17675719.

Schmeida, M., & McNeal, R. (2009). Demographic differences in telehealth policy outcomes. In Lazakidou, A., & Siassiakos, K. (Eds.), *Handbook of research on distributed medical informatics and e-health* (pp. 500–508). Hershey, PA: Medical Information Science Reference.

Schmeida, M., McNeal, R., & Mossberger, K. (2007). Policy determinants affect telehealth implementation. *Journal of Telemedicine and e-Health, 13*(2), 101-108.

Selwyn, N. (2004). Reconsidering political and popular understandings of the digital divide. *New Media & Society*, *6*(3), 341–362. doi:10.1177/1461444804042519.

Senate Hearing 103-515. (1993). *Reinventing government: Using new technology to improve service and cut costs.* 103rd Congress.

Stanley, L. (2003). Beyond access: Psychosocial barrier to computer literacy. *The Information Society*, *19*(5), 407–416. doi:10.1080/715720560.

Stover, S. (1999). *Rural internet connectivity.* Rural Policy Research Institute. Retrieved June 21, 2000, from http://www.rupri.org

Stover, S., Chapman, G., & Waters, J. (2004). Beyond community networking and CTCs: Access, development, and public policy. *Telecommunications Policy*, *28*(7-8), 465–485. doi:10.1016/j.telpol.2004.05.008.

Thomas, J., & Streib, G. (2003). The new face of government: Citizen-initiated contacts in the era of e-government. *Journal of Public Administration: Research and Theory*, *13*(1), 83–102. doi:10.1093/jpart/mug010.

Tong, R. (2007). Gender-based disparities east/west: rethinking the burden of care in the United States and Taiwan. *Bioethics*, *21*(9), 488–499. doi:10.1111/j.1467-8519.2007.00594.x PMID:17927625.

Van Dijk, J., & Hacker, K. (2003). The digital divide as a complex and dynamic phenomenon. *The Information Society*, *19*(4), 315–326. doi:10.1080/01972240309487.

West, D. (2004). E-government and the transformation of service delivery and citizen attitudes. *Public Administration Review*, *64*(1), 15–27. doi:10.1111/j.1540-6210.2004.00343.x.

West, D. (2005). *Digital government: Technology and public sector performance*. Princeton, NJ: Princeton University Press.

West, D., & Miller, E. (2006). The digital divide in public e-health: Barriers to accessibility and privacy in state health department Web sites. *Journal of Health Care for the Poor and Underserved*, *17*, 652–666. doi:10.1353/hpu.2006.0115 PMID:16960328.

ADDITIONAL READING

Bennett, M. D. (2003). *A broadband world: The promise of advanced services*. Washington, DC: Alliance for Public Technology & the Benton Foundation.

Bertot, J., & Jaeger, P. (2008). The E-government paradox: Better customer service doesn't necessarily cost less. *Government Information Quarterly*, *25*(3), 134–154.

Bimber, B. (1999). The Internet and citizen communication with government: Does the medium matter? *Political Communication*, *16*(4), 409–428. doi:10.1080/105846099198569.

Bimber, B. (2003). *Information and American democracy: Technology in the evolution of political power*. New York, NY: Cambridge University Press. doi:10.1017/CBO9780511615573.

Dugdale, A., Daly, A., Papandrea, F., & Maley, M. (2005). Accessing e-government: Challenges for citizens and organizations. *International Review of Administrative Sciences*, *71*(1), 109–118. doi:10.1177/0020852305051687.

European Commission. (2004). eEurope 2005 broadband. Retrieved July 19, 2005, from http://ec.europa.eu/information_society/eeurope/2005/all_about/broadband/index_en.htm

Evans, D., & Yen, D. (2006). E-government: Evolving relationships of citizens and government, domestic, and international development. *Government Information Quarterly*, *23*, 207–235. doi:10.1016/j.giq.2005.11.004.

Fountain, J. (2001). *Building the virtual state: Information technology and institutional change*. Washington, DC: Brookings Institution Press.

Fountain, J. (2008). Bureaucratic reform and e-government in the United States: An institutional perspective. In Chadwick, A., & Howard, P. N. (Eds.), *Routledge handbook of internet politics* (pp. 99–113). New York, NY: Routledge.

Goldsmith, S., & Eggers, W. (2004). *Governing by network: The new shape of the public sector*. Washington, DC: Brookings Institution Press.

Hargittai, E., & Hinnant, A. (2008). Digital inequalities: Differences in young adults' use of the Internet. *Communication Research*, *35*(5), 602–621. doi:10.1177/0093650208321782.

Ho, A. T.-K. (2002). Reinventing local governments and the e-government initiative. *Public Administration Review*, *62*(4), 434–444. doi:10.1111/0033-3352.00197.

Kernaghan, K. (2005). Moving toward the virtual state: Integrating services and service channels for citizen-centered delivery. *International Review of Administrative Sciences*, *71*(1), 119–131. doi:10.1177/0020852305051688.

Kettl, D. (2002). *The transformation of governance: Public administration for twenty-first century America*. Baltimore, MD: The Johns Hopkins University Press.

Lenhart, A., Purcell, K., Smith, A., & Zichuhr, K. (2010). *Social media & mobile use among teens and young adults*. PEW Research Center. Retrieved October 24, 2011, from http://pewinternet.org/Reports/2010/social-media-and-young-adults.aspx

Levy, F., & Murnane, R. (1996, May). With what skills are computers a complement? *The American Economic Review*, *86*(2), 258–262.

Mayer-Schonberger, V., & Lazer, D. (Eds.). (2007). *Governance and information technology: From electronic government to information government*. Cambridge, MA: MIT Press.

McNeal, R., Hale, K., & Dotterweich, L. (2008). Citizen-government interaction and the internet: Expectations and accomplishments in contact, quality and trust. *Journal of Information Technology & Politics*, *5*(2), 213–229. doi:10.1080/19331680802298298.

Norris, P. (1999). *Critical citizens: Global support for democratic governance*. Oxford: Oxford University Press.

Ong, C., & Wang, S. (2009). Managing citizen-initiated email contacts. *Government Information Quarterly*, *26*(3), 498–504. doi:10.1016/j.giq.2008.07.005.

Rappoport, P. N., & Kridel, D. J., & Taylor, L.D. (2002). The demand for broadband: Access, content, and the value of time. In R.W. Crandall & J.H. Alleman, (Ed.), Broadband: Should we regulate high-speed internet access? (pp. 57-82). Washington, DC: AEI Brookings Joint Center for Regulatory Studies.

Rose, W., & Grant, G. (2010). Critical issues pertaining to the planning and implementation of e government initiatives. *Government Information Quarterly*, *27*(1), 26–33. doi:10.1016/j.giq.2009.06.002.

Servon, L., & Nelson, M. (2001). Community technology centers: Narrowing the digital divide in low income urban communities. *Journal of Urban Affairs*, *23*(3-4), 279–290. doi:10.1111/0735-2166.00089.

Thomas, J. C. (1982). Citizen-initiated contacts with government agencies: A test of three theories. *American Journal of Political Science*, *26*(3), 504–522. doi:10.2307/2110940.

Thomas, J. C., & Melkers, J. (1999). Explaining citizen-initiated contacts with municipal bureaucrats Lessons from the Atlanta experience. *Urban Affairs Review*, *34*(5), 667–690. doi:10.1177/10780879922184130.

Tolbert, C., Mossberger, K., & McNeal, R. (2008). Innovation and learning: Measuring e-government performance in the American states 2000-2004. *Public Administration Review*, *68*(3), 549–563. doi:10.1111/j.1540-6210.2008.00890.x.

Walsh, E. (2001). The truth about the digital divide. In Compaine, B. (Ed.), *The digital divide: Facing a crisis or a myth?* (pp. 279–284). Cambridge, MA: MIT Press.

KEY TERMS AND DEFINITIONS

America Recovery and Reinvestment Act of 2009: A $787 billion economic stimulus package signed into law by U.S. President Obama.

Community Technology Center (CTC): A public building including schools and libraries where citizens can go for computer access and training.

Digital Divide: Persistent gaps in Internet access based on demographic factors such as age, income and education.

Electronic Government (E-Government): The delivery of information and services online through the Internet or other digital means.

E-Rate: Created by the passage of the Telecommunications Act of 1996, this federal program was set up as a $2.25 billion annual fund to help defray the cost of Internet service to schools and libraries by providing discounts for connectivity costs for the Internet.

Information Literacy: The ability to determine which information found on the Internet is appropriate for a specific task.

Medicaid: Public health insurance program sponsored by the U.S. government for the impoverished of all age groups, for the blind, disabled, and medically needy considered impoverished. It is the second largest U.S. public health insurance program.

Medicare: Public health insurance program sponsored by the U.S. government for persons under 65 years and certain disability, age 65 or older, and all age groups with End-State Renal Disease. It is the largest U.S. public health insurance program.

Technical Competency: Necessary skills to use hardware and software, such as typing and using a mouse.

Chapter 5
Trust Measures for Implementers of E-Government Adoption: A Confirmatory Factor Analysis

Gabriel Puron-Cid
Centro de Investigacion y Docencia Economicas, Mexico

ABSTRACT

Trust is a critical factor for e-government adoption that has been extensively studied from the citizen´s perspective. This study explores the multiple dimensions of trust, but from the perspective of those inside of government responsible to implement and adopt it. As in previous studies of citizen trust, the nature of trust of those inside of government is also complex and multi-dimensional. A confirmatory factor analysis was conducted to uncover the multiple dimensions of trust inside of government. The data come from a questionnaire applied over government officials who participated in a contemporary case of e-government. The questionnaire includes inquiries about different dimensions of trust found in the literature. The main motivation of this study is to extend our understanding of multiple dimensions of trust as possible enablers and inhibitors during e-government adoption inside of government. Derived from the analysis, five practical advises are suggested as trust-building mechanisms during e-government adoption.

INTRODUCTION

Trust is one of the most influential factors for e-government success (Chan & Pan, 2008; Heeks, 2006; Puron-Cid, 2010; Scholl, 2009). In particular, Colesca (2009, p. 8) commented that "Trust in e-government is an abstract concept that underlies a complex array of relationships, so the method used to quantify trust in e-government should therefore account for this abstract nature." The literature points out different types of trust related to e-government adoption: trust of internet, trust of government, perceived usefulness of technology, perceived quality of e-government services, and disposition to trust (Belanger & Carter, 2008; Colesca, 2009). These categories of trust usu-

DOI: 10.4018/978-1-4666-4173-0.ch005

Copyright © 2013, IGI Global. Copying or distributing in print or electronic forms without written permission of IGI Global is prohibited.

ally have placed the adoption of technology in the middle of the relationship between citizens and government. However, the impact of trust of those involved in e-government implementation is sparse and rare. This study focuses on the dimensions of trust among actors inside of government responsible of adopting e-government initiatives into their organizational contexts.

In order to explore the dimensions of trust among actors who participate inside of government, this study argues that it is necessary to consider the different structures and disciplines enacted in practice while adopting a particular e-government initiative. The structures and dimensions of trust involved in e-government projects depend on the type of the initiative and the context in which they are embedded. In this respect, Puron-Cid (2010; 2012) indicates that e-government projects are usually interdisciplinary in nature. The term "interdisciplinary" for this study means "a group of people from different professional backgrounds, knowledge, and expertise usually collaborate for the adoption of the e-government initiative into their work routines." (Puron-Cid, 2012). This article sustains that during the implementation of e-government projects, groups of professionals with different backgrounds and expertise usually collaborate. Depending on the type of e-government, Puron-Cid (2010; 2012) suggests to consider other relevant dimensions of e-government from other disciplines that are present when these groups of professionals collaborate in practice that consequently need to be considered in theory. The approach here is to consider the type of e-government project to subsequently analyze the multiple dimensions of trust involved elicited not only from the information systems, but from other disciplines. The purpose of this study is to consider the interdisciplinary nature of e-government implementation into the study of trust from the perspective of those inside of government.

This paper claims that trust among actors inside of government are usually embedded in collaboration among participants from different disciplinary fields and areas. Therefore, this study uses an IT-enabled budget reform in Mexico as a case study to complement the information systems' structures with other disciplinary components (in this case budgeting). By using this case as an interdisciplinary example of a common e-government project, this paper examines the multiple dimensions of trust among actors inside of government who are responsible of adopting the e-government initiative. This case not only helps to understand the role of information systems over the trust structures involved in e-government adoption, but also is useful to identify other critical structures of trust from the field of budgeting interacting in the same project. The field of budgeting has been subject of several applications of e-government (2010). Various technological tools and information systems have been central components of budgeting operations in government because of the intensive informational content and technological use in the budget process (Joyce et al., 2004; Melker & Willoughby, 2001; OECD, 2007; Puron-Cid, 2012).

This study conducted a confirmatory factor analysis to identify the different dimensions of trust among actors inside of government responsible of adopting the e-government initiative into their organizational routines based on the answers of the questionnaire over the adoption of this IT-enabled budget reform. The questionnaire was applied over 1,482 federal and state government officials who participated in the initiative. With a response rate of 14.9% (221 respondents), the goal of the questionnaire was to evaluate a variety of dimensions of trust found critical in the literature, but from the perspective of public officials who adopt the initiative into their work routines. The main motivation of this study is to derive useful results for extending our understanding about the dimensions of trust among government officials involved in a successful adoption of e-government. The purpose is that e-government community of practitioners and scholars use these findings for advising trust developing and management mechanisms for this type of initiatives. From the analysis, a selection of 5 "practical advices" was identified as useful for a successful adoption of e-government. The structure of the paper is organized in five sections including these introductory remarks. The second reviews the literature about the multiple factors of trust involved in e-government. The third and fourth sections state this study's research question and hypotheses. The fifth section presents details of this research design and methods. The sixth section details the results of the factor analysis. The seventh section discusses 5 "practical advises" resulting from the analysis which we believe are useful for a successful adoption of e-government. The eighth section provides conclusions on the results of this questionnaire.

BACKGROUND OF TRUST

Trust is a critical success factor for any e-government initiative (Dirks & Ferrin, 2001; Gil-Garcia & Pardo, 2005; Gil-Garcia, 2005; Mayer et al., 1995, Zaheer et al., 1998). For this reason, different theoretical and disciplinary lenses have been examined to understanding the role of trust in e-government adoption (Colesca, 2009; Belanger & Carter, 2008). Colesca (2009) has identified some of the diverse disciplinary approaches to study trust, from the sociological, political and economical views to the managerial, technological, and human-computer interaction perspectives. In the field of information systems, several theoretical perspectives have also placed trust at the center of the analysis (see Table 1). Due to this variety of theoretical lenses and disciplinary perspectives, trust has been examined extensively and defined differently (Belanger & Carter, 2008). Colesca (2009, p. 8) reviewed several definitions of trust across various disciplinary traditions. Table 2 entails some of these definitions related to information systems and e-government, but the list is larger if including terms from other fields. This variety of concepts reflects the lack of consensus about the complex nature and wide range of the dimensions of trust in social contexts (Belanger & Carter, 2008; Colesca, 2009; Gefen et al., 2003; Johnson-George & Swap, 1982; Mayer et al., 1995; McKnight et al., 2002; Zucker, 1986).

Based on these definitions and theoretical frameworks, a significant number of dimensions of trust have been developed to study e-government. It is important to emphasize that these dimensions particularly concentrate on the interaction enabled by technology and internet between citizens and government (Akkaya et al., 2012; Belanger & Carter, 2008; Gefen et al., 2002; Heimbut et al., 2012). Table 3 presents some of the most common dimensions of trust in the literature explored in e-government initiatives: trust of internet, trust of government, perceived usefulness, perceived quality of e-government services, and disposition to trust. The nature and complexity of these dimensions have been operationalized differently in the literature and some combinations of several models like the ones listed in Table 1 are common in the study of trust in e-government. These dimensions and derived indicators have served to capture the different aspects of trust in e-government adoption in general from the citizen's perspective.

These efforts have contributed to our understanding of the role of trust in e-government. In particular, the role of trust has been widely examined in the context of the trust relationship between citizens and governments enabled technology or internet (Belanger & Carter, 2008). This study presents a different standpoint. I argue that these trust dimensions are useful to understand

Table 1. Theoretical frameworks of trust in information systems

Theoretical Framework	Authors
Complexity Theory	Ninghui et al., 2005
Critical realism theory	Reed, 2001
Diffusion of innovation theory	Colesca, 2009
Game theory	Jarvenpaa, Knoll, & Leidner, 1998; Jarvenpaa & Leidner, 1999
Organizational knowledge creation	Levin & Cross, 2004
Punctuated equilibrium theory	Jarvenpaa, Shaw, & Staples, 2004
SERVQUAL	Parasurama, Berry, & Zeithaml, 1985; 1988; 1991
Technology acceptance model	Belanger & Carter, 2008; Gefen, Karahanna, & Straub, 2003; Gefen et al., 2002; Horst, Kuttschreuter, & Gutteling, 2007; Wang & Benbasat, 2005; Warkentin et al., 2005
Transaction cost economics	Bunduchi, 2005

Source: Own preparation

Table 2. Trust definitions

Author	Definitions of Trust
Grandison and Sloman (2000)	Trust is the firm belief in the competence of an entity to act dependably, securely, and reliably within a specified context
Mui et al. (2002)	Trust is a subjective expectation an agent has about another's future behavior based on the history of their encounters.
McKnight et al. (2002)	Trust of a user is previous to experiencing the service. This is called initial trust that refers to trust in an unfamiliar trustee. Initial trust is required in a relationship in which the citizen does not yet have credible or meaningful information about the e-service provider.
Olmedilla et al. (2005)	Trust of a party A to a party B for a service X is the measurable belief of A in that B behaves dependably for a specified period within a specified context (in relation to service X)

Source: Adapted from Colesca (2009) and Belanger & Carter (2008)

citizen trust, but they are not functional to understand the dimensions of trust among actors inside of government who are responsible of implementing and adopting e-government initiatives in the first place.

The studies that focused on the dimensions of trust inside of government are rare and sparse. In this sense, some of these efforts have timidly characterized the dimension of trust among public officials and other actors inside of government in different ways. Chan and Pan (2008) have found different groups of stakeholders inside of government whose levels of trust differ according to their experience, interests, and technological capabilities in adopting new technology. Gupta, Dasgupta, and Guptac (2008) emphasize the concept of trust in terms of the type of collaboration between organizations in government based on intra-organizational and inter-organizational arrangements. Similar observation was made by Gil-Garcia, Chengalur-Smith, and Duchessi (2007) at the level of interoperability of information systems between agencies as representative of the level of trust among government agencies Other studies indicate trust among actors inside of government in terms of the level of organizational learning and creativity among those participating in the implementation of e-government initiatives (Moon & Norris, 2005; Phang, Kankanalli, & Ang, 2008).

In order to explore the dimensions of trust among actors who participate inside of government, this study proposes a consideration of the different structures and disciplines enacted in practice while adopting a particular e-government initiative. In other words, the structures and dimensions of trust involved in e-government projects depend on the type of initiative and the context in which they are embedded. The approach of this article is to consider the different disciplines (interdisciplinary view) involved in the e-government implementation to subsequently analyze the multiple dimensions of trust. Puron-Cid (2012) has observed that this interdisciplinary view occurs

Table 3. Dimensions of trust

Author	Trust dimensions
Trust of internet	This type of trust is labeled as institution-based trust that refers to an *individual's perceptions of the institutional environment, including the structures and regulations that make the environment feel safe* (McKinght et al., 2002). According to Shapiro (1987) institution-based trust refers to trust of internet in the following indicators: trust in the security measures, safety and performance structures of the electronic channel
Trust of government	Trust in the agency has a strong impact on the adoption of technology in government (Gefen et al., 2005). Before endorsing e-government initiatives, citizens must believe government agencies possess the astuteness and technical resources necessary to implement and secure these systems (Belanger & Carter, 2008). So, trust of government refers to *one´s perception regarding the integrity and ability of the agency providing the service* (Becerra & Gupta, 1999; McKnight et al., 2002; Jarvenpaa, Knoll, & Leidner, 1998). Among some indicators of trust, Belanger & Carter (2008) refer to citizen confidence in the ability of an agency to provide online services; protection and respect of private data; honesty from government officials and employees; e-services for the purpose of benefiting, not monitoring; and non-fraudulent interaction.
Perceived usefulness	Perceived usefulness is based on the individual's perception of risks and benefits of using a particular technology (in this case e-services provided by government), not per se on the actual risks and benefits. Perceived usefulness then refers to *the degree to which a person believes e-government or e-services provided by government would enhance their performance or individual situation* (Horst, Kuttschreuter, & Gutteling, 2007). Perceived usefulness is a concept that originally came for the technology acceptance model. Other terms have similar applications as the perceived usefulness, but have different connotations such as perceived risk defined as the *citizen's subjective expectation of suffering a loss in pursuit of a desired outcome* (Belanger & Carter, 2008; Warkentin et al., 2002).
Perceived quality of e-government services	The importance of e-government services has been emphasized as being perceived as secure (Tassabehji, Elliman, & Mellor, 2007; Lee & Rao, 2007). Some of the dimensions of the perceived quality of e-services imply individual concerns about security and confidence in services provided electronically by governments (Cremonini & Valerie, 2003).
Disposition to trust	Disposition of trust is defined as *one´s general propensity to trust others* (Belanger & Carter, 2008; Mcknight et al., 2002). This dimension refers to a more psychological aspect of trust beyond the immediate control of any government agency (Belanger & Carter, 2008). Colesca (2009) characterizes this dimension as propensity to trust which indicates that people who have more propensity to trust, in general, are more likely to trust in e-government or e-services provided by government.

Source: Own preparation

naturally in practice that also needs to be built in theory. The interdisciplinary approach considers the different disciplines involved during the adoption of the e-government initiative. As a result, the dimensions of trust among actors inside of government depend on the different disciplines involved in the design, development and implementation of the technologies and information systems applied in a particular field of government.

This section summarizes some dimensions of trust among those involved inside of government identified in the literature in the fields of information systems and budgeting. The nature of the case study involves the review of the literature of these fields, but more comprehensive reviews in future research may include other fields such as management and accounting. The dimensions for trust identified in the literature for those who participate inside of government are: clarity of roles and responsibilities, previous experience knowledge, creating incentives, knowledge sharing experience, and teamwork experience. These dimensions integrate the research model for trust among those inside of government involved in the implementation and adoption of the e-government initiative (see Figure 1).

Clarity of roles and responsibilities builds trust across participants inside of government when the roles and responsibilities of the project are clearly divided between partners from different organizations. In information systems, the clarity of roles and responsibilities is measured by the level of autonomy of each organization participating in the e-government project (Dirks & Ferrin,

Figure 1. Research model

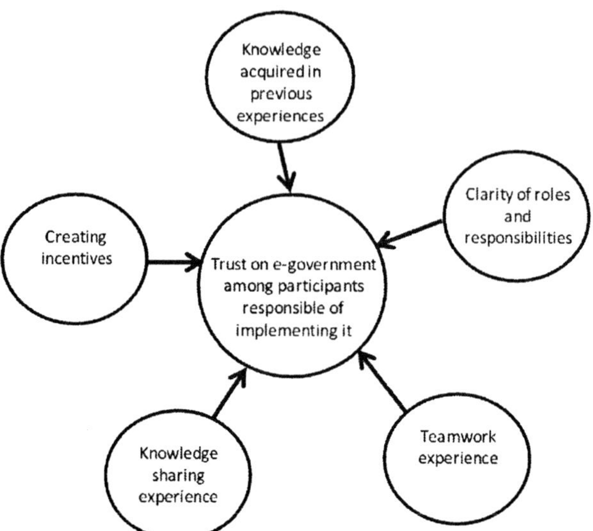

2001; Elgarah et al., 2005; Hart & Saunders, 1997; Hirscheim & Adams, 1991; Kumar et al., 1998; Gulati, 1995; Mayer et al., 1995; Nidumolu, 1989; Pardo et al., 2004; Powell et al., 1996; Smith et al., 1995; Williams, 1994; Zaheer et al., 1998). Another way in the field to measure clarity of roles and responsibilities is through a well instrumented network of communication and collaboration between partners from different organizations (Cohen & Prusak, 2001; Cunningham, 2002; Nahapiet & Ghoshal, 1998; O'Toole & Meier, 1999). In budgeting, clarifying roles and responsibilities has also been identified as influential for building trust across participants during the implementation of the initiative (Dirks & Ferrin, 2001; Pardo et al., 2004; Puron-Cid, 2010; 2012).

Knowledge acquired in previous experiences is related in the information systems field in terms of work experience in previous projects of e-government and official training have significant effect on the confidence of individuals in adopting the initiative into their organizational routines (Burt, 1992; Cross & Cummings, 2004; Gulati, 1995; Kostova & Roth, 2003; Larson, 1992; Ring & Van de Ven, 1994; Szulanski, 1996).

Creating incentives has also been identified as influential for e-government success (Behn, 2002; Grizzle & Pettijohn, 2002; Puron-Cid, 2010; 2012; Shick, 2008). In information systems, incentives such as economic incentives, resource flexibility and decentralization, and public recognition are critical for adopting e-government. In the budgeting field, the perception of individuals is that if they receive an economic incentive, they can operate fairly independent and confident through their local boards and overhead budgetary authorities. Other authors have found that public recognitions to valuable members of the project may increase trust among participants during the adoption of the budget reform (Behn, 2002; Grizzle & Pettijohn, 2002; Jones, 1992; Larkey, 1995; Lynn, 1998; OECD, 1997; Schick, 1998).

Knowledge sharing experience is considered in the field of information systems as influential as well in terms of the interaction, mechanisms, and dialogue to share different disciplinary knowledge, content and information between different participants (Davenport & Hall, 2002; Pardo et al., 2006; Puron-Cid, 2010). In budgeting, previous experience are represented in the forms of previous conflict or success while working with participants from other areas or staffs (Lüder, 1992; Melkers & Willoughby, 2004; Van Reeth, 2002).

Teamwork experience suggests that the proper mechanisms of participants to work together in projects or initiatives such as e-government or budget reforms. Puron-Cid (2010; 2012) found teamwork experience as critical for building trust and consequently for a successful adoption of IT-enabled budget reform.

RESEARCH QUESTION

As previously discussed, trust is a critical factor that influences e-government success, in particular, from the citizen's perspective. However, there are multiple dimensions of trust among actors inside of government identified in the literature that this paper attempts to test using a confirmatory factor analysis. The main focus of this paper is about the following research question: What dimensions of trust among actors inside of government are implied in e-government success?

HYPOTHESIS

This paper tests if the chosen set of variables of the applied questionnaire fairly represents the multiple dimensions of trust among actors inside of government identified in the literature for e-government success. This study claims that confirmatory factor analysis is a useful technique to test the soundness and reliability of the questionnaire design based on the multiple dimensions of trust found in the literature. The confirmatory factor analysis technique should exhibit the expected number of factors and how each variable loads significantly or not on each factor (Gorsuch, 1983; Kano, 2007). Based on these technical criteria and the research question, this study proposed two hypotheses by which to evaluate the technical soundness of the questionnaire design as representative of the multiple dimensions of trust:

H1: The influence of trust among actors inside of government on e-government success can be described by the dimensions of clarity of roles and responsibilities, previous experience knowledge, creating incentives, knowledge sharing experience, and teamwork experience.

H2: The set of questions included in the questionnaire reliably represents the dimensions of trust among actors inside of government that were identified in the literature.

RESEARCH DESIGN AND METHODS

This research was conducted over the case of an IT-enabled budget reform in Mexico which is considered as a contemporary e-government initiative. The data was collected using a questionnaire applied to public officials who participated in this e-government initiative. The questionnaire served to gather the opinion of our participants about several dimensions of trust influencing a successful adoption of the PbR-SED initiative into their organizations. The questionnaire integrates 9 questions used as indicators of trust identified in the literature review section. The names of these variables and codes by which they were abbreviated in this study are shown in Table 4. In order to test the hypotheses, a confirmatory factor analysis using iterative confirmatory factor extraction was performed using STATA 11.1 SE version as statistical package.

This research applied a questionnaire to a total of 1,482 civil servants from various ministries and government agencies of the federal and state governments. The data of participants were collected from the lists of staff who participated in the official training of the PbR-SED initiative provided during 2009 and 2010 and

Table 4. Questions, variables and dimensions

• **t1:** My role and responsibilities were clear when I participated in the PbR-SED Project in my organization [*Clarity of roles and responsibilities*] • **t2:** The role and responsibilities of other organizations that participate in the PbR-SED project were clear to me [*Clarity of roles and responsibilities*] • **t3:** The content of the official PbR-SED training was useful for a better adoption of the initiative in my organization [*Previous experience knowledge*] • **t4:** The acquired knowledge in previous initiatives of reform was valuable for a successful adoption of the PbR-SED in my organization [*Previous experience knowledge*] • **t5:** I had attractive incentives to participate in the PbR-SED initiative [*Creating incentives*] • **t6:** My effort of implementing the PbR-SED in my organization was recognized [*Creating incentives*] • **t7:** Knowledge sharing with participants from other areas such as budgeting, information systems, and management were valuable for adopting the PbR-SED in my organization [*Knowledge sharing*] • **t8:** Previous experience working with other areas such as budgeting, information systems, and management was valuable for a better adoption of the PbR-SED in my organization [*Previous teamwork experience*] • **t9:** The members of the PbR-SED team in my organization have worked well together in previous experiences [*Previous teamwork experience*]

* Note: This is an English translation of the original Spanish version applied.

contact information of public executives from official websites of government. A total of 2,048 potential participants were first invited to participate in the questionnaire during the month of June 2011. 566 emails were not valid or rejected by security measures from their organizations. Only 1,482 emails were sent back and valid. 221 questionnaires were completed with a response rate of 14.9%. However, there are sections of the questionnaire that reported lower rates of response (in particular the last sections of the questionnaire). This rate is considered normal in the application of questionnaires via online tools (Bryman, 2004).

The questionnaire was designed and developed using an electronic tool called SurveyMonkey. The tool offers a platform to make the questionnaire available online for participants. The questionnaire contains 9 trust-related questions (t1-t9). Each question represents an indicator of a particular dimension of trust. The 9 questions use a 7-points Likert scale (from "totally agree" to "totally disagree" options) in order to explore the opinion of participants about different statements related to trust discussed in the literature. The questionnaire registered the opinion of public officials at different levels of responsibility in the areas of budget, management programs, information systems, and other areas.

Figure 2 details the participation of respondents by type of staffs in the organization. Respondents from the areas of planning, budget & finance, management, and information systems were the most participative during the period of response of the questionnaire. The option "other" registered other ascription areas such as evaluation, management, internal control and auditing. The most common levels of education were undergraduate and graduate level mainly in the fields of accounting, economics, management, information systems, law and various engineering fields. The average age of respondents is 45 (with a minimum of 25 years and a maximum of 69 years). Gender of respondents was reported as 33.6% women and 66.4% men.

CASE BACKGROUND

Since late 1980s, Mexican federal government has reformed its budget system involving new information systems and budgetary techniques. The last of these reforms, known as PbR-SED for its Spanish abbreviation of "Budgeting based on Results-Performance Evaluation System,"

Figure 2. Staffs involved in the initiative (206 responses)

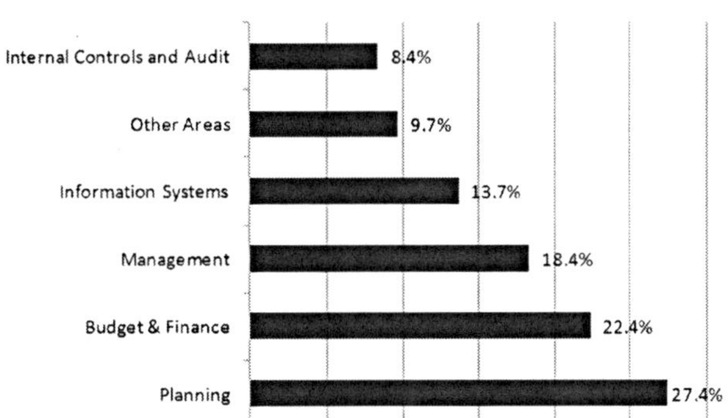

was recently designed and enacted in 2008. Its purpose is to transform the way agencies spend public resources based on results, performance information, and cost savings. The PbR-SED condenses the multiple dimensions of trust of actors inside of government in the context of an ongoing and complex e-government transformation in the information systems and budgeting areas.

The PbR-SED integrates different actors from inside of government in order to collaborate for the adoption of the e-government project: reformer agencies and implementer agencies. Reformer agencies are the Ministry of Finance (SHCP[1]), the Comptroller's Office (SFP[2]) and the National Council of Social Policy Evaluation (CONEVAL[3]). All these control agencies are responsible of the design the PbR-SED tools, techniques and information systems at the federal level. The SHCP serves as the responsible of the budgetary process, the SFP as the auditor and evaluator of budget and programs, and the CONEVAL as the evaluator of social programs. These three organizations were and are engaged in an obligated collaborative relationship around this initiative, but only the SHCP is responsible of coordinating the PbR-SED implementation across implementer agencies. The rest of agencies and state and local governments perform the role of implementers and are responsible to adopt the PbR-SED tools, techniques and information systems into their daily routines and operations.

In any case, reformer or implementer agencies usually integrate interdisciplinary teams that are in charge of implementing the initiative into the organization. As a constant of all these efforts, professionals from different areas and professional backgrounds have collaborated together to adopt the PbR-SED project by collecting and reporting performance information using information systems into their own operations and contexts.

RESULTS

This section presents the results in two sections. A brief section of descriptive statistics is provided and the results of the confirmatory factor analysis are presented.

Descriptive Statistics

The first step of the analysis consists in analyzing the means and standard deviations of these indicators. Table 5 shows the descriptive statistics for the indicators of trust. Indicators t1, t2, t3, t4, 7, and t8 show similar pattern of centrality above 5 and similar pattern deviation between ±1.2 and ±1.4. However, the indicators t5, t6 and t9 show lower patterns of centrality (less than 5) and more dispersed deviation than the first group of indicators (above ±1.5).

Table 6 indicates the correlation among indicators. The table suggests that indicators t1, t2, t3, t4, 7, and t8 are highly correlated to each other with around 60%. Indicators t5 and t6 present the lower estimates of correlation with the rest of indicators, below 50%. Except for indicators t5 and t6, the indicator t9 shows correlations between 50-60% with respect to the rest of indicator variables. These patterns of correlation may represent a limitation or a clearer pattern of loadings later on the developing of the confirmatory factor analysis.

Factor Analysis

In spite of the low correlations of indicators t5, t6 and t9, the study applies the confirmatory factor analysis by computing a unrotated iterated principal factor (ipf) estimation. The first evaluation of factors should be done by analyzing the eigenvalues. According to Kaiser, Hunka, and Bianchini (1971), only factors with an eigenvalue greater than one are meaningful. This method is called Kaiser test. Table 7 provides the eigenvalues generated by the unrotated version of the ipf estimation. This statistic shows the presence of only one factor with an eigenvalue of 5.2558. This factor accounts for 73.09% of the common variance among the nine indicators. The second most significant factor is close to 1 with an Eigenvalue of 0.8724 and a cumulative proportion of 12.13% of common variance. Between the first two factors, the cumulative explained variation is 85.22% of total variance using the unrotated factor model. An alternative method to the Kaiser test is the graphical approach or Scree plot that determines the number of meaningful factors by considering the ones above the flat line (Cattell, 1966). Figure 3 shows the Scree plot graph confirming the presence of two factors as well. This graphical analysis indicates that two factors load heavily, and then the rest of factors remain flat. The first factor aggregates all indicators as representative of the multiple dimensions of trust while the second

Table 5. Means and standard deviations

Indicators	Obs.	Mean	Std. Dev.	Max.	Min.
t1	152	5.43	1.374	1	7
t2	152	5.15	1.418	1	7
t3	152	5.06	1.368	1	7
t4	152	5.09	1.357	1	7
t5	152	4.10	1.655	1	7
t6	152	4.14	1.649	1	7
t7	152	5.66	1.202	1	7
t8	152	5.26	1.285	1	7
t9	152	4.74	1.546	1	7

Table 6. Correlation matrix (143 obs.)

t	1	2	3	4	5	6	7	8	9
1	1								
2	0.78	1							
3	0.62	0.67	1						
4	0.64	0.70	0.78	1					
5	0.46	0.41	0.49	0.44	1				
6	0.36	0.30	0.42	0.41	0.69	1			
7	0.62	0.52	0.62	0.56	0.36	0.36	1		
8	0.74	0.68	0.65	0.67	0.43	0.46	0.67	1	
9	0.56	0.53	0.52	0.61	0.47	0.40	0.52	0.62	1

Table 7. Eigenvalues of the unrotated factor model (143 obs.)

	Eigenvalue	Proportion
Factor 1	5.2558	0.7309
Factor 2	0.8724	0.1213
Factor 3	0.3555	0.0494
Factor 4	0.3092	0.0430
Factor 5	0.1988	0.0277
Factor 6	0.1283	0.0178
Factor 7	0.0547	0.0076
Factor 8	0.0166	0.0023
Factor 9	-0.0003	0.0000

Figure 3. Scree plot of the unrotated factor model

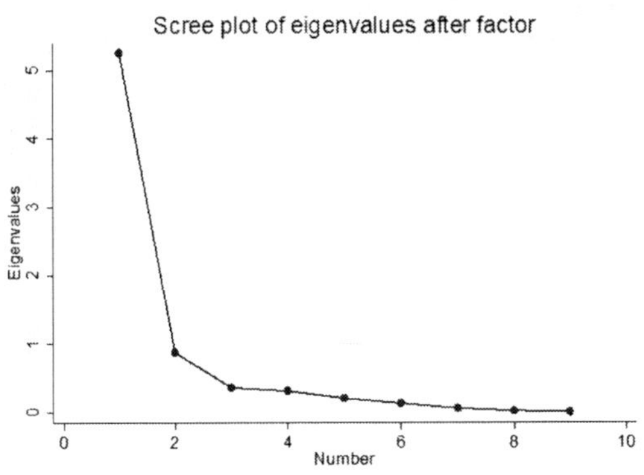

factor accounts only for the indicators t5 and t6 as representative of the dimension of "creating incentives."

The next step of the confirmatory factor analysis is to examine the factor loadings (patterns) which are actually correlation coefficients. The closer to ±1, the more highly correlated an indicator variable is with the factor. Table 8 provides the factor loadings from the ipf solution for the unrotated version. For the purpose of presentation, only the first five factors are shown since the rest of factors shown not to be significant. The interpretation of the first five factors patterns indicates no clear solution for the different dimensions of trust suggested in the literature. All indicators (t1-t9) heavily load on the first factor (T1) making difficult the analysis of the multiple dimensions of trust. In addition, indicator variables t5 and t6 load heavily on the second factor (T2). It is also important to consider that indicators t6, t7 and t9 present a certain level of unique variation of around 30%. This unique variation remains unexplained by using the unrotated model. This is an indication that significant variation is caused by something else different from these indicators' variation. This is a criterion for researchers to caution over the use of these indicators for further statistical analysis. Table 9 shows the squared multiple correlation (SMC) of indicator variables. The SMC also demonstrates that indicator variables 1-9 are highly correlated with each other deriving on the one-factor loading pattern. However, indicator variables t5, t6, t7 and t9 weight relatively low with the rest of variables' variance (between 50-57%). This SMC pattern is an indication of why the loading structure of the unrotated factor model version presents two factors.

Table 10 shows the raw residuals correlations between indicator variables showing zero correlation. This is evidence of an orthogonal relationship between the first two factors. The term orthogonal means that factors are uncorrelated to one another. Another way to detect orthogonal relationships between factors is to estimate the correlation

Table 8. Factor loadings and unique variance of the unrotated factor model (143 obs.)

	Factor 1	Factor 2	Factor 3	Factor 4	Factor 5	Uniqueness
t1	0.8362	-0.1995	0.2818	-0.1621	-0.1051	0.1298
t2	0.8078	-0.2553	0.0454	-0.3078	-0.0221	0.1709
t3	0.833	-0.0812	-0.3685	0.0306	-0.1798	0.1209
t4	0.8372	-0.131	-0.3053	-0.0415	0.1709	0.1373
t5	0.6466	0.5987	0.0372	-0.1666	-0.0336	0.1689
t6	0.581	0.5943	0.0107	0.0809	-0.0326	0.2622
t7	0.7258	-0.1289	0.0791	0.338	-0.1499	0.2981
t8	0.8473	-0.1223	0.1799	0.1687	0.044	0.1661
t9	0.7134	0.0212	0.0701	0.0923	0.3149	0.3546

Table 9. Squared multiple correlation of the unrotated factor model (143 obs.)

	SMC
t1	0.7146
t2	0.6991
t3	0.6899
t4	0.6979
t5	0.5668
t6	0.5277
t7	0.5475
t8	0.6945
t9	0.4953

between factors. Table 11 details the correlation between Factor 1 and Factor 2 showing a very low correlation of 0.70%. This is strong evidence that these factors are orthogonal and a varimax rotation is potentially needed the solution to better understand the multiple dimensions of the trust inside of Factor 1 and Factor 2.

In sum, the unrotated factor model resulted into a loading structure supporting the presence of one meaningful factor, but with a potential structure of two orthogonal factors. Figure 4 illustrate the biplot graph of the two orthogonal factors estimated by this unrotated version. In spite that this two-factor structure shows certain consistency about what the dimensions are for trust, it does not clearly capture the different dimensions of trust identified in the literature. Therefore, the results of analysis are not useful to reveal the dimensions of trust for e-government success. Thus, the confirmatory factor analysis has the option to rotate the axes with the purpose of getting a better fit. In this case due to the orthogonal nature of factors, the axes were rotated using an orthogonal varimax rotation.

The varimax option keeps the factors orthogonal to one another by moving the factor loadings in a position that is closer as possible to one factor and little as possible to the rest of factors. The varimax rotation solution resulted into five factors allowing for more dimensions of trust. Table 12 indicates the eigenvalue structure by factor of the varimax model solution. A better and clearer structure of factors resulted out of this varimax rotation estimation: four factors revealed meaningfully structured. The four factors account for a total 89.82% of cumulative variance. The first factor explains 29.76% of common variance. The second and third factors explained similar variation of 25.33% and 23.10% of common variance, respectively. Finally, the fourth factor explains 11.63% of common variance.

The varimax rotation model presents a more clear structure of factors, but it is not free from

Table 10. Squared multiple correlation of the unrotated factor model (143 obs.)

I	1	2	3	4	5	6	7	8	9
1	1								
2	0.0	1							
3	0.0	0.0	1						
4	0.0	0.0	0.0	1					
5	0.0	0.0	0.0	0.0	1				
6	0.0	0.0	0.0	0.0	0.0	1			
7	0.0	0.0	0.0	0.0	0.0	0.0	1		
8	0.0	0.0	0.0	0.0	0.0	0.0	0.0	1	
9	0.0	0.0	0.0	0.0	0.0	0.0	0.0	0.0	1

Table 11. Squared multiple correlation of the unrotated factor model (143 obs.)

	Factor 1	Factor 2
Factor 1	1.0000	
Factor 2	-0.0070	1.0000

Figure 4. Biplot graph of the unrotated factor model

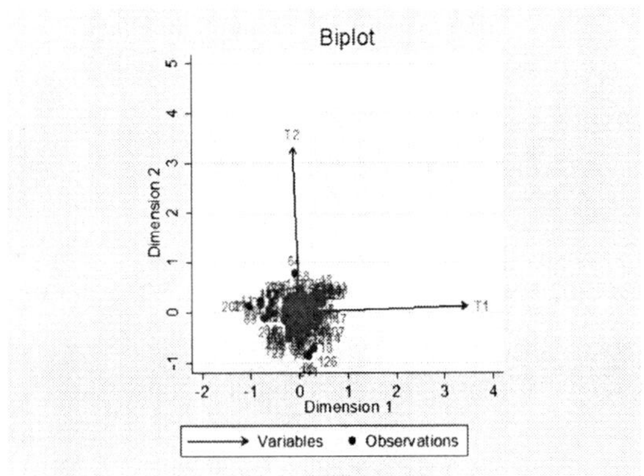

the complexity of the multidimensional nature of trust in e-government success. Table 13 details the factors loadings for the first five factors for the interest of space and since the first four factors shown to be significant. The varimax solution presents a more distinctive loading pattern for the dimensions of trust. No indicator loads significantly in more than one factor. However, t9 loads meaningfully on the first factor, instead of the fifth factor along with the indicator t9 that together measure the intended dimension of previous teamwork experience. This represents a limitation to build a more robust factor model that fairly represents the dimensions of trust. In particular, indicators t1, t2 and t9 load heavily on Factor 1 (T1a) showing evidence of the dimension of *clarity of roles and responsibilities*. Indicators t3 and t4 weight significantly on Factor 2 (T2a) presenting evidence of the dimension of *previous experience knowledge*. Indicators t5 and t6 integrate Factor 3 (T3a) as evidence for the dimension of *creating incentives*. Indicator t7 load meaningfully on Factor 4 (T4a) as a representative of the dimension of *knowledge sharing experience*. Finally, indicator t10 loads on Factor 5 (T5a) as representative of the dimension of *teamwork experience*.

These results show three important findings. First, trust in e-government success is in fact a multidimensional phenomenon. Figure 5 precisely depicts the multiple dimensions that can be drawn from the data representing the different expressions of trust in e-government adoption. Second, the factor loading structure of the varimax rotated version corresponds with the multiple dimensions of trust in e-government success identified in the literature. People participating in e-government initiatives build trust based on clarity of roles and responsibilities, previous experience knowledge, incentives for participation, knowledge sharing experience, and previous teamwork experience. Third, the indicator t9 for previous teamwork experience load meaningfully for Factor 5, but 35% of its variation is not explained by this factor structure. This is a moderate, but significant level of unique variance that is not caused by the proposed trust's factor structure.

Table 12. Eigenvalues: varimax factor model (143 obs.)

	Eigenvalue	Proportion
Factor 1	2.14003	0.2976
Factor 2	1.82160	0.2533
Factor 3	1.66119	0.2310
Factor 4	0.83645	0.1163
Factor 5	0.45482	0.0632
Factor 6	0.16774	0.0233
Factor 7	0.08227	0.0114
Factor 8	0.02717	0.0038

Table 13. Factor loadings and unique variance of the varimax factor model (143 obs.)

	Factor 1	Factor 2	Factor 3	Factor 4	Factor 5	Uniqueness
t1	0.8043	0.2704	0.2235	0.2839	0.1061	0.1298
t2	0.7529	0.4520	0.1539	0.0570	0.1156	0.1709
t3	0.3374	0.7743	0.2686	0.2807	0.0203	0.1209
t4	0.4081	0.7257	0.2130	0.1166	0.2673	0.1373
t5	0.2406	0.2002	0.8330	0.0574	0.1313	0.1689
t6	0.1022	0.1889	0.7735	0.1747	0.0356	0.2622
t7	0.3667	0.3565	0.1769	0.6254	0.1310	0.2981
t8	0.5607	0.3424	0.2431	0.4175	0.2356	0.1661
t9	0.3588	0.3127	0.2958	0.2469	0.5169	0.3546

In order to refine the varimax factor model, a new estimation was conducted by excluding the indicator t9 due to its low factor loading (51.69%) and high level of unique variance above all indicators (35.46%). The refined varimax solution without the indicator t9 resulted in four meaningful factors or dimensions of trust. Table 14 presents the eigenvalues for each factor of the refine varimax rotation version. The new estimation shows a four-factors structure that accounts for 97.23% of cumulative variation.

By excluding the indicator t9, the refined version provides a clearer factor loadings structure of four factors (see Table 15). Indicators t1, t2 and t8 load heavily on Factor 1 (T1b) as representing the dimension of *clear of roles and responsibilities*. Indicators t3 and t4 load meaningfully on Factor 2 (T2b) as an approximation for *previous experience knowledge*. Indicators t5 and t6 weight significantly on Factor 3 (T3b) as part of the dimension of *creating incentives*. Finally, indicator t7 loads on Factor 4 (F4b) as representing the dimension of *knowledge sharing experience*.

The indicator t8 was designed to capture the value of previous experience of participants working with other areas such as budgeting, information systems, and management in order to build trust in the adoption of e-government in the organization. However, the indicator t8 shares more common variance with the indicators designed to capture the dimension of *clear of roles and responsibilities*, than with the indicator designed for the dimension of *teamwork experience*. In other words, the indicator t8 designed to reflect teamwork experience do not covariate meaningfully for a separate dimension of trust as suggested in the literature. Instead, the results of the refined varimax rotation model indicate that teamwork experience is part of the dimension of clarity of roles and responsibilities. The factor patterns of the revised model also confirm the multidimensional nature of trust in e-government success. Figure 6 illustrates the multidimen-

Figure 5. Biplot graph of the varimax factor model

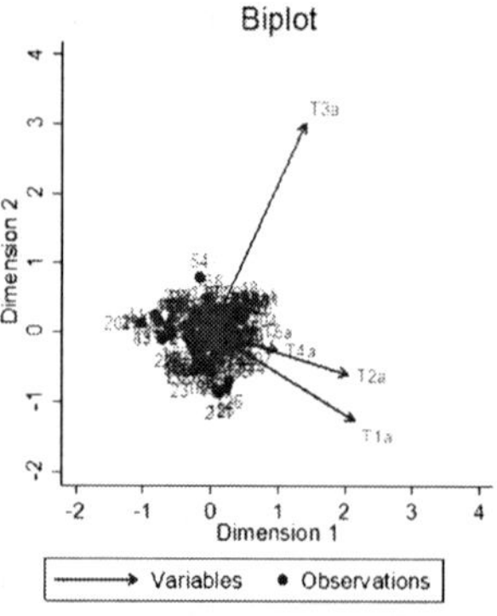

Table 14. Eigenvalues: refined varimax factor model(152 obs.)

	Eigenvalue	Proportion
Factor 1	2.1193	0.3339
Factor 2	1.6486	0.2598
Factor 3	1.5572	0.2454
Factor 4	0.8461	0.1333
Factor 5	0.1270	0.0200
Factor 6	0.0358	0.0057
Factor 7	0.0130	0.0021

sional nature of trust using a biplot graph of factors.

The correlations between factors computed in the revised varimax rotated model (without t9) reinforce the idea that the structure of factors is orthogonal. Thus, the varimax rotation was adequate for this analysis. Table 16 shows the correlations between the factors found in the revised varimax solution using the first eight indicator variables. The correlations between factors (T1b-T4b) are less than 15% suggesting that factors are orthogonal. Finally, Cronbach's α was calculated over the set of indicator variables that loaded on each factor as measures of reliability. The Cronbach's α ranges from 0 to 1. The closer to 1 the more reliable the set of indicator variables is for the factor they are loading to. Table 17 shows the Cronbach's α estimated by factor for each rotated and unrotated models. The results show high levels of reliability in all models. For the unrotated factor model with 9 indicator variables, the results show that the first factor (T1) is reliable with 0.9114. For the rotated varimax version, the Cronbach's α for the three-factors structure using 9 variables also shows levels of reliability above 80%. Indicator t8 and t9 were intended to capture the dimension of teamwork experience, but the results present a lack of correspondence with this dimension. Instead, the indicator t9 presented a level of unique variance around 35% and indicator t8 showed a meaningful covariance with the rest of indicators. These results support the decision of excluding the indicator t9 as part of the dimension of trust. By excluding these variables, the revised unrotated varimax version using only eight variables still maintain acceptable levels for reliability above 80% in each of the four factors (see Table 17).

DISCUSSION

The confirmatory factor analysis was useful for testing the two hypotheses set in this study. First, it was a valuable tool to reveal the dimensions of

Table 15. Factor loadings and unique variance of the refined varimax factor model (152 obs.)

	Factor 1	Factor 2	Factor 3	Factor 4	Factor 5	Uniqueness
t1	0.8075	0.2537	0.2213	0.3049	-0.0542	0.1322
t2	0.7698	0.4433	0.1506	0.0731	0.0601	0.1703
t8	0.5744	0.3408	0.2621	0.4724	0.2586	0.1951
t3	0.3505	0.7680	0.2639	0.2692	-0.0484	0.138
t4	0.4526	0.6872	0.2317	0.1639	0.1461	0.2038
t5	0.2621	0.2136	0.7936	0.0574	-0.0963	0.2381
t6	0.1091	0.1797	0.7940	0.1851	0.1415	0.2651
t7	0.3694	0.3629	0.1822	0.6228	-0.0243	0.3102

Figure 6. Biplot graph of the revised varimax factor model

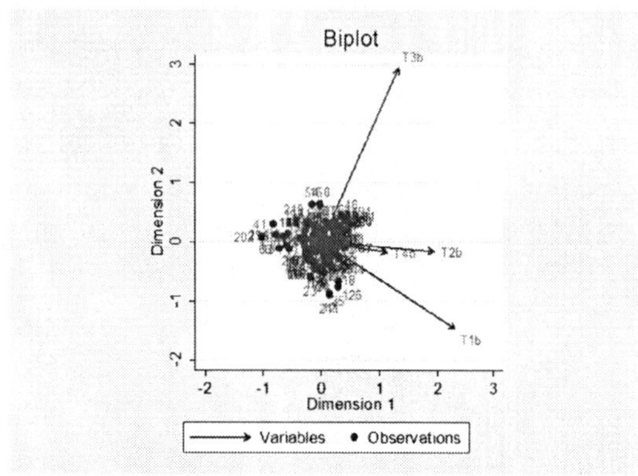

trust for e-government success among participants inside of government. Second, the results of the confirmatory factor analysis yield several implications for the reliability of the questionnaire design for future studies.

Testing Hypothesis 1 (H1)

The results of the confirmatory factor analysis confirm the acceptance of the following dimensions trust among participants inside of government: clear roles and responsibilities, previous experience knowledge, creating incentives, and knowledge sharing experience. However, this study rejects the acceptance of previous teamwork experience as a clear dimension of trust among participants inside of government.

The results of the unrotated model indicate that the grouping of the 9 indicator variables applied in the questionnaire loaded more efficiently on one factor. This is indicative of the presence of trust as one significant dimension of e-government adoption inside of government. The first nine indicators capture different types of trust hypothesized in the literature (clear roles and responsibilities, previous experience knowledge, creating incentives, knowledge sharing experience, and previous teamwork experience). The factor structure of the unrotated version only suggests a significant covariance of these indicators with respect to the dimension of trust among participants inside of government. However, this factor loading is not useful to examine these dimensions of trust as identified in the literature. In other words, the different types of trust represented for this set of indicators load heavily on the first factor as representative of one dimension of trust, but not clearly loading on the different dimensions of trust identified in the literature. This is an important finding in terms of the consistency of the indicators used for the analysis of trust dimensions. Among all measurements, indicator t9 showed a significant level of unique variance indicating the possibility that t9 is not representative of any dimension of trust, but of something else.

In addition, the analysis of the unrotated version also found evidence of an orthogonal relationship between factors. The term orthogonal means that factors are uncorrelated to one another. This is a critical finding that derived into the type of rotation conducted in the study. According to the confirmatory factor analysis, an orthogonal relationship between factors requires a varimax rotation (Gorsuch, 1983). Table 11 details the correlation between Factor 1 and Factor 2 showing a very low correlation of 0.70%. This is strong evidence that these factors are orthogonal and a varimax rotation is potentially needed the solution to better understand the multiple dimensions of the trust inside of Factor 1. Based on these criteria, the decision of continuing the confirmatory factor analysis was made by focusing the analysis over the first factor using a varimax rotation. The results over the first factor using a varimax rotated

Table 16. Correlation matrix (143 obs.)

	T1b	T2b	T3b	T4b
T1b	1			
T2b	0.1252	1		
T3b	0.0337	0.0674	1	
T4b	0.1440	0.1089	0.0607	1

Table 17. Reliability indicators for each factor model

Factor	Factor Name	# of Vars on Scale	Cronbach's α
Unrotated Factor Model (9 Indicator Variables)			
T1	Trust	9 (t1-t9)	0.9114
Rotated Factor Model (9 Indicator Variables)			
T1a	Clear roles and responsibilities	3 (t1-t2-t8)	0.8915
T2a	Previous experience knowledge	2 (t3-t4)	0.8734
T3a	Creating incentives	2 (t5-t6)	0.8156
T4a	Knowledge sharing experience	1 (t7)	Unspecified
T5a	Previous teamwork experience	1 (t8-t9)	0.7605
Revised Rotated Factor Model (8 Indicator Variables)			
T1b	Government Knowledge	3 (t1-t2-t8)	0.8915
T2b	Budget Knowledge	2 (t3-t4)	0.8734
T3b	Information Technology Knowledge	2 (t5-t6)	0.8156
T4b	Management Knowledge	1 (t7)	Unspecified

model show a more consistent set of dimensions for trust according to the dimensions identified in the literature. However, the factor structure using the varimax rotated version with all 9 indicators showed only four significant dimensions: clear roles and responsibilities, previous experience knowledge, creating incentives, knowledge sharing experience. Again the indicator t9 presented a significant unique variance above 35%. Table 10 shows how the indicator t8 presented a more meaningful covariance with the dimension of clear roles and responsibilities (56.07%) than the covariance with the dimension of teamwork experience (23.56%).

The results of the varimax rotated version using all 9 indicators show a significant four-factor structure representing the dimensions of clear roles and responsibilities, previous experience knowledge, creating incentives, and knowledge sharing experience. The indicators for the dimension of teamwork experience (t8 and t9) appear to have contrasting results: indicator t8 loads heavily with the first factor along with indicators t1 and t2 and indicator t9 again presents loads heavily on factor 5 and presents a significant level of unique variance above 35%. Table 10 shows how the indicator t8 presented a more meaningful covariance with the dimension of clear roles and responsibilities (56.07%) than the covariance with the dimension of teamwork experience (23.56%). Thus, the use of indicators t8 and t9 as measures for the trust dimension of teamwork experience needs caution from researchers.

For this study, the analysis excluded the indicator t9 for a refined rotated version due to its significant level of unique variance of above 35%, and considered the indicator t8 as part of the dimension of clear roles and responsibilities. The results of the refined varimax rotated version present clearer factor structure. In this version, the indicators load heavily and clearer a four-factors structure representing the dimensions of *clear of roles and responsibilities, previous experience knowledge, creating incentives, and knowledge sharing experience*. These four factors represent meaningfully four dimensions of trust among participants inside of government that were identified in the literature with high levels of reliability measures. Only the dimension of *teamwork experi-*

ence was rejected as hypothesized dimension of trust due to its poor loading structure.

In sum, these results confirm that trust for a successful adoption of e-government among actors inside of government is a significant dimension. This dimension is multifaceted. Building trust across participants inside of government requires multiple indicators. In the context of an IT-enabled budget reform, participants had to understand not only the information and technology aspects of the project, but also the trust-building components of the initiative. Puron-Cid (2010) commented that the implementation of e-government initiatives should consider trust-building mechanism across participants. This study identified the need of considering four types of trust building: *clear definition of roles and responsibilities, consideration of previous experience, creation of incentives for participation, and developing mechanisms for knowledge sharing*. These mechanisms to build trust among those responsible of adopting e-government are not usually considered important tools. This study clearly shows that this is a common mistake of reformers and policy makers. Trust among participants inside of government matters. So, caution should be paid in order to design the proper tools of building trust according to the dimensions identified in this study for a successful adoption of e-government.

The dimension of *teamwork experience* was not significant in this study. However, the indicator t8 as a measure of teamwork experience loaded meaningfully on the dimension of clear roles and responsibilities. This is an interesting finding since participants from different areas and professional backgrounds usually collaborate in the adoption of e-government. Reformers should design clearer sets of roles and responsibilities across different areas and staff members for a successful adoption of the e-government initiative. This study found that only 13.7% of participants of the PbR-SED are part of the information technology team. In other words, more than 86% of participants come from different areas and professional backgrounds. This is an important evidence that reformers and designers of e-government initiatives need to think about when developing tools and mechanisms for building trust among participants from different areas and staffs involved in the initiative. Current mechanism such as official training material and manuals are mostly designed for information technology literates. These materials and training sessions are usually reluctant of the multidisciplinary teamwork of the project in the other areas such as: information systems, budgeting, management, planning, evaluation, management, internal control, and auditing.

Testing Hypothesis 2 (H2)

Only the first 8 questions included in the questionnaire reliably represents several dimensions of trust identified in the literature. The indicator i9 presented high unique variance and low reliability indicating further studies over the inclusion or exclusion of teamwork experience as a trust dimension. This results needs caution from researchers since it these results may be resulted from a misspecification of the questions. The one-factor representation of data presented in the unrotated model fairly indicates the presence of a significant factor structure for trust in the questionnaire. Further, the results show that reliability measures for the unrotated and rotated versions were significant with levels above 80% considered acceptable in the literature (Bryman, 2004).

Researchers should exercise caution when interpreting the data collected. In this case the data was collected from the questionnaire which was derived from the dimensions of trust found in the literature. This approach defined the dimensions of trust based on a deterministic way. The results of the confirmatory factor analysis show that teamwork experience is a separate dimension than the rest of indicator variables that measure trust. In other words, using empirically derived weights is more useful in producing meaningful data with the purpose of evaluating the multifaceted phenomena of trust, than just conducting these studies with only intuitive or conceptual data schemes (even if they come from previous empirical studies).

FIVE PRACTICAL ADVISES

The results of the confirmatory factor analysis indicate four critical dimensions of trust: *clear definition of roles and responsibilities, consideration of previous experience, creation of incentives for participation, and developing mechanisms for knowledge sharing*. The dimension of *teamwork experience* was no significant but highly correlated with the clear definition of roles and responsibilities. Based on these results 5 "practical advises" are recommended for a successful adoption of e-government managing and building trust among participants inside of government in the process of e-government adoption. The first recommendation cautions about the importance of the dimensions of trust among those who are responsible of adopting e-government inside of government. The second recommendation advices about the significance of clarifying roles and responsibilities inside of participants and organizations in government when adopting e-government initiatives. The third recommendation suggests the critical role of previous knowledge and expertise of participants inside of government for adopting projects like e-government. The fourth recommendation advocates different types of incentives, not only economic to motivate participation among actors inside of government in this type of projects. Finally, the fifth recommendation points out that enhancing trust may traduce itself as an opportunity to share knowledge among participants inside of government.

1. Official presentations, enacting laws and regulations, developing information systems, and official training are usually considered the unique tools available to build trust among those who are responsible of adopting e-government into their organizations. The results of this study confirm that participants acquired different types of trust in various ways. This study identifies some different trust-building mechanisms in which participants develop more confidence for adopting the e-government initiative. In the case of IT-enabled budget reforms, building trust involves a clear definition of roles and responsibilities, consideration of previous experience, creation of incentives for participation, and developing mechanisms for knowledge sharing.
2. Defining clear roles and responsibilities among participants during the adoption of the initiative represents an important dimension of trust related to e-government success. Participants of e-government initiatives require clear roles and responsibilities in order to be more successful in adopting the initiative into their organizational routines. Reformers should pay attention to define clearer the roles and responsibilities of the intended areas and staff involved in the project.
3. The knowledge and expertise developed by participants in previous experiences in the past related to similar projects or initiatives imposes a baseline for present and future confidence of assuming e-government. In other words, the knowledge acquired in previous experiences influences the confidence of participants in adopting the e-government initiative into their organizational routines. Reformers and designers of e-government need to consider the experience of participants in past e-government initiatives for a successful adoption of the e-government initiative.
4. Creating incentives for participation in the e-government initiative is critical for building trust among participants. Reformers should consider a clear set of incentives,

economic or not, for the participants while adopting e-government. Traditional designs of e-government projects usually consider the participation as a responsibility of public officials while in reality is seen as an extra load of responsibilities.

5. Traditional e-government projects do not consider the possibility of knowledge sharing mechanisms in which participants have the opportunity not only to share information, but to learn new abilities and knowledge across participants from different professional and area backgrounds. Reformers should consider knowledge sharing mechanisms as a way to increase confidence and knowledge among participants who are responsible of adopting the e-government into their organizational routines.

FUTURE TRENDS

The literature of e-government traditionally has focused on citizen trust neglecting the dimensions of trust from those responsible of implementing and adopting e-government inside of government. This study was able to reveal a consistent and significant group of dimensions of trust of e-government, but from the perspective of those who directly participate in the adoption of the project into their organizations and routines. Future studies may continue this effort in order to confirm these dimensions or to reveal other dimensions of trust among those inside of government. This study applied confirmatory factor analysis, but other research may apply other quantitative or qualitative techniques to examine the trust phenomenon inside of government. An additional research direction may examine the potential mechanisms to distribute clear roles and responsibilities, creating incentives, knowledge from previous experiences, and knowledge sharing. This research will have the purpose to uncover these mechanisms in practice across participants inside of government who are responsible of adopting e-government initiatives.

CONCLUSION

By using confirmatory factor analysis, this study was able to reveal a consistent and significant group of dimensions of trust of e-government adoption among those who directly participate in the adoption of the project into their organizations and routines. This finding represents a critical turn from previous studies of trust that usually focused on trust relationship between citizen and government. This study focused on the trust dimensions of those responsible who implement and adopt the e-government initiative inside of government. The evidence shows that trust among participants inside of government matters a lot for a successful adoption of e-government.

The results of this research also indicate four critical significant dimensions of trust: *clear definition of roles and responsibilities, consideration of previous experience, creation of incentives for participation, and developing mechanisms for knowledge sharing*. The dimension of *teamwork experience* was no significant but highly correlated with the clear definition of roles and responsibilities. In other words, the results show one meaningful structure of trust consistent with the set of dimensions identified in the literature for actors inside of government. According to the analysis, four dimensions loaded heavily among actors inside of government: clear roles and responsibilities, previous experience knowledge, creating incentives, knowledge sharing experience.

These dimensions show that building trust for a successful adoption of e-government is not one-discipline task inside of government actors. These proofs demonstrate that trust inside of government works through different mechanisms, such as distribution of roles and responsibilities, previous experience, incentives, knowledge sharing, and teamwork. Therefore, building trust across participants responsible of implementing e-government projects in agencies requires several actions that need to be taken for a successful adoption of e-government such as a clear definition of roles and responsibilities, consideration of previous experience, creation of incentives for participation, and developing mechanisms for knowledge sharing.

Participants of e-government had to understand not only the information and technology aspects of the project, but also need clear set of roles and responsibilities, clear set of incentives, previous knowledge and experience in this type of initiatives, and multi-disciplinary knowledge. Based on these results, this paper suggests five advises that basically retrieve the dimensions of trust in order to recommend practice. In general, these recommendations warn policy makers and reformers about potential trust building mechanisms for a successful adoption of e-government from inside of government.

The confirmatory factor analysis also proved to be a useful methodological tool to examine the dimensions of trust among actors inside of government in two ways. First, the analysis allowed us to reveal and to examine the dimensions of trust from the perspective of those responsible of e-government adoption inside of government. Second, the study allowed measuring the level of reliability of the indicators used for the analysis.

REFERENCES

Akkaya, C., Wolf, P., & Krcmar, H. (2012). Factors influencing citizen adoption of e-government services: A cross-cultural comparison. Research in progress presented at *the 45th Hawaii International Conference on System Sciences*.

Becerra, M., & Gupta, A. K. (1999). Trust within the organization: Integrating the trust literature with agency theory and transaction costs economics. *Public Administration Quarterly*, *23*(2), 177–203.

Behn, R. D. (2002). The psychological barriers to performance management: Or why isn't everyone jumping on the performance-management bandwagon? *Public Performance and Management Review*, *26*(1), 5–25. doi:10.2307/3381295.

Belanger, A., & Carter, L. (2008). Trust and risk in e-government adoption. *The Journal of Strategic Information Systems*, *17*, 165–176. doi:10.1016/j.jsis.2007.12.002.

Bryman, A. (2004). *Social research methods*. Oxford University Press.

Bunduchi, R. (2005). Business relationships in internet-based electronic markets: The role of goodwill trust and transaction costs. *Information Systems Journal*, *15*(4), 321. doi:10.1111/j.1365-2575.2005.00199.x.

Burt, R. S. (1992). *Structural holes: The social structure of competition*. Cambridge: Harvard Univ. Press.

Cattell, R. B. (1966). The Scree test for the number of factors. *Multivariate Behavioral Research*, *1*(2), 245–276. doi:10.1207/s15327906mbr0102_10.

Chan, C. M. L., Lau, Y. M., & Pan, S. L. (2008). E-government implementation: A macro analysis of Singapore's e-government initiatives. *Government Information Quarterly*, *25*(2), 239–255. doi:10.1016/j.giq.2006.04.011.

Cohen, D., & Prusak, L. (2001). *In good company: How social capital makes organizations work*. Boston: Harvard Business School Press. doi:10.1145/358974.358979.

Colesca, S. E. (2009). Understanding trust in e-government. *Engineering Economics*, (3).

Cremonini, L., & Valeri, L. (2003). *Benchmarking security and trust in Europe and the US*. Rand Monograph Report MR-1763, Europe.

Cross, R., & Cummings, J. N. (2004). Tie and network correlates of individual performance in knowledge-intense work. *Academy of Management Journal*, *47*(6). doi:10.2307/20159632.

Cunningham, I. (2002). Developing human and social capital in organizations. *Industrial and Commercial Training*, *34*(3), 89–94. doi:10.1108/00197850210424926.

Davenport, E., & Hall, H. (2002). Organizational knowledge and communities of practice. *Annual Review of Information Science & Technology*, *36*, 171–222.

Dirks, K. T., & Ferrin, D. L. (2001). The role of trust in organizational settings. *Organization Science*, *12*(4), 450–467. doi:10.1287/orsc.12.4.450.10640.

Elgarah, W., Falaleeva, N., Saunders, C. S., Ilie, V., Shim, J. T., & Courtney, J. F. (2005). Data exchange in interorganizational relationships: Review through multiple conceptual lenses. *The Data Base for Advances in Information Systems*, *36*(1). doi:10.1145/1047070.1047073.

Gefen, D., Karahanna, E., & Straub, D. W. (2003). Trust and TAM in online shopping: An integrated model. *Management Information Systems Quarterly*, *27*(1), 51–90.

Gefen, D., Rose, G. M., Warkentin, M., & Pavlou, P. A. (2005). Cultural diversity and trust in IT adoption: A comparison of USA and South African e-voters. *Journal of Global Information Management*, *13*(1), 54–78. doi:10.4018/jgim.2005010103.

Gefen, D., Warkentin, M., Pavlou, P., & Rose, G. (2002). *E-government adoption*. Paper presented at the *Americas Conference on Information Systems (AMCIS)*. Paper 83 of the AIS Electronic Library (AISeL).

Gil-Garcia, J. R. (2005). *Enacting state websites: A mixed method study exploring e-government success in multi-organizational settings*. (Unpublished Doctoral Dissertation). University at Albany, State University of New York, Albany, NY.

Gil-Garcia, J. R., Chengalur-Smith, I. N., & Duchessi, P. (2007). Collaborative e-government: Impediments and benefits of information sharing projects in the public sector. *European Journal of Information Systems*, *16*(2), 121–133. doi:10.1057/palgrave.ejis.3000673.

Gil-Garcia, J. R., & Pardo, T. A. (2005). E-government success factors: Mapping practical tools to theoretical foundations. *Government Information Quarterly*, *22*(2), 187–216. doi:10.1016/j.giq.2005.02.001.

Gorsuch, R. L. (1983). *Factor analysis* (2nd ed.). Hillsdale, NJ: Lawrence Erlbaum.

Grandison, T., & Sloman, M. (2000). A survey of trust in internet applications. *IEEE Communications Survey and Tutorials*, 3.

Grizzle, G.A., & Pettijohn, C. D. (2002). Implementing performance-based program budgeting: A system-dynamics perspective. *Public Administration Review*, January/February 2(X)2, *62*(1).

Gulati, R. (1995). Social structure and alliance formation patterns: A Longitudinal analysis. *Administrative Science Quarterly*, *40*, 619–653. doi:10.2307/2393756.

Hart, P., & Saunders, C. (1997). Power and trust - Critical factors in the adoption and use of electronic data interchange. *Organization Science*, *8*(1), 23–42. doi:10.1287/orsc.8.1.23.

Heeks. (2006). *Implementing and managing e-government. An International Text*. London: Sage Publications.

Heimbur, Y.V., Wolf, P., & Krcmar, H. (2012). *E-government monitor 2012*. Report from TNS Infratest.

Hirschheim, R., & Adams, D. (1991). Organizational connectivity. *Journal of General Management, 17*(2), 65–76.

Horst, M., Kuttschreuter, M., & Gutteling, J. M. (2007). Perceived usefulness, personal experiences, risk perception and trust as determinants of adoption of e-government services in The Netherlands. *Computers in Human Behavior, 23*, 1838–1852. doi:10.1016/j.chb.2005.11.003.

Jarvenpaa, S. L., Knoll, K., & Leidner, D. E. (1998). Is anybody out there? Antecedents of trust in global virtual teams. *Journal of Management Information Systems, 14*(4), 29.

Jarvenpaa, S. L., & Leidner, D. E. (1999). Communication and trust in global virtual teams. *Organization Science, 10*(6), 791. doi:10.1287/orsc.10.6.791.

Jarvenpaa, S. L., Shaw, T. R., & Staples, D. S. (2004). Toward contextualized theories of trust: The role of trust in global virtual teams. *Information Systems Research, 15*(3), 250–267. doi:10.1287/isre.1040.0028.

Johnson-George, C., & Swap, W. (1982). Measurement of specific interpersonal trust: Construction and validation of a scale to assess trust in a specific other. *Journal of Personality and Social Psychology, 43*(6), 1307–1317. doi:10.1037/0022-3514.43.6.1306.

Jones, L. R. (1992). Public budget execution and management control. In Rabin, J. (Ed.), *Handbook of public budgeting* (pp. 147–164). New York: Marcel Dekker.

Joyce, P. G., Lee, R. D., & Johnson, R. W. (2004). *Public budgeting systems* (7th ed.). Jones and Bartlett Publishers.

Kaiser, H. F., Hunka, S., & Bianchini, J. C. (1971). Relating factors between studies based upon different individuals. *Multivariate Behavioral Research, 6*(4), 409–422. doi:10.1207/s15327906mbr0604_3.

Kano, Y. (2007). Selection of manifest variables. In *Handbook of latent variable and related models*. Oxford, UK: North-Holland.

Kostova, T., & Roth, K. (2003). Social capital in multinational corporations and a micro-macro model of its formation. *Academy of Management Review, 28*(2), 297–317.

Kumar, K., & Van Dissel, H. G. (1996). Sustainable collaboration: Managing conflict and cooperation in interorganizational systems. *Management Information Systems Quarterly, 20*(3), 279–300. doi:10.2307/249657.

Larkey, P. D. (1995). *Good budgetary decision processes*. (Unpublished manuscript). Carnegie Mellon University.

Larson, A. (1992). Network dyads on entrepreneurial settings: A study of the governance of relationships. *Administrative Science Quarterly, 36*, 76–104. doi:10.2307/2393534.

Lee, J., & Rao, H. R. (2007). Perceived risks, counter-beliefs, and intentions to use anti-counter-terrorism websites: An exploratory study of government–citizens online interactions in a turbulent environment. *Decision Support Systems, 43*, 1431–1449. doi:10.1016/j.dss.2006.04.008.

Levin, D. Z., & Cross, R. (2004). The strength of weak ties you can trust: The mediating role of trust in effective knowledge transfer. *Management Science, 50*(11), 1477–1490. doi:10.1287/mnsc.1030.0136.

Lüder, K. G. (1992). A contingency model of governmental accounting innovations in the political-administrative environment. *Research in Governmental and Nonprofit Accounting, 7*, 99–127.

Lynn, L. E., Jr. (1998). *Requiring bureaucracies to perform: What have we learned from the U.S. Government Performance and Results Act (GPRA)?* Working paper no. 98-3, The Harris School, University of Chicago.

Mayer, R. C., Davis, J. H., & Schoorman, F. D. (1995). An integrative model of organizational trust. *Academy of Management Review*, *20*, 709–734.

McKnight, D. H., Choudhury, V., & Kacmar, C. (2002). Developing and validating trust measures for e-commerce: An integrative approach. *Information Systems Research*, *13*(3), 334–359. doi:10.1287/isre.13.3.334.81.

Melkers, J.E., & Willoughby, K.G. (2001). Budgeters' view of state performance-budgeting systems: Distinctions across branches. *Public Administration Review*, January/February, *61*(1).

Moon, M. J., & Norris, D. (2005). Does managerial orientation matter? The adoption of reinventing government and e-government at the municipal level. *Information Systems Journal*, *15*, 43–60. doi:10.1111/j.1365-2575.2005.00185.x.

Mui, L., Mohtashemi, M., & Halberstadt, A. (2002). A computational model of trust and reputation. In *Proceedings of the35th Hawaii International Conference on System Sciences* (pp. 2431- 2439).

Nahapiet, J., & Ghoshal, S. (1998). Social capital, intellectual capital, and the organizational advantage. *Academy of Management Review*, *23*(2), 242–266.

Nidumolu, S. R. (1989). The impact of interorganizational systems on the form and climate of seller-buyer relationships: A structural equations modelling approach. In *Proceedings of the 10th International Conference on Information Systems* (pp. 289-304).

Ninghui, L., Mitchell, J. C., & Winsborough, W. H. (2005). Beyond proof-of-compliance: Security analysis in trust management. *Journal of the ACM*, *52*(3), 474–514. doi:10.1145/1066100.1066103.

O'Toole, L. J., & Meier, K. J. (1999). Modeling the impact of public management: Implications of structural context. *Journal of Public Administration: Research and Theory*, *9*(4), 505–526. doi:10.1093/oxfordjournals.jpart.a024421.

OECD. (1997). *In search of results: Performance management practices*. Paris: PUMA/OECD.

OECD. (2007). *Performance Budgeting in OECD Countries*. Paris, France: Organisation for Economic Co-operation and Development.

Olmedilla, D., Rana, O., Matthews, B., & Nejdl, W. (2005). Security and trust issues in semantic grids. In Proceedings of the Dagsthul Seminar, *Semantic Grid: The Convergence of Technologies*, volume 05271.

Parasuraman, A., Berry, L. L., & Zeithaml, V. A. (1985). A conceptual model of service quality and its implications for future research. *Journal of Marketing*, *49*(4), 41–50. doi:10.2307/1251430.

Parasuraman, A., Berry, L. L., & Zeithaml, V. A. (1988). SERVQUAL: A multiple-item scale for measuring consumer perceptions of service quality. *Journal of Retailing*, *64*(1), 12–40.

Parasuraman, A., Berry, L. L., & Zeithaml, V. A. (1991). Refinement and reassessment of the SERVQUAL scale. *Journal of Retailing*, *67*(4), 420–450.

Pardo, T. A., Cresswell, A. M., Dawes, S. S., & Burke, G. B. (2004). Modeling the social and technical processes of interorganizational information integration. Paper presented at *HICSS2004, 37th Hawaiian International Conference on System Sciences*.

Pardo, T. A., Cresswell, A. M., Thompson, F., & Zhang, J. (2006). Knowledge sharing in cross-boundary information systems development. *Journal of Information Technology Management*, *7*(4).

Powell, W. K., Koput, K. W., & Smith-Doerr, L. (1996). Interorganizational collaboration and the locus of innovation: Networks of learning in biotechnology. *Administrative Science Quarterly*, *41*, 116–145. doi:10.2307/2393988.

Puron-Cid, G. (2010). *Extending structuration theory: A study of an IT-enabled budget reform in Mexico*. (Doctoral Thesis). University at Albany, State University of New York, Albany, New York.

Puron-Cid, G. (2012). Interdisciplinary application of structuration theory for e-government: A case study of an IT-enabled budget reform. Accepted for publication at *Government Information Quarterly*.

Reed, M. I. (2001). Organization, trust and control: A realist analysis. *Organization Studies*, *22*(2), 201. doi:10.1177/0170840601222002.

Ring, P. S., & Van de Van, A. H. (1994). Developmental processes of cooperative interorganizational relationships. *Academy of Management Review*, *19*(1), 90–118.

Schick, A. (1998). Why most developing countries should not try New Zealand reforms. *The World Bank Research Observer*, *13*(1), 123. doi:10.1093/wbro/13.1.123.

Schick, A. (2008). Getting performance budgeting to perform. *Paper presented at the Conferencia Internacional de Presupuesto por Resultados, Mexico City*.

Scholl, H. J. (2009). Electronic government: A study domain past its infancy. In Scholl, H. J. (Ed.), *Electronic government: Information, technology and transformation*. M.E. Sharpe Armonk.

Shapiro, S. P. (1987). The social control of impersonal trust. *American Journal of Sociology*, *93*(3), 623–658. doi:10.1086/228791.

Smith, K. G. et al. (1995). Intra- and Interorganizational Cooperation: Toward a Research Agenda. *Academy of Management Journal*, *38*(1), 7–23. doi:10.2307/256726.

Szulanski, G. (1996). Exploring internal stickiness: Impediments to the transfer of best practice within the firm. *Strategic Management Journal*, 17.

Tassabehji, R., Elliman, T., & Mellor, J. (2007). Generating citizen trust in e-government security: Challenging perceptions. *International Journal of Cases on Electronic Commerce*, *3*(3). doi:10.4018/jcec.2007070101.

Van Reeth, W. (2002). *The bearable lightness of budgeting. An explorative research on the uneven implementation of performance oriented budget reform*. (Doctoral Degree Thesis). Catholic University of Leuven, Leuven, Germany.

Wang, W., & Benbasat, I. (2005). Trust in and adoption of online recommendation agents. *Journal of the Association for Information Systems*, *6*(3), 72–101.

Warkentin, M., Gefen, D., Pavlou, P. A., & Rose, G. (2002). Encouraging citizen adoption of egovernment by building trust. *Electronic Markets*, *12*(3), 157–162. doi:10.1080/101967802320245929.

Williams, L. R. (1994). Understanding distribution channels: An interorganizational study of EDI adoption. *Journal of Business Logistics*, *15*(2), 173–203.

Zaheer, A., McEvily, B., & Perrone, V. (1998). Does trust matter? Exploring the effects of interorganizational and interpersonal trust on performance. *Organization Science*, *9*, 141–158. doi:10.1287/orsc.9.2.141.

Zucker, L.-G. (1986). Production of trust: Institutional sources of economic structure, 1840–1920. *Research in Organizational Behavior*, *8*, 53–111.

ADDITIONAL READING

Bouckaert, G., & Van de Walle, S. (2001). Government performance and trust in government. *Paper for the Permanent Study Group of Productivity and Quality in the Public Sector. EGPA Annual Conference*, Vaasa, Finland, 5-89 September.

Fukuyama, F. (1995). *Trust: The social virtues and the creation of prosperity*. Harmondsworth: Penguin Books.

Galindo, F. (2002). *E-government trust providers. In the Electronic government: Design, applications and management*. IGI Global.

Gambetta, D. (1988). *Trust: Making and breaking cooperative relationships*. Oxford: Basil Blackwell.

Mezgar, I. (2006). *Trust in e-government services. In the Encyclopedia of e-commerce, e-government, and mobile commerce*. IGI Global.

Misztal, B. A. (1996). *Trust in Modern Societies*. Cambridge, MA: The Polity Press.

Riegelsberger, J., Sasse, M. A., & McCarthy, J. D. (2005). The mechanisms of trust: A framework for research and design. *International Journal of Human-Computer Studies*, *62*(3), 381–422. doi:10.1016/j.ijhcs.2005.01.001.

KEY TERMS AND DEFINITIONS

Citizen Trust: In the context of e-government adoption, is the personal belief or disposition that a particular information, interaction, transaction or service is certain and reliable.

Confirmatory Factor Analysis (CFA): Is a statistical technique that is used to test whether measures of a construct are consistent with a researcher's understanding of the nature of that construct (or factor). The CFA serves to test whether the data fit a hypothesized measurement model.

E-Government: Is the use of information and communication technologies in order to transform relations with citizens, businesses, and other arms of government.

Interdisciplinary Perspective to Study E-Government: Is a conceptual framework that serves to understand the multiple structures interacting in e-government, but detected from other disciplines different than information systems.

IT-Enabled Budget Reform: Is the use of information technology to enabled interaction, transactions, accountability and transparency in the process of public spending among actors inside and outside of government.

Mexico: Is a country with a democratic, republican and federal regimen divided in three levels of government: federal, 32 states, and 2,457 municipal governments. Each level of government is autonomous, but there are different levels of authority and coordination among them. Most of government reforms have been conducted from the federal government with impact on the other two levels.

Trust among Actors inside Government: In the context of e-government adoption, is the personal belief or disposition based on clear roles and responsibilities, previous experiences, knowledge, and incentives to collaborate or participate in a particular e-government project.

ENDNOTES

1. SHCP stands for the Spanish acronym of *Secretaria de Hacienda y Credito Publico.*
2. SFP stands for the Spanish acronym of *Secretaria de la Funcion Publica*.
3. CONEVAL stands for the Spanish acronym of *Consejo Nacional de Evaluación de la Política de Desarrollo Social*.

Chapter 6
Implementation of Information and Communications Technologies for Financial Inclusion in Programs to Alleviate Poverty in Brazil, Colombia and Mexico

Judith Mariscal
Centro de Investigación y Docencia Económicas, Mexico

César Rentería
Centro de Investigación y Docencia Económicas, Mexico

ABSTRACT

Implementation of ICT in policies targeted to alleviate poverty, specifically in conditional transfer programs (CTP), offers two opportunities. On one side, it contributes to improve delivery efficiency to beneficiaries, diminishing transfer costs with better control over beneficiaries' registry. On the other side, ICT incorporation on CTP helps to reduce costs of receiving funds and, from a broader scope, it contributes to social and digital inclusion of poor; this is especially relevant with the emergence of mobile banking.

Almost every country in Latin America employs CTP programs as a social policy. Approximately 100 million of people are beneficiaries of CTP in Latin America, which accounts for about half of the people living in poverty in the region. Hence, improving administration of this kind of policy implies for the Latin-American countries, not only savings based on efficiency, but the opportunity of broaden the benefits.

The main objective of this chapter is to analyze innovative ICT implementation on CTP in three countries in the region: Bolsa Familia (Brazil), Oportunidades (Mexico) and Familias en Acción (Colombia). These three countries are implementing pilot programs that include ITC. These experiences may important insights for future successful implementation of ICT for CTP in other countries.

DOI: 10.4018/978-1-4666-4173-0.ch006

Copyright © 2013, IGI Global. Copying or distributing in print or electronic forms without written permission of IGI Global is prohibited.

1. INTRODUCTION

Information and communications technologies (ICTs) have become a strategic focus in countries' development plans. Ensuring that the majority of the population has access to ICT services has become a fundamental public policy objective for both economic and social reasons. In terms of the economy, various studies document how ICTs increase productivity and contribute to economic growth by making the adoption of more efficient business processes possible and maximizing the effective use of resources (Katz, 2009; Qiang & Rossotto, 2009; Karner & Onyeji, 2007). They also contribute to speeding up innovation through the introduction of new applications and services (such as new varieties of commerce and financial intermediation).

In terms of social impact, various studies have identified the positive effect of the adoption of mobile telephony by the poorest sections of the population (Horst & Miller, 2005; Bar et al., 2007; Ling, 2008). The poorest sections of the population generally operate within the informal sector and survive with high transaction costs. There is also a growing literature documenting the role of ICTs as tools with productive uses, for finding employment, strengthening small businesses and contributing to the integration of the inhabitants of remote areas (Waverman et al., 2001; Galperin, 2005; DIRSI, 2007; LIRNE, 2006; Jackson, 2008).

This chapter analyzes three cases where e-government solutions have been implemented to strengthen programs designed to alleviate poverty. Additionally, these solutions aim to endow beneficiaries with additional capacities through financial inclusion and technology adoption. Even if it is still early to draw conclusions, the paper offers an exploration and an analysis of the key elements to provide the reader with valuable lessons regarding opportunity areas for e-government implementation in poverty alleviation programs. The studied cases reveal critical strategies for successful administration of similar interventions.

Common to the cases studied in this work is the two-fold benefit from using ICT's. The main objective is to make poverty alleviation policies more efficient and effective through the implementation of ICT's. In addition, considering that one of the characteristics of the conditional transfer programs (CTP's) lies in its capacity to incorporate financial inclusion strategies in daily processes, ICT's can also be used as a tool to promote financial inclusion through CTP's natural functions, as an additional objective. A distinction must be made on the fact that ICT implementation for CTP's does not serve as a public policy and that the beneficiaries technological adoption due to the programs payoffs is a consequential benefit of the financial inclusion strategies and not an established goal itself.

CTP's can benefit by reducing its operation costs and increasing its effectiveness in selecting beneficiaries, reinforcing government's current operative challenges of improving public policy performance. However, beyond the benefits derived from ICT to improve government functions and program efficiency and effectiveness standards through e-management (Galindo, 2002; Gil-García & Luna Reyes, 2006), ICT's can be used as tools that reinforce policies that help reduce the challenges facing disadvantaged segments in Latin American in terms of poverty alleviation and social exclusion. According to Amartya Sen (1999), escaping poverty is a matter of building capabilities. Poverty is a limited assets trap (education, capital, information and health); if these are available, they generate increased assets. The poor are faced with numerous obstacles in their daily lives and they require access not only to resources but to information, knowledge and skills. The creation and accumulation of specific assets is a direct means of generating capabilities.

A crucial variable for asset creation is the opportunity to create savings, because it makes it possible to transform financial assets into productive assets, which facilitate self-development. In other words, savings are an essential foundation of the accumulation processes that makes it possible to escape from the poverty trap.[1]

Empirical evidence shows that poor households do indeed save and borrow as strategies for dealing with emergencies and for investing in human capital (for example, to educate children) as well as for starting small businesses. When the poor segments of society are offered access to financial services and are provided with training in its use, they make productive use of their bank deposits.[2]

ICTs provide a route that is more direct and less expensive than traditional delivery of financial services through several strategies, e.g. mobile banking, electronic pocketbooks, etc. For example, the ubiquity of mobile telephony, even among the lowest income deciles of the population, makes it possible for applications associated with a service, such as mobile banking, to become accessible to a growing number of cellular phone users. Another example is the use of electronic government payments to beneficiaries (known as G2P) which allows government to reduce its operative costs and beneficiaries to access their aid in a faster and safer way, spending less time and money at it.[3]

In terms of public policy, in addition to promoting an environment suitable for the development of ICT (and especially mobile banking models), government can play a proactive role in this area. There are pilot projects in Latin America and other regions where governments encourage, through technology based innovative schemes, access to savings by poor people by providing financial inclusion mechanisms in social transfer programs. This kind of intervention includes more than just facilitating account openings; it also includes financial education programs to assure the effective use of the banking system by the poor.

The link between social transfer programs and ICT's, such as mobile telephony platforms, can promote innovation in financial services for the poor. Thus, government would fulfill the role of "first mover" and boost access to banking systems among those currently excluded, making the most of the opportunities offered by ICTs.

The objective of the present work is to explore recent alternatives that incorporate ICT to improve social policies performance, particularly for financial inclusion. After this introductory section, it will present an overview of the state of access to telecommunications and the financial markets in Latin America. The third section shows the progress of welfare programs to address poverty while the fourth maps three programs that have begun to use ICTs as banking tool to introduce its beneficiaries to financial services. The cases chosen were the *Familias en Acción* program in Colombia, Brazil's *Bolsa Familia* and *Oportunidades* in Mexico, which as will be explained in detail in the fourth section, were selected because they are the biggest programs in the region and each one of them has launched a pilot program aimed to include beneficiaries of those programs to financial sector. In the fifth section, presents highlights of relevant lessons from the cases studied; while the sixth and last section present conclusions about the implementation of ICT's as a way to efficiently address the challenges of financial inclusion in the region.

This paper seeks to identify the advantages of using ICTs a tool for strengthening policies to address poverty, specifically in CTP's, whose features provide a window of opportunity to implement actions moving towards a process of financial inclusion. This window offers further prospects for the poor to escape the poverty trap. However, it is important to point out that these are recent initiatives that cannot be evaluated yet. Therefore, the objective of this analysis is to identify innovative improvement mechanisms for CTP's and to explore its benefits and key components.

2. ASSESSMENT OF CONNECTIVITY AND FINANCIAL INCLUSION IN LATIN AMERICA

In the past decade, Latin America experienced significant growth in ICT penetration (fixed telephony, mobile telephony and broadband Internet). In some of these technologies, there is a degree of maturity, which implies a certain level of stability in current penetration. This is the case with landlines, which have only increased marginally from 2000 to 2011, stabilizing at a level of penetration of approximately 19 lines *per capita* (see Figure 1).

On the other hand, mobile penetration in Latin America has grown rapidly from 10 connections per 100 inhabitants in 2000 to 112 in 2011. This indicates that the mobile industry is becoming consolidated as one of the region's strongest windows of opportunity with regards to development opportunities. In contrast to other regions, there is significant deployment in Latin America, whereas in the other developing regions such as Asia and Africa, the average level of penetration was 53 per 100 inhabitants (ITU, 2012). However, if we break down the level of penetration of mobile telephony in the major countries of the region, there is significant variation in the level of penetration, for example, four countries (Uruguay, Argentina, Chile and Brazil) display over 120 penetration, while other countries have a relatively low level of penetration, Bolivia and Mexico being the lower cases (see Figure 2).

There has been a more or less linear growth in the number of Internet users over the last decade; however, the level of penetration is still low. The low level of Internet penetration is even more remarkable in terms of the average level of penetration of broadband and its low growth rate. On average, the level of broadband penetration in Latin America is 6.8%, with Uruguay (11.4%), Chile (11%) and Mexico (10.9%) being the countries with higher levels of penetration in the region. In contrast, the average penetration of broadband in OECD countries is 25.1%. Netherlands has the highest penetration (38.5%) with Chile, Mexico and Turkey being the countries with the lowest penetration (10%) among this group of countries.[4]

The coverage and the current pace of growth of mobile telephony and to a lesser extent, Internet access make these two communications technologies a bulwark for their use in other areas of the economy, given their nature as general purpose technologies. The banking sector, with its window of opportunity for progress in mobile banking systems, is one of the sectors that could benefit the most from the possibilities of technological convergence. This is especially valuable in the case of Latin America, owing to the regional overview of access to financial services.

The level of access to financial services in Latin America is very low compared to developed countries. In none of the countries in the region apart from Chile do more than 50% of the population use banking services, in other words, the level of penetration of banking services is less than half

Figure 1. Penetration of ICTs in Latin America, 2000-2011

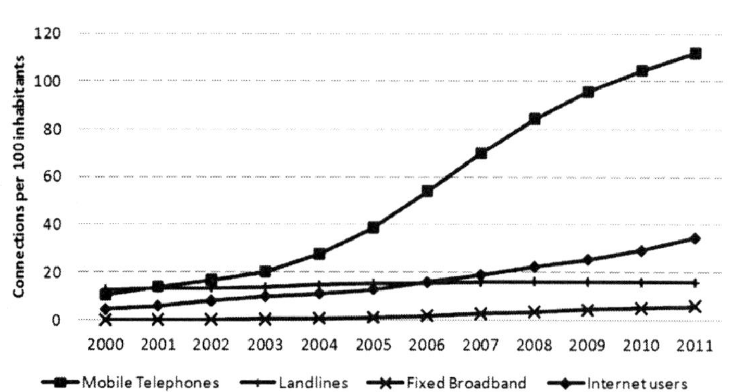

Source: ITU, 2012

Figure 2. Penetration of mobile telephony in Latin America, 2011

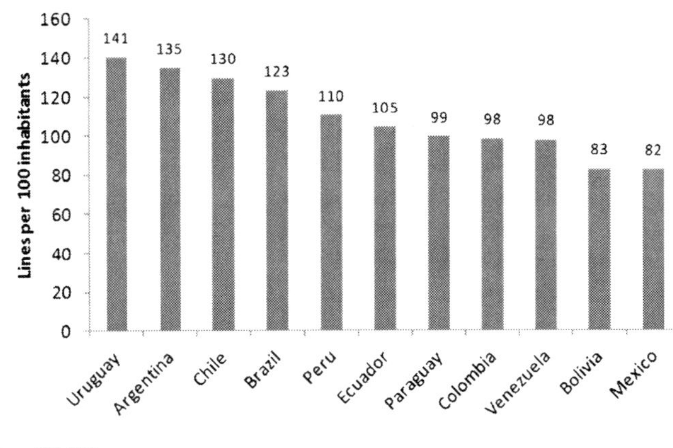

Source: ITU, 2012

that of developed countries such as Spain and the United States (see Figure 3). The most extreme case is Nicaragua, where only about 5% of the population use banking services. Other cases with a low percentage of bank users (less than 30%) are Mexico, Honduras, Peru, El Salvador, Venezuela, Argentina and the Dominican Republic.

Financial inclusion policies in the region face strong restrictions on access to banking services, particularly access to bank branches, but above all, access to ATMs. This hinders the possibilities of inclusion via electronic cards. ATMs are not the only option for financial transactions in remote areas, since branchless banking, business partners and other operators may be found. The evaluation of geographic and demographic ATM coverage provides an overview of the challenges facing banking coverage in the region. Compared with the United States and Spain, ATM coverage in Latin American countries is low. While the former have a level of demographic coverage of over 120 ATMs per 100,000 inhabitants, of Latin American countries only Chile has over 20 ATMs per 100,000 inhabitants, which implies a five-fold difference in the level of coverage (see Figure 4).

Another challenge facing the countries of the region in terms of financial inclusion is the limited bank coverage in geographical terms, which means that it is harder to provide financial services in remote areas. In general, except for small countries such as Guatemala, Costa Rica, El Salvador and the Dominican Republic, the level of coverage is less than 5 ATMs for every 1,000 square kilometers, in contrast to over 110 in Spain.

3. PROGRAMS FOR ALLEVIATING POVERTY IN LATIN AMERICA

Social policy was implemented for many years on the basis of providing basic social rights such as education, health and housing (Cordera, 2007). Other areas were added such as labor policies that established decent working conditions for workers (e.g. minimum wage and severance pay) as well as policies to strengthen the agricultural sector (Solimano, 2005). In terms of specific strategies for combating poverty, these were characterized by the pursuit of short-term solutions with a strong welfare and paternalistic element, such as handing out resources in kind, food subsidies and services, as well as the construction of basic facilities in households (latrines, concrete floors, drains, drinking water wells and so on).

In the context of economic reforms that included a process of structural adjustment, social policy faced a drastic reduction in resources devoted to solving the problems of poverty. In

Figure 3. Access to formal financial services as a percentage of the population, 2009

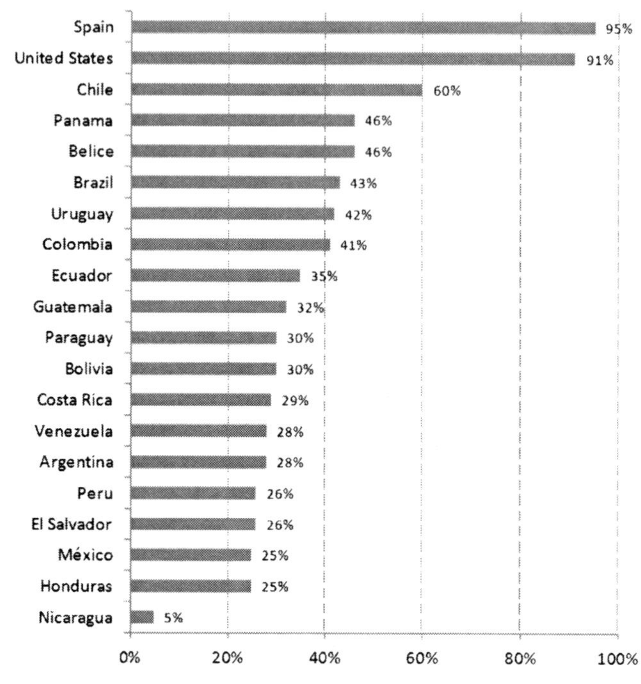

Source: ITU, 2012

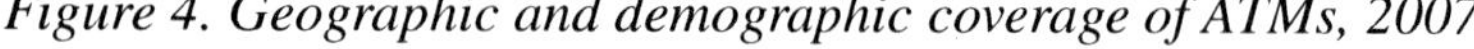

Figure 4. Geographic and demographic coverage of ATMs, 2007

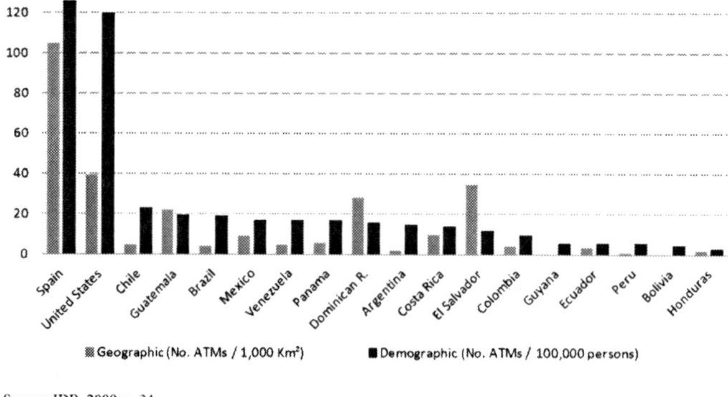

Source: IDB, 2009, p. 34

the early 1990s the foundations began to be laid for the current approach shared by the region's main social policy programs, with the following principal aspects (Solimano, 2005; Cabrera, 2007):

1. Targeting criteria were established to select social groups with certain characteristics (e.g. poor people, the elderly and disabled persons) as direct beneficiaries of programs designed to offer them *ad hoc* assistance.
2. Subsidies were removed from basic consumer goods to avoid distortion in market prices.
3. There was a shift from assistance criteria to a subsidy model.[5]

Conditional Transfer Programs

Under the previous rules, targeted programs began to take shape in Latin America aimed at the poorest people with a combination of material support to alleviate poverty in the short-term, with mechanisms for the accumulation of human capital that would address the causes of poverty in the long-term (ECLAC, 2007). These practices subsequently resulted in an innovative scheme of cash transfers conditional on investment in the development of human capital known as CTPs. Such programs have spread across the region so that CTPs have been consolidated as the main tool for combating poverty in Latin America (ECLAC, 2007; Cabrera, 2007; Maldonado, 2011). It is estimated that approximately 110 million people in Latin America are beneficiaries of a CTP, which accounts for about half of all people living in poverty in the region (220 million) (Solimano, 2005, p. 46; Maldonado, 2011, p. 15).[6]

CTPs involve the provision of monetary transfers to assist families living in chronic poverty or as a result of catastrophic events. This component represents a solution to short-term symptomatic problems, but not the causes of poverty (ECLAC, 2007). However, the conditionality component brings to CTPs the factor of investment in the development of individual skills that is necessary, but not sufficient, to break the intergenerational transmission of poverty, to avoid falling into poverty traps.

This new approach represents a clear trend towards the implementation of social policies that prioritize the delivery of individual benefits instead of a community approach, which are based on the "empowerment of the poor" as a key mechanism to improve the quality of public services of education and health (Fox, 2007, p. 5 and 15).

The proliferation of CTPs in Latin America has led to variations from one country to another and an understanding that each country faces particular social problems. However, in general terms, these policies share a common conceptual basis including the following four points (ECLAC, 2007, p. 5):

1. The pursuit of a simultaneous attack on the causes and the consequences of poverty. This means that the transfers have an enormous potential to maintain the basic levels of consumption, while making this guarantee conditional on beneficiaries' investing in developing their individual capacities.
2. The pursuit of efficiency and correction of market failures. This implies that the price effect of conditioning should give individuals an incentive to decide to invest part of their resources in the development of individual skills of their own free will.
3. The promotion of family responsibility. This principle relates to the need to implement the subsidy component in social policy, such that beneficiaries are proactive agents in promoting their own development.
4. The use of multidimensional interventions. Implies widening the impact of these programs, beginning with design, on the one hand through simultaneous intervention at several levels of human capital, and on the other, through institutional joint working by different government agencies.

Opportunities to Implement ICTs in CTPs

As mentioned above, CTPs are based on the selection of beneficiaries for the transfer of grant money. The programs that exist in the region define the household as the basic unit of economic transfer, with families in poverty and in extreme poverty being the recipients of targeted support (ECLAC, 2007; Maldonado, 2011). Targeting criteria are established, based on the specific objectives of each program and are usually rigid, but in recent years in some countries the eligibility criteria have tended to become more flexible, for example, in Mexico, Brazil and Chile (ECLAC, 2007). The rigidity of targeting criteria is of particular interest in ICT implementation, since as these become more rigid, the need for monitoring and supervision to ensure the proper selection of beneficiaries' increases.

After defining the selection criteria, programs need information about the socioeconomic conditions of families. To this end, mechanisms are used for collecting information such as inscriptions and surveys with different sample stratification strategies (ECLAC, 2007). The information subsequently focuses on databases and is processed according to the selection criteria to produce a register of beneficiaries. In some countries, a stage of beneficiary register validation is performed afterwards where selected families are visited to verify the information. In other countries, such as Peru and Mexico, community meetings are held to validate the register of beneficiary families (ECLAC, 2007). These complementary strategies are carried out in order to reduce errors of inclusion in the registers. Inclusion errors are inevitable, above all in top-down targeting policies directed by central government. It is, however, important to minimize this error for two reasons: 1) to avoid tension in community relations that bear the waste of social capital, and 2) to increase targeting efficiency and, therefore, the program's impact on poverty alleviation (Cordera, 2007; ECLAC, 2007). At this point ICTs represent a window of opportunity to reduce potential data collection errors while preparing the databases.

Another important CTP process is the monitoring system by means of which compliance with the beneficiaries' conditions is checked (ECLAC, 2007). Monitoring systems are also the basis for additional analysis of the program and for strengthening the transparency with which these programs operate. One of the points where at which ICTs could have most impact is in the process of program monitoring. A monitoring system capable of generating and processing accurate and fresh information would make it possible to improve program impact assessment, to issue payments faster and offer protection against the possibility of corruption and manipulation of the beneficiary register (ECLAC, 2007).

Finally, the last CTP process that could be improved through the implementation of ICTs is the funds transfer process. In many cases it is difficult to make effective cash transfers to beneficiaries as a result of the limited state of development and access often faced by beneficiary families living in marginal and inaccessible locations. Moreover, resource transfer implies a significant wastage of resources to cover the high transaction costs involved in this process. Because of the inaccessibility of most of the localities in which the beneficiaries reside, with a limited presence of public or private institutions, governments generally have to rely, for the effective delivery of the resources, on temporary coverage strategies in partnership with financial institutions (Maldonado, 2011).

Means of payment may be divided into three classes as follows (Maldonado, 2011): 1) cash payments, 2) electronic pocketbooks and 3) savings accounts. Initially the programs were based on cash payments, so that programs incurred substantial costs transporting and protecting the money while considerable time was spent counting it, putting it in envelopes and delivering it (Maldonado, 2011). For beneficiaries, the scheme also represents a significant expense, since it is costly to receive the aid, as it often involves the beneficiaries moving from their place of origin and dedicating several hours of the day to the receipt of the cash (Maldonado, 2011). Currently, electronic credits are the most widespread means of payment, accounting for about 56% of program payments in Latin America, while cash transfers represent 17% of payments made in this region (Maldonado, 2011, p. 20).

Also for CTPs, the transition to an electronic payments scheme opens the possibility of introducing complementary banking programs for the beneficiary families. This would allow much of the population without access to financial services to be able to save, to manage deposits, to process remittances and transfers as well as to access micro-credits. There is a great deal of literature on the impact of banking services as a means of reducing poverty in marginalized areas. Based on the above, this study considers four critical aspects in the CTP flow chart in which the implementation of ICTs could have a significant impact on strengthening these programs. Below are the four elements in the order in which they occur (see Figure 5):

1. Tools for generating information on families' socio-economic circumstances
2. Mechanisms for validating information and reducing inclusion errors
3. Monitoring and evaluation systems
4. Money transfer mechanisms

These processes are grouped according to their characteristics into two categories, to simplify their analysis in the case studies. The first three processes relate to information systems management, while the fourth process is a technological and logistical challenge for the transfer of financial incentives, as well as the synergies that can be achieved by adding additional elements such as financial inclusion policies. The first category is called Integrated Social Information Systems, information management tools for social policy administration. The second category refers mainly to the implementation of ICTs to mitigate transaction costs, although from a broader perspective it can be considered a Financial Inclusion strategy.

4. CASE STUDIES

At the end of 2011 there were active CTPs in Latin America. Of course there are great differences between these in terms of coverage and program maturity (ECLAC, 2011). Except for the pioneering programs in Mexico, Brazil and Ecuador, all the programs began in the 2000s, the most recent being the *Bono 10,000* program in Honduras, launched in 2010. The programs with the widest coverage remain in Brazil (which covers 50 million people) and Mexico (which covers 27 million people) but in terms of proportionality to each country's population, the programs of Colombia, Ecuador and Guatemala have a coverage equal to or greater than those of Brazil and Mexico (see Table 1) (Maldonado, 2011, p. 54).

To select cases for study in this paper, it was decided to choose the biggest programs in the region. This criterion stands for the number of beneficiaries that has each program. In this manner, the biggest programs are Brazil (49 million),

Figure 5. Flow chart of the critical CTP processes

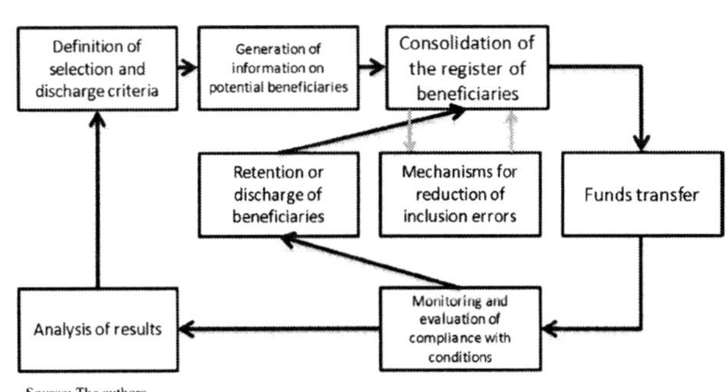

Table 1. CTP performance in Latin America, 2010

Country	Conditional Transfer Programs	Start	Coverage				Program expenditure as a percentage of GDP
			Total (in millions of persons)	Percentage of the total population	Percentage of the poor population	Percentage of the indigent population	
Argentina	1) Children's welfare; 2) *Ciudadanía Porteña "Con todo derecho"* Program	1) 2009; 2) 2005	3.400	8.3	46.4	100	0.20
Bolivia	1) *Bono Juancito Pinto*; 2) *"Juana Azurduy"* mother/child payment	1) 2006; 2) 2009	0.340	17.5	32.4	50.7	0.33
Brazil	*Bolsa Familia*	2003	49.614	26.4	84.6	100	0.47
Chile	*Chile Solidario*	2002	0.332	6.8	51.7	100	0.11
Colombia	1) *Familias en Acción*; 2) *Red Juntos*; 3) Subsidies conditional on school attendance	1) 2001; 2) 2007; 3) 2005	11.650	25.2	56.5	100	0.39
Costa Rica	*Avancemos*	2006	0.185	3.3	17.4	52.2	0.39
Ecuador	*Bono de Desarrollo Humano*	2003	6.100	44.3	100	100	1.17
El Salvador	*Comunidades Solidarias Rurales*	2005	0.508	8.2	17.1	38.7	0.02
Guatemala	*Mi Familia Progresa*	2008	3.253	22.6	39.7	70.5	0.32
Honduras	*Bono 10.000*	2010	0.409	17.2	S. D.	S, D.	0.24
Mexico	*Oportunidades*	1997	27.246	24.6	62.8	100	0.51
Panama	*Red de Oportunidades*	2006	0.371	10.9	39.5	81.0	0.22
Paraguay	1) *Tekporá*; 2) *Abrazo*	1) 2005; 2) 2005	0.554	8.6	13.9	25.2	0.36
Peru	*Juntos*	2005	0.490	7.6	21.2	60.6	0.14
Dominican Republic	*Solidaridad*	2005	2.168	21.2	46.3	89.0	0.51
Uruguay	*Asignaciones Familiares*	2008	0.377	11.6	84.6	100	0.45

Source: The authors based on data from ECLAC, 2011 and Maldonado, 2011

Mexico (27 million), and Colombia (11 million). However, aiming to consider countries with lower population, the authors reviewed this criterion as percentage of beneficiaries according national population, finding the following results: Ecuador (44.3%), Brazil (26.4%), Mexico (24.6%), and Colombia (25.2%).

The second criterion was the existence of fund transfer systems that contribute to the financial inclusion of beneficiaries as an emergent collateral goal of the program. Based on a review of each country ordered by the size of program (in terms of beneficiaries), the authors decided to select the cases of Brazil, Mexico and Colombia given that, besides of being the biggest programs in the region, each one of them have developed recently a pilot program to implement mechanisms of financial inclusion for their beneficiaries. Those programs bring an enormous opportunity of learning from their innovative initiatives.

Nevertheless, it should be noted that this does not imply that important lessons cannot be drawn from the information management systems of other programs. However, space restrictions meant it was strategic for the authors to focus on examining information systems in a small number of cases. For this reason it is hoped a priori that the countries chosen will provide important lessons for the handling of complex CTP information management systems.

5. METHODOLOGY

The investigation's objective is to compile information that focuses solely on the payment mechanisms of the conditional transfer programs. Additionally, the document emphasis is on the analysis of the improvements of these programs. In methodological terms, the case of Mexico is a distinct case as it presents an analysis of the implementation of a pilot project while the cases of Colombia and Brazil present and analysis of the recent adjustments undertaken in transfer programs.

For each case study a documentary investigation was undertaken by means of interviews and data analysis. The documentary revision included a literature review, program evaluations, and analysis of official documents such as operating procedures, decrees, legislation, operation and user manuals, etc. The interviews were made to officials directly responsible of the programs operation and both program operators and international organizations reviewed the collected official data.

Colombia

Familias en Acción Program Description

The *Familias en Acción* (Families in Action, or FA) program is a national government initiative created in 2000. It operates through the Ministry of Health and Social Protection in order to help families living in extreme poverty to maintain or increase their investment in human capital building. The specific program objectives are as follows:

1. Reduce truancy and dropout rates of students in elementary and middle school.
2. Supplement the income of families with children younger under seven living in extreme poverty in order to increase the food budget.
3. Increase health care for children under seven years of age.
4. Improve child care practices in areas such as health, nutrition, early childhood stimulation and prevention of interfamily violence.

In order to achieve these objectives, the program is mainly based on conditioned transfers to families with children who are under 18. In this regard, the program has two components: the Nutrition Subsidy and the Education Subsidy. The first is targeted at families with children under 7. This subsidy is contingent on the family's participation in medical monitoring of growth and development, and provides COP$50,000 for each two-month period (Maldonado, 2011). This subsidy is designed to reduce the malnutrition rate among children so that they can remain healthy and improve their academic performance.

The second subsidy is designed for families with children between 7 and 18. A subsidy was given for each child in this age range who is attending elementary school or middle school. Every two months, a subsidy of 15,000 pesos is granted to children in elementary school and between 15,000 and 60,000 pesos for children attending middle school (Maldonado, 2011).[7] This subsidy is contingent on school attendance (A minimum 80% attendance in each two-month cycle). The specific objectives of the Education Subsidy are the following:

1. Reduce the truancy and dropout rate.
2. Increase the average level of education in the targeted areas.
3. Provide an incentive to return to school for school-age children who have dropped out.

Selection Mechanisms

Selection criteria are brought into line with the rest of social protection policies in Colombia. This means that all of the demand-based subsidy programs share the same selection mechanism. This mechanism is the Social Program Beneficiary Information System (SISBEN), a tool for identifying beneficiaries of Colombian social policy programs. The SISBEN calculates the population's standard of living based on designated variables that capture the capacity of the families in the continuous current expenditure. To this end, local governments across the nation administer a general survey every three years.

The target populations of the program are the families enrolled in the SISBEN 1,[8] displaced families who are registered in the Displaced Population System (SIPOD) and indigenous families registered in the indigenous census. Once they become part of the target population, the eligibility criteria stipulate that families who access the program must: have children under 11 or children between 11 and 18 years of age. In the first stage, the FA program covered nearly 315 thousand families in 691 municipalities, mainly in the country's rural areas (Maldonado & Tejerina, 2010). By 2010, the program covered 1093 out of 1098 municipalities and served a population of over 2.5 million Colombians (Maldonado, 2011, p. 175).

The following conditions have been established for accessing the subsidies:

- All children within the nuclear family must attend growth and development appointments.
- Beneficiary mothers must attend the meeting and training spaces.
- Beneficiary mothers must attend the care seminars that are scheduled by the municipality.
- The children must attend at least 80% of their classes.

Payment System

The program has had three payment systems. Initially, the payment system was operated directly by the Presidential Agency for Social Action and International Cooperation (Social Action) with the support of the commercial banking system and consisted of directly delivering the money, in cash, to the beneficiaries. This is why the Families in Action Information System (SIFA) was created, which is responsible for managing the database of the program beneficiaries, verifying compliance with the conditions and determining which beneficiaries could receive the support. Once payment was approved, resources were transferred from the Bank of the Republic to the commercial banks, which served as the last link in delivering the money. Beneficiary payments could be cashed using the following methods:

1. Payment in the beneficiary municipality. These were made in the municipalities where the participating commercial banks have branches.[9] The money was delivered through the teller over a 20-day period that had been established previously by the banks.
2. Payment through a temporary teller. In municipalities without bank branches, the payment may be made by installing an *ex profeso* temporary bank branch in a location provided by the municipal government. Due to difficulties related to movements and personnel restrictions, the payment was made on a specific date for each cycle.

3. Payment in a neighboring municipality. The payments of beneficiaries residing in municipalities without bank coverage were channeled toward neighboring municipalities that did have coverage (or a temporary bank branch).

These methods experienced various problems in making the payment; for example, the branches were overwhelmed with users (who had to wait an average of up to 3 hours) (DNP, 2011). The temporary branch operations incurred higher operating costs because of the need to transport personnel and money (the latter in armored trucks or helicopters) to areas that were difficult to access. Likewise, the beneficiaries who were unable to be present on the payment day for whatever reason were unable to receive their subsidy for that cycle (DNP, 2011). The third method substantially increased transaction costs for the families and increased the number of beneficiaries who were unable to collect the subsidy.

Since these three plans encountered many obstacles, the payment system was later modified to allow transfers through a card with an electronic purse. In this system, the beneficiaries received an electronic card called the *Tarjeta Eficaz*, which was automatically credited with the amount of the allotted transfer every two months. One of the greatest benefits of this transaction was the opportunity to collect through an ATM and thus avoid bottlenecks in the branches. In addition, the use of the card constituted the first effort to include banking services for the beneficiaries. These were limited at first, however, because since the card was not linked to a savings account, banking services were limited to the possibility of withdrawing the subsidy in authorized automatic tellers and terminals. Likewise, the operations regulations provided no incentive to save money, because if the transfers were not withdrawn, the beneficiaries lost the amount without collecting each cycle (DNP, 2011).

Later, in order to solve the abovementioned problems and to promote financial inclusion, the government instituted, through a Banking Plan, the association of a Banco Agrario savings account (a publicly owned financial institution) with the FA *Tarjeta Eficaz*.[10] The Banking Plan is based on Decrees 4590 and 4591 in 2008 that established the basic regulations for low amount electronic savings accounts designed for low income families. Based on this regulation, the Banco Agrario savings account was designed for the beneficiaries, and offered the following benefits:

- Savings accounts with remote subsidy payments
- No account service fees
- Transactions may be completed through cards, cellular phones, automatic teller machines, branch tellers, branchless banking and business partners of Banco Agrario
- At least two cash withdrawals per month and an account balance inquiry may be made without generating service fees
- No minimum deposit is required to open the account (in fact, the FA program operators open it automatically), and no minimum balance is required to maintain it
- Accounts are exempt from the financial transaction tax (known as 4x1000)
- Allows cash back of two VAT decimal points in purchases made with the card

There are additional services offered that are designed to cover the financial services needs that fit the general profile of the beneficiaries such as receiving remittances, the national deposit service, sending tax remittances and purchase of insurance (Maldonado, 2011). The Banking Plan is also considering the future expansion of services for these types of accounts such as mortgage, educational and productive loans, and insurance acquisition (DNP, 2011).

Families in Action Information System (SIFA)

The design of the SIFA includes the following eight modules to manage information from the program: 1) enrolling families; 2) recording new developments; 3) verifying compliance; 4) settlements, payments and reconciliation; 5) complaints; 6) follow-up; 7) administration; and 8) frameworking.

There is a five-stage process for inputting and updating the information contained in the SIFA, which is outlined below:

1. Identification of eligible families for the enrollment process
2. Subsidy settlement for the first payment
3. Subsidy settlement for subsequent payments
4. Academic update
5. Verification of commitments

In the first stage, eligible families are identified using the SISBEN database in order to extract a register of families located in the first category (SISBEN 1). This is used to create a register that is used as a base to launch the invitation and initiate the enrollment process. The second stage begins with the eligible families filling out the SIS forms to update the family information in the original SISBEN database. This means that for its internal operations, the SIFA updates and expands the database that it extracted from the SISBEN. Afterward, a report is prepared and distributed to the network of beneficiaries that details the amount to be paid to each one. The payment is made by municipality.

Once the payments are made, after the established payment period, the completed payments are reviewed and reconciled. Afterward, a report for generating the following payment is prepared and the files are generated to export to the banks. Likewise, in every cycle an update of the academic status of the members of the beneficiary families is reviewed and their compliance with the commitments is verified.

Currently, the Banca de las Oportunidades,[11] with the support of the IDB Korea Fund and USAID, carried out a pilot project using mobile banking to pay monetary transfers to the FA beneficiaries. The pilot program began in August 2011 during the third payment period of the FA program, with the participation of four banks in 17 municipalities and an initial stratification of 22,634 families.

So far, the two preliminary evaluations that have been performed indicate that the initiative has been fairly well received by the beneficiaries;[12] the evaluation results indicate, in general terms, that nearly half the beneficiaries invited to use mobile banking accepted the invitation. Of these, nearly all were able to collect their subsidies without any problems. Likewise, an increase was also noticed in the use of mobile banking for other purposes (such as transactions or balance inquiries). In spite of the fact that the results of the pilot program have been relatively successful, for the time being the initiative has retained its pilot program status; it is uncertain whether this initiative may eventually be applied to the entire FA beneficiary population.

Brazil

Bolsa Familia Program Description

Conditional transfer programs in Brazil began in the mid-1990s with policies such as the Program for the Eradication of Child Labor (PETI), School Stipend, Food Stipend, Cooking Fuel Supplement and Food Card. In 2003, the federal government decided to merge the last four programs into one, called the *Bolsa Familia* (Family Purse, or BF), to unify federal government expenditure in aid to families living in poverty and extreme poverty. *Bolsa Familia* is a conditional transfer program coordinated by the Ministry of Social Development and the Alleviation of Hunger (MDS). It is an integral part of the *Fome Zero* (Zero Hunger) program, designed to enforce the human right to proper nutrition. The design of the BF program makes the participation of various institutions indispensable, highlighting the importance of the coordination process. Municipal governments are responsible for the operations section of the program, based on the registration systems provided by the *Caixa Econômica Federal* (Federal Savings Bank, or CEF),[13] the selection criteria stipulated by the MDS and the control and validation mechanisms implemented by the same institution. The program has three main areas: cash transfer for immediate poverty alleviation, conditionality for improving access to basic social rights and complementary programs for overcoming the conditions that lead to vulnerability (MDS, 2012).

The program's target public includes families living in poverty and extreme poverty. Brazil has not adopted an official poverty line, so the establishment of the target public was based on the minimum wage (Lindert, 2007). Thus, the target public includes families with per capita monthly incomes of less than R$140, who have children less than 17 years of age or expectant or nursing mothers (Maldonado, 2011).

Beneficiary Selection Mechanisms

It is important to mention that the MDS is able to establish the eligibility criteria for being a BF program beneficiary mainly by setting income caps and determining how many subsidies may be granted in each municipality (municipal quotas) (Lindert, 2007). There are two beneficiary selection mechanisms: subsidies are allotted by geographic measurement and family evaluation. The first measures geographic information that identifies targeted geographic areas for setting the subsidy allotment quotas designated by the MDS at the regional level. This means that the MDS is able to determine the number of subsidies that will be distributed in each region according to the geographic information that permits identification of poverty maps (Lindert, 2007). Based on this, a census of potential beneficiary families is carried out based on a Single Registry known as the *Cadastro Único*. The *Cadastro Único* is operated and controlled by the CEF, but receives input from the studies organized by the municipal governments (who are free to register as many families as they consider necessary) and is supervised and validated by the MDS.

The program is characterized, therefore, by the participation of various actors in its implementation. While the targeting is technically the responsibility of the CEF (through the *Cadastro Único*), the MDS plays an important role in controlling the quality of the registration and logistics required to make the payments. This is possible thanks to a contract between the MDS and the CEF based on results that allow the MDS to supervise the work of the CEF (Lindert, 2007). The contract obliges the CEF to generate 17 performance indicators so that the MDS may supervise the quality of the services (Lindert, 2007). Likewise, municipal governments are responsible for collecting information. Each municipality has the freedom to design the survey according to its capacities and needs, and is responsible for the task of registering the families who express an interest at any time; this is to avoid selective and strategic use of the registration survey (see Figure 6).

Payment System

Payments are made through the CEF, which delivers the subsidy through an electronic card each month known as the *Caixa Fácil*. The card is an electronic wallet associated with a bank account from the same institution (CEF). Payments are supervised by the MDS and made by the CEF. The MDS supervises and validates the list of BF beneficiaries and calculates the amount of the monthly benefit for each family according to their compliance with the conditionalities and the various benefits they are entitled to. Once payments are validated by the MDS, the *Tesouro Nacional*

Figure 6. Registration process for the Cadastro Único

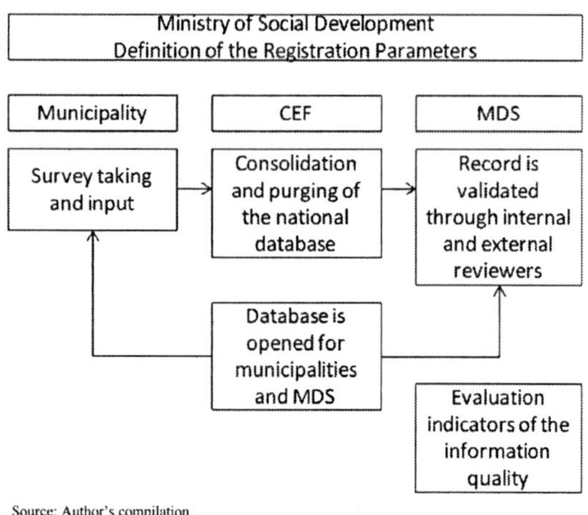

Source: Author's compilation

transfers the funds directly to the CEF to make the corresponding payroll payment.

The CEF is also responsible for producing and distributing the electronic cards and distributes them through its branches and recently (beginning in 2006) through the postal service (Lindert, 2007). The CEF operates through more than 2,000 branches throughout the country and has approximately 9,000 Lotería points[14] and 2,000 branchless banking operators, in addition to having a network of 16,281 ATMs (Lindert, 2007). There is an additional agreement in force between the MDS and the CEF that requires the CEF to submit a diagnosis to the MDS on the quality of the payments and logistics in the operation (Lindert, 2007).

Since 2008, the federal government launched a financial inclusion program with the purpose of linking a bank account with all low income residents. In terms of the BF program, the CEF was responsible for the process of replacing the electronic wallet card that was used previously with the *Caixa Fácil*, an electronic card linked to a bank account. In operational terms, the payment periods, availability of end withdrawal points and the logistical processes mentioned above remained the same. The advantages gained through this new bank account included (Maldonado, 2011):

1. It allows traditional banking service transactions such as deposits, withdrawals and purchases with the card.
2. No account fees.
3. Free, unlimited balance inquiries and deposits.
4. Free withdrawals and bank statement inquiries for the first four transactions.
5. The possibility of obtaining a loan (*Crédito Caixa Fácil Rotativo*) for a maximum of R$200 at a monthly rate of 2%.

Currently, the Brazilian financial inclusion strategy does not include subsidy transfer mechanisms for BF beneficiaries through mobile banking. If the Brazilian government, after observing successful implementations in other countries, is in fact considering implementing a mobile banking pilot program for the BF payments, the model faces great challenges in the entity. For example, in spite of the fact that users may transfer air time between them, the Central Bank of Brazil does not allow mobile telephone operators to implement a payment system using air time, because fees may vary over time, as well as between operators (Diniz, Fingermann, & Best, 2011). For the present, the MDS has initiated the first stage of an eventual pilot program, inviting banks and operators to design a project for delivery of the BF program transfers (Diniz, Fingermann, & Best, 2011). In addition, the United Nations Development Program announced three projects to strengthen financial inclusion strategies for the BF program, financial education and the improvement of payment logistics.

Mexico

Oportunidades Program Description

The *Oportunidades* ("Opportunities," previously known as *Progresa*, "Make Progress") program was launched in Mexico in 1997 and is managed by the Ministry of Social Development (SEDESOL).

The program objectives are: 1) to help reduce extreme poverty; and 2) to promote equality of opportunities and expand capabilities.

The program's design is based on acknowledging that populations in extreme poverty must play an active role in transforming their own lives. Therefore, the transformation mechanism must, in principle, grant the beneficiaries greater freedom in terms of how to spend their cash transfers, and more responsibility to take the necessary steps to obtain the funds (Levy, 2006, p. 17).

Conditioned transfers are delivered every two months; the support components in money and cash total approximately US$35 per person according to certain behaviors and commitments from the population. Half the support is a cash transfer for education, 35% is to support nutrition, 4% for medicine and 10% for other services. Beginning in 2007, the federal government also included an energy component consisting of a MXN$55 (approximately US$4) subsidy to compensate for increased fuel prices. The amount increases depending on the number of children in the household to a maximum of US$153 per month.

The program's recipient population is responsible for improving family health, especially that of children, and commits to helping children finish elementary, middle and high school, and to improving the nutritional content of the family diet. The mothers, in whose name the benefits are distributed and who receive the cash transfers, must take their children to their designated health centers on a regular basis to receive medical evaluations, vaccines, preventive treatments and nutritional supplements. They must also actively participate in community workshops on the subjects of health, nutrition and addictions. In terms of education, children under 18 must be enrolled and attending school in order to receive support from the program. Those with an attendance rate of at least 85% in the school year receive a stipend 10 months of the year. The cash transfer amounts increase according to the academic level, and is higher for girls beginning middle school, when their dropout rate is highest.

In terms of coverage, the program was conceived and designed to be applied in rural settings, where there is a higher degree of marginalization and poverty. The goal for 2010 was to provide support for 5.7 million families, in addition to 650 thousand families in the *Programa de Apoyo Alimentario* (Food Support Program, or PAL), which has also been managed by the *Oportunidades* Coordinating Office since 2010. This means that it is the most important measure for alleviating poverty in Mexico and ranks among the largest populations receiving support anywhere in the world.

Selection Mechanisms

The first stage of the program begins after selecting the urban and rural communities where *Oportunidades* may operate – based on the National Population Council Marginalization Index (CONAPO) and statistical information at the local level – and a validation of the accessibility and care capacities of the health and educational services in those communities. The next step involves collecting, capturing, processing, backing up and analyzing the families' socioeconomic information to identify those living in extreme poverty and who are therefore eligible for inclusion in the program. In order to determine household eligibility, a point system based on quantifiable demographic characteristics is used that is recorded in an individual sheet that includes the socioeconomic data for each family member and their housing features.

The socioeconomic information for applying the point system is collected at service and information tables available in the communities; later, through a "sweep system" of house to house visits, households are surveyed to identify possible beneficiaries in order to corroborate the information provided. Each household's information is recorded on individual data sheets (through the ENCASEH survey in the rural communities and the ENCASURB in urban and semi-urban communities), and each house and its members is assigned identification numbers to ensure the confidentiality of the information.

Once they are included in the program, beneficiaries are guaranteed *Oportunidades* support for three years. After that time, a recertification process is carried out using the same point system to assess whether they will continue in the program or, if their socioeconomic situation has improved, they are no longer eligible to continue receiving support.

Payment System

Beneficiaries receive a bi-monthly payment with prior validation of the information linked to the conditionality components (health and education) with data from 115,000 schools and 17,000 health clinics (Gómez Hermosillo, 2011, p. 8). Based on this information, a list is drawn up with the amounts corresponding to each family once the conditions are complied with. The National Savings and Financial Services Bank (BANSEFI) is responsible for making the payment with partner institutions such as *Telecomunicaciones de Mexico* (TELECOMM), a decentralized public entity, stores belonging to DICONSA, another public company, and 283 branches of *Crédito Popular*.[15]

BANSEFI's payment strategy had to undertake resource dispersion by electronic means due to the provisions established in the federal expenditure budget of 2010 that established that all subsidy programs' payments to their corresponding beneficiaries would have to be made electronically by December 2012.[16]

At this point, BANSEFI started to pilot programs between November 2008 and March 2009 in which it would disperse *Oportunidades* aid to thousands of beneficiaries. The dispersion was divided in two types of groups, beneficiaries in urban zones (more than 20 thousand people) and those in rural zones, where one pilot program corresponding to each. For the beneficiaries of urban zones, a card associated to a BANSEFI account was given which could be used in any ATM machine or branchless banking operator.

However, the dispersion challenge lies in those locations that do not have access to financial services, which is the case of transfers in rural zones. To resolve this problem, BANSEFI implemented point of sale (PoS) terminals in DICONSA stores so that its beneficiaries can effectively make use of payments made electronically through a branchless banking scheme. Also, beneficiaries were provided with a BANSEFI bank account associated to the card through which they receive the money. Branchless banking operators, aside from acting as the programs dispersal agents, act as a BANSEFI's branchless banking that allow users to receive deposits, pay for services, withdraw cash, consult their balance, etc.

One of the challenges that have surged from this payment scheme is the lack of sufficient liquidity in DICONSA stores to deal with the program's massive payments, making it necessary to rely on cash transport routes to procure payment every two months. In addition the low availability of commercial shops where card payments can be made limits card use to merely a form of identification.

BANSEFI's model faces a greater challenge derived from the Mexican financial system security measures for financial transactions that establishes that all transactions must be made on-line and in real time. This regulation excludes from the program all DICONSA stores found in a zone with no connectivity. To solve this problem, BANSEFI is currently working on an offline financial transaction scheme through PoS mobile terminals that can be updated every two days by moving to connectivity zones.

One of the pilot project innovations was that the beneficiaries had their digital print associated to the electronic card, providing additional security to the payment scheme and avoiding double payments. Additionally, since the card is associated to a bank account, beneficiaries can receive deposits from anyone through any banking institution, national or international, broadening the remittances transfer mechanisms.

The model sought to mitigate the operation costs of transporting cash to beneficiaries without the necessity of additional infrastructure. The model focused on hiring networks with initial infrastructures such as DICONSA, incorporating through commissions. For example, for the aid dispersion, a service contract is made in which BANSEFI pays a commission for each transaction, while the banking service is done through merchant commissions in which the beneficiary has to pay a commission for each transaction (except deposits).

The pilot programs have provided satisfactory results for BANSEFI, where 593 million MXN were dispersed to a total of 209,700 beneficiaries in urban zones and 179 million MXN to 33,200 beneficiaries in rural zones (Seira et al., 2010). It is estimated that the savings for government if all *Oportunidades* transfers were made through electronic means would rise to 8,300 million MXN (0.1% del PIB) (BBVA Research, 2011). In terms of the beneficiary, it is estimated that the costs from receiving the aid are reduced from 77 to 2.80 MXN (Seira, 2010, p. 14). In terms of savings, an experiment carried out in 320 communities showed that 22% of *Oportunidades* income was invested by receptor families. The most recent result from the program's implementation of ICT's in *Oportunidades* was that in June 23, 2012 the UN granted BANSEFI the Recognition to Public Service 2012 for the project.

Given these results, a complete migration was initiated in 2010 having currently 6.5 million beneficiaries with access to electronic transfers (see Figure 7). BANSEFI is still seeking to broaden its correspondent's network; currently it has managed to link a network of credit unions and is working on a pilot project with gas stations.

6. ANALYSIS

The national cases analyzed here have two components in common that provide a better understanding of the potential benefits of the use of ICTs in CTPs. On the one hand, these are the largest conditioned transfer programs in Latin America, which poses a challenge when trying to provide resources in a flexible, targeted manner. On the other hand, they three of the five largest countries in the region with a high percentage of

Figure 7. Monetary transfers in México: Oportunidades y PAL by millions of beneficiaries, 2006-2012

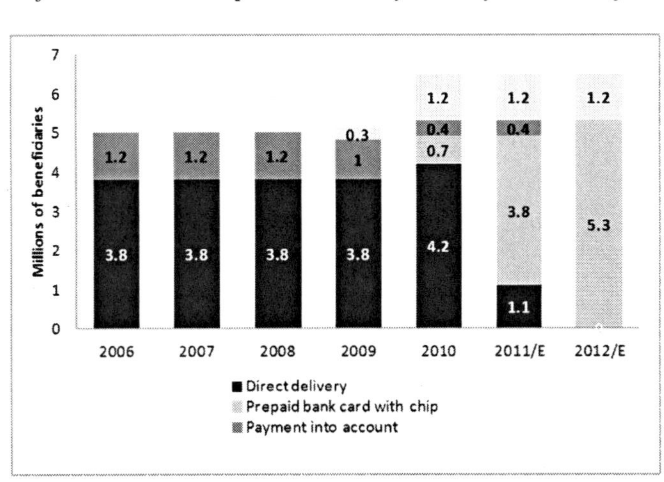

Source: BBVA Research, 2011

un-accessible geographic areas, which makes the subject of transaction costs a critical feature in the operation of these programs.

In all three cases, governments are implementing mechanisms to reduce the transaction costs of the subsidy payments through banking strategies and ICT investment. In terms of banking strategies, CTPs are identified as powerful channels for expanding financial coverage in each of these countries. The association of a banking plan with CTPs is a model strategy that positively impacts two objectives: on the one hand, it facilitates the financial inclusion process so that families living in poverty and extreme poverty have access to loans and savings; and on the other, it expedites the payment process of the CTPs and provides an important reduction in the transaction costs incurred both by the government and the beneficiaries. In this regard, Mexico, Colombia and Brazil have taken important steps. Mexico had to design a system that linked banking accounts to an electronic card in order to comply with the aperture and flexibility requisites. Mexico's case provides important lessons in terms of overcrowding schemes, in both affiliation and dispersion of supports; the issue with overcrowding is paired with specific recipes for improving transference security, avoiding double payments, generating better internal information for improved accountability and, mainly, as an austerity measure for public spending.

Colombia initiated a banking process in 2008, with modifications to the regulatory framework for promoting access to financial services through low amount electronic accounts (Decrees 4590 and 4591 in 2008). Another regulatory action benefiting financial inclusion progress occurred in 2006 with Decree 2233, which allowed financial entities to offer their services through branchless banking operators.[17] By implementing payment using electronic cards linked to a bank account in the *Familias en Acción* program, the government has reaped savings of approximately 10.5% in the program's management.[18]

Brazil's case is interesting because of its horizontal accountability system in terms of the quality of the payment system. Although CEF is responsible for managing all the information from the BF program (because it controls the *Cadastro Único* registration and the payment system), the MDS plays a key role in improving payment speed and quality. This is achieved by signing a collaboration contract (under which the CEF is responsible for making the payments) in a results-based system that grants the MDS monitoring and evaluation powers over the CEF performance both in the compilation of the beneficiary census as well as in the payment process. Its monitoring functions based on an information system that captures data for 17 variables about the process.

Mexico's case offers valuable experience in the "fragmentation" process of financial services through its advances in a model, which is still at the pilot stage, of resource transfer through stores that have coverage in the remotest regions. This model implies the double function of being a branchless banking operator and a point of sale terminal to access loans, cash withdrawals or purchase of goods with the card.

The most important lessons from these cases have to do with the way in which critical aspects for the successful dispersion of electronic payments are addressed. The first of them has to do with the geographic coverage among its agents; BANSEFI sought to make its support's electronic dispersion effective through external distribution networks which allowed the bank to avoid the need to invest in infrastructure. Yet a problem that remains unsolved is the payment agents' limited liquidity when dealing with the program's massive payments in remote communities. Another remaining challenge that remains is procuring payment agents in communities with no connectivity.

The second has to do with the contracting strategies to make alliances with other dispersion networks. BANSEFI offers economic incentives to each of the agents that form part of the network that manages *Oportunidades* payments and offers branchless banking services. Finally, BANSEFI's possibility to receive payments from any bank, be it national or international, should be remarked.

Based on the foregoing, it is evident that the focus of these countries is accompanying ICT investment with institutional and regulatory modifications to optimize the use of these tools. These experiences also clearly indicate the search for strategies to increase financial services coverage sufficiently to be able to transfer the CTP payment system toward automatic mechanism with immediate and ubiquitous availability. This focus will surely entail the need to implement banking strategies that use mobile telephony, as is already occurring with a pilot program in Colombia. In 2011 Colombia inaugurated a pilot program to provide FA program beneficiaries with banking services through mobile telephones with results that are just beginning to be measured, but that indicate relative success. This mechanism implies substantial changes in the regulation of the financial and telecommunication sectors to permit their implementation. It also requires extending enabled terminals to operate mobile telephone-based payment systems.

Also, ICT implementation is relevant in the management of the enrollment process of the beneficiaries in a census. The experiences in the region in this regard are numerous and quite consolidated; however, the countries studied in this document offer valuable experiences for improving the beneficiary registration systems.

The concept of a single registration model for targeted social programs is common in the region, but Colombia's case offers an important lesson in the efforts to consolidate a registration system (SISBEN) with interoperability qualities among other information systems used in the policy operating, monitoring or evaluation processes. The success of the interoperability of these systems may be observed insofar as the registration systems work effectively, not only as a tool for consolidating a census of beneficiaries in a program, but also as fundamental inputs for their very operation.

Brazil's case offers an important lesson in the benefits that arise from designing accountability mechanisms in information management, with which the Brazilian *Cadastro Único* registry has obtained the best evaluations in terms of targeting and inclusion errors (Lindert, 2007). For its part, Mexico has implemented ICTs in the information gathering process from the beneficiary census that has achieved the following: 1) significant reductions in the costs of feeding its model, 2) expediting the information collection and sending time; and 3) making this phase of the process more transparent by eliminating the intermediaries between the beneficiary population and the program operators.

7. FUTURE RESEARCH DIRECTIONS

The use of ICT in poverty alleviation programs is recently emerging. There are still no rigorous evaluations available on how e-government innovations undertaken by some countries are generating benefits for government itself and for society. Future investigation on the topic will be particularly beneficial for conditioned transference policies in Latin American countries since it is the region in which this type of programs is more extended. The practical implications of this type of studies allow knowledge development to have a direct impact on the efficiency and effectiveness of these programs.

On the other side, this article indicates that financial inclusion, mainly in remote zones, is a pending issue of the State in several Latin American countries. Also, it is presumed that mobile telephony, due to its high penetration, represents an opportunity for social programs to reach its beneficiaries in a more agile and efficient way. These ingredients strengthen the need to provide solutions for financial inclusion based on technology platforms. Due to the previously mentioned and in view of the lack public policy recipe to improve the CTP or increase financial inclusion through ICT's, the room for research remains open to increase our knowledge about what initiatives are ICT's incorporating to improve poverty alleviation programs and financial inclusion.

CONCLUSION

Latin American countries have initiated the role of a driver in the implementation of mobile banking models that target the poor. These initiatives expand the benefits to marginalized groups of the population by using CTP programs as mediums to promote financial inclusion through the use ICTs. Additionally, the use of ICT in these programs diminishes transactions costs and improves the efficiency in their operation. The large and diverse information that is required in the process of registry and monitoring of the population covered may be systematized through digitalization thus reducing the resources employed.

Very little time has elapsed since the CTPs in the countries studied here have used ICTs in the process of distributing resources to their beneficiaries. Even though the benefits may be glimpsed in terms of reducing transaction costs in this process, we still know little about the direct impact on the quality of life of the beneficiaries. It is important to develop research agendas to evaluate the evolution of the use of ITC in these programs that would generate knowledge about best practices that could feed in the design of policies in this area.

Even though there are studies that document the benefits of banking the poor, there are few evaluations on the impact of access to mobile banking in transforming the lives of marginalized populations. This vacuum must be filled with rigorous studies that document why and how financial inclusion of unbanked populations through ICTs offers new opportunities to satisfy existing needs in the daily lives of the poor. For example, we need to identify whether access to the financial market has an impact on the diversification of self-employment, or the adoption of agricultural techniques, among others. Research strategies should include surveys as well as in-depth interviews and social experiments. In other words, both qualitative and quantitative indicators, as well as interdisciplinary perspectives, should be used to achieve robust results.

REFERENCES

Bar, M., Aminoff, E., Mason, M., & Fenske, M. (2007). The Units of tought. *Hippocampus, 17*(6), 420–428. doi:10.1002/hipo.20287 PMID:17455334.

BBVA Research. (2011). *Avanza el pago electrónico de programas sociales en América Latina y el Caribe*. México City: BBVA Research.

Cabrera, J. (2007). Política social: cambio y resultados. In Cordera, R., & Cabrera, J. (Eds.), *La política social en México: tendencias y perspectivas* (pp. 67–94). Mexico City: UNAM.

CGAP. (2009). Banking the poor via G2P payments. *Focus Note*, 1-24.

Cordera, R. (2007). Mercado y equidad: de la crisis del Estado a la política social. In Cordera, R., & Cabrera, J. (Eds.), *La política social en México: tendencias y perspectivas* (pp. 25–66). Mexico City: UNAM.

Diniz, E., Fingermann, N., & Best, N. (2011). *Banca Móvil y programas de transferencia monetarias condicionadas*. En Breve.

DNP. (2011). *Evaluación de la gestión y la operación de la bancarización a través del programa Familias en Acción*. DNP.

ECLAC. (2007). Las transferencias condicionadas en América Latina: Luces y Sombras. In CEPAL, *Seminario Internacional*. In *Evolución y desafíos de los programas de transferencias condicionadas* (pp. 1–44). Brasilia: ECLAC.

ECLAC. (2011). *La Trayectoria de los programas de transferencias con corresponsabilidad (PTC) en América Latina y el Caribe.*

Fox, J. (2007). El acceso a la rendición de cuentas: ¿voces individuales o colectivas? In *Documento presentado al Seminario Internacional sobre Candados y Derechos*. Protección de Programas Sociales y Construcción de Ciudadanía.

Galperin, H. (2005). Wireless networks and rural development: Opportunities for Latin America. *Information Technologies and International Development*, *2*(3), 47–56. doi:10.1162/1544752054782420.

Gates Foundation. (2009). *Diconsa: financial services for the rural poor. Grantee profile.*

González de la Rocha, M. (2008). La vida después de Oportunidades: Impacto del Programa a diez años de su creación. In SEDESOL, Evaluación Externa del Programa Oportunidades 2008. A diez años de intervención en zonas rurales (1997-2007). SEDESOL.

Horst, H., & Miller, D. (2005). From kinship to link-up: The cell phone and social networking in Jamaica. *Current Anthropology*, *46*, 755–778. doi:10.1086/432650.

IDB. (2009). *Telefonía Móvil y Desarrollo Financiero en América Latina*. Barcelona: Editorial Ariel.

IICA. (2009). *Mujeres Ahorradoras en Acción. Una sistematización de la mirada de sus protagonistas*. Bogotá: IICA - Acción Social.

Karner, J., & Onyeji, R. (2007). *Telecom private investment and economic growth: The case of African and Central & East European countries*. Jonkoping University.

Katz, R. (2009). *El papel de las TIC en el desarrollo. Propuesta de América Latina a los retos económicos actuales*. Barcelona: Ariel.

Levy, S. (2006). *Progress against poverty. Sustaining the Progresa-Oportunidades program.* Washington, DC: Brookings Institution Press.

Levy, S. (2007). *Productividad, crecimiento y pobreza en México: ¿Qué sigue después de Progresa-Oportunidades?* Banco Interamericano de Desarrollo.

Lindert, K. (2007). *The nuts and bolts of Brazil's Bolsa Familia Program: Implementing conditional cash transfers in a descentralized context.* The World Bank.

Ling, R. (2008). *New tech, new ties: How mobile communication is reshaping social cohesion.* Cambridge: MIT Press.

Maldonado, J. (2011). *Los programas de transferencias condicionadas: ¿hacia la inclusión financiera de los pobres en América Latina?* Ottawa: International Development Research Centre.

Maldonado, J., & Tejerina, L. (2010). *Investing in large scale financial inclusion: The Case of Colombia*. Banco Interamericano de Desarrollo.

McKinsey México. (2009). *Creating change at scale through public-private partnerships. Lessons from an innovative financial inclusion partnership in Mexico. A case study prepared for the Clinton Global Initiative.* Working Paper.

McNamara, K. S. (2003). *Information and Communication Technologies, Poverty and Development: Learning from Experience. Ginebra*. The World Bank.

MDS. (2012). *Ministério do Desenvolvimento Social e Combate à Fome*. From www.mds.gov.br.

Mina, L. (2011). *La efectividad de las redes de protección social: el rol de los sistemas integrados de información social en Colombia*. Banco Interamericano de Desarrollo.

Mir Cervantes, C. (2008). Evaluación operativa y de la calidad de los servicios que brinda Oportunidades. In SEDESOL, Evaluación Externa del Programa Oportunidades 2008. A diez años de intervención en zonas rurales (1997-2007). SEDESOL.

Parker, S., & Berham, J. (2008). Seguimiento de adultos jóvenes en hogares incorporados desde 1998 a Oportunidades: impactos en educación y pruebas de desempeño. In SEDESOL, Evaluación Externa del Programa Oportunidades 2008. A diez años de intervención en zonas rurales (1997-2007). SEDESOL.

Romero, S. (2008). *Evaluación de Consistencia y Resultados 2007. Programa de Desarrollo Humano Oportunidades*. CONEVAL.

Sariego, J. (2008). Cobertura y operación del Programa Oportunidadesen regiones interculturales indígenas. In SEDESOL, Evaluación Externa del Programa Oportunidades 2008. A diez años de intervención en zonas rurales (1997-2007). SEDESOL.

Seira, E., Parker, S., Silva, P., Marcué, E., & Cárdenas, C. (2011). *Estudio para el H. Congreso de la Union en cumplimiento del artículo 55 BIS 2 de la Ley de Instituciones de Crédito. Banco del Ahorro Nacional y Servicios Financieros, Sociedad Nacional de Crédito, Institución de Banca de Desarrollo*. BANSEFI.

Sen, A. (1999). *Development as freedom*. New York: Oxford University Press.

Solimano, A. (2005). Hacia nuevas políticas sociales en América Latina: Crecimiento, clases medias y derechos sociales. *Revista de la CEPAL*, 45-60.

United Nations Development Program. (2003). *Reporte de Desarrollo Humano 2003*. New York: Oxford University Press.

Waverman, L., Meschi, M., & Fuss, M. (2005). The impact of telecoms on economic growth in developing countries. In Africa: The Impact of Mobile Phones: Moving the Debate Fordward. The Vodafone Policy paper series, No. 2.

ADDITIONAL READING

Cominos, A., Esselaar, S., Ndiwalana, A., & Stork, C. (2008). M-banking the unbanked. *Series Towards Evidence-Based ICT and Regulation*, 1. Policy Paper 4.

Dermish, A., Kneiding, C., Leishman, P., & Mas, I. (2011). Branchless and mobile banking for the poor: A survey. *Innovations*, 6.

Francke, P., & Cruzado, E. (2009). *Transferencias Monetarias Condicionadas e Instrumentos Financieros en la lucha contra la Pobreza*. Proyecto Capital.

IDB. (2009). *Telefonía móvil y desarrollo financiero en América Latina*. Barcelona: Editorial Ariel.

Lindert, K. (2007). *The nuts and bolts of Brazil's Bolsa Familia Program: Implementing conditional cash transfers in a descentralized context*. The World Bank.

Maldonado, J. (2011). *Los programas de transferencias condicionadas: ¿hacia la inclusión financiera de los pobres en América Latina?* Ottawa: International Development Research Centre.

Maldonado, J., & Tejerina, L. (2010). *Investing in large scale financial inclusion: The Case of Colombia*. Banco Interamericano de Desarrollo.

Pickens, M., Porteous, D., & Rotman, S. (2009). *Banking the poor via G2P Payments*. CGAP.

World Bank. (2011). *The mobile financial services development report*. Geneva: World Economic Forum.

KEY TERMS AND DEFINITIONS

Branchless and Mobile Banking: Are schemes of providing financial services in a cheaper way than traditional franchise banks. The use of these schemes is intended to expand financial services more efficiently.

Conditional Cash Transfers: A scheme of funds transfers to alleviate poverty widely used by Latin American governments. Conditionality is a key aspect of these programs, given that in order to receive funds, beneficiaries have to accomplish certain conditions attached to education, nutrition, etc.

Financial Inclusion: Consists in broaden the offer of financial services to people that previously could not access to those services for economic or geographic reasons.

G2P Payments: G2P, for "Government to People," include all payments made by government to individuals, such as subsidies (e. g. conditional cash transfers), government's payroll, or government's providers. Recently, G2P payments are subject of innovative ideas of channeling these payments in order to improve efficiency and accountability.

ENDNOTES

1. See: www.proyectocapital.org.
2. Evidence taken from Proyecto Capital's initiatives. See: www.proyectocapital.org.
3. While there is 70% mobile phone penetration in Latin America, only 30% of the population has access to financial services. See www.proyectocapital.org.
4. 2012 data with OECD information from Communications Outlook, 2011 and World Bank, 2011. See SCT, 2012.
5. Subsidizing means giving people the basic elements for individual development to ensure that they exercise their abilities fully, on the understanding that human development contributes not only to improving people's quality of life, but also to improving the productive capacity of individuals.
6. In 2002, approximately 44% of the region's total population was in poverty, which means that the CTPs administer to 22% of the total population of Latin America (Solimano, 2005).
7. This figure varies inversely according to the size of the place of residence and directly according to the academic level being studied.
8. The SISBEN 1 category corresponds to the group of Colombians with the most difficult living conditions who are registered in the system.
9. The program launch included the following Banks: Banagrario, Banco Popular, Davivienda, Banco de Bogota, Bancolombia, BBVA and Banco de Occidente.
10. Banco Agrario covers 81% of the municipalities through its 738 branches. It also has a network of 298 branchless banking operators and a network of 2,067 ATMs as a result of its deal with Grupo Aval.
11. The Bank of Opportunities Investment Program (Programa de Inversión Banca de las Oportunidades) is a Colombian policy designed to extend financial coverage in the country.
12. Please see Plan Piloto Banca Móvil (Mobile Banking Pilot Program) at www.bancadelasoportunidades.gob.co.
13. CEF is a publicly owned financial institution focused on offering financial services for all

sectors, with a special emphasis on social coverage (see Decree 759 from 1969).

14. CEF is responsible for managing lottery games and their points of sale.

15. The participation of these entities is part of a business partnership with BANSEFI known as "L@ Red de la Gente" (The People's Network).

16. Diario Oficial de la Federación, December 24, 2009

17. This allowed a reduction from 309 municipalities without a financial presence in 2006 to only four municipalities in 2010 (Banca de las Oportunidades, 2010).

18. Calculation performed by CGAP based on the average cost of six CTPs (from Argentina, Brazil, Colombia, India, Mexico and South Africa). See CGAP, 2009.

Section 2
Asia and Australia

Chapter 7
Developing E-Government Readiness Factors:
A Bottom-Up Approach

Lei Zheng
Fudan University, China

ABSTRACT

E-government readiness is critical and fundamental to e-government success. This paper reviews and differentiates the definitions of e-readiness, e-government readiness and e-government maturity, and examines the literatures on current assessment practices to identify issues, controversies and problems. The chapter then proposes a bottom-up approach to develop a field-based E-government readiness assessment method and factors that could be usable and applicable for a specific local government with its own unique e-government priorities and goals, and then tests the approach in a city government in China and receives positive feedbacks. As a result of this new approach and methods, a set of specific readiness assessment factors, rather than predefined all-size-fits-all criteria, are derived. The method takes both qualitative and quantitative approaches, and collects both primary and secondary data.

INTRODUCTION

Since the emergence of e-government, a number of e-government assessment surveys and rankings have been conducted throughout the world to evaluate the success of e-government. However, these surveys are evaluating different aspects of e-government success with various methods. Some attempt to carry out global or regional benchmarking and rankings, some intend to implement national assessment across states, provinces or cities, and some are simply evaluating one specific local government. To make the assessment meaningful and useful, different as-

DOI: 10.4018/978-1-4666-4173-0.ch007

Copyright © 2013, IGI Global. Copying or distributing in print or electronic forms without written permission of IGI Global is prohibited.

sessment purposes may and should take different approaches and methods. The chapter will discuss the approach of assessing e-government readiness with a local government.

E-government readiness assessment (ERA) evaluates how ready a country, a city, or a particular government agency is to develop e-government. E-readiness assessment can be an effective tool to carry out planning, monitoring and evaluation of the initiatives toward Information Society in general and e-Government in particular (Ojo, Janowski, & Estevez, 2007). It can serve as a useful starting point, because when deciding where to go, one must first know where it is now. Thus, the assessment could "provide a firm base upon which to make strategy, plan, policy and decisions" (Dada, 2006). Through ERA, a government can assess its stage of readiness, identify its gaps, and then redesign its e-government strategy. Therefore, E-government readiness is critical to e-government success and is especially relevant for a government at its preliminary or intermediate development stage of e-government. Particularly, e-readiness assessment can help developing countries to measure and plan for ICT integration. It can help them focus their efforts from within, and identify areas where external support or aid is required (Rahman, 007). In short, it is of great importance to establish a useful and feasible framework, methods and factors of ERA.

The chapter starts with reviewing and clarifying the definitions of e-readiness, e-government readiness and e-government maturity. Next, the chapter examines the literatures on current e-government readiness assessment practices with regard to their features, issues and problems, followed by suggestions for improving current practices. Based on the literature review, the chapter proposes a bottom-up approach to develop a field-based E-government readiness assessment method and factors that could be applicable for a specific local government with its own unique e-government priorities and goals. Furthermore, the study also applied the approach in a city government in China. The detailed procedures of the experiment are illustrated and lessons learned are shared. In the end, the chapter is concluded with discussions about the strengths and weaknesses of this approach.

EXAMINING CURRENT E-GOVERNMENT READINESS INDEX

Differentiating E-Readiness, E-Government Readiness and E-Government Maturity

The section will first differentiate three related but different concepts--e-readiness, e-government readiness and e-government, while all three concepts are essential for e-government success. Currently, there does not exist a standard and universal definition for e-government readiness. According to Ojo, Janowski, and Estevez (2007), E-readiness measures the extent to which a society is prepared to reap the opportunities from the information and communication technologies. The notion of e-readiness broadly covers political, regulatory, organizational, cultural, communication and technological factors. "To comply with e-Governance, one must first be e-Ready" (Rahman, 2007), and e-Readiness is the ability to use ICT to develop one's economy and to foster one's welfare (Rahman, 2007).

Some scholars have clearly differentiated e-readiness assessment for particular themes, such as e-commerce or e-government, from e-readiness assessment for general purpose without focusing on any particular aspects of government society. One example of the former is the World Economic Forum Networked Readiness, and examples of the latter includes the United Nations Department of Economic and Social Affairs (UN-DESA) e-government survey and the Economist Intelligence Unit E-readiness Index which focuses on e-commerce (Economist Intelligence Unit, 2005).

Kachwamba and Hussein (2009) further distinguish e-government readiness from e-government maturity. According to the authors, E-government readiness comprises of all prerequisite necessary to implement e-government and e-government maturity refers to the actual level of e-government progress a country has attained. Ayanso et al. (2011) argued that E-government readiness index is aimed to assess the preparedness of various nations to make the transformation to electronic governance, and is meant to alert specific strengths and weaknesses that could be addressed to deliver e-governance in a country. Therefore, the critical difference between e-readiness indices and other related indices is that the former focuses on preparedness rather than proven E-government capabilities. The United Nation E-Government Survey in 2010 published by the UN Department of Economic and Social Affairs (UNDESA) also replaces the term "e-government readiness," which was adopted in its previous reports, with the term "e-government development." The reason is that the term "e-government development" describes "how far governments have actually advanced in e-government," while "e-government readiness" describes how ready or able they might be to do so (UNDESA, 2010). The term of "e-government development" remain to be used in the 2012 Survey (UNDESA, 2012). This research will focus on the e-government readiness assessment method.

Assessing E-Government Readiness or E-Government Maturity?

So far, only a few globally or regionally surveys assess e-government, such as UNDESA e-readiness Index (UNDESA, 2004), the Brown University e-government ranking (West, 2005), and overall Maturity Index (Accenture, 2003). These indices adopt different sets of indicators, and many of them are actually evaluating e-government maturity, with focuses on the features of government websites and online services, instead of e-government readiness. For example, West' e-government ranking (West, 2005) assesses the features of national government websites, and the Accenture E-government Maturity Index (Accenture, 2003) evaluates the e-government service maturity, delivery maturity and citizen voice. Among them, the UNDESA e-government readiness survey explicitly uses the term "readiness" until 2008 (UNDESA, 2008). However, in its 2010 survey, the notion of "e-government readiness" was replaced by the term of "e-government development" to describe what governments have actually advanced in e-government (UNDESA, 2004).

The UNDESA conducted e-government surveys since 2001. The UNDESA e-readiness survey considers a relatively comprehensive assessment of e-government including both general and specific indicators, while other indices only consider the indicators regarding e-government applications or government websites (Ojo, Janowski, & Estevez, 2007). Its E-government Readiness Index is a comprehensive scoring of the willingness and capacity of national administrations to use online and mobile technology in the execution of government functions. The conceptual framework of these surveys was derived from the vision of human development provided by the UN Millennium Declaration (UNDESA, 2005). The conceptual question behind e-readiness assessment is how ready states are to take advantage of the opportunity provided by advances in information technology (UNDESA, 2008).

The UNDESA survey is comprised of four indices. First, Online Service Index (named Web Measure Index in earlier years) is based on a comprehensive survey of 192 countries' national website as well as the websites of the ministries of education, labor, social services, health and finance. The survey evaluates countries based on the four-stage web maturity model of e-government development: emerging online presence, enhanced presence, transactional presence, and connected presence. The second index, the telecommunication infrastructure index, is a composite of five indicators: number of personal computers per 100 persons, number of Internet users per 100 persons, number of telephone lines per 100 persons, number of mobile cellular subscriptions per 100 persons and number of fixed broadband subscribers per 100 persons. Thirdly, the human capital index is a composite of two indicators: adult literacy rate and the combined primary, secondary, and tertiary gross enrollment ratio. The forth one, the e-participation Index focuses on the use of the Internet to facilitate "e-information," "e-consultation," and "e-decision making" (UNDESA, 2010).

When assessing the UNDESA e-government readiness indices against the difference between the e-government readiness and maturity, it seems that the UNDESA survey's first and forth indices, online service index and e-participation index, are in fact assessing the e-government maturity of a nation instead of its readiness. Only the rest two indices, human capital index and the telecommunication infrastructure index, seem to meet the requirements of e-readiness assessment.

Issues, Problems, and Suggestions for Improvement

Since its launch in 2001, the UNDESA e-government readiness assessment has received great attention as well as many critiques with regard to its underlying assumption, assessment strategy and approach, level of assessment, index framework, indicator selections, data collection and analysis methods. Altman (2002) argued that there was no direct link between countries with high readiness and those with actually broad use of e-government. Many studies also challenged the top-down and all-size-fits-all approach of current global benchmarking surveys which ignore the unique characteristics of individual countries, and their different people, contexts, and purposes (Data, 2006). Furthermore, Khalil (2011) found that E-government readiness varies significantly across nations, and national culture values and practices correlated negatively and positively with E-government readiness. Particularly, gender egalitarianism, institutional collectivism, performance orientation and uncertainty avoidance values were found to be key determinants of E-government readiness. Potnis and Pardo (2011) further argued that the developing nations have very different priorities compared to developed nations, and developed nations have better leverage over developing nations due to their established socio-economical and political conditions, while disadvantaged populations in developing nations are still struggling for survival. Therefore, governments in developing nations face a very difference set of challenges in terms of acquiring technologies and offering e-governance to citizens.

Some also argued that the UNDESA Surveys confined themselves to central government website assessments alone. Several benchmarking indices are available at the macro level primarily for ranking countries. However, what appears on the macro level can hide wide heterogeneity among organizations, local areas, and individuals, therefore, micro-level measurable criteria needs to be developed (Rahman, 2007).

Some other researchers further asserted that the readiness indices of UNDESA e-government survey offered an over-simplistic solution to a complex task. One study argued that adult literacy, one of the Human Capital Index indicators, is not enough to take advantage of e-Government initiatives. Citizens must achieve technical acquaintances in order to be benefited from e-Governance initiatives (Potnis & Pardo, 2008). Bannister (2003) pointed out that some easily available quantitative and statistical indicators of e-readiness tend to be superficial and do not necessarily represent the true nature of the situation, while the more complex and significant measures often cannot be quantified easily and are subsequently omitted. In terms of the survey's data collection methods, it might be inconsistent across countries as many different researchers are involved in gathering, retrieving and processing data (Potnis & Pardo, 2011).

A number of studies have attempted to improve or expand the index framework for e-government readiness assessment. Some researchers present a general framework which comprises six key factors to implement any E-government initiatives: Organizational Readiness, Governance and leadership Readiness, Customer Readiness, Competency Readiness, Technology Readiness and Legal Readiness (Al-Omari & Al-Omari, 2006). Janssen, Rotthier and Snijkers (2004) analyzed 18 international eGovernment benchmarking studies and summarized indicators into five categories, which include Input indicator, Output indicators, Usage/Intensity indicators, Impact/Effect indicators, and Environmental/Readiness indicators. According to the authors, the Environmental indicators do not measure eGovernment itself, but instead measure the preconditions and surrounding environment of eGovernment, such as ICT infrastructure, ICT skills, trust in ICT and the legal environment. These environment indicators seem to be assessing e-readiness. One study identified a number of core e-government readiness variables, which account for the wide disparity between the 'top ready' and 'not ready' countries. The results show that e-government readiness is determined by mature online presence characterized by full transactional services, support for citizens' engagement in consultation and decision-making, and availability of the requisite access infrastructure (Ojo, Janowski, & Estevez, 2007). However, the first two measures seem to be e-maturity indicators rather than e-readiness indicators. Shareef et al. (2008) concluded that designing readiness assessment frameworks requires clear specification of the assessment purpose and designing concrete instruments explicitly based on the information requirements. Usually, these information needs are modular and can be satisfied by any instrument composed from the required set of assessment components. Therefore, they proposed an assessment framework consisting of a set of assessment perspectives. Each of these perspectives is mapped to a corresponding set of concrete assessment components, satisfying the information requirements of these perspectives, allow for easy substitution or specialization of specific components to suit different contexts or assessment scenarios. Aysnso et al. (2011) argued that UNDESA surveys rely on a simple mathematical average of the values of the variables measured and proposed alternative indices based on principal components analysis. Four different versions of the index and ranking results are presented to compare with the existing ranking.

Rahman (2007) also suggested that although a number of e-readiness assessment tools and methods have measured ICT connectivity, ICT use and integration, training, human capacity, government policies and regulations, infrastructure, security and economy, the consequences of socio-political-cultural economical stages of a country needs to be studied as well. Thus, an extensive study is desired at the lower level government in formulating EGR performance indicators. Rahman (2007) pointed out that lack of technical skills and policy building capacity are barriers to establish effective e-government at the grass roots. InfoDev (2005b) argued that e-readiness assessment needs to become more focused and action-oriented, and moves from the simple measurement to concrete action by looking at both micro and the macro level. Simply having an environment that is supportive of these technologies is not enough, in order to gain benefits from ICTs, an organization must first be willing to accept, adopt and internalize these new technologies, therefore, a integrated model should consider both the organizational factors that influence a user's acceptance of the technology, and the environmental readiness factors that create an enabling environment for technology including the perceived performance expectancy, effort expectancy, social influence etc (Dada, 2006). Madon (2004) argued that evaluation criteria should come from the field and reflect felt needs and priorities of the users of the project rather than the fined objective criteria.

The 2010 UNDESA E-government Survey also acknowledged that E-readiness is not fostered in a digital vacuum, but rather in a complex web of social, cultural, economic and political factors, ultimately driven by the usage imperative and proposed a number of suggestions for future assessment (UNDESA, 2010). Particularly, E-government development is often impeded by constraints in public sector capacity including the fragmented information systems that accompany organizational complexity, the ICT skills, the mindset and behaviors of work force in the public sector, the existence and effectiveness of a supportive institutional framework such as government-wide chief information officer for coordinating national e-government policy, and the work processes. The 2010 UNDESA report further suggests that future work on measuring e-government capacity need to expand beyond ICT infrastructure and human resource issues to cover the design of institutional machinery, laws, regulations, policies and standards. Furthermore, capacity constraints are very much present on the demand side of the e-government equation as well, while the currently UNDESA national capacity indicators do not provide breakdowns by population segment.

Berntzen and Olsen (2009) compares the evolution of indicators used by three widely referenced international e-government studies, the UNDESA survey, the Accenture repot and the Brown University report. They pointed out that one problem with the three studies is that they all target electronic services at national level. In practice, many services are the responsibility of lower levels of government. All studies are primarily based on observation, which does not reveal what is behind the facade. Observation requires fluency in the languages used. A large number of observers may also cause problems, since observers may have different conceptions of what they observe.

In sum, the current global benchmarking e-government assessment frameworks, methods and indices mainly have the following limitations: 1) take a top-down approach; 2) focus on national level; 3) rely heavily on macro and often quantitative indicators; 4) base on theoretical assumptions which do not necessarily fit the development goals and strategies of a specific country, especially developing countries; 5) some indicators are actually measuring the maturity rather than the readiness of e-government; 6) With the observation method, the back-office operation is ignored and the consistency of assessment is threatened. Therefore, a predefined, top-down and one-size-fits-all ERA methods which is originally designed for ranking countries may not be applicable for a specific local government, especially that in a developing country, to assess its e-government readiness. Thus, this study attempts to develop and test an assessment framework and methods with a different approach.

PROPOSING A BOTTOM-UP APPROACH

This paper attempts to take a bottom-up approach to develop a field-based E-government Readiness Assessment method that could be applicable for a specific local government with its own unique e-government priorities and goals. With this approach, a set of specific readiness assessment indicators, rather than a set of predefined one-size-fits-all criteria, will be derived. The method takes both qualitative and quantitative approaches, collects both primary and secondary data, and comprises of the following steps:

Developing Field-Based E-Government Readiness Indicators

The study suggests a bottom-up approach to assess e-government readiness. With this approach, the assessment team should first conduct in-depth interviews and focus groups with relevant leaders, mangers and staff to identify assessment indicators from the field, a specific local government or a particular government agency. The purpose of collecting field data is to identify specific e-government goals and priorities of the government, external constraints and enablers as well as internal advantages and disadvantages that could impact the effectiveness of this local government to achieve their e-government goals. The external readiness factors refer to the variables outside the government, and the internal readiness factors refer to factors inside the government. Meanwhile, the team should also collect secondary data from relevant government documents and statistics to investigate the external and internal readiness factors.

The collected data will then be coded and classified with qualitative approach to identify repeated common patterns. Factors that appear frequently in the data will be recognized as indicators of e-government readiness for this specific government or agency. Next, those indicators recognized in qualitative analysis will be developed into a systematic indicators framework, which will then be turned into questionnaires for quantitative assessment.

Conducting Pilot Test

Before the formal readiness assessment starts, the questionnaires developed from the field should be tested with a few samples to examine their relevance, applicability and feasibility. The objective of the pilot study is to modify and improve the indicators' framework and the questionnaires. Some indicators could be added and removed base on the test results.

Starting Assessment

Finally, the revised questionnaires can be applied for assessing the readiness of this specific local government or agency. Other than conducting surveys in a quantitative approach, in-depth interviews and focus groups should also be conducted to assess the readiness with qualitative data. Those qualitative data could provide richer and more in-depth findings, and help to cross-check the results of quantitative surveys to improve the quality of assessment. In the end, the data collected will be analyzed to develop an assessment report.

METHODOLOGY: TESTING THE METHOD IN A LOCAL GOVERNMENT

The above assessment method also has the opportunity to be applied to a city government in China in summer 2009. The detailed procedures are described as follows:

Sample City

City Z, located in the middle of China, is at intermediate stage of e-government development. E-government readiness assessment is commonly considered to be more suitable for regions and governmental departments at preliminary and intermediate stage of e-government; therefore City Z provides an ideal case for testing the assessment methods. Thirty government agencies at City Z, mainly being responsible for delivering public services and social management, participated in the e-government readiness assessment project. The assessment also includes four governments at district or county level in City Z to test the applicability of method at different level of government. The assessment experiences learned from City Z might be valuable for other similar cities and for improving the methods of e-government readiness assessment.

Tailoring a Specific Indicators' Framework

Four government agencies at City Z were first selected in a pilot study to develop a tailored indicators' framework for City Z. The four agencies have different and supplementary characteristics so as to enhance the representativeness of participants in the pilot study. Semi-structured interviews were conducted with IT leaders and business leaders in the four agencies, and focus groups were targeted at staff from both IT department and business departments. In each agency, at least one leader in charge of e-government initiatives was interviewed for 30-60 minutes, and around 15-20 government staff from both IT department and business departments were invited to attend a focus group lasting for approximately one hour. The questions asked in the interviews and focus groups include:

1. Please briefly describe the e-government development and major achievement of your agency in the last five years.
2. What are the major external enablers and barriers for e-government development in your agency in the last five years? Why?
3. What are the major internal strength and weakness for e-government development in your agency in the last five years? Why?
4. What are the e-government goals and priorities of your agency in the next five years?
5. In order to achieve these e-government goals, what external and internal issues and problems should be addressed and revolved in the next five years?

Developing Indicator's Framework

Through this bottom-up approach, an indicators' framework was developed by analyzing, coding and classifying the data collected. Meanwhile, the assessment team also reviewed some existing well-recognized ERA methods to identify indicators that did not stand out in the qualitative analysis from the field but might be relevant to E-government in City Z. These indicators identified in current ERA practices were also added into the framework, in order to cover universal as well as specific indicators.

By combining the indicators identified in the field as well as those derived from current best practices, the assessment framework becomes more comprehensive and complete (see Table 1). A number of first-level and second-level indicators are identified (see Table 1). The framework includes two major building blocks, the external environment e-readiness indicators and the internal government e-readiness indicators. The external environment readiness comprises of social ICT infrastructure and social and human environment. The internal government readiness is composed of managerial framework, leadership, investment, workforce capability, internal IT infrastructure, information safety, and legal and regulatory environment.

Designing Assessment Instruments

The assessment framework was then turned into questionnaires for assessment. Two questionnaires were developed for different samples. Questionnaire A was designed for leaders and staff from IT department with a focus on IT infrastructure-related data, and Questionnaire B was designed for business leaders and staff from business department to investigate factors that are not directly related to IT infrastructure and are more associated with institutional, organizational and social factors.

Semi-structured questions were also designed into the questionnaires to assess the readiness of City Z with a qualitative approach. The same set of interview questions used in 4.2 was included into the questionnaire, and was also used for conducting interviews and focus groups with leaders and staff respectively in each participating agency. The questionnaires developed were then tested with the four agencies to examine their applicability and feasibility, and were modified and improved accordingly.

Table 1. E-government readiness assessment indicators developed in city Z

	First-level Indicators	Second-level Indicators
External Environment Readiness	Social ICT infrastructure	Penetration of PCs
		Penetration of cell phones
		Penetration of fixed telephone
		Penetration of broadband usage
		Penetration of internet
		Density of internet cafe
		Coverage of mobile telecommunication
	Social and Human Environment	Average education level of citizens
		Illiteracy rate
		Availability of IT courses offered at primary and secondary schools
		Availability of IT training centers in society
		Age structure of citizens
Internal government Readiness	Managerial framework	Governance structure
		Availability of Information department
		Availability of Information leaders
		Role and Responsibility of Information department and leaders
		Staff number of Information department
	Leadership	Leader's Perception and Knowledge of Information-related work
		Leaders' Implementation Capability
	Investment	Source of Investment
		Execution of Investment
	Workforce Capability	Technological and Professional Capability of IT workforce
		Perception and Capability towards Information of Staff in business departments
		Effectiveness of IT Training
	Internal IT infrastructure	Penetration of PCs
		Network Coverage
		Broadband Width
		Infrastructure Maintenance and Upgrade
	Information Safety	Staff Perception towards information Safety
		Policy for Safety and Confidentiality
		Technological Infrastructure for safety
	Legal and regulatory environment regarding information	Open Government Status
		Conflicts between laws related to information
		Implementation of other information-related Laws

Carrying Out Full Assessment

In the full assessment, all thirty four participating agencies and districts were asked to fill up the questionnaires. Interviews and focus groups were also conducted with relevant leaders, manager and staff respectively in each participating agency. In addition to primary data, secondary data were also collected from City Z to investigate the city's e-government strategies, priorities and current status, such as the City Z Statistics Year Book, E-government development plans, and other government reports related to e-government initiatives. The data collected for assessment was analyzed with qualitative and quantitative methods. Based on the analysis, a final report was developed and submitted to the government of City Z.

Lessons Learned

Some lessons are learned through the process of testing the method in City Z in China. Accordingly, some suggestions about adjusting and improving assessment methods are raised.

First, the assessment team found some discrepancy in results between the qualitative data collected through questionnaires and quantitative data collected through interviews and focus groups. The qualitative data seems to more close to the truth, especially when the topic or issue is sensitive. The possible reason is that even though participants had been informed at the beginning of the assessment that the survey is anonymous, many participants were still very cautious about the consequence of telling the truth and regarded the assessment as a ranking of agencies' e-government development, so many participants tended to score their agency highly when filling up the questionnaires. The effect is especially obvious when participants were required to fill up the questionnaire before the focus group discussions. The assessment team also noticed that usually after an interview or focus group started for about 15-20 minutes, participants started to talk in a more comfortable and relaxed way and were willing to tell more truth. This may explain why the qualitative data collected through interviews and focus groups seem to be more real than the quantitative data collected through the questionnaire. Therefore, in future assessment, we suggest asking participants to fill up the survey questionnaires after the interview and focus groups are finished when participants feel more relaxed and comfortable.

Second, we suggests separating agency leaders from their subordinates during focus group discussions, as it is observed that subordinates tended not to speak up when their leaders were presented in the same room.

During the data collection procedure, it occurred that some leaders presented at the focus group which was originally arranged for general staff. During such situations, the head of the assessment team stood up and invited the leaders to a separate room for individual interviews. The team head explained to the leaders that some special questions to the leader needed to be asked separately in an individual interview. During the assessment, most leaders accepted such invitations and left the room following the assessment team head. The rest of the assessment team then stayed with the general staff to continue the focus group discussion.

DISCUSSIONS AND CONCLUSION

E-government readiness is critical and fundamental to e-government success. The chapter reviewed and differentiating the definitions of e-readiness, e-government readiness and e-government maturity, examined the literatures on current assessment practices to identify issues, controversies and problems. The chapter then proposed a bottom-up approach to develop a field-based E-government readiness assessment method and factors for a specific local government with its own unique e-government priorities and goals, and then tested the approach in a city government in China.

After systematic analysis, the final indicators' framework developed from the field in City Z turned out to be a quite comprehensive set of assessment criteria, which addresses both external social environment and internal government environment, covers technological, managerial, legal and social factors, and considers both attitude and capability of leaders and staff. It should also be emphasized that the framework developed in City Z in Table 1 is just an example of the result developed with this method in City Z, rather than fixed all-size-fits-all criteria for all situations.

The results of the assessment method in City Z suggest that this bottom-up assessment method could serve as a quite useful, flexible and applicable tool for a specific local government to measure its e-government readiness according to its own e-government goals and priorities. The method does not intend to deliver a "fish," a set of fixed predefined indicators; instead, it is aimed at developing a set of "fishing" skills that could be used by any local governments to assess their e-government readiness by creating a set of by-the-local and for-the-local assessment indicators. Therefore, this local-specific and bottom-up assessment approach is significantly different from other top-down and universal assessment methods. However, this approach also has some limitations. For example, it is more time-consuming and effort-consuming compared to a top-down approach, and the assessment indicators developed out of a location-specific context may not be generalizable to different conditions.

REFERENCES

Accenture. (2003). *eGovernment leadership report: The citizen's view.* Retrieved May 11, 2012, from http://www.accenture.com/us-en/Pages/insight-egovernment-2003-summary.aspx

Al-Omari, A., & Al-Omari, H. (2006). E-Government readiness assessment model. *Journal of Computer Science*, *2*, 841–845. doi:10.3844/jcssp.2006.841.845.

Altman, D. (2002). Prospects for e-government in Latin America: Satisfaction with democracy, social accountability and direct democracy. *International Review of Public Administration*, *7*, 201–219.

Ayanso, A. et al. (2011). E-government readiness index: A methodology and analysis. *Government Information Quarterly*, *28*, 522–532. doi:10.1016/j.giq.2011.02.004.

Bannister, F. (2003). Deep e-government. *EGPA 2004 Annual Conference*. Slovenia. Retrieved May 11, 2012, from http://scholar.google.com.hk/scholar_url?hl=zh-CN&q=http://citeseerx.ist.psu.edu/viewdoc/download%3Fdoi%3D10.1.1.118.1451%26rep%3Drep1%26type%3Dpdf&sa=X&scisig=AAGBfm1gZi5rQWXIc-O-ggj9xs_mikCFEg&oi=scholarr&ei=XpOtT_rFPK2tiQeMyK3sCA&ved=0CBwQgAMoATAA

Berntzen, L., & Olsen, M. G. (2009). Benchmarking e-government: A comparative review of three international benchmarking studies. *Proceedings of the 2009 Third International Conference on Digital Society*, 77-82.

Dada, D. (2006). E-readiness for developing countries: Moving the focus from the environment to the users. *The Electronic Journal on Information System in Developing Countries*, *27*, 1–14.

Economist Intelligence Unit. (2009). *E-readiness rankings 2009: The usage imperative.*

Economists Intelligence Unit. (2005). *The 2005 E-readiness rankings, a white paper from the economists intelligence unit.* Retrieved May 11, 2012, from http://graphics.eiu.com/files/ad_pdfs/2005Ereadiness_Ranking_WP.pdf

Guerrini, A. W., & Aibar, E. (2007). Towards a network government? A critical of current assessment methods for e-Government. *EGOV*, 330-341.

InfoDev. (2005b). *e-Ready for what? E-Readiness for developing countries: Current status and prospects toward Millennium Development Goals*. Retrieved May 11, 2012, from http://www.infodev.org/en/Publication.3.html

Jassen, A., Rotthier, S., & Snijkes, K. (2004). If you measure it they will score: An assessment of international eGovernment benchmarking. *Information Polity*, *9*, 121–130.

Kachwamba, M., & Hussien, A. (2009). Determinants of e-government maturity: Do organizational specific factors a atter? *Journal of US-China Public Administration*, *6*(50).

Khalil, O. (2011). E-Government readiness: Does national culture matter? *Government Information Quarterly*, *28*, 522–532. doi:10.1016/j.giq.2010.06.011.

Madon, S. (2004). Evaluating E-governance projects in India: A focus on micro-level implementation. *Department of Information Systems Working Paper Series*. London School of Economics and Political Science.

Ojo, A., Janowski, T., & Estevez, E. (2007). Determining progress towards e-Government – What are the core indicators? *United Nation University – International Institute for Software Technology Report*, No. 360.

Potnis, D., & Pardo, T. (2011). Mapping the evolution of e-Readiness Assessments. *Transforming Government: People. Process and Policy*, *5*(4), 345–363.

Rahman, H. (2007). E-government readiness: From the design to table to the grass roots. *Proceedings of the 1st International Conferences on Theory and Practices of Electronic Governance* (pp. 225-232). ACM Press.

Shareef, M., et al. (2008). A readiness assessment framework for e-Government Planning – Design and Application. *Proceedings of the 2nd International Conferences on Theory and Practices of Electronic Governance* (pp. 403-409). ACM Press.

UNDESA. (2002). *Benchmarking e-government: A global perspective: Assessing the progress of the UN member States*. Retrieved May 11, 2012, from http://unpan1.un.org/intradoc/groups/public/documents/un/unpan021547.pdf

UNDESA. (2003). *UN global e-government survey: E-government at the crossroads*. Retrieved May 11, 2012, from http://www.unpan.org/egovkb/global_reports/08report.html

UNDESA. (2004). *Global e-government readiness report 2004: Towards access for opportunity*. Retrieved May 11, 2012, from http://www.unpan.org/egovkb/global_reports/08report.htm

UNDESA. (2005). *Global e-government readiness report: From e-Government to e-Inclusion*. Retrieved May 11, 2012, from http://www.unpan.org/egovkb/global_reports/08report.htm

UNDESA. (2008). *United Nations e-government survey: From e-government to connected governance*. Retrieved May 11, 2012, from http://www.unpan.org/egovkb/global_reports/08report.htm

UNDESA. (2010). *United Nations e-government survey: Leveraging e-government at a time of financial and economic crisis*. Retrieved May 11, 2012, from http://www.unpan.org/egovkb/global_reports/08report.htm

West, D. M. (2005). *Global E-government*. Retrieved May 11, 2012, from http://www.insidepolitics.org/egovtdata.html

KEY TERMS AND DEFINITIONS

Bottom-Up Assessment Approach: It refers to the approach of developing E-government Readiness Assessment Indicators with field-based methods and factors that could be usable and applicable for a specific local government with its own unique particular e-government priorities and goals.

E-Government Maturity: It refers to the actual level of progress in e-government that a government has achieved. Therefore, the critical difference between e-readiness indices and other related indices is that the former focuses on preparedness rather than proven E-government capabilities.

E-Government Readiness: It refers to e-readiness assessment with a particular focus on e-government including all conditions regarding the preparedness for a government to achieve electronic governance. E-government readiness is critical and fundamental to e-government success.

E-Government Readiness Assessment: Methods and indicators adopted to assess the readiness of e-government.

E-Government Readiness Indicators: Measures that can suggest and be used to assess the preparedness of e-government.

E-Readiness: The extent to which a society is prepared to take advantage of the opportunities in the information age.

Top-Down Assessment Approach: It refers to the approach of developing E-government Readiness Assessment Indicators with standardized one-size-fits-all index, based on theoretical assumptions which do not necessarily fit the development goals and strategies of a specific government.

Chapter 8
Urban Community Grids Management in Metropolitan China:
A Case Study on Factors Contributing to Mobile Governance Success

Shuhua Monica Liu
Fudan University, China

Qianli Yuan
Fudan University, China

ABSTRACT

Promoted by demands for a more responsive government, local governments across China are exploring the utility and feasibility of Urban Community Grids Management (UCGM) featuring mobile interaction and working. It is believed to provide not only innovative means for local public operations, but new channels for government-citizen communication and public service delivery (Chen, 2006). Though UCGM is generally perceived as one of the most recent innovation success and has great potential in public management on the level of municipal government in China (Jiang, 2009), current research offers little support in understanding factors that contribute to the wide success of UCGM (Liu et al., 2011).

Based on empirical data collected from Beijing, Shanghai and Wuhan, the authors will analyze the use of UCGM in public services delivery in three different cities. Aiming to evaluate and compare the impact of UCGM on local government operations, this paper is to develop a theoretical model that help to explain the success of mobile government in cities of different scales in China. Extracting commonalities of best practices, the authors attempt to dig deeper on social, organizational, and technological challenges each local government is facing when using m-technology to facilitate public service delivery.

DOI: 10.4018/978-1-4666-4173-0.ch008

Copyright © 2013, IGI Global. Copying or distributing in print or electronic forms without written permission of IGI Global is prohibited.

INTRODUCTION

Due to demands for a more responsive government, local governments across China have recognized the potential of using mobile and wireless technology (m-technology) for urban community management (Xu, 2007). They are exploring the utility and feasibility of Urban Community Grids Management (UCGM). UCGM refers to the management of government assets and public service delivery based on grids constructed artificially on electronic maps.

Featuring mobile interaction, UCGM not only provides innovative means for local public operations such as government asset management and internal operation efficiency and effectiveness improvement, but also serves as a new channel for government-citizen communication and public service delivery (Chen, 2006). According to official data, by the year of 2008, 52 Chinese cities headed by Beijing municipal government have adopted UCGM in urban public affair management (Wang et al., 2007). It is generally perceived as one of the most recent innovation success cases in public management on the municipal level in China (Jiang, 2009).

However, despite of the great potential and positive expectations about this trend in urban affairs management, current research offers little support in understanding the factors that contributed to the success of UCGM in China. Most academic papers published so far are of descriptive nature, and rarely provide any solid explanations for the UCGM's wide success (Liu et al., 2011). Thus, both academics and practitioners are facing problems when they try to theorize UCGM as the most recent innovation success in China's public operation management. Bearing this in mind, this research aims to provide a better understanding of the following questions:

- How do Chinese public agencies define the role of UCGM?
- What factors are contributing to UCGM's successful adoption in Chinese cities?
- What challenges do cities adopting UCGM face when they rely on UCGM to provide public services?

FACTORS CONTRIBUTING TO E-GOVERNMENT SUCCESS

Following the years of development of e-government projects worldwide, e-government evaluation and measurement are becoming increasingly important tools in understanding the benefits and challenges government innovations bring to traditional administration. Different methods have been employed by different scholars in the evaluation of e-government projects (Alshawi & Alalwany, 2009; Heeks, 2002; Gil-Garcı´a & Pardo, 2005), and critical issues and factors have been identified in many academic publications (Evans & Yen, 2005; Reffat, 2006; Becker et al., 2004; Park, 2008). These are described in the next two sections.

Measurements

Hard Measurements

Hard measurements refer to those that are relatively easy to gauge, because of their quantifiable and less ambiguous nature. Many scholars have developed hard measurements for e-government developments. Gupta and Jana (2003) identified hard measurements for e-government evaluation. They used tangible aspects including cost benefit analysis and benchmarks in e-government evaluation. They also introduced indicators and analytic tools such as return on investment (Sakowicz, 2004), cost benefit analysis (Kertesz, 2003), payback period, and present worth (Alshawi & Alalwany, 2009). Jain (2001) and Glazer (2002) also emphasized that cost benefit analysis is fundamental and critical for e-government project success.

Sorin Kertesz (2003) identified three basic elements for cost and benefit analysis. He suggested that when adopting a new electronic government project, one had to consider pre-implementation cost, implementation cost and operational cost, while balancing them against benefits for governmental agencies, citizens or customers.

Marcin Sakowicz (2004) paid more attention to "return on investment" tool. He considered three key variables: (1) application and service relevance; (2) citizens and business satisfaction; and (3) preservation of public trust (Meskell, 2003; Carratta, 2006).

In comparison to the mentioned academic investigations, IBM is putting more emphasis on the business benefits introduced by e-government projects. IBM insisted that evaluation of e-government should be divided into three parallel parts, namely, input, output, and outcome (Torres, 2005).

However, different variations of cost benefit analysis have been widely criticized. These approaches have been criticized for targeting only direct tangible costs and benefits, missing the fact that investments are based on accounting and financial instruments (Farbey et al., 1995). Critics have also noted that these approaches lack the capability of identifying and measuring intangible and hidden costs and benefits in the implementation of e-government projects (Smithson, 2000; Hochstrasser, 1992).

Soft Measurements

Soft measurements are supplementary to hard measurements, because these measurements cannot be employed in a quantifiable way (Gupta & Jana, 2003). Researchers used scoring method, identified stages of e-government, and analyzed the success of e-government projects from a sociological angle. A four-stage e-government evolution model has been widely adopted by scholars and practitioners in this type of evaluations: (1) cataloguing (Online Presence, Catalogue Presentation, and Downloadable Forms), (2) transaction (Services and forms are online, Working database supporting online transactions), (3) vertical integration (Local systems linked to higher level system), (4) horizontal integration (Systems integrated across different functions, real one-stop shopping for citizens) (Kunstelj & Vintar, 2004; Gupta & Jana, 2003; Reffat, 2003; Layne & Lee, 2001; Akman et al., 2005).

Citizen-centric approach has been also prevalent among researchers. It relies heavily on citizen feedback when evaluating impacts of e-government projects (Wang et al., 2005). Wang (2005) proposed that aspects like performance of Web-based information seeking, citizen's preference, characteristics of information task and government website should be taken into consideration when evaluating e-government projects. In addition, Filgueiras (2004) emphasized usability evaluation of e-government, underlined the importance of human-computer interface and ease of use for e-government project success.

Elements from the social sciences have also contributed to soft measurements. Social and political context for successful e-government adoption and its value for citizen are the key indicators used by Eschenfelder and Miller (2005). Similarly, Shan (2011) proposed an evaluation model based on socio-technical analysis. They considered four interdependent social and technical categories of variables: actors, structure, technology, and task. Their model integrated fifteen variables relevant to output, input and outcome of e-government.

Technology Acceptance Model (TAM) and Diffusion of Innovation (DOI) have been also widely used in e-government project assessment (Davis, 1989; Rogers, 1995). Those methods evaluate performance of e-government by gauging its acceptance level (Carter & Belanger, 2005). Based on the TAM, DOI and trustworthiness models, Carter and Belanger (2005) proposed an evaluation model that includes multiple indicators: compatibility, relative advantage, complexity, perceived ease of use, perceived usefulness and trust of Internet and government.

Other proposals for measurements are composed of various indicators. With regard to e-government system evaluation, Alshawi and Alalwany (2009) proposed that technical performance and accessibility, economic issues, openness, trust, perceived ease of use and perceived usefulness should be considered. Similarly, Park (2005) stated that e-government evaluation should be conducted against two objectives: means objectives and fundamental objectives. While means objective refers to the factors like public trust, information access, public accessibility and quality of service, fundamental objectives include time saving, efficiency of service, service to citizens and social awareness.

In a different vein, Kunstelj and Vintar (2004) concluded that indicators for egov success can be categorized into four groups: (1) e-readiness, (2) back-office, (3) front-office and (4) effects and impacts in evaluation of e-government (Altameem et al., 2006; Reffat, 2006). While back-office approach evaluates adoption and use of different information systems including data sharing and exchanging technologies, effect and impact evaluation assessed the impact of e-government on economic, social and democracy process (Sakowicz, 2004; Dugdale et al., 2005).

Factors Contributing to Success of E-Government

Many key factors contributing to e-government success have been proposed in the literature (Ebbers et al., 2007; Gil-Garcı´a & Pardo, 2005; Reffat, 2006; Altameem et al., 2006). Some of them are technical in nature and others are organizational.

Technical Factors

The model proposed by DeLone and McLean (2003) illustrated six aspects that are critical to e-government information system success: (1) system quality, (2) information quality, (3) use, (4) user satisfaction, (5) individual impact, and (6) organizational impact (Wang & Liao, 2008).

Alshawi and Alalwany (2009) proposed that information accessibility and communication capability are critical for success of e-government. According to Terry Ma and Zaphiris (2003), accessibility means an effective and efficient user interface that is inclusive for more people with better user satisfaction (Jaeger & Thompson, 2003).

Evans and Yen (2005) suggested that interoperability is a key for future information update in e-government communication. Reffat (2006) concluded that e-government needs to make sure that large volume of data from different sources can be easily integrated for a wider audience to satisfy dynamic information needs of different administrative departments (Brown & Brudney, 2003; Davis, 1989; Jaeger & Thompson, 2003). Technological compatibility with traditional administrative system is also vital for implementation and operation of e-government (Dawes, 1996; Chengalur-Smith & Duchessi, 1999; Brown, 2001; Landsbergen & Wolken, 2001)

Organizational and Management Factors

Organizational and managerial factors are critical for implementation and operation success of e-government too (Gil-Garcı´a & Pardo, 2005; Evans & Yen, 2005; Becker et al., 2004).

Strong, consistent and active leadership commitment is constantly discussed due to its importance in pushing e-government project forward (Rose & Grant, 2010; Reddick & Frank, 2007; Gagnon, 2001). Sabrina Ching Yuen Luk (2009) illustrated the impact of leadership on the success of e-government service. In addition to the commitment of leadership and senior bureaucrats, technical staff and professional IT, employees are also a key factor in project success (Huang & Bwoma, 2003). Thus system familiarity and training of public employees in the use of information and communication technology are very critical (Huang & Bwoma, 2003; Ebbers & Dijk, 2007; Altameem et al., 2006).

Besides the technological factors that contribute to the success of e-government, business process re-engineering and change management were identified as the key factors by Altameem (2006), Jaeger and Thompson (2003) and Reffat (2006). They suggested that to successfully promote e-government projects, work processes and information flow need to be realigned according to the key organizational values and principles. Gant and Gant (2002) agreed that special attention should be paid to the changes in the organization processes and the organization structure that are brought by ICT implementation (Dugdale et al., 2001). A suitable organization structure can facilitate successful implementation of e-government (Altameem et al., 2006; Al-khamayseh et al., 2006; Becker et al., 2004).

Performance evaluation and incentive are other major elements that are vital for e-government project success (Gupta & Jana, 2003; Jaeger & Thompson, 2003; Altameem et al., 2006). Performance evaluation and incentive system can measure milestone and benchmarks of e-government evolution and alter stakeholders' action by recognizing and appreciating their contributions. In order to create e-government services that account for the needs of citizens, assessments should examine citizens' needs, capacity to find, digest and use relevant information (Jaeger & Thompson, 2003).

Coordination among different levels of government can have a significant impact on the success of e-government efforts as well (Jaeger & Thompson, 2003; Altameem et al., 2006). Vertical and horizontal integration is critical for e-government project evolution (Gupta & Jana, 2003; Reffat, 2003; Huang & Bwoma, 2003). Yang and Maxwell (2011) argued that inter-personal, intra-organizational, and inter-organizational information sharing is fundamental for the integration of public administration systems. Along with integration within governmental organizations, clear delineation of responsibility and accountability for all information and services is needed. This would prevent e-government from the problem of lessening responsiveness of government officials (Jaeger & Thompson, 2003).

Organizational environment and strategy factors also matter in e-government programs (Huang & Bwoma, 2003; Al-khamayseh et al., 2006; Becker et al., 2003). Strategy and planning employed in organizations when information and communication technology is introduced have great impact on success and failure of the system. Before adopting a new technology, the government should develop a strategy to motivate main stakeholders to participate (Altameem et al., 2006). Evans and Yen (2005) argued that planning can help administrative staff to share a common picture and estimate potential challenges and obstacles in the implementation process.

Consistent funding is another major factor. Budgetary funding and money spent on e-government programs are critical for IT infrastructure building, employee training, and system design for e-government development (Evans & Yen, 2005; Becker, 2004; Ebbers & Dijk, 2007). Kamal (2006) even argued that financial support and resources are one of the strongest predictors of innovation success.

Organization's culture and awareness are also viewed as vital factors for e-government success. Awareness of e-government refers to communicating e-government initiatives to the appropriate stakeholders and providing means for individuals to understand projected e-government benefits and challenges (Altameem et al., 2006; Gil-Garcı´a & Pardo, 2005). Increasing awareness about the information systems and their value would motivate administrative staff to accept e-government model in the long term (Jaeger & Thompson, 2003; Ebbers & Dijk, 2007).

RESEARCH DESIGN AND METHODOLOGY

Theoretical Framework: Structuration Theory

"Structuration" theory is a meta-theory. Its principal goal is to connect human actions with a structural explanation in social analysis (Giddens, 1979; Reily, 1983). Though not yet explicitly used to study interactions between urban community grid management and city public affairs management, structuration approach has been widely applied to study applications of ICT and its influence on institutional, organizational environments as well as individuals' behavior related to ICT use (Orlikowski & Robey, 1991; Rose, 1998).

Structuration approach is different in nature from structuralism and functionalism (where individuals' behavior is largely determined by their class structure) and hermeneutics and phenomenology (where human agents are the primary actors in and interpreters of social life). It forsakes the dichotomy between structure and human agencies in social analysis (Giddens, 1984; 1989). Instead, by emphasizing the importance of structuration process, Giddens (1979) argues that the focus of social analysis should be on the interactions between structure and human agency (Rose, 1998, p. 2). Evolving as one major product of these interactions, stabilized and institutionalized sets of rules, routines and relationships over time have the structural properties (Giddens, 1989). These rules, routines and relationships would further influence and interact with knowledgeable human agents in their social activities, in this case their reliance on urban grids as major tools in management urban public affairs. These social activities include defining roles of individuals/teams/organizations when employing urban grid for urban affair management. This process of production and reproduction of urban community and affair management systems through knowledgeable agents' application of generative rules and use of urban community grid management system can be perceived as the structuration process (Giddens, 1984).

Thus an exploratory, qualitative research based on structuration approach was taken in this study, seeking to understand the interactions between urban grid management system and public affair management efforts in China. The study specifically focused on the research questions list below. By combining these different dimensions, we hope to achieve a better understanding of China's urban grid management system:

- How do Chinese public agencies define the role of UCGM?
- What factors are contributing to UCGM's successful adoption in Chinese cities?
- What challenges do cities face when they rely on UCGM to provide public services?

Data Analysis Guided by Grounded Approach

Data analysis and theory development in qualitative research have always been the point of discussion and sometimes where critiques are originated (Glaser, 1992; Anselm & Corbin, 1998). Comparing to classical theories, some of which were developed deductively, the grounded approach is derived inductively, a methodology comprising a number of single techniques. Its main purpose is to bridge the gap between theoretically uninformed empirical research and empirically uninformed theory (Frank & Riedl, 2004). Emphasizing new discovery and "focusing on the process of generating theory rather than a particular theoretical content" (Patton, 2002), grounded theory is often used in areas where little is known or to put existing knowledge into a new perspective (Goulding, 1999).

Strauss and Corbin [32] elaborated on the strength of this approach when they defined the term grounded theory:

What do Strauss and Corbin mean when they use the term 'grounded theory'? They mean theory that was derived from data systematically gathered and analyzed through the research process. In this method, data collection, analysis and eventual theory stand in close relationship to one another. A researcher doesn't begin a project with a preconceived theory in mind (unless his or her purpose is to elaborate and extend existing theory). Rather, I begin with an area of study and allow the theory to emerge from the data. Theory derived from data is more likely to resemble the 'reality' than is theory derived by putting together a series of concepts based on experience or solely through speculation (how one thinks things ought to work). Grounded theories, because they are drawn from data, are likely to offer insight, enhance understanding and provide a meaningful guide to action (Anselm & Corbin, 1998, p. 12).

Beginning with basic descriptions, Grounded Theory moves to conceptual ordering ("...organizing data into discrete categories 'according to their properties and dimensions and then using description to elucidate those categories," (Ibid, p19)) and then theorizing ("...conceiving or intuiting ideas --concepts–then also formulating them into a logical, systematic and explanatory schemes...)" (Ibid, p. 21).

Thus the research team decided that techniques based on grounded theory are instrumental for studying interactions between urban grid management system and city public affair management in China. This would help to challenge presumably sound knowledge, and to avoid a tunnel-viewed perspective on a particular phenomenon. We aim to develop and fine-tune theories about the use of urban grids and urban public affair management in China. Guided by these two approaches, our data collection and analysis thus started.

Data Collection, Data Sources, and the Filtering Process

Drawing on secondary sources the data we collected were included in formal publications since 1990, we collected three types of data:

1. Academic papers published in leading Chinese academic databases since 1990,
2. Official reports produced by the Chinese government and international organizations and a number of government databases, and
3. Project progress reports and case study reports collected from individual government agencies.

Selection of Journals, Databases, and Typical Cities

The study relied on high-quality government reports and Chinese academic papers on Urban Grid management system and public affair management in urban China. For academic publications, we chose the largest database of China, the China National Knowledge Infrastructure (CNKI, www.cnki.net), which contains 6642 types of domestic academic journals, including 2460 types of core journals and important databases. This database contains 99% of all the journals published in China and 99.9% of the papers written in the Chinese language. Given the completeness of this database, we chose core journals in this database as the main source for academic publications to further investigate.[1] In this research, core journals particularly refer to journals listed in the list "Main list of the Chinese core journals" which is being developed and published by Peking University Library every four years. Google Scholar was also employed to search for English papers by scholars centering on Urban Grid management in China.

To collect government reports, we searched websites of major central government agencies such as the Ministry of Science and Technology, which involved them actively in the promotion of urban grid management initiative since 2003 (Chen, 2006). We also collaborated with local government seeking for internal project and progress reports on Local Urban Grid management system. During this process, we also compared and selected representative cities as typical cases that can best demonstrate the current development and impact of UCGM in contemporary China. Beijing, Shanghai and Wuhan were later selected as leading examples for further data collection and system analysis. Beijing, the capital of China, is where the urban community grid management movement originated (Chen, 2006). To investigate how UCGM was introduced and widely promoted, we should definitely start from here. Shanghai, crowned as the economic capital of China by some, is currently developing one of the most service-oriented urban grid management systems in China (Zhang et al., 2006). With the heavy investment from Shanghai municipal government, it also has the most developed UCGM system (Zhang et al., 2006). Wuhan, different from Beijing and Shanghai, is the representative of the second tier cities in China. Located in mid-China, Wuhan's UCGM offered a unique example that can be replicated by cities that are less developed in the middle and mid-west China in the coming years (Tu et al., 2005).

Selection of Papers and Reports

To narrow and secure core papers that can directly inform our study, we searched for papers and reports published since 1990 in the databases, search engines and government websites mentioned above. Combinations of different key words we used included: (1) urban grid management + Beijing/Shanghai/Wuhan; (2) grid management + Beijing/Shanghai/Wuhan; (3) urban community grid management + Beijing/Shanghai/Wuhan; (4) community grid management + Beijing/Shanghai/Wuhan; (5) grid management; (6) urban grid management; (7) urban community grid management; (8) community grid management.

The first round of documents search retrieved 1197 academic papers, 1083 reports, 564 government bulletins, one governmental research report and two introductions to urban grid management from technology corporation website.

Our preliminary review of these documents found that most academic papers collected in the first round were not relevant. In fact, a high number of these papers were relevant to electricity grid, computer system grid, or Internet grid. One-page bulletin articles and advertisements were also filtered out because of their low quality.

The same filtering procedure was performed on official government reports and progress case reports. As a result, a total of 212 papers and 398 government reports were selected for study. The research team then coded each paper separately according to the classification schemes to be explained later. During the coding process, we re-evaluated each paper for its relevance to urban community grid management and city affair management in China. After the coding process, the research team met to discuss the coding scheme and to finalize it.

Multifaceted Coding Methods

The research team extracted data from different academic papers and government reports and assembled them onto a network to facilitate cross-case comparison. Owing to its interdisciplinary nature, the topic *urban community grid management in China* encompassed an array of rich research ingredients. This required us to conduct a multifaceted coding of the papers and reports we had selected.

After the first round of discussions among the research team members, we identified various aspects and ingredients of urban grid management system for public affair management in China. Special attentions were paid to: *the paper/report's source, the public affair and city management issue discussed, the stage of the project, the goals for adopting UCGM, the functions UCGM played, the impact/effects generated*, and *challenges for UCGM*. The reasons and purposes of setting these aspects and their application are as follows:

1. **The paper/report's source:** How heavy should we rely on data extracted out of the paper/report?
2. **The public affair and city management issue discussed:** We would try to outline the project scale, including why UCGM was introduced, which area of public affairs was discussed, what changes were brought in, and what was the results of the actions.
3. **The stage of the project:** How mature is UCGM in city affair management? Has it been widely integrated into the city's daily operation management?
4. **The goals of adopting UCGM:** Why did the city government decide to introduce UCGM?
5. **The functions UCGM played:** The functions of UCGM in the city affair management.
6. **The impact/effects generated by UCGM in the daily city operation management:** What was the actual impacts/influence of UCGM in each city? How did the civil servants and citizens evaluate UCGM?
7. **The challenges:** What were the challenges of adopting, using, and integrating UCGM in daily city management in China? What challenges UCGM brought to China's public administration system?

FINDINGS

What is Urban Community Grid Management?

There is no definition of Urban Community Grid Management that has been universally agreed upon. But it seems that all urban community grid management system feature operations and information flow to be described below (Wang, 2009; Xie & Ren, 2007; Qi et al., 2008; Yan, 2006):

1. To employ urban community grid management system, the city or the district has to artificially segment the area into grids on electronic maps. Each grid size about 100*100 square meters. So UCGM is also called 10,000 meter-grid-based community management systems (Jiang & Ren, 2007; Wang et al., 2007).
2. All public assets such as manhole covers, public telephone booths, traffic lights or utility boxes in each grid are uniquely identified, coded and recorded in computer database (Chen, 2006; Liu, 2009; Zhang et al., 2008).
3. A mobile grid supervisor is assigned to each grid. Each supervisor is equipped with smart/mobile devices and is in charge of inspection, uncovering and reporting problems associated with public assets in the grid assigned to him/her (Jiang, 2009). With the help of 3S technology (Geographic Information System (GIS), Global Positioning System (GPS) and Remote Sensing (RS) technology) and a video camera, they can quickly register problems with each public asset on e-maps and fill in predesigned e-forms called "work order request form" (Zhang et al., 2006; Zeng et al., 2009).
4. A call center, the Supervision Center for City Management (SCCM), is specifically set up to coordinate among different public agencies participating in UCGM (Yuan, 2007; Liu et al., 2006). Agents in the call center are trained to take calls from mobile supervisors and citizens. Integrating photos and work orders request forms sent by mobile grid supervisors or information from citizens into one work order, the call center agents will contact the Management Commission of City Affairs (MCCA) (Cheng & Zhang, 2007; Fan, 2009).
5. MCCA will then forward the work order to the corresponding public service agency. The agency is requested to ensure the problem is solved within a certain time range depending on the priority level of the work order. The

more urgent the problem is, the less time the corresponding public service team has (Zhu, 2009).

6. Once the task is finished, the service agency will provide a work order report to MCCA, which will then forward the report to SCCM. SCCM agents will then send the report to the mobile grid supervisor for results verification (Li, 2007; Wang et al., 2006). Once mobile grid supervisors confirm that the problem has been addressed, the case is closed. But if the mobile grid supervisor still has concerns about the work order, the individual who provided the service will be identified and requested to go back to the work site to redo the job. Individuals who constantly are held accountable for low quality tasks will get low performance evaluation (Peng et al., 2008; Xu, 2007).

Technical Backbones of UCGM

Three types of technologies are critical for a successful UCGM system. The first type is technologies like 3S (GIS, GPS, and Remote Sensing) capable of acquiring, storing, manipulating, and analyzing geological and location data have been widely adopted (Gao & Meng, 2011; Yang, 2008; Lu & Zhang, 2008). On one hand, they can simulate geographic data. Combining with urban attribute data, they can vividly demonstrate the geographic characteristics of certain areas in the city (Zeng et al., 2009). On the other, real time data transmission and integration can ensure real time monitoring of the city ecological system (Wang, 2009).

Geocoding is the second major technology applied in UCGM (Yang, 2008; Dong & Liu, 2009; Cheng, 2007). By assigning a unique serial numbers to each city asset, such as a traffic light or a utility box in a certain area, the system is able to record functions, locations and attributes of all public assets (Kong et al., 2008). Paralleling these serial numbers with their positioning data, city managers are able to recreate the city life on e-maps (Qiu & Zhang, 2008). Furthermore, combining data collected from different government agencies and formatting them in a standard and unified fashion creates a more solid basis for decision making in urban affair management (Wang et al., 2006).

The third type of technology that is indispensable for UCGM is the use of smart mobile devices such as Personal Digital Assistant (PDA) (Kong et al., 2008). These specially designed PDAs serve as major tools for information collection, information sharing, and communications among mobile grid supervisors, SCCM, MCCA and public service workers (Xu, 2007; Zhang, 2006; Zhang et al., 2008).

Success in Changing Cities' Governance Structure and Urban Affair Management

The wide adoption of UCGM in urban affair management also introduced substantive changes in the governance structure of most cities. As an example, Figure 1 shows the old governance structure of Dongcheng District, Beijing before UCGM was initiated (Chen, 2006).

As we can see from Figure 1, before UCGM was introduced for urban affair management, city affairs, especially public service provision was guided by a government-centric perspective (Zhang et al., 2008; Guo, 2011; Li et al., 2009; Pi, 2008). For both citizens and the mass media, their major role was to uncover and report problems associated with the public infrastructures (Wang, 2007; Wang, 2009). Citizens had to investigate and submit requests for service directly to the administrative office in charge of a specific type of public service (Jiang & Liang, 2008; Tian, 2010; Pi, 2008). Once requests for public service were sent, the only option left for the public and the media was to wait for the government agencies to respond. They had no control over how long they had to wait, who and when to contact, and,

Figure 1. The traditional governance structure of urban affair management

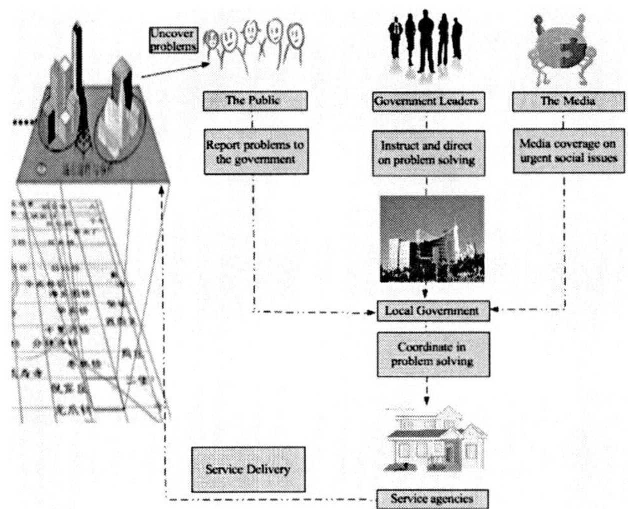

how and when the services would be provided (Zhang et al., 2008; Yang & Pi, 2011). In addition, they had no power in holding any individual accountable even when the services provided were unsatisfactory. Special difficulties arose when citizens were not familiar with the government structure and operation. Their requests were often rejected because they had contacted a person in the wrong level in the bureaucratic hierarchy or in the wrong government agency (Yang & Pi, 2011; Chen, 2005). To have their request addressed then, they would have to go through a trial and error process till they find the right person (Zhu & Yuan, 2011; Qiu & Zhang, 2008; Wu et al., 2011). This lack of transparency in government operations and service provision incurred high dissatisfaction and distrust among the citizens towards local government and especially towards service agencies (Zhu, 2009; Cheng & Zhang, 2007).

After the UCGM had been introduced, a service-oriented perspective featuring accountability was planted in the public administration system (Qi et al., 2008; Zhang, 2006; Fang, 2006). The city administration was divided into two different but interdependent Axises (See Figure 2 for details) (Yuan, 2007; Liu et al., 2006; Cheng & Zhang, 2007; Fan, 2009). While one part is responsible for service provision, the other part is paying more attention to supervision and accountability.

This new administration model clearly differentiates between service agencies and supervision offices, and some humorously referred to it as separating between roles of referees and athletes (Fan, 2009; Gao et al., 2007; Zhang et al., 2006). This model has also helped reduce potential corruptions and bureaucratic cover-up to certain extent (Cheng, 2007; Yan, 2006; Peng et al., 2008). In addition, different from the traditional administration model, citizens do not have to climb through the bureaucratic hierarchy to search for the appropriate agencies for public services. All they need to do is to dial and contact the SCCM agents in the call center (Zhang, 2008; Wang et al., 2010). SCCM agents will contact MCCA, which will then efficiently assign tasks to relevant service agencies or administrative offices (Cheng, 2007; Zhang et al., 2006). After the services are delivered to citizens, the public has a new choice of evaluating service quality and providing feedback to SCCM (Figure 3). These feedback messages are integrated into organizational performance evaluation (Chen, 2006; Yang & Pi, 2011) and help SCCM and MCCA in identifying the

Figure 2. The governance structure manifested by UCGM in Dongcheng District, Beijing

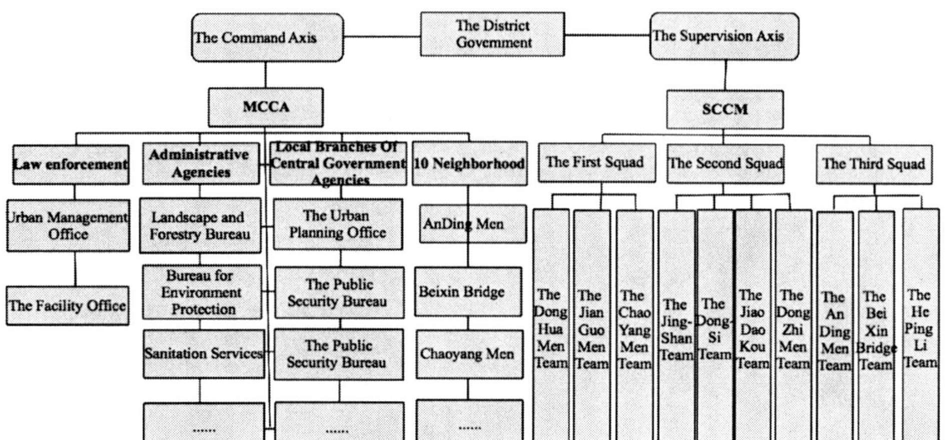

individual service workers who will be held accountable if service is rated as unsatisfactory by clients (Zhang et al., 2006; Gao & Meng, 2011).

Public servants in the agencies under the Supervision Axis who perform specific functions need to (Yan, 2006; Qiu & Zhang, 2008; Wu et al., 2011; Kong et al., 2008; Wu, 2005; Cheng & Bai, 2008):

- Collect real time information on problems associated with the city infrastructure and different service or administrative agencies.
- Maintain an all-time supervision system on service quality and problem solving.
- Serve as a third-party inspector in providing a relatively objective evaluation of public servants' performance.
- Communicate with the public constantly in collecting citizens' feedback and suggestions on public affair management, actively involving stakeholders in optimal decision making and service quality improvement.

The agencies under the Command Axis are the direct service providers. Their roles center around three leading functions (Yan, 2006; Qiu & Zhang, 2008; Wu et al., 2011; Pi, 2008; Li, 2011):

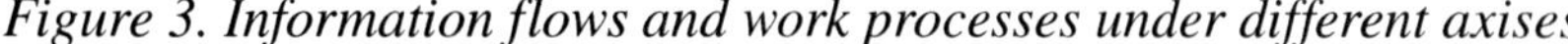

Figure 3. Information flows and work processes under different axises

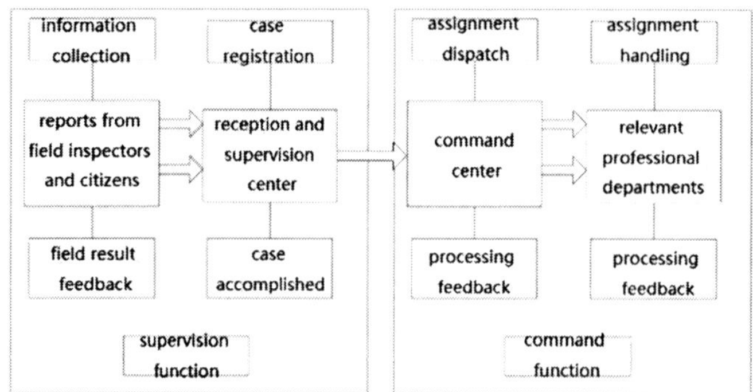

- Coordinate among service agencies and administrative offices for efficient collaborations and service provision,
- Streamline the information flow among service provision agencies, government leaders and facility management agencies for optimal resource allocation and coordination,
- Integrate information collected from different parties for better decision making, planning and implementation.

Success in Process Reengineering, Promoting Agency Collaboration and Coordination

As we briefly touched upon earlier, the use of mobile and wireless technology in urban affair management unavoidably brought changes in information flow, work processes as well as in mechanisms for agency collaboration (Zhang et al., 2008; Yan, 2006; Wang, 2007; Li, 2009; Li, 2006). Before UCGM was introduced, government field operations were largely a black box that kept citizens guessing and wondering. After UCGM was brought in, fieldworkers' work processes and information flow were becoming increasingly transparent (Luo, 2006; Jiang, 2007; Jiang & Ren, 2007).

From a management perspective, work processes in public service provision can be separated into seven phases (Jiang & Ren, 2007) (see Figure 4).

This work process change mirrored also a change in the information flow, which is the backbone for a successful process change backed up by new information technology use in an organization (Davenport, 1993) (see Figure 5).

Changes in both work processes and information flow also facilitate the development of a new mechanism for agency collaboration and coordination (Zhu, 2009; Chen et al., 2007; Jiang & Liang, 2008). Traditionally, agency collaboration and coordination in public service provision have always been a problem for both civil servants and the public because there was no coordinating organizational set-up (Ma, 2007; Zhang et al., 2008). Each government agency operated according to its own schedule and functions without really understanding how other agencies worked. With new organizations such as MCCA and SCCM set up, problems associated with agency collaboration and coordination are increasingly being addressed with high efficiency and effectiveness (Hu et al., 2010; Cheng, 2007). In particular, many agencies saw a stable increase in both service attitude and quality after feedback responses from the public on individual civil servants' performance in the field had been integrated into organizational performance evaluation (Zhu, 2009; Zhang et al., 2008; Pan, 2007).

Figure 4. Work processes in public service provision

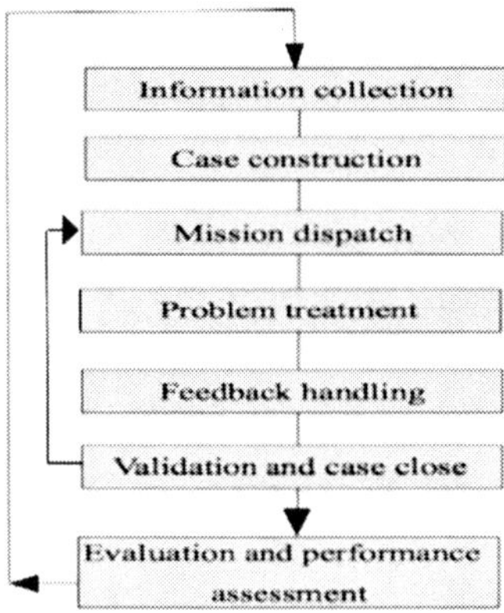

Figure 5. Information flows in public service provision

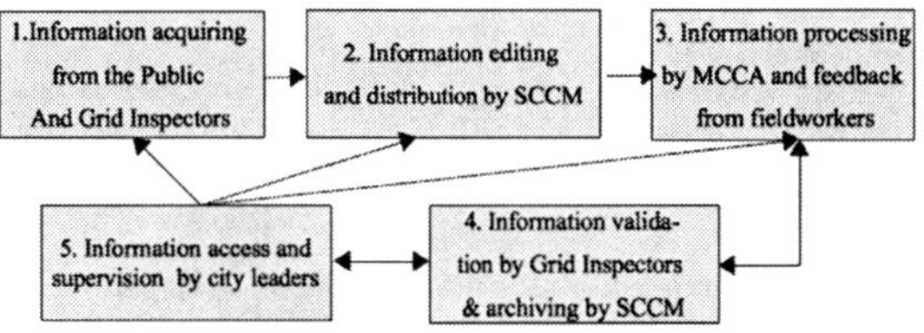

Success in Linking Field Workers' Performance and Feedback from the Public to their Rewards

One of the most significant changes on the individual level was the new link created between field workers' performance evaluation and feedback from the public (Qi, 2008; Wang, 2007; Wang, 2009). Before UCGM was introduced, the public generally had no way to address the quality of civil servants' service (Yan, 2006; Chen et al., 2007). While some chose to complain to the individual department to which individual worker belonged, it was not surprising for them when the department or office did not return to them (Gao & Meng, 2011).

After UCGM was introduced, like the grid supervisor, each field worker was assigned to one or several grids. The worker had to respond to requests from the public for service in the assigned grid(s) (Zhang et al., 2006; Zeng et al., 2009). This not only helped clarify each individual's responsibility and rights, and it also helped each fieldworker to develop a sense of responsibility and attachment to "their grids" (Qi et al., 2008). In addition, feedback from the public was also being integrated in their performance review (Jiang, 2009; Chi et al., 2008; Zhou, 2011). The government does not have specific regulations on how people who constantly get low rating should be reprimanded, but it was clear that in most cases peer pressure served as one of the most efficient lever in correcting fieldworkers' behavior and attitude (Gao et al., 2007). Last but not the least, the separation between the command axis and the supervision axis, caused a mutual supervision system to slowly develop and help prevent collaborative cover-up that traditionally was a persistent problem (Yuan, 2007; Chen, 2008; Li et al., 2007).

From the public's perspective, by actively getting themselves involved in the new work processes, they had more opportunities to participate in public affair management (Li et al., 2006; Chen, 2008). Specifically, by actively providing feedback to SCCM and MCCA, they were facilitating the advancement of better pubic services and cultivating a customer-oriented culture in the public sector (Xu, 2007).

Furthermore, with citizens increasingly involving themselves voluntarily in online discussions on urban affair management using the open platform provided by UCGM, city leaders found themselves interacting more frequently with citizens, whether actively or passively (Wang et al., 2010).

DISCUSSIONS: WHAT IS CONTRIBUTING TO THE SUCCESS OF UCGM IN METROPOLITAN CHINA?

Based on statistics provided by academic papers and government reports, UCGM in urban China is increasingly becoming more attractive to local leaders and civil servants. Up until January 2011-headed by Beijing municipal government--about two thirds of Chinese cities have adopted UCGM in public utility management, government asset management, and emergency response (Chen, 2008). In addition, our analysis of these documents clearly presented factors that contributed to the successful development of UCGM in China. These factors can be divided into three vertical levels: the micro level, team and organizational level, and the macro level.

The Micro Level

The successful operations of UCGM relied on support and active participation of members of civil servants and the public. Most grid supervisors were rehired by the city for operations around UCGM after they had lost previous jobs when their previous positions were eliminated (Chen, 2006). As a result, this group demonstrated a high level of motivation to zealously contribute to accurate data collection, work initiation and the successes of UCGM. They tirelessly patrolled around grids assigned to them and reported emergencies associated with city infrastructure (Sun, 2010; Li et al.,

2009; Liu et al., 2006). After each task was accomplished, most of them tried to provide objective evaluations that acted as key informational components for organizational performance evaluation (Fan, 2009; Jiang, 2009; Chi et al., 2008). Data accumulated by these grid supervisors via smart devices and wireless transmission help establish systematic organizational memory and knowledge for both short term service improvement and long term fieldwork planning. Each month some MCCAs awarded top grid supervisors who reported most incidents by posting their names on the bulletin board (Ma, 2009). This further boosted grid supervisors' determination to contribute to the success of UCGM.

Improved technical and informational capability of government employees in the past five years for those involved in UCGM (grid supervisors, call center agents and service field workers) is an essential factor that helped make UCGM success possible (Yan, 2006; Qiu & Zhang, 2008; Wu et al., 2011). As the new mechanism introduced to urban affair management, UCGM mandated individual government employees to improve their ability to operate and work efficiently within it. Challenges were on two independent but inter-connected dimensions: Employees' technical operation capability and informational capability. While technical operational capability was improved with training and frequent use, the latter was much harder to enhance (Zhou, 2011; Qiu & Zhang, 2008; Cheng & Zhang, 2007). Informational capability generally refers to human beings' capability to recognize, seek, identify, select, retrieve, secure, apply, and even inherit useful information to increase performance (Bharadwaj, 2000). Interestingly, in the case of UCGM, because of its innovative nature and the use of newest technology in city affair management, government employees generally demonstrated a high level of curiosity to learn and cope with a steep learning curve (Qi et al., 2008; Chen, 2005).

Active participation and contribution by the citizens is yet another factor that help refine government operations and decision making, thus making the success of UCGM possible. In the past ten years, Chinese government saw a rapid enhancement of citizens' awareness in participating in public affair management and decision-making (Li et al., 2006; Chen, 2008). When UCGM was launched in each city, citizens were generally invited as external feedback providers and service quality monitors (Jiang & Ren, 2007). Different from before, citizens' calls to the call center and service receivers' feedback became a vital part of government operations. After information and feedback contributed by the public was used in field operations, service agencies made special efforts to publicize and award these voluntary actions and detailed feedback provision (Li, 2008; 2011). This signal of appreciation in turn inspired more citizens to participate in information collection and feedback provision (Ma, 2007). Constant information exchange between the public and government agencies not only helped service agencies to further improve service quality but ease the previously tense relationship between government agencies and the citizens. This then helped to amend the plagued problems of distrust and lack of satisfaction associated with local affair management.

Leaders' commitment and constant financial support provided the institutional and financial means for UCGM to be successful in urban China. Before UCGM was introduced, local leaders and the public had to trust that each government agency would try their best to serve the public interest. There was no efficient mechanism to ensure the quality of public service (Wu, 2005; Tu et al., 2010). In addition to daily reports leaders received from their subordinates, the introduction of UCGM had provided a newer and more efficient, in fact, almost real time, information collection tool (Luo, 2006; Liu et al., 2011). For city leaders, efficient information collection and compilation meant far more than just informed decision-making. It also provided a powerful tool for them to monitor and quickly uncover anomaly such as collaborative cover-up or even corruptions in subordinating government agencies. This hence stimulated local leaders' interests in patronizing and sponsoring the development of UCGM in each city (Tu et al., 2005).

The Team and Organizational Level

When it comes to field operation of teams and government agencies, tailored integration of UCGM by motivated stakeholders with existing operational framework helps reduce resistance to new changes critical for the success of UCGM. Be it an individual field operation team or a government agency, UCGM provided innovative means to empower these teams and agencies in their daily work (Qi et al., 2008; Xie & Ren, 2007). These empowered teams and agencies then developed great loyalty and helped tailor UCGM according to local context. The interconnections and interdependences between existing operational framework and new tools, processes and data flows promoted by UCGM were strengthened and thus successfully established.

Unlike private sectors, the public sector lacks financial means when it comes to employee motivation. Government service provision agencies can only rely on civil servants' good will in delivering high quality public services. Performance evaluation tools were introduced to different agencies for service quality improvement purpose. However they were quite often limited by the scope of each evaluation and possible means to implement consequence of the evaluation because of government agencies' commitment to lifelong employment.

In addition, before UCGM was introduced individual government employees had to rely on performance evaluations solely from their supervisors. It helped promote a supervisor-oriented instead of citizen-centric culture in service agencies. But after UCGM was introduced, each fieldworker was assigned of his/her own grid. Grid supervisors, call center agents, service team leaders and fieldworkers collaboratively provided public support for citizens in each grid (Zhang et al., 2006; 2009). They quickly developed a strong sense of ownership for "his/her grid" and competed healthily with each other (Qi et al., 2008). Team leaders and city managers were actively using peer pressure and sense of ownership as two most efficient motivating mechanisms UCGM endorsed in each city. Passion to promote UCGM is now widely shared among city managements. This further facilitated civil servants to adopt UCGM in different domains of city affair management tailored towards local context and thus contribute inevitably to the wide success of UCGM in different local contexts.

Furthermore, for individual field workers, their performance evaluation package is now composed of feedback from multiple sources (Jiang, 2009; Chi et al., 2008; Zhou, 2011). Intentional distortion on individual fieldworkers' performance evaluation is less possible with the support of solid data from different stakeholders. Thus it is not surprising to see the surge of service-oriented culture in government agencies, which in turn helped make UCGM even more successful.

With UCGM local government can monitor city affair management around the clock (Wang et al., 2010). This control of real time information empowered the public and supervision agencies greatly. Agencies were no longer passive information receiver and inactive disaster responders. They can take a more proactive role in initiating quality check and preventing greater problem to emerge before it is too late. When emergencies do occur, they can quickly compile, analyze and identify the origin of those emergencies, and take appropriate and immediate action to prevent further deterioration (Jiang & Liang, 2008; Li et al., 2009; Tian, 2010). Decision making quality and accuracy are also greatly improved. UCGM also helps to efficiently prevent corruptions associated with loose inspection and collusion because information is accessible at any time and to all who are authorized (Zhang, 2008; Chen, 2006).

Improved organizational communication, division of work (professionalism) and common picture sharing among all agencies introduced by the adoption of UCGM further nurtured an environment that in turn contribute to its wide success.

The biggest impact of UCGM on the team and organizational level was the way it has changed organizational communication, division of work, information sharing and agency coordination. A flatter hierarchy is also slowly emerging in local government (Cheng & Zhang, 2007; Chen et al., 2007). Before UCGM was widely used for city affair management, individual public employees were each assigned and took charge of a specific subarea such as manhole cover repair or water hydrant replacement. These individuals each operated on their own and lacked meaningful communication with others (Cheng & Bai, 2008; Cheng & Zhang, 2007). But once UCGM was put in place, the traditional wall of communication was automatically torn down. Today, grid supervisors, call center agents, fieldworkers, SCCM agents and local leaders each works as a node on the information flow network (Cheng & Zhang, 2007; Cheng, 2007; Jiang & Ren, 2007). By contributing to central database and information warehouse, they not only provide data needed for government operations, but collaboratively present a comprehensive picture of the whole operation. Individual agents were not constrained by traditional division of work. Instead, they were equipped with convenient learning tools and channels to communicate and collaborate with colleagues from other offices. Especially during city emergencies, different offices can quickly align and cooperate in identifying roots of the problem and entities or individuals that are accountable.

The Macro Level

Informed decision making and strategic public asset management promoted by UCGM help establish its crucial position in sustainable government asset management. Although Chinese cities developed rapidly in the past decade, the traditional public asset management still featured a passive response model (Gao et al., 2007; Guo, 2011). In the past the fieldworkers were the main caretakers of each city's public assets. Instead of projecting and preparing for future emergencies, they were used to passively remedy damages to city infrastructure when they happened (Jiang & Liang, 2008). This created an enormous pressure on fieldwork planning and strategic public asset management (Gao et al., 2007).

In contrast, the promotion and wide adoption of UCGM mandated city government to carefully plan and schedule fieldwork based on real time data (Wang et al., 2010). This helped SCCM to save cost by reducing random driving hours and dispatching appropriate fieldworkers to targeted location. Furthermore, accumulated data formed basis for in depth analysis and identification of weak spots in city public asset system. The local government then proactively planned and scheduled maintenance fieldwork that extended the duration of service time of different equipment and infrastructure (Chen, 2006).

Corresponding institutional arrangements made to match and facilitate the development of UCGM provides institutional setup that is vital for UCGM to succeed. Two types of government agencies such as MCCA and SCCM were reorganized and reformed specifically to serve the need for UCGM adoption. Their roles were clearly differentiated, defined and sustained by new organizational rules, regulations and routines (Liu et al., 2006; Wang et al., 2007). At the same time the wellbeing of each agency was also closely related to the performance of other agencies. A healthy ecosystem was developed in the sense that internally all public agencies were fulfilling their roles while providing continuous support for each other. Externally, nonprofit organizations and the public were also engaged in urban affair management and contributed to the success of UCGM (Yan, 2006). A service attitude emphasizing the need of the citizens instead of that of the government slowly emerged in the public sector.

Challenges Ahead

In spite of all the benefits associated with UCGM for public service quality control, the challenges faced by local governments are still enormous.

First, on the individual level, data quality and accuracy in the mobile and wireless monitoring system is still an issue (Li & Qian, 2009; Wang et al., 2006). While automatic data provided by remote sensors or satellites are more unbiased, they only form a basis for information accumulation and further analysis. Individual public employees' efforts are still highly needed to improve the agency's performance and decision-making. But these are still largely hindered by individuals' different levels of familiarity with the system, willingness to share information and power, and capability to absorb more information for accurate decision-making.

Second, the level of maturity of the technology in China presents additional challenges. In the past decade, the advances in mobile and wireless technology in China made it possible for wireless information collection and transmission. It is the technological foundation for the success of UCGM (Xu, 2007; Dong & Liu, 2009). However, the development of mobile and wireless technologies in China is unbalanced (Liu et al., 2011). In smaller cities and remote villages in the vast area of the huge country, UCGM is still facing overwhelming challenges. In particular, the lack of public support and civil servants' sympathy for the new technology in these areas are a major obstacle (Zhuang, 2011). But with national initiative headed by bigger cities and developed areas, some smaller cities are forced to adopt this new trend. Especially when local government leaders are catering to national initiatives and desperately seeking for better personal performance evaluation for them, it is not surprising to see taxpayers' money wasted and project failing on the way.

Third, fieldworkers are still unfamiliar with the new work mechanism and are reluctant to share key quality control information with the supervision agencies (Cheng & Zhang, 2007; Qiu & Zhang, 2008; Yi, 2006). It is not surprising therefore that most of them lack the motivation to install mobile and wireless devices for quality control purposes. While concerns about privacy and security are publicly offered as an issue by most civil servants, an anonymous insider explained that if current service quality control regulations were enforced, no single office would be able to reach the criteria set up by the government (Private Communication in 2011). This is mainly due to the excessive workload and limited training conducted in some local offices. Fieldworkers, especially senior fieldworkers have great difficulty in quickly adjusting to the new tool and communication speed mandated by UCGM (Zhou, 2011). Thus, how to balance the public's living standard with civil servants' needs to survive and perform is definitely an issue faced by many local governments. Especially when in disruption with some local leaders' personal pursuit of performance evaluation and promotion for themselves, local service supervision agencies are left with little space for taking action.

In relation to this the legal and regulatory environment for service quality control that currently exists in China is loose. At present, most local governments still rely heavily on regulations drafted by different local agencies to contain civil servants and government officials' wrongdoings (Jiang & Ren, 2007). Except for several capital cases that have experienced national outcry, most of the offenders can successfully and quickly escape criminal charges with financial fines. Some scholars are calling for government agencies, law makers, and the public to collaborate in making better laws and taking stronger control of the situation (Zhuang, 2011; Chen, 2008). However, little progress has been made in this aspect so far.

CONCLUSION

Based on second hand data from academic publications and empirical data collected from Beijing, Shanghai and Wuhan, we analyzed the use of UCGM in public services delivery and city affair management in metropolitan China.

Extracting commonalities of best practices, we explored deeper the social, organizational and technological challenges local governments face when they employ UCGM to facilitate public service delivery. After evaluating the impact of UCGM on local government operations, we presented our findings that help to explain the success of UCGM in cities of different scales in China. Our analysis showed that the success of new e-government initiatives is far more than changes in technologies or individual task performance. Instead it is the outcomes of interactions among existing technological infrastructure, individual performance, team and organizational collaboration, work process and information flows and governance model. Thus a successful adoption of UCGM stresses the maturity of all different layers, factors and collaborations among all stakeholders.

This study contributes to the current discussion of comparative mobile governance. Furthermore, since findings of this research are grounded in actual government field work operations, emergency response and daily business practices, it offers insightful guidelines for the development of mobile governance, public fieldwork operations and business process redesign. Further investigations of the generality of these guidelines will soon be conducted to validate with wider audience, geographic distribution and economic status.

ACKNOWLEDGMENT

We want to thank multiple funding agencies for their generous support to this research: China National Social Science Foundation (Project ID: KRB3056068), Shanghai Pujiang Program (Project ID: KBH3056609), New Faculty Member Start- up Programs, China Ministry of Education (Project ID: JJH3056008), Fudan 985 Program (Project ID: 2011SHKXZD013)

REFERENCES

吴倚天 (2005). 网格下的城市——北京市东城区依托信息技术探索城市管理新模式. 信息化建设, 2005(8), 24-26. Retrieved from http://d.g.wanfangdata.com.cn/Periodical_xxhjs200508008.aspx

涂亚卓, 张新, 梅智云 (2005). 武汉?点城市网格化管理江汉区建成投入试?行. http://news.sina.com.cn/c/2005-10-21/06447225553s.shtml

陈平 (2005a). 解读万米单元网格城市管理新模式. 城乡建设, 2005(10), 10-13. Retrieved from http://d.g.wanfangdata.com.cn/Periodical_cxjs200510004.aspx

陈平 (2005b). 依托数字城市技术, 创建城市管理新模式. 中国科学院院刊, 20(3), 220-222. Retrieved from http://d.g.wanfangdata.com.cn/Periodical_zgkxyyk200503011.aspx

陈平 (2006). 数字化城市管理模式探析. 北京大学学报(哲学社会科学版), 2006(1), 142-148. Retrieved from http://www.cqvip.com/qk/81274x/2006001/21149564.html

罗建宾 (2006). 谈谈数字化城市管理模式. 中国城市经济, 2006(2), 74-75. Retrieved from http://d.g.wanfangdata.com.cn/Periodical_zgcsjj200602026.aspx

阎耀军(2006). 城市网格化管理的特点及启示. 城市问题 2006(2), 76-79. Retrieved from http://d.wanfangdata.com.cn/Periodical_cswt200602017.aspx

刘文清, 廖齐梅, 黄明钢, 杜夏雨, 秦斌 (2006). 深圳:数字化城市管理建设?实. 中国建设信息, 2006(24), 25-28. Retrieved from http://10.55.100.201/kns50/detail.aspx?QueryID=51&CurRec=1

方家平 (2006). "网格化管理"试水江城. 上海信息化, 2006(5), 43-45. Retrieved from http://d.g.wanfangdata.com.cn/Periodical_shxxh200605008.aspx

伊凡(2006).解读数字城市.城建档案,2006(5), 5-8. Retrieved from http://d.g.wanfangdata.com.cn/Periodical_cjda200605002.aspx

张超, 吴丹, 范况生 (2006). 城市网格化管理. 城建档案 2006(7), 8-12. Retrieved from http://d.wanfangdata.com.cn/Periodical_cjda200607003.aspx

李立明, 张骥, 傀乔 (2006). 网格化城市管理应急与非应急统一模式研究. 城市管理与科技, 2007(1), 18-22. Retrieved from http://d.g.wanfangdata.com.cn/Periodical_csglykj200701005.aspx

王喜, 杨华, 范况生 (2006). 城市网格化管理系统的关?技术及示范应用研究. 测绘科学 31(4), 117-119. Retrieved from http://d.wanfangdata.com.cn/Periodical_chkx200604041.aspx

张大维 (2006a). 城市网格化管理"数字化为民"工程. 社区, 2006(17), 12-13. Retrieved from http://10.55.100.201/kns50/detail.aspx?QueryID=238&CurRec=1

张大维 (2006b). 城市网格化管理模式的创新研究——以武汉市江汉区为例. 理论与改革, 2006(5), 56-57. Retrieved from http://10.55.100.201/kns50/detail.aspx?QueryID=284&CurRec=1

姜爱林, 任志儒 (2007). 网格化:现代城市管理新模式——网格化城市管理模式若干问?初探. 上海城市规划 2007(1), 9-11. Retrieved from http://d.wanfangdata.com.cn/Periodical_shcsgh200701003.aspx

程艳秋 (2007). 数字化城管:提升行政执行力的有力推手. 中国建设信息, 2007(10X), 10-12. Retrieved from http://www.cqvip.com/qk/83587x/200710x/25751982.0.html

蒋荣 (2007). 数字化城市管理项目现?与趋? 中国信息界 2007(11), 38-47. Retrieved from http://d.wanfangdata.com.cn/Periodical_zgxxj200711011.aspx

徐波 (2007). 移动?用服务现代城市管理. 系统?真技术 2007(2), 121-123. Retrieved from http://www.cqvip.com/qk/88720x/200702/1000960150.html

高琦, 赵铁汉, 马玉梅 (2007). 城市管理新模式在应对突发公共事件中的作用. 城市与减? 2007(3), 2-4. Retrieved from http://www.cqvip.com/qk/91118a/200703/24525133.html

王保森(2007).网格化管理:城市社区管理模式的创新. 规划师, 2007(5), 46-49.

程方升, 张敏娜 (2007). 网格化管理:数字时代城市治理的新取向——城市网格化管理模式问?的探究. 科协?坛(下半月), 2007(5). Retrieved from http://d.g.wanfangdata.com.cn/Periodical_kxlt-x200705031.aspx

李德仁,李宗华,彭明军,邵振峰(2007).武汉市城市网格化管理与服务系统建设与应用.测绘通报, 2007(8), 1-4. http://d.g.wanfangdata.com.cn/Periodical_chtb200708001.aspx

陈云, 周曦民, 王浣尘 (2007). 政府网格化管理的现状与展望. 科技管理研究, 27(5), 40-41. Retrieved from http://d.g.wanfangdata.com.cn/Periodical_kjglyj200705013.aspx

潘兴? (2007). 浅谈网格化城市管理模式. 中共宁波市委党校学报, 29(3), 41-46. Retrieved from http://d.g.wanfangdata.com.cn/Periodical_zgnbswdxxb200703008.aspx

吴海涛, 陈亚萍, 孙海浩 (2007). 市政专业网格化管理平台开?建设研究. 管理论坛 29(4), 140-143. Retrieved from http://d.wanfangdata.com.cn/Periodical_szjs201104044.aspx

王金诚,陈晓岚,翁裔(2007).上海市城市网格化管理的技术实现.测绘与空间地理信息,30(4),71-77. Retrieved from http://d.g.wanfangdata.com.cn/Periodical_dbch200704019.aspx

谢伟文, 任福 (2007). 基于空间基本网格的城市公共管理体系. 地理空间信息, 5(3), 28-29. Retrieved from http://d.g.wanfangdata.com.cn/Periodical_dlkjxx200703010.aspx

李林 (2007). 深圳市数字化城市管理模型探析. 福建工程学院学报, 5(6) 581-585. Retrieved from http://d.g.wanfangdata.com.cn/Periodical_fjgcxyxb200706006.aspx

袁翱 (2007). 城市万米网格化管理的思考——结合成都市数字化城市管理建设的探讨. 城市管理与科技 9(4), 45-48. Retrieved from http://d.wanfangdata.com.cn/Periodical_csglykj200704012.aspx

卢廷玉, 张忠岩 (2008). 地理信息系统在城市网格化管理中的应用. 交通科技与经? 10(3), 68-69. Retrieved from http://d.wanfangdata.com.cn/Periodical_jtkjyjj200803028.aspx

承建文 (2008). 城市网格化管理机制完善的理性思考——以上海为例. 上海城市管理职业技术?院学? 17(3), 2-5. Retrieved from http://d.wanfangdata.com.cn/Periodical_shcsglzyjsxyxb200803019.aspx

皮定均 (2008). 朝阳区利用网格化管理的实践与创新. 中国行政管理, 2008(S1), 108-110. Retrieved from http://10.55.100.201/kns50/detail.aspx?QueryID=97&CurRec=1

齐国生, 李立明, 曹杰峰, 朱光宇 (2008). 城市管理的"网格化"——从政务网格到行业网格再到公务网格. 中国行政管理 2008(S1), 79-81. Retrieved from http://10.55.100.201/kns50/detail.aspx?QueryID=142&CurRec=1

张冲, 徐飞, 夏建磊 (2008). 基于万米单元网格管理法的数字城管新模式. 光盘技术 2008(2), 20-22. Retrieved from http://d.wanfangdata.com.cn/Periodical_gpjs200802006.aspx

张勇进 (2008). 基于网格空间的城市管理创新. 行政论坛 2008(3), 83-86. Retrieved from http://d.wanfangdata.com.cn/Periodical_xingzlt200803020.aspx

池忠仁, 王浣尘, 陈云 (2008). 上海城市网格化管理模式探讨. 科技进步与对策, 25(1), 40-43. Retrieved from http://d.g.wanfangdata.com.cn/Periodical_kjjbydc200801011.aspx

杨宏波 (2008). 网格化的城市危机管理研究. 凯里学院学? 26(6), 62-64. Retrieved from http://d.g.wanfangdata.com.cn/Periodical_qdnmzsfgdzkxxxb200806022.aspx

程述, 白庆? (2008). 网格技术?示及网格化城市管理机制研究. 情报?志, 27(10), 56-59. Retrieved from http://d.g.wanfangdata.com.cn/Periodical_qbzz200810018.aspx

邱春霞, 张亚南 (2008). 城市网格化管理系统平台初步?计. 西安科技大学学报 28(1), 96-99, 127. Retrieved from http://d.wanfangdata.com.cn/Periodical_xakyxyxb200801021.aspx

孔凡敏, 苏科华, 朱欣焰 (2008). 城市网格化管理系统框架研究. 地理空间信息, 6(4), 28-31. Retrieved from http://d.g.wanfangdata.com.cn/Periodical_dlkjxx200804010.aspx

姜金贵, 梁静国 (2008). 基于网格化管理的突发事件应急管理机制研究. 情报?志2008(6), 26-28. Retrieved from http://www.cqvip.com/qk/90226x/20086/27608083.0.html

彭程, 李京, 廖通逵, 刘纯波, 蔡洪春 (2008). 基于SIG 的城市网格化管理与服务系统. 计算机工程 34(13), 245-247. Retrieved from http://d.wanfangdata.com.cn/Periodical_jsjgc200813088.aspx

江绵康 (2009). 上海市:网格化在数字城管中的实践. 建设科技, 2009(21), 38-40. Retrieved from http://d.wanfangdata.com.cn/Periodical_jskj200921012.aspx

董云铮, 刘瑜 (2009) 城市网格化管理系统技术框研究. 浙江纺织服装?业技术?院学?, 2009(3), 57-61. DOI: 10.3969/j.issn. 1674-2346.2009.03.014

朱彤(2009). 网格化城市管理技术与方法研究. 科技创新导?2009(30), 4-5. http://d.wanfangdata.com.cn/Periodical_kjzxdb200930003.aspx

马龙 (2009). 对数字化城市管理系统的再思考. 信息化建设 2009(7), 19-22. Retrieved from http://d.wanfangdata.com.cn/Periodical_xxhjs200907007.aspx

范况生 (2009). 现代城市网格化管理新模式探讨. 商丘师范学院学报, 25(12), 111-115. Retrieved from http://www.cqvip.com/qk/97536b/200912/32713566.html

李平, 全斌 (2009). "网格化"城市管理系统中城市部件数字化采集方法的探讨. 测绘标准化, 25(4), 11-14. Retrieved from http://10.55.100.201/kns50/detail.aspx?QueryID=3&CurRec=1

王立(2009). 城市网格化管理与安全社区建设. 安全 30(10), 8-11. Retrieved from http://d.wanfangdata.com.cn/Periodical_aq200910003.aspx

刘静 (2009). 浅谈城市网格化管理中的部件采集. 测绘与空间地理信息, 32(1), 98-101. Retrieved from http://d.g.wanfangdata.com.cn/Periodical_dbch200901030.aspx

李国明, 孟现? 徐志强, 王长春 (2009). 浅谈城市网格化管理. 测绘与空间地理信息, 32(6), 141-143. Retrieved from http://d.g.wanfangdata.com.cn/Periodical_dbch200906045.aspx

王爽 (2009). 城市网格化管理模式研究. 软件导刊 8(3), 115-116. Retrieved from http://10.55.100.201/kns50/detail.aspx?QueryID=188&CurRec=2

曾绍炳, 洪中华, 周世健 (2009). 城市网格化管理关键技术与系统构成. 铁道勘察35(5), 39-42. Retrieved from http://d.wanfangdata.com.cn/Periodical_tlhc200905014.aspx

汪云峰, 白庆? 田欣 (2010). 城市突发公共事件管理的网格化:控制结构的功能障碍及其突破. 情报?志 2010(4), 31-35. Retrieved from http://www.cqvip.com/qk/90226x/201004/33504785.html

田依林 (2010). 基于网格化管理的突发事件应急资源管理研究. 科技管理研究 30(8), 135-137. Retrieved from http://d.wanfangdata.com.cn/Periodical_kjglyj201008046.aspx

胡春凌, 钱杰, 杨学军 (2010). 城镇?地网格化管理模式探讨. 城市管理与科技12(2), 49-51. Retrieved from http://d.wanfangdata.com.cn/periodical_csglykj201002014.aspx

李鹏(2011). 我国城市网格化管理研究的拓展. 城市发展研究, 18(2), 114-118. Retrieved from http://d.g.wanfangdata.com.cn/Periodical_csfzyj201102018.aspx

祝小宁, 袁何俊 (2011). 基于网格化管理的突发公共事件预警机制探析. 中国行政管理 2006(10), 102-105. Retrieved from http://www.cqvip.com/qk/81961x/200610/22945833.html

周莉 (2011). 上海浦东新区城市网格化管理的建设探析. 中小企业管理与科技(上旬刊), 2011(22), 184. Retrieved from http://d.g.wanfangdata.com.cn/Periodical_xzqykj201122167.aspx

郭苗苗 (2011). 非常规突发事件网格化管理研究. 商业文化 2011(5). Retrieved from http://www.cnki.com.cn/Article/CJFDTOTAL-SYWH201105054.htm

刘淑华, 詹华, 袁千里, 武明戈 (2011). 移动政务与中国城市治理. 电子政务 2011(6), 2-12. Retrieved from http://www.cqvip.com/qk/94368c/201106/38203077.html

庄毅 (2011). 中小城市网格化管理的有益探索—以晋江市为例. 中国集体经济, 2011(9), 40-41. Retrieved from http://d.g.wanfangdata.com.cn/Periodical_zgjtjj201119022.aspx

高淑华, 孟庆海 (2011). 3G无线?频?控系统在城市管理领域的成功应用. 城市管理与科技 13(2), 50-51. Retrieved from http://www.cqvip.com/qk/93666a/201102/37764886.html

Akman, I., Yazici, A., Mishra, A., & Arifoglu, A. (2005). E-Government: A global view and an empirical evaluation of some attributes of citizens. *Government Information Quarterly*, *22*(2), 239–257. doi:10.1016/j.giq.2004.12.001.

Al-khamayseh, S., Lawrence, E., & Zmijewska, A. (2006). Towards understanding success factors in interactive mobile government. *ColleCTeR Europe*, *2006*, 129.

Alshawi, S., & Alalwany, H. (2009). E-government evaluation: Citizen's perspective in developing countries. *Information Technology for Development*, *15*(3), 193–208. doi:10.1002/itdj.20125.

Altameem, T., Zairi, M., & Alshawi, S. (2006). Critical success factors of e-government: A proposed model for e-government implementation. *Proc. Innovations in Information Technology Conference*. IEEE. Retrieved from http://ieeexplore.ieee.org/stamp/stamp.jsp?tp=&arnumber=4085489

Anselm, S., & Corbin, J. (1998). *Basics of qualitative research: Techniques and procedures for developing grounded theory*. Thousand Oaks, California: Sage Publication.

Arpaci, I. (2010). E-government and technological innovation in Turkey: Case studies on governmental organizations. *Transforming Government: People. Process and Policy*, *4*(1), 37–53. doi: doi:10.1108/17506161011028795.

Barki, H., Rivard, S., & Talbot, J. (1993). Toward an assessment of software development risk. *Journal of Management Information Systems*, *10*(2), 203–223. Retrieved from http://dl.acm.org/citation.cfm?id=1189679.

Becker, J., Niehaves, B., Algermissen, L., Delfmann, P., & Falk, T. (2004). e-Government Success Factors. EGOV Lecture Notes in Computer Science, 3183, 503–506. doi: doi:10.1007/978-3-540-30078-6_87.

Bharadwaj, A. S. (2000). A resource-based perspective on information technology capability and firm performance: An empirical investigation. *Management Information Systems Quarterly*, *24*(1), 169–196. Retrieved from http://www.jstor.org/stable/3250983 doi:10.2307/3250983.

Bhatnagar, S. (2002). E-government: Lessons from implementation in developing countries. *Regional Development Dialogue*, 24, 1–9 (Autumn). Retrieved from http://www.iimahd.ernet.in/~subhash/pdfs/RDDAutumn2002.pdf

Brown, M. M. (2001). The benefits and costs of information technology innovations: An empirical assessment of a local government agency. *Pubic Performance and Management Review*, *24*(4), 351–366. doi:10.2307/3381224.

Brynjolfsson, E., & Hitt, L. M. (1998). Beyond the productivity paradox. *Communications of the ACM*, *41*(8), 49–55. Retrieved from http://www.jstor.org/stable/3381224 doi:10.1145/280324.280332.

Burbridge, L. (2002). Accountability and MIS. *Public Performance and Management Review*, *25*(4), 421–423. doi:10.1177/15357602025004013.

Carratta, T., Dadayan, L., & Ferro, E. (2006). ROI analysis in e-government assessment trials: The case of Sistema Piemonte. *5th International Conference, EGOV 2006, Poland. Computers & Society*, *4084*, 501–505. doi: doi:10.1007/11823100_29.

Carter, L., & Bélanger, F. (2005). The utilization of e-government services: Citizen trust, innovation and acceptance factors. *Information Systems*, *15*(1), 5–25. doi:10.1111/j.1365-2575.2005.00183.x.

Chen, Zhou, & Wang. (2007). Griddling management and its research progress. *Science and Technology Management Research*, *27*(5), 40–41.

Chen. (2005a). Ten-thousand meter unit network--New mode of city management. *Urban and Rural Development, 10*, 10-13.

Chen. (2005b). Developing a new approach of urban management on the basis of digital city technology. *Bulletin of Chinese Academy of Sciences, 20*(3), 220-222.

Chen. (2006). An analysis on digital urban management model. *Journal of Peking University, 1*, 142-148.

Cheng & Bai. (2008). Implications of ICT use and urban grid management. *Journal of Information*, *27*(10), 56–59.

Cheng & Zhang. (2007). Urban city management: A new direction in modern city governance. *Science and Technology Association Forum, 5*.

Cheng. (2007). *Digital city management: A powerful engine for administrative operation*. Paper presented at China Construction Information, 2007(10X). Retrieved from http://www.cqvip.com/qk/83587x/200710x/25751982.0.html

Cheng. (2008). Rational thoughts on ways to refine mechanisms in urban city management- A case study in Shanghai. *Journal of Shanghai Polytechnic College of Urban Management, 17*(3), 2-5.

Chi, Wang, & Chen. (2008). Thoughts on Shanghai municipal management model. *Technology Advancement and Strategy*, *25*(1), 40–43.

Davenport, T. (1993). *Process innovation: Reengineering work through information technology*. Harvard Business School Press.

Davis, F. D. (1989). Perceived usefulness, perceived ease of use and user acceptance of information technology. *Management Information Systems Quarterly*, *13*, 319–330. Retrieved from http://www.jstor.org/stable/249008 doi:10.2307/249008.

Dawes, S. S. (1996). Interagency information sharing: Expected benefits, manageable risks. *Journal of Policy Analysis and Management*, *15*(3), 377–394. doi:10.1002/(SICI)1520-6688(199622)15:3<377::AID-PAM3>3.0.CO;2-F.

Dawes, S. S., & Nelson, M. R. (1995). Pool the risks, share the benefits: Partnerships in IT innovation. In Keyes, J. (Ed.), *Technology trendlines. Technology Success Stories from Today's Visionaries. New York7 Van Nostrand Reinhold*.

Dawes, S. S., & Pardo, T. (2002). Building collaborative digital government systems. In McIver, W. J., & Elmagarmid, A. K. (Eds.), *Advances in digital government. Technology, human factors, and policy*. Norwell, MA: Kluwer Academic Publishers. doi:10.1007/0-306-47374-7_16.

DeLone, W., & Mclean, E. (1992). Information systems success: The quest for the dependent variable. *Information Systems Research*, *3*(1), 60–95. doi:10.1287/isre.3.1.60.

DeLone, W., & Mclean, E. (2003). The DeLone and McLean Model of information systems success: A ten year update. *Journal of Management Information Systems*, *19*(4), 9–30.

Dingjun. (2008). Urban grid management in Chaoyang district, Beijing. *China Public Administration Review,* (S1), 108-110.

Dong & Liu. (2009). A research on the technological structure of urban grid management system. *Zhejiang Fabrics and Clothing Professional School Journal*, (3), 57-61.

Duchessi, P., & Chengalur-Smith, I. (1998). Client/server benefits, problems, best practices. *Communications of the ACM*, *41*(5), 87–94. doi:10.1145/274946.274961.

Dugdale, A., Daly, P. A. F., & Maley, M. (2005). Accessing e-government: Challenges for citizens and organizations. *International Review of Administrative Sciences*, *71*(1), 109–118. doi:10.1177/0020852305051687.

Ebbers, W. E., & van Dijk, J. A. G. M. (2007). Resistance and support to electronic government, building a model of innovation. *Government Information Quarterly*, *24*(3), 554–575. doi:10.1016/j.giq.2006.09.008.

El Kiki, T., & Lawrence, E. (2006). Government as a mobile enterprise: Real-time, ubiquitous government. Information technology: New Generations, 2006. *ITNG 2006. Third International Conference* (pp.320-327). 10-12 April 2006. doi: 10.1109/ITNG.2006.68

Ernst, C., & Young (2004). Online availability of public services: How is Europe progressing? (Web-based Survey on Electronic Public Services: Report of the Fourth Measurement, October 2003). European Commission DG Information Society.

Eschenfelder, K. R., & Miller, C. (2005). *The openness of government websites: Toward a sociotechnical overnment website evaluation toolkit*. MacArthur Foundation/ALA Office of Information Technology Policy Internet Credibility and the User Symposium, Seattle, WA.

Evans, D., & Yen, D. C. (2005). E-government: An analysis for implementation: Framework for understanding cultural and social impact. *Government Information Quarterly*, *22*(3), 354–373. doi:10.1016/j.giq.2005.05.007.

Fan. (2009). An investigation of new management models in modern city grid management. *Shangqiu Normal School Journal, 25*(12), 111-115.

Fang. (2006). Urban grid management is testing water in Jiangcheng. *Shanghai Informatization,* (5), 43-45.

Farbey, B., Land, F., & Targett, D. (1993). *How to assess your IT investment: A study of methods and practice*. Oxford: Butterworth-Heinemann Ltd..

Filgueiras, L., Aquino, P. Jr, Tokairim, V., Torres, C., & Barbarian, I. (2004). *Usability evaluation as quality assurance of e-government services* (*Vol. 146*, pp. 77–87). IFIP International Federation for Information Processing. doi:10.1007/1-4020-8155-3_5.

Frank, D., & Riedl, P. (2004). Theoretical foundations of contemporary qualitative market research Forum: An overview and an integrative perspective. *Qualitative Social Research, 5*(2), 30. Retrieved from http://www.qualitative-research.net/index.php/fqs/article/view/596/1294

Gagnon, Y.-C. (2001). The behavior of public managers in adopting new technologies. *Pubic Performance and Management Review, 24*(4), 337–350. Retrieved from http://www.jstor.org/stable/3381223

Gant, J. P., & Gant, D. B. (2002). Web portal functionality and state government eservice. System Sciences, 2002. HICSS. *Proceedings of the 35th Annual Hawaii International Conference* (pp. 1627- 1636). doi: 10.1109/HICSS.2002.994073

Gao, Zhao, & Ma. (2007). The role of urban grid management in emergency response. *Cities and Disaster Relief,* (3), 2-4.

Gao & Meng. (2011). The successful implementation and use of the third generation wireless video monitoring system in urban management. *City Management and Science and Technology, 13*(2), 50–51.

Giddens, A. (1979). *New rules of sociological method*. London: Hutchinson.

Giddens, A. (1984). *The constitution of society*. Cambridge: Polity Press.

Giddens, A. (1989). In Held, D., & Thompson, J. B. (Eds.), *A reply to my critics' in Social theory of modern societies: Anthony Giddens and his critics* (pp. 249–305). Cambridge: Cambridge University Press. doi:10.1017/CBO9780511557699.013.

Glaser, B. G. (1992). *Emergence vs. forcing: Basics of grounded theory*. Mill Valley, CA: Sociology Press.

Glazer, A., Kanniainen, V., & Niskanen, E. (2002). Bequests, control rights, and cost–benefit analysis. *European Journal of Political Economy*, *19*(1), 71–82. doi:10.1016/S0176-2680(02)00130-1.

Goulding, C. (1999). *Grounded theory: Some reflections on paradigm, procedures and misconceptions*. Working paper series, WP006/99, Wolverhampton: University of Wolverhampton

Guo. (2011). Research on the use of grid management in irregular emergency response. *Commercial Culture,* (5).

Gupta, M. P., Debashish Jana. (2003). E-government evaluation: A framework and case study. *Government Information Quarterly*, *20*(4), 365–387. doi:10.1016/j.giq.2003.08.002.

Gupta, M. P., & Jana, D. (2003). E-Government evaluation: A framework and case study. *Government Information Quarterly*, *20*(4), 365–387. doi:10.1016/j.giq.2003.08.002.

Heeks, R. (2003). *Most e-government for development projects fail: How can risks be reduced*? I-Government, Working Paper Series, Paper no. 14.

Heintze, T., & Bretschneider, S. (2000). Information technology and restructuring in public organizations: Does adoption of information technology affect organizational structures, communications, and decision making? *Journal of Public Administration: Research and Theory*, *10*(4), 801–830. Retrieved from http://jpart.oxfordjournals.org/citmgr?gca=jpart;10/4/801 doi:10.1093/oxfordjournals.jpart.a024292.

Hochstrasser, B. (1992). Justifying IT investment. *Proceedings of the Advanced Information Systems Conference; The New Technologies in Today's Business Environment*, (pp. 17–28). UK.

Holden, S. H., Norris, D. F., & Fletcher, P. D. (2003). Electronic government at the local level: Progress to date and future issues. *Public Performance and Management Review, 26*(4), 325–344. Retrieved from http://www.jstor.org/stable/3381110

Hu, Qian, & Yang. (2010). The use of urban grid management model in city greenbelt. *Urban Governance and Technology*, *12*(2), 49–51.

Huang, Z., & Bwoma, P. O. (2003). An overview of critical issues of E-government. *Issues in Information Systems*, *4*(1), 164–170. Retrieved from http://iacis.org/iis/2003/HuangBwoma.pdf.

Jaeger, P. T., & Thompson, K. M. (2003). E-government around the world: Lessons, challenges, and future directions. *Government Information Quarterly*, *20*, 389–394. doi:10.1016/j.giq.2003.08.001.

Jiang & Liang. (2008). Emergency management employing urban grid management model. *Journal of Intelligence,* (6), 26-28.

Jiang & Ren. (2007). Grid management: New mode of modern urban management—Research on certain questions of urban grid management mode. *Shanghai Urban Planning Review*, (1), 9-11.

Jiang. (2007). The current status and trend in urban grid management projects. *China Information Times,* (11), 38-47.

Jiang. (2009). Shanghai: Practice of gradding urban management in the digital city. *Construction Science and Technology,* (21), 38-40.

Kamal, M. M. (2006). IT innovation adoption in the government sector: Identifying the critical success factors. *Journal of Enterprise Information Management, 19*(2), 192–222. doi:10.1108/17410390610645085.

Kaylor, C., Deshazo, R., & Eck, D. V. (2001). Gauging E-government: A report on implementing services among American cities. *Government Information Quarterly, 18*(4), 293. doi:10.1016/S0740-624X(01)00089-2.

Ke, W., & Wei, K. K. (2004). Successful e-government in Singapore. *Communications of the ACM, 47*(6), 95–99. doi:10.1145/990680.990687.

Kertesz, S. (2003). *Cost-benefit analysis of e-government investments.* Cambridge: Harvard University Press.

Khan, M. Y., & Jain, P. K. (2001). Capital budgeting: Principles and techniques. In *Financial Management* (pp. 171–273). New Delhi: Tata McGraw-Hill Publishing Company.

Kong, Su, & Zhu. (2008). Framework of urban grid management systems. *Geospatial Information, 6*(4), 28–31.

Korteland, E., & Bekkers, V. (2007). Diffusion of E-government innovations in the Dutch public sector: The case of digital community policing. *Information Polity, 12*(3), 139–150. Retrieved from http://iospress.metapress.com/content/7PH50Q3771845628

Kunstelj, M., & Vintar, M. (2004). Evaluating the progress of e-government development: A critical analysis. *Information Polity, 9*(3-4), 131–148. doi: doi:10.1007/978-3-540-74444-3_22.

Landsbergen, D. J., & Wolken, G., Jr. (1998, October). *Eliminating legal and policy barriers to interoperable government systems.* Paper presented at the Annual Research Conference of the Association for Public Policy Analysis and Management. New York.

Layne, K., & Lee, J. (2001). Developing fully functional e- Government: A four stage model. *Government Information Quarterly, 18*(2), 122–136. doi:10.1016/S0740-624X(01)00066-1.

Li, et al. (2007). The construction and application of Wuhan urban grid management and service system. *Bulletin of Surveying and Mapping,* (8), 1-4.

Li, et al. (2009). Discussion on the urban grid management. *Geomatics & Spatial Information Technology, 32*(6), 141–143.

Li, Zhang, & Kui. (2006). Study about emergency and non-emergency unified pattern of griding management. *Urban Management Science and Technology,* (1), 18-22.

Li & Quan. (2009). Urban digitalization and data collection in urban grid management systems. *Surveying and Mapping Standardization, 25*(4), 11–14.

Li. (2007). Analysis of Shenzhen's digital city management model. *Journal of Fujian University of Technology, 5*(6), 581-585.

Li. (2011). The Chinese urban grid management and research. *Urban Studies, 18*(2), 114-118.

Liu, et al. (2006). Implementation of urban grid management in Shenzhen. *China Construction Information,* (24), 25-28.

Liu., et al. (2011). Mobile governance and city management in China. Electronic Government, (6), 2-12.

Liu. (2009). Components acquisition on the urban grid management. *Geomatics and Spatial Information Technology, 32*(1), 98-101.

Lu & Zhang. (2008). The integration of GIS in urban grid management system. *Transportation Technology and Economy*, *10*(3), 68–69.

Luk, S. C. Y. (2009). The impact of leadership and stakeholders on the success/failure of e-government service: Using the case study of e-stamping service in Hong Kong. *Government Information Quarterly*, *26*(4), 594–604. doi:10.1016/j.giq.2009.02.009.

Luo. (2006). Talking about urban grid management model. *China Urban Economy,* (2), 74-75.

Ma. (2009). Rethinking about urban grid management system. *Informatization*, (7), 19-22.

Mahler, J., & Regan, P. M. (2002). Learning to govern online: Federal agency Internet use. *American Review of Public Administration*, *32*(3), 326–349. doi:10.1177/0275074002032003004.

Meskell, D. (2003). High payoff in electronic government: Measuring the return on e-government investment. Washington, DC: Federation of Government Information Processing Councils.

Moon, M. J. (2002). The evolution of e-government among municipalities: Rhetoric or reality? *Public Administration Review*, *62*(4), 424–433. doi:10.1111/0033-3352.00196.

Moore, A. (2005). Implementing e-government portals, technical and organizational issues: Montgomery county (USA) portal. *Proceedings of the E-Gov VC Series Under Joint Economic Research Program of the Government of Kazakhstan and the World Bank, World Bank Video Conference*.

Norris, D. F., & Moon, M. J. (2005). Advancing e-government at the grassroots: Tortoise or hare? *Public Administration Review*, *65*(1), 64–75. doi:10.1111/j.1540-6210.2005.00431.x.

Orlikowski, W. J., & Robey, D. (1991). Information technology and the structuring of organizations. *Information Systems Research*, *2*(2), 143–169. doi:10.1287/isre.2.2.143.

Pan. (2007). When it comes to urban grid management model. *Journal of the Party School of CPC Ningbo Municipal Committee, 29*(3), 41-46.

Park, R. (2008). Measuring factors that influence the success of e-government initiatives. *Proceedings of the 41st Hawaii International Conference on System Sciences – 2008* (pp. 218). doi: 10.1109/HICSS.2008.244

Patricia, R. (1983). A structrationist accounts of political culture. *Administrative Science Quarterly*, *28*(3), 414–437. Retrieved from http://www.jstor.org/stable/2392250 doi:10.2307/2392250.

Patton, M. Q. (2002). *Qualitative research and evaluation methods*. Thousand Oaks, California: Sage Publications.

Peng, et al. (2008). Grid management and service system in city based on SIG. *Computer Engineering*, *34*(13), 245–257.

Pollitt, C. (2001). Clarifying convergence: Striking similarities and durable differences in public management reform. *Public Management Review*, *3*(4), 471–492. doi:10.1080/14616670110071847.

Qi, et al. (2008). Urban gridization in modern city management. *China Public Administration Review,* (S1), 79-81.

Qiu & Zhang. (2008). Design of city-grid management system platform. *Journal of Xi'An University of Science and Technology*, *28*(1), 96–99.

Ramo'n Gil-Garcı'a, J., & Pardo, T. A. (2005). E-government success factors: Mapping practical tools to theoretical foundations. *Government Information Quarterly*, *22*(2), 187–216. doi:10.1016/j.giq.2005.02.001.

Reddick, C. G., & Frank, H. A. (2007). The perceived impacts of E-Government on U.S.cities: A survey of Florida and Texas city managers. *Government Information Quarterly*, *24*(3), 576–594. doi:10.1016/j.giq.2006.09.004.

Reffat, R. M. (2006) Developing a successful e-government. *Electronic Government, an International Journal, 2*(3), 247-276. Retrieved from http://www.imamu.edu.sa/Scientific_selections/files/DocLib/E16.pdf

Rogers, E. M. (1995). *Diffusion of innovations* (4th ed.). New York, NY: The Free Press.

Rose, J. (1998). *Evaluating the contribution of structuration theory to the information systems discipline*. Presented at 6th European Conference on Information Systems, Aix-en-Provence. Retrieved from http://folk.uio.no/patrickr/refdoc/ECIS1998-Rose.pdf

Rose, W. R., & Grant, G. G. (2010). Critical issues pertaining to the planning and implementation of E-Government initiatives. *Government Information Quarterly, 27*(1), 26–33. doi:10.1016/j.giq.2009.06.002.

Sakowicz, M. (2004). How to evaluate e-government? Different methodlogies and methodes. In *NISPAcee occasional papers, V*(2), 18-26. Retrieved from http://unpan1.un.org/intradoc/groups/public/documents/NISPAcee/UNPAN009486.pdf

Seitz, N. E. (1989). *Capital budgeting and long term financing decision*. Hindsdale, IL: Dyden Press.

Serafeimidis, V., & Smithson, S. (2000). Information systems evaluation in practice: A case study of organizational change. *Journal of Information Technology, 15*(2), 93–105. doi:10.1080/026839600344294.

Shan, S., Wang, L., Wang, J., Hao, Y., & Hua, F. (2011). Research on e-Government evaluation model based on the principal component analysis. *Information Technology Management, 12*(2), 173–185. doi:10.1007/s10799-011-0083-8.

Srivastava, S. C. (2011). Is e-government providing the promised returns? A value framework for assessing e-government impact. *Transforming Government: People. Process and Policy, 5*(2), 107–113. doi: doi:10.1108/17506161111131159.

Terry Ma, H., & Zaphiris, P. (2003). *The usability and content accessibility of the e-government in the UK*. London: Centre forHuman-Computer Interaction Design, City University. Retrieved October, 2007, from http://www.soi.city.ac.uk/~zaphiri/Papers/HCII2003/HCII2003-Accessibility.pdf

Tian. (2010). Research on emergency resource management based on urban grid management model. *Science and Technology Management Research*. Retrieved from http://d.wanfangdata.com.cn/Periodical_kjglyj201008046.aspx

Torres, L., Pina, V., & Acerete, B. (2005). EGovernment developments on delivering public services among EU cities. *Government Information Quarterly, 22*(2), 217–238. doi:10.1016/j.giq.2005.02.004.

Tu, Zhang, & Mei. (2005). *Urban grid management in Jianghan district in Wuhan city*. Retrieved from http://news.sina.com.cn/c/2005-10-21/06447225553s.shtml

Van de Ven, A. H., Polley, D., Garud, R., & Venkataraman, S. (1999). *The innovation journey*. New York: Oxford University Press.

Vintar, M., Kunstelj, M., Decman, M., & Bercic, B. (2003). Development of e-government in Slovenia. *Information Polity, 8*(3,4), 133–149. Retrieved from http://iospress.metapress.com/content/ARCQJ62E942M2PEY

Wang, Bai, & Tian. (2010). Grid management of city emergencies. *Journal of Intelligence,* (4), 31-35.

Wang, Chen, & Weng. (2007). Technological implementation of city grid management of Shanghai. *Geomatics and Spatial Information Technology*, *30*(4), 71–77.

Wang, L., Bretschneider, S., & Gant, J. (2005). Evaluating web-based e-government services with a citizen-centric approach. *Proceedings of the 38th Hawaii International Conference on System Sciences*. doi: 10.1109/HICSS.2005.252

Wang, S. (2009). Research on urban grid management models. *Software and Educational Technology*, *8*(3), 115–116.

Wang, Yang, & Fan. (2006). Study on the key technologies and demonstrating application of urban griddization management system. *Science of Surveying and Mapping*, *31*(4), 117–119.

Wang, Y.-S., & Liao, Y.-W. (2008). Assessing eGovernment systems success: A validation of the DeLone and McLean model of information systems success. *Government Information Quarterly*, *25*(4), 717–733. doi:10.1016/j.giq.2007.06.002.

Wang. (2007). Urban grid management: Innovation in urban community management model. *Planner,* (5), 46-49.

Wang. (2009). Urban grid management and safe community construction. *Safety, 30*(10), 8-11.

West, D. M. (2003). *Global e-government 2003, Centre for Public Policy*. Brown University, Providence. Retrieved from http://www.InsidePolitics.org

West, J. P., & Berman, E. M. (2001). The impact of revitalized management practices on the adoption of information technology: A national survey of local governments. *Pubic Performance and Management Review, 24*(3), 233–253. Retrieved from http://www.jstor.org/stable/3381087

Wu, Chen, & Sun. (2007). Study on development and construction of grid management platform of municipal professional. *Management Forum, 29*(4), 140-143.

Wu. (2005). Urban Grid management in Dongcheng district in Beijing. *Informatization Construction*, (8), 24-26.

Xie & Ren. (2007). Urban management system based on urban grids. *Geospatial Information*, *5*(3), 28–29.

Xu. (2007). Mobile applications are serving the needs of modern city management. *System Simulation and Technology,* (2), 121-123.

Yan. (2006). The nature and implication of urban grid management. *City Issues,* (2), 76-79.

Yang, T.-M., & Maxwell, T. A. (2011). Information-sharing in public organizations: A literature review of interpersonal, intra-organizational and inter-organizational success factors. *Government Information Quarterly*, *28*(2), 164–175. doi:10.1016/j.giq.2010.06.008.

Yang. (2008). City emergency management employing grids. *Journal of Kaili University, 26*(6), 62-64.

Yi. (2006). Interpreting digital city. *The Urban Construction Archive Magazine,* (5), 5-8.

Yuan. (2007). Reflection on urban ten-thousand-meter basic grid management—Discussion be combined with construction of Chengdu digital urban management system. *Urban Management Science and Technology, 9*(4), 45-48.

Zeng, Hong, & Zhou. (2009). Key technology and system composition of urban grid management. *Railway Investigation and Surveying*, *35*(5), 39–42.

Zhang, Danwu, & Fan. (2006). Urban grid management. *The Urban Construction Archive Magazine,* (7), 8-12.

Zhang, Feixu, & Xia. (2008). The new urban management model based on ten thousand meter unit grid. *CD Technology,* (2), 20-22.

Zhang. (2006a). Urban grid management: A project serving the people digitally. *Community,* (17), 12-13.

Zhang. (2006b). Innovation on urban grid management- A case study in Jianghan district in Wuhan city. *Theory and Reform,* (5), 56-57.

Zhang. (2008). Innovation in city management based on urban grids. *Administrative Forum,* (3), 83-86.

Zhou. (2011). Investigations of urban grid management innovation in Pudong district in Shanghai. *Management and Technology in SME,* (22), 184.

Zhu & Yuan. (2011). Public crisis and emergency preparation mechanisms based on urban grids. *China Public Administration Review,* (10), 102-105.

Zhu. (2009). Urban management technology and methods research. *Science and Technology Innovation Herald,* (30), 4-5.

Zhuang. (2011). Exploration of urban grid management development in small cities—A case study in Jinjiang. *China State Economy,* (9), 40-41.

ENDNOTES

1. Core journals in China are generally referred to journals that have accumulatively published a great number of papers, and have high paper citations and high academic influence.

Chapter 9
E-Government in Singapore: Critical Success Factors

Huong Ha
University of Newcastle, Singapore

ABSTRACT

In Singapore, e-Government has been developed more than 10 years ago, concurrently with the re-invention of the Public Administration. Technologically, e-Government initiatives in Singapore have been supported by the launch of seven national strategic ICT plans since 1980. The success of Singapore's e-Government has been internationally recognised.

This chapter aims to (i) discuss the current e-Government framework in Singapore, (ii) examine factors affecting the success of e-Government in Singapore, and (iii) make policy recommendations on how to improve the effectiveness and efficiency of e-Government.

This chapter is significant as it will provide better insights for further research in e-Government, given the high demand for good governance and better delivery of public services. The lessons drawn from Singapore's e-Government, in terms of how to achieve a balance between technology adoption, citizen engagement and effective public administration, can be further developed into an e-Government model applicable to other neighbouring countries.

INTRODUCTION

E-Government has been adopted by many countries to improve public services and improve the relationship between government and other groups of stakeholders (OGS), including citizens, businesses, civil servants, and various national and international government agencies. The USA, the UK, Canada and Australia have been pioneers in adopting an electronic platform and ICT applications in the 1990s to improve the flows of information and knowledge exchange within and among government agencies, as well as between government and OGS. E-Government is one of the tools to enhance democracy as it facilitates open and two-way communication between government and citizens, and allows collective participation (Chadwick & May, 2003). According to McDaniel (2003), Yong (2003), Tapscott (2009), and Alghamdi, Goodwin, and Rampersad

DOI: 10.4018/978-1-4666-4173-0.ch009

Copyright © 2013, IGI Global. Copying or distributing in print or electronic forms without written permission of IGI Global is prohibited.

(2011), e-Government facilitates government's efficiency, effectiveness and progress. ICT applications help government improve managerial and administrative capability, integrate inter-governmental processes (for example, tax filing reporting, payment), enhance law implementation and enforcement. E-Government can reduce the time lag, and distance is not an issue to recipients of e-services who reside in different geographical locations. Chadwick and May (2003) argued that power inequalities have existed within government, and between government and other stakeholders. The adoption of ICT new technologies, in fact, has fostered this type of pre-existing power inequity due to digital divide (McNamara, 2003). Nevertheless, the benefits of e-Government are universally undeniable.

Singapore is selected for this project due to the following reasons. Singapore is a very small city-state in Southeast Asia. However, effective management of physical and social resources has been considered one of the critical success factors of national survival. The success of Singapore has not only been demonstrated via economic achievements, but also via several achievements in e-Government. In Singapore, e-Government has been launched many years ago. Singapore's e-Government aims to reinvent government and public administration via better delivery of public services and closer interaction between government and OGS. The Singapore government has launched seven national Infocomm plans since 1980 to support the development and implementation of e-Government. Singapore has been recognised for its success in e-Government, and it has received many awards and has been ranked in the top places for its e-Government by many international organizations, such as the UNDP, the World Economic Forum, etc. Therefore, the lessons learnt from Singapore's successful e-Government may benefit other city-states which have similar socio-economic conditions and legal frameworks to the ones in Singapore.

This chapter aims to (i) discuss the current e-Government framework in Singapore, (ii) examine factors affecting the success of e-Government in Singapore, and (iii) make policy recommendations on how to improve the effectiveness and efficiency of Singapore's e-Government which, in turn, can enhance the delivery of public services.

This study has adopted secondary research. The secondary data for this study have been obtained from academic and non-academic (government websites, annual reports, etc.) literature. As this is an explorative research project, content analysis approach has been employed to examine, analyse and evaluate the current e-Government activities and programs implemented in Singapore and critical success factors of e-Government.

This chapter is significant since it will provide better insights for further research in e-Government and governance given the high demand for good governance and better public services. The lessons drawn from Singapore's successful e-Government, in terms of how to achieve a balance between technology adoption, citizen engagement and effective public service, can be further developed into an e-Government model applicable to other neighbouring countries.

BACKGROUND

Concepts of E-Government

E-Government refers to the delivery of public services to citizens via information technology (IT), such as the Internet (Shailendra, Palvia, & Sharma, 2007; World Bank, 2011). E-Government has been considered as one of the effective instruments to improve the delivery of public services, enhance transparency and accountability, prevent corruption, engage citizens and improve interactions with businesses, citizens and among government agencies (Heeks, 2005; Evans & Ye, 2006; Rotchanakitumnuai, 2008; Angelopoulos, Kitsios, & Papadopoulos, 2010; Latre et al., 2010). Therefore, e-Government can change the nature of the relationship between government and other groups of stakeholders in the private sector and civil society. However, in order to reap the benefits of e-Government and IT, factors affecting the effectiveness of e-Government initiatives must be identified and addressed satisfactorily.

Factors Affecting the Implementation of E-Government

E-Government initiatives can only be successful if they allow public services to be delivered in a speedy, interactive and cost-effective manner. Also the information must be accurate, timely and of high quality (Angelopoulos et al., 2010). Literature suggests that the success and efficiency of e-Government initiatives is affected by the following key variables, namely (i) managerial, (ii) technical, (iii) financial, and (iv) human behavioural factors (Ndou, 2004; Chen & Knepper, 2005; Rashid & Rahman, 2010).

Regarding managerial factors, Singh (2003), Coursey and Norris (2008), Rashid and Rahman (2010), and Council for Excellence in Governance (2011) explained that leadership committment and competency is a prerequisite for any e-Government program to be developed and implemented. Without leadership commitment in terms of policy making and implementation, resource allocation and investment in technology and manpower, it is impossible for a government agency to adopt e-Government successfully. In addition, leaders who are not competent will not be able to make appropriate decisions. Bonham, Seifert, and Thorson (2001), Koh, Ryan, and Prybutok (2005), Wescott (2007) and Rashid and Rahman (2010) found that administrative arrangements and organisational structure are positively co-related with the effectiveness of an e-Government initiative. Administrative arrangements refer to the establishment of institutes which are responsible for the development and implementation of e-Government; whereas organizational structure will help relevant government agencies to implement the strategies and achieve the objectives of e-Government initiatives. Rashid and Rahman (2010) also discussed the important of institutions in developing and implementing e-Government. In other words, institutions must be in place to implement, monitor, evaluate and revise e-Government initiatives. Ebrahim and Irani (2005), Wescott (2007), and Ha (2011, 2012) explored the critical role of security and privacy in the design of e-Government systems. They elaborated that users will not want to adopt e-services if they do not feel secure in the online environment. According to Ha and Cghill (2006), Ojo et al. (2007), Prananto and McKemmish (2007) and Zheng et al. (2012), insufficient financial and human resources have been considered as glaring barriers to e-Government adoption. In addition, educational level and technological knowledge of users and system operators have been variables affecting the effectiveness and efficient of the adoption of e-Government (Sharma & Gupta, 2002; Vintar et al., 2003; Ebrahim & Irani, 2005; Sipior & Ward, 2005). Users with low level of education and IT skills may not be confident to receive public services and obtain information via government online portals. Hermana and Sulfianti (2011) identified another critical factor influencing the user acceptance of e-Government, i.e. the affordability of Internet access and computers/laptops.

MAIN FOCUS OF THE CHAPTER

E-Government in Singapore

Singapore's e-Government aims to provide public services rapidly, cost-effectively and inclusively. The current e-Government framework, e-government master plans, institutional arrangement and e-services in Singapore will be examined in the following section.

Singapore's E-Government Framework

The proposed framework for e-Government worldwide is customized, i.e. provision of what users need and want, as e-Government is generic in nature and not limited to a single geographical location's use (Rabaiah & Vandijck, 2009). In Singapore, the current e-Government framework revolves around the provision of comprehensive government information and e-services for all users on a single portal, and to allow enhanced efficiency and convenience in government transactions (Infocomm Development Authority of Singapore, 2006). The basic framework of e-Government focuses on easy and convenient transactions between the government and OGS. E-Government also emphasizes the provision of high quality government information to citizens, and allows commercialized transactions to be carried out online. This will help with removing the tiresomeness of travelling between numerous offices to conduct transactions with government.

Singapore's E-Government Master Plans

So far, Singapore has launched six e-Government master plans, supported by seven national Infocomm programs. In 2000, the first master plan of e-government in Singapore was launched. This plan was supported by five initiatives, namely (i) enhancement of electronic service delivery, (ii) expansion of capabilities and capacity through innovation, (iii) leveraging the public and private sectors, (iv) developing though leadership on e-government, and (v) spreading the value of e-Government by popularizing usage of its services. This plan centres on the close relationship between government and OGSs (Baum et al., n.d.).

The key goal of the action plan is the evolution of public services through evaluation of all aspects of government to refine the government interaction with citizens. This can be done via providing customer-centric integrated electronic services, being proactive through a consensus and responsive approach, using ICT to build new capabilities and capacities to greatly boost public service delivery (Wong & Cha, 2009).

In 2000-2003, e-Government Action Plan I was launched with the aim to deliver as many public services online as possible. The second e-Government Action Plan, launched from 2003 to 2006, emphasized the provision of top quality e-services across the nation. It also aimed at increasing connection between the government and its citizens (Infocomm Development Authority of Singapore, 2011). The purposes of this plan were to make customers delighted when going online, to better connect with citizens and to implement networked government. It also strives for a strong Infocomm sector. Altogether, these action plans aimed at increasing public awareness, cost-effective and speedy access, active citizen participation, and effective government machinery (Chung, 2007).

In 2006, iGov2010, a $2 billion five-year plan was inaugurated to further increase the efficiency of e-government via integration of back-end processes throughout the government agencies to reach the peak of e-service delivery. The eventual goal is an integrated e-Government which provides customer satisfaction and connects citizens through Infocomm applications (Infocomm Development Authority of Singapore, 2006). Following these above plans, the new target would be to surpass organizational structures and the evolution of operating procedures, creating a user-centric government (Infocomm Development Authority of Singapore, 2011).

The recent e-Government Master Plan 2011-2015 (iN2015) has provided a new opportunity for enhanced relationship between government and citizens, from a government-to-you paradigm to a government-with-you model regarding governance (Ha, 2012). The e-Government plans have been well strategized in a way that each of them has been supported by a national Infocomm plan. In other words, the Infocomm plans have laid a strong foundation in terms of technical, physical and social capital for each e-Government plan (Chung, 2007).

Compared with Hong Kong, Singapore's e-Government plans have been updated more frequently. Hong Kong launched its first "Digital

21" IT Strategy in 1998, and this plan was revised in 2001. Three years later, this plan was revised again by the Commerce, Industry, and Technology Bureau (CITB) (Ching, 2009). Similar to Singapore, Hong Kong's e-Government initiatives also focus on provision of e-services to citizens (G2C), businesses (G2B), employees in the public sector (G2E), and other governments (G2G).

Taiwan's e-Government has been implemented through the launch of a centralized government portal (www.gov.tw), which allows government services and information to be integrated in one online portal. This portal provides information in both English and Chinese, whereas the information on e-citizen website in Singapore is only in English (Yong, 2003). Thus, people who do not read and write English may not be access to information on government websites. The government of South Korea has also established an online government for citizen (G4C) portal (www.egov.go.kr) to provide e-services. Apparently, the number of public services provided only is only 400, much less than the number of e-services provided by Singapore's e-Government (Yong, 2003). Nevertheless, it is difficult to assess the quality of such e-services.

Institutional Arrangements and Implementation Mechanisms

In terms of institutional arrangements, the Ministry of Finance (MOF) is the owner of Singapore's e-Government system. The Infocomm Development Authority (IDA) of Singapore is in charge of developing and maintaining the competitive Infocomm industry. The IDA is a government agency which seeks to achieve the role of the Infocomm industry champion. It has been involved in planning and developing the national Infocomm master plans (iN2015 Master plan), and has been the Government Chief Information Officer (Lim & Koh, 2008).

Regarding the implementation of e-Government, the Public Service Infrastructure (PSi) is a platform for the deployment of dynamic, user friendly government e-services for both citizens and corporations, in collaboration with the NCS (National Computer Systems Pte Ltd), *Ecquaria* (providing e-Government consultancy and infrastructure solutions), and the IDA (Infocomm Development Authority of Singapore, 2010). PSi has since been commercialized into the Ecquaria Service-Oriented Platform with more than 80 government agencies hosting over 2,000 services for consistent provision of e-services to citizens and businesses regardless of time and location (Infocomm Development Authority of Singapore, 2006).

In 2005, IDA collaborated with Singapore Infocomm Technology Federation (SiTF) and Nanyang Polytechnic (NYP) to set up the Service Oriented Architecture (SOA) Centre. SiTF is the premier Infocomm industry association in Singapore with more than 400 corporate members which are MNCs and local companies. NYP's School of Information Technology's Centre for IT Innovation (CITI) is another platform for firms to collaborate with leading IT providers and vendors. NYP has developed partnerships with "technology leaders such as IBM, Microsoft, Cisco Systems, Oracle, SAP to spearhead the development of technologies in the areas of web services, enterprise solutions, RFID integration, mobility solutions, business rules solutions, IP convergence and grid computing" (Lim & Koh, 2008, p. 580). The main goal of the SOA Centre is to provide a single point of contact to address key issues associated with the development of e-Government, and the adoption of e-Government by the industry and enterprises in Singapore. Stakeholders are urged to be part of the SiTF, and accelerate SOA adoption to create business value and innovation (Lim & Koh, 2008).

The Singapore government has also worked closely with the private sector to tap on their expertise in new technology. E-services are administered by different government departments, working with various private enterprises. In other words, Public-private partnership (PPP) has been adopted by the Singapore government to implement e-Government. For example, *Ecquaria* is technically responsible for the Online Business Licensing Service, while *Elixir Technology* has been engaged to implement the high powered Intelligent Fool Approval and Safety Tracking System (iFAST). This system processes over a million business permits annually. *Netrust* has implemented the PKI-based (Public Key Infrastructure) authentication and verification systems which have been used to administer newly introduced biometric e-passports (Infocomm Development Authority of Singapore, 2006).

E-Services

Singapore's e-Government has been developed to cater to the needs of different groups of users. Firstly, e-Government for citizens has been implemented via the e-Citizen Centre which provides one-stop online information and services. Non-residents can also find necessary information on this website. The information and services have been identified and classified according to the popular themes which citizens are interested in, and several aspects of citizen welfare. The e-Citizen Centre has offered more than 1,700 out of the 2,600 services which are possibly delivered via electronic means (Department of Economic and Social Affairs Division for Public Administration and Development Management, 2008). The new objective of the e-Citizen Centre is to enhance the e-service experience of users. This can be done by cooperation with grass-root organizations and private enterprises. This also aims to promote e-Government among citizens, and increase accessibility through the e-Citizen Helper Partnership initiative. E-services have helped users save time, efforts and money through compaction of services. For instance, citizens and permanent residents can apply for their Singapore Personal Access (SingPass), a personal user identification which allows users to conveniently access to government e-services. SingPass holders can use their SingPass to e-file income tax returns, check their CPF (Central Provident Fund) accounts, renew road taxes as well as access to other personal confidential information online (Infocomm Development Authority of Singapore, 2006). The operation of the e-Citizen portal has been maintained by the PSi which can minimise red tape by allowing access to existing transaction templates. To allow greater interaction with citizens, the Feedback Unit offers an online portal where citizens can express their views in a constructive manner on many issues, including national policies and politics (Rabaiah & Vandijck, 2009). This is a very radical initiative of the government to interact with citizens so that they can design and deliver services which meet citizens' needs and wants.

Secondly, e-Government for business has been implemented via the business centre on the Singapore Government Online Portal, such as Enterpise One (http://www.enterpriseone.gov.sg), and the Accounting and Corporate Regulatory Authority's (ACRA) one-stop business services portal (www.bizfile.gov.sg). These portals have adopted a customer centric approach to providing e-services. Local and international business communities can utilize a complete range of e-services to obtain information for their business activities. Service-Wide Online Procurement is also available to allow cost cutting. The Government Electronic Business Centre (GeBiz) (www.gebiz.gov.sg) has provided easy access for local and international suppliers to search for procurement opportunities in the public sector. This portal allows business to trade with the government online. Business registration has been simplified as new local companies can register their business and enlist electronically via the Registry of Companies and Businesses portal of the ACRA (www.acra.gov.sg). Existing businesses can also make statutory disclosure requirements online (Rabaiah & Vandijck, 2009).

Firms can reap the benefits from business-related e-Government initiatives, such as the Online Business Licensing Service, a sub-section of the EnterpriseOne's system (https://licences.

business.gov.sg) which allows applications, renewals or terminations for one or more licenses at the same time. This results in greater efficiency as companies do not have to go through as much red tape by dealing directly with various government agencies (Infocomm Development Authority of Singapore, 2006). Generally, the development of government-to-business includes business permit registration, access to information regarding laws of business practice, government regulations and guidelines, filling corporate tax returns, and tendering for government contracts online. The government has also promoted the growth of local online businesses in international markets through innovative applications of technology (Baum et al., 2006).

Thirdly, e-Government for employees in the public sector has been implemented mainly via the use of ICTs to increase the quality and confidentiality of government communication to employees, and readily accessible and easily updated relevant content online (Baum et al., n.d.). The Government Access Infrastructure (www.egov.gov.sg) has allowed authorised public officers to access to the government network at any time and place through a kaleidoscope of channels. The broadband infrastructure has allowed the public sector to choose its own Internet services. It has been complemented by the Service-Wide Technical Architecture, which creates common infrastructures and architectures for various government agencies. These platforms serve to reduce operation boundaries across public agencies. Instruments and tools used by the public sector, such as the Public Sector Smart Card, Government Email system and Government Intranet have created interconnectivity among public sector agencies. These mechanisms and tools have also allowed various public services to be integrated. As a result, government-to-employee links streamline information flows within the machinery of government. A People Matter Management System to implement better central human resource policies has also been developed to support the specific human resource needs in the public sector (Rabaiah & Vandijck, 2009). For example, the Infocomm Education Programme has been launched to equip government officers with the required expertise so that they can work well within an e-Government system. Public servants can also take advantage of the opportunities to create novel e-services via e-Government (Baum et al., n.d.). In 2001, the Knowledge Management Experimentation Programme (KM-EP) was introduced to forge a knowledge-based workplace in the public service to leverage on knowledge management in the public sector (Singapore Ministry of Finance and Infocomm Development Authority of Singapore, 2001).

Assessment of Outcomes

So far, about 1,700 public services suitable for online delivery have been available online, at the click of a mouse (Infocomm Development Authority of Singapore, 2006). Compared to many newly developed countries, Singapore has made early and great strides in adopting e-Government to improve its governance and public administration. At the early stage, most e-Government websites in Singapore have only provided information to users. Later, they have gradually made online transactions available. From a one-way communication, i.e. users search for information on government websites, Singapore's e-Government facilitates two-way interaction between government and other groups of stakeholders (Teo, Srivastava, & Jiang, 2009).

Many research studies have indicated that Singapore was among the top ten nations in terms of the variety of available information and services on government websites. Singapore has also been cited as one of the e-Government leaders in Asia (United Nations Department of Economic and Social Affairs, 2012). Singapore has received many international awards for its e-Government initiatives, such as the Stockholm Challenges Awards (2010, 2008), the Commonwealth Association of Public Administration and Management International Innovations Awards (2010, 2008, 2006), the UN Public Service Awards (2005, 2006, 2007, 2008 and 2010), and the United Nations e-Government Survey 2010 Special Awards (Department of Economic and Social Affairs Division for Public Administration and Development Management, 2008; Ha, 2012; United Nations Public Administration Network, n. d.).

Singapore has also topped (i) the WEF's Networked Readiness Index (2002 -2006), (ii) the Accenture 2007 Ranking regarding public service. It was ranked in the seventh and the second positions in terms of e-Government Readiness and e-Government Participation in the UN's 2005 e-Government Readiness Report, respectively (Ha, 2012). Singapore was among the top 35 countries in the Web Measurement Assessment in 2008 (Department of Economic and Social Affairs Division for Public Administration and Development Management, 2008). The World Economic Forum Global Information Technology Report ranked Singapore the second in 2010 in terms of Networked Readiness Index. Again, Singapore has also topped the Waseda University World e-Government ranking list in 2012 (Dutta & Mia, 2011; Infocomm Development Authority of Singapore, 2012a). Various government agencies in Singapore have also received awards and/or high ranks for their online portals.

Critically, it is not about the awards and the high ranks which make Singapore's e-Government accepted and successful. It is the level of acceptance and satisfaction of users of e-Government that counts as the adoption of e-Government will depend on the public and political acceptability. About 80% of participants, both enterprises and individuals, in the e-Government Perception Survey 2006 were pleased with the quality of e-services (Infocomm Development Authority of Singapore, n. d.).

However, some have argued that the achievements of Singapore's e-Government are due to its small territorial size since "larger countries often face more diverse socio-economic conditions especially across urban and rural communities;" and thus they may have to deal with different issues associated with the utilization and development of e-Government (Department of Economic and Social Affairs Division for Public Administration and Development Management, 2008, p. 87). Although Singapore received relatively high scores for the two measures of e-Information and e-Consultation in 2008, the score for its e-Decision-making was only 18.75 out of 100. This may be interpreted that Singapore's e-Government has not reached the technical-matured level that can help users to make informed decisions (Department of Economic and Social Affairs Division for Public Administration and Development Management, 2008). Also, given the substantial proportion of the residents in Singapore are Muslim, Singapore may have to introduce e-Syariah to support the operations of Syariah courts, similar to what Malaysia's e-Government has offered (Ahmad, 2006).

Singapore can also learn from South Korea in terms of good practice in public administration via e-Government. A good example of accountability and transparency via the adoption of e-Government is the South Korea's Online Procedures Enhancement for Civil Application (OPEN) system. This system has demonstrated how corruption in the public sector can be mitigated via e-Government. Online discussion boards, Government Information Agency websites and Regulations.gov portal are some other good illustrations of how citizens can be engaged and participated via submission of their feedback and comments online (Schwester, 2009).

Critical Success Factors of E-Government in Singapore

Some factors affecting the success of an e-Government system have been identified by various authors, namely leadership, seamless government services, technical skills, citizen participation. PPPs, perception of risk, and monitoring and evaluation processes (McDaniel, 2003; OECD, 2003; Ahmad, 2006; Ching, 2009; Schwester, 2009; Alghamdi et al., 2011). In the case of Singapore, the following critical success factors have been identified and classified into four main groups, namely managerial, technical, financial and human behaviour factors.

Managerial Factors

Managerial aspects include visions, objectives, strategic planning, leadership, collaboration, and government networking. Vision, objectives and strategies are very important since the e-Government vision is driven by the unique social, political and economic factors and requirements of Singapore (Rabaiah & Vandijck, 2009). Vision and strategy must be articulated to gain public acceptability and support (OECD, 2003). The strategic objectives justify the huge resources invested in e-Government initiatives. Every amount of tax-payers counts as the approval of the parliament must be obtained to fund e-Government initiatives. Hence, the e-Government committee must strive to convince decision makers that investment in e-Government will reap huge benefits for the public and the nation. Justification of critical and strategic objectives of e-Government is the focus on user-orientation, and this is also one of the government's goals. These objectives affect the design of an e-Government framework (Rabaiah & Vandijck, 2009). The vision of Singapore's e-Government is to provide customer-focused e-services for the benefits of all users. Therefore, it has gained momentum, and gain political and public acceptability.

Regarding planning, strategic plans provide directions to develop e-Government from the current state to the desired state in the future (Lee, 2010). However, Ke and Wei (2006) explained that too much formal planning may be too rigid. Flexibility is needed as adjustments are necessary over the time as the project progresses. In Singapore, the master plans have been introduced and modified every three to five years, so that any changes in both internal and external environments can be incorporated in the new plans. E-Government master plans have been supported by several ICT plans. This aims to provide skills, knowledge to civil servants so that they can perform their tasks competently, and to build physical and social infrastructure for e-Government. In Singapore, the central agency with legitimate power and authority to develop the vision, to manage e-Government master plans and strategies has contributed to the success of its e-Government (Tan, Pan, & Cha, 2008)

Another critical successful variable of Singapore's e-Government is effective leadership since strong leadership can expedite the development and implementation process of e-Government (Cook et al., 2002; OECD, 2003; Suan, 2003). Committed and capable leaders make sure that "work is getting done correctly and leadership is needed to help identify the right things to do" in the right way (Streib & Navarro, 2008, p. 40). In Singapore, governmental agencies and competent leaders have closely worked with each other to cross traditional boundaries to improve the delivery of public services, and to meet the needs of the citizens. Governmental bodies have also communicated the vision of e-Government, and the benefits of e-Government adoption to other stakeholders via a number of campaigns and programs.

A clear framework to legalize e-transactions would facilitate the adoption of e-Government. Many countries, for instance the USA, Canada and Australia, have enacted legislation regarding information collection, storage, use and dissemination by government agencies, and how such information is shared with other agencies, the media and the citizenry. Although the legal framework in Singapore is clear, and enforcement mechanisms are stringent and effective, Singapore does not have any privacy laws, especially for e-transactions. However, the government of Singapore has been in the process to introduce new privacy law in the near future (Warkentin et al., 2002; Tan et al., 2008).

In addition, government should create a conducive environment to encourage coordination and collaboration within and between governmental agencies (Cook et al., 2002; Ha & Coghill, 2008; McDaniel, 2003). The benefit of collaboration is the sharing of information, good practices and experience between government agencies at different levels (Reddick, 2009). In the case of Singapore, many government agencies and statutory boards, such as Ministry of Trade and Finance and other ministries, the IDA, the then National Computer Board (NCB), the Inland Revenue Authority of Singapore (IRAS), the Central Provident Fund (CPF) board, NYP, etc. have been involved in the development and/or implementation of e-Government. The private sector has also been active in this aspect. For example, many private enterprises, namely *Ecquaria, Elixir Technology and Netrust*, have been engaged by government bodies and statutory boards to provide technical services. Inter-governmental and inter-sectoral collaboration is necessary for e-Government development due to the nature of cross-border of the online environment. The impact of collaboration among organisations includes efficient use and sharing resources, and avoidance of overlapped activities and processes by providing one-stop shops.

Technical Factors

Apart from service delivery, internal efficiency and government networking, one of the top focus areas of e-Government is the development of IT infrastructure (Rabaiah & Vandijck, 2009). IT Infrastructural development has taken a front seat in Singapore as public investments in IT infrastructure are intense, especially at the initial stage when technical development is extremely important to the diffusion of e-Government. A successful e-Government initiative requires that suitable IT infrastructures to support information systems and applications must be established before an e-Government program can be deployed. Many e-Government initiatives from developing countries fail due to being unable to establish a solid IT infrastructure for e-Government deployment (World Bank, 2006). IT infrastructure for e-Government includes hardware and software, the architecture models and the operations of e-Government systems, connectivity and accessibility, privacy and security (Tan et al., 2008; West, 2004).

Singapore has done well in this aspect by investing adequate resources to develop its technical foundation. For instance, *SQLView's* KRIS, an electronic registry system, has been deployed to enable various government institutions in different ministries and industries to create a world class e-Government structure (Infocomm Development Authority of Singapore, 2006). Singapore has enjoyed a healthy state of connectivity with 100.8% mobile phone penetration rate, and 82% of the households (2010) in Singapore have been connected to the Internet (Infocomm Development Authority of Singapore, 2012b). The extremely high mobile phone penetration percentage allows public services to be delivered not only via the Internet, but also via mobile phone. A good illustration is the launch of the mPAL service by the CPF. SMEs with fewer than 10 employees can submit their CPF contribution information via this service, using mobile phone (Bakry, 2004; Gilbert, Balestrini, & Littleboy, 2004; Tan et al., 2008).

In order to address the issue of accessibility to e-services, Singapore has introduced several IT training programs, including programs for senior citizens, to equip participants with necessary IT skills to go online (Tan et al., 2008). The government of Singapore has also introduced many training programs to civil servants, and foreign ICT professionals have been employed to mitigate the shortage of skilled manpower. Additionally, local universities and polytechnics have offered new ICT related courses, and ICT has been incorporated in the curriculums offered at public schools. New technical institutes, such as the German-Singapore Institute and the Japan-Singapore Institute, have been set up to train lower-level skilled IT technicians, while the Institute of Systems Science has been established to train high-ranked government officials and business senior executives in the usage of ICT (Tan et al., 2008).

An important critical successful construct of an e-Government architecture is security (Ha, 2011; Ha & Coghill, 2006). Users will go online if they are assured that their personal information is kept confidential and secure (Schwester, 2009). Government must take a holistic approach to ensure a secure online environment since "the political risks of security breaches in government are often perceived to be far more serious than proportionally similar risks in the private sector context" (Department of Economic and Social Affairs Division for Public Administration and Development Management, 2008, p. 89). The main reason is that government agencies are holding a significant amount of personal and sensitive information, and information relating to national security. Singapore has engaged three providers of IT security solutions to ensure the security of its e-Government infrastructure. They are *e-Cop, Frontline Solutions* and *Opus IT.* The first system, *e-Cop*, is a provider of security service to protect the Infocomm security of various government agencies against any potential cyber threats. *Frontline Solutions* provides security expertise to detect and control malware affecting the key desktop firewall of the public sector. *Opus IT* is a provider of forensics security solutions for networks. It can help client investigate security and policy breaches and enhance the network performance (Infocomm Development Authority of Singapore, 2006).

Financial Factors

Financial and human capital investments need to be adequate for e-Government to flourish. The development and maintenance of e-Government initiatives require both physical and social capitals, and thus sufficient funds must be available. Resources must also be allocated in a manner which can save tax-payers' money, and can help resource allocators achieve the set objectives (Enyon & Dutton, 2007).

The Singapore government has invested $2 billion to develop the iGov2010 master plan. This aimed to enhance the quality and capability of Singapore's e-Government and the Infocomm industry to create an integrated government which can meet citizens' demand and needs and can link up government with all groups of stakeholders (World Bank & National Institute of Education (NIE), 2008). Another $13.5 billion has also been spent on R&D activities via the Science and Technology 2010 plan (iN2015 Steering Committee, 2006). Apparently, adequate funds have been set aside to develop Singapore's e-Government and national Infocomm plans. This is critical for (i) the acquisition of the required and important ICT infrastructure, (ii) training and development of ICT professionals and employees in the public sectors in terms of ICTs knowledge and skills, (3) encouragement of technological innovations and creativity to produce new products and services to enhance e-Government applications and adoption, and (iv) provision of measures to close the digital divide for the groups of the residents who were marginalised from the implementation of e-Government (Tan et al., 2008).

Human Behavioural Factors

It is impossible for e-Government to thrive without the change in the mind-set of both providers (the public sector) and users. Human behavioural factors affecting the success of e-Government initiatives encompass the level of citizen trust to the government and to technology, the perceived ease of use and usefulness of e-Government, the level of awareness of the benefits and problems with the adoption of e-services, and the acceptability of e-Government as a new platform to deliver public services (Steyaert, 2004; Tan et al., 2008).

First of all, government is considered a monopolist in the country in terms of delivery of public services via e-Government, and thus it is critical for citizens to trust the ICT systems and the integrity of governmental agencies adopting e-Government (Teo et al., 2008). Due to the intensive inter-governmental competition and the urge for an increase in productivity and cost-effectiveness, some governmental agencies may implement e-Government initiatives in a manner that boosts operational effectiveness and efficiency at the expense of transparency, accountability and social embracement inclusion (Grimsley & Meehan, 2007). In order to subdue the effects of such technological and socio-political impediments to e-Government, it is necessary to build public trust in e-Governments (Bélanger & Carter 2008).

The government has initiated a number of educational and training programs which cater to the needs of various groups of users. For example, IDA has launched the Silver Infocomm Initiative and other programs to close the gaps in digital divide among senior citizens aged 50 and above since 2007 (Infocomm Development Authority of Singapore, 2012c) Such programs aim to educate senior citizens on how to use the computer, access to the Internet and obtain public services online. IRAS has deployed volunteers to different locations in order to assist tax-payers with tax e-filing (Alkhatib, 2012). Generally, the government has tried to promote e-Government and encourage citizens to receive public services and to communicate with government agencies via the online portals.

In Singapore, the tax *E-filing* system launched by the IRAS has received overwhelming responses with 62% (or 961,806) of the tax-payers submitting their income statements online in 2010 (Inland Revenue Authority of Singapore, 2010). Companies have also e-filled their returns. The auto-inclusion scheme has been supported by 6,576 organizations (11% of all companies in Singapore) (Inland Revenue Authority of Singapore, 2010). This successful E-Filing system provides better insights into how a statutory board has exploited ICTs via e-Government to advance a trusting relationship between government agencies and their customers (Lim et al., 2011). Trust will enhance the level of public acceptance of e-Government as a new channel of communication with government, and a new form of receipt of public services.

The way the websites of governmental agencies is designed and the navigation of government websites also affect user acceptability. For example, the CPF board has introduced CPF e-Withdrawal portal which allows senior citizens above 55 years old to manage their money contributed to the CPF online. They can transfer the money withdrawn from their CPF account to their bank accounts directly and electronically. The interface of this portal has several user-friendly features for senior citizens. For examples, the font size is large, there are many colours to make the navigation easy, and the buttons are placed in locations where they are easy to see (Phang et al., 2006). Hence, senior users do not mind trying to access the information, and to conduct transactions online.

Policy Recommendations

The above critical success factors can be classified into two main groups, namely demand side and supply side. The demand side refers to public awareness and the willingness of citizens to adopt e-services due to trust to e-Government and acceptability of the availability and benefits of e-services. The supply side includes vision, strategies, leadership commitment, the extent to which government agencies collaborate and work with each other, technical infrastructure, and resources, which are required during the preparation, development and implementation stages. From the above critical success factors, a number of policy recommendations to enhance the effectiveness and efficiency of e-Government are discussed in Table 1.

The supply side must be stimulated, developed and advanced to meet the on-going changing external environment. Firstly, vision, objectives

Table 1. Critical success factors of e-government in Singapore and policy recommendations

Determinants	Sub-determinants	Policy recommendations
Managerial	Vision, objectives	Clearly set mission, vision, objectives and time frame
	Strategic planning	Adopt an approach of advance and long-term planning
	Leadership commitment	Demonstrate strong leadership commitment and competency
	Collaboration, coordination and networking	Encourage collaboration, coordination and networking among government agencies, and between the public sector with other sectors
Technical	Technical infrastructure Technical development	Invest in infrastructure Ensure reliable and secure networks Invest in training and development Provide low cost access to the Internet
	Security	Provide measures to ensure security in the online environment Provide training to enhance public awareness of online incidents and how to deal with such incidents
Financial	Resources	Have available resources Encourage public-private partnerships
Human behavioural	Mind-set	Enhance public awareness and willingness to adopt e-Government via public education Provide information about the benefits of adoption of e-Government
	Trust in government and user acceptability	Enhance trust via timely and accurate information and friendly-user websites Encourage citizen participation

Source: By the author

and strategies of e-Government initiatives must be clearly set to provide directions for development and implementation of such initiatives. There must be clear development directions and focuses of each stage. Guiding principles define the general themes of e-Government projects. The most common guiding principles of e-Government are efficiency and active participation from the constituents. Achieving internal efficiency is the core of a responsive government which endeavours to provide improved public services. Secondly, political leaders must demonstrate strong leadership commitment to invest in e-Government in order to enhance the relationship between government and citizens. Thirdly, government should encourage collaboration, coordination and networking among government agencies, and between the public sector with other sectors. E-Government should be treated as a whole system where all parts of the system must function simultaneously in order to achieve the set objectives. Coordination and collaboration will help operators avoid duplication of activities and waste of scare resources.

In terms of technical factors, an e-Government project cannot be deployed successfully without the basic infrastructure. Also, government should invest in training and development to equip operators and users with technical skills and knowledge to manage the implementation of e-Government.

For instance, Singapore's e-Government has been developed via three stages. In the initial stage, e-users can access government information online. The flow of information is uni-linear from government to users, and there is no or very little interaction between government and OGS in the online platform. In the second stage, e-users can conduct transactions with government via online portals. The principal mechanisms for interaction are mainly one-stop business services and one-stop shops for citizens to receive public services online. This fits into the first model of interaction in e-Government discussed by Chadwick and May (2003), i.e. a managerial model. The key defining logic is to deliver public services and present policy. In this stage, Singapore has focused on digitalized as many public services as possible in order to achieve effective and efficient government. In the third stage, the nucleus of e-Government development is to improve the quality of e-services via technical accuracy.

Overall, in the preparation stage, provision of infrastructure, availability and allocation of resources, and raising IT and Internet awareness are imperative (Yong, 2003). In the development stage, institutions must be in place to administer the operations of e-Government system, and governments should keep the costs of e-Government adoption and development affordable. In the implementation stage, government agencies need to make the delivery of e-services more attractive than the conventional physical means, for example, visiting the office of a government department, so that citizens will switch to use e-services (Yong, 2003). Information is not static, and the acquisition of information and knowledge is a dynamic process. Thus, information must be frequently updated on government's websites.

In order to encourage citizens to receive public services and interact with the public sector online, government should provide measures to ensure security in the online environment. The provision of fast, reliable and secure nation-wide network would facilitate the adoption of e-Government. Government should also work with relevant groups of stakeholders to provide training programs to enhance public awareness of online incidents and how to deal with such incidents. If citizens are confident with the online platform, they would actively adopt e-services.

Referring to financial factors, physical and social capital must be available and frequently upgraded to ensure technology is not obsolete, and e-Government can help the public sector to meet the requirements of future trends of governance and public administration. R&D can help government agencies and enterprises to fulfil this task. Yet, R&D activities are usually costly, and it requires a huge amount of capital to invest in e-Government initiatives.

Government agencies can collaborate with private sector, such as Internet providers, to work out a solution for affordable broadband and/or wireless packages to individual and business users so that everybody can have access to the Internet whenever they need. Private Internet providers may not have sufficient capabilities to invest in technology, infrastructure and human capital, and thus PPPs (public-private partnerships) would help to address this issue. Government should engage all groups of stakeholders in different stages of e-Government development since e-users can play the role of promoters of e-Government if they perceive e-services are good, cost-effective, speedy and secure.

For example, Thailand launched the 'People's PC' campaign in May 2003 to facilitate the ownership of PC at an affordable price. The 'Used-PC' project is another initiative by the Thai government which allows people to trade-in their old PCs for new ones. The old PCs are then redistributed to schools in different provinces nationwide (Young, 2003). In India, all computers have been exempted from excise duty which encourages individuals to own a computer so that they can go online (Yong, 2003).

Regarding the demand side, to address the factors relating to human behaviour, the following suggestions are proposed to change users' mindset and to enhance public acceptability and trust in e-Government. Although the current research indicates a positive outlook for e-services, it should not be mistakenly concluded that everyone is interested and willing to use online services. Citizens may be ignorant of the available options for doing things besides the traditional ways.

Citizens may also doubt the security of making transactions online (Rabaiah & Vandijck, 2009). Thus, governments should have policies and practices in place to stimulate the demand side. The level of awareness of users of e-services can be enhanced through various promotional campaigns and educational programs. Educational initiatives by both the public and private sectors can also help participants acquire necessary IT skills. Public communication is vital since it helps to alleviate any public concerns associated with security and privacy in the online environment (Yong, 2003). Promotion of local language content and development applications in local languages would enable citizens to adopt e-services, especially senior citizens and those who cannot read and write in English (Yong, 2003). Information about the benefits of adoption of e-Government should be widely and timely diffused via various communication channels, including social media.

In addition, trust is an important factor in the demand side to promote the adoption of e-services. In order to build trust with stakeholders, information and services available on governmental agencies' websites must be accurate, easy to be navigated and used. The following measures can be employed to enhance the level of public trust, namely, (i) engagement of all groups of stakeholders (Azad & Faraj, 2008; Chan & Pan, 2008), (ii) establishment of performance benchmarks and measurements (e.g., Irani et al., 2008), (iii) encouragement of intra- and inter-organizational acceptance and support (Gupta, Dasgupta, & Guptac, 2008), (iv) ensuring service interoperability across various governmental agencies at all levels (Gil-Garcia, Chengalur-Smith, & Duchessi, 2007), and (v) nurturing a corporate environment that enables and promotes organizational learning and creativity (Moon & Norris, 2005; Phang, Kankanalli, & Ang, 2008). Regarding citizen participation, the return of investment of e-Government is to the enhancement of government-citizen relationship via better connection, improvement of democracy via citizen engagement. Another important variable in the supply side is universal access, as investment in cutting edge technology is not worthy if only a few can access its benefits (Rabaiah & Vandijck, 2009). Hence, e-Government deployment should benefit as many users as possible.

FUTURE RESEARCH DIRECTIONS

The public sector needs to guard against the trap of implementing e-Government for the sake of fashion in new public management, i.e. "deploying the latest tools, solutions or services simply because the technology is available or because other economies are doing it" (Yong, 2003, p. 7). E-Government deployment must achieve its objectives, which can improve the delivery of public services, meet the needs of citizens and enhance public participation. In the case of Singapore, the social, economic, technological and cultural conditions together with the legal framework have facilitated the implementation of e-Government and contributed to the success of e-Government initiatives. Thus, the above critical success factors may apply only to Singapore and/or to other city-states where the political, socio-economic and technical conditions are similar to those in Singapore. The critical success factors of e-Government may be different in other countries where the social conditions and legal frameworks are different from those in Singapore. Hence, an e-Government system must be modified to suit the contingencies of the country where it is adopted. The future directions of research should focus on (i) other critical success factors of e-Government in different contexts, and (ii) how different models of e-Government can be applied to different countries where political, socio-economic, technological, legal and environmental conditions are different.

CONCLUSION

This chapter has discussed the state of e-Government in Singapore. It has examined Singapore's e-Government framework, including the master plans, institutional arrangements and implementation mechanisms. The Singaporean government has developed e-Government to enhance the delivery of information and public services to citizens, businesses, civil servants and other governments. As of now, more than 1,700 public services have been delivered online. E-Government in Singapore has gained popularity and public acceptability due to efficient and effective e-services.

Determinants affecting the success of e-Government in Singapore include clear vision and strategic plans, leadership commitment and competency, adequate funds and physical resources, well-prepared human capital. In other words, Singapore has successfully implemented e-Government due to clear vision and objectives, clear and forward strategies, strong leadership commitment, adequate financial resources, investment in advanced technology and infrastructure. The adoption rate of e-Government in Singapore is high due to public awareness of and experience in the benefits of e-Government via educational and training campaigns. Nevertheless, a number of shortcomings of Singapore's e-Government have been identified. They are technical immature in the degree of public participation in e-decision making, insufficient online services catering to different groups of citizens, and lack of content in local language. In other words, Singapore still has to improve the delivery of e-services in order to meet the needs of its citizens, businesses, and civil servants.

This chapter has also made several policy recommendations on how to improve the performance of an e-Government system. It is essential that all groups of stakeholders have to collaborate to promote the availability, affordability and benefits of e-services, and to enhance public awareness of e-Government. Yet, the future of e-Government development and deployment in a country depends on many external and internal conditions.

REFERENCES

Ahmad, M. B. H. J. (2006). Implementation of electronic government in Malaysia: The status and potential for better service to the public. *Public Sector ICT Management Review*, *1*(1), 1–9.

Alghamdi, I. A., Goodwin, R., & Rampersad, S. (2011). E-government readiness assessment for government organizations in developing countries. *Computer and Information Science*, *4*(3), 3–17. doi:10.5539/cis.v4n3p3.

Alkhatib, S. (2012). IRAS says 78% of taxpayers have filed tax returns. Retrieved September 14, 2012, from http://www.channelnewsasia.com/stories/singaporelocalnews/view/1050329/1/.html

Angelopoulos, S., Kitsios, F., & Papadopoulos, T. (2010). New service development in e-government: Identifying critical success factors. *Transforming Government: People. Process and Policy*, *1*(1), 95–118.

Azad, B., & Faraj, S. (2008). Making e-government workable: Exploring the evolution of frames. *The Journal of Strategic Information Systems*, *17*(1), 75–98. doi:10.1016/j.jsis.2007.12.001.

Bakry, S. H. (2004). Development of e-Government: A STOPE view. *International Journal of Network Management*, *14*(5), 339–350. doi:10.1002/nem.529.

Baum, S., Yigitcanlar, T., Mahizhnan, A., & Andiappan, N. (2006). Singapore government online: A consideration of e-government outcomes. *Journal of E-Government*, *3*(4), 65–84. doi:10.1300/J399v03n04_04.

Baum, S., Yigitcanlar, T., Mahizhnan, A., & Andiappan1, N. (n.d.). ICTs and e-governance in Singapore. Retrieved March 14, 2012, from http://unpan1.un.org/intradoc/groups/public/documents/un-dpadm/unpan043267.pdf

Bélanger, F., & Carter, L. (2008). Trust and risk in e-government adoption. *The Journal of Strategic Information Systems*, *17*(2), 165–176. doi:10.1016/j.jsis.2007.12.002.

Bonham, G., Seifert, J., & Thorson, S. (2001). *The transformational potential of e-government: At the role of political leadership*. Paper read at the 4th Pan European International Relations Conference, University of Kent.

Chadwick, A., & May, C. (2003). Interaction between states and citizens in the age of the internet: "e-Government" in the United States, Britain, and the European Union. *Governance: An International Journal of Policy, Administration and Institutions*, *16*(2), 271–30. doi:10.1111/1468-0491.00216.

Chan, C. M. L., & Pan, S. L. (2008). User engagement in e-government systems implementation: A comparative case study of two Singaporean e-government initiatives. *The Journal of Strategic Information Systems*, *17*(2), 124–139. doi:10.1016/j.jsis.2007.12.003.

Chen, Y. C., & Knepper, R. (2005). Digital government development strategies. Lessons for policy makers from a comparative perspective. In Huang, W., Siau, K., & Kwok, K. W. (Eds.), *Electronic government strategies and implementation* (pp. 394–420). Hershey, PA: Idea Group Publishing.

Ching, Y. L. S. (2009). The impact of leadership and stakeholders on the success/failure of e-government service: Using the case study of e-stamping service in Hong Kong. *Government Information Quarterly*, *26*, 594–604. doi:10.1016/j.giq.2009.02.009.

Chung, M. K. (2007). *Singapore e-government experience*. Paper presented at Asia e- Government Forum 2007, 20 September 2007, Seoul, Korea.

Cook, M. E., LaVigne, M. F., Pagano, C. M., Dawes, S. S., & Pardo, T. A. (2002). *Making a case for local e-government*. Retrieved April 26, 2007, from http://www.ctg.albany.edu/ publications/guides/making_a_case/making_a_case.pdf

Council for Excellence in Governance. (2001). *E-Government, the next American revolution*. Washington, DC: Council for Excellence in Governance.

Coursey, D., & Norris, D. (2008). Models of e-Government: Are they correct? An empirical assessment. *PAR*, *68*, 523–536.

Department of Economic and Social Affairs Division for Public Administration and Development Management. (2008). *United Nations e-government survey 2008: From e-Government to Connected Governance*. New York: United Nations.

Dutta, S., & Mia, I. (2011). *Global information technology*. Geneva: World Economic Forum.

Ebrahim, Z., & Irani, Z. (2005). E-government adoption: Architecture and barriers. *Business Management Process*, *11*(5), 589–611. doi:10.1108/14637150510619902.

Enyon, R., & Dutton, W. H. (2007). Barriers to networked governments: Evidence from Europe. *Prometheus*, *25*(3), 225–242. doi:10.1080/08109020701531361.

Evans, D., & Yen, D. C. (2006). E-government: Evolving relationship of citizens and government, domestic, and international development. *Government Information Quarterly*, *23*(2), 207–235. doi:10.1016/j.giq.2005.11.004.

Gil-Garcia, J. R., Chengalur-Smith, I., & Duchessi, P. (2007). Collaborative e-government: Impediments and benefits of information sharing projects in the public sector. *European Journal of Information Systems*, *16*(2), 121–133. doi:10.1057/palgrave.ejis.3000673.

Gilbert, D., Balestrini, P., & Littleboy, D. (2004). Barriers and benefits in the adoption of e-government. *International Journal of Public Sector Management*, *17*(4), 286–301. doi:10.1108/09513550410539794.

Grimsley, M., & Meehan, A. (2007). E-government information systems: Evaluation-led design for public value and client trust. *European Journal of Information Systems*, *16*(2), 134–148. doi:10.1057/palgrave.ejis.3000674.

Gupta, B., Dasgupta, S., & Guptac, A. (2008). Adoption of ICT in a government organization in a developing country: An empirical study. *The Journal of Strategic Information Systems*, *17*(2), 140–154. doi:10.1016/j.jsis.2007.12.004.

Ha, H. (2011). Security and privacy in e-consumer protection in Victoria, Australia. In Wakeman, I. et al. (Eds.), *IFIPTM 2011, IFIP AICT 358* (pp. 240–252). Berlin, Heidelberg: Springer-Verlag. doi:10.1007/978-3-642-22200-9_19.

Ha, H. (2012). A new SWOT analysis of e-government systems in Singapore. In C-P., Rueckemann (Ed.), Integrated information and computing systems for natural, spatial, and social sciences (pp. 75-96). USA: IGI Global.

Ha, H., & Coghill, K. (2006). E-government in Singapore: A SWOT and PEST analysis. [APSSR]. *Asia-Pacific Social Science Review*, *6*(2), 103–130.

Ha, H., & Coghill, K. (2008). Online shoppers in Australia: Dealing with problems. *International Journal of Consumer Studies*, *32*(1), 5–17.

Heeks, R. (2005). e-Government as a career of context. *Journal of Public Policy*, *25*, 51–74. doi:10.1017/S0143814X05000206.

Hermana, B., & Sulfianti, W. (2011). Evaluating e-government implementation by local government: Digital divide in internet-based public services in Indonesia. *International Journal of Business and Social Sciences*, *2*(30), 156–163.

iN2015 Steering Committee. (2006). *Innovation. Integration. Internationalisation*. Singapore: Infocomm Development Authority of Singapore.

Infocomm Development Authority of Singapore. (2006). *Singapore: A world class e-government*. Singapore: Singapore Government.

Infocomm Development Authority of Singapore. (2010). *Realising the iN2015 vision. Singapore: An intelligent nation, a global city, powered by Infocomm*. Singapore: Singapore Government.

Infocomm Development Authority of Singapore. (2011). *Singapore eGov: Connecting people – enriching lives*. Singapore: Singapore Government.

Infocomm Development Authority of Singapore. (2012a). *Accolades and awards*. Singapore: Singapore Government.

Infocomm Development Authority of Singapore. (2012b). *Singapore Infocomm statistics at a glance*. Retrieved March 22, 2012, from http://www.ida.gov.sg/Publications/20061130175201.aspx

Infocomm Development Authority of Singapore. (2012c). *Factsheet: Silver Infocomm Initiative*. Singapore: Infocomm Development Authority of Singapore.

Infocomm Development Authority of Singapore. (n.d.). *Singapore's e-Government journey*. Singapore: Singapore Government.

Inland Revenue Authority of Singapore (IRAS). (2010). *Annual report 2009/10*. Singapore: Singapore Government.

Irani, Z., Love, P. E. D., Elliman, T., & Jones, S. (2008). Learning lessons from evaluating eGovernment: Reflective case experiences that support transformational government. *The Journal of Strategic Information Systems*, *17*(2), 155–164. doi:10.1016/j.jsis.2007.12.005.

Ke, W., & Wei, K. K. (2006). Understanding e-government project management: A positivist case study of Singapore. *Journal of Global Information Technology Management*, *1*(2), 45–61.

Koh, C. E., Ryan, S., & Prybutok, V. R. (2005). Creating value through managing knowledge in an e-government to constituency (G2C) environment. *Journal of Computer Information Systems*, *45*, 32–41.

Latre, M. A., Lopez-Pellicer, F. J., Nogueras-Iso, J., B'ejar, R., & Muro-Medrano, P. R. (2010). Facilitating e-government services through SDIs, an Application for Water Abstractions Authorizations. In Andersen, K. N., Francesconi, E., Grönlund, A., & van Engers, T. M. (Eds.), *Electronic government and the information systems perspective. Verlag* (pp. 108–119). Berlin, Heidelberg: Springer. doi:10.1007/978-3-642-15172-9_11.

Lee, Y. N. (2010). *E-government application*. UN-APCICT. Retrieved March 10, 2012, from http://www.unapcict.org/academy

Lim, L., & Koh, A. (2008). *The acceleration of SOA adoption in Singapore: Challenges and issues*. Paper read at The 19th Australasian Conference on Information Systems, 3-5 Dec 2008, Christchurch.

Lim, T. K. E., Tan, C-W., Cyr, D., Pan, S. L., & Xiao, B. (2011). Advancing public trust relationships in electronic government: The Singapore e-filing journey. *Information Systems Research*, Article in Advance, 1-21.

McDaniel, E. M. (2003). Facilitating cross-boundary leadership in emerging e-government leaders. IS2003 Proceedings. *Informing Science*.

McNamara, K. S. (2003). *Information and communication technologies, poverty and development: Learning from experience*. A Background Paper for the infoDev Annual Symposium December 9-10, 2003, Geneva, Switzerland. Washington, DC: The World Bank.

Moon, J. M., & Norris, D. F. (2005). Does managerial orientation matter? The adoption of reinventing government and e-government at the municipal level. *Information Systems Journal*, *15*(1), 43–60. doi:10.1111/j.1365-2575.2005.00185.x.

Ndou, V. (2004). E-government for developing countries: Opportunities and challenges. *Electronic Journal of Information Systems in Developing Countries*, *18*, 1–24.

Ojo, A., Janowski, T., Estevez, E., & Khan, I. K. (2007). *Human capacity development for e-government*. UNU-IIST Report No. 362 T. Yokyo: United Nations University, International Institute for Software Technology.

Organization for Economic Co-operation and Development (OECD). (2003). *Checklist for e-Government leaders*. Paris: OECD.

Phang, C. W., Kankanalli, A., & Ang, C. (2008). Investigating organizational learning in egovernment projects: A multi-theoretic approach. *The Journal of Strategic Information Systems*, *17*(2), 99–123. doi:10.1016/j.jsis.2007.12.006.

Phang, C. W., Sutanto, J., Kankanhalli, A., Li, Y., Tan, B. C. Y., & Teo, H. H. (2006). Senior citizens' acceptance of information systems: A study in the context of e-government services. *IEEE Transactions on Engineering Management*, *53*(4), 555–569. doi:10.1109/TEM.2006.883710.

Prananto, A., & McKemmish, S. (2007). *Critical success factors for the establishment of e-government*. RISO Working Paper. Melbourne, Victoria: Faculty of Information and Communication Technologies, Swinburne University of Technology.

Rabaiah, A., & Vandijck, E. (2009). A strategic framework of e-government: Generic and best practice. *Electronic. Journal of E-Government*, *7*(3), 241–258.

Rashid, N., & Rahman, S. (2010). An investigation into critical determinants of e-government implementation in the context of a developing nation. In K. N. Andersen, Francesconi, E., Grönlund, A., & van Engers, T. M. (Eds.), Electronic government and the information systems perspective (pp. 9-21). Verlag, Berlin and Heidelberg: Springer.

Reddick, C. G. (2009). Factors that explain the perceived effectiveness of e-government: A survey of United States city government information technology directors. *International Publication of Electronic Government Research*, *5*(2), 1–15. doi:10.4018/jegr.2009040101.

Rotchanakitumnuai, S. (2008). Measuring e-government service value with the E-GOVSQUAL-RISK model. *Business Process Management Journal*, *14*(5), 724–737. doi:10.1108/14637150810903075.

Schwester, R. W. (2009). Examining the barriers to e-government adoption. *Electronic. Journal of E-Government*, *7*(1), 113–122.

Shailendra, C., Palvia, J., & Sharma, S. S. (2007). E-government and e-governance: Definitions/domain framework and status around the world. In Agarwal, A., & Ramana, V. V. (Eds.), *Foundations of E-government* (pp. 1–12). India: Computer Society of India.

Sharma, S., & Gupta, J. (2002). *Transforming to e-government: A framework*. Paper presented at the 2nd European Conference on E-Government, Public Sector Times (pp. 383-390). 1-2 Oct 2002, St. Catherine's College Oxford, United Kingdom.

Singapore Ministry of Finance and Infocomm Development Authority of Singapore. (2001). *E-government 2001: Accelerating, integrating, transforming public services*. Singapore: Singapore Government.

Singh, S. H. (2003). Government in the digital era and human factors in e-governance. Paper read the Regional Workshop on e-Government, 1-3 Dec 2003, Sana'a.

Sipior, J., & Ward, B. (2005). Bridging the digital divide for e-Government inclusion: A United States Case Study. *The Electronic. Journal of E-Government*, *3*(3), 137–146.

Steyaert, J. C. (2004). Measuring the performance of electronic government services. *Information & Management*, *41*(3), 369–375. doi:10.1016/S0378-7206(03)00025-9.

Streib, G., & Navarro, I. (2008). City managers and e-government development: Assessing technology literacy and leadership needs. *Journal of Electronic Government Research*, *4*(4), 37–53. doi:10.4018/jegr.2008100103.

Suan, B. H. (2003). Making e-governance happen—a practitioner's perspective. In Yong, J. S. L. (Ed.), *Enabling public service innovation in the 21st century: e-Government in Asia* (pp. 366–391). Singapore: Times Editions.

Tan, B. C. C., Pan, S. L., & Cha, V. (2008). The evolution of Singapore's government Infocomm plans: Singapore's e-government journey from 1980 to 2007. Singapore: Singapore eGovernment Leadership Centre and School of Computing, National University of Singapore.

Tapscott, D. (2009). *Grown up digital: How the net generation is changing your world*. New York: McGraw-Hill.

Teo, T. S. H., Srivastava, S. C., & Jiang, L. (2009). Trust and electronic government success: An empirical study. *Journal of Management Information Systems*, *25*(3), 99–131. doi:10.2753/MIS0742-1222250303.

United Nations Department of Economic and Social Affairs. (2012). *United Nations e-government survey 2012: E-government for the people*. New York: United Nations.

United Nations Public Administration Network. (n.d.). United Nations e-government survey 2010 special awards. New York: United Nations.

Vintar, M., Kunstelj, M., Decman, M., & Bercic, M. (2003). Development of e-government in Slovenia. *Information Polity*, *8*, 133–149.

Warkentin, M., Gefen, D., Pavlou, P. A., & Rose, G. M. (2002). Encouraging citizen adoption of e-government by building trust. *Electronic Markets*, *12*(3), 157–162. doi:10.1080/101967802320245929.

Wescott, D. (2004). E-government and the transformation of service delivery and citizen attitudes. *Public Administration Review*, *64*(1), 15–27. doi:10.1111/j.1540-6210.2004.00343.x.

West, D. M. (2004). Equity and accessibility in e-Government: A policy perspective. *Journal of E-Government*, *1*(2), 31–43. doi:10.1300/J399v01n02_03.

Wong, P., & Cha, V. (2009). *The evolution of government Infocomm plans: Singapore's e-government journey (1980 – 2007)*. Singapore: Institute of Systems Science, National University of Singapore.

World Bank. (2006). *Information and communications for development 2006: Global trends and policies*. Washington, DC: The World Bank.

World Bank. (2011). *Definition of e-government*. Retrieved September 14, 2012, from http://web.worldbank.org/wbsite/external/topics/extinformationandcommunicationandtechnologies/extegovernment/0,contentMDK:20507153~menuPK:702592~pagePK:148956~piPK:216618~theSitePK:702586,00.html

World Bank and National Institute of Education (NIE). (2008). *Toward a better future: Education and training for economic development in Singapore since 1965*. Washington, DC: The International Bank for Reconstruction and Development/The World Bank.

Yong, J. S. L. (2003). *Enabling public service innovation in the 21st century: e-Government in Asia*. Singapore: Times Editions.

Zheng, D., Chen, J., Huang, L., & Zhang, C. (2012). E-government adoption in public administration organizations: Integrating institutional theory perspective and resource-based view. *European Journal of Information Systems* (Advance online publication 19 June 2012).

ADDITIONAL READINGS

Das, J., DiRienzo, C., & Burbridge, J. (2009). Global e-government and the role of trust: A cross country analysis. *International Journal of Electronic Government Research*, *5*(1), 1–18. doi:10.4018/jegr.2009010101.

Kannabiran, G., Xavier, M. J., & Banumathi, T. (2008). E-governance and ICT enabled rural development in developing countries: Critical lessons from RASI project in India. *International Journal of Electronic Government Research*, *4*(3), 1–19. doi:10.4018/jegr.2008070101.

Li, H., Detenber, B. H., Lee, W. P., & Chia, S. (2004). E-government in Singapore: Demographics, usage patterns, and perceptions. *Journal of E-Government*, *1*(3), 29–54. doi:10.1300/J399v01n03_03.

Wahid, F. (2011). Explaining history of e-government implementation in developing countries: An analytical framework. *International Federation for Information Processing*, *6848*, 38–49.

KEY TERMS AND DEFINITIONS

Citizen Engagement: The degree of involvement of citizens in public affairs and the inputs from citizens in the policy making process.

E-Government: The provision of public services and diffusion of government information to stakeholders through various electronic means, mainly the Internet.

E-Government System: A system adopting ICT applications in an integrated manner to deliver public services and to allow multi-way communication between various groups of stakeholders and government.

E-Participation: The level of involvement of citizens in country affairs and in the decision making process via electronic means.

E-Services: Public services which are delivered through electronic means.

Public Trust: The degree of trust and confidence which citizens have in the public sector as a result of effective governance and pubic administration.

Singapore: A republic country in Southeast Asia, a small nation with limited natural and human resources.

Chapter 10
Users' Experiences of Internet-Based Systems in Malaysian Research Universities:
Success Factors and Barriers as Starting Points to Best Practices in a Developing Country

Mohd Azul Mohamad Salleh
The National University of Malaysia, Malaysia

ABSTRACT

Internet-based systems are providing more interactive and collaborative forms of participation in many kinds of organizations, particularly with the spread of the Internet and Web 2.0 technology. They have been designed to enhance organizational communications processes, information management and staff interaction. This qualitative study explores employees' experiences in Malaysian research universities, and particularly strives to understand successes and problems in the implementation of Internet-based systems. Based on in-depth interviews with officers and academics at four research universities, the study found that employees were most concerned with three issues that determined success or failure in this scenario: technological features of the systems; social and human factors; and organizational initiatives. Organizations such as universities and senior management may improve employees' satisfaction with Internet-based systems as e-government applications by implementing several recommendations arising from this study's analysis.

DOI: 10.4018/978-1-4666-4173-0.ch010

Copyright © 2013, IGI Global. Copying or distributing in print or electronic forms without written permission of IGI Global is prohibited.

INTRODUCTION

The public and private sectors have realised the importance of using information and communication technology (ICT). The use of Internet-based systems has been significant in ensuring more flexible and efficient forms of communication and organizational management. This chapter discusses the successes and challenges in using Internet-based systems as experienced by employees at four research universities in Malaysia. The Malaysian government encourages the country's universities to use ICT and online systems to improve the effectiveness and efficiency of their services, and to close the communication gaps between faculties and departments, and provide quicker information services. For example, in order to support the implementation of ICT, the Malaysian government has allocated an ICT-specific budget outlay as part of the Malaysian National Plan and the Country's Annual Budget (Kaliannan, Raman, & Dorasamy, 2009).

Internet-based systems have grown exponentially in universities due to the government implementing ICT-related policies and a strategic plan, such as the Multimedia Super Corridor (MSC) in 1996 (Hashim, 2008). The most heavily promoted project under MSC is e-government which aims to accelerate ICT development by focusing on the digital environment in terms of government-to-government and government-to-public communication (Abdullah, Kaliannan, Mohamed Ali, & Bakar, 2006). It is important to implement and develop Internet-based systems because the e-government platform intends to transform the way that government agencies operate and deliver better services. The objective of raising Malaysia's national profile means developing an information society that understands the basics of: interoperability, better information sharing, and collaborating internationally with other organizations or countries.

In order to transform Malaysia's higher education institutions into better functioning organizations, the Ministry of Higher Education (MOHE) is playing an important role in creating innovative communities and workplaces. According to Othman, Ismail and Md Raus (2009), the implementation of online systems in universities is important for improving the management and use of data, information and records. In order to implement these, the research universities should design their strategic plans so that they include electronic governance systems and e-government applications that are 'world class' and allow Malaysia's premier universities to be internationally competitive (Hadi, Jelas, Mokhtar, & Abdul Aziz, 2002).

Internet-based systems or applications in research universities now incorporate important web technologies that manage and distribute information to their staff, students and other stakeholders. This type of online system is designed not only to share information and make collaboration between stakeholders in research universities possible, but functions to support the implementation of e-government flagship in Malaysia. It is important for the research universities to continue using Internet-based systems in managing information and resources so that their performance and productivity is enhanced and makes the education sector competitive. In addition, from the e-government perspective, Internet-based systems are also important in reconnecting citizens to government agencies in order to change the way governments communicate with their citizens (Schwester, 2009).

This chapter discusses the findings based on a qualitative research study of employees at four pioneer research universities in Malaysia, incorporating in-depth interviews with academic and officer personnel. It emerges that these employees are concerned with three issues: systems' technological features, social and human factors, and organizational initiatives in using Internet-based systems. In order to succeed in the democratization of information exchange and communication in higher education, especially universities, the current study suggests significant solutions to improve end users' perceptions and satisfaction in using the systems. Therefore, I employ the ideas generated in this case study to develop recommendations for enhancing and supporting the Malaysian government's implementation of Internet-based systems as e-government platforms.

BACKGROUND

In order to become 'world class' higher education institutions and to develop a knowledge-based society by 2020, the Malaysian government established four research universities in 2006 (Mohd Majzub, 2008): University of Malaya (UM), University Science Malaysia (USM), The National University of Malaysia (UKM), and University Putra Malaysia (UPM). In 2010, a fifth university, University Technology Malaysia (UTM), was also designated as a research university. According to Mohd Majzub (2008) these universities were selected because they already excel in teaching and learning, research activities and academic publications. This higher education transformation plan is an important initiative to create innovative academic communities of practices, to produce smart human capital for the nation and to enhance the higher education sector in Malaysia. As a research university, each institution must use information technology to execute administrative tasks in order to improve the acquisition of data and information exchange (Othman, Ismail, & Md Raus, 2009). This will help them obtain a competitive advantage (Un Jan & Contreras, 2011) in the global education industry.

Furthermore, the Malaysian government also encourages its public agencies to use ICT applications in order to modernise their delivery systems (Salman, 2009), transform the way people work, and develop a knowledge-based economy and society (Abdul Karim, 1999). To date ICT in Malaysia has witnessed tremendous growth and this is because of the deliberate government policy and program of developing e-government platform (Abdul Karim & Mohd Khalid, 2003). In government agencies, the use of e-government applications is needed to improve communication and support information distribution and marketing of services in order to enhance their strategic goals (Mohamed, Hussin, & Hussein, 2009).

The earliest steps taken in employing e-government initiative in Malaysia came with the launch of the National IT Council (NITC) and National IT Agenda (NITA) in 1996 (Kit Siang, 2001). These strategic plans were important in reinforcing the initiatives so that the master plan for developing a national information technology system could transform the country into one comprising ICT-based businesses, services and industries (Hashim, 2008). A main pillar of the master plan is the MSC which has seven flagship applications (Abdul Karim, 1999), whereby e-government is the most important project undertaken for creating government agency-operated Internet-based systems. The ultimate goal of the e-government applications is to support collaboration between citizens with government agencies or across government agencies (Mohamed, Hussin, & Hussein, 2009).

This Internet-based system is fostering more efficient online platforms of audience communication and interaction within various kinds of organizations (Bekkers, 2003), especially among employees in universities. Internet-based systems open up greater accessibility to online services through computer networks and Internet technologies (Wan Mohd Isa, Suhami, Safie, & Semsudin, 2011) in order to support the development of e-government. From the education point of view, it is necessary to implement Internet-based systems to support the universities in managing records and resources that are available to their students (O'Brien, 2002) and human resources management functions.

Furthermore, Internet-based systems in research universities have become important web-based technologies that support the implementation of e-government. The rapid changes and developments occurring in e-government applications are leading to several advantages, for example multi-users' access to online data and information, and flexibility in accessing systems at anywhere and at anytime via the Internet. Government policies, programs and initiatives are contributing to the implementation of new systems in the research universities. Table 1 summarises some of the many Internet-based systems in each research university.

TECHNOLOGY ACCEPTANCE AND USAGE

According to Stone, Good, and Baker-Eveleth (2007), information systems and other applications provide effective communication platforms, information management, improve how individuals work and enhance levels of productivity in the workplace. Questions still remain, however, concerning the significant factors and barriers that characterise the systems. For example, the question has never been asked whether individual experiences tend to influence employees' use of Internet-based systems, particularly in Malaysia's research universities. Most studies about system usage, technology acceptance and adoption have been done in Western countries, particularly the U.S.A. (Wong & Teo, 2009). Wong and Teo state that only a few studies have been conducted in Eastern cultures and so our understanding of users' experiences and perceptions here is very limited. The findings from other countries may be inconsistent and/or not applicable to organizations and the cultural context of Malaysia, and specifically in its research universities.

In the education sector, most studies concentrated on Malaysia where several applications such as digital and online libraries have been

Table 1. Examples of Internet-based systems

Research University in Malaysia	Example of IBIMS
University of Malaya	• E-Attendance (Intranet) • UM Conference Management System • Responsibility Centre Information System (UMRCIS) • University of Malaya Management Information system (UMMIS) • UM e-Senate (Intranet) • UM e-Meeting
University Science Malaysia	• University Information System – Staff (SMU-S) • Human Capital Management System (HCMS) • Online Attendance (Kehadiran Online) • Travelling Claims (e-Tuntutan) • E-Leave System (e-cuti) • Electronic Insurance (e-insurance)
The National University of Malaysia	• Sistem Maklumat Penilaian Kakitangan (Staff Assessment Information System) • Sistem Maklumat Kakitangan (Staff Information System) • Sistem Permohonan ke Luar Negara (Overseas Application System) • Sistem e-cuti (e-leave System) • Sistem e-Tiket (e-ticket System) • Sistem Maklumat Eksekutif (Executive Information System)
University Putra Malaysia	• UPM Payment Portal • Sistem Cuti Belajar (Study Leave System) • Sistem Perjalanan Luar Negara (Overseas Application System) • Aplikasi Cuti Online (Online Leave Application) • Aplikasi Keluar Masuk Pejabat (Login and Logout Application) • Aplikasi Tempahan Bilik (Room Reservation Application)

introduced (Teow & Zainab, 2003). Furthermore, collaborative learning (Measin, Mansor, Shafie, & Nayan, 2009) and e-learning (Ali & Bahroom, 2008) have been examined. In other environments several studies have focused on the acceptance of online banking systems (Sohail & Shanmugham, 2003), ICT usage (Wong & Teo, 2009), multipurpose smartcards (Loo,Yeow, & Chong, 2009), electronic ticketing (Sulaiman, Ng, & Mohezar, 2008), mobile personal computers (Ramayah & Mohd Suki, 2006), wireless Internet using mobile devices (Parveen & Sulaiman, 2008), and electronic medical records (Mohd & Syed Mohamad, 2005).

There are many key factors that explain the resistance to using technology or to understanding users' attitudes towards online systems,for example: usefulness of the system and ease of use (Davis, 1989), positive usability of the system (Preece, 2001) and information system quality (Lin, Fan, & Zhang, 2009). Other studies have examined technology acceptance, usage and adoption through Theory of Reasoned Action (TRA), Theory of Planned Behavior (TPB) and Innovation Diffusion Theory (IDT) (Mitchell, Gagne, Beaudry, & Dyer, 2012). However, the Technology Acceptance Model (TAM) has been one of the most heavily employed models for examining user acceptance and various other information systems (Park, Son, & Kim, 2012, p. 378). Azmi and Bee (2010) also reveal that TAM was a widely accepted model for examining how organizations utilized technology. TAM explains that actual systems acceptance is determined by perceived ease of use and usefulness. With reference to this, Davis and colleagues contend that end users' acceptance of new technology and systems is strongly influenced by their attitudes and behaviour (Davis, Bagozzi, & Warshaw, 1989). Thus, ease of use, usefulness and attitudes of individual people will affect behavioural intention and what they actually do.

Chen and Yen (2004) stress that interactivity features of the system constitute one of the key elements that have a positive impact on users' behavioural intentions and attitudes to their use of web sites and online chat rooms. On this theme, Fiore (2008) states that interactivity is one of the key factors influencing end users' interaction with information and content appearing on web sites, and at the same time enhancing user satisfaction. However, Gleason and Lane (2009) state that technological features, user experiences and content all have a direct impact on interactivity and user satisfaction when these systems are being used. All of these explain why interactive elements are important to influencing user perception and satisfaction with technology, and in increasing people's familiarity with Internet-based systems (Thong, Hong, & Tam, 2004).

DeLone and McLean's IS Success Model has emerged as one of the most successful models for understanding the acceptance of technology in organizations. This model contributes to overall user satisfaction and system use in terms of the individual and the organization (DeLone & McLean, 1992). In a later study these same authors emphasised the importance of information system quality (information quality, system quality and service quality) to enhance user satisfaction and positively influence the acceptance of online systems (DeLone & McLean, 2003). Their conclusions have been supported by various studies where this model has been employed to evaluate system usage and acceptance in any type of business environment (Lin & Lee, 2006; Petter, DeLone & McLean, 2008; Lin, Fan, & Zhang, 2009).

However, according to Dawson (1994) there are several internal and external factors that affect end user's use of new technology in the workplace, for example society and people, economics, government rules and regulations, and political influences. Furthermore, Schwester (2009) indicates that one potential barrier which influences people when using e-government applications is organizational or staff resistance. In their research, Susanto and Goodwin (2010) indicate several important issues that influence citizens' acceptance of SMS-based e-government services such as ease of use, efficiency of time and distance, value for money, usefulness, responsiveness, convenience, relevance, quality and reliability of the information, trust, risk to user privacy and availability of device and infrastructure. The key success factors in acceptance of technology and its usage cannot only be investigated by examining the technical features such as interface, content, and ease of use, but also by understanding social perspectives and organizational factors as perceived by the system user.

It is therefore necessary to take advantage of what can be learned from in-depth research using the qualitative approach to understand end users' feelings and experiences when utilising Internet-based systems in order to support the development of e-government applications. Justifications from the end user's point of view are needed to show the potential of e-government applications in providing new technology and online communication tools to employees and citizens. In the context of technology acceptance and usage, it is important to investigate the factors that lead to success and/or failure that users experience when they operate online or Internet-based systems in their organization. A better understanding of end user success factors and barriers will improve our knowledge of technology acceptance, adoption and usage of e-government applications such as Internet-based systems.

METHODOLOGY

A qualitative method was developed to provide a deep understanding that will assist in developing our knowledge of the successes and challenges when using Internet-based systems. The data collection method consists of semi-structured in-depth interviews. According to Myers (1997), qualitative research methods make it possible to explain information systems research. Markus and Lee (2000) also suggest that existing researchers in information systems should use a qualitative method in order to better comprehend the phenomenon under study. In addition, Ekdahl, Karlsson, Wigertz, and Forsum (2000) confirm that a qualitative approach can answer the research objectives. The following paragraphs describe in more detail the interview process.

Firstly, the author developed important questions to measure the topic, using the acceptance model based on: firstly, Davis's (1989) theory of TAM; and secondly, the important interactivity features inherent in Outcome Interactivity Theory as suggested by Gleason and Lane (2009). Then the respondents were asked questions that referred to usability, system quality, information quality, service quality, and information system quality (Koohang & Ondracek, 2005; DeLone & McLean, 2003). Specifically, some of the interview questions were:

- Do you think ease of use is a key factor in your satisfaction with Internet-based information management systems?
- Do you think usefulness is a key factor in your satisfaction with Internet-based information management systems?
- How important are interactivity features to you when using Internet-based information management systems?
- What are the main features of Internet-based information management systems that contribute to your overall satisfaction?
- How important is information system quality to your online communication satisfaction?
- Do you always use Internet-based information management systems as required by your institution?
- What are the other factors that influence your use of Internet-based information management systems in your office?

Following the development of these questions, human ethics approval was granted by the University of Adelaide for one year from 2nd November 2010 until 30th November 2011 to conduct the interviews in Malaysia. Further ethics approval was received in a formal letter by the Director-General of the Department of Higher Education, MOHE in order to ensure the integrity, anonymity and confidentiality of the respondents/informants, information and organizations involved in this study. After that, the interviews were conducted to obtain each respondent's personal feelings, opinions and experiences of IBIMS. The researcher took one week to contact all the target respondents in each university to discuss the available date and venue for the interview. When people did agree to participate, the interview objectives were explained so that they understood what this study was about. The interviews were held in participants' offices or a more convenient venue, and they were recorded using a digital audio recorder, but no names were used in any of the reports or publications. The respondents' participation was on a voluntary basis. The interviews were conducted in four pioneer research universities in Malaysia within a period of one and half months from 17 January 2011 to 2 March 2011 with twenty-one respondents comprising 10 academic staff and 11 executive officers.

The next step involved transcribing the audio recordings and then coding and analyzing them. This study uses NVivo version 9.0 to encode all the data. In the early parts of this phase of the research process, audio data from digital recorder (interviews) was copied to the researchers' personal computer for safety and confidentiality reasons. The audio data was transcribed into Microsoft Word format. The transcriptions were done after the field trip and entered into NVivo. At this stage, the researcher qualitatively analysed the responses and phrases categorised to make sense of the interview texts and the topics they covered. The author concentrated on meaningful data generated by a discussion of specific topics or themes in order to document the successes and problems concerning the use of the systems.

FINDINGS: FACTORS CONCERNING SUCCESS AND PROBLEMS

The purpose of this study was to understand employees' experiences, successes and problems or barriers when utilising Internet-based systems. Table 2 summarizes the issues that employees at research universities in Malaysia feel to be important. These findings highlight the three themes that are the focus here: technological features, social and human factors, and organizational initiatives.

The following section describes several solutions and recommendations so that the technological features, social and human factors, and organizational initiatives are employed successfully.

DISCUSSIONS, SOLUTIONS, AND RECOMMENDATIONS

This section highlights several solutions and recommendations so that the systems are used more efficiently in the research universities. These findings can then be generalized to other teaching universities and government agencies when they are implementing e-government applications. It is necessary to recognize solutions that help improve and encourage staff to use Internet-based systems and e-government applications in their daily tasks.

To understand the success factors and barriers in using Internet-based systems, a system development team should focus on quality when developing software or application so that end users have access to better technology. For example, this study found the importance of technological features in the Internet-based system. Technological features should consist of accurate and

Table 2. Successes and problems

Themes	Success factors	Problems
Technological features	• Ease of use and usefulness • Interactivity features • Accurate and up-to-date information • Relevant content, link and navigation • User friendly and simple to use • Reliable and current (online) • Flexibility and accessibility • Safety and security of the systems • Provide interactivity features • Integrated with other systems	• Down time (off-line) • Slow internet speed • System not fully integrated • Information and content (limitation, over loaded, misunderstanding and not up-to-date) • System not flexible • Difficult to use and not user friendly • Lack of online help
Social and human factors	• Support from friends, peers and administrators (management) • Employees' needs • Positive motivation in using them (satisfy, enjoy, love and prefer to use) • Generation or age	• Negative perception of user's age • Lack of knowledge • Time constraints and late responses by other people • Negative perception about information, security and transparency • Negative attitudes to use and change
Organizational initiatives	• Introduce and promotion program • Technical support • Skills and training • Enforcement by organization and senior management	• Negative feelings concerning enforcement • Lack of promotional information • Not enough special skills and training • Lack of technical support for systems • Lack of facilities and infrastructure • Management still needs paper-based instructions for online applications

up-to-date information, ease and simplicity of use, better interactivity features and provision of relevant content, links and navigation aids. In addition, instructions and descriptions of the content in the systems should be well explained and easy to understand. The developer should also improve the quality of interface design to enhance ease of use and interaction processes between employees and electronic systems. Azmi and Bee (2010) in their study emphasize the importance of ease of use when people are utilising electronic systems in their everyday work. With further reference to this, content and information require simple words, jargon-free sentences, instructions and descriptions, and a minimum of technical terms and unfamiliar words. Indeed, Mohamed, Hussin, and Hussein (2009) claim that content format and accuracy of information systems constitute one of the key contributors to end users being satisfied and used with online systems.

This study indicates that each university needs to provide end users with reliable connectivity, especially to enhance the capacity to stay online and connected to the systems. This reveals that the consistency of the system (uptime) is the key indicator in supporting greater systems accessibility. The systems should be operating 24/7 without any down time or offline periods of time. This indicates the need to develop open access systems where employees can access them from anywhere and anytime (Susanto & Goodwin, 2010). In other words, the system should be accessible in terms of its intranet and extranet environment for 24 hours to support full accessibility and timeliness. Timeliness is the key to enhancing the success of an Internet-based system because it is important to ensure an end user's ability to access and receive up-to-date information immediately (Mohamed, Hussin, & Hussein, 2009).

Next, to improve the accessibility and navigational capabilities, the systems need to be well integrated through Intranet and extranet technologies. This will enable end users to use more than one system at the same time with the same username and password. It will enhance end users' flexibility in accessing more than one system to do their work. Thus, system developers need to develop integrated Internet-based systems that assist people in changing their attitudes and improving their sense of satisfaction when using and accessing online systems. This point is stressed by Mohamed, Hussin, and Hussein (2009), who contend that the organization needs to improve the capability and interoperability whereby stakeholders can access government agencies' integrated online systems. It is evident that universities sometimes fail to provide an international standard of facility and infrastructure to support greater access to their systems. For example, it emerged in this study that some universities did not install enough wireless hotspots to support wireless connection through broadband wireless fidelity (WI-FI).

In relation to systems accessibility, the overarching organization plays an important role in budgeting to improve the network and Internet infrastructure so that faster access connections exist on campus. Susanto and Goodwin (2010) indicate the importance of devices and infrastructure being available so that e-government services were positively perceived. Therefore, to achieve better efficiency in accessing online systems, these universities or other organizations for that matter should provide high speed Internet connections and broadband technology and in this way improve system interoperability. These initiatives will help organizations to improve system quality so that accessibility, integration and interoperability of the e-government platform in each university or government agency are sustained.

It is necessary for system analysts and system developers to clearly communicate with employees about their needs. Clear and concise communication processes between developers and end users are important to provide a high quality of information in system development processes. For example, software development groups must conduct end user requirements and feasibility analyses to understand what they want or what works best for them. Schwester (2009) notes the importance of end users' technical needs if e-government applications are to be accepted and used. In other words, the organization and development team should be willing to invite employees (end users) to join in the software development process so that the basic features and technological needs of an e-government application such as an Internet-based system are understood.

To increase usage of online systems, universities should ensure that people are confident in and trust system security and safety. This factor has a significant influence on employees' perceptions and trust in online environment services. According to Susanto and Goodwin (2010), some people do not use e-government services because they do not trust the level of security. They also worry about the risk to their information privacy if the organization does not provide a secure network. In order to increase people's trust and perceptions of security, the organization needs to focus on several dimensions of security, i.e. confidentiality of information and message, authentication to verify only authorized people can engage with the systems, the integrity of the message, and authorization and permission to access the systems. In using an Internet-based system to manage government internal operations, the most relevant security and safety issues are to protect the integrity of data, to ensure the privacy of end users, and regulate access to the information. Authentication can be consolidated via the use of smart cards, fingerprints, retina scans, voice recognition or other biometric technologies. Currently online systems can be secured through firewalls, passwords, a digital certificate and Internet transmission via Secure Sockets Layer (SSL) encrypted security in order to protect data and information from hackers and unauthorized users (Azmi & Bee, 2010).

This study found that there may not be enough technical staff to assist those faculty members who experience problems when using online systems. To overcome this, universities should provide enough supervisory officers and technical support staff through one stop helpdesk centers in each faculty or department. The universities should also create online support in the form of online help, online manuals or online guides for the system. This online support will help employees who experience problems as long as such a assistance is always available. According to Azmi and Bee (2010), organizations need to develop and create web-based tutorials or online videos to teach end users how to use the system in order to increase its user-friendliness. From the e-government perspective, government agencies should run 24-hour technical and online support, and it must readily available to ensure the consistent and effective use of Internet-based systems. Furthermore the organizations could also increase their online support through SMS-based services to provide a 24-hour- service.

Social and human factors have important 'push-and-pull' factors that support the acceptance and usage of Internet-based systems in the universities. For example, motivation and encouragement from other people may help new users to understand the objectives in using the system. Workers' peers and senior management should help in order to improve employees' motivation, perceptions and satisfaction. Susanto and Goodwin (2010) suggest creating an awareness programme to enhance people's knowledge about the usefulness, user-friendliness, functions, and existence of an innovation. For example, to increase the awareness and usage of e-government platforms and other online services, organizations should initiate intensive marketing and advertising campaigns to make sure employees and other end users are aware of the benefits of the systems (Susanto & Goodwin, 2010). It may be possible to set up a Publicity and Promotion Unit under the Department of Information Technology, and focus on how to promote and market the systems and applications in their organizations.

In terms of know-how and popularity of the systems, organizations and their management are the most important elements that drive employees to adopt technological innovations. The Department of Information Technology in each university can introduce the systems through several in-house marketing campaign programs and 'road shows' to improve end user's awareness, motivation, expectations and perceptions of technological innovations. These programs should involve interpersonal communications and channels so that all the target users are informed about the systems by system developers and other relevant experts. Roger (2003) claims that successful adoption of an innovation depends on communication channels and how the information is distributed. In terms of communication channels, he states that mass media channels, interpersonal methods, media and the Internet are the best avenues for informing people (Roger, 2003). Interpersonal communication can explain the relative advantages of the systems in order to deliver better service to employees and an organization's clients.

However, individuals who lack knowledge about the systems and computer skills may remain dissatisfied with Internet-based systems in their workplace duties. Specifically, this study found that two major reasons for this problem are: (1) employees are not personally briefed about new systems; and (2) there are too many systems in their universities, and this makes them confused about the purpose of the systems. In general, this study also found that some employees tend to abandon the systems when they did not know how to use them, each system had unclear objectives, not relevant to their daily work and there was insufficient information about them. To solve these problems, system administrators and developers should provide enough information to all university staff through informal and formal communication media (information talks, bulletins and portals) to help them understand the systems better. Susanto and Goodwin (2010) claim that if the system in the organization is relevant and satisfies end users' needs, they will accept it. In short, in order for the system to be accepted by individual users, the system should meet the needs of the target users (Susanto & Goodwin, 2010).

In addition, this study found that some university employees do not have enough time to attend training and information sessions. For example, academic staff are busy with their teaching and learning duties, research and publication commitments. To improve employees' participation in training sessions, the Department of Information Technology should conduct its training programs during semester breaks when academic staff members have time to attend. On the other hand, particular departments, such as a Training Unit from the Human Resources and Development Section in each university, need to provide sufficient training not only in using Internet-based systems, but skills in using computers generally to increase their level of confidence and expertise.

Finally, in Table 2, it is also evident that employees can become dissatisfied with the universities' policy which requires them to print and submit paper-based forms for some online transactions and other applications. The reasons why people in organizations love to use online systems or e-government applications are because they believe that the systems are paperless, easy to use and user friendly. Employees may use the systems when they perceive the simplicity in submitting their forms without printing it out and communicating with the person. To ensure the simple implementation of Internet-based systems or e-government applications, organizations should be clear about the means to do so. Organization (university) policy needs to focus on the greater potential of online systems to provide services where forms can be submitted anytime and anywhere, and try to avoid paper-based duplication.

CONTRIBUTIONS OF THE STUDY

This study on users' experiences of Internet-based systems in four Malaysian universities has contributed several significant findings and has theoretical implications for best practice in Malaysia. We can use the findings from Table 2 to develop a strategic plan for technological changes and their adoption in the research universities.

The positive acceptance and usage of the Internet-based applications are important in creating a virtual environment, collaborative medium and e-government platform. For example, Internet-based systems are having a positive impact on university work, such as communication processes and integrated information management. These greater advantages will assist organizations and senior management in a virtual environment and world class universities in Malaysia in utilizing systems and other e-government applications. With reference to Internet-based systems, this study reveals that their implementation will succeed when employees are satisfied with their technological features, human/social factors and organizational initiatives.

This study also shows the importance of a qualitative approach to understanding end users' experiences of technology. The concept of technology acceptance and use was developed by Davis (1989) in TAM and other models/theories in explaining the factors which influence employees' attitudes and behaviour. The qualitative approach in this study is not only important for auditing the implementation of Internet-based systems in research universities, but it also serves as a suitable approach to understanding the acceptance of e-government applications in Malaysia. In terms of theoretical contribution, it provides new external key factors (social and human factors, and organization initiatives) to enhance TAM in the field of technology acceptance.

It is evident that building on the acceptance, adoption and use of Internet-based systems in universities, requires these and other kinds of organizations to re-educate, reinforce and re-engineer all employees. The goal is for technological changes to be more effectively implemented by senior management and administrative staff. In this study, most employees revealed that the most influential factor in using online systems was the mandatory requirement emanating from senior management. Therefore, we should integrate the importance of social and human factors, and organizational initiatives with technological features in order to improve individual end users' satisfaction with the systems in their workplaces.

FUTURE RESEARCH DIRECTIONS

There are several limitations of this study. First, the data was collected in only four research universities in Malaysia. The research findings may vary from a research university to a teaching university. The results also may vary from one developing country to another. The success and problems in using Internet-based systems may significantly differ between universities and countries, depending on relative advantages, systems implemented and cultural differences. Future research is required to examine and confirm these sorts of findings for different universities, government agencies, private organizations and countries employing Internet-based systems in the form of e-government applications.

Second, the data was collected from professional and management groups (officer staff), and academics (lecturers). The perspective of the study was that of officers and academics in Malaysia's research university environment. Further suggestions for future research are needed to understand how other types of administration personnel perceive online technologies. In order to improve this study, longitudinal case studies or critical analysis studies are needed to investigate different aspects of employees' attitudes, system developer practices and organizational initiatives. For example, a SWOT (Strength, Weakness, Opportunity and Threat) analysis could be done on various universities' ICT policies, strategic plans and system development processes. These are important in that they will highlight significant issues in technology usage and e-government implementation initiatives.

Finally it is necessary to examine the role of leadership in project management, especially in the software development life cycle. A study could also examine the effects of changes in management and technology and how these influence employees in their acceptance of Internet-based systems. These approaches may contribute new findings and insights that make technology implementation successful, specifically for higher education institutions that are carrying out e-government applications in Malaysia.

CONCLUSION

Users' experiences of any type of e-government applications such as Internet-based systems differ from one individual to another, from one system to another, and from one technology to another. However, they all want to achieve similar goals. Several advantages and disadvantages for Internet-based systems users have been discussed in this chapter and the findings have implications for the implementation of e-government applications in various government sectors, especially higher education and business. This chapter not only highlighted the advantages and disadvantages of using Internet-based systems, it also emphasized three categories experienced by employees in research universities in Malaysia. First, the technological features of the systems to accommodate quality features as well as infrastructure to support end users with reliable platforms in accessing the systems were investigated. Then, the importance of human factors in encouraging other people to use and choose the best technology in their daily task was looked at. Finally, the organizational initiatives to ensure staff receive good information and knowledge, skills and training, and access to suitable infrastructure in dealing with the systems were examined. This chapter argues that, to succeed in the implementation of Internet-based systems in the form of e-government applications, these three issues need to be integrated.

REFERENCES

Abdul Karim, M. R. (1999). *Reengineering the public service leadership and change in an electronic age. Subang Jaya Selangor: Pelanduk Publications (M)*. Sdn. Bhd.

Abdul Karim, M. R., & Mohd Khalid, N. (2003). E-government in Malaysia. Kuala Lumpur: Pelanduk Publications (M) Sdn. Bhd.

Abdullah, H.Z., Kaliannan, M., Mohamed Ali, A.J., & Bakar, A.N. (2006). eGoverment in evolution an evaluation survey of government websites in Malaysia. *e-Gov,* 8-12.

Ali, A., & Bahroom, L. (2008). Integrated e-learning at Open University Malaysia. *Public Sector ICT Management Review*, *2*(2), 33–39.

Azmi, A. C., & Bee, N. G. (2010). The acceptance of the e-filing system by Malaysian taxpayers: A simplified model. *Electronic. Journal of E-Government*, *8*(1), 13–22. Retrieved from http://www.ejeg.com.

Bekkers, V. (2003). E-government and the emergence of virtual organizations in the public sector. *Information Polity*, *8*, 89–101.

Chen, K., & Yen, D. C. (2004). Improving the quality of online presence through Interactivity. *Information & Management*, *42*, 217–226. doi:10.1016/j.im.2004.01.005.

Davis, F. D. (1989). Perceived usefulness, perceived ease of use, and user acceptance of information technology. *Management Information Systems Quarterly*, (September): 318–340.

Davis, F. D., Bagozzi, R. P., & Warshaw, P. R. (1989). User acceptance of computer technology: A comparison of two theoretical models. *Management Science*, *35*(8), 982–1002. doi:10.1287/mnsc.35.8.982.

Dawson, P. (1994). *Organizational change: A processual approach*. London: Paul Chapman Publishing.

DeLone, W. H., & McLean, E. R. (1992). Information system success: The quest for the dependent variable. *Information Systems Research*, *3*(1), 60–95. doi:10.1287/isre.3.1.60.

DeLone, W. H., & McLean, E. R. (2003). The Delone and McLean model of information systems success: A ten-year update. *Journal of Management Information Systems*, *19*(4), 9–30.

Ekdahl, C., Karlsson, D., Wigertz, O., & Forsum, U. (2000). A study of the usage of a decision-support system for infective endocarditis. *Medical Informatics and the Internet in Medicine*, *25*(1), 1–18. doi:10.1080/146392300298229 PMID:10757478.

Fiore, A. M. (2008). The digital consumer: Valuable partner for product development and production. *Clothing & Textiles Research Journal*, *26*(2), 177–190. doi:10.1177/0887302X07306848.

Gleason, J. P., & Lane, D. R. (2009). *Interactivity redefined: A first look at outcome interactivity theory*. Retrieved from http://people.eku.edu/gleasonj/Outcome_Interactivity_Theory.pdf

Hadi, A. S., Jelas, Z. M., Mokhtar, M., & Abdul Aziz, Y. F. (2002). *Universiti Kebangsaan Malaysia, The national university with an international reach: Opportunities and challenges in the 21st century*. Paper presented at The 16th Australian International Education Conference. Hobart.

Hashim, J. (2008). Factors influencing the acceptance of web-based training in Malaysia: Applying the technology acceptance model. *International Journal of Training and Development*, *12*(4), 253–264. doi:10.1111/j.1468-2419.2008.00307.x.

Kaliannan, M., Raman, M., & Dorasamy, M. (2009). ICT in the context of public sector service delivery: A Malaysian perspective. *WSEAS TRANSACTIONS on SYSTES*, *8*(4), 543–556.

Kit Siang, L. (2001). IT and governance in Malaysia. In Becker, J., & Hashim, R. (Eds.), *internet M@laysia* (pp. 159–169). Universiti Kebangsaan Malaysia, Malaysia: Department of Commmunication.

Kong, H., Ogata, H. C., Arnseth, C. K. K., Chan, T., Hirashima, F., & Klett, J. H. M. Yang. (Eds.). (n.d.). *Paper presented at the 17th International Conference on Computers in Education*, Hong Kong. Retrieved from http://www.apsce.net/ICCE2009/pdf/C6/proceedings784-791.pdf

Koohang, A., & Ondracek, J. (2005). Users' views about the usability of digital libraries. *British Journal of Educational Technology*, *36*(3), 407–423. doi:10.1111/j.1467-8535.2005.00472.x.

Lin, H., Fan, W., & Zhang, Z. (2009). A qualitative study of web-based knowledge communities: Examining success factors. *International Journal of e-Collaboration, 5*(3). Retrieved from http://find.galegroup.com/itx/infomark.do?&contentSet=IAC- Documents&type=retrieve&tabID=T002&prodId=AONE&docId=A203129230&source=gale&srcprod=AONE&userGroupName=adelaide&version=1.0

Lin, H. F., & Lee, G. G. (2006). Determinants of success for online communities: An empirical study. *Behaviour & Information Technology*, *25*(6), 479–488. doi:10.1080/01449290500330422.

Loo, W. H., Yeow, P. H. P., & Chong, S. C. (2009). User acceptance of Malaysian government multipurpose smartcard applications. *Government Information Quarterly*, *26*, 358–367. doi:10.1016/j.giq.2008.07.004.

Markus, M. L., & Lee, A. L. (2000). Special issue on intensive research in information technology: Using qualitative, interpretative, and case methods to study information technology-Foreword. *Management Information Systems Quarterly*, *23*(1), 35–38.

Measin, A., Mansor, M., Shafie, L. A., & Nayan, S. (2009). A study of collaborative learning among Malaysian undergraduates. *Asian Social Science*, *5*(7), 70–76.

Mitchell, J. I., Gagne, M., Beaudry, A., & Dyer, L. (2012). The role of perceived organizational support, distributive justice and motivation in reactions to new information technology. *Computers in Human Behavior*, *28*, 729–738. doi:10.1016/j.chb.2011.11.021.

Mohamed, N., Hussin, H., & Hussein, R. (2009). Measuring users' satisfaction with Malaysia's electronic government systems. *Electronic. Journal of E-Government*, *7*(3), 283–294. Retrieved from http://www.ejeg.com.

Mohd, H., & Syed Mohamad, S. M. (2005). Acceptance model of electronic medical record. [from http://www.health-informatics.kk.usm.my/pdf/JAIMS.pdf]. *Journal of Advancing Information and Management Studies*, *2*(1), 76–92. Retrieved August 15, 2010

Mohd Majzub, R. (2008). *The challenge of Research Universities: A SWOT Analysis*. Paper presented at the ASAIHL International Conference 2008. Nonthaburi, Thailand.

Myers, M. D. (1997). Qualitative research in information systems. *Management Information Systems Quarterly*, 241–242. doi:10.2307/249422.

O'Brien, J. (2002). *Management information systems: Managing information technology in the e-business enterprises* (5th ed.). Boston, MA: McGraw-Hill Irwin.

Othman, M., Ismail, S. N., & Md Raus, M. I. (2009). The development of the web-based Attendance Register System (ARS) for higher academic institution: From feasibility study to the design phase. *International Journal of Computer Science and Network Security*, *9*(10), 203–208.

Park, Y., Son, H., & Kim, C. (2012). Investigating the determinants of construction professionals' acceptance of web-based training: An extension of the technology acceptance model. *Automation in Construction*, *22*, 377–386. doi:10.1016/j.autcon.2011.09.016.

Parveen, F., & Sulaiman, A. (2008). Technology complexity, personal innovativeness and intention to use wireless internet using mobile devices in Malaysia. *International Reviews of Business Research Papers, 4*(5), 1-10. Retrieved July 8, 2010, from http://www.bizresearchpapers.com/1[1].%20Ainin.pdf

Petter, S., DeLone, W., & McLean, E. (2008). Measuring information system success: Models, dimensions, measure, and relationships. *European Journal of Information Systems, 17*, 236–263. doi:10.1057/ejis.2008.15.

Preece, J. (2001). Sociability and usability in online communities: Determining and measuring success. *Behaviour & Information Technology*, *20*(5), 347–356. doi:10.1080/01449290110084683.

Ramayah, T., & Mohd Suki, N. (2006). Intention to use mobile PC among MBA students: Implications for technology integration in the learning curriculum. *UNITAR E-Journal, 1*(2). Retrieved from http://ejournal.unirazak.edu.my

Salman, A. (2009). ICT, the new media (internet) and development: Malaysian experience. *The Innovation Journal: The Public Sector Innovation Journal, 15*(1).

Schwester, R. W. (2009). Examining the barriers to e-government adoption. *Electronic. Journal of E-Government*, *7*(1), 113–122. Retrieved from http://www.ejeg.com.

Sohail, M. S., & Shanmugham, B. (2003). E-banking and customer preferences in Malaysia: An empirical investigation. *Journal Information Sciences-Informatics and Computer Science, 150*(3-4), 207-217. Retrieved June 29, 2010, from http://www.sciencedirect.com/science/article/pii/S002002550200378X

Stone, R. W., Good, D. J., & Baker-Eveleth, L. (2007). The impact of information technology on individual and firm marketing performance. *Behaviour & Information Technology*, *26*(6), 465–482. doi:10.1080/01449290600571610.

Sulaiman, A., Ng, J., & Mohezar, S. (2008). E-ticketing as a new way of buying tickets: Malaysian perceptions. *Journal of the Social Sciences, 17*(2), 149–157.

Susanto, T. D., & Goodwin, R. (2010). Factors influencing citizen adoption of SMS-based e-government services. *Electronic. Journal of E-Government*, *8*(1), 55–71. Retrieved from http://www.ejeg.com.

Teow, P. L., & Zainab, A. N. (2003). Access to online database at private colleges and universities in Malaysia. *Malaysian Journal of Library & Information Science*, *8*(1), 91–101.

Thong, J. Y. L., Hong, W., & Tam, K. Y. (2004). What lead to user acceptance of digital libraries? *Communications of the ACM*, *47*(11), 79–83. doi:10.1145/1029496.1029498.

Un Jan, A., & Contreras, V. (2011). Technology acceptance model for the use of information technology in universities. *Computers in Human Behavior*, *27*, 845–851. doi:10.1016/j.chb.2010.11.009.

Wan Mohd Isa, W. A. R., Suhami, M. R., Safie, N. I., & Semsudin, S. S. (2011). Assessing the usability and accessibility of Malaysia e-government website. *American Journal of Economics and Business Administration*, *3*(1), 40–46. doi:10.3844/ajebasp.2011.40.46.

Wong, S.L., & Teo, T. (2009). Determinants of the intention to use technology: Comparison between Malaysia and Singaporean female student teachers.

ADDITIONAL READING

Asiimwe, E. N., & Lim, N. (2010). Usability of government websites in Uganda. *Electronic. Journal of E-Government*, *8*(1), 1–12.

Cohen, J. E. (2006). Citizen satisfaction with contacting government on the Internet. *Information Polity*, *11*, 51–65.

Enyon, R., & Dutton, W. H. (1998). Barriers to networked governments: Evidence from Europe. *Prometheus*, *25*(3), 225–242. doi:10.1080/08109020701531361.

Fang, Z. (2002). E-government in digital era: Concept, practice, and development. *International Journal of the Computer, the Internet and Management*, *10*(2), 1-22.

Gil-Garcia, J. R., & Martinez-Moyano, I. J. (2007). Understanding the evolution of e-government: The influence of systems of rules on public dynamics. *Government Information Quarterly*, *24*, 266–290. doi:10.1016/j.giq.2006.04.005.

Gil-Gargia, J. R., & Pardo, T. A. (2005). E-government success factors: Mapping practical tools to theoretical foundations. *Government Information Quarterly*, *22*, 187–216. doi:10.1016/j.giq.2005.02.001.

Gilbert, D., Balestrini, P., & Littleboy, D. (2004). Barriers and benefits in the adoption of e-government. *International Journal of Public Sector Management*, *17*(4), 286–301. doi:10.1108/09513550410539794.

Helbig, N., Gil-Garcia, J. R., & Ferro, E. (2009). Understanding the complexity of electronic government: Implication from the digital divide literature. *Government Information Quarterly*, *26*, 89–97. doi:10.1016/j.giq.2008.05.004.

Jain, R., Jain, S., & Raju, V. S. (2011). Study of success and failure of e-governance. *Journal of Advances in Development Research*, *2*(2), 299–302.

Kifle, H., & Cheng, P. L. K. (2009). e-Government implementation and leadership – the Brunei case study. *Electronic. Journal of E-Government*, *7*(3), 271–282.

King, S. F., & Burgess, T. F. (2008). Understanding success and failure in customer relationship management. *Industrial Marketing Management*, *37*, 421–431. doi:10.1016/j.indmarman.2007.02.005.

Luarn, P., & Huang, K. (2009). Factors influencing government employee performance via information systems use: An empirical study. *Electronic. Journal of E-Government*, *7*(3), 227–240.

Taylor, S., & Todd, P. (1995). Assessing IT usage: The role of prior experience. *Management Information Systems Quarterly*, *19*(4), 561–570. doi:10.2307/249633.

Yonazi, J., Sol, H., & Boonstra, A. (2010). Exploring issues underlying citizen adoption of eGovernment initiatives in developing countries: The case of Tanzania. *Electronic. Journal of E-Government*, *8*(2), 176–188.

KEY TERMS AND DEFINITIONS

Extranet: A computer network that allows access from outside.

Innovation Diffusion Theory (IDT): A theory developed by Everett Rogers in 1962 to explain how an innovation is spread and is communicated through communication channels to members of society.

Internet-Based System: A web-based application that allows people to access web browsers through the Internet.

Intranet: A computer network to share, receive and distribute information within an organization.

Multimedia Super Corridor (MSC): The program was launched in 1996 by former Prime Minister of Malaysia, Tun Dr Mahathir Mohamed to accelerate the development of information and communication technology and to transform Malaysia into a knowledge-based society by the year 2020.

National IT Agenda (NITA): The foundation and framework to accelerate and utilise the advantage of information and communication technology so that Malaysia is a highly developed nation by 2020.

National IT Council (NITC): The National Information Technology Council of Malaysia strategically manages information and communication technology in the interests of the nation.

NVivo: A qualitative data analysis computer software and application produced by QSR International.

Research University: Research-intensive university that concentrates on research and innovations, publications, undergraduate and postgraduate programmes in order to be a world class university.

Technology Acceptance Model (TAM): This model was developed by Fred Davis in 1989 to explain how individual people come to accept and use a technology. He claimed that two main factors influence people to decide their acceptance and use of a technology; perceived usefulness and perceived ease of use.

Theory of Planned Behavior (TPB): A theory that explains the relationship between attitudes and behavior, developed by Icek Ajzen in 1985.

Theory of Reasoned Action (TRA): A theory for the prediction of behavioral intention, prediction of attitude, and prediction of behavior. This theory was developed by Martin Fishbein and Icek Ajzen (1975 & 1980).

Chapter 11
E-Government in Australia:
A Usability Study of Australian City Council Websites

Ritesh Chugh
Central Queensland University Melbourne, Australia

Srimannarayana Grandhi
Central Queensland University Melbourne, Australia

ABSTRACT

The adoption of e-government signifies a positive way to move ahead in the 21st century with enhanced quality, cost effective government services and a superior relationship between different stakeholders. E-government provides new opportunities to both government and its citizens. The wider acceptance of new communication technologies are helping governments and their agencies worldwide to serve citizens, businesses and other governments with greater efficiency.

This chapter looks at e-government development statistics globally before narrowing down to Internet usage and e-government adoption in Australia. Opportunities and challenges of e-government adoption are presented. The chapter then focuses on the current state of e-government in Australian city councils and seeks to evaluate council websites to understand their usability characteristics. Seven Australian capital city council websites have been chosen and evaluated based on factors such as navigation, searchability, layout and visual clarity, information content, communication methods, and transactional services.

The research indicates that e-government in Australia is in its early stages and there is scope for further improvement and growth. The high incidence of web presence indicates that government entities, such as city councils are pursuing cyber strategies. Although the majority of government entities utilise websites to disseminate information to the public, optimal use of ICT in the public sector is ad hoc and in infancy albeit growing rapidly. This chapter provides a concise and holistic understanding of issues that can be encountered when exploiting the Internet and ICT for providing e-government services.

DOI: 10.4018/978-1-4666-4173-0.ch011

Copyright © 2013, IGI Global. Copying or distributing in print or electronic forms without written permission of IGI Global is prohibited.

1.0 INTRODUCTION

The wide proliferation of Internet for conducting business has impacted almost everyone in today's global world. The usage of Internet in other fields has amplified the expectation of citizens (or netizens) that government organisations will provide services similar to those in private organisations with the same efficacy and proficiency. Electronic government (e-government) provides new opportunities to government for providing services to its citizens through electronic means. New technologies, Internet being the key, in this area are helping governments and their agencies to serve citizens, business organisations and other governments both locally and globally. Providing services online is useful for governments' various stakeholders owing to the ubiquitous nature of the Internet. These services can be accessed around the clock and remove time and spatial limitations (Kašubienė & Vanagas, 2007).

Undoubtedly in today's Internetworked world, e-government plays an important role in the delivery of services yet some of the city councils in Australia are slow in utilising technology to serve their citizens. In order to make the transition many city councils in Australia have adopted a 'clicks and bricks' (use of an online channel in addition to a traditional channel for carrying out business activities) strategy to serve citizens in their constituency. This obviously sounds a good way to move forward as it complements other existing strategies of serving their customers e.g. citizens, organisations and other agencies. Since the survival and sustenance of an organisation depends on its capability to redefine and adopt continuous goals, purposes and way of doing things (Malhotra, 2001), it is important that government organisations are not laggards in this area. The Internet and Information and Communication Technology (ICT) are an important way of improving the quality and responsiveness of the services that governments provide to their citizens, increasing the geographic reach and accessibility of their services and providing a faster and more transparent way of access to different government services.

The existing literature (Burt & Sparks, 2003; Sharma & Sheth, 2004; Bocij, Chaffey, Greasley, & Hickie, 2006) focusses upon the potential of the Internet for enhancing efficiency, cost reduction, improvement in the quality of services, flexibility and convenience. So far, in the current literature, there is limited research (O'Toole, 2007; Walsh, 2007) on the state of e-government in Australia, with restricted focus on the overall adoption of e-government by city councils. A lot of literature on e-government in Australia is fragmented and incoherent so this chapter will provide a clear insight into the adoption of e-government by city councils. Therefore, the purpose of this chapter is to examine the extent of the utilisation of the Internet and ICT in providing e-government services by 7 city councils in Australia. This chapter outlines the state of e-government in Australia before specifically focussing on city council websites. It is important to assess the usability of website deployment as a platform for e-government (Wood et al., 2003). Hence an analysis of the usability of 7 Australian capital city council websites has been carried out and factors relating to navigation, searchability, layout and visual clarity, information content, communication methods, transactional services and others pertaining to online web browsers support and Really Simple Syndication (RSS) feeds have been assessed. The usability analysis is based on evaluation carried out by experts who scrutinize and use a website to discover usability problems that they believe will affect end users (Nielsen, 1994). Various authors have suggested that usability is still one of the main problems that influences and hinders users' interaction and adoption of e-government services worldwide (Al-Sobhi, Weerakkody, & Al-Shafi, 2010; Asiimwe & Lim, 2010; Donker-Kuijer, Jong & Lentz, 2010) and there exists a lack of specific research of usability in an e-government context (Huang & Brooks, 2011).

The remainder of the chapter is divided into seven sections. The following section defines e-government and provides a brief insight into the Australian government structure. The third section explores the opportunities and challenges in electronic government. Section four delves into global adoption of e-government. The fifth section outlines Internet accessibility and the state of e-government in Australia. Section six outlines the research methodology that was adopted for data collection. Findings and discussion then follow to provide an analysis of the usability of city council websites. Finally, the conclusion section summarises the key points, outlines the limitations of this chapter and suggests directions for future research. The key purpose of this research is to assess usability characteristics of Australian city councils websites and the intention is not to provide rankings of the chosen websites. This research makes no implication that one council's website is better than another. The chapter is a useful source of information for managers, administrators and other government professionals who need to understand the opportunities and challenges of e-government in order to harness the advantages of this rapidly growing phenomenon.

2.0 ELECTRONIC GOVERNMENT AND THE AUSTRALIAN GOVERNMENT STRUCTURE

The advent of the World Wide Web has left almost no business untouched and governments are no exception to this phenomenon. It is plausible that governments have been slow to embrace the fast galloping World Wide Web phenomenon but nevertheless now are poised to provide government services online. The use of the Internet and ICT has transformed the way people live, communicate and work. E-government is certainly transforming the way people communicate with their government entities.

Definitions of e-government include:

The use of information systems to provide citizens, organisations and other Governmental agencies with information about and access to public services (Valacich & Schneider, 2010, p.593).

e-government involves the use of information and communication technologies to transact the business government" (Kašubienė & Vanagas, 2007, p. 68).

application of information and communications technology (ICT) to enable the better delivery of services and better government administration (Australian Government Information Management Office, 2006, p.4).

As evident from the definitions above, there are minor subtleties but the fundamental meaning is still the same – e-government is the provision of information and services using technology. To eliminate any further ambiguity, this chapter proposes a definition that has summarised different aspects of e-government: "the use of the Internet and ICT to electronically empower governments to provide information and services to a diverse range of stakeholders."

The adoption of communication technologies in public administration is changing the way government entities provide services to its citizens. E-government services can take different forms ranging from a website that acts as an information portal to an interactive gateway that provides integrated services to different stakeholders (Rorissa, Demissie, & Pardo, 2011). Undoubtedly, the Internet is playing a vital role in providing connectivity between government and its citizens, private organisations and other governments. E-government has existed for several years mainly in the form of Government to Citizens (G2C) to serve its citizens (Clift, 2002). However new relationships such as Government to Business (G2B) and Government to Government (G2G) have come to exist that offer economies of scale for both suppliers and governments by reducing operational timelines and supply chain costs.

As mentioned above, there are 3 different forms of e-government, Government to Citizens (G2C), Government to Businesses (G2B) and Government to Government (G2G) (Stair, Reynolds, & Chesney, 2008). G2C allows interactions between national, regional and local governments and their constituents. G2B allows interactions between government and businesses, in which government streamlines its supply chain by purchasing materials or procuring services directly from its suppliers. G2G allows interactions between countries or different levels of government within a country. This is to allow other government entities to access information regarding laws and regulations relevant to national requirements (Valacich & Schneider, 2010).

Two most common Internet strategies are 'Clicks & Bricks' and 'Clicks only'. 'Clicks and Bricks' or 'Clicks and Mortar' strategy refers to having an online channel in addition to a traditional channel for communication and carrying out business activities (Brown, Dehayes, Hoffer, Martin, & Perkins, 2009). 'Clicks only' strategy refers to communicating and carrying out business activities through electronic means only (Laudon & Laudon, 2010). Some of the benefits with this approach include cost savings relating to inventory and storage. These savings can be transferred to customers in the form of online discounts (The Economist, 2010). 'Clicks only' strategy would be most suitable for commercial organisations as these organisations are not obliged to offer goods and services through traditional channels. Although this might seem an efficient and cost saving method, government entities such as city councils in Australia cannot adopt "Clicks Only" strategy as they have an obligation to offer services to all its citizens regardless of their ability to use the Internet (Randall, 2010). Therefore city councils maintain both a physical presence through offices and an online presence through websites to serve their citizens.

Australia is a democratic (representative democracy) country with constitutional monarchy. It has three levels/tiers of government - federal, state and local (Commonwealth of Australia, 2009). It has six states and two territories. The government in each level has different responsibilities. The federal government(highest one) is responsible for introducing laws in the areas of customs, defence, immigration, taxation, telecommunications, money, copyrights and patents, trade, social security, the territories and industrial relations that cover more than one state (Australian Electoral Commission, 2010). The state and territory governments(middle tier) are responsible for providing education, transport, family services, housing, water, industrial relations and urban planning for its people (Commonwealth of Australia, 2010). The local governments/city councils(lowest tier) are established by the state governments and are responsible for approving development applications, garbage collection, waste management, local parks and reserves, roads and pathways, and most areas to do with local amenities (Demand Media, 2010). Local governments are generally referred to as councils. The local government operates via a local council structure in municipal and shire areas. In most cases, the terms city, municipal or shire have a geographic interpretation. Municipality generally refers to councils governing urban areas whereas shire refers to councils governing rural areas (Australian Government, 2012a). The powers of local government are defined by the state or territory government which establishes them (Australian Government, 2012b).

This chapter focusses on the local government/city council level because local governments/city councils are closer to citizens and constitute the main representation of government at a local level.

The link of citizens and local authorities tends to be one based on geographical closeness, and the city councils play a vital role in addressing several issues such as public services, urban planning and development, education, public transport, environmental concerns and local politics. As can be expected with the adoption and use of any technology, there are inherent lacunae and forte so before progressing any further it is vital to explore the opportunities and challenges of e-government.

3.0 OPPORTUNITIES AND CHALLENGES OF E-GOVERNMENT

As e-government offers the prospective of reforming the delivery of government activities and processes, increasing transparency, forging stronger relationships between citizens and the government, it is important to explore the opportunities and challenges of e-government adoption.

Government websites can act as a platform to disseminate information (Alonso, 2009) and enable them to be more transparent to citizens and businesses. Governments implement e-government services for many reasons including improved service efficiency and a reduction in transaction costs (Alshawi & Alalwany, 2009; Kašubienė & Vanagas, 2007). However, this is not the case with every nation, as they have different needs. Some nations such as India use e-government to fight corruption and to reduce bureaucrats along the service chains as it allows faster service delivery and minimal face-to-face interaction (Jenkins, 2002). It also allows citizens to report corrupt practices to the relevant authority without revealing their identity (United Nations Educational, Scientific and Cultural Organisation, 2005). Singh, Pathak, Naz, & Belwal (2010) in their research paper on electronic government in India, Ethiopia and Fiji, also point out that e-government helps in reducing corruption by allowing transparency between government and its citizens. Although it is debatable in terms of actual figures relating to corruption in these countries, electronic government will certainly allow some level of transparency.

Through e-government, government entities and agencies can allow interactions with its citizens and allow online transactions, such as online payments for council rates, parking fines and so forth. Such additional capabilities not only help improve the efficiency and effectiveness of the functions of government, including the delivery of public services, but also enhance their flexibility (Ciborra, 2005). Alter (2002) points out that electronic communication systems such as email, voice mail, instant messaging and chat rooms help people work together by exchanging or sharing information in many different forms. These systems have also largely been adopted by governments although their uptake is segmented. Turban, McLean, and Wetherbe (2004) have asserted that e-government provides opportunities to both its citizens and local businesses to provide feedback to government agencies and to participate in democratic institutions and processes, which may facilitate fundamental changes in the relationships between citizens and governments and the way they operate.

E-government also provides flexibility to its citizens by offering additional services such as online license renewal, e-tax, e-visa, online payments and so forth (Laudon & Laudon, 2010). These services will not only offer flexibility but also provide economies of scale, increase collections and lead to a reduction in mailing and handling costs for paper statements too (Talaga, 2009). Bhuiyan (2011) has indicated that the provision of electronic services by governments will enable them to generate more revenue while citizens will benefit from prompt and improved service delivery.

Apart from the various advantages that e-government provides, it does not come without pitfalls. There are various challenges in the development and adoption of e-government services. It is always a challenge to select what information needs to be presented on websites. It is important to provide a wide variety of information to suit the needs of website visitors (Bovee & Thill, 2007). In addition, informational websites need to be organised to enhance visibility and accessibility.

Government websites can support openness and a transparent environment, if these are designed to meet the expectations of the stakeholders (Ahmed, 2008). Visitors of the government websites are general public (citizens), private organisations and other government agencies. It might be possible to understand the users' expectations by allowing them to leave feedback. Feedback can be gathered through the use of discussion forums, online surveys, social networks, emails, and chat rooms. Feedback gathered through these methods can further be analysed easily to improve services.

By the end of 2009, it is expected that the number of mobile phone users around the world will rise to 4.4 billion (Riley, 2009). However current figures indicate that the number of mobile phone users have already risen to 5.6 billion in 2011 (How many are there, 2012), which is equivalent to 79.86 percent of the total world population. Although South Korea and Japan are leading the list of top 10 countries in active mobile broadband subscriptions per 100 inhabitants, Australia is ranked fourth with 82.7 percent (dotMobi, 2012). In Australia, out of 11.6 million Internet users 47 percent are mobile wireless broadband connections (Australian Bureau of Statistics, 2012). As more and more citizens are using mobile devices to access web content, governments can utilise this opportunity to reach their citizens by delivering key e-government services to mobile devices. In order to achieve this multichannel delivery, it is suggested to develop mobile versions of their sites which as a trade-off might increase the cost of delivering services. Also, since multiple and diverse users participate in accessing and exchanging information, it is important for the government entities to create websites that can be accessed with most commonly used web browsers. Website accessibility from a variety of different devices (laptops, tablets, smart phones) should also be assessed since users use different devices now especially ones that promote portability.

The cost of developing, operating and maintaining online services can be prohibitive too. There are several factors that need to be considered, such as website development, choice and purchase of hardware and software, hiring skilled staff and maintenance of the system. In most instances, operating cost is more than the development costs thus can be a reason for withdrawal (Stair & Reynolds, 2010). Research by Schwester (2009) has shown that municipalities with higher operating budgets, more full time information technology staff and technical resources are more likely to have a comprehensive e-government platform.

Introducing technology is only half the job done. City councils may need to reengineer their current processes to provide services online as these services needed to be integrated into the current business processes. For example, city councils might need to offer the same information that is being offered through traditional channels. Sometimes streamlining of operational processes may become necessary, if the underlying data needs to be extracted from multiple sources or databases (Singh et al., 2010).

According to O'Brien and Marakas (2011), in addition to the benefits technology provides, there are detrimental effects on society and people. Government entities need to secure their websites from hacking, cyber theft, viruses, worms, adware, spyware and other malicious programs to minimise the detrimental effects and optimize their beneficial effects, as it is important to protect its citizens' data. Also privacy laws in Australia and other countries regulate the collection and use of personal data by business corporations and Government agencies so it is important to secure organisational data.

Digital divide refers to the inequalities in people's access to information technologies. This divide is because of several factors which include age, gender, disability, lower income and being located outside metro regions (Atkinson, Black, & Curtis, 2008). It is important to have Internet accessibility not only in suburban areas but also in rural areas for e-government to be successful. E-government services cannot often be extended to rural areas because of the unavailability of Internet access (Aman & Kasimin, 2011). Usually rural areas are not equipped with the latest technology, posing accessibility and connectivity issues, and providing Internet accessibility to rural areas poses significant technology challenges (Velaga, Beecroft, Nelson, Corsar, & Edwards, 2012). However, government initiatives to implement adequate infrastructure in rural areas can help improve citizens' participation rate in e-government. Apart from rural areas, the uptake of e-government services among people over 65 years of age is low (AGIMO, 2011). Governments need to explore ways of providing this age group with better skills and training so the adoption of e-government services increases. Ignoring the digital divide can lead to social exclusion (Margetts & Dunleavy, 2002) as some people with whom governments deal are often likely to be alienated because of the inability to access e-government services.

Although city council websites are not necessarily aimed at increasing councils' revenue, there are possibilities of resistance from its users. Bureaucracy and unwillingness to change the public domain have created a lot of criticism regarding the government services leading to low trust between the government and its citizens (Dawes, 2008; Singh, 2010). There are inherent socio-cultural barriers also that hinder the adoption of online services. Some socio-cultural barriers are a lack of transactional trust, no social interaction, and poor understanding of language and content (Lawrence & Tar, 2010).

The major challenge for governments is to ensure that community needs and expectations are met while also ensuring cost effectiveness. There is a shifting trend where governments are not only focussing on the technical aspects of website provision but moving towards having an integrated e-government solution (Mishra & Mishra, 2011). Luna-Reyes, Gil-Garcia, and Romero (2012) have developed a model that can guide governments in making decisions about their current and future e-government initiatives. It is suggested that such a model is used and the challenges identified in this section are addressed to facilitate improved services.

4.0 GLOBAL ADOPTION OF E-GOVERNMENT

A report initiated by the Australian Government Information Management Office (AGIMO) in 2011 found that there has been a steady growth in the use of e-government services in Australia. Over the past three years, two thirds of Australians have used e-government channels to contact government, confirming the prominence of providing convenient and efficient e-government services (AGIMO, 2011). It could be argued that Australia is a regional leader in the adoption of e-government services. Before looking at the adoption of e-government in Australia, this section dwells on the state of e-government development globally so that an informed comparison can be made.

Africa

Tunisia, Mauritius, Egypt and South Africa are the top four ranked countries with e-government development index value close to the world average of 0.4406 (United Nations, 2010). Few nations in the African region have adequate resources or proper infrastructure to offer government services online. As a result some African nations (Burkina Faso, Ghana, Mali, Tanzania, Uganda, and Zambia) are slow in implementing new technologies and offering e-government services to their citizens (i4d, 2005). Some of the key reasons for not implementing e-government services in African nations are low human development, low literacy rates, less affordability and political instability in these regions (Kitaw, 2006). Other reasons include inefficient public administration, corruption, limited capability and very few trained or qualified personnel (Schuppan, 2008).

Asia

The Republic of Korea, Singapore, Bahrain and Japan are the top four ranked countries in the Asian region with an e-government development index value that is much higher than the world average of 0.4406 (United Nations, 2010). In Southern Asia, India ranks fourth with the Maldives topping the list whilst in Eastern Asia, China ranks fourth in e-government development. The United Nations (2010) survey also revealed that in Southern Asia most portals and websites have remained stagnant since 2008 in terms of developing new features.

A survey of 121 public sector officials from eight Asia pacific region countries indicated that Asian countries will continue to deploy e-government services in the coming years (Phang, 2010). Increase in broadband Internet accessibility and affordability is making more citizens to utilise e-government services. As a result these nations are focussing more on designing and deploying services to improve two-way communication and the use of social media to interact with their citizens (Yeo, 2011).

Europe

All European sub-regions excel in the e-government development index and achieve high scores far above the world average (United Nations, 2010). This proves the point that high-income developed countries are ahead of others and also have well developed technological infrastructure that can support e-government services to their citizens (United Nations, 2010). Governments in these nations have identified extensive possibilities of reaching their citizens through government websites to provide content and electronic services. E-government sites in the European Union facilitate two-way interaction and are fully transactional (Ding, Wang, & Ye, 2008) allowing users to not only access the content on their websites and complete electronic forms but also make online payments.

The Americas

The status of e-government development in Northern America is far ahead of other American regions. United States of America and Canada are the top two ranked countries in the Americas with an e-government development index value almost double the world average of 0.4406 (United Nations, 2010). Very well designed government portals can help reach their citizens, allow citizens to participate in decision making processes and to get feedback on several issues prior to deciding on policies. This is particularly true in North America, as both United States and Canada have created a favourable environment that helps e-government thrive.

In Central America, Mexico enjoys the top ranking whereas in the Americas, it ranks ninth (United Nations, 2010). The United Nations (2010) survey also revealed that the e-government development index value and scoring for Central America declined below the world average in comparison to their previous survey in 2008.

5.0 INTERNET ACCESSIBILITY AND STATE OF ELECTRONIC GOVERNMENT IN AUSTRALIA

Internet accessibility and availability of technology to citizens is a critical factor and determines the success of e-government adoption. According to the Australian Bureau of Statistics (2009), in 2008-09, 72 percent of Australian households had home Internet access and from 1998 to 2008-09, household access to the Internet at home has more than quadrupled from 16 percent to 72 percent. The quadrupling of household access to the Internet at home prompts the need for local governments to provide their services online. Socio-economic characteristics of households influence the rate of computer, Internet and broadband connectivity across Australia. The Australian Bureau of Statistics (2008) also reported that 64 percent of Australian homes had access to the Internet in 2006-2007 compared to 35 percent in 2001 which demonstrates a substantial growth in the usage of Internet as a way of accessing information and communicating. By the end of 2008 around 43 percent of Internet users had switched from dial-up to Broadband, which provided advantages in accessing websites with greater speeds (Bushell-Embling, 2008). As of 2011, Australia had 11.6 million Internet subscribers and 96 percent of these Internet connections were broadband as dial-up connections are being phased out (Australian Bureau of Statistics, 2012). Nearly half of the current broadband connections in Australia are currently mobile wireless (Australian Bureau of Statistics, 2012). The growth of mobile wireless represents an important change as it adds more mobility and makes Internet access truly ubiquitous. These broadband Internet technologies allows users to download larger files and web pages with graphics and videos thus providing more opportunities for local governments to create sites that can provide such content.

In 1997 the Australian prime minister's office released the Investing for Growth policy statement that became a catalyst for future online innovations. In 2000, the Australian government's 'Government Online-The Commonwealth Government's Strategy' was released and aimed to assist agencies to deliver all appropriate services online and encourage government operations to go online. A report by DMR Consulting (2003) for the National Office for the Information Economy recommended that increased utilisation of government online services can be achieved through more accessible information and services, better cross channel integration and the ability to complete more of the transactions online. The AGIMO (2006) report outlined four strategic priorities to guide government agencies: meet users' needs, establish connected service delivery, achieve value for money and enhance public sector capability through the use of ICT. Australia is currently in the process of rolling out a National Broadband Network (NBN) that utilises optic fibre, fixed wireless and next-generation satellite aimed at providing every Australian with faster, more reliable broadband access. The NBN will enable Australia to become one of the world's leading digital economies. One of the key goals of the NBN is to provide improved online government service delivery and engagement (Department of Broadband, Communications and the Digital Economy, 2011). It is anticipated that the NBN will provide government with greater flexibility in delivering better services to people and streamline their existing operations. Undoubtedly the adoption of e-government services in Australia has come a long way from 1997 and government agencies have achieved significant progress in implementing their online programs. The advantages of online service provision have been recognised by the federal government for some time. Over the past ten years, federal government in Australia has started using the web as a major way of information provision and service delivery. Thus, accessibility and quality come to the forefront of online service deployment for e-government.

According to the United Nations (2010), in the Oceania region Australia leads ahead of New Zealand whilst Australia ranks eighth out of the top twenty countries in e-government development. So it is apparent that Australia is a leader in the adoption of e-government services in the Oceania region. Although there is a strong commitment from local, state and federal governments in Australia to offer services to their citizens through web communication technologies, most of the services offered online are complementing rather than replacing traditional government service delivery (Berryman, 2004), as the majority of the government websites do not allow two way interactive communication. As mentioned earlier clicks & bricks strategy is the best way to move forward for city councils.

Over the past five years Australians have continued to embrace the Internet as a way of interacting with government. 46 percent of Australians have indicated a preference for using the Internet over other communication channels to contact government (AGIMO, 2011). In 2011, 65 percent of people in Australia used e-government services to contact government. Australians' use and satisfaction with e-government services also indicates that use of e-government services has been stable since 2008, and overall satisfaction with the outcome of the service received is 86 percent (AGIMO, 2011). In spite of the stability indicated by the AGIMO (2011) report, there is potential room for improvement as 7 percent of Australians reported that they would prefer to make contact with government using the Internet, but were unable to do so because of inadequate access to the Internet (AGIMO, 2011). The report by AGIMO (2011) also indicated that people would prefer to use e-government channels against mail and in person channels. All these are very promising signs for e-government sustenance and further development of e-government services in Australia.

6.0 RESEARCH METHODOLOGY

Australia is comprised of six states (New South Wales, Queensland, South Australia, Tasmania, Victoria, and Western Australia) and two territories (Australian Capital Territory and Northern Territory). All six states and the Northern Territory have dedicated capital city councils while in the Australian Capital Territory, the local government plays the dual role of a city council and a territory government. Hence it was not considered appropriate to include the Australian Capital Territory in this evaluation as the scale and features of its site would be different. As there are 563 Australian city councils in the six states and Northern Territory, it was practically impossible to investigate each one of them. So to limit the scope, a total of 7 city council websites were chosen i.e. a council of the capital city from the six states and Northern Territory. Details of the chosen capital city councils are included in Table 1.

Table 2 indicates the current number of city councils in each state and Northern Territory.

Out of the 73 city councils in Queensland 2 city councils did not maintain an online web presence while four city councils, out of 74, in South Australia did not have an online web presence either. All other city councils in Victoria, New South Wales, Tasmania, Northern Territory and Western Australia maintained 100 percent web presence.

Table 1. Chosen capital city councils

Council Name	Web Address	State
City of Melbourne	http://www.melbourne.vic.gov.au	Victoria
City of Sydney	http://www.cityofsydney.nsw.gov.au	New South Wales
Brisbane City Council	http://www.brisbane.qld.gov.au	Queensland
Adelaide City Council	http://www.adelaidecitycouncil.com	South Australia
Hobart City Council	http://www.hobartcity.com.au	Tasmania
City of Perth	http://www.cityofperth.wa.gov.au	Western Australia
City of Darwin	http://www.darwin.nt.gov.au	Northern Territory

Table 2. Number of city councils by state/territory

State/Territory	Number of City Councils	Source
Victoria	79	State Government of Victoria (2012)
New South Wales	152	NSW Government (2012)
Queensland	73	Queensland Government (2012)
South Australia	74	Local Government Association of South Australia (2012)
Tasmania	29	Tasmania Government (2012)
Western Australia	140	Government of Western Australia (2012)
Northern Territory	16	Northern Territory Government (2012)

This study analysed website usability through heuristic evaluation (Kantner & Rosenbaum, 1997). This evaluation method is based on evaluation carried out by experts who scrutinize and use a website to discover usability problems that they believe would affect end users (Nielsen, 1994). The evaluation may include site layout and structure, navigation tools, search function, fonts and colours, and so forth (Wood et al., 2003).The seven capital city council websites were analysed using a quantitative web evaluation survey that contained 24 close ended questions. The process of developing the questionnaire balanced the needs of validity, reliability and practicality. Evaluation and re-evaluation was carried out to establish the reliability of the survey. There was zero difference between the evaluation and re-evaluation scores indicating 100 percent reliability of the instrument. The questions in the survey helped in determining factors relating to navigation, searchability, layout and visual clarity, information content, communication methods, transactional services and others pertaining to online web browsers support and RSS feeds. The collated results of the survey have been presented in Table 2.

Website evaluation was conducted in March 2012. In order to ensure consistency of results, specifically for the load times of the websites, all evaluations were carried out at the researchers' workplace with Internet that uses fibre optic backbone @ 100mbits with dedicated virtual private network tunnelling. The evaluation was conducted by the researchers who are skilled ICT professionals. Many online website load testing tools were evaluated but most tools only offer page loading estimates by downloading a limited amount of data. Pingdom (2012) downloads the entire page providing an accurate picture of the download time. Thus, Pingdom was selected to test the load time of the retailers' homepage.

7.0 FINDINGS AND DISCUSSION

All the capital city councils maintained an online web presence and are searchable through search engines like Google and Bing. The analysis (refer to Table 3 for the collated results) has revealed that all the Australian capital city councils have maintained an effective online web presence, which indicates the importance of online connectivity in public administration. All these websites provide information relating to the particular services they offer. All these websites are dynamic and designed to disseminate informational content to the public, government departments and businesses. Some of these websites provide basic information relating to the department or office, and list the links where further detailed information can be obtained. It is evident that the prime focus of these sites was the provision of information content.

All the sites were clearly laid out and visually appealing. Coincidentally all the city councils' websites used blue colour as the background. All

Table 3. Collated results of the survey

	Navigation			Searchability		Layout & Clarity		Information Content								
City Council Name	Ease of navigation	Load time(in seconds)	Ease of finding information	Search Function	Site Map	Entry Splash page	Visual Clarity	Council Background(About us)	Attractions and Events	Online Career/Recruitment	Privacy Policy	Security Policy	Links to other Government websites	G2G- Info for other Government entities	G2B-Info for Businesses
City of Melbourne	Y	10.44	Y	Y	Y	N	Y	Y	Y	Y	Y	N	Y	N	Y
City of Sydney	Y	4.37	Y	Y	Y	N	Y	Y	Y	Y	Y	N	Y	N	Y
Brisbane City Council	Y	3.73	Y	Y	Y	N	Y	Y	Y	Y	Y	N	Y	N	Y
Adelaide City Council	Y	2.11	Y	Y	Y	N	Y	Y	Y	Y	Y	N	Y	N	Y
Hobart City Council	Y	8.16	Y	Y	Y	N	Y	Y	Y	Y	Y	N	Y	N	Y
City of Perth	Y	5.99	Y	Y	Y	N	Y	Y	Y	Y	Y	N	Y	N	Y
City of Darwin	Y	15.57	Y	Y	Y	N	Y	Y	Y	Y	Y	N	Y	N	Y

	Communication Methods			Transactional Services				Others	
City Council Name	Feedback Mechanism(email, phone)	Chat Function	Follow us (Social forums like Facebook, Twitter, YouTube, Flickr)	Online Booking Facilities	G2B-Online Tender/Application Submission	Bill Pay options (Credit card, Bpay, Bank Transfer)	Online Account/Registration	Web browsers supported(IE, Netscape, Mozzilla, Safari)	RSS feeds
City of Melbourne	Y	N	N	Y	Y	Y	Y	Y	N
City of Sydney	Y	N	Y	N	N	Y	N	Y	Y
Brisbane City Council	Y	N	Y	N	Y	Y	N	Y	Y
Adelaide City Council	Y	Y	N	Y	N	Y	N	Y	N
Hobart City Council	Y	N	Y	N	Y	Y	N	Y	Y
City of Perth	Y	N	N	N	Y	Y	Y	Y	Y
City of Darwin	Y	N	N	N	N	Y	N	Y	N

of them avoided unnecessary animation, especially at the site entry point, since it is often frustrating for consumers to look at an entry splash page. The websites are standardised with basic colours and minimal or no graphics requiring users to have very minimal Internet connection speeds hence reducing the digital divide too. Interestingly none of the websites had animations at the entry point, which helped to reduce web page loading time. This design feature might be helpful in addressing inequalities of access by preventing page loading issues. Also, in most instances the councils' websites used the home page to display images relating to popular places and/or community activities, which are easily loadable on all the web browsers, even with minimum Internet download speeds.

The load time of the councils' website home page was also determined. Three tests were performed at different times of the day (between 9-10am, 1-2pm and 4-5pm) to ascertain the average load for each site. The average load time for the seven sites was 7.20 seconds. The fastest site to load was Adelaide city council at 2.11 seconds whilst the slowest site to load was city of Darwin at 15.57 seconds. Figure 1 details the load time of the councils' website home pages.

Ease of navigation is one factor that determines the revisits of users. All the websites were easily navigable. City of Darwin and Perth used text links as their navigation style while all the other sites had organised their information in the form of drop-down menus, which can be expanded by pointing at the tab. The drop-down menu navigational style is very easy and convenient when there is a huge amount of information that needs to be made available to the visitors (Hochheiser & Shneiderman, 2000). Drop-down menus allow visitors to reach subsections with ease and eliminate unnecessary clicks. Hence it is recommended that city of Darwin and Perth also adopt drop-down menus for improved navigation capabilities.

Under the searchability category, all the chosen websites had an in-site search tool. Most of the sites used Google for searching the contents on their website and for performing a custom search. However sitemaps were also available on the sites that complement the search function and

Figure 1. Load time for the councils' website home pages

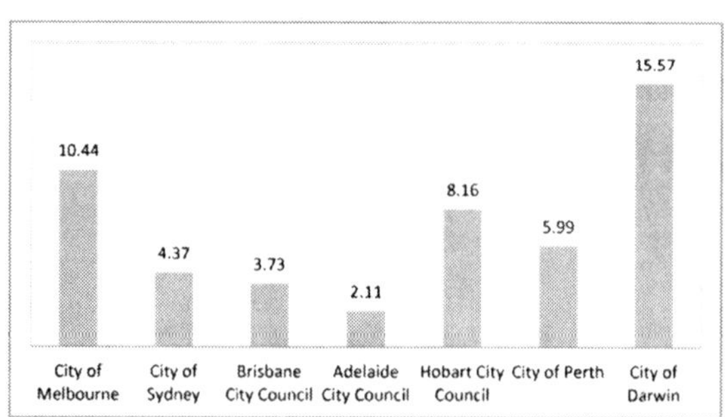

help in finding information more easily. All the surveyed websites had a sitemap, which provided a hierarchical listing of pages linked to the home page. Apart from helping users locate the site's content, site maps can also improve search engine optimisation by ensuring that all the web pages in the site can be found.

All the councils used their site as a platform to communicate with their citizens by providing city council information through their 'About Us' page. The type of information communicated by city councils includes brief history, vision, mission, council members, framework, service charter and current projects. Although all the websites had information relating to "Attractions and Events" in their city councils, only 2 websites had provisions for online booking. All the councils provided links to relevant government laws, where necessary.

All the city councils dedicated a page on their websites for careers and recruitment. Information provided on these sites includes future prospects at city council, working conditions, pay, current vacant positions and selection process. However, two sites (Hobart and Darwin) did not allow online (through the website) submission of applications and applications could only be made through email or post.

All the city councils except Adelaide and Perth had dedicated privacy policies displayed on their website. Adelaide and Perth councils had included elements of a privacy statement in their website disclaimers. Alarmingly none of these councils had separate security policies, although most had embedded security information within their privacy policy, which warrants some uniformity. The privacy policy generally outlined the type of personal information the site collected, how the information is used, how the information collected can be accessed and the security measures the council takes to protect personal information. Visitors will feel more confident in doing online transactions with any website when the security policy provides some assurance about the steps and procedures taken to protect business assets and their confidential information (Mistry, 2001). To provide a sense of security to the site visitors, it is recommended that separate security policies are provided on websites.

Only the Brisbane city council utilised their website to gather visitors' feedback through an online questionnaire. Adelaide city council was quite ahead of other city councils in utilising web functions to allow two-way interaction with its citizens by creating an online chat option. However, this service is restricted to working hours only. It is hard to contemplate why other city councils have not provided a chat function which although easy to develop and implement can be expensive to resource. Other feedback mechanisms that were openly promoted on all websites were email, phone and postal delivery.

Three sites provided an option for its online visitors to follow them on social networks like Facebook, Twitter and so forth. Online social networking can help businesses to make new contacts, contact potential customers, market themselves and most importantly disseminate key information to their members. Hence its usage in the current organisational environment is very vital. The popularity of social networks is an indication for the other four sites to follow suit and adopt them to keep in regular touch with their citizens.

Only 2 sites allowed its constituents to make online bookings i.e. book function rooms, grounds and other community facilities. 100 percent of the websites had information for its suppliers or other businesses, however only 4 websites allowed tender (e-tender) submission on-line. Apart from convenience, this e-tendering option would help to reduce their costs and speed up the tendering process. All the websites offered a multitude of online payment options like credit cards, BPAY service, online bank transfers and so forth. Offering different ways of payment mechanisms makes it easier for people to pay their rates, fines and other taxes.

All the seven chosen city councils adopted the first two forms of e-government (G2C and G2B) to serve their citizens and local businesses. However, none of these city councils made provisions for the third form of E-government (G2G) to serve other local, state and federal government or Government agencies. Accommodating and offering information and services for other governments might help build relationships among city councils, develop emergency response systems with other government agencies like State Emergency Services, detect crime and improve homeland security (Evans & Yen, 2006).

Cross browser compatibility checks were carried out in four different browsers (Microsoft's Internet Explorer, Mozilla's Firefox, Google's Chrome and Apple's Safari) that customers are more likely to use. All the sites had a consistent look and the homepage loaded uniformly across the browsers. This proves that web designers develop sites that are supported by multiple browsers.

Four of the seven surveyed sites offered visitors the opportunity to subscribe to RSS feeds. RSS is an easy way through which subscribers can choose to receive updates and news from different websites. Subscribing to RSS feeds negates the need for people to visit each site individually.

Hence providing its constituents access to various information and services online is useful for the city councils as the Internet is ubiquitous in nature. These sites can be accessed 24/7 and remove time and spatial limitations. As described earlier, apart from being beneficial to the constituents, these sites are also advantageous for the city councils. As with any website, these sites also pose security and trust issues that need to be assessed by all the involved stakeholders before deciding to either offer the services or before using them. City councils should not lag behind in the process of technology adoption and commercial reinvention in order to reap the benefits of the Internet and ICT.

CONCLUSION

E-government has the potential to change the level and quality of interactions citizens have with their governments. High Internet adoption rates in Australia can point towards the possible number of citizens participating in electronic government activities. It is also clear that the high web presence among city councils indicates the rising importance of e-government. This research study has provided an insight into e-government development globally and has outlined key challenges and opportunities of e-government adoption. An assessment of the usability of seven capital city councils' websites was carried out. This led to further discussion about their key functionality.

As with any other research, this research also has its limitations. One city council in each state or territory does not represent the whole government sector. As it is impractical to include a greater number of city councils, the research was limited to seven capital city council websites. It was not practical to collect and analyse a large number of usability factors, so the questionnaire was limited to 24 questions that were deemed to have significant influence on usability. This study has also neglected an analysis of citizen/user needs, wishes, and behaviours towards e-government. This calls for further study to better understand citizen behaviour and e-government adoption patterns in Australia. This study has not looked at the number of hits that these councils' websites get to prove their popularity but that could be the focus of another study. Also, whilst this chapter focuses largely through personal interest in e-government and website usability in Australia, a similar study can also be initiated for analysing the e-government adoption in other countries or by initiating a cross-comparison of e-government adoption between developing and developed countries. Similar studies could also be initiated for assessing the usability of federal government sites.

However in spite of these limitations, the results obtained from the current study are promising and advance our knowledge of the state of e-government adoption in Australia. Analysis of the websites indicates that Australian city councils are utilising ICT to interact with its stakeholders.

In addition to this, it was found that new services such as the ability to make online payments, online tenders and initiate online contact with the city councils provides greater flexibility to both citizens and businesses. E-government provides opportunities to both governments and its citizens. However users require Internet accessibility, minimum hardware and software resources to access these sites and these can be a caveat for some of its populace.

Thus, in conclusion, e-government will allow city councils to work smarter and provide their citizens a ubiquitous channel to facilitate transactions. E-government undoubtedly has the capacity to transform the way councils conduct their daily operations and make it a win-win situation. The surveyed city councils have well developed websites that act as information portals, in most cases, only offering one way interactions; thus do not truly offer two way interactions and optimal online transactional services. As can be seen from this case of city councils, it is imperative that the online medium is fully exploited to enable city councils to operate more efficiently without changing the fundamental way of doing business. Successful e-government has the potential to offer greater choice and a better match between what their citizens want, what they are offered, and how quickly it is offered to them.

REFERENCES

i4d. (2005). *e-Governance in Africa*. Retrieved on March 20, 2012, from http://www.i4donline.net/dec05/knowledge.pdf

Ahmed, M. A. (2008). Developing parliamentary web portals for citizens, MPs and related groups — Challenges and proposed solutions. *IEEE International Symposium on Technology and Society,* 26-28 June 2008, 1-7, Fredericton, NB (Online Xplore).

Al-Sobhi, F., Weerakkody, V., & Al-Shafi, S. (2010). The role of intermediaries in facilitating egovernment diffusion in Saudi Arabia. *Proceedings of the European and Mediterranean Conference on Information Systems*, 1-17.

Alonso, A. L. (2009). E-Participation and local governance: A case study. *Theoretical and Empirical Researches in Urban Management, 3*(12), 1–14.

Alshawi, S., & Alalwany, H. (2009). E-government evaluation: Citizen's perspective in developing countries. *Information Technology for Development, 15*(3), 193–208. doi:10.1002/itdj.20125.

Alter, S. (2002). *Information systems: The foundation of e-business* (4th ed.). New Jersey: Pearson Education, Inc..

Aman, A., & Kasimin, H. (2011). E-procurement implementation: A case of Malaysia government. *Transforming Government: People. Process and Policy, 5*(4), 330–344.

Asiimwe, E., & Lim, N. (2010). Usability of government websites in Uganda. *Electronic. Journal of E-Government, 8*(1), 1–12.

Atkinson, J., Black, R., & Curtis, A. (2008). Exploring the digital divide in an Australian Regional City: A case study of Albury. *The Australian Geographer, 39*(4), 479–493. doi:10.1080/00049180802419203.

Australian Bureau of Statistics. (2008). *8146.0 - Household Use of Information Technology, Australia, 2007-08*. Retrieved on March 12, 2012, from http://www.abs.gov.au/AUSSTATS/abs@.nsf/0/A6CCA61410C0B988CA25768D0021D429

Australian Bureau of Statistics. (2009). *8146.0 - Household Use of Information Technology, Australia, 2008-09*. Retrieved on March 12, 2012, from http://www.abs.gov.au/AUSSTATS/abs@.nsf/0/5B15663305C2B5DCCA25796600153023?opendocument

Australian Bureau of Statistics. (2012). *8153.0 - InternetActivity, Australia, Dec 2011*. Retrieved on March 12, 2012, from http://www.abs.gov.au/ausstats/abs@.nsf/Lookup/8153.0Chapter3Dec%20 2011

Australian Electoral Commission. (2010). *Fact sheet: Three levels of government*. Retrieved on March 14, 2012, from http://www.aec.gov.au/About_AEC/Publications/Fact_Sheets/three_lvls.htm

Australian Government. (2012a). *Local government national report 2008-2009*. Department of Regional Australia, Local Government, Arts and Sport. Retrieved on July 9, 2012, from http://www.regional.gov.au/local/publications/reports/2008_2009/LGNR_2008-09.pdf

Australian Government. (2012b). *Local government (councils)*, Retrieved on July 9, 2012, from http://australia.gov.au/about-australia/our-government/local-government-councils

Australian Government Information Management Office (AGIMO). (2006). *Responsive government a new service agenda 2006 e-government strategy*. Retrieved on April 12, 2012, from http://www.finance.gov.au/publications/2006-e-government-strategy/docs/e-gov_strategy.pdf

Australian Government Information Management Office (AGIMO). (2011). *Interacting with Government: Australians' use and satisfaction with e-government services*. Retrieved on March 25, 2012, from http://www.finance.gov.au/publications/interacting-with-government-2011/docs/interacting-with-government-2011.pdf

Berryman, J. (2004). *E government: Issues and implications for public libraries, a report on trends and themes in the literature*. Retrieved on March 20, 2012, from http://www.sl.nsw.gov.au/services/public_libraries/docs/egov_issues_implications_pln.pdf

Bhuiyan, M. S. H. (2011). Public sector eservice development in Bangladesh: Status, prospects and challenges. *Electronic. Journal of E-Government*, *9*(1), 15–29.

Bocij, P., Chaffey, D., Greasley, A., & Hickie, S. (2006). *Business information systems: Technology, development & management for the e-business* (3rd ed.). Harlow: Prentice Hall.

Bovee, C., & Thill, J. (2007). *Business communication essentials* (3rd ed.). New Jersey: Pearson Education, Inc..

Brown, V. C., Dehayes, D. W., Hoffer, J. A., Martin, E. W., & Perkins, W. C. (2009). *Managing information technology* (6th ed.). New Jersey: Pearson, Inc..

Burt, S., & Sparks, L. (2003). E-commerce and the retail process: A review. *Journal of Retailing and Consumer Services*, *10*(5), 275–286. doi:10.1016/S0969-6989(02)00062-0.

Bushell-Embling, D. (2008). *Dial-up fading, DSL still King*. IDG Communications. Retrieved on March 14, 2012, from http://www.pcworld.idg.com.au/article/261414/dial-up_fading_dsl_still_king/

Ciborra, C. (2005). Interpreting e-government and development: Efficiency, transparency or governance at a distance? *Information Technology & People*, *18*(3), 260–279. doi:10.1108/09593840510615879.

Clift, S. (2002). *E-Governance to e-democracy: Progress in Australia and New Zealand toward information-age democracy*. Retrieved on March 14, 2012, from http://www.publicus.net/articles/aunzedem.html

Commonwealth of Australia. (2009). *Australian citizenship: Our common bond*. Retrieved on March 15, 2012, from http://www.citizenship.gov.au/learn/cit_test/_pdf/australian-citizenship-nov2009.pdf

Commonwealth of Australia. (2010). *Our government*. Retrieved on March 15, 2012, from http://australia.gov.au/about-australia/our-Government

Consulting, D. M. R. (2003). E-government benefits study (Commonwealth of Australia ed.). Canberra (Australia): National Office for the Information Economy.

Dawes, S. S. (2008). The evolution and continuing challenges of e-governance. *Public Administration Review*, *68*, 86–102. doi:10.1111/j.1540-6210.2008.00981.x.

Demand Media. (2010). *The Australian government structure: An outline of the 3 levels of government in Australia and their respective responsibilities*. Retrieved on March 15, 2012, from http://www.essortment.com/all/australiangover_rbpt.htm

Department of Broadband, Communications and the Digital Economy. (2011). *National digital economy strategy: Leveraging the national broadband network to drive Australia's digital productivity*. Canberra. Retrieved on July 12, 2012, from http://www.nbn.gov.au/files/2011/05/National_Digital_Economy_Strategy.pdf

Ding, F., Wang, Y., & Ye, X. (2008). E-government for the people: Learn from North America and European Union. *IEEE/WIC/ACM International Conference on Web Intelligence and Intelligent Agent Technology* (vol. 3, pp. 211-214). 9-12 Dec (Online Xplore).

Donker-Kuijer, M. W., Jong, M., & Lentz, L. (2010). Usable guidelines for usable websites: An analysis of five e-government heuristics. *Government Information Quarterly*, *27*, 254–263. doi:10.1016/j.giq.2010.02.006.

dotMobi. (2012). *Global mobile statistics 2012: All quality mobile marketing research, mobile Web stats, subscribers, ad revenue, usage, trends*. Retrieved on March, 25, 2012, from http://mobithinking.com/mobile-marketing-tools/latest-mobile-stats

Evans, D., & Yen, D. C. (2006). E-government: Evolving relationship of citizens and government, domestic, and international development. *Government Information Quarterly*, *23*(2), 207–235. doi:10.1016/j.giq.2005.11.004.

Government, N. S. W. (2012). *Local government directory - Local councils*. Division of Local Government - Department of Premier and Cabinet. Retrieved on July 16, 2012, from http://www.dlg.nsw.gov.au/dlg/dlghome/dlg_LocalGovDirectory.asp?index=1&mi=2&ml=2

Government of Western Australia. (2012). *Local government directory*. Department of Local Government. Retrieved on July 16, 2012, from http://www.dlg.wa.gov.au/Content/Directory/Default.aspx

Hochheiser, H., & Shneiderman, B. (2000). Performance benefits of simultaneous over sequential menus as task complexity increases. *International Journal of Human-Computer Interaction*, *12*(2), 173–192. doi:10.1207/S15327590IJHC1202_2.

How many are there? (2012). *How many mobile phone users in the world*. Retrieved on March, 25, 2012, from http://www.howmanyarethere.org/how-many-mobile-phone-users-in-the-world/

Huang, Z., & Brooks, L. (2011). Credibility and usability evaluation of e-governments: Heuristic evaluation approach. *Transforming Government Workshop*, 1-15.

Jenkins, G. (2002). *Observations from the trenches of electronic government*. Retrieved on March, 25, 2012, from http://ubiquity.acm.org/article.cfm?id=504686

Kantner, L., & Rosenbaum, S. (1997). Usability studies of WWW sites: Heuristic evaluation vs. laboratory testing. *Proceedings of the 15th Annual International Conference on Computer Documentation*, Salt Lake City, UT, 153-60.

Kašubienė, L., & Vanagas, P. (2007). Assumptions of e-government services quality evaluation. *The Engineering Economist*, *55*(5), 68–74.

Kitaw, Y. (2006). *E-Government in @frica: Prospects, challenges and practices*. Retrieved on March 20, 2012, from http://people.itu.int/~kitaw/egov/paper/EGovernment_in_Africa.pdf

Laudon, K. C., & Laudon, J. P. (2010). *Management information systems: Managing the digital firm* (11th ed.). New Jersey: Pearson Education, Inc..

Lawrence, J. E., & Tar, U. A. (2010). Barriers to ecommerce in developing countries. *Information. Social Justice (San Francisco, Calif.)*, *3*(1), 23–35.

Local Government Association of South Australia. (2012). *Councils*. Retrieved on July 16, 2012, from http://www.lga.sa.gov.au/site/page.cfm?u=210

Luna-Reyes, L. F., Gil-Garcia, J. R., & Romero, G. (2012). Towards a multidimensional model for evaluating electronic government: Proposing a more comprehensive and integrative perspective. *Government Information Quarterly*, *29*(3), 324–334. doi:10.1016/j.giq.2012.03.001.

Malhotra, Y. (2001). *Enabling next generation e-business architectures: Balancing Integration and Flexibility for Managing Business Transformation*. Portland, Oregon: Intel Corporation.

Margetts, H., & Dunleavy, P. (2002). Cultural barriers to e-government. In *Better public services through e-government: Academic article in support of better public services through e-government*. National Audit Office Report by the Comptroller and Auditor General, HC 704-III Session 2001-2002, 4 April.

Mishra, A., & Mishra, D. (2011). E-government: Exploring the different dimensions of challenges, implementation, and success factors. *The Data Base for Advances in Information Systems*, *42*(4), 23–37. doi:10.1145/2096140.2096143.

Mistry, J. (2001). *Developing security policies for protecting corporate assets*. SANS Institute, Version 1.2d, Retrieved on July 13, 2012, from http://www.sans.org/reading_room/whitepapers/policyissues/developing-security-policies-protecting-corporate-assets_490

Nielsen, J. (1994). Heuristic evaluation. In Nielsen, J., & Mack, R. L. (Eds.), *Usability inspection methods*. New York, NY: Wiley.

Northern Territory Government. (2012). *Council information*. Department of Housing, Local Government and Regional Services. Retrieved on July 16, 2012, from http://www.localgovernment.nt.gov.au/council_information

O'Brien, J., & Marakas, G. (2011). *Management information systems* (10th ed.). New York: McGraw Hill.

O'Toole, K. (2007). E-Governance in Australian local government: Spinning a web around community? *International Journal of Electronic Government Research*, *3*(4), 58–75. doi:10.4018/jegr.2007100104.

Phang, R. (2010). Asian e-government in 2010. Retrieved on March 20, 2012, from http://www.futuregov.asia/articles/2010/jul/13/asian-e-government-2010/

Pingdom. (2012). *Pingdom tools - Full page test*. Retrieved on March 1, 2012, from http://tools.pingdom.com/

Queensland Government. (2012). *Search the local government directory*. Department of Local Government. Retrieved on July 16, 2012, from http://www.dlgp.qld.gov.au/local-government-directory/search-the-local-government-directory.html

Randall, S. (2010, September 18). Why bricks and clicks don't always mix. *New York Times*. Retrieved on March 20, 2012, from http://www.nytimes.com/2010/09/19/business/19digi.html

Riley, J. (2009). *The world now has 4 billion mobile phone users*. ITWire, Retrieved on March, 25, 2012, from http://www.itwire.com/it-industry-news/market/27107-the-world-now-has-4-billion-mobile-phone-users

Rorissa, A., Demissie, D., & Pardo, T. (2011). Benchmarking e-government: A comparison of frameworks for computing e-Government index and ranking. *Government Information Quarterly*, *28*(3), 354–362. doi:10.1016/j.giq.2010.09.006.

Schuppan, T. (2008). E-Government in developing countries: Experiences from sub-Saharan Africa. *Government Information Quarterly*, *26*(1), 118–127. doi:10.1016/j.giq.2008.01.006.

Schwester, R. W. (2009). Examining the barriers to e-government adoption. *Electronic. Journal of E-Government*, *7*(1), 113–122.

Sharma, A., & Sheth, J. N. (2004). Web-based marketing: The coming revolution in marketing thought and strategy. *Journal of Business Research*, *57*(7), 696–702. doi:10.1016/S0148-2963(02)00350-8.

Singh, A. (2010). Role of information technology in enabling e-governance. *The IUP Journal of Systems Management*, *8*(1), 7–14.

Singh, G., Pathak, R. D., Naz, R., & Belwal, R. (2010). E-governance for improved public sector service delivery in India, Ethiopia and Fiji. *International Journal of Public Sector Management*, *23*(3), 254–275. doi:10.1108/09513551011032473.

Stair, R., & Reynolds, G. (2010). Principles of business information systems (9th ed.). Course Technology, CENGAGE Learning, USA.

Stair, R., Reynolds, G., & Chesney, T. (2008). *Principles of business information systems*. Cengage Learning, USA: Course Technology.

State Government of Victoria. (2012). *Find your local council*. Department of Planning and Community Development. Retrieved on July 16, 2012, from http://www.dpcd.vic.gov.au/localgovernment/find-your-local-council#councils

Talaga, J. (2009). Online payments in the new retail environment. *Healthcare Financial Management*, *63*(3), 86–91. PMID:20669848.

Tasmania Government. (2012). *Local government directory*. The Department of Premier and Cabinet. Retrieved on July 16, 2012, from http://www.dpac.tas.gov.au/divisions/lgd/local_government_directory

The Economist. (2010). *Online retailing in China: Clicks trumps bricks*. Retrieved on March 20, 2012, from http://www.economist.com/node/15955376

Turban, E., McLean, E., & Wetherbe, J. (2004). *Information technology for management: Transforming organisations in the digital economy* (4th ed.). USA: John Wiley & Sons, Inc..

United Nations. (2010). World e-government rankings. *United Nations E-Government Survey*. Retrieved on March 20, 2012, from http://unpan1.un.org/intradoc/groups/public/documents/undpadm/unpan038848.pdf

United Nations Educational, Scientific and Cultural Organisation. (2005). *Examples of e-governance*. Retrieved on March 25, 2012, from http://portal.unesco.org/ci/en/ev.php-URL_ID=6616&URL_DO=DO_TOPIC&URL_SECTION=201.html

Valacich, J., & Schneider, C. (2010). *Information systems today: Managing in the digital world* (4th ed.). USA: Pearson Education, Inc.

Velaga, N. R., Beecroft, M., Nelson, J. D., Corsar, D., & Edwards, P. (2012). Transport poverty meets the digital divide: Accessibility and connectivity in rural communities. *Journal of Transport Geography*, *21*, 102–112. doi:10.1016/j.jtrangeo.2011.12.005.

Walsh, L. (2007). *Darebin eForum Evaluation Report*. Report commissioned by Darebin City Council. Centre for Citizenship & Human Rights, Deakin University, Melbourne Australia. Retrieved on July 12, 2012, from http://www.darebin.vic.gov.au/Files/Darebin_eForum_Evaluation_090807.pdf

Wood, F., Siegel, E., LaCroix, E., Lyon, B., Benson, D., Cid, V., & Fariss, S. (2003). A practical approach to e-government web evaluation. *IT Professional*, *5*(3), 22–28. doi:10.1109/MITP.2003.1202231.

Yeo, V. (2011). *Asia speeds up e-government efforts*. Retrieved on March 20, 2012, from http://www.zdnetasia.com/asia-speeds-up-e-government-efforts-62300717.htm

KEY TERMS AND DEFINITIONS

Clicks & Bricks (a.k.a. Clicks and Mortar): This strategy refers to having an online medium in addition to a traditional medium for conducting business processes.

Clicks Only (a.k.a. Pure Online): This strategy refers to having only an online medium for conducting business processes.

E-Government: The use of the Internet and ICT to electronically empower governments to provide information and services to a diverse range of stakeholders.

Government to Businesses (G2B): This model refers to online activities in which the government deals with other businesses such as suppliers.

Government to Citizens (G2C): This model refers to online activities in which the government provides access to information and services to its citizens.

Government to Government (G2G): This model refers to online activities in which the government conducts activities between different government agencies.

Information and Communication Technology (ICT): A broader term that refers to technologies which help to gain access to a variety of information and enable communication. ICT covers broad range of technologies including, but not limited to, mobile phones, communication mediums, software, hardware and networks.

Netizen: An avid user of the Internet.

Really Simple Syndication (RSS): A web feed format for delivering the latest content from sites that interest people by not having to visit each site individually.

Chapter 12
Local E-Government and Citizen Participation:
Case Studies from Australia and Italy

Julie Freeman
University of Canberra, Australia

ABSTRACT

This chapter explores local e-government and the provision of online spaces for citizen participation. It highlights how different approaches to e-government development and implementation contribute to the likely success of participatory practices in informing decision-making and enhancing civic engagement with government. A comparative examination is drawn from the experiences of two local governments – the City of Casey in Australia and the Italian City of Bologna. The City of Casey's e-government prioritises service delivery, with opportunities for participation largely restricted. In contrast, the City of Bologna facilitates two-way online citizen discourse and deliberation, which is used to enhance public policy. This chapter highlights that institutional contexts, including insufficient policies and the understandings and motives of political actors, affect the development of participatory e-government and the use of citizen contributions in decision-making. It suggests that successfully facilitating civic participation and engagement through e-government requires strong policy frameworks guiding online content and applications, and a broader change in governmental culture so that representatives are receptive to civic views.

INTRODUCTION

Throughout the world, governments are developing their use of information and communication technologies (ICTs) for e-government practices. New technologies, particularly the Internet, can aid information dissemination, enhance service delivery, and enable greater transparency and accountability of government operations. The success of e-government ventures will vary depending on the specific aims of individual initiatives, the government body and its citizenry, and the sup-

DOI: 10.4018/978-1-4666-4173-0.ch012

Copyright © 2013, IGI Global. Copying or distributing in print or electronic forms without written permission of IGI Global is prohibited.

porting frameworks in place. This chapter focuses on the capacity of local e-government to foster, stimulate and support citizen participation online.

Local e-government initiatives often lag behind applications implemented by state and federal authorities due to resource limitations or a lack of recognition of the potential value of advanced online practices (Seifert, 2006; Cohen, van Geenhuizen, & Nijkamp, 2005). Local governments frequently prioritise one-way online practices and increased service delivery functions, which offer the greatest economic rewards for councils (see Beynon-Davies & Martin, 2004). Many councils are, however, now recognising the need to advance their online initiatives to take advantage of two-way possibilities for exchange, sharing and collaboration. This chapter highlights how different approaches to e-government development impact upon citizen participation practices. It suggests that, to be effective, online participation must inform decision-making processes, as it is this that facilitates greater engagement with government.

This chapter details the experiences of two local governments – the City of Casey (Casey) in Australia and the Italian City of Bologna (Bologna) – and the way each has developed online practices. Casey and Bologna were selected because each has taken a different approach to e-government with substantial variations in the intended use of online communications, but both began their online development at a similar time. Casey's e-government has followed a linear transition, initially using a website for greater transparency of government information, then progressing to enable limited interactivity and improved service delivery. While the council is beginning to recognise the need to include opportunities for dialogue and exchange with citizens through e-government, current forms of two-way online involvement appear largely tokenistic and do not yet facilitate citizen participation in decision-making processes. In contrast, Bologna began its e-government development with a strong focus on local democracy and the need for citizen contributions to inform public policy. While the government faced many challenges to its online development, it continues to provide and continually updates spaces for civic inclusion, and offers a sound example of how to effectively facilitate civic engagement through e-government. This chapter suggests that, to successfully develop its e-government practices to facilitate increased citizen participation and engagement as Bologna has done, Casey will require both stronger policy frameworks guiding the development of its online content and applications, and a change in its governmental culture to be more receptive and responsive to civic input. First, however, this chapter offers a discussion of the importance of local e-government specifically, and provides a distinction between the concepts of ICT-enabled interaction, participation and engagement.

BACKGROUND

While there are numerous understandings and definitions of electronic government, it is broadly understood as the use of networked ICTs such as the Internet and mobile telephony in government operations (see Mayer-Schönberger & Lazer, 2007; Moon, 2002). Early perspectives on e-government often focused on the potential of new technologies to facilitate information dissemination and improved service delivery, viewing citizens as clients or customers (see, for example, Silcock, 2001; Ho, 2002; Kunstelj & Vintar, 2004). More recently, there has been a shift away from the bureaucratic focus of e-government initiatives towards more citizen-centric applications (Norris, 2005; Homburg, 2008; Luna-Reyes, Gil-Garcia, & Celorio Mansi, 2011). Emphasis has been placed on the capacity of e-government to facilitate two-way communication between citizens and governments (Norris, 2005). Such functions have been recognised as producing broader effects on governmental processes, such as increased transparency of government operations, greater accountability of decision-making, and helping to build civic trust in governments (see Eggers, 2005; Wong & Welch, 2004; Bertot, Jaeger, & Grimes, 2012; Griffin & Halpin, 2005; Bonsón, Torres, Royo, & Flores, 2012). Furthermore, the concept of 'engagement' enabled by e-government has emerged as a key research area (Reece, 2006).

This chapter focuses on the way that local governments can facilitate citizen participation and engagement through e-government practices. Neo-liberal tendencies in Western developed economies have meant that the majority of local e-government initiatives followed the path of e-commerce (Graham & Aurigi, 1997; Margolis & Moreno-Riaño, 2009; Homburg, 2008). Local government websites initially offered increased access to information, and then slowly progressed to incorporate and capitalise on the Internet's interactive nature, primarily to enable administrative and financial transactions (Ho, 2002; Flamm, Chaudhuri, et al., 2006). While many e-government websites commonly remain in this state today, the pervasiveness of ICTs in citizens' everyday lives, enabling greater exchange and collaboration, is creating a demand for governments to adapt their practices to incorporate more two-way participation methods through, for example, discussion boards, wikis and blogs. Such spaces act as contexts for the articulation of citizen involvement to action (Couldry, Livingstone, & Markham, 2007), enabling citizen participation to influence democratic decision-making and facilitating increased engagement with representatives.

Local governments offer a useful setting for the development of such online spaces for citizen participation (Sandoval-Almazan & Gil-Garcia, 2012). As the closest democratic representatives to citizens, local governments are responsible for enhancing citizenship practices by offering improved methods for civic participation (Pratchett, 1999). This task is aided by increased knowledge of the needs and concerns of local citizens, existing infrastructure, and of the issues directly affecting the local area and population. Couldry and Langer (2005) note that citizens perceive democratic participation to exist primarily at the local level. The increased sense of immediacy and familiarity with local issues encourages active involvement because citizens can see the direct implications and relevance of political participation for their everyday lives (Margolis & Moreno-Riaño, 2009). Local e-government practices can therefore draw from the common understandings and experiences of distinct community groups to drive online participation (see Graham & Aurigi, 1997). Online discourse and deliberation is also more manageable on a smaller scale than that which takes place through state or federal governments (see Jimenez, Mossberger, & Wu, 2012). These observations suggest that local governments hold a key position for targeted, participatory e-government development.

Despite these advantages, local governments are often the slowest to adapt their practices through the use of new technologies and struggle to cope with rapid changes in the communications environment (see Seifert, 2006; Gil-Garcia & Martinez-Moyano, 2007; Edmiston, 2003; Norris, 2007). Local governments may lack the necessary skills, resources and knowledge to develop participatory e-government practices (Cohen et al., 2005). Existing organisational tendencies are reinforced through the frequent prioritisation of online service delivery improvements, which offer the greatest chance of economic gains to councils by, for example, minimising the number of staff hours needed for customer services (see Beynon-Davies & Martin, 2004; Hale, Musso, & Weare, 1999; Shackleton, Fisher, & Dawson, 2005). But this focus results in online initiatives that fail to provide "opportunities for citizens to participate and exert influence on local issues and decisions" (Leach & Pratchett, 2005, p. 323).

This chapter suggests how e-government practices that facilitate citizen participation can be successfully developed and implemented at the local level. It outlines the autonomous development of online practices by two local governments – Casey and Bologna – highlighting the limitations and benefits of the approaches used for increased citizen participation and engagement. First, however, it is important to distinguish between the concepts of interaction, participation and engagement, as each is often ill-defined and used interchangeably for analytical purposes.

Interaction, Participation and Engagement

Technological developments bring new possibilities for interaction, participation and engagement through e-government practices. Interaction can be understood as an exchange function of any available communication process (mediated or non-mediated), although it is often only associated with new communications technologies, particularly the Internet, as they provide substantially more avenues for interaction than previous technologies (see Kiousis, 2002; Stromer-Galley, 2000).

Stromer-Galley (2004) identifies the differences between the types of interactivity available through ICTs. She ascertains that 'interactivity-as-product' occurs between people and computers or networks (user and technology), and that 'interactivity-as-process' occurs between multiple people with the aid of computers (human interaction).[1] In the context of e-government, Stromer-Galley's (2004) distinction illustrates that current government ICT use that focuses on e-services can be considered as interactivity-as-product. In terms of service delivery, interactivity-as-product substantially reduces the need for government officials or administrators to deal extensively or interpretively with enquiries. As such, interactivity-as-product applications are more attractive to governments than interactivity-as-process as they reduce the number of staff hours needed to deal with citizen enquiries. Increasing interactivity-as-product does not, however, equate with improved forms of participation. Interactivity-as-process helps to provide a stronger connection between citizens and their representatives through the aid of communications technology, and it is this form of interaction that relates to civic participation and engagement mechanisms.

Interaction may not equate with participation, but interaction is needed in order for participation to occur. The forms of interaction enabled by different communication technologies shape the way participation takes place. Yet, the concept of political participation itself exists independently of the communication medium that enables it. For example, postal voting, voting at a polling booth and e-voting can be considered the same type of political participation but these occur through different means. A citizen paying rates can do so in person, over the telephone or online, but they are still undertaking the same practice. However, as technological capacity for interaction increases so do opportunities for additional forms of direct participation. This point highlights the importance of using networked digital communications technologies to facilitate more direct avenues of two-way civic participation. In terms of local community-based participation, Burns, Heywood, Taylor, Wilde, and Wilson (2004) indicate that participation can be understood as citizens playing an active part in the decisions that affect their lives, requiring a significant degree of power to exert influence (see also Margolis & Moreno-Riaño, 2009).

In a broad sense, the concept of civic engagement can be considered in terms of citizens paying attention to politics and being provided with opportunities to become actively involved in public issues (Couldry et al., 2007). Norris (2001) outlines three specific dimensions to civic engagement:

1. *Political Knowledge – what people learn about public affairs;*
2. *Political Trust – the public's orientation of support for the political system and its actors; and*

3. *Political Participation – activities designed to influence government and the decision-making process. (Norris, 2001, p. 217)*

ICTs can be used to develop each of these engagement dimensions through e-government. For example, knowledge of political issues and public affairs can be spread through websites, trust is built through new forms of connection between citizens and their representatives, and ICTs facilitate two-way dialogue, which can be used in decision-making. Online civic engagement therefore involves the availability of information, service delivery and participatory practices, coupled with citizens' trust and willingness to use online mechanisms (see Chen & Dimitrova, 2008). While Norris' (2001) three dimensions of civic engagement interrelate, the participation component, being directly concerned with citizens' capacity to influence government decision-making, is the primary focus of this chapter's examination of local e-government, given that participation itself requires both knowledge and trust. Conversely, Damodaran, Olphert, and Balatsoukas (2008) highlight that participation aids in building both knowledge and trust. The following section details the methodological approach of this research.

METHODOLOGY

Research into the Australian local government, the City of Casey, followed a grounded methodological approach, which privileges the formation of theoretical analysis from empirical data collection (Glaser & Strauss, 1967). A variety of research methods were used to aid broad understanding into local e-government and to ensure the validity of findings by enabling analytical comparisons between different research methods.

The City of Casey's online practices were examined to establish the one-way or two-way nature of the initiatives employed for citizens and statistical evidence of Casey's website usage was provided by the local government. Document analysis of Casey's policies and strategies was undertaken to illustrate the impact of official documents on council operations and the development and implementation of e-government practices (see Ritchie, 2003; Esmark & Triantafillou, 2007). As the City of Casey does not have an e-government or Internet policy (to-date) that specifically governs its online content and applications or that guides future development, it was necessary to more broadly look at council documents to determine how (if at all) they influence local e-government. Documents were selected for examination if they related to council operations, infrastructure development, government-citizen communications, ICT in general, or citizen participation. Documents within these themes were determined the most likely to impact e-government within the municipality, enabling explanation of existing practices and theorisation of potential improvements.

In-depth, semi-structured interviews were conducted with five of Casey's eleven councillors during 2008 to uncover their understandings and experiences in relation to both e-government practices and the importance of citizen participation in local political processes (see Lindlof & Taylor, 2002).[2] Each participant had at least three years of experience on council, with two interviewees having served as representatives for more than a dozen years. Four of the five interviewed councillors had held the position of City of Casey Mayor, and each represented a different ward within the municipality. There was also at least one representative interviewed from each of the three political parties on council (Labor, Liberal, and Independent).[3] Whilst a small sample size, the experience and diversity of the interviewees allows for broad insight and understanding into the factors impacting on Casey's e-government.

In Australia, the Federal Government is investing in the ubiquitous provision of high-speed broadband Internet infrastructure through optic fibre, fixed wireless and satellite technologies (see www.nbn.gov.au). In order to capitalise on this improved infrastructure, the government developed a *National Digital Economy Strategy* (Department of Broadband, Communications, & the Digital Economy (DBCDE), 2011). In terms of e-government, an aim of this strategy is to have four out of five Australians choosing to engage with governments online by the year 2020. This is a significant goal given that the infrastructure needed to achieve it is not scheduled for completion until the same year. This goal recognises that local governments hold a key position in driving greater digital engagement in communities (DBCDE, 2011). However, the Federal Government has not provided any suggestions or recommendations to local authorities on how to advance their online practices to facilitate greater engagement. Opportunities for online participation through local e-government are currently largely limited within Australia, with the bulk of local initiatives focused on improved information dissemination and service delivery (see, for example, O'Toole, 2007; 2009; Tiecher & Dow, 2002). In order to progress online practices to meet the goal set by the Federal Government, Australian local governments can draw from experiences elsewhere to help ensure that new online opportunities facilitate increased citizen engagement. For this reason, an international comparison was necessary for this investigation as it provides beneficial insight into the development of well-established and successful online engagement opportunities.

Bologna's *Iperbole* e-government project offers an early instructive example of government ICT use, which has been well documented and is widely recognised as an innovative local initiative that emphasises administrative transparency and encourages civic participation in public policy to enhance local democracy (see, for example, Di Maria & Rizzo, 2005; Guidi, 2009; Nesti & Valentini, 2010).[4] Bologna specifically developed *Iperbole* for its citizens, the site undergoes continual development to facilitate new mechanisms for civic input, and it was the first project in Italy to focus on local e-democracy and the second of its kind in Europe, following Amsterdam's *Digital City* (Nesti & Valentini, 2010). Because of its success and reputation throughout Europe, Bologna's *Iperbole* is one of the most frequency referenced examples of a local initiative and has won multiple European awards (Aurigi, 2000; 2005b). Bologna's drive to facilitate improved mechanisms for online civic participation in policy-making also positioned the local government to offer its expertise on other e-government initiatives. For example, Bologna coordinates the development of Web 2.0 applications in partnerships created with five other municipalities from the wider Emilia Romagna region. Bologna has also been involved with larger projects such as the European Union's *Delphi Mediation Online System*, in which Bologna implemented the first online prototype for civic consultation (Di Maria & Rizzo, 2005). The developmental processes and experiences of the City of Bologna in offering online opportunities for civic engagement therefore offer an invaluable source of information for municipalities seeking to advance their online practices to facilitate two-way civic participation.

While other local e-government initiatives that are progressive and socially inclusive were considered for comparison with this empirical study of the City of Casey, Bologna was selected as its online practices are managed by the local government itself, with no private influences such as occurs in cities like Amsterdam and Bristol. Both Casey and Bologna are well-positioned financially to trial and implement e-government initiatives, an advantage not held by all authorities. Bologna is an economically affluent area; the government won the funds to set up *Iperbole* and has subsequently gained outside grants to continually develop it (Tambini, 1997). The City of Casey's 2009-2010 financial year budget was approximately AU$198 million, with an estimated expenditure on its e-government practices of AU$10,000 (Freeman, 2011). Casey is in a favourable position to develop its e-government as it has a staff member in its communications department who is dedicated to online communications, has undertaken university training in website development, and creates and updates the local government's web content. Few Australian local governments have such a valuable resource and must outsource the development and maintenance of their e-government practices, increasing both the cost of e-government and the time required to update information. This means that Casey is in an optimal position to further develop e-government engagement opportunities and, if it does so, may subsequently provide an exemplar to other Australian local governments seeking to improve their online practices to meet the Federal Government's online engagement goal.

Casey's current website was predominantly the result of an increased need for the government to manage communications in the digital age and aid citizen access to information. Bologna's emphasis on public participation, administrative transparency and the enhancement of local democracy offers a suitable contrast in terms of ICT-enabled civic participation. In Bologna, a universal right to connectivity was viewed as a political right of citizenship and recognised as a necessary precondition for civic inclusion and participation in e-democracy (Tambini, 1997). The local government subsequently initially prioritised the provision of ICT infrastructure for civic access, which offers a useful parallel to the infrastructure currently being installed throughout Australia. However, Bologna offered free Internet access to its citizens to help ensure social inclusion and prevent the emergence of an uninformed underclass (Tambini, 1997). Australian citizens will continue to be required to pay for Internet access, and the cost is likely to partially inhibit online participation. Casey does, however, provide free public access terminals in local libraries and community centres for citizen use, as Bologna has done. While governance processes in Italy and Australia vary, much can be learned from a comparison of different contexts rather than by examining similar case studies. This comparison helps in identifying recommendations for the development and implementation of participatory e-government both in Casey and for local governments at a similar stage of development.

Evidence of the City of Bologna's e-government development has been taken from secondary sources. The use of secondary sources was necessary due to language barriers that inhibited direct examination of the government's online practices. While several sources have been used to highlight Bologna's e-government development, the work of Guidi (2009) and Aurigi (2000; 2005a; 2005b; 2006) particularly inform this chapter. The reasoning for this is that Guidi offers invaluable insight from the perspective of an official from the municipality itself, providing evidence of the local government's online practices and future aims for increasing citizen participation through additional ICT innovation. Aurigi's work provides an extensive in-depth empirical investigation (spanning eight years) of *Iperbole*, which began during *Iperbole's* early stages of development and includes website analysis and interviews with local politicians and officials. The evidence drawn from Aurigi's investigation therefore parallels both Casey's current e-government practices and this chapter's evaluation of Casey's development through in-depth interviews with local councillors. As such, evidence from Bologna provides vital insight into the ways that Casey may progress its online practices to facilitate increased civic participation and engagement.

LOCAL E-GOVERNMENT AND CITIZEN PARTICIPATION

The City of Casey

The Australian municipality of the City of Casey is located to the south-east of metropolitan Melbourne. It was proclaimed in 1994 after forced amalgamations and the restructuring of local governments throughout the State of Victoria.

Casey covers 400 square kilometres and is home to approximately 256,000 citizens, making it the seventh largest Australian local government in terms of population (Australian Bureau of Statistics, 2010). The council faces some limitations in terms of infrastructure access in rural areas and in suburbs that have undergone rapid development where existing infrastructure is insufficient to keep up with demand. Many of these problems will, however, be addressed under the Australian Federal Government's plan to implement improved broadband infrastructure to all Australian premises (see www.nbn.gov.au).

The council's website is its primary form of e-government (www.casey.vic.gov.au). The site is continually updated and successfully increases information dissemination, offering transparency of government documents. It contains an immense array of information on the local area, services, events, the council itself, and contains copies of policies, strategies and budgets. The site facilitates minimal two-way transactions, for example, to pay infringement notices and rates. As previously suggested, this type of website that privileges one-way service delivery over opportunities for two-way exchange is common amongst Australian local governments (see O'Toole, 2009). Casey also uses social media including *Facebook* and *Twitter* to further spread messages to the public. However, the two-way nature of these platforms is largely overlooked. Instead, they are predominantly used to post the headlines of media releases with links to the full reports on the council's website. This observation confirms Jimenez et al.'s (2012) finding that social media are largely underused by local governments, with their use employed primarily for increased access to information.

A civic networking site has been developed by the City of Casey (www.caseyconnect.net.au), which enables local clubs, groups and association to produce a webpage free of charge to help recruit new members. Interaction through this site is limited to downloadable forms and hyperlinks to external websites and email addresses. The site does not facilitate citizen communication with the local government itself. In November 2010, the council launched another website called *Casey Conversations* (caseyconversations.com.au), which provides discussion boards on key advocacy issues. *Casey Conversations* is a promising development that suggests the government has recognised the need to offer more participatory practices for citizens. However, the discussion topics available primarily concern issues where the final responsibility rests with state or federal authorities, rather than locally-decided issues. There is also no indication that local representatives visit the website or read citizens' comments, meaning citizen contributions through this site may have little impact.

An example of an advocacy campaign run through *Casey Conversations* is a discussion forum regarding the capacity of the water authority's drainage system.[5] This forum was launched in mid-June 2011 after heavy rains brought flash flooding to Casey communities, resulting in emergency evacuations and many losses of homes and businesses. The forum contains 29 posts (until June 2012), which highlight how local residents were affected by the floods and suggest potential action to prevent future flooding. Citizens also posted information about community-run groups that were set up to offer support to those affected, and the forum has been viewed over 1,200 times. The council was slow to respond to comments, with four responses in total over a 12-month period, and the only posts to citizens by a Casey administrator were generic 'thank you for your feedback' replies. Citizens began to question use of the website to communicate with the local government. For example, on 19 July 2011, part of one citizen's post was: "I believe this site is more of a front to stop us calling and bothering the Casey, Seriously will we get any feed back from this?" (Peterk, errors in original). This comment received a generic thank you response from the Casey administrator. This advocacy campaign did not influence the operation of either the water authority in improving the drainage systems and retarding basins or the local government, which could have addressed many of the citizens' suggestions such as building additional footbridges and clearing drains along roadways. In June 2012, large parts of the municipality again flooded, this time it was the worst flooding that many areas had seen in half a century. Emergency evacuations again occurred and further homes and businesses (as well as many that had previously been affected) received substantial damage. Many citizens did, however, receive a general letter of apology from Melbourne Water for having their properties inundated with water.

Casey's e-government therefore currently remains predominantly restricted to service delivery and tokenistic forms of participation, rather than spaces for discourse and deliberation (see Freeman & Hutchins, 2009). Casey, like many local governments, is grappling in the midst of a realisation of the need to incorporate more participatory elements into its online operations to suit the changing communications environment and the new forms of sharing, collaboration and exchange inscribed through the interactive nature of ICTs. This realisation has not yet led to the effective implementation of online mechanisms that facilitate, stimulate and support active online civic participation where citizen involvement informs decision-making processes.

The hesitation to create more online participatory practices that can influence local decisions appears to be resulting from existing political problems behind the technology. Jensen's (2009) investigation into citizens' online interactions with local governments and the impact on policy-making highlights that government ICT use is politically shaped. While Casey is a relatively newly established council, it has received a substantial amount of negative news media coverage, making both state and national headlines, and has been labelled the State's "most dysfunctional council" (Rolfe, 2012, p. 18). The actions of Casey councillors have been the subject of several Ombudsman investigations and on multiple occasions the police have been called into council meetings to expel unruly councillors. Corruption, misconduct, leaking of information, death threats, threats of poisoning pets, sexual harassment law suits, and accusations of intimidation and bullying are nothing new for this local government. Each interviewee spoke of other councillors' transgressions, particularly regarding misconduct during meetings, leaking of information and attempted manipulation of the election process. The political culture of Casey council has resulted in the formation of strategic alliances, which heavily influence the outcomes of local decisions.[6] Opening additional channels for communication with citizens in such a culture is likely to present unnecessary risks for representatives to demonstrate greater accountability for their actions.

Shin's (2012) study of the determinants behind e-government reveals that individual understandings and attitudes towards both technology and public service work shape e-government at the local level. There were substantial variations between interviewees in relation to ICT-knowledge and the value placed on citizen participation. The interviews revealed that the limited nature of Casey's e-government practices is the result of two key factors: the influence of political actors unwilling to trial new methods of communicating with citizens, and insufficient and ineffective policy frameworks guiding the council's online content and applications.

The interviewees' comments surrounding the value of civic views in decision-making reflected the council's reluctance to employ participatory e-government practices. The interviewees indicated that the only form of citizen participation that may influence councillors' decisions is direct contact with representatives (through face-to-face, letters, telephone or email), given enough people contacted their representatives with the same concern. However, it is unlikely that citizen participation actually shapes decision-making. In reference to a local road development issue, citizens created an action group, an online petition, wrote numerous letters-to-the-editor in local newspapers, and had direct contact with representatives at purposely held public meetings. When asked about citizens' comments surrounding this issue, Councillor Red stated that they had no influence on the council's decision. Councillor Black confirmed that, even though it was "terribly controversial... [the decision] never really got down to the citizens' influence." These comments suggest that neither online or offline methods for civic participation in Casey are currently considered in the council's decision-making processes. Another interviewee indicated that citizen participation is often uninformed and too emotional to be considered in decision-making, and is unnecessary when representatives have been elected to make decisions for their citizens:

Eleven people have been elected to make the decision. If you put it back to the web and everyone may put their hand up and make the decision, then why have eleven councillors? And the other thing also is the people who are going to respond to this question, how well informed are they? That would be the real issue... Unfortunately, I think most times people make an emotional decision about things without having the facts in front of them. (Councillor White)

In contrast to this councillor's comment, Pratchett (1999) highlights that it is part of the role of local government to keep citizens informed on issues to build democratic consciousness. Additionally, Pantti and van Zoonen (2006) suggest that emotion is needed in order to encourage participation in political activities. The flooding issue outlined earlier provides evidence of an emotional issue for citizens. Common suggestions for action on the *Casey Conversations* forum include sealing dirt roads, building footbridges, developing additional retarding basins, ensuring drains are cleared of rubbish, and using mobile-based emergency notifications. These are hardly irrational comments by local citizens.

If councillors are disinclined to use citizen participation to inform their decision-making, then it is of little surprise that the government's online practices do not facilitate increased engagement. Councillors' understandings and decisions regarding citizen involvement shape the ICT-enabled practices implemented. This point was evident in the interviewees' comments regarding a motion to webcast council meetings. In this instance, councillors who were opposed questioned whether anyone would watch webcasts, viewed it as a waste of money (it was estimated to cost Casey less than 0.01 percent of its yearly budget; Freeman, 2011), and were concerned about potential legal issues that could arise from having full deliberations webcast to the public. Jimenez et al. (2012) highlight that the participatory features of local e-government are largely underdeveloped as the result of political and legal issues. Officially, the motion to webcast Casey council meetings failed due to unnecessary cost and potential legal concerns. However, Councillor Red stated that, "The true underlying meaning is that several councillors wouldn't want to have been put under the pump of having their actions broadcast... I think for certain councillors, fear of being recorded would've been too much." In this instance, the increased mediated visibility (Thompson, 2005) associated with webcasting was seen as a potential threat to councillors' political viability. The strategic alliances on the council also shaped the outcome of the webcasting motion. Councillor Blue indicated that the decision not to webcast meetings was the result of the "climate of division" on the council and suggested that, "After the election we might be able to do it [webcast], if we get a few more councillors in that are a bit more amenable to those sort of things." This webcasting example affirms Norris' (2010) argument that technology application is dependent on the people and institutions that develop and implement its use.

In addition to shaping policy decisions, council divisions influence the effectiveness of current policies: "If you've got the numbers on the council, you can totally disregard that policy" (Councillor Red). This comment suggests that Casey's current policy frameworks may be ineffective if they are not in line with the views of the stronger alliance, which potentially impacts on all areas of Casey's development. Equally alarming is the fact that the council does not have an e-government or Internet policy guiding its online content and applications; no councillor interviewed was aware of this fact. Inadequate policy guidance means that Casey's e-government development is undertaken in an ad hoc manner. These findings are a concern for potential future engagement mechanisms, particularly as the decisions made according to alliances may not always be fully informed.

Casey's communications department was asked to produce a report outlining the potential use of social media for more two-way communication with citizens. The report outlined the costs, risks and threats of implementing more participatory online practices, but failed to provide any suggestions of possible benefits. Based on its recommendations, the council voted against using the interactive applications of social media platforms, instead deciding to restrict online communication to one-way forms that it can control: "The key concern for Council when using social networking sites is the ability to *control* information that is placed on these sites" (City of Casey, 2009, p. 64, emphasis added). When the interests of the council are prioritised over advanced forms of communication with citizens, there is little hope that the City of Casey will facilitate greater online engagement. The following section details the Italian City of Bologna's approach to e-government and citizen participation.

The City of Bologna

The Italian City of Bologna governs approximately 380,000 citizens within 140 square kilometres. In contrast to Casey, the local government has long been established, having existed for well over a century. It was not, however, until 1995 that the council and mayor began to be elected by popular vote. This date coincided with the development of the council's *Iperbole* Internet project, an initiative that emphasises the importance of public involvement in government decisions (see www.comune.bologna.it). *Iperbole* itself was specifically designed to promote e-democracy through public participation in decision-making and engagement with government.

Iperbole is a free wireless civic network and community portal set up by the local government, which is designed to promote social cohesion and local development by enhancing public participation in decision-making. The initiative aims to provide equal opportunities to access the Internet, and enable direct relationships between citizens and the local area's administration (Aurigi, 2005b). The City of Bologna recognised that the "involvement of citizens in the decision-making process and in designing (and monitoring) service activities is increasingly mandatory if the quality of public policy is to be enhanced" (Guidi, 2009, p. 262). Bologna has several broad aims for *Iperbole*:

- *Allow more direct citizen participation in consultation and decision-making processes;*
- *Renew citizens' interest in areas of dwindling political participation;*
- *Build a more solid consensus around the choices planned;*
- *Foster an ongoing dialogue to ensure balanced power and voices;*
- *Promote transparency in the public administration;*
- *Provide more direct and equal access to information, knowledge and services;*
- *Reduce discretionary administrative practices;*
- *Reduce the various 'divides' and gaps in order to empower citizens' status and competences;*
- *Improve the quality of life and the economy; and*

- *Inject social knowledge/capital into the public administration and counter the natural entropy of such complex and vertical organisations. (Guidi, 2009, p. 262)*

Communication is encouraged both between citizens and with the government, and *Iperbole* is supported by a set of policies that aim to increase usage of the site through inclusiveness and participation. These include policies addressing connectivity, public access, and citizens' socio-economic differences (see Aurigi, 2000). The initiative aims to provide all of Bologna's residents with access to the Internet in order to empower citizens (Tambini, 1997). The *Iperbole* website provides newsgroups and discussion forums for civic consultation. Drafts of government proposals are placed on the site so that citizens have a chance to contribute their views and inform public decision-making (Biasiotti & Nannucci, 2004). Citizens of Bologna are therefore provided with the opportunity to participate in online deliberation, contributing to the council's decision-making processes and leading to engagement with government.

Bologna faced many challenges during the early stages of *Iperbole's* development. The initial success of *Iperbole* was limited, with issues of civic access to the Internet and computer literacy found to be contributing factors to *Iperbole's* slow uptake and use for political participation (see Tambini, 1997). The council attempted to counter these problems by providing free Internet connections and a small number of public access terminals where assistance with Internet use could be attained. A dramatic increase in users indicated that this was a successful policy measure. However, online public discourse on policy matters remained limited. Aurigi (2005b) highlights that Bologna needed to combine public participation policies with wider strategies for urban and community development to ensure successful online public debate. This approach would have capitalised on citizens' increased interest in local issues (see Margolis & Moreno-Riaño, 2009). Instead, the council's emphasis on public discourse weakened. Focus was placed on online services, with online participation mechanisms still present, but in the background (Aurigi, 2005b).

The online civic participation that did take place in *Iperbole's* early years was often not taken into consideration in the council's decision-making processes: "due to the poor contents of the discussion groups, these were rarely taken into account or used to improve the way the Council worked" (Aurigi, 2005b, p. 124). Online discussions often focused on leisure and entertainment, with debates on local politics and municipal issues few and far between (Aurigi, 2005b). Aurigi undertook an empirical investigation into Bologna's *Iperbole* project between 1997 and 2004, which included interviewing local politicians and government officials. His work suggests that, during the early stages of *Iperbole's* development, local politicians did not use online public participation to inform their decisions or actions. A local politician stated that, "I believe that for the moment there is no influence whatsoever from Iperbole on decision-making processes" (Interviewee quoted in Aurigi, 2000, p. 40). Another one of the local policy-makers indicated that, "If I told you that we have learnt something from there [Iperbole] that would allow us to change municipal organisation for the better, I would be just silly" (Interviewee quoted in Aurigi, 2000, p. 40). Additionally, online discussions were not moderated so conversations often became chaotic and dominated by a few local interest groups and protestors (Millham & Eid, 2009).

In addition to limited civic access and poor public discourse, Bologna encountered other problems that could have easily deterred the council from continuing its online initiatives. For example, Bologna was sued by four local Internet service providers over loss of profits, due to the local government's provision of free Internet access for citizens. Funding and ownership issues also resulted from the council winning the funds to develop *Iperbole* (Aurigi, 2005b). While these issues contributed to criticism of *Iperbole*, Bologna continued to develop its e-government practices.

Not dissuaded from the initial limited success of *Iperbole*, the City of Bologna continued to provide the contexts needed for online civic deliberation and involvement with government. Bologna also persistently updated *Iperbole* to accommodate changes in the networked communications environment. For example, *Iperbole* is accessible via a smart phone optimised web application, is on *Twitter* – '*Twiperbole*' – and Bologna has launched an *Iperbole* 2.0 project. This project is an experimental platform that utilises the open source nature of Web 2.0 tools (such as wikis, blogs and user-generated content) to facilitate increased interactivity, social sharing and personalised customisation of online practices (see Guidi, 2009). As a result of Bologna's continued drive for online innovation, *Iperbole* now receives 500,000 visits daily (Guidi, 2009), which is a notable feat for any local government. Online discourse has also significantly grown through *Iperbole* and its associated initiatives. For example, Bologna recently sought civic input into the development of its digital agenda. More than 70 applications were lodged online and there have been over 700 tweets with the agenda's hashtag. In the long-term, therefore, *Iperbole* has been a successful initiative in fostering and supporting online citizen participation. Other Italian municipalities including Rome, Venice, and Milan have since followed Bologna's lead (Biasiotti & Nannucci, 2004).

The success of Bologna's *Iperbole* project is arguably the result of the broader attitudes towards online engagement held by the local government, which shaped both *Iperbole's* development and the use of citizen participation in decision-making. While, initially, local politicians suggested that poor online public discourse was not used to inform decision-making, the local government's continual drive for innovation has created thriving discourse and debate on local issues that is both rational and structured (Nesti & Valentini, 2010). A gradual process was, however, required to facilitate such effective online opportunities and public dialogue. Aurigi's study highlights that the desire to provide improved opportunities for citizen participation was a key driver behind the development of Bologna's e-government practices. An interview with a local government official illustrates the importance placed on citizen participation: The "citizen is much more than customer or client, because people must not be restricted to consuming services, but they should intervene in the decision making processes" (Interviewee quoted in Aurigi, 2006, p. 20). The promotion of e-democracy was viewed as necessary to help develop the capacity of the government to listen to the community (Di Maria & Rizzo, 2005). Bologna's approach was therefore shaped by its primary emphasis on open government that sought to increase participation and consensus building (Aurigi, 2005a; Di Maria & Rizzo, 2005), rather than improve service delivery per se.

Facilitating Civic Engagement

E-government initiatives should not solely address citizens as customers needing improved service delivery methods, but as key participants in the policy processes that shape civil society. The effectiveness of future e-government initiatives will depend upon each government's willingness and capacity to recognise the needs of its citizens and implement networking tools that permit civic participation. While the types of representative democracy present in Australia and Italy are different, Casey and Bologna provide useful case studies of the autonomous development of local e-government. At this stage, the City of Casey has prioritised the development of one-way information dissemination and service delivery practices. In contrast, Bologna has used ICTs to actively seek out two-way citizen participation and engagement, recognising that community involvement in decision-making enhances public policy (Guidi, 2009). While both councils capitalise on the interactive capabilities of ICTs to enhance their operations, Casey is yet to recognise the value of including civic views in decision-making and has not taken full advantage of e-government tools to facilitate citizen participation and engagement. The different approaches to e-government development undertaken by Casey and Bologna have had noticeable effects on the participatory nature of their e-government practices.

Bologna's initial e-government development largely focused on improving access to infrastructure, with citizen use also facilitated through public terminals. Ensuring equal access to sufficient ICT infrastructure is an important policy measure. This is a common and necessary course for many local governments, particularly during early stages of development (Cohen et al., 2005). Other local governments throughout the world have also addressed the need to offer improved access to ICT infrastructure for the advancement of social, cultural, and economic endeavours as well as political activities. Often these developments take place in municipal areas that cover large cities. For example, municipal broadband networks have been developed in over 300 cities in the United States of America, including San Francisco, Chicago, Atlanta, Los Angeles and Houston (Mossberger, Tolbert, & McNeal, 2008).

Not all local governments are in a position to advance infrastructure as Bologna and other select councils have done. In Australia, for example, the dispersed geographical nature of many local governments requires substantial resources to implement improved infrastructure, which creates a difficult task for rural and remote local governments with limited finances and small populations to govern. Many Australian infrastructure developments also lie outside the control of local authorities, with state and federal bodies responsible for developments. On this note, the Federal Government's planned broadband infrastructure developments will provide a useful resource throughout the country. It is, however, up to the discretion of local governments to offer public access terminals and educational programs to enhance civic adoption and use of ICTs. The City of Casey provides complimentary public Internet access terminals in local libraries and community centres, and the libraries run free Internet education classes on an ad hoc basis. The cost of providing these terminals and training programs may not be feasible for some local governments, and there may be a failure amongst local governments in recognising the various needs of users (Cohen et al., 2005). In Casey, there was evidence that some councillors had limited understandings of new technologies. For example, when asked about the availability of broadband Internet, Councillor White responded:

I think broadband is available, but everyone keeps talking about broadband and whatever the other one is called, dial up... Depending on what you do, and what your needs are, I don't know whether broadband is a must have. So if you've got one or the other, I don't really think it matters if you've got the time to use it. (Councillor White)

This comment reaffirms Tate, Hynson, and Toland's (2007) argument that many local authorities are experiencing a disconnection between expectations for ICT use and the necessary knowledge and capabilities to meet these expectations.

Damodaran, Nicholls, Henny, Land, and Ferby (2005) highlight that, in addition to a gap in knowledge and skills in local councils, e-government principles are not embedded in local government processes, resulting in little emphasis on e-participation. A cohesive approach that combines federal resources and local practices may be needed to facilitate online citizen participation and engagement through e-government in certain countries (see Flowers, Tang, Molas-Gallart, & Davies, 2006). Jaeger and Thompson (2003) highlight that in order "to achieve effective e-governance, the different levels of government in a nation must work in cooperation to develop and implement an e-government strategy" (2003, p. 391). Federal resources and guidance can aid infrastructure developments and enhance digital literacy amongst local government officials. Conversely, local governments possess the necessary knowledge about particular areas, citizen groups and local issues needed to ensure infrastructure developments and online spaces for engagement are the most effective for citizens and locales. Bologna illustrates that local governments are often well positioned to recognise citizens' needs and address socio-economic and skill divisions to ensure civic access to and use of the Internet. Additionally, Bologna highlights that, given sufficient resources, local governments are capable of implementing effective online spaces for citizen participation. Local policies may therefore play a crucial role in the development of participatory e-government practices (Graham & Aurigi, 1997).

In their analysis of Dutch cities, Cohen et al. (2005) highlight the importance of using local policies that address infrastructure improvements, enhance civic adoption and use, and more broadly guide the provision of online spaces for citizen discourse and deliberation. To facilitate participation in decision-making and enhance civic connection and engagement through e-government, such a holistic approach to ICT policy is needed. E-government policy-makers therefore need to recognise the importance of utilising strong policy guidance to ensure democratic application of the technologies. Casey is yet to recognise the benefits of using ICT policies to guide the development and implementation of its online practices. Despite the initial focus on infrastructure and use, Bologna did not fall into the predicament of equating improved access with increased participation, and recognised that spaces for direct online involvement needed to be provided. Moreover, Bologna was prepared to allow online discourse to inform decision-making.

The right to participate in government processes lies at the heart of a democratic society. Citizens are not, however, required to participate in deliberative democratic practices (see Barber, 1984). Opportunities for participation should still be provided by governments. Participatory e-government practices need to evolve continually with changes in the communications environment to offer new opportunities for citizens and to bolster and support online engagement. Bologna recognised the importance of this, continually advancing and adapting its online initiatives to changing communicative practices, and providing citizens with developed contexts and ample opportunities for participation. Moreover, e-government was integrated into the councils' everyday practices, with improved services and advanced participation complementing each other. Internet technologies have become a part of many citizens' everyday experiences (Green, 2008). E-government, then, in principle should be routine, not separated from the normal duties of governments but incorporated and integrated into everyday operations. The City of Casey facilitates excellent transparency of information and continues to develop its online presence. It has taken innovative e-government steps in its establishment of a civic networking website and a website for citizen views on advocacy issues. However, these sites do not operate within a government Internet domain. The development, maintenance and moderation of *Casey Conversations* are also outsourced from the local government. These observations suggest that Casey is reluctant to integrate these e-government initiatives into their everyday practices, potentially mitigating the impact of online citizen participation.

Online engagement is a gradual process that takes effort on the part of both politicians and constituents. The impact of current methods for citizen participation on decision-making in the City of Casey is negligible, at best. Additional online opportunities may be futile until there is a change in the governmental culture of Casey council to allow citizens to inform local decisions. By following the example of Bologna, Casey may be able to open their representation by being receptive to civic views. At present, evidence from Casey suggests that broader attitudes towards civic participation and the political will of representatives shape the inclusion of, and responsiveness to, civic views (see also Jensen, 2009; Gauld, Gray, & McComb, 2009). Local governments do not necessarily possess all the knowledge necessary to make every decision effectively for locales (Aurigi, 2005a). Citizen involvement adds an information source and enriches debate. In Casey, it is the politics behind the technology, rather than the online tools and participation methods offered, that limit the use of citizen participation in decision-making and hinder civic engagement with representatives. Institutional settings play a powerful role in developing online engagement through e-government (Chadwick, 2011). Civic engagement is a long-term exercise and should not be inhibited by short-term politics. Therefore, changing the culture of government is as important for the success of participatory e-government as the updating of practices to suit new technological developments.

FUTURE RESEARCH DIRECTIONS

This chapter highlights that current limitations to online engagement at the local level are often the result of institutional influences behind the application of the technologies. The use of technology in government operations is moulded by various factors (Millham & Eid, 2009). Some of the factors highlighted here include the impact of councillors' understandings of the value of civic participation, limited digital literacy amongst representatives, insufficient and ineffective policy frameworks, and the impact of political machinations and short-term politicking. The success of future participation initiatives will depend upon recognising and addressing these types of limitations for each authority, citizenry and locale, as problems will vary across governments and areas. Moreover, the diverse nature of e-government – internal and external communications, alterations to service delivery, broader administrative reform, and changing notions of democracy and citizenship – means that measures for success will vary depending on the goal of each initiative. For this reason, it is important for governments to develop and utilise strong policy frameworks and learn from lessons of other government bodies to enhance the approaches undertaken. The experience of Bologna, for example, highlights the initial need for a well co-ordinated approach that combines online participation initiatives with community development issues in order for facilitate citizen discourse and deliberation (Aurigi, 2005b).

While this chapter has used the views of local government officials to examine citizen participation through e-government, there is also a need for greater research into citizens' perspectives. There is little point in governments implementing new online opportunities for participation if the platforms developed do not appeal to citizens. Moreover, if the goal is to enhance citizen engagement, it is important to uncover the types of issues with which citizens want to be involved. Governments can speak to, for example, interest groups or citizen advisory committees to gain an understanding into the practices desired by citizens. This knowledge can be used to frame the development of e-government practices to suit citizens and increase the chance of successful engagement.

CONCLUSION

The varying approaches to e-government development and implementation undertaken by Casey and Bologna have had marked impacts on the success of their participatory projects. Bologna initially set out to encourage e-democracy whereas Casey followed the typical evolution of e-government by beginning with information dissemination and basic e-commerce functions (see Margolis & Moreno-Riaño, 2009). Both local governments developed their online practices autonomously from other levels of government, but Casey's online applications have been implemented in an ad hoc manner without the aid of any guiding policy documentation. Bologna, by comparison, had specific aims for *Iperbole's* space for online dialogue and its incorporation into decision-making. In Casey, citizen involvement scarcely informs the views of policy-makers. Broader institutional contexts and political factors, such as affiliations and councillors' divergent understandings of ICTs and the role of citizens in the democratic process, contribute to a reluctance to cede control of political messages in the online environment, which presently restricts the council's development of participatory e-government practices.

These local government examples highlight the varying emphasis placed on service delivery and civic participation in e-government initiatives, and how institutional contexts directly shape opportunities for civic engagement. If Casey is to offer more participatory mechanisms as Bologna has done, the local government will need to make greater use of guiding policy documentation, further educate local representatives on the potential benefits of online civic involvement, and undergo a broader change in governmental culture so that representatives are receptive to citizen input. Such strategies are needed if Casey's e-government is to progress to effectively facilitate civic participation and enable contributions to inform decision-making processes.

As communicative and democratic practices change, e-government holds a vital position for the future of citizen participation. Local governments offer a key context for the provision of online spaces that enable increased civic engagement and connection with representatives. The success of such spaces largely depends upon effective political frameworks being in place that allow citizen participation to influence government decision-making. If e-government is to facilitate online civic engagement, focus needs to be shifted away from the 'e' in e-government – away from the technologies and the increased efficiency they enable – and towards the government actions, policies and outcomes that support the 'e'.

REFERENCES

Aurigi, A. (2000). Digital city or urban simulator? In Ishida, T., & Isbister, K. (Eds.), *Digital cities: Technologies, experiences, and future perspectives* (pp. 33–44). Berlin: Springer. doi:10.1007/3-540-46422-0_4.

Aurigi, A. (2005a). Competing urban visions and the shaping of the digital city. *Knowledge, Technology & Policy*, *18*(1), 12–26. doi:10.1007/s12130-005-1013-z.

Aurigi, A. (2005b). *Making the digital city: The early shaping of urban internet space*. Aldershot, Hampshire: Ashgate Publishing Limited.

Aurigi, A. (2006). New technologies, same dilemmas: Policy and design issues for the augmented city. *Journal of Urban Technology*, *13*(3), 5–28. doi:10.1080/10630730601145989.

Australian Bureau of Statistics. (2010). *Regional population growth, Australia (No. 3218.0)*. Canberra, Australian Capital Territory: Australian Bureau of Statistics.

Barber, B. R. (1984). *Strong democracy: Participatory politics for a new age*. Berkeley, California: University of California Press.

Bertot, J. C., Jaeger, P. T., & Grimes, J. M. (2012). Promoting transparency and accountability through ICTs, social media, and collaborative e-government. *Transforming Government: People. Process and Policy*, *6*(1), 78–91.

Beynon-Davies, P., & Martin, S. (2004). Electronic local government and the modernisation agenda: Progress and prospects for public service improvement. *Local Government Studies*, *30*(2), 214–229. doi:10.1080/0300303042000267245.

Biasiotti, M. A., & Nannucci, R. (2004). Learning to become an e-citizen: The European and Italian policies. In M.A. Wimmer (Ed.), *Knowledge Management in Electronic Government, 5th IFIP International Working Conference, KMGov 2004* (pp. 269-280). Krems: Springer.

Bonsón, E., Torres, L., Royo, S., & Flores, F. (2012). Local e-government 2.0: Social media and corporate transparency in municipalities. *Government Information Quarterly*, *29*(2), 123–132. doi:10.1016/j.giq.2011.10.001.

Bruns, A. (2008). *Blogs, wikipedia, second life, and beyond: From production to produsage*. New York: Peter Lang Publishing, Inc..

Burns, D., Heywood, F., Taylor, M., Wilde, P., & Wilson, M. (2004). *Making community participation meaningful: A handbook for development and assessment*. Bristol: Policy Press.

Chadwick, A. (2011). Explaining the failure of an online citizen engagement initiative: The role of internal institutional variables. *Journal of Information Technology & Politics*, *8*(1), 21–40. doi: 10.1080/19331681.2010.507999.

Chen, Y., & Dimitrova, D. V. (2008). Civic engagement via e-government portals: Information, transactions, and policy making. In Norris, D. (Ed.), *E-Government research: Policy and management* (pp. 205–209). Hershey, Pennsylvania: IGI Global.

City of Casey. (2009). *Council meeting agenda*. October 20, 2009, City of Casey, Victoria: City of Casey. Retrieved December 7, 2011, from http://www.casey.vic.gov.au/meetings/article.asp?Item=14187

City of Casey. (2012). *Casey connect: Connecting communities online*. Retrieved January 20, 2012, from http://www.caseyconnect.net.au

City of Casey. (2012). *Casey conversations*. Retrieved March 2, 2012, from http://caseyconversations.com.au

City of Casey. (2012). *City of Casey*. Retrieved February 8, 2012, from http://www.casey.vic.gov.au

Cohen, G., van Geenhuizen, M., & Nijkamp, P. (2005). ICT as a contributing factor to urban sustainable development: Policymaking in Dutch cities. In van Geenhuizen, M., Gibson, D. V., & Heitor, M. V. (Eds.), *Regional development and conditions for innovation in the network society* (pp. 99–117). West Lafayette, Indiana: Purdue University Press.

Comune de Bologna. (2012). *Iperbole: La rete vivica di Bologna*. Retrieved January 20, 2012, from http://www.comune.bologna.it/

Couldry, N., & Langer, A. I. (2005). Media consumption and public connection: Towards a typology of the dispersed citizen. *Communication Review*, *8*(2), 237–257. doi:10.1080/10714420590953325.

Couldry, N., Livingstone, S., & Markham, T. (2007). *Media consumption and public engagement: Beyond the presumption of attention*. Basingstoke, Hampshire: Palgrave Macmillan. doi:10.1057/9780230800823.

Damodaran, L., Nicholls, J., Henney, A., Land, F., & Farbey, B. (2005). The contribution of sociotechnical systems thinking to the effective adoption of e-government and the enhancement of democracy. *The Electronic Journal of E-Government*, *3*(1), 1–12.

Damodaran, L., Olphert, W., & Balatsoukas, P. (2008). Democratizing local e-government: The role of virtual dialogue. In. T. Janowski & T.A. Pardo (Eds.), *Proceedings of the 2nd international conference on theory and practice of electronic governance (ICEGOV'08)* (pp. 388-393). New York: ACM.

Department of Broadband, Communications and the Digital Economy (DBCDE). (2011). *#au20 national digital economy strategy: Leveraging the national broadband network to drive Australia's digital productivity*. Canberra, Australian Capital Territory: DBCDE.

Department of Broadband, Communications and the Digital Economy (DBCDE). (2012). *National broadband network: Empowering Australia*. Retrieved January 20, 2012, from http://www.nbn.gov.au/

Di Maria, E., & Rizzo, L. S. (2005). E-democracy: The participation of citizens and new forms of the decision-making process. In E. Di Maria & S. Micelli (Eds.), *On line citizenship: Emerging technologies for European cities* (pp. 71-106). New York: Springer Science+Business Media, Inc.

Edmiston, K. D. (2003). State and local e-government: Prospects and challenges. *American Review of Public Administration*, *33*(1), 20–45. doi:10.1177/0275074002250255.

Eggers, W. D. (2005). *Government 2.0: Using technology to improve education, cut red tape, reduce gridlock, and enhance democracy*. Lanham, Maryland: Rowman & Littlefield Publishers, Inc.

Esmark, A., & Triantafillou, P. (2007). Document analysis of network topography and network programmes. In Bogason, P., & Zølner, M. (Eds.), *Methods in democratic network governance* (pp. 99–124). Basingstoke, Hampshire: Palgrave Macmillan.

Flamm, K., & Chaudhuri, A. et al. (2006). The internet, the government, and e-governance. In Hernon, P., Cullen, R., & Relyea, H. C. (Eds.), *Comparative perspectives on e-government: Serving today and building for tomorrow* (pp. 331–348). Lanham, Maryland: Scarecrow Press Inc.

Flowers, S., Tang, P., Molas-Gallart, J., & Davies, A. (2006). Contrasting approaches to the adoption of e-government: The UK and the Netherlands. *Journal of E-Government*, *2*(3), 51–83. doi:10.1300/J399v02n03_04.

Freeman, J. (2011). *Local e-government: Politics and civic participation*. (Unpublished doctoral thesis). Monash University, Australia.

Freeman, J., & Hutchins, B. (2009). Balancing the digital democratic deficit? E-government. *Media International Australia*, *130*, 17–27.

Gauld, R., Gray, A., & McComb, S. (2009). How responsive is e-government? Evidence from Australia and New Zealand. *Government Information Quarterly*, *26*(1), 69–74. doi:10.1016/j.giq.2008.02.002.

Gil-Garcia, J. R., & Martinez-Moyano, I. J. (2007). Understanding the evolution of e-government: The influence of systems of rules on public sector dynamics. *Government Information Quarterly*, *24*(2), 266–290. doi:10.1016/j.giq.2006.04.005.

Glaser, B. G., & Strauss, A. L. (1967). *The discovery of grounded theory: Strategies for qualitative research*. Chicago: Aldine Publishing Company.

Graham, S., & Aurigi, A. (1997). Virtual cities, social polarization, and the crisis in urban public space. *Journal of Urban Technology*, *4*(1), 19–52. doi:10.1080/10630739708724546.

Green, L. (2008). Is it meaningless to talk about 'the internet'? *Australian Journal of Communication*, *35*(3), 1–14.

Griffin, D., & Halpin, E. (2005). An exploratory evaluation of UK local e-government from an accountability perspective. *The Electronic Journal of E-Government*, *3*(1), 13–28.

Guidi, L. (2009). Participation at the municipal level in Italy: The case of Bologna. In Organisation for Economic Co-operation and Development (OECD) *Focus on citizens: Public engagement for better policy and services* (pp. 261–266). Paris: OECD Studies on Public Engagement.

Hale, M., Musso, J., & Weare, C. (1999). Developing digital democracy: Evidence from Californian municipal web pages. In Hague, B. N., & Loader, B. D. (Eds.), *Digital democracy: Discourse and decision making in the information age* (pp. 96–115). London: Routledge.

Ho, A. T.-K. (2002). Reinventing local governments and the e-government initiative. *Public Administration Review*, *62*(4), 434–444. doi:10.1111/0033-3352.00197.

Homburg, V. (2008). *Understanding e-government: Information systems in public administration*. New York: Routledge.

Jaeger, P. T., & Thompson, K. M. (2003). E-government around the world: Lessons, challenges, and future directions. *Government Information Quarterly*, *20*(4), 389–394. doi:10.1016/j.giq.2003.08.001.

Jensen, M. J. (2009). Electronic democracy and citizen influence in government. In Reddick, C. G. (Ed.), *Handbook of research on strategies for local e-government adoption and implementation: Comparative studies* (pp. 288–305). Hershey, PA: Information Science Reference. doi:10.4018/978-1-60566-282-4.ch015.

Jimenez, B. S., Mossberger, K., & Wu, Y. (2012). Municipal government and the interactive web: Trends and issues for civic engagement. In Manoharan, A., & Holzer, M. (Eds.), *E-governance and civic engagement: Factors and determinants of e-democracy* (pp. 251–271). Hershey, PA: Information Science Reference. doi:10.4018/978-1-4666-1740-7.ch006.

Kiousis, S. (2002). Interactivity: A concept explication. *New Media & Society*, *4*(3), 355–383.

Kunstelj, M., & Vintar, M. (2004). Evaluating the progress of e-government development: A critical analysis. *Information Polity*, *9*(3/4), 131–148.

Leach, S., & Pratchett, L. (2005). Local government: A new vision, rhetoric or reality? *Parliamentary Affairs*, *58*(2), 318–334. doi:10.1093/pa/gsi025.

Lindlof, T. R., & Taylor, B. C. (2002). *Qualitative communication research methods* (2nd ed.). Thousand Oaks, California: Sage.

Luna-Reyes, L. F., Gil-Garcia, J. R., & Celorio Mansi, J. A. (2011). Citizen-centric approaches to e-government and the back-office transformation. In *Proceedings of the 12th annual international conference on digital government research* (pp. 213-218). New York: ACM.

Margolis, M., & Moreno-Riaño, G. (2009). *The prospect of internet democracy*. Farnham, Surrey: Ashgate Publishing Limited.

Mayer-Schönberger, V., & Lazer, D. (2007). From electronic government to information government. In Mayer-Schönberger, V., & Lazer, D. (Eds.), *Governance and information technology: From electronic government to information government* (pp. 1–14). Cambridge, Massachusetts: MIT Press.

Millham, R., & Eid, C. (2009). Digital cities: Nassau and Bologna – A study in contrasts. In *Proceedings of the IEEE Latin-American Conference on Communications, IEEE Communications Society* (pp. 1-6). Medllin, Colombia: LATINCOM. Retrieved January 20, 2012, from http://ieeexplore.ieee.org/xpls/abs_all.jsp?arnumber=5305144

Moon, M. J. (2002). The evolution of e-government among municipalities: Rhetoric or reality? *Public Administration Review*, *62*(4), 424–433. doi:10.1111/0033-3352.00196.

Mossberger, K., Tolbert, C. J., & McNeal, R. S. (2008). *Digital citizenship: The internet, society and participation*. Cambridge, Massachusetts: MIT Press.

Nesti, G., & Valentini, C. (2010). E-democracy and Italian public administration: New media at the service of citizens. In Ardizzoni, M., & Ferrari, C. (Eds.), *Beyond monopoly: Globalization and contemporary Italian media* (pp. 151–170). Plymouth, UK: Lexington Books.

Norris, D. F. (2005). E-government at the American grassroots: Future trajectory. In *Proceedings of the 38th Hawaii International Conference on System Sciences (HICSS'05)* (pp. 125-132). Washington: Computer Society Press.

Norris, D. F. (2007). Electronic democracy at the American grassroots. In Norris, D. F. (Ed.), *Current issues and trends in e-government research* (pp. 164–179). Hershey, Pennsylvania: IGI Global. doi:10.4018/978-1-59904-283-1.ch008.

Norris, D. F. (2010). E-government... not e-governance... not e-democracy: Not now! Not ever? In J. Davies & T. Janowski (Eds.), *Proceedings of the 4th international conference on theory and practice of electronic governance (ICEGOV'10)* (pp. 339-346). New York: ACM.

Norris, P. (2001). *Digital divide: Civic engagement, information poverty, and the internet worldwide*. New York: Cambridge University Press. doi:10.1017/CBO9781139164887.

O'Toole, K. (2007). E-governance in Australian local government: Spinning a web around community? *International Journal of Electronic Government Research*, *3*(4), 58–75. doi:10.4018/jegr.2007100104.

O'Toole, K. (2009). Australia local government and e-governance: From administration to citizen participation? In Khosrow-Pour, M. (Ed.), *E-government diffusion, policy, and impact: Advanced issues and practices* (pp. 174–184). Hershey, Pennsylvania: IGI Global.

Pantti, M., & van Zoonen, L. (2006). Do crying citizens make good citizens? *Social Semiotics*, *16*(2), 205–224. doi:10.1080/10350330600664797.

Pratchett, L. (1999). New technologies and the modernization of local government: An analysis of biases and constraints. *Public Administration*, *77*(4), 731–750. doi:10.1111/1467-9299.00177.

Reece, B. (2006). E-government literature review. *Journal of E-Government*, *3*(1), 69–110. doi:10.1300/J399v03n01_05.

Ritchie, J. (2003). The applications of qualitative methods to social research. In Ritchie, J., & Lewis, J. (Eds.), *Qualitative research practice: A guide for social science students and researchers* (pp. 24–46). London: Sage.

Rolfe, P. (2012, April 15). The case against Casey council. *Herald Sun* (pp. 18-19).

Sandoval-Almazan, R., & Gil-Garcia, J. R. (2012). Are government internet portals evolving towards more interaction, participation, and collaboration? Revisiting the rhetoric of e-government among municipalities. *Government Information Quarterly*, *29*(Supplement 1), S72–S81. doi:10.1016/j.giq.2011.09.004.

Seifert, J. W. (2006). E-government in the United States. In Hernon, P., Culleen, R., & Relyea, H. C. (Eds.), *Comparative perspectives on e-government: Serving today and building for tomorrow* (pp. 25–54). Lanham, Maryland: Scarecrow Press, Inc..

Shackleton, P., Fisher, J., & Dawson, L. (2005). From dog licenses to democracy: Local government approaches to e-service delivery in Australia. In D. Bartmann, F. Rajola, J. Kallinikos, D. Avison, R. Winter, P. Ein-Dor, J. Becker, F. Bodendorf, & C. Weinhardt (Eds.), *Proceedings of the thirteenth European conference on information systems* (pp. 724-735). Regensburg, Germany: ECIS Standing Committee.

Shin, E. (2012). Attitudinal determinants of e-government technology use among U.S. local public managers. In *Proceedings of the 45th Hawaii Conference on System Science* (pp. 2613-2622). Washington: Computer Society Press.

Silcock, R. (2001). What is e-government? *Parliamentary Affairs*, *54*(1), 88–101. doi:10.1093/pa/54.1.88.

Stromer-Galley, J. (2000). Online interaction and why candidates avoid it. *The Journal of Communication*, *50*(4), 111–132. doi:10.1111/j.1460-2466.2000.tb02865.x.

Stromer-Galley, J. (2004). Interactivity-as-product and interactivity-as-process. *The Information Society*, *20*(5), 391–394. doi:10.1080/01972240490508081.

Tambini, D. (1997). Civic networking and universal rights to connectivity: Bologna. In Tsagarousianou, R., Tambini, D., & Bryan, C. (Eds.), *Cyberdemocracy: Technology, cities and civic networks* (pp. 84–109). London: Routledge.

Tate, M., Hynson, R., & Toland, J. (2007). The disconnect between the current orthodoxy of local government and the promise and practices of information technology management: An illustrative case study. *Electronic Government: An International Journal*, *4*(4), 509–526. doi:10.1504/EG.2007.015041.

Teicher, J., & Dow, N. (2002). E-government in Australia: Promise and progress. *Information Polity*, *7*(4), 231–246.

Thompson, J. B. (2005). The new visibility. *Theory, Culture & Society*, *22*(6), 31–51. doi:10.1177/0263276405059413.

Wong, W., & Welch, E. (2004). Does e-government promote accountability? A comparative analysis of website openness and government accountability. *Governance: An International Journal of Policy, Administration and Institutions*, *17*(2), 275–297. doi:10.1111/j.1468-0491.2004.00246.x.

ADDITIONAL READING

Borge, R., Colombo, C., & Welp, Y. (2009). Online and offline participation at the local level: A quantitative analysis of the Catalan municipalities. *Information Communication and Society*, *12*(6), 1–30. doi:10.1080/13691180802483054.

Brants, K., Huizenga, M., & van Meerten, R. (1996). The new canals of Amsterdam: An exercise in local electronic democracy. *Media Culture & Society*, *18*(2), 233–247. doi:10.1177/016344396018002004.

Brown, M. M. (2007). Understanding e-government benefits: An examination of leading-edge local governments. *American Review of Public Administration*, *37*(2), 178–197. doi:10.1177/0275074006291635.

Chen, P., Gibson, R., Lusoli, W., & Ward, S. (2007). Australian governments and online communication. In Young, S. (Ed.), *Government communication in Australia* (pp. 161–180). Port Melbourne, Victoria: Cambridge University Press.

Coleman, S., & Blumler, J. G. (2009). *The internet and democratic citizenship: Theory, practice and policy*. New York: Cambridge University Press. doi:10.1017/CBO9780511818271.

Coursey, D., & Norris, D. F. (2008). Models of e-government: Are they correct? An empirical assessment. *Public Administration Review*, *68*(3), 523–536. doi:10.1111/j.1540-6210.2008.00888.x.

Cullen, R. (2005). E-government, a citizens' perspective. *Journal of E-Government*, *1*(3), 5–28. doi:10.1300/J399v01n03_02.

Downes, E. J., & McMillan, S. J. (2000). Defining interactivity: A qualitative identification of key dimensions. *New Media & Society*, *2*(2), 157–179. doi:10.1177/14614440022225751.

Fountain, J. E. (2001). *Building the virtual state: Information technology and institutional change*. Washington: Brookings Institutional Press.

Hacker, K. L., & van Dijk, J. (Eds.). (2000). *Digital democracy: Issues of theory and practice*. London: Sage.

Hague, B. N., & Loader, B. D. (Eds.). (1999). *Digital democracy: Discourse and decision making in the information age*. London: Routledge.

Hernon, P., Cullen, R., & Relyea, H. C. (Eds.). (2006). *Comparative perspectives on e-government: Serving today and building for tomorrow*. Lanham, Maryland: Scarecrow Press Inc.

Kingston, R. (2007). Public participation in local policy decision-making: The role of web-based mapping. *The Cartographic Journal*, *44*(2), 138–144. doi:10.1179/000870407X213459.

Lowndes, V., Pratchett, L., & Stoker, G. (2001). Trends in public participation: Part 1 – local government perspectives. *Public Administration*, *79*(1), 205–222. doi:10.1111/1467-9299.00253.

Lowndes, V., Pratchett, L., & Stoker, G. (2001). Trends in public participation: Part 2 – citizens' perspectives. *Public Administration*, *79*(2), 445–455. doi:10.1111/1467-9299.00264.

Morphet, J. (2009). E-government and local government. In Budd, L., & Harris, L. (Eds.), *E-governance: Managing or governing?* (pp. 197–212). New York: Routledge.

Norris, D. F., & Moon, M. J. (2005). Advancing e-government at the grassroots: Tortoise or hare? *Public Administration Review*, *65*(1), 64–75. doi:10.1111/j.1540-6210.2005.00431.x.

Pavlichev, A., & Garson, G. D. (Eds.). (2004). *Digital government: Principles and best practices*. Hershey, Pennsylvania: Idea Group Publishing.

Reddick, C. G. (2005). Citizen interaction with e-government: From the streets to servers? *Government Information Quarterly*, *22*(1), 38–57. doi:10.1016/j.giq.2004.10.003.

Reddick, C. G. (2011). Citizen interaction and e-government: Evidence for the managerial, consultative, and participatory models. *Transforming Government: People. Process and Policy*, *5*(2), 167–184.

Scott, M., Russell, P., & Redmond, D. (2007). Active citizenship, civil society and managing spatial change in the rural-urban fringe. *Policy and Politics*, *35*(1), 163–190. doi:10.1332/030557307779657702.

West, D. M. (2004). E-government and the transformation of service delivery and citizen attitudes. *Public Administration Review*, *64*(1), 15–27. doi:10.1111/j.1540-6210.2004.00343.x.

West, D. M. (2005). *Digital government: Technology and public sector performance*. Princeton, New Jersey: Princeton University Press.

Wiklund, H. (2005). A Habermasian analysis of the deliberative democratic potential of ICT-enabled services in Swedish municipalities. *New Media & Society*, *7*(5), 701–723. doi:10.1177/1461444805056013.

Wilhelm, A. (2000). *Democracy in the digital age: Challenges to political life in cyberspace*. New York: Routledge.

KEY TERMS AND DEFINITIONS

Citizens: Individuals with the political right to reside in a region, vote and be represented by a government.

Councillors: Elected representatives of local governments.

E-Government: Use of information and communication technologies as the interface for government-citizen communications.

Engagement: The active involvement of citizens in political issues, with the ability to exert influence on government decision-making.

Information and Communications Technologies (ICTs): Information and communications technologies that combine computing with telecommunications, such as the Internet and World Wide Web.

Interaction: The exchange function of communication processes, mediated or non-mediated.

Local Government: An administrative level of government concerned with the civic affairs of a designated region.

Participation: Citizens' political involvement with government.

ENDNOTES

1. Similarly, Bruns (2008) distinguishes between politics-as-product and politics-as-process. The former is concerned with winning votes and elections, and the latter emphasises ongoing participation, which enables public policy to be continually revised.
2. In accordance with university ethics requirements, councillors cannot be identified by name in this research. To distinguish between councillors, each has been assigned a colour: Councillors Black, Blue, Red, White and Yellow.
3. There has been a local government election since the interviews were conducted with Casey councillors, which has altered the representatives on council. However, the issues impacting on local e-government that are identified later in this chapter, such as ICT knowledge, ineffective policy documents, lack of responsiveness to citizens, and councillor corruption and misconduct, persist within the government.
4. The acronym *Iperbole* stands for 'Internet per Bologna e L'Emilia Romagna' – Internet for Bologna and Emilia Romagna (Aurigi, 2005b).
5. Melbourne Water manages water drainage throughout the municipality jointly with the local government.
6. Interestingly, these alliances do not entirely align with political parties as may be expected. There has, however, been an instance where a mayor has changed political parties to maintain an alliance.

Section 3
Europe

Chapter 13
Critical Success Factors for E-Government Infrastructure Implementation

Marijn Janssen
Delft University of Technology, The Netherlands

Mark Borman
The University of Sydney, Australia

ABSTRACT

Effective digital government infrastructures are needed to support the policy and strategy of governments. ICT Infrastructures provide generic functionalities that are shared and used by large numbers of users. Typically, many stakeholders are involved in the implementation of the infrastructure and the infrastructure is shaped by the interactions among stakeholders. The management of the development of such infrastructures is complicated. Multiple competing agendas and needs have to be reconciled. One approach for managing and guiding its development is based on critical success factors (CSFs). CSFs are those areas that need to be given attention and are perceived to be most important to the success of the infrastructure development. The aim of the research described in this chapter is to identify CSFs for guiding shared infrastructure implementation. This research is conducted by identifying CSFs for Surfnet - which is a public organization providing a digital infrastructure for researchers, teachers and students. This infrastructure enables them to collaborate with each other. The framework of Borman and Janssen (2012) was used which classified CSF in outcome, process and operating environment characteristic categories. The CSFs suggest a need to have a well-developed infrastructure implementation strategy. It is argued that taking a CSF-based approach is suitable for guiding complex projects, but they should be revisited regularly as they might change over time.

DOI: 10.4018/978-1-4666-4173-0.ch013

Copyright © 2013, IGI Global. Copying or distributing in print or electronic forms without written permission of IGI Global is prohibited.

INTRODUCTION

To inspire and support e-government developments, governments from all over the world create national digital government infrastructures (or e-government infrastructure) to provide generic functionalities that can be used by different public agencies to develop electronic services (M. Janssen, Chun, & Gil-Garcia, 2009). Infrastructures provide the base foundation for IT capabilities and are shared throughout the organizations (Weill, Broadbent, & Butler, 1996). Infrastructures serve as the foundation for building new services on top of it, in this way enabling the fast and easy development of new services. Infrastructures are typically not the primary source of an organization's competitive advantage, rather they are necessary conditions and provides a facilitating capability to create value. Generic functionalities such as identification and authentication mechanisms, centralized registries, secure exchange facilities and portals have been set up (Klievink & Janssen, 2009). These generic functionalities (or services) can be used by a large number of users (M. Janssen et al., 2009) and provide generic support to often multiple different activities. The facilities that make up these infrastructures function as a kind of building blocks that can be reused by other public organizations. The concept of infrastructures is based on the idea that basic services are developed that can be shared and used by many organizations (ibid). Hence organizations do not have to develop nor maintain the services themselves. They are provided over the web and others parties are in charge of running and operating the infrastructure. Shared infrastructures are considered to hold considerable benefits for businesses and governments enabling information sharing, reducing costs of already existing interactions and enabling new ones (Hanseth & Lyytinen, 2010).

The development of an infrastructure is not easy as it is a result of the technology used, the needs of and interactions among different stakeholders. Infrastructures are used by a large number of users and its services are shared among members. Shard services can be defined as "the concentration of dispersed service provisioning activities in a single organizational entity" (Marijn Janssen, Joha, & Zuurmond, 2009, p. 16). Infrastructures are not static, but dynamic and evolve due to advances in technology as well as changes in the social system. Hanseth et al. (1996) name infrastructures 'information infrastructures' in order to emphasize the holistic, socio-technical and evolutionary nature. They put the combined social and technical complexity at the center of an empirical scrutiny.

An infrastructure offers only value to its users after a certain critical mass of users has been reached (M. Janssen et al., 2009). In such infrastructure the installed base is of particular importance (Hanseth, Ciborra, & Braa, 2001). An infrastructure is never developed from scratch, but is built on top of an existing base of technical and non-technical elements. The installed base refers to the institutionalized technical, organizational, legal and other elements that determines the further development of the information infrastructure (Hanseth et al., 2001). The installed base represents "sunk costs," that is, huge investments (in terms of investments, development, training, education and habits) are made only be earned back over a pre-longed period of time. These sunk costs make it attractive to continue current practices and not replacing them with entirely new and more up-to-date solutions. The evolution of infrastructures is path-dependent due to the installed base, which can be viewed as the "living legacy" (Hanseth, Monteiro, & Hatling, 1996).

The technical complexity and the decentralized control which involves many stakeholders having their own requirements makes the development of a public infrastructure difficult. Some stakeholders might have less resources than others, might have less ICT-expertise and might have legacy systems which results in a heterogeneous landscape of stakeholders. Iindividual organizations make their local design decisions, which in turn influence the further development of the infrastructure. Path-dependencies play a major role in infrastructure related development. *Path-dependencies* are related to available alternatives (Eisenhardt & Martin, 2000). They take into account past decisions and the associated repertoire of procedures and routines, which can constrain or enable changes. Decision-makers are confronted by the challenge of fostering bottom up development but at the same time avert fragmentation of systems in a top-down manner (Veenstra & Janssen, 2012).

Citizen's and government's needs are dynamic as conditions, practices, needs and expectation change due to rapid technology development which also affect society. User expectations and needs change over time and new technologies needs to be adopted. As such, there is a need for having flexible infrastructure that are able to adopt to changing circumstance. *Flexibility* is the general ability to react to changes (Li & Zhao, 2006). The continuous flux of changes results in an environment in which it is not easy to manage the infrastructure development. Recognition of the complexity and risk and of the broad range of stakeholders involved rules out the use of traditional control and management approaches. The CSF approach represents an alternative and accepted approach for strategic planning (Boynton & Zmud, 1984; Rockart & Morton, 1984). In a prescriptive manner CSF can be used to prioritize development projects and identify those aspects that address critical concerns (Boynton & Zmud, 1984). CSFs can be used to identify those areas which need to be careful management to ensure success. This results in the premise that taking a CSF approach will also be suitable for managing complex infrastructure development.

While there have been several CSF studies in e-government research domain, including mobile applications (Al-Hadidi & Rezgui, 2009), websites (Sagheb-Tehrani, 2010), innovation adoption (Kamal, 2006), services (Mahrer & Brandtweiner, 2004) and e-government practices and theory (Gil-Garcia & Pardo, 2005), there has been limited work specifically examining infrastructure aspects and the use of taking a CSF approach for managing infrastructure development. The goal of this paper is to identify CSFs which can guide infrastructure implementation. The paper is structured as follows. In the next section the background about infrastructures and success factors will be presented, which will be followed by the research approach. Next an in-depth case study will be presented and CSF will be identified. This is followed by a discussion of the findings and by an overview of further research directions. Finally, conclusions will be drawn.

BACKGROUND

Rockart (1979) popularized the concept of critical success factors (CSFs) defining them as the few key areas in which favorable results will ensure successful competitive performance. He also pointed out that there is a need that the CSF reach the appropriate decision-makers and that the current state should be continually monitored. The intention was to identify the structural variables that most contribute to the attainment of an organization's strategic goals and objectives. The CSF approach was originally developed to assist managers determine their information needs – but has since been ported to a wide variety of contexts. From a decision making perspective a focus on CSFs will help organizations identify those factors that they perceive to be most important to the success of any move to introduce shared infrastructure in their organization and determine whether they are present or not. The work of Rockart (1979) was further taken forward by Bullen and Rockart (1981). Bullen and Rockart (1981) concentrated on uncovering *what areas* are important to success.

CSFs are often identified without looking at the various types of CSFs that can be identified, whereas several researchers have suggestions categorization of CSFs (Borman & Janssen,

2012b; Bullen & Rockart, 1981; Gil-Garcia & Pardo, 2005). Gil-Garcia and Pardo (2005) scanned 5-years of literature in information systems research to identify factors found to influence the success of IT initiatives. They identify information and data, information technology, organizational and managerial, legal and regulatory and institutional environmental categories of challenges. Recently a new categorization of CSF was introduced by merging various streams in literature (Borman & Janssen, 2012a; 2012b). We adopted this categorization which includes the following three categories.

1. **Outcome based CSF:** Success requires identification of the levers – or outcomes – required to realize the desired objective together with an understanding of the key contributors to the delivery of those outcomes within a particular organizational context. An example of outcome based CSF is data standards for electronic data interchange (EDI) enabling information sharing among organizations (Angeles, Corritore, Basu, & Nath, 2001). Data standards are necessary to ensure interoperability and should as a result be the outcome of the project. Without developing any standards the project is failed as interoperability with other partners will be hampered.
2. **Process CSF:** These concern factors associated with the process of implementation of a system or initiative. Literature have generally examined implementation in a specific context – for example an enterprise resource planning system (Somers & Nelson, 2001), a global information system (Biehl, 2007) or an inter-organizational information system (Lu, Huang, & Heng, 2006) – and have sought to identify factors that will be *common* across all such initiatives. A typical example of process CSF is top management support (Nah, Lau, & Kuang, 2001).
3. **Operating environment characteristic:** These characteristics concert path-dependencies are related to available alternatives (Eisenhardt & Martin, 2000). Context includes the shaping influence of the environment - especially aspects of the economic environment such as competition - and institutions - rules, regulations, norms - on the possible and acceptable actions available to an organization. These CSFs are different from the previous categories in the sense cannot be easily influenced and changed (Borman & Janssen, 2012b). A typical example of operating environment characteristic is the arrangement of working relationships with trading partners (Angeles et al., 2001).

The overview and relationship between the CSF is visually depicted in Figure 1. The separation of outcome and process CSFs - *while including them within a single analysis* - should add clarity regarding what is needed to deliver the desired objective and the requirements for its successful implementation. In contrast operating environment CSF are important for infrastructure as the environment, including existing infrastructure and parties, is often given and cannot be easily changed. The environment can be influenced and change might take a very long time. Operating environment CSFs are the basis for the process and the outcome. We will use these three categories to classify the CSFs found in the case study.

Figure 1. Three categories of critical success factors (based on Borman & Janssen, 2012a)

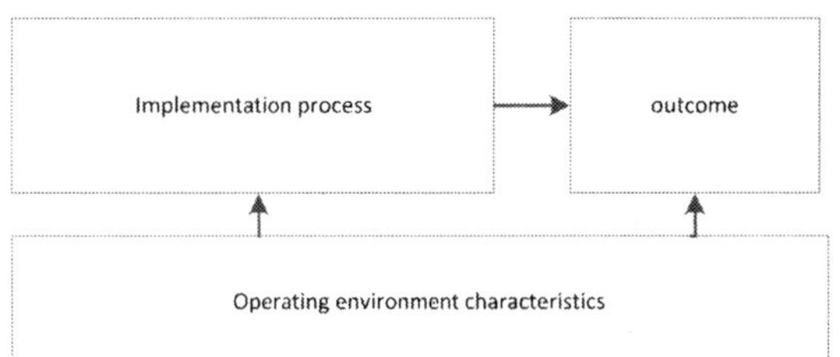

RESEARCH APPROACH

The aim to seek to identify and classify CSFs. A qualitative – case study based – approach was determined to be appropriate (Benbasat, Goldstein, & Mead, 1987; Strauss & Corbin, 1990). A case enabled us to investigate the CSFs in detail and to develop an understanding of why factors were considered to be contributing to the success. The research was primarily oriented towards exploring, understanding and identifying CSFs rather than the process by which they were decided upon. The public organization SURFnet was chosen as the case study, as much information is publicly available. and they operate and develop a public infrastructure. SURFnet provide an infrastructure and innovation capabilities for a situation having many stakeholders and involving many new technology developments. SURFnet started as a project organization and developed into an organization operating and developing a shared infrastructure for higher educational organizations. The SURFnet infrastructure evolved from providing basic connectivity to an advanced infrastructure providing services and collaboration support. The SURFnet case study was investigated by studying, documents and reports and interviewing four persons. In this way a retrospective picture about the history and developments was created and CSFs were identified. The documents and reports were used to understand its historical context and developments over time, whereas the interviews were focused on identifying CSFs. This enabled us to understand how CSFs were put in place over time. Interviews were conducted with the CIO of SURFnet and three ICT managers of higher education institutions. The latter are interviewed as representatives of the user organizations and the management of the shared service organization. The interviews lasted between one and one and a half hours and were semi-structured. Elements related to the history and the CSF in the three categories were addressed during the interviews. The questions concerning the CSF were open-ended and no suggestions for certain CSF were made, in this way, avoiding bias in certain direction.

In the next section the case description will start with the history of the cases to provide a context. Thereafter the objectives will be described followed by the CSFs identified by interviewees categorized along the dimensions of outcome, process and operating environment characteristic (Borman & Janssen, 2012a). The CSFs are derived from the perceptions of the interviewees about what was important. This is in line with the philosophy of interpretivist research - which suggests actions are guided by perceptions (Yin, 1981). A factor was only considered as critical if it was viewed as such by the majority of interviewees. In case there was no consensus if a factor would be a CSF, it was left out.

CASE: SURFNET

Introduction

There are many professional and academic education institutes in the Netherlands. SURFnet is a publicly funded organization that was initiated some 25 years ago and supports Dutch researchers, teachers and students to collaborate using ICT (http://nl.wikipedia.org/wiki/SURFnet). SURFnet was initiated as a response to the lagging behind of the use of ICT by higher education institutions in the Netherlands. Initially SURFnet comprised several projects to accelerate the ICT developments - the first being to develop a research network infrastructure. Whereas the initial focus was on executing projects to develop an infrastructure, the focus gradually shifted toward maintaining and operating the infrastructure. While these initial initiatives developed in isolation a longer term view has emerged towards developing *and* maintaining an underlying supporting infrastructure.

History

The first activities were initiated at the end of 1986 and resulted in the development of the SURFnet1 infrastructure which was released in 1988. Over the years various versions and updates of SURF-net were developed and since 2006 SURFnet6 is in place. This network provides internet and options to create your own optical network to avoid any communication delay. The network is updated regularly and currently a next version under development. This clearly shows the need to continuously deal with changes and to adopt new technologies.

The use of ICT in education and research resulted in the foundation of SURFdiensten (services). Procuring and developing low-cost services by profiting from the combined mass of all organizations was a primarily objectives. Currently, there are over 150 contracts with more than 100 vendors. Furthermore the scope has expanded to the Flemish part of Belgian. In 2012 the name was changed into SURFmarket.

Initially the focus was on innovation and not on control and maintenance or user supported. These aspects gained more and more attentions over the years which resulted in the founding of the SURF-share in 2010. SURFshare maintains services likes Studiekeuze123 (www.studiekeuze123.nl) and Studielink (www.studielink.nl/) which guarantees continuity and quality of service.

In 2012 SURFnet gained structural funding for a prolonged period of time to further develop a research infrastructure, which has significantly influenced the organizational structure. Nowadays the organization consists of three main business units; SURFnet (infrastructure), SURFMarket (procurement of software, hardware and services) and SURFshare (new innovation and development projects for higher education). Over time the scope has expanded and more and more services have been included. There are over a million students, lecturers and researchers who are making use of the infrastructure. The value of the infrastructures comes from the cooperating among higher educational organizations who share investments and services and in this way profit from economics of scale and synergy effects. Furthermore by bundling the capacity a better negotiation position towards software and hardware vendors is accomplished.

Mission, Services and Capabilities

SURFnet's main mission is "*To improve higher education and research by promoting, developing, and operating shared ICT facilities that are not offered by the market of its own accord*" (http://www.surfnet.nl/), SURFnet is a subsidiary of the SURF organization, in which Dutch universities, universities for applied sciences and research centres collaborate nationally and internationally with regard to the development and deployment of innovative ICT infrastructures and supporting facilities. The focus is on three areas: a hybrid end-to-end network, trusted identity and a pioneering collaboration environment. SURFnet is a long established initiative and recently introduced a focus on shared services. There has been incremental growth of services over time.

Services provided include SURFconext, SURFcontact, SURFfederatie, SURFgroepen, SURFmedia and SURFteams, Two services (SURFgroepen and SURFmedia) will be terminated at the end of 2012 to adapt to changes. Innovative developments for online collaboration infrastructure are developed within the SurfWorks innovation program. The goal is to develop a safe and secure environment in which students and lecturers can work together, but also will enable collaboration with persons outside these boundaries (national and international). This infrastructure enables to connect and integrate collaboration services from diverse providers and facilitates multiple devices and platforms. Traditionally a variety of devices are supported as each higher education organization has their own devices, this makes it easy to support the new trend to Bring Your Own Device (BYOD). Other innovation projects include the development of 4K video, which is four times the format of high definition television. Also new applications in higher educations of these new technologies are sought for. Another project is the filesender which is similar to dropbox but is aimed at overcoming the security concerns that dropbox has. Other projects include identity management, video sharing, unified communication (integrating email, instant messaging, voice and video conferencing) and a diversity of projects aimed at spotting new technologies and trends and piloting and prototyping new opportunities. Many of the innovations are driven by the explosion of data resulting in data-driven research and home-based education.

A key capability is the take up of new developments in the existing infrastructure. The SUFRnet infrastructure is whenever possible based on available open standards. When there are no standards available, the innovation projects should contribute to the development of open standards. This is accomplished by giving presentations and actively participating in standardization committees and communities. SURFnet activities have contributed to the establishment of the Amsterdam Internet Exchange, one of the most used internet junctions in the world.

The principal objective of developing and maintaining shared services at SURFnet is to be a driving force behind ICT-based innovation in higher education and research in the Netherlands. In the current financial climate, the additional objective of efficiency has been added driven by opportunities such as cloud computing.

Innovation is required to ensure that our customers can use shared services. This is the basis, which ultimately will result in more efficiency. The objective is more about the shared service business model that is important then how it will be delivered as the latter might change over time.

This states the need to innovate and at the same time align the innovation with users' needs. SURFnet has to deal with a large and varied user base having a high degree of autonomy in making their own decisions and often have their own systems. Educational organizations have their own budgetary control and can make independent IT investment decisions. As such SURFnet need to attract and retain users by providing an infrastructure and accompanying services at the edge of the newest development. This is a field to which many of the success factors are related. In the following subsection the outcome, process and environmental success factors will be elaborated.

Outcome Critical Success Factors

A variety of CSF were found as necessary to deliver the outcomes. These CSF are in place now, but it should be noted that they have been gradually developed over time. In the initial SURFnet many of them were not in place, but they are developed based on experiences and several iterations over time.

- **Transaction based service offering:** The necessary technology need to be in place to ensure secure transmission and to support the identification and authentication. This should ensure a safe and secure network which is the cornerstone for development of the infrastructure. The basis facilities are necessary for gaining trust in the infrastructure.
- **Standardised processes:** The risk is that heterogeneous processes will be created to support stakeholders' having a variety of requirements and interests. Variety results in higher costs and a decline of the benefits originating from economies of scale. As such it is key to standardize processes based on the inputs from different stakeholders, while still fulfilling customer needs. This might require negotiations and changes. At the end one process or a few processes should be selected, defined as

best practice, and delivered consistently across the organisations. Indeed a process might be configurable to support the local conditions and variety in needs and requirements.

- **Common IT applications:** Stakeholders have often their own platforms and there are often multiple initiatives at higher education institutions which aimed to develop similar services. Single solutions should be implemented replacing the heterogeneous systems previously used by the multiple users. This should result in the selection of common IT applications. Each time new technologies and ideas appear which will likely result in various processes and applications that need to be standardized.
- **Meeting users' needs:** A main risk is that standardization results in not fulfilling the needs of the users and even might alienate them. History shows that there is a constant struggle with retaining users while adopting the newest technologies. Users might view the infrastructure as old-fashioned or not supporting their needs. Therefore the infrastructure should adapt to the latest technology and support a variety of user needs. At some time the old infrastructure might need to be replaced by gradually removing old components and adding new components or a large part of the infrastructure might need to be phased out and substituted by a new part. To some extend this might look conflicting with the success factor standardize processes, but it is not as standardized processes might also support a variety of needs.
- **Retain expertise:** Expertise about the users' needs and newest technology developments is essential for ensuring continuous innovations that meets the user needs. The local level often initiates innovation, whereas at the more centralized level (Surfnet) it is integrated in the existing infrastructure and maintained. Central implementation should utilize the local knowledge. To some extent this was achieved, but on some areas this proved to be difficult and the challenge is to balance this.

Process Critical Success Factors

The process is aimed at guiding the evolution of the infrastructure. The past experiences resulted in a consistent view regarding what was required and what factors were considered as contributing to the success by the interviewees.

- **Committed senior leadership:** Active commitment of senior leaders of higher education organizations to ensure that resources are freed and commitment is given to new innovations. Commitment is also necessary regarding the role of and relationship with Surfnet from higher educational institutions.
- **Evolutionary approach to roll out:** Incremental and step by step implementation are a key aspects for the services provided, the stakeholders (types) targeted and the geographic location. An evolutionary approach should ensure that the various stakeholders have a say in the evolvement of the infrastructure. Backward compatibility is key as not all users move to newer versions at the same time.
- **Delivery of comprehensive training:** Although some users are frontrunners and stimulate innovation, most of the users are lagging behind. Adoption and use of new services is confronted with a lack of knowledge by users and often requires a need to change work processes causing resistance. Training and education is a key element for adoption by a broader audience. Ultimately the adoption of a large userbase should results in the creation of economies of scale.

- **Community and change support:** The evolutionary development is supported by a community in which experiences can be shared and questions posted. In addition other material and support can be provided to ensure smooth adoption of new services which are built on top of the infrastructure. Early adopters can share their experiences and the opportunities provided by new services and their benefits. The community consists of experts and representatives from all stakeholders involved.
- **Help desk:** New innovations might contain failures or might not work smoothly from the start resulting in questions by users. A one stop shop helpdesk for providing support and quickly answering user questions and solving user problems is a key aspect for ensuring adoption. Furthermore analysing questions allows for understanding the user problems which are used as input for continuously improvement.
- **Exploiting emerging technology:** New technology should be spotted and evaluated which requires monitoring new technology, understanding it and managing the translation to the requirements and needs of users. In this way technology is matched with the user needs. At a certain stage the exploration of new technology should be turned in exploitation of these new technologies in customer-oriented business processes.

Operating Environment Characteristic Critical Success Factors

Some of the operating environment factors were absent at the beginning, but most of them are available now. The main reason for this is that SURFnet was started as a temporary organizational aimed at exploring new technologies, whereas over time their exploitation function became more and more important. The initial project organization was changed in a professional service organization having all kind of governance mechanisms in place.

- **Management structure:** Over time a professional and standardized management and relationship structure was developed between SURFnet and its users. There are various departments which are responsible for account management, marketing and communication and community support.
- **Centralized and decentralized governance:** Literature indicates that centralized/decentralized is a main challenges in governance (Peterson, 2004; Sambamurthy & Zmud, 1999). In the case study this is confirmed as much of the governance is outside the control of SURFnet and based on the willingness, goodwill and trust of the participants of the user organizations. This concerns the allocation of responsibilities, budgeting, evaluation, and investment decisions. Therefore managing these relationships using the management structure and creating ties with the environment is key. All stakeholders are involved in decision-making groups to ensure that the decisions made are accepted by a broad range of stakeholders.
- **Sharing and distribution of IT-costs:** Benefits and gains are typically unequally divided among participants and the division of benefits and costs is an issue that need to be addressed for every shared infrastructure implementation. Sometimes long-term negotiations among stakeholders are necessary and different revenue models are employed (pay-per-use, investments based and free for use etc.). Although attention is given to this, there is not method or proven model for this.
- **Relationship management:** Relationships are a key factor when developing services that are remotely used and managed.

Research pinpoints already that the level of trust, cooperation and satisfaction increased between collaborating parties (M. Janssen, Joha, & Weerakkody, 2007). Account management should ensure close relationships between SURFnet and the key stakeholders in the user organizations. Furthermore, annual newsletters, leaflets of new projects, and information about development are distributed and new services are disseminated. If needed workshops and sessions are organized to discuss the newest developments or to ensure a wider acceptance and knowledge of infrastructure functionality and services.

The CSFs found provide a consistent set which are aimed at the management of the evolvement of the infrastructure in which both exploration and the exploitation plays a major role and need to be constantly balanced. In total 15 CSF were found evenly distributed over the outcome, process and operating environment characteristic categories as summarized in Table 1.

Table 1. Overview of success factors categories and factors found

CSF category	CSF found
Outcome	1. Transaction-based service offerings 2. Standardized processes 3. Common IT applications 4. Meeting users' needs 5. Retain expertise
Process	6. Committed leadership 7. Evolutionary approach to roll out 8. Delivering of comprehensive training 9. Community and change support 10. Helpdesk 11. Exploiting emerging technology
Operating environment characteristics	12. Management structure 13. Centralized and decentralized governance 14. Sharing and distribution of IT-costs 15. Relationship management

DISCUSSION AND FINDINGS

The infrastructure development is a cumbersome process as new technologies arise, there might be different user needs and economies of scale needs to be achieved by creating a large user base. In total 15 success factors were found which are relevant for the development of the SURFnet infrastructure over time. The infrastructure have been expanded and developed over time. The infrastructure can be characterized by a number of elements which all adds to the complexity and uncertainty and makes the management difficult.

- **Sunk cost:** Investments are made which need to be earned back over a pre-longed period of time. The large investments might block progress, but are needed to keep the infrastructure up-to-date.
- **Installed base:** A large installed base of users is necessary to make the infrastructure work. Yet it makes innovation more difficult, as more stakeholders having a diversity of interested and needs need to be involved. Also the installed base likely change over time; it might be extended to other domains (more and different higher education institutions, even across the country boundaries), but also current players might step out as it might not fulfil their needs anymore.
- **Designed and emerging parts:** Several parts are designed consciously, whereas other emerged over time. The infrastructure needs to be flexible enough to be updated on a regular basis. Initiatives emerging at the local level and are adopted at the national level.
- **Co-evolution:** There are multiple users which might have different and even opposing requirements. The infrastructure exists within their own environment, and they are also part of that environment which is a typical characteristics of a com-

plex (adaptive) system (Auyang, 1998). As their environment changes, the infrastructure needs to be changed to ensure a best fit. But because infrastructures are part of their environment, they do change their environment when they change to better fit the environment. In this way a constant process of change is made.

- **Openness, dynamics and uncertainty:** New developments and new users need to be incorporated. How users will use the infrastructures is uncertain and the use will likely change over time (for example the amount of communication). The infrastructure should have a long term focus and adaptive enough to support future development as well as a broad range of current users.

Some elements of the SURFnet infrastructure have been designed centrally and implemented in a top-down manner, whereas other parts have emerged in a decentralized way as the educational organizations created their own systems bottom-up. Together these form the infrastructure that evolves as a results of these centralized and decentralized initiatives. The strategy to stimulate development of facilities and let them emerge or become obsolete by the selection of public organizations has led to a number of successful initiatives in the past. Also the top-down strategy to replace the existing infrastructure by new components has been successful in the past. We argue that the combination of bottom-up and top-down development generates the added value. From the CSF this becomes visible as many of them are related to the process of bottom-up and top-down development. Furthermore many of the CSFs are related to the elements listed above.

There are differences between process, outcome, and environmental results in clarity regarding what is needed to deliver on the desired objective and the requirements for its successful implementation. At the beginning many of the environmental factors were not in place. Over time the right conditions were shaped. Especially having the right management structure, governance mechanisms and relationship management in place is essential for survival of these type of infrastructures.

For development and gaining economies of scale and scope the standardization of processes and services and having a common IT applications are key success factors. Standardization needs to be balanced with the need for providing customized services to ensure that customers' needs are fulfilled. These two aspects need to be continuously balanced. Often at the start of new innovations there are more customized applications and over time the needed functionality gets clearer resulting in more standardized processes and ultimately in the development of a single, common IT application. To gain economies of scale a large user base is necessary and standardization on a limited number of processes and applications. Therefore factors like committed leadership, evolutionary approach to roll out, delivering of comprehensive training, community and change support and Helpdesk (process) and relationship management (operating environment) are all contributing to the gaining a larger user base.

CSFs are hardly used for managing the development process and guiding it. The CSF approach can be further extended to be used it in a prescriptive manner and guide the development of the infrastructure. An appealing benefit of taking a CSF approach is that it can be done with relatively limited efforts and nevertheless by managing CSFs it can have a tremendous effect on success. Taking a CSF approach can result in a number of relatively simple principles guiding infrastructure development. A key challenge is to create a set of principles that merely sets the direction for the future, ensures uptake of emerging initiatives, and is ready to adapt and evolve as the environment changes such as the one outlined by Janssen and Kuk (2006). CSF provides a useful starting point for deriving principles and CSF and principles might be complimentary to each other.

FUTURE RESEARCH DIRECTONS

The CSF approach can be extended in various directions. The CSF approach was used in the case study to manage the development process and focus on the aspects expected to contribute to success. Markus and Robey (1988) suggested that specific implementations will have some unique qualities that impact which factors are seen as critical. Consequently many factors are not universal, but might be case dependent. Furthermore the key areas that need to be managed will likely change over time and as such regularly re-assessment is necessary. The key areas identified needs to be monitored and information about the CSFs should be distributed to the relevant stakeholders. In this way the stakeholders are aware of the factors, can act upon them, and can identify new ones when they arise. We recommend to research the use of CSF for public infrastructure development in different countries and also investigate different types of infrastructures.

Another development is the integration of the infrastructure development and CSF approaches. A combination of them yields likely more benefits than a single approach. An important issue that need to be resolved is how the CSF can be used in a prescriptive manner. Is only identifying and communicating the factors sufficient, or should they be used in a more intrusive manner and become part of development methodologies and even resulting in separate developing activities? The latter will utilize more resources but might result in a higher likelihood of success. Research into the use of CSF in a prescriptive manner is necessary.

A remaining question is if utilizing a CSF approach will result in more success. In other words will addressing the CSF help to ensure success or at least improve the change to successfully develop a digital government infrastructure? CSFs are sometimes used in a prescriptive manner (see for example Boynton & Zmud, 1984), but there is hardly any data available about their effectiveness. This would require the use of the CSF method in different situations and the comparison with situations without its use. More research is necessary into the effectiveness of CSF for managing such complex situation and how they can be of help.

Public infrastructures are not static and keep on developing with new developments like open linked data, big data, semantic web. This new developments will be integrated in the infrastructures which results in completely new types of infrastructure. The take up of these new developments will be gradually and the development will evolve over time. CSF approaches can be used to shape the evolvement of these infrastructures and ensure that the infrastructure will develop successfully. New developments should adhere to the CSFs with have appeared and developed over time. The identified CSFs are likely useful for other infrastructures developments, but might be executed in different ways and customized to the specific situation at hand. Even at SURFnet the CSFs might change over time and new developments might need other CSFs. The influence of new developments on the CSF should be researched.

CONCLUSION

Digital government infrastructure development is a complex process having many uncertainties and in which many stakeholders are involved. This makes the development of such an infrastructure difficult. An approach based on CSFs can be used to concentrate on a limited number of aspects to guide its evolution. In this chapter, CSFs were identified by investigating a public organization developing infrastructure for use by researchers, teachers and students. The case demonstrates that CSFs can be used as a suitable approach for managing complex infrastructure development projects. With relatively limited efforts the critical areas can be identified, which subsequently can be managed to improve the success rate. In this contexts CSFs should be viewed as a kind of heuristics for infrastructure developments, as the CSF might change over time and new critical areas might emerge they need to be continually updated.

CSF is an area which has received much research attention, however, current literature did not address CSF as a means to guide infrastructure development. This study is a first attempt in this research domain and revealed 15 CSFs, including transaction-based service offerings, standardized processes, common IT applications, meeting users' needs, retaining expertise, committed leadership, evolutionary approach to roll out, delivering of comprehensive training, community and change support, helpdesk, exploiting emerging technology, management structure, centralized and decentralized governance, sharing and distribution of IT-costs and relationship management. The CSF were identified using a classification of Borman and Janssen (2012a, 2012b) in outcome, process and operating environment characteristic categories. Outcome based CSF identifies the levers required to realize the desired objective together with an understanding of the key contributors to the delivery of those outcomes within a particular organizational context, process CSF are derived from the implementation processes and operating environment characteristic are given and relate to the path-dependencies and available alternatives. The classification helped to manage a larger number of CSF better and proved to be useful to identify a variety of factors. In the case most of the success factors are dealing with the life-cycle of extending and modifying the infrastructure by spotting new developments, developing them to make them ready for a large audience and ensuring adoption to gain economies of scale and scope. To support the evolutionary nature of the infrastructure development the areas is indicated by the success factors needs to be addressed. More research is necessary into the use of the CSF for a variety of infrastructure and the effectiveness of CSF for managing such complex situation and how they can be of help.

REFERENCES

Al-Hadidi, A., & Rezgui, Y. (2009). *Critical success factors for the adoption and diffusion of m-government services: A literature review*. Paper presented at the 9th European Conference on e-Government.

Angeles, R., Corritore, C. L., Basu, S. C., & Nath, R. (2001). Success factors for domestic and international electronic data interchange (EDI) implementation for US firms. *International Journal of Information Management*, *21*, 329–347. doi:10.1016/S0268-4012(01)00028-7.

Auyang, S. Y. (1998). *Foundations of complex-system theories in economics, evolutionary biology, and statistical physics*. New York: Cambridge University Press.

Benbasat, I., Goldstein, D. K., & Mead, M. (1987). The case study research strategy in studies of information systems. *Management Information Systems Quarterly*, *11*(3), 369–386. doi:10.2307/248684.

Biehl, M. (2007). Success factors for implmenting global information systems. *Communications of the ACM*, *50*(1), 53–58. doi:10.1145/1188913.1188917.

Borman, M., & Janssen, M. (2012a). *Critical success factors for shared services: Results from two case studies*. Paper presented at the HICSS2012.

Borman, M., & Janssen, M. (2012b). Reconciling two approaches to critical success factors: The case of shared services in the public sector. *International Journal of Information Management*. doi: doi:10.1016/j.ijinfomgt.2012.1005.1012.

Boynton, A. C., & Zmud, R. W. (1984). An assessment of critical success factors. *Sloan Management Review*, *25*(4), 17–27.

Bullen, C. V., & Rockart, J. F. (1981). *A primer on critical success factors*. Sloan School of Management, Massachusetts Institute of Technology.

Eisenhardt, K., & Martin, J. A. (2000). Dynamic capabilities: What are they? *Strategic Management Journal*, *21*, 1105–1121. doi:10.1002/1097-0266(200010/11)21:10/11<1105::AID-SMJ133>3.0.CO;2-E.

Gil-Garcia, J. R., & Pardo, T. A. (2005). E-government success factors: Mapping practical tools to theoretical foundations. *Government Information Quarterly*, *22*(2), 187–216. doi:10.1016/j.giq.2005.02.001.

Hanseth, O., Ciborra, C., & Braa, K. (2001). The control devolution. ERP and the side effects of globalization. *The Data base for advances in information systems. Special issue: Critical Analysis of ERP systems, 32*(4), 34-46.

Hanseth, O., & Lyytinen, K. (2010). Design theory for adaptive complexity in information infrastructures. *Journal of Information Technology*, *25*(1), 1–19. doi:10.1057/jit.2009.19.

Hanseth, O., Monteiro, E., & Hatling, M. (1996). Developing information infrastructure: The tension between standardization and flexibility. *Science, Technology & Human Values*, *21*(4), 407–442. doi:10.1177/016224399602100402.

Janssen, M., Chun, S. A., & Gil-Garcia, J. R. (2009). Building the next generation of digital government infrastructures. *Government Information Quarterly*, *26*(2), 233–237. doi:10.1016/j.giq.2008.12.006.

Janssen, M., Joha, A., & Weerakkody, V. (2007). Exploring relationships of shared service arrangements in local government. *Transforming Government: People. Process & Policy*, *1*(3), 271–284.

Janssen, M., Joha, A., & Zuurmond, A. (2009). Simulation and animation for adopting shared services: Evaluating and comparing alternative arrangements. *Government Information Quarterly*, *26*(1), 15–24. doi:10.1016/j.giq.2008.08.004.

Janssen, M., & Kuk, G. (2006, 5-7 January). *A complex adaptive system perspective of enterprise architecture in electronic government.* Paper presented at the Hawaii International Conference on System Sciences (HICSS-39).

Kamal, M. M. (2006). IT innovation adoption in the government sector: Identifying the critical success factors. *Journal of Enterprise Information Management*, *19*(2), 192–222. doi:10.1108/17410390610645085.

Klievink, B., & Janssen, M. (2009). Realizing joined-up government. Dynamic capabilities and stage models for transformation. *Government Information Quarterly*, *26*(2), 275–284. doi:10.1016/j.giq.2008.12.007.

Li, L., & Zhao, X. (2006). Enhancing competitive edge through knowledge management in implementing ERP systems. *Systems Research and Behavioral Science*, *23*(2), 129–140. doi:10.1002/sres.758.

Lu, X.-H., Huang, L.-H., & Heng, M. (2006). Critical success factors of inter-organizational information systems - A case study of Cisco and Xiao Tong in China. *Information & Management*, *43*, 395–408. doi:10.1016/j.im.2005.06.007.

Mahrer, H., & Brandtweiner, R. (2004). Success factors for implementing e-government services: The case of the Austrian e-government service portal. *International Journal of Information Technology and Management*, *3*(2-4), 235–245. doi:10.1504/IJITM.2004.005034.

Markus, M. L., & Robey, D. (1988). Information technology and organizational change: Causal structure in theory and research. *Management Science*, *34*(5), 583–598. doi:10.1287/mnsc.34.5.583.

Nah, F. F., Lau, J., & Kuang, J. L. (2001). Critical factors for successful implementation of enterprise systems. *Business Process Management Journal*, *7*(3), 285–296. doi:10.1108/14637150110392782.

Peterson, R. (2004). Crafting information technology governance. *Information Systems Management*, *21*(4), 7–22. doi:10.1201/1078/44705.21.4.20040901/84183.2.

Rockart, J. F. (1979). Chief executives define their own data needs. *Harvard Business Review*, (March-April): 81. PMID:10297607.

Rockart, J. F., & Scott Morton, M. S. (1984). Implications of changes in information technology for corporate strategy. *Interfaces*, *14*(1), 84–95. doi:10.1287/inte.14.1.84.

Sagheb-Tehrani, M. (2010). A model of successful factors towards e-government implementation. *Electronic Government, an International Journal*, *7*(1), 60-74.

Sambamurthy, V., & Zmud, R. W. (1999). Arrangements for information technology governance: A theory of multiple contingencies. *Management Information Systems Quarterly*, *23*(2), 261–290. doi:10.2307/249754.

Somers, T. M., & Nelson, K. (2001, 3-6 January). *The impact of critical success factors across the stages of enterprise resource planning implementation.* Paper presented at the 34th Hawaii International Conference on Systems Sciences, Maui, Hawaii.

Strauss, A., & Corbin, J. (1990). *Basics of qualitative research: Grounded theory procedures and techniques*. Newbury Park: Sage.

Veenstra, A. F. V., & Janssen, M. (2012). Policy implications of top-down and bottom-up patterns of e-government infrastructure development. In E. T.M. & D. C. Mehos (Eds.), Inverse infrastructures. Disrupting networks from below: Edward Elgar.

Weill, P., Broadbent, M., & Butler, C. (1996). *Exploring how firms view IT infrastructure. Melbouren*. Melbourne Business School, the University of Melbourne.

Yin, R. (1981). The case study crisis: Some answers. *Administrative Science Quarterly*, *26*, 58–65. doi:10.2307/2392599.

ADDITIONAL READING

Chen, T. (1999). Critical success factors for various strategies in the banking industry. *International Journal of Bank Marketing*, *17*(2), 83–91. doi:10.1108/02652329910258943.

Gil-Garcia, J. R. (2005). Exploring the success factors of state website functionality: An empirical investigation. In *Proceedings of the 2005 national conference on Digital government* (pp. 121-130).

Gil-Garcia, J. R. (2006). Enacting state websites: A mixed method study exploring e-government success in multi-organizational settings. In: *Proceedings of the 39th Annual Hawaii International Conference on Systems Sciences* (HICSS 2006).

Guimaraes, T., & Igbaria, M. (1994). Exploring the relationship between IC success and company performance. *Information & Management*, *26*(3), 133–141. doi:10.1016/0378-7206(94)90037-X.

Guynes, C. S., & Vanecek, M. T. (1996). Critical success factors in data management. *Information & Management*, *30*(4), 201–209. doi:10.1016/0378-7206(95)00053-4.

Holland, C. P., & Light, B. (1999). A critical success factor model for ERP implementation. *IEEE Software*, *16*(3), 30–36. doi:10.1109/52.765784.

Janssen, M., & Joha, A. (2006). Motives for establishing shared service centers in public administrations. *International Journal of Information Management*, *26*(2), 102–116. doi:10.1016/j.ijinfomgt.2005.11.006.

Lee, J. H., & Shim, H. J. et al. (2011). Critical success factors in SOA implementation: An exploratory study. *Information Systems Management*, *27*(2), 123–145. doi:10.1080/10580531003685188.

Leidecker, J. K., & Bruno, A. V. (1984). Identifying and using critical success factors. *Long Range Planning*, *17*, 23–32. doi:10.1016/0024-6301(84)90163-8.

Natalie Helbig, J.R., Gil-García, & Ferro, E. (2009). Understanding the complexity of electronic government: Implications from the digital divide literature. *Government Information Quarterly*, *16*(1), 89–97. doi:10.1016/j.giq.2008.05.004.

Rosacker, K. M., & Olson, D. L. (2008). Public sector information system critical sector factors. *Transforming Government: People. Process and Policy*, *2*(1), 60–70.

Wixom, B., & Watson, H. (2001). An empirical investigation of the factors in data warehousing success. *Management Information Systems Quarterly*, *25*(1), 17–24. doi:10.2307/3250957.

Younga, R., & Jordan, E. (2008). Top management support: Mantra or necessity. *International Journal of Project Management*, *26*(7), 713–725. doi:10.1016/j.ijproman.2008.06.001.

KEY TERMS AND DEFINITIONS

Critical Success Factors: The collection of areas that need to be given attention to enable success (based on Rockart, 1979).

Digital Government Infrastructures: Basic and generic facilitates enabling connectivity and providing shared services to a large number of users (based on Janssen, Chun, & Gil-Garcia, 2009).

Information Infrastructures: A term used to emphasize a holistic, socio-technical and evolutionary perspective on infrastructure (Hanseth et al., 1996).

Infrastructure Flexibility: The general ability to react to changes (based on Li & Zhao, 2006).

Path-Dependencies: Path-dependencies are related to available alternatives and take into account past decisions and the associated repertoire of procedures and routines, which can constrain or enable change (Eisenhardt & Martin, 2000).

Shared Service Center: "The concentration of dispersed service provisioning activities in a single organizational entity" (Janssen, Joha, & Zuurmond, p. 16).

Shared Services: The provisioning of pre-agreed services to multiple users.

Sunk Cost: Investments made that can only be earned back over a pre-longed period of time (Hanseth et al., 1996).

Chapter 14
Social Media and Public Administration in Spain: A Comparative Analysis of the Regional Level of Government

J. Ignacio Criado
Universidad Autónoma de Madrid, Spain

Francisco Rojas-Martín
Universidad Autónoma de Madrid, Spain

ABSTRACT

The chapter investigates the employment of digital social media by Spanish regional administrations: its presence, the factors that determine that presence, as well as the self-perception of those responsible for its management. This study raises the following questions: What are the key factors that explain the use of social media in public administrations? What is the self-perception of those responsible for the management of digital social media about its current level of development within their organisations? What are the main inhibitors-facilitators for the development of digital social media in public administrations? What are the next steps to promote digital social media in the sphere of public organisations? This chapter is based on a questionnaire that was responded to by those responsible for the management of digital social media in the Spanish regional administrations. This research shows that Web 2.0 tools are more oriented to explore potential changes in the relations between the public administrations and citizens, than to innovate the functioning of public sector organisations. In sum, this chapter offers a relevant analysis, although it is of an exploratory character because of the almost total absence of systematic studies about the diffusion of digital social media within Spanish public administrations.

DOI: 10.4018/978-1-4666-4173-0.ch014

Copyright © 2013, IGI Global. Copying or distributing in print or electronic forms without written permission of IGI Global is prohibited.

INTRODUCTION

Recently, the debate about the diffusion of digital social media in public administrations has intensified. This chapter addresses some of the key aspects related to the diffusion of these technological innovations within the public sector, with the aim of throwing light on a reality that is still under construction, but that attracts great social and academic interest. Specifically this study focuses on regional level government in Spain, whose public administrations are increasingly adopting digital social media. However, very little is known about the most widely used tools, the reasons for their use, the factors that inhibit-facilitate their establishment, as well as the areas forecast for development in the future. The following pages present an exploratory analysis that is based on data drawn from a questionnaire responded to by those responsible for the management of digital social media in regional Spanish administrations. This work also seeks to contribute to understanding the role that digital social media are already playing in the construction of public administrations that are both more open and in closer contact with citizens.

This study is framed within a collective effort that aims to identify and characterise the consequences and results of the diffusion of Web 2.0 tools within public administrations. The interest is twofold: on the one hand to understand the implications for the functioning of organisations that make up the public sector; and on the other to explore potential changes in the relations between the public administrations and citizens that flow from its establishment. With this in mind, the introduction of digital social media in the public sector can be analysed by following some of the patterns employed in previous studies on the use of Information and Communication Technology (ICT) and the Internet within public administrations. This work departs from the opposition to the technological determinism that is commonly found in many of the works undertaken in this area of academic study (Gil-García, 2012; Heeks & Bailur, 2006; Yildiz, 2007).

This study assumes that Web 2.0 represents a qualitative leap forward in the role of ICT and the Internet within public administrations. This advance has been made possible thanks to the existence of new tools and applications that allow citizens to become active participants in the creation, organisation, publication, combination, exchange, commentary and evaluation of public web content, which has created a network through which people can interact and link up among themselves or with government institutions (AGIMO, 2009; Chun et al., 2010). Consequently, digital social media offer a new area of academic interest that must be addressed, without forgetting the history of the use of ICT and the Internet in public administrations, but at the same time particularly focusing on a new generation of technologies with some unique functionality.

The interest of the Spanish regional administrations in ICT derives from their growing political power and the increase in the volume of responsibilities assigned to them. Spanish regional governments are political structures that manage some of the largest areas of public activity (in terms of budgetary size), particularly in the areas of health and education. Regional governments also therefore have a 'superior weight' in comparison with other levels of government (central and local) in terms of the number of public employees. For these reasons, this collection of organisations are of enormous interest in understanding the technological dynamics that are developing around the adoption, use and diffusion of digital social media in the Spanish public sector.

At the same time the interest that has been generated by digital social media in public administrations is not surprising. The use of digital social media has rapidly grown in recent years, incorporating 77% of Internet users in Spain (ONTSI, 2011). The same study situates Spain in third position in the world ranking that calculates the use of digital social media. Specifically, the tools that are most used in Spain are *Facebook*, *Tuenti* and *Twitter*. The former has around 850 million users across the globe, with 15 of these in Spain. *Tuenti* specialises in youth and has around 11 million users in Spain. Finally, *Twitter* had achieved around 2.8 million users by 2011, but it is additionally experiencing a particularly rapid diffusion within the public administrations.

The object of study of this research focuses on the adoption, use and diffusion of the digital social media in Spanish regional administrations. At this time it is assumed that the development of these types of tools in the Spanish public sector is still at an embryonic stage. On the other hand, there are some highly successful cases and applications that make this research worthwhile. Hence, this chapter is oriented to address the key factors that explain the use of social media in public administrations, the self-perception of those responsible for the management of digital social media about its current level of development within their organisations, and the main inhibitors-facilitators for the development of digital social media in public administrations.

Methodologically, the data in this study is drawn from a questionnaire given to those responsible for the management of digital social media across the 17 Spanish regional administrations. The questionnaire consists of 20 questions aimed at investigating its development level in-depth, identifying the factors for its successful adoption, the strategies for its application and future possibilities for the development of these types of tools. The design of this questionnaire is based on two previous studies. On the one hand, the survey takes into account the 'eight essential elements' of the policies for the users of digital social media in public administrations, as defined by Hrdinová et al. (2010). In second place, we have followed the content of the questions designed for the *National Survey of Social Media Use in State Government* by Bailey and Singleton (2010). The employment of these questions is an opportunity to both take advantage of an instrument that has been previously validated in another context, and to also increase the future comparative potential of the results.

The results of this chapter have both a theoretical and empirical relevance. From a theoretical perspective, this chapter offers some conclusions of interest with respect to the growing area of research into digital social media in the public sector. From an empirical perspective, the current study provides primary data derived from an ongoing piece of doctoral research about the use of digital social media within the public sector of Spain and the United Kingdom. In sum, this chapter can be placed within an international dynamic that seeks to understand the next steps in the diffusion of digital social media in the public sector of diverse countries.

The chapter is structured as follows. The following two sections respectively seek to define the theoretical and analytical framework of the study. In the fourth part of this chapter we undertake data analysis from the questionnaire given to those responsible for the digital social media of the regional administrations, with the aim of providing responses to the questions posed in this research. The fifth part of the chapter provides a discussion of the results, drawing on the analysis of the contributions. A series of conclusions are then put forward concerning the applicability of this study and proposals for future lines of research.

THEORETICAL FRAMEWORK: FROM E-GOVERNMENT TO GOVERNMENT 2.0

The study of social media is recent and multi-disciplinary. It includes areas of computing, business, law, sociology, politics, and public administration, among others. The rapid diffusion of social media in public agencies around the world has promoted the specific interest for this phenomenon from the perspective of public administration. At the same time, the study of social media in the public sector needs to pay close attention to previous processes of technology diffusion in bureaucracies, in order to facilitate the understanding of this new wave of innovation. In fact, some authors suggest the idea of a transition from traditional electronic government (e-government) to government 2.0, as a result of the adoption, use, and diffusion of social media tools in the public sector.

During the last decades, the study of ICT in public administration (or e-government) has become a well-established discipline. A short review of e-government scholars identifies a variety of issues, methodologies, and scopes (Calista & Melistky, 2007; Danziger & Andersen, 2002; Gil-García, 2012; Heeks & Bailur, 2006; Hood & Margetts, 2007; Yildiz, 2007). The study of web portals for electronic services delivery (using rankings and evolutionary models), the exchange of data and information between public administrations (inter-agency collaboration and interoperability), or impact of the digitalization of administrative tasks and activities (both internally in public management areas, and externally addressing the interaction with the citizenry) have concentrated some of the most prominent contributions within this academic field.

Social media have arrived on the public sector modernization agenda, potentially favouring the engagement between citizens and public administrations in a sort of a dialogue. Social media may be defined as "a group of Internet-based applications ideologically and technologically grounded from the creation of Web 2.0, and that leads to the creation and exchange of user-generated content" (Kaplan & Haenlein, 2010, p. 61). Another definition of social media is focused on users: "web-based services that allow individuals to (1) construct a public or semi-public profile within a bounded system, (2) articulate a list of other users with whom they share a connection, and (3) view and traverse their list of connections and those made by others within the system" (Boyd & Ellison, 2007).

Thus, founded on the Web 2.0 philosophy, social media do not only entail interactive elements, but also collaborative attitudes and behaviours in line with the many-to-many approach. Unlike previous e-government, social media may contribute to implement a bidirectional communication between the public sector and the citizenry, and to create virtual communities, among other interactive innovations. To put it in other words, social media platforms may facilitate governments to get into the final stage of e-government evolution, as suggested by Chun et al. (2010). This final station (government 2.0) is characterized as the promotion of shared governance to transform how the government operates, in terms of seamless information flows and collaborative decision-making processes using Web 2.0 technologies (see Table 1).

Social media cover different Web 2.0 tools such as microblogging (e.g., *Twitter*), multimedia sharing (e.g., *YouTube*), virtual worlds (e.g., *Second life*), mashups and open data applications (e.g., *Data.gov*), questioning Tools (e.g., *Quora*), crowdsourcing (e.g., *Mechanichal Turk,*), collaboration tools (e.g., *Peer to patent* and *WikiGovernment*), social networking (*Facebook*), blogs, among others. The analysis of these different

Table 1. Comparison between traditional electronic government and government 2.0

Comparison between Traditional Electronic Government vs Government 2.0	
Traditional digital government	Social media-based digital government (Gov 2.0)
Information provision (information sink) model	Information source (creation) model
Service provision model	Service demand model
Policy enforcement model	Policy making and negotiation model
Agency internal decision making/governance model	Shared governance

Source: Adapted from Chun et al. (2010)

strategies and applications in public settings is important to understand how the exchange of information between governments and citizens may significantly transform the way in which the public sphere operates, create new ways of governing, and/or enhance different forms of participation. In other words, social media applications have the potential to transform the mediation process between government actors, institutions, and citizens (Bailey & Singleton, 2010; Bertot et al., 2012; Bonsón et al., 2012; Criado et al., 2011; Dixon, 2010). During the last few years, different public agencies across the world have made advances in this field.

Some studies have suggested that government-citizens interactions may be significantly transformed using social media tools. These instruments are oriented to improve administrative transparency, as the citizens collaborate in the agenda-setting process (Meijer & Thaens, 2010). Grassroots mobilization regarding to public policy is becoming of importance for public agencies' reputation, authority, and impact (Heidinger et al., 2010). Besides, social media facilitate the processes of public services co-production with the citizens, not only by giving opinions or making suggestions; additionally, they enhance citizen's collaboration with new contents and services requiring their proactivity (Chun & Warner, 2010).

In sum, using social media in government facilitates the interaction with citizens in an unexplored way so far (Cerrillo Martinez, 2010). They make a difference from traditional mass media as they "*relies on user-generated content, which refers to any content that has been created by end users or the general public*" (Bertot et al., 2012). At the same time, from the citizens' perspective social media provide a platform for direct participation in decision-making. Thus, Ramon (2010, p. 160) states that "*public participation would cease to be intermediated by structures and institutions and would become a direct citizen action.*" Complementary, social media allows the communication of citizens' views in a simpler, faster, and more direct way, creating a better informed, more innovative, and more citizen-centric government (Bonsón et al., 2012). In Nam's words citizens can collectively create public information, provide service, and take part in policy processes (Nam, 2012).

Fewer evidences exist about the results of social media in public sector management dimensions. Hrdinová *et al.* (2010) distinguish, at least, two different social media uses in public administrations. On the one hand, public employees using social media tools on behalf of the public administration to express contents previously agreed with the organization's officials. On the other, public employees using social media for personal purposes related to professional activities. Here, they provide their own personal opinions about professional issues, not expressing the organizational view. Professional interactions using these tools exist outside formal organizations (Cerrillo & Martinez, 2010). These processes highlight the potential of social media as a management tool that also facilitates knowledge networks and information-sharing processes inside public bureaucracies.

ANALYTICAL STRATEGY: WHO USES; WHY AND WITH WHAT INTENSITY THE DIGITAL SOCIAL MEDIA IN PUBLIC ADMINISTRATIONS?

This section presents the analytical strategy that has guided the study. The objective of this research consists in investigating various aspects of the employment of digital social media by Spanish regional administrations: its presence, the factors that determine that presence, as well as the self-perception of those responsible for its management. With the aim of achieving this objective, this chapter raises the following questions: What are the key factors that explain the use of social networks in public administrations?

What is the self-perception of those responsible for the management of digital social media about its current level of development within their organisations? What are the main inhibitors-facilitators for the development of digital social media in public administrations? What are the next steps to promote digital social media in the sphere of public organisations? We have designed the following research strategy with the aim of seeking a response to these questions.

In first place, our universe of study is the 17 Spanish regional administrations. For context, it is worth mentioning that these are a group of public administrations that were created during the establishment of the Constitution in 1978, and their resources and personnel have expanded from that time to manage an increasingly broad range of decentralised public services including health, education and social services. In fact, they now represent more than 50% of public expenditure and of the personnel that work in the Spanish public sector. For that reason, their need to interact with citizens and to innovate administratively has grown signifcantly in recent years. On the other hand, this group of regional administrations has adopted the functional structure of the central administration of the Spanish State. That means it has the Napoleonic-Mediterranean style of administration and incorporates some Neo-Weberian innovations. Among other aspects, this implies the reaffirmation of the role of the state as the main facilitator of solutions for societal problems, the preservation of the idea of a public service with a distinctive status, culture, terms, and conditions, and the reaffirmation of the role of the administrative law in preserving the basic principles pertaining to the citizen-state relationship (Pollit & Bouckaert, 2011, p. 118). Also, regional administrations have a level of employment of ICT that is equivalent to other administrations in the European environment (Criado, 2009).

This study seeks to undertake an exploratory analysis of the diffusion of digital social media within this group of regional administrations, by analysing who is behind this process and how it is led. For that reason we have identified both the unit that is responsible for the management of the digital social media within each of the regional administrations, and the person responsible. One of the first conclusions drawn from this work was that all the public bodies analysed have a unit in which the management of the digital social media of the whole administration are centralised, although in an unequal way. Also, the names of units or potential results vary appreciably.

Once these details were identified a strategy of information collection was undertaken (regarding digital social media in the administrations under study) by specifically focusing on a questionnaire. This work is based on an analysis of the data drawn from a questionnaire that was developed by the authors. This tool has allowed us to obtain primary data from the opinions of those responsible for the management of the digital social media of the 17 regional administrations under study. Furthermore, the questionnaire has enabled us to access information on manager's opinion and personal perceptions concerning the use of the networks, a goal that would have not been possible to achieve using any other type of tool.

The main areas of interest in the management of digital social media were also identified and used as a source of information for the questionnaire employed in this study. The questionnaire was carried out during March and April 2012. The response rate was 100%, and all 17 regional managers responded within the established time frame.

The dimensions analysed in this questionnaire focused on the research questions that have guided this study.

- **Use of the digital social media:** Although the use of social networks within public administrations is still in its early stages, it is necessary to study the motivations that are guiding the processes of technological diffusion (Bonson et al., 2012). In general it is believed that the factors that make public administrations use digital social media are more tied to improvements in citizen relations than to innovations in internal aspects of management.

- **Strategies or plans about the use of the digital social media:** This chapter deals with the existence of plans about the use of the digital social media within public administrations (AGIMO, 2009). Specifically, interest in this area focuses on understanding the extent to which public administrations are employing digital social media by employing some kind of policy or formalised and/or explicit strategy. This serves as an indicator about the level of evolution of digital social media within public administrations, as well as the degree of sophistification in their management.
- **Self-perception about the development of digital social media:** The initial developments in the use of digital social media within public administrations are strongly linked to those responsible for their management. It is expected that those in charge of the digital social media have an optimistic view of their potential and that they are promoters of their rapid inclusion in public organisations (Bailey & Singleton, 2010).
- **Main inhibitors to the development of digital social media:** One of the aspects that has attracted least attention in studies of digital social media relates to inhibitors to their introduction within organisations. As with previous technologies, it is expected that the primary barriers within public administrations to the use of digital social media are related to cultural questions and a lack of understanding about their potential to achieve improvements.
- **Main facilitators to the development of digital social media:** In addition to inhibitors, facilitators are also of interest to study social media adoption in public administration. In other words, identify the variables that interact to produce greater acceptance of social media in public administration is important. Previous diffusion processes of other technological innovations suggest that, among others, experience with a technology or technology-trained human capital are variables explaining acceptance (Criado & Rojas-Martin, 2012; Gil-Garcia, 2012).
- **The future of digital social media in public administrations:** Digital social media are still in their initial expansion phase, so one of the key questions relates to areas of future growth. The 'next steps' need to be investigated as there is currently no clear information about development tendencies; so in this case we seek to obtain exploratory information.

In sum, this study is supported by data on each of the aforementioned dimensions, as well as an analysis that allows us to infer some conclusions, which are all exploratory. This chapter offers a general approximation to the use and diffusion of the digital social media within Spanish public administrations, although it particularly focuses on regional level government. Consequently, the conclusions of this work must be interpreted with caution, in particular in their extrapolation to other spheres.

MANAGEMENT OF, USES OF, AND PERCEPTIONS ABOUT DIGITAL SOCIAL MEDIA IN SPANISH REGIONAL ADMINISTRATIONS

This section provides statistical data on the diffusion of digital social media in Spanish regional administrations. It is worth highlighting the fact that 13 of the cases analysed changed their government team following the May 2011 elections, and therefore some of them have renewed teams for the management of ICT within their administrations. At the same time, the introduction of digital social media in Spanish public administrations has been undertaken recently, and therefore the interpretation of the data offered below must take these circumstances into account. Each of the following sections presents descriptive statistical data, through simple frequencies, about: (a) the units that manage the digital social media (b) the formalisation of policies or user guides (c) the principal tools employed (d) the reasons for their use (e) perceptions about their evolution (f) inhibiting factors for their use (g) facilitating factors for their introduction and (h) the next steps to consolidate digital social media in future.

The Units that Manage the Digital Social Media

The first dimension of analysis relates to the departments that manage the introduction of digital social media within the administrations under study (see Figure 1). Within this section we seek to identify the area of regional government that is responsible for digital social media, as well as the specific name of the units that are in charge in each of the 17 regional administrations.

Figure 1. Units responsible for the management of the digital social media

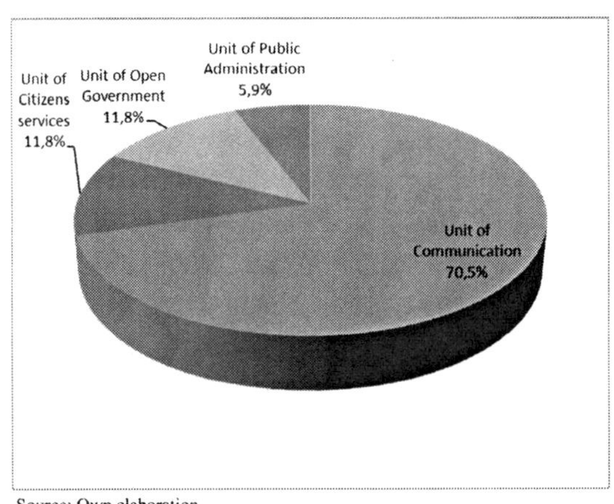

Source: Own elaboration

Question 15: Please, indicate your regional government and unit, your name, and job title. (N=17).

Firstly, 70.5% of those responsible for the management of social networks in the administrations under study are located within regional government's communication departments, and are primarily responsible to the office of the presidency. Specifically, 12 of the 17 units manage social networks through communication departments, another two in their general department for citizen information (11.8%) and one within the department of public administration (5.9%). Finally it is worth highlighting the cases of the Basque Country and Navarra, whose governments have created a management unit that specialises in open government, and which have an overall vision about the management of digital social media, as well as other tools related to administrative transparency and accountability.

These results show that the majority of regional governments have placed their trust, for the first stage in the management of digital social media, in departments or units of communication. This can be interpreted as a move by these organisations to offer more information to citizens. At the same time, it also implies a focus that puts into second place the dimensions of participation and collaboration with citizens. As we shall see below, these results are of great interest, given that there apparently exists a dysfunction between, on the one hand, the reasons that they give as motivations to employ digital social media and, on the other, the management units that take responsibility for leading this function within public administrations.

The Introduction of Policies or Guidance for the Use of Digital Social Media

One of the indicators that shows the degree of maturity of digital social media within public administrations relates to the existence of a

Figure 2. The existence of a user's guide for digital social media

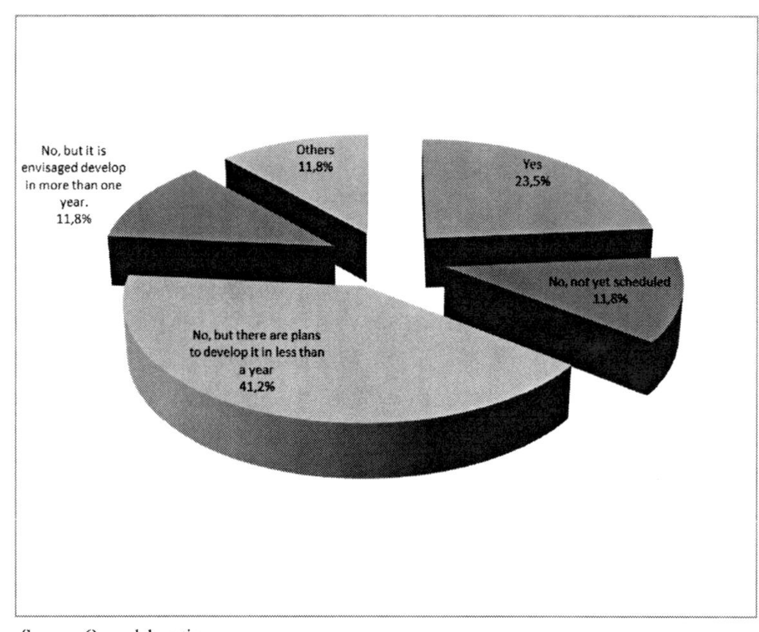

Source: Own elaboration

formalised policy, or a 'normalised document', to define and regulate its use. In recent years the diffusion of digital social media in some public administrations has been accompanied by the creation of a user's guide, in which the main aspects that affect its management are included. The existence of this type of document does not determine the level of evolution of digital social media within the organisation, but it is an indicator of both work and previous reflection on the purpose and orientation of its adoption and use.

Question 3: Please, indicate if you have developed a guide of digital social media use in your administration. (N=17).

As can be seen in Figure 2, five situations have been identified regarding the availability of a digital social network user's guide. Firstly, seven regional administrations (41.2%) confirm that, despite not currently having a document of this type, *they are planning to develop it in less than a year,* while another two *plan to develop it in more than a year* (11.8%). In addition to these situations, another two regional administrations *do not plan to adopt this instrument* (another two reported other types of circumstances). On the other hand, four administrations (23.5%) have a user's guide for digital social media: the regional governments of Catalonia, Valencia, Castilla y León, and the Basque Country.

Each user's guide exhibits differential aspects however the four regional communities demonstrate a common intention of those in charge to progressively introduce digital social media within their administrations. The concept of a *user's guide for digital social media* is in constant development due to its novelty within public administrations. The Catalan regional government, without seeking to provide a universal definition, conceptualises its own document in the following way: "*The Guide contains the procedure recommended to open email accounts or create accounts and profiles for any department, service or brand in spaces where relationship building and par-*

ticipation take place. The Guide also lists different social networking tools, the diverse uses and objectives of each one, recommendations for an appropriate and fruitful presence [on digital social media], as well as criteria for the communicative style that is most adequate for each tool" (Generalitat de Cataluña, 2012).

On the other hand, the Basque country has written a user's guide (Basque Government, 2011) that can be considered as a reference point in the field due to its structure and content, as well as forming part of one of the most advanced Spanish projects in electronic government. *The User's Guide of the Basque Government* was presented in May 2011, which chronologically makes it the second to appear in Spain, following that of the Catalan regional government that was created one year previously. The analysis of the Basque government document can take into account the work by Hrdinová et al. (2010) and the eight essential elements for policies in the use of digital social media in public administrations (access for public employees, management of accounts, acceptable use, behaviour of public employees, content, security, legal aspects and behaviour of citizens), and therefore confirms its high level of interest. As a result, the *User's Guide of the Basque Government* deals with the eight aspects in a comprehensive way, and their government has taken a first step towards the formulation of a public policy for digital social media.

In sum, the *User's Guide of the Basque Government* represents an example of where a strategy to promote the use of digital social media within public administrations should head. An analysis of its content allows us to identify the basic elements to bear in mind. At the same time, the formulation of a strategy or public policy in this sphere requires greater specification, as well as consideration of further dimensions, such as: objectives, actors, criteria of evaluation, budget, etc.

Principal Tools Employed

There is a great diversity of digital social media, and regional administrations have a broad presence in them, although some have drawn particular interest. Firstly, the administrations under study have commonly organised their digital social media in an exogenous way, that is, they have been developed by private companies that offer their services free of charge to their users. Specifically, Spanish regional administrations have most employed *Facebook* and *Twitter* in their relationship with citizens (see Figure 3). *Facebook* is the leading social network in terms of the number of users across the world, as it allows simple interaction among its users by means of texts, photographs and videos, in an instantaneous and free way. On the other hand *Twitter* is the digital social network that has experienced the most rapid growth in recent years, numerically situating itself in second place. *Twitter* is an outstanding "*microblogging*" tool, as it enables the exchange of information and conversation in real time. Together with these two examples, the level of use of *YouTube* (88.2%) or *Flickr* (64.7%) is also relatively high, as these digital social media, respectively, specialise in videos and photographs, and they can also enable an increase in communication and interaction between public administrations and citizens.

Question 5: Please, indicate the digital social media tools used by your regional government (Multi-answer) (N=17).

As can be seen in Figure 3 the administrations, taken together, have tried out a broad range of digital social media, although in some cases in a small way compared to the applications mentioned above. These networks offer very heterogeneous tools, some of which are very specialised, such as: *LinkedIn*, which is orientated towards the creation of professional and employment links, as well as recruitment processes; *Dropbox*, which offers a virtual space to store documents and

Figure 3. Principal digital social media employed

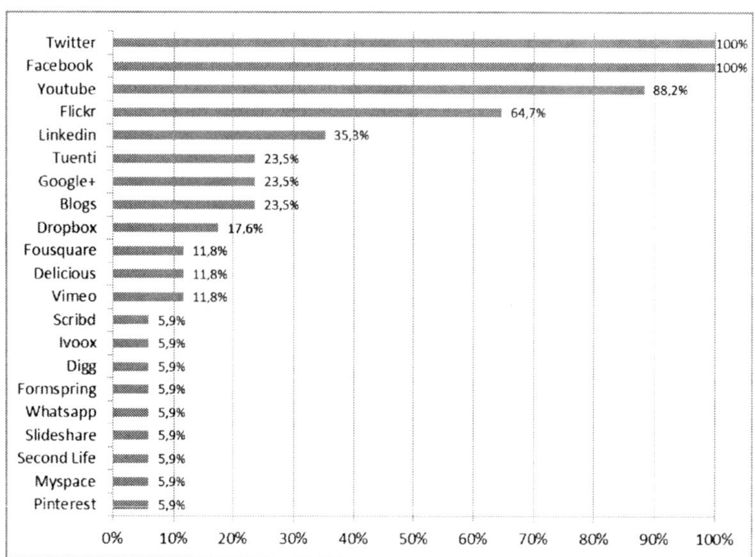

work cooperatively; and *Foursquare*, with a more fun orientation, but linked to the use of mobile devices and localisation applications. In sum, the public administrations under analysis have gone to where the users of the digital social media are most present in Spain (ONTSI, 2011), even though there still is a margin for improvement to take advantage of the full potential of each of them within the public sector.

Motivations for the Use of the Digital Social Media

The fourth aspect of interest raised in this analysis relates to the motivations for the use of digital social media within public administrations. There is an absolute concensus among those responsible for their management in Spanish regional administrations when they are asked to identify the main reasons for its introduction. Specifically, they emphasise three motivations: *to promote participation, increase transparency* and *provide information to citizens*. In fact 16 of the 27 regional managers (94.1%) emphasise that these are the main reasons for its use (see Figure 4).

This confirms that those responsible for digital social media prioritise reasons that focus on external dimensions of the organisation, against improvements of the internal dimension. In other words, the main reasons to employ digital social media are to do with improving relations with citizens, while in second plane are questions linked to the potential *improvement in processes* (29.4%) a *reduction in the amount of resources necessary for the functioning of the administration* (23.5%) or *employees engagement* (23.5%). In sum, there is still room for digital social media to have a much greater organisational impact, above all, via applications that can provide greater efficiency in the workplace, facilitate the management of procedures and services, improve recruitment systems and/or broaden channels of internal communication.

Question 8: What are the main reasons to use digital social media in your government? (Multi-answer). (N=17).

Finally, it has been highlighted above that these results must take into account the units responsible

Figure 4. Motivations for the use of digital social media

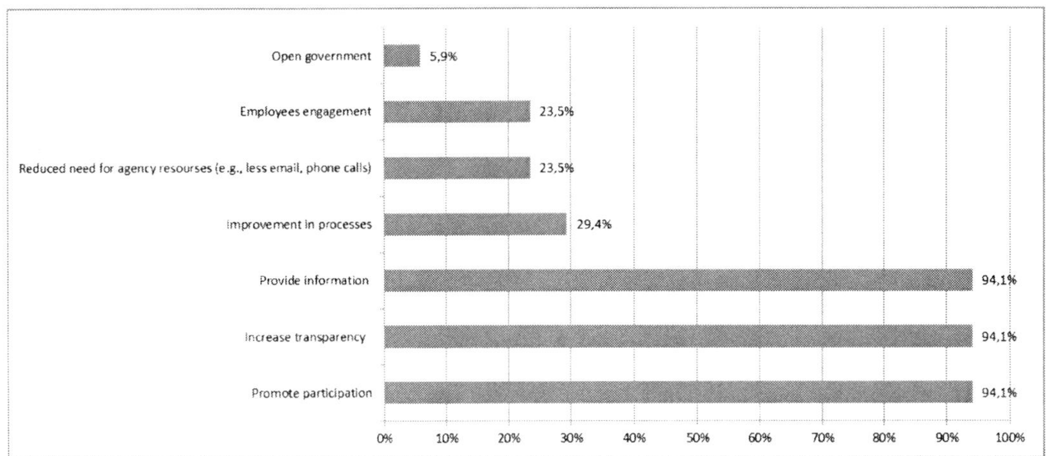

Source: Own elaboration

for the management of the digital social media in the administrations under study. The fact that it is communication departments that are at the forefront of this new area of public administration activity adds weight to the idea that it is strengthening the provision of information and improvements in communications with citizens. However, it is not at all clear that communication departments can promote participation or improve administrative transparency, as these are much more substantive questions, of a more political character, that require a more ambitious management focus. In any case, this point requires further research in order to confirm and develop the conclusions reached above.

Perception about the Level of Development of Digital Social Media

One of the points that generates most interest in technological innovation processes, such as the appearance of digital social media, has to do with the identification of evolutionary levels within public administrations. In this study an approximation has been made through the opinion of those responsible for digital social media in Spanish regional administrations, taking into account that this is a phenomenon that is at an incipient stage and without clear external reference points. Firstly, it is significant that all the Spanish regional administrations have made use of some type of social network in their daily activity. However the limited range of that use, and the lack of other studies, has led us to employ manager's perceptions in order to establish the various levels of development.

Question 12: Despite foregoing risks and concerns, how would you characterize the level of current development of digital social media in your regional government? (N=17).

The data show a high level of optimism among managers in regional administrations when they were asked to locate their organisations on an evolutionary scale with four levels (see Figure 5). Firstly, 64.7% of those responsible for the digital social media stated that they are *advancing rapidly* in their development. In second place, 23.5% affirm that they are *acting with precaution, given that these tools have value, but there is still a lot that is not known about them.* Only one regional administration recognises that they are *starting,* and one other that *they have done a little, because*

Figure 5. Perception about the level of development of digital social media

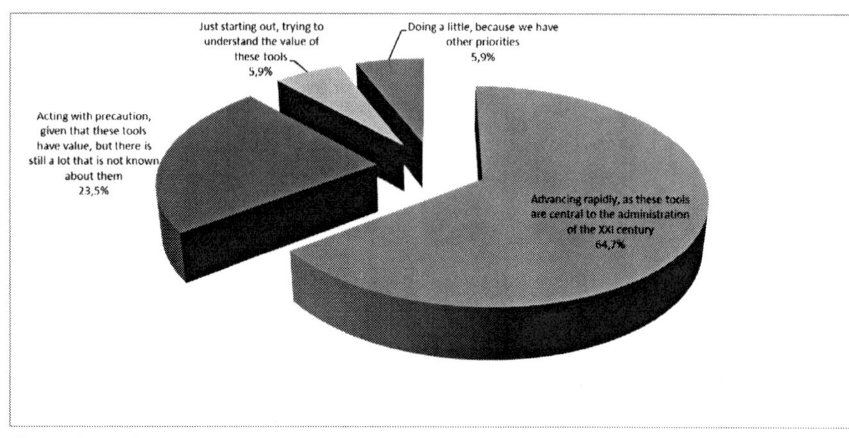

Source: Own elaboration

they have other priorities. Therefore there is a generally positive vision about the situation of administrations under study regarding the level of establishment of digital social media within them.

In conclusion, beyond the optimism expected in those who lead this new aspect of activity in public organisations, the data confirm that public administrations think about digital social media as a project for the future. Or in other words, not only are Spanish regional administrations making use of these tools, but a significant proportion also consider digital social media to be *fundamental administration tools of the XXI century*. Although this perception cannot be generalised to the whole public sector, there is no doubt that an increasingly strong will exists to promote their diffusion and extend them rapidly.

Inhibitors of the Use of the Digital Social Media

The next aspect of interest relates to the identification of inhibitors to the use of social networks in public administrations. As can be seen in Figure 6, those responsible for the management of digital social media in Spanish regional administrations identify four points as being key barriers to the diffusion of these technological tools within their organisations: the lack of an adequate *organisational culture*, *security* risks, the *absence of a framework of governance* and the *absence of resources for control and evaluation*. Although each factor can have its own logic, perhaps it is especially interesting that culture is identified as a fundamental barrier, together with security, because it signals a lack of maturity and experience in the employment of these types of technological innovations.

Question 9: The following issues have commonly constrained broader the use of digital social media in government. Please, indicate your level of concern in each area (0 is very low and 5 is very high). (N=17).

On the other hand, Figure 6 also offers results that are of interest, as it highlights factors that act as inhibitors of lesser importance: such as the fact that regional administrations manage their social networks by employing applications principally developed and organised by third parties, namely *Facebook* and *Twitter*. The data obtained through the questionnaire show that those responsible for digital social media do not distrust the *absence of control over the providers* of these applications, as it is the inhibitor that generates the least concern.

Figure 6. Inhibitors to the use of digital social media

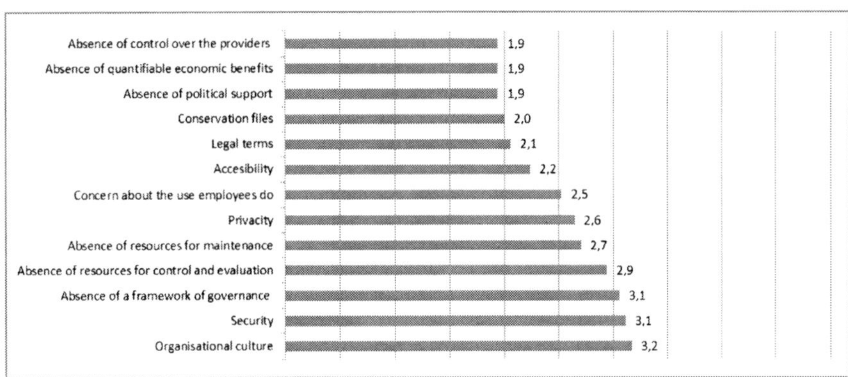

Source: Own elaboration

Additionally, it is interesting to highlight the fact that among the most important inhibitors are not the *absence of political support*, nor the *absence of quantifiable economic benefits*. This could signify that there currently is explicit *political support* for the introduction of digital social media, or that significant investment is not necessary for its deployment. At the same time, as has been suggested above, it is also worth noting that digital social media are not perceived as having a strategic and/or political character within public administrations, or that they require a significant investment for their consolidation.

Facilitators of the Use of Digital Social Media

This study also seeks to analyse the key facilitating factors for the diffusion of digital social media within public sector organisations. It has already been pointed out that all the public administrations under study can be considered users of digital social media, however, as with the process of diffusion of other technological innovations, it is important to identify the variables that interact to produce greater acceptance. For that reason, it is of great interest to know the perspective of those responsible for their management, so that the principal facilitators that promote the use of digital social media within these public organisations can be identified.

Question 11: What would facilitate the advance in the use of digital social media at your regional government? (Multi-answer). (N=17).

Various interesting conclusions can be drawn from this dimension. The most significant facilitating factor among those identified by managers in Spanish regional administrations is to *accumulate user experience,* with 64.7%; this highlights the importance given to the need to extend the use of these tools within the public sector (see Figure 7). On the other hand, *to generate teamwork* (58.8%), as well as *to provide case studies with statistics* (52.9%), are another two points highlighted as facilitating factors. In the former case, it seems that the need for shared work is inherent to digital social media. In the latter, the accent is put on the importance of evaluating these types of processes of technological diffusion within public administrations.

On the other hand, it is interesting to find that other factors are considered to have lesser importance. Both the *capacitation of public employees* and the *development of a public policy or user's guide* are not considered to be such critical factors by those responsible for digital social media. The latter point is particularly significant because it

Figure 7. Facilitators of the use of digital social media

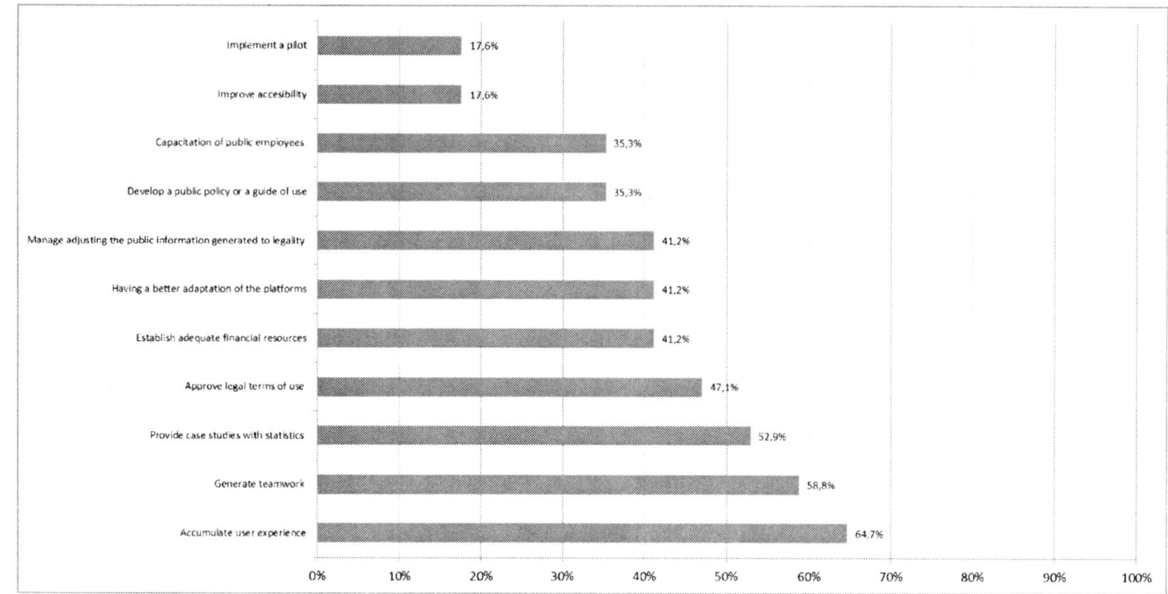

Source: Own elaboration

reflects the idea of a lack of interest in the strategic/political factors linked to the diffusion of these types of technological tools within public administrations.

Next Steps for Digital Social Media

The majority of public managers that collaborated in this research agreed that digital social media will be key tools in public administrations in the XXI century. However, at the same time, it is necessary to know from a forecasting perspective how they believe their use will be orientated. For this reason, the interviewees were asked about the next steps that their public administrations are planning to advance their implementation.

Question 14: What are your next steps as digital social media tools evolve and products are introduced? (Multi-answer). (N=17).

Those responsible for the digital social media confirmed that they are going to initiate projects, above all, in two areas. On the one hand, they seek to achieve *greater integration of the digital social media* (58.8%), as well as *aggregation of the digital social media on the web portal* (52.9%). On the other hand, a *generation of services based on localisation* is expected (52.9%), as well as the *creation of advanced applications for mobiles* (52.9%) (see Figure 8). As might be suspected, the former two aspects are oriented towards the integration of communication tools, while the latter two focus on the development of the use of digital social media by means of mobile devices.

On the other hand, it is also worth emphasising some of the aspects that have not been considered in such detail as areas for future development. In particular, it is worth highlighting the role of the *exploitation of user's data* in digital social media, given that this is already a sphere in which significant advances are taking place, linked to disciplines such as *data mining*. These lines of work may result in a true transformation in the capacity of public administrations to monitor user's activity, to achieve a deeper knowl-

Figure 8. Next steps for the digital social media

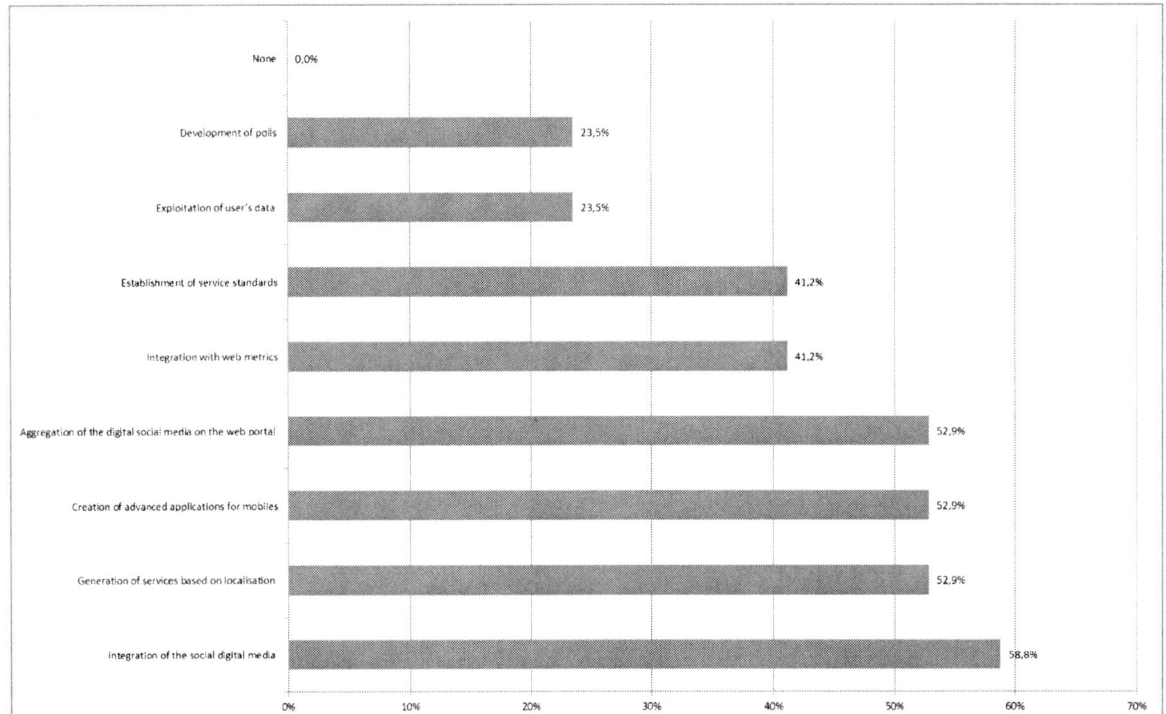

Source: Own elaboration

edge of the environment in which they operate, as well as to facilitate the adoption of better public decisions. At the same time, the data available confirm that we find ourselves before an open type of technological innovation whose development is pending, not only the policies that those responsible for public administrations adopt in the future, but also the decisions of citizens that interact with them.

FUTURE RESEARCH DIRECTIONS

Overall, it is worth highlighting that the analysis drawn from this study are located in the regional sphere of Spanish government and in no case seek to be generalised to the whole of the public sector in Spain. To deepen the results of this research it would also be of interest to develop comparative studies with, on the one hand, other levels of government in Spain and other regional administrations at international level. Moreover it would also be important to go deeper into the study of the diffusion of digital social media in different sectors of public policy or specific areas of management. In this way some of the results derived from the data analysis that has been put forward in this chapter could be contrasted.

This study may be expanded studying other levels of government in Spain and other regional administrations at international level. The former implies addressing the differences among the three layers of government in Spain (local, regional, and national). While they share the Napoleonic-style of public sector management, they have their own agendas and priorities. The later is based on the scarcity of studies about the regional level in the international e-government community. In both cases, future research should focus on differences/

continuities through different layers of government or groups of countries.

Besides, the study of the diffusion of digital social media in different public policy sectors or specific areas of management will be of importance. Here, it is expected that governments will use more intensively social media tools within policy fields in which up-to-date information and communication are more useful for citizens/public administrations (emergencies, police, etc.). At the same time, variations in the use of social media through management functions (human resource management, organizational communication, strategic planning, etc.) is also of interest, because of the need of knowledge about the challenges of social media use in the organizational dimension of public management.

DISCUSSION AND CONCLUSION

This section provides the main findings of this research. The dimensions of analysis employed have been selected for their descriptive/explanatory value, as well as for their potential to inspire new lines of work. This chapter provides information about the role that digital social media are playing in Spanish regional administrations, through an empirical analysis about its current level of use and diffusion. The study has sought to investigate the key questions which have guided this study: What are the main factors that explain the use of digital social media in public administrations? What is the self-perception of those responsible for the management of digital social media about their level of development within their organisations? What are the key inhibitors-facilitators for the development of digital social media in public administrations? What are the next steps to promote digital social media in the sphere of public administrations?

Firstly, we have confirmed that all the Spanish regional administrations have adopted these technological innovations, albeit in an incipient way. This development has led them to establish departments that specialise in the management of digital social media. In their majority, these management units pertain to the area of communication, except in specific cases where administrations have created management units that are more specifically related to open government. This point allows us to infer a still incipient use of digital social media, oriented towards boosting the informative dimension of public administrations, more than facilitating processes of citizen participation or of 'collaboration with society'. It should not be forgotten that the boost given to these latter aspects allows us to confirm that digital social media strengthen government 2.0 and not only an informative model of digital administration (Chun et al., 2010).

This argument reinforces the still limited presence of policies or user guides for the use of digital social media in the public administrations under study. As has been pointed out above, the user guides are only an indicator of the existence of both work and previous reflection on their adoption. However, only a limited number of regional administrations have these types of documents (the majority of the remainder have stated that they will approve them in less than one or two years). By means of an example, the administrations of the regional governments of Catalonia or the Basque Country have demonstrated a greater will to formulate a strategy with greater reach in the management of digital social media through their user's guides (Generalitat de Catalunya, 2012; Basque Government, 2011). Besides the style guides or communicative factors, these documents relate to more substantive dimensions such as, among others, the access given to different types of public employees, the management of accounts, or the type of content that is permitted. However, there are further steps to take in order to stop them simply being 'normalising good practice mechanisms' or informative points of reference for public employees/citizens, and to transform them into instruments with greater political and strategic weight.

Facebook and *Twitter* are two digital social media that have achieved the highest level of diffusion within the Spanish administrative sphere, as is confirmed by the fact that they are already present in all regional administrations. Those who are responsible for their management argue that they are essential instruments for public administrations in the future. This leads us to believe that these organisations are backing the development of digital social media, above all, with the object of improving spaces of interaction with citizens, in line with that already highlighted in previous studies in the Spanish case (Criado et al., 2011). In reality, this group of public administrations clearly intends to tie themselves to those ICT tools that have the most societal penetration.

The motivations behind the adoption and use of digital social media are intimately related to the ideas mentioned above. This study has confirmed that other networks have a lower level of presence in the public sector (for example, *YouTube*, *Flickr*, blogs, etc.), but the adoption of *Facebook* and *Twitter* allows public administrations to be closer to citizens in the digital sphere, which is essential to strengthening governments by focusing more on citizens (Bonson et al., 2012). This is also undertaken in order to generate a co-production of public services (Bertot et al., 2012), as well as to promote closer collaboration in the process of developing public policies (Nam, 2012). In other words, this opens up a path which can deliver better information, increase transparency and promote citizen participation.

Another of the axes that has guided this study relates to the main inhibitors-facilitators to the development of digital social media in public administrations. Among the inhibitors, cultural factors (*organisational culture*) are still the main barrier that impedes this type of technological innovation becoming more widespread, together with a perception of a lack of security and the absence of a framework for adequate governance. Consequently, digital social media still find themselves faced with significant barriers both within and outside public administrations. The former barrier is due, above all, to its recent adoption, as well as to the low level of accumulated use during recent years. In fact, it can be stated that technological innovations must be integrated more into the daily activities of employees if there is to be a greater level of diffusion within the public sector.

That said, it is not surprising that the main facilitator of digital social media is accumulation of user experience, followed by the generation of team-work linked to them. Social networking tools can clearly be orientated towards improving interaction with citizens, however it is also important to emphasise their potential to innovate the internal activity of public administrations. This latter dimension has not been explored in the studies undertaken to date, that have been highly focused on the external projection of digital social media. Consequently it is necessary to investigate deeper into the internal organisation of administrations in future lines of research.

It is also worth highlighting the fact that the evolution of digital social media in public administrations represents an object of study of growing interest. Firstly, these types of technological diffusion processes probably respond to the same patterns as previous technologies. In particular, one of the key ideas refers to the inexistence of closed and/or predetermined results regarding the future of digital social media within public administrations. In any case, this work has thrown light on some of the incipient concerns about the future and, above all, the integration of digital social media, as well as public web portals. These areas are key to achieving seemless public administrations, which are increasingly integrated and more oriented to a shared model of governance with society.

The current context of digital social media in the public sector is characterised by various aspects. On the one hand, those who are politically in charge support the idea of extending their diffusion. At the same time there is a lack of knowledge about their current and potential impact in the future functioning of public administrations. This is a consequence of both the lack of systematic research in this area, and the need for the existence of a more passionate, rather than rational, debate about the next steps to promote digital social media in the sphere of public organisations.

On the other hand, it is important to point out that this work is based on a methodological effort linked to a content analysis of the Internet, a questionnaire that was responded to by those responsible for the management of digital social media in the Spanish regional administrations, together with a documental analysis of the most recent publications in this area. This chapter contributes a relevant analysis, although it is of an exploratory character because of the almost total absence of systematic studies about the diffusion of digital social media within Spanish public administrations. It is therefore necessary to broaden this research by strengthening the data available, for example, through in-depth interviews, that will facilitate a more specific investigation into the qualitative factors, complementary to the information obtained through questionnaires. Equally, within the context of consolidating research techniques linked to the analysis of digital social media, one could put the focus on the content generated by the interaction between public administrations and citizens through these new digital social media.

REFERENCES

AGIMO. (2009). *Engage. Getting on with Government 2.0*. Report of the Government 2.0 Taskforce. Australian Government Information Management Office. Retrieved September 15, 2010, from www.finance.gov.au

Bailey, C., & Singleton, R. (2010). *National survey of social media use in state government*. Lexington: NASCIO.

Bertot, J. C., Jaeger, P. T., & Hansen, D. (2012). The impact of polices on government social media usage: Issues, challenges, and recommendations. *Government Information Quarterly*, *29*(1), 30–40. doi:10.1016/j.giq.2011.04.004.

Bonsón, E., Torres, L., Royo, S., & Flores, F. (2012). Local e-government 2.0: Social media and corporate transparency in municipalities. *Government Information Quarterly*, *29*, 123–132. doi:10.1016/j.giq.2011.10.001.

Boyd, D. M., & Ellison, N. B. (2007). Social network sites: Definition, history, and scholarship. *Journal of Computer-Mediated Communication*, *13*(1), 11. doi:10.1111/j.1083-6101.2007.00393.x.

Calista, D. J., & Melitski, J. (2007). e-Government and e-Governance: Converging constructs of public sector information and communications technologies. *Public Administration Quarterly*, *31*(1), 87–120.

Cerrillo i Martínez, A. (2010). Web 2.0 y la participación ciudadana en la transparencia administrativa en la sociedad de la información. In Cotino, L. (Ed.), *Libertades de expresión e información en Internet y las redes sociales: ejercicio, amenazas y garantías*. Valencia: Publicacions de la Universitat de València.

Chun, S. A., Shulman, S., Sandoval, R., & Hovy, E. (2010). Government 2.0. Making connections between citizens, data and government. *Information Polity: The International Journal of Government & Democracy in the Information Age*, *15*, 1–9.

Chun, S. A., & Warner, J. (2010). Finding information in an era of abundance: Towards a collaborative tagging environment in government. *Information Polity. The International Journal of Government & Democracy in the Information Age*, *15*, 89–103.

Criado, J. I. (2009). *Entre Sueños Utópicos y Visiones Pesimistas. Internet y las TIC en la Modernización de las Administraciones Públicas*. Madrid: Instituto Nacional de Administración Pública.

Criado, J. I., Martín, Y., & Camacho, D. (2011). *Experiences using social networks in Spanish public administration*. Paper presented at the meeting of the 1st International Workshop on Social Data Mining for Human Behaviour Analysis. Songndal, Norway.

Criado, J. I., & Rojas-Martin, F. (2012). *Strategies and realities of social media diffusion in the public sector. Evidence from the regional government in Spain*. Paper presented at the annual meeting of the European Group of Public Administration. Bergen, Norway.

Danziger, J. N., & Andersen, K. V. (2002). Impacts of information technology on public administration: An analysis of empirical research from the "Golden Age" of transformation. *International Journal of Public Administration*, *25*(5), 591–627. doi:10.1081/PAD-120003292.

Dixon, B. E. (2010). Towards e-Government 2.0: An assessment of where e-government 2.0 is and where it is headed. *Public Administration & Management*, *15*(2), 418–454.

Generalitat de Cataluña. (2012). Guía de usos y estilo en las redes sociales de la Generalitat de Cataluña. Retrieved May 13, 2012, from http://www.gencat.cat/web/meugencat/documents

Gil-García, J. R. (2012). *Enacting electronic government success: An integrative study of government-wide websites, organizational capabilities, and institutions*. New York: Springer. doi:10.1007/978-1-4614-2015-6.

Gobierno Vasco. (2011). Guía de Usos y Estilos del Gobierno Vasco. Retrieved May15, 2001, from http://www.irekia.euskadi.net/assets/a_documents/

Heeks, R., & Bailur, S. (2006). Analyzing e-government research. Perspectives, philosophies, theories, methods, and practice. *Government Information Quarterly*, *24*(2), 243–265. doi:10.1016/j.giq.2006.06.005.

Heidinger, C., Buchmann, E., & Böhn, K. (2010). Impact assessment in public policy: Towards a Web 2.0 application. *Information Polity: The International Journal of Government & Democracy in the Information Age*, *15*(1-2), 33–50.

Hood, C., & Margetts, H. (2007). *The tools of government in the digital age*. London: Palgrave.

Hrdinová, J., Helbig, N., & Peters, C. S. (2010). *Designing social media policy for government: Eight essential elements*. Albany: The Research foundation of State University of New York. Retrieved February 20, 2012, from http://www.ctg.albany.edu/publications

Kaplan, A. M., & Haenlein, M. (2010). Users of the world, unite! The challenges and opportunities of social media. *Business Horizons*, *53*(1), 59–68. doi:10.1016/j.bushor.2009.09.003.

Meijer, A., & Thaens, M. (2010). Alignment 2.0: Strategic use of new internet technologies in government. *Government Information Quarterly*, *27*(2), 113–121. doi:10.1016/j.giq.2009.12.001.

Nam, T. (2012). Dual effects of the internet on political activism: Reinforcing and mobilizing. *Government Information Quarterly*, *29*(1), 90–97. doi:10.1016/j.giq.2011.08.010.

ONTSI. (2011). *Informe Anual de la Sociedad de la Información en España*. Industria y hábitos de consumo. Retrieved April 20, 2012, from http://www.ontsi.red.es/ontsi/es/estudios-informes/

Pollit, C., & Bouckaert, G. (2011). *Public management reform: A comparative analysis* (3rd ed.). Oxford: Oxford University Press.

Ramón, F. (2010). La red social como ejemplo de participación: casos y cuestiones. In Cotino, L. (Ed.), *Libertades de expresión e información en Internet y las redes sociales: ejercicio, amenazas y garantías*. Valencia: Publicacions de la Universitat de València.

Yildiz, M. (2007). E-government research. Reviewing the literature, limitations, and ways forward. *Government Information Quarterly*, *24*(3), 646–665. doi:10.1016/j.giq.2007.01.002.

ADDITIONAL READING

Axelsson, K., Ulf, M., & Lindgren, I. (2010). Exploring the importance of citizen participation and involvement in e-government projects. Practice, incentives, and organization. *Transforming Government: People, Process and policy*, 4, 299-321.

Bannister, F., & Connolly, R. (2012). *The great theory hunt: Does e-government really have a problem?* Paper presented at the EGPA Annual Conference. Bergen. Norway.

Bernhard, I., & Wihlborg, E. (2012). Regional e-Governance opens up to entrepreneurial behavior in public administration. In Johansson, B., Karlsson, C., & Stough, R. R. (Eds.), *Agglomeration, clusters, and entrepreneurship: Studies in regional development*. London: Edward Elgar Publications.

Bovaird, T., & Loeffler, E. (2010). User and community co-production of public services and public policies through collective decision-making: The role of emerging technologies. In Brandsen, T., & Holzer, M. (Eds.), *The future of governance*. Newark, NJ: National Center for Public Performance.

Claes, N. J., Hurley, C., & Stefanone, M. A. (2012). *Do me a solid? Information asymmetry, liking, and compliance gaining online*. Paper presented at the 45th Hawaii International Conference on System Sciences. Hawaii.

Dunleavy, P., Margetts, H., Bastow, S., & Tinkler, J. (2005). New public management is dead – long live digital-era governance. *Journal of Public Management Research and Theory*, *16*, 467–494. doi:10.1093/jopart/mui057.

Grönlund, Å., & Andersson, A. (2006). e-Gov research quality improvements since 2003: More rigor, but research (perhaps) redefined, electronic government. LNCS, 4084,1-12. Springer, Heidelberg.

Heeks, R. (1999). *Reinventing government in the Information Age – International practice in IT-enabled public sector reform*. London: Routledge. doi:10.4324/9780203204962.

Heeks, R. (2006). *Implementing and managing e-government: An international text*. Thousand Oaks, CA/London: Sage Publications.

Ilshammar, L., Bjurström, A., & Grönlund, Å. (2005). Public e-services in Sweden: Old wine in new bottles? *Scandinavian Journal of Information Systems*, *17*(2), 11–40.

Irani, Z., Love, P., & Montazemi, A. (2007). E-government: Past, present and future. *European Journal of Information Systems*, *16*(2), 103–105. doi:10.1057/palgrave.ejis.3000678.

Jun, K.-N., & Weare, C. (2011). Institutional motivations in the adoption of innovations: The case of e-government. *Journal of Public Administration: Research and Theory*, *21*(3), 495–519. doi:10.1093/jopart/muq020.

Lee, J. (2012). *Active e-participation in local governance: Citizen participation values and social networks*. Paper presented at the EGPA Annual Conference. Bergen. Norway.

Lee, J., & Kim, S. (2011). Exploring the role of social networks in affective organizational commitment: Network centrality, strength of ties, and structural holes. *American Review of Public Administration*, *41*, 205–223. doi:10.1177/0275074010373803.

Löfgren, K., & Meijer, A. (2012). *Why do governments not copy successful technological practices? A study of the transfer of a technology for citizen participation from the Netherlands to Denmark.* Paper presented at the EGPA Annual Conference. Bergen. Norway.

Luna-Reyes, L. F., & Gil-Garcia, J. R. (2011). Using institutional theory and dynamic simulation to understand complex e-Government phenomena. *Government Information Quarterly*, *28*(3), 329–345. doi:10.1016/j.giq.2010.08.007.

Margetts, H. (2009). Public management change and e-government: The emergence of digital era governance. In Chadwick, A. (Ed.), *Routledge handbook of internet politics* (pp. 99–113).

Pignato, V. (2012). *How to read development lines of e-government in the Public Administrations? Towards the construction of an interpretative model.* Paper presented at the EGPA Annual Conference. Bergen. Norway.

Seebach, C. (2012) *Searching for answers -knowledge exchange through social media in organizations.* Paper presented at the 45th Hawaii International Conference on System Sciences. Hawaii.

Stieglitz, S., & Dang-Xuan, L. (2012). *Political communication and influence through microblogging--An empirical analysis of sentiment in Twitter messages and Retweet behavior.* Paper presented at the 45th Hawaii International Conference on System *Sciences. Hawaii.*

Suh, A., & Shin, K.-S. (2012). *Self discrepancy, perceived privacy rights, and contribution in virtualcommunities.* Paper presented at the 45th Hawaii International Conference on System *Sciences. Hawaii.*

Togo, T., & Enomoto, K. (2011). Consideration of regional informatization practices in Japan: A case study on a civic organization operating community media. *Journal of Business Studies*, *58*(2), 237–255.

Walsham, G. (2012). Are we making a better world with ICTs? Reflections on a future agenda for the IS field. *Journal of Information Technology*, *27*(2), 87–93. doi:10.1057/jit.2012.4.

Yang, T. M., & Maxwell, T. A. (2011). Information-sharing in public organizations: A literature review of interpersonal, intra-organizational and inter-organizational success factors. *Government Information Quarterly*, *28*, 164–175. doi:10.1016/j.giq.2010.06.008.

KEY WORDS AND DEFINITIONS

E-Government: The utilization of digital governmental mechanism for delivering information and services to the citizens and for improving efficiency, effectiveness and transparency in Government and Public Administration.

ICT: Information and communications technology.

Micro-Blogging: A broadcast medium in the form of blogging. Here, the content is smaller, both in actual or and aggregate size. It allows the users to exchange small elements of content, including short text, but also images, videos, etc. Today, the most extended micro-blogging platform is Twitter.

Regional Level of Government in Spain: Group of seventeen administrative units with political autonomy and powers.

Social Media: A group of Internet-based applications ideologically and technologically grounded from the creation of Web 2.0, and that leads to the creation and exchange of user-generated content.

Social Media Manager or Community Manager: A new type of manager in the public sector who is in charge of fostering the utilization, sharing, and diffusion of social media in the organization. At the same time, he/she engages, involves and facilitates the participation of the public with the organization.

User's Guide (For Social Media): It is a 'normalized document' of variable size and form intended to define and regulate the use of social media within the organization. In some cases, it also guides the organization in how to manage the interaction with the public within the social media dimension.

Chapter 15
A Country Level Evaluation of the Impact of E-Government: The Case of Italy

Walter Castelnovo
University of Insubria, Italy

ABSTRACT

Despite considerable investments made worldwide in e-government initiatives in the past years, whether e-government succeeded in achieving the expected benefits in terms of increased efficiency, effectiveness and quality in the delivery of services is still under discussion. This chapter proposes an evaluation of the outcomes of the National Action Plan (NAP) for the diffusion of e-government at the local level in Italy. The evaluation considers whether the implementation of the projects funded under the action plan determined positive effects at the country level in terms of an increase in the value generated for different stakeholders. The discussion of data from both national and international secondary sources shows that during the period in which the benefits of the NAP should have become apparent no positive effects have emerged with evidence. The chapter argues that this depends on some of the principles the NAP has been based on that limited its capability of achieving the expected results.

INTRODUCTION

During the last two decades considerable resources have been invested worldwide in supporting innovation in public administration. Most of these resources have been devoted to e-government, which is the use of Information and Communication Technologies (ICT) to achieve better policy outcomes, higher quality services and greater engagement with citizens (OECD, 2003). In the countries of the European Union, the policies for the diffusion of e-government have mainly been coordinated at the Community level within the frameworks defined by the member governments and implemented by the action plans set up by the European Commission. The more recent ministerial declaration on e-government is the Malmö declaration in which the joint vision is stated that by 2015:

DOI: 10.4018/978-1-4666-4173-0.ch015

Copyright © 2013, IGI Global. Copying or distributing in print or electronic forms without written permission of IGI Global is prohibited.

European governments (...) use e-government to increase their efficiency and effectiveness and to constantly improve public services in a way that caters for users' different needs and maximizes public value, thus supporting the transition of Europe to a leading knowledge-based economy. (EU, 2009a, p. 1)

In order to achieve these objectives, in the Malmö declaration some priorities have been defined; namely:

- Citizens and businesses empowerment by means of e-government services,
- Implementation of seamless e-government services to support mobility in the single market,
- Achieve efficiency and effectiveness through the use of e-government to reduce the administrative burden and improve organisational processes,
- Establish the legal and technical preconditions that make possible the implementation of the policy priorities (EU, 2009a, p. 2).

All these priorities, as well as some of the specific actions devised to achieve them, were already included in the previous EU action plans for e-government. Actually, citizens' centricity, efficiency, effectiveness, transparency, responsiveness and accountability of governments have been at the centre of the e-government initiatives from the very beginning. However, under the current global financial crisis, the achievement of those objectives is even more crucial than in the past. Indeed, according to a survey run by the Organization for Economic Co-operation and Development (OECD) in 2009, almost all the member countries report that e-government is seen as a contribution to the economic recovery (OECD, 2009; Ubaldi, 2011). This is mainly due to the expectation that e-government investments will provide significant cost-savings both directly, in terms of improved efficiency and effectiveness of government organizations, and indirectly, in terms of better quality of the services delivered and reduction of administrative burden on citizens and enterprises. However, this expectation is uncertain; indeed, after more than a decade of investments in e-government a discussion is still going on worldwide concerning whether the policies for the diffusion of e-government implemented so far succeeded in achieving the expected results.

This chapter discusses this problem by considering the case of Italy, with a specific focus on the evaluation of the outcomes of the policies for the diffusion of e-government at the local level established in the Italian National Action Plan for e-government (NAP). The evaluation is based on a holistic approach and it is performed at the country level using secondary data sources (Alalwan & Thomas, 2011; Srivastava & Teo, 2007; 2010), including surveys conducted by both national and international organizations and data provided by the Italian National Institute of Statistics (ISTAT) and the European Institute of Statistics (EUROSTAT). On the basis of the data considered, in the chapter it is claimed that at the moment no positive effects at the country level have emerged with evidence yet as a result of the NAP, neither for the citizens as such (in terms of an increase of the country's global wellbeing), nor for citizens as taxpayers (in terms of the reduction of the global cost of local government), for citizens as public servants (in terms of the increase of their human capital) and for citizens as entrepreneurs (in terms of the reduction of the administrative burdens on enterprises).

The chapter concludes that this scarce impact of the NAP depends on some of the principles it has been based on rather than on the way the funded projects have been implemented.

BACKGROUND

In broad terms, e-government aims at the transformation of government through the pervasive use of ICT. As such, e-government should be considered as a system innovation; this means that the evaluation of the policies implemented for the spreading of e-government cannot be simply based on the possible success of single projects implemented at the local level (best practices). Rather, what is needed is a holistic approach allowing an evaluation of the impacts of those policies at the level of the whole system of government (Srivastava & Teo, 2007; 2010; Castelnovo, 2010; Alalwan & Thomas, 2011).

The whole system of government should be considered as a system of systems, that is a strictly interconnected system of components in which the activities performed by one of the components impact on the behavior of other components, not necessarily those more directly connected to it. In such a strictly interconnected system the "optimization" of one of the components can be achieved through actions successfully implemented locally. However, these actions could determine unforeseen "long-distance effects" that could impact negatively on other components of the system. Hence, positive effects shown locally not necessarily determine positive results at the level of the whole system. This is what typically happens when a government body (usually one belonging to a higher institutional level, for instance a ministry) implements solutions that while improving its performances put a further burden on other government bodies (for instance the municipalities that have to interact with that ministry). For this reason, although a single e-government project can be evaluated even simply considering the effects it generates locally, in the evaluation of general policies for the diffusion of e-government at the local level a holistic approach should be taken, considering the effects they can possibly determine at the level of the whole system of local government, and more generally at the level of the whole country development (Srivastava & Teo, 2007; 2010). In this chapter such a holistic approach will be assumed in the evaluation of the outcomes of the national policies for the diffusion of e-government implemented in Italy in the past decade. Since citizens (user) centricity is one of the leading principles of e-government, the discussion will start by considering what citizens centricity could mean in a holist approach to e-government evaluation.

The concept of public value is becoming increasingly popular in the discussions about the evaluation of e-government policies, even outside the limits of the academic debate (Castelnovo & Simonetta, 2007; 2008; Codagnone & Undheim, 2008; Benington, 2009; Misuraca, Alfano, & Viscusi, 2011; Karunasena & Deng, 2010; 2012). However, such an interest toward public value is quite recent, at least in the European Union policies for e-government. Actually, the first time the term "public value" occurs within the EU Ministerial Declarations on e-government is in the Malmö declaration. This follows the shift observed in the 2009 report on the progress of the i2010 E-Government Action Plan prepared for the European Commission:

> *All of the five Action Plan objectives report a shift over the last few years in underlying requirements and developments. There is increasing focus on user centricity and empowering citizens and businesses, on benefits and impacts, and with a longer term concern for improving performance and public value.* (EU, 2009c, p. 8)

In a broad sense, public value refers to the value created by government through services, laws, regulations and other actions. Public value provides a broader measure than is conventionally used within the new public management literature, covering outcomes, the means used to deliver them as well as trust and legitimacy. It addresses issues such as equity, ethos and accountability (Kelly, Mulgan, & Muers, 2002; Castelnovo & Simonetta, 2007; 2008; Grimsley & Meehan, 2008; Harrison et al., 2011; Karunasena & Deng, 2010; 2012) and focuses on a "wider range of value than public goods; more than outputs; and what has meaning for people, rather than what a public-sector decision-maker might presume is best for them" (Alford & O'Flynn, 2009, p. 176).

As pointed out by Karunasena and Deng (2010, p. 287), the popularity of the concept of public value is because it provides an inclusive framework for examining the performance of public services from the perspective of citizens. However, the delivery of services is just one of the elements through which governments can generate public value. Public value can also be generated through a better use of public resources by governments; a more responsive and trustworthy government; the improvement of the citizens wellbeing and the development of public trust.

The close relation between public value and e-government has been pointed out byKearns (2004) that refers to the work of Kelly, Mulgan, and Muers (2002) in a critical discussion about the excessive emphasis given to online services as the central element of e-government systems. Public Administration aims at producing value for citizens; thus, the use of ICT to improve government can be considered as a means to improve the production of public value. From this point of view, an e-government system can be evaluated by considering the possible increasing of public value deriving from the adoption of that system (Castelnovo & Simonetta, 2007; 2008; Yu, 2008; Codagnone & Undheim, 2008).

Since E-Government aims at a citizen centered vision of government, also the evaluation of an e-government system as regards the public value produced should be based on a citizen-centered approach (Bannister, 2002; Alford, 2002; Alshawi & Alalwany, 2009). Discussing the value of ICT for Public Administration, Bannister (2002) underlines that the definition of value reflects the fact that citizens interact with Public Administration, which creates public value, playing different roles as e-government stakeholders (Scholl, 2001; Alalwan & Thomas, 2011; Rowley, 2011). A possible classification of the citizens' roles as e-government stakeholders is the following:

- **Citizen as such:** Any person having the right of citizenship;
- **Citizen as taxpayer:** Person who, through taxation, finances public administration;
- **Citizen as user/consumer:** Person who "buys" a service from public administration, thus obtaining private value (for himself);
- **Citizen as beneficiary:** Person who receives a service from public administration without having to buy it;
- **Citizen as entrepreneur:** Person who benefits from the services of public administration as economical subject;
- **Citizen as participant:** Person participating in democratic processes;
- **Citizen as policy maker:** Person playing the role of policy maker within public administration;
- **Citizen as civil servant:** Person working for public administration;
- **Citizen as delegate agent:** Person working on behalf of Public Administration without being an operator of public administration;
- **Citizen as supplier:** Person who, as economic subject, supplies goods and services to public administration. (Castelnovo & Simonetta, 2007)

These roles correspond to some modalities of interaction between citizens and public administration. Some of these modalities concern relations between public administration and subjects that are external to it (external stakeholders): they correspond to roles in which citizens receive a value from public administration as users of services or participants in democratic processes (user/consumer, beneficiary, entrepreneur, participant).

Other modalities of interaction, by contrast, concern internal relations (internal stakeholders): they correspond to relations between public administration and citizens playing a direct or indirect role in the processes for the production of value (policy maker, civil servant). In these roles citizens receive a private value from public administration (in terms of political or economical reward). Nevertheless, as these roles are responsible, on different levels, for the functioning of the organization, they might also receive a public value, for instance in terms of good functioning of public administration itself.

To these two kinds of roles a third one can be added, which includes roles external to public administration and yet involved on different levels in the production of public value, as it is the case of Networked Government. Examples of such "mixed" roles are the role of delegate agent and of supplier, in particular of service supplier (for instance an outsourcer).

In considering the classification of the citizen roles above it should be borne in mind that an individual can play many different roles simultaneously. Thus, for instance, an individual can simultaneously be a taxpayer that "funds" public administration, a consumer that uses the services delivered by public administration and a civil servant working in a public administration organization. This can generate a conflict of interests that must be considered in evaluating public administration from the point of view of the public value it delivers to citizens. Actually, as a user of the services a citizen would like to receive more and better services from the public administration. However, this could determine a higher cost for service delivery (at least on the short term), which could mean that the citizen has either to pay a higher cost for accessing the services or to be prone to incur in a higher level of taxation. Similarly, as a civil servant a citizen might want a higher wage, that is a private value for him; however, this could mean that public administration has to spend more for salaries and this, as a consequence, could force public administration either to invest less in improving the quality of the services (which means less value for the citizen as user) or to higher the level of taxation (which means less value for the citizen as taxpayer).

In the next sections of the chapter it will be considered whether the policies for the diffusion of e-government at the local level in Italy succeeded in delivering value to citizens, as they play some of the roles considered in the taxonomy described above. More specifically, by following a holistic and role based approach to the evaluation of e-government, it will be considered whether the implementation of the NAP determined positive effects for the citizens as such, as tax payers, as entrepreneurs (considering the case of small to medium enterprises) and as public servants.

THE DEVELOPMENT OF E-GOVERNMENT IN ITALY: AN OVERVIEW

In the past decade many investments have been made in Italy for the modernization of the public sector through the deployment of ICT. These investments involved both the central government and the whole system of local government of Italy, which includes 8092 municipalities, 110 provinces and 20 regions. This modernization effort has been supported with investments both from the central government and from the regional governments, sometimes in an uncoordinated way. Actually, it was only in 2002 that a coherent framework has been established by means of the definition of the national action plan for e-government, which set up a set of modernization objectives coherent with the EU's strategy for the information society.

The Italian Action Plan for E-Government (NAP)

The Italian National Action Plan for e-government has been launched in 2002 with a first announcement for the co-financing of innovation projects with the aim of:

- Using ICTs in order to achieve a significant increase in quality and efficiency of the services delivered to citizens and enterprises,
- Promoting the creation, or the transformation, of the services delivered by local

government into online services, or anyway services accessible through multiple channels.

The first announcement was followed by the presentation of 377 projects, whose overall value was € 1200 Mln. Out of these 377 projects, 134 have been co-financed with € 120 Mln, for an overall value of about € 500 Mln (CNIPA, 2007). Those projects involved about 5000 public bodies, 3574 of which were municipalities (or aggregations of municipalities), covering an overall population of about 38 million citizens (out of the 59 million inhabitants of Italy in 2007, the year in which all the projects have been concluded).

The funded projects, that mainly concerned the implementation of online services for citizens and for enterprises, started in the spring 2003, after the signing of all the agreements for their activation, and should have ended within 24 months. At the end of 2007, 2 projects had never been started, 121 projects were completed, in the sense that all the planned services had been released, whereas the remaining 11 projects were closed without having released all the services that had been planned.

With a delay of about 30 months, the first phase of the NAP can be considered as concluded at the end of 2007 (so it was considered by the National Center for IT in Public Administration (CNIPA) that was responsible for the monitoring of the projects funded under the NAP programme).

The NAP also included a second phase that has been launched in 2004, based on 4 specific lines for the funding of projects with the aim of:

Line 1: Implementing the "Sistema Pubblico di Connettività e Cooperazione" (Public Connectivity and Cooperation System), that is a technical and organizational nationwide system for network communication, basic interoperability, cooperation and security services among administrations.

Line 2: Extending local availability of services for citizens and enterprises through the re-use of the systems funded under the first phase of the NAP.

Line 3: Including small municipalities (municipalities with less than 5000 inhabitants) in the diffusion of e-government at the local level.

Line 4: Promoting ICT projects aiming to allow democratic citizen participation in public decision-making (e-democracy).

Under the line 1, 56 projects that involved all the 20 regions of Italy have been funded with € 32 Mln, for an overall value of about € 97 Mln (co-financed with resources from the regions). The line 2 involved 36 projects submitted by aggregations of municipalities that have been funded with € 37 Mln (out of the € 60 Mln originally available). Under the line 3, 43 projects have been funded with € 14,5 Mln, for an overall value of about € 41 Mln. These projects involved almost 4000 municipalities, out of which more of 3000 are small municipalities, covering almost 18 Mln inhabitants. Finally, the line 4 funded 57 projects, out of the 127 submitted, with € 9,5 Mln, for an overall value of about € 41 Mln.

At the moment a complete analysis of the impact of the NAP is still missing (an exception is (CNIPA, 2008) that considers only 20 of the 134 projects funded during the first phase of the NAP), also due to the fact that many of the projects funded under the second phase of the NAP started only in 2009. Actually, although the second phase of the NAP was launched in 2004, the funding for the projects based on the lines 2 and 3 was delivered to the municipalities only in 2009.

However, since the first phase of the NAP ended in December 2007 it is reasonable to expect that, after more than 4 years, the investments made under the first phase of the that programme have already started spreading their benefits. Moreover, it should be observed that (as reported by CNIPA (2007)), the release of services to citizens and enterprises began long before December 2007.

The projects funded under the second phase of the NAP that have a direct impact on the delivery of services to citizens and enterprises are those based on the lines 2 and 3. As observed above, those projects started only in 2009 and at the moment there are no complete data available concerning their progression (see Ferro & Sorrentino (2010) for a discussion of the impact of line 3 on small municipalities). However, since they concern the same services implemented with the projects of the first phase of the NAP, it seems reasonable to assume that they will show a similar progression pace. Concerning the first phase of the NAP, CNIPA (2007) reports that after 30 months from the beginning of the funded projects the earned value was 91% and about 70% of the total number of the planned services had already been released. From this point of view, it could be expected that also the projects of the second phase of the NAP should already be contributing, at least partially, to increase the efficiency and effectiveness of the Italian local government, to improve public services and to maximize the public value delivered to citizens and enterprises.

The Results Achieved

As observed above, a complete and detailed evaluation of the outcomes of the policies for the development of e-government at the local level implemented in Italy is still lacking. However, some country level data are available that are usually considered as indicators that measure a country's progress toward e-government. In this section some of these data are reported that will then be commented in the next section.

Coherently with the objectives stated by the eEurope 2002 and the eEurope 2005 Action Plans the NAP pursued the objective of developing modern public services (available online) and a favorable environment for e-business through the widespread availability of broadband access and secure information infrastructures. Figure 1 reports data concerning the availability and use of online services both for citizens and enterprises. Those data can be considered as a direct output of the NAP since the implementation of online services was the main objective for most of the projects funded under the NAP.

The NAP also aimed at increasing the availability of broadband connections in Italy both directly, by funding projects for the establishment of local infrastructures, and indirectly, by using online services as a driver to increase the need for broadband connections, thus making the private investments in broadband infrastructures

Figure 1. Online services availability and use (source: EU Digital Agenda Scoreboard (2011))

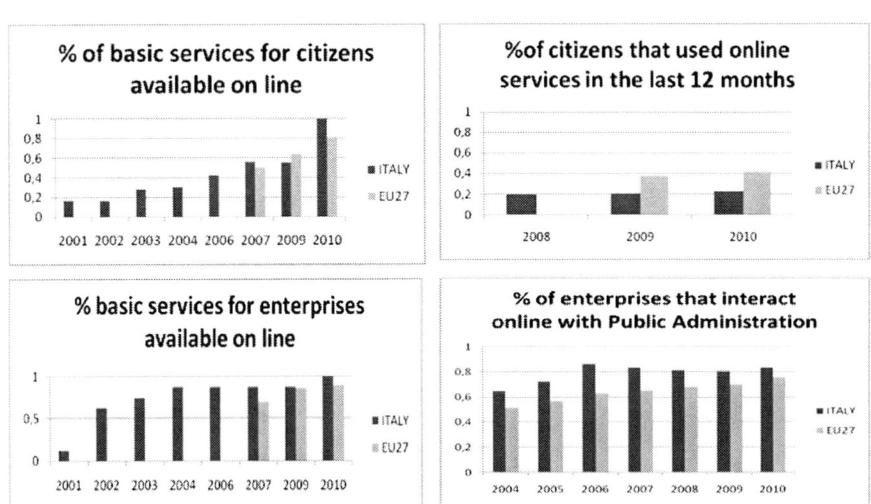

more attractive. Figure 2 reports data on the availability of broadband connections in Italy.

A significant amount of the funding delivered by the NAP has been devoted to increase the availability of ICT within the Italian municipalities. Figure 3 compares the availability of ICT in the Italian municipalities from 2005 to 2009 (the last year for which official data are available), based on the data reported by the Italian National Institute of Statistics (ISTAT, 2006; 2008; 2010).

A HOLISTIC AND ROLE-BASED EVALUATION OF E-GOVERNMENT

In this section an evaluation of the impact of the NAP at the country level will be introduced that is based on the holistic and role based approach described above.

The more general role in the taxonomy introduced above is the role of citizen as such, that is a person simply having the right of citizenship. Under this role there is not a specific value a

Figure 2. Availability and use of broadband lines (source: EU Digital Agenda Scoreboard (2011))

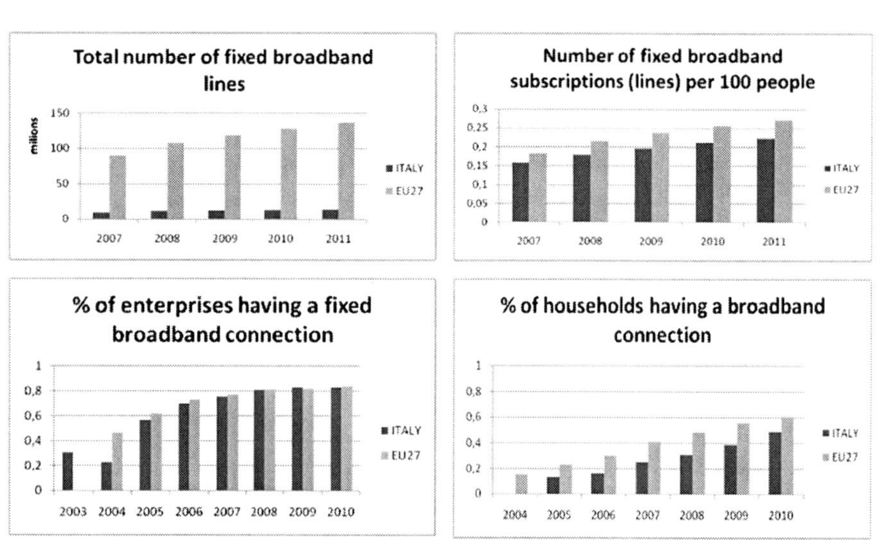

Figure 3. ICT in the Italian municipalities (source: ISTAT, 2006; 2008; 2010)

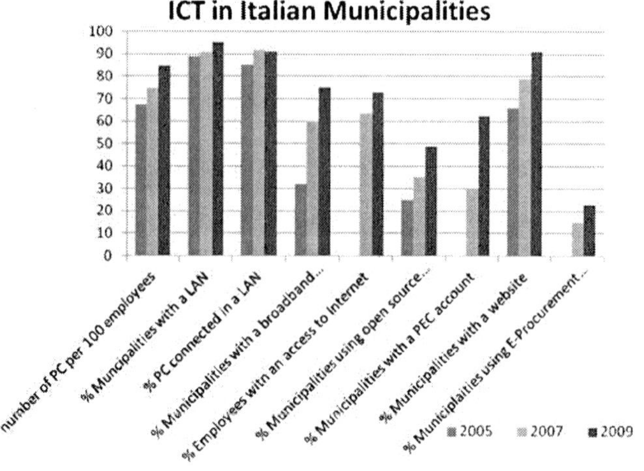

citizen can get from government, but the one that derives from living in a developed and wealthy country. Seen from this point of view, the NAP can be evaluated by considering its possible contribution to the increasing of the wealth of Italy, due to the effect of the transformation of government it should have determined. In doing so an approach similar to that advocated by Srivastava and Teo (2007, 2010) can be assumed, that suggests examining the payoffs from e-government in the form of national performance.

Figure 4 reports data concerning indicators frequently used to measure a country's wealth and performance (comparing Italy and the EU17 and EU27 countries), as well as the position of Italy in some well known international rankings.

The indicators considered in Figure 4 are:

- The Gross Domestic Product per capita, as an indicator of a country's standard of living, expressed in Purchasing Power Standards (PPS) (source: EUROSTAT: http://epp.eurostat.ec.europa.eu/tgm/table.do?tab=table&init=1&plugin=1&language=en&pcode=tec00114)
- The Gini coefficient, as a measure of inequality; the higher the index, the more is the level of inequality (source: EUROSTAT -http://epp.eurostat.ec.europa.eu/tgm/table.do?tab=table&init=1&plugin=0&language=en&pcode=tessi190)
- The United Nations E-government Development index (EGDI), as a comprehensive scoring of the willingness and capacity of national administrations to use online and mobile technology in the execution of government functions; the higher is a country's ranking, the lower is its capacity (source: UN E-Government Survey - http://www.unpan.org/egovkb/global_reports/08report.htm)
- The Digital Economy index (DEI), to assess the quality of a country's ICT infrastructures and the ability of its consumers, businesses and governments to use ICT to their benefit; the higher is a country's ranking, the lower is its capacity to support digital economy (source: Economist Intelligence Unit - http://graphics.eiu.com/upload/EIU_Digital_economy_rankings_2010_FINAL_WEB.pdf)
- The Ease of Doing Business index (EDBI), as a measure of a country's capability of setting up an environment favorable to business in terms of better, usually simpler, regulations for businesses and stronger protections of property rights; the higher is a country's ranking, the less it is easy to do business in it (source: World Bank - http://www.doingbusiness.org/data)
- The Global Competitiveness index (GCI), to measure the institutions, policies, and factors that set a country's sustainable current and medium-term levels of economic prosperity; the higher is a country's ranking, the lower is its competitiveness (source: World Economic Forum - http://www.weforum.org/issues/global-competitiveness/index.html)
- The United Nations Human Development index (HDI), as a comparative measure of life expectancy, literacy, education and standards of living and a measure of the impact of economic policies on quality of life (source: United Nations Development Programme - http://hdrstats.undp.org/en/countries/profiles/ITA.html)

As highlighted by the data reported in Figure 4, in the period under consideration (2007-2011), the Italy's global wealth has not improved. Rather, it seems that there has been a general worsening of the living conditions in Italy. Actually, the only values that show some improvement are the Gini coefficient and the GCI. The Gini coefficient gives a better result in 2010 than in 2007 and 2009 (that means a reduction of inequalities), although it is worse than it was in 2008. In 2011, Italy scores

Figure 4. General indicators of Italy's wealth in the past decade

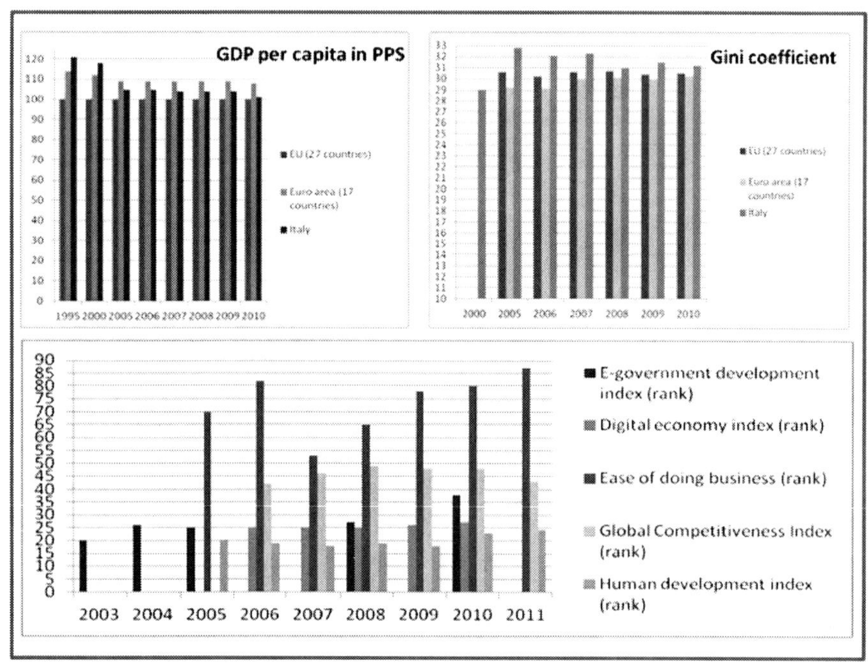

better in the GCI ranking than in 2007; however, this ranking is still worse than it was in 2006. Of course, these results are likely to depend on the negative effects of the global crisis and cannot be simply ascribed to national policies (including the policies for the diffusion of e-government). However, since all the indicators that more directly depend on the E-Government policies (EGDI, DEI and EDBI) show negative results, it seems reasonable to conclude at least that the NAP did not positively contribute to reduce the negative effects of the global crisis. Hence, the NAP does not seem to have been able to generate a value for citizens as such.

Efficiency in government is one of the main goals of e-government. Efficiency does not mean simply the reduction of the costs of government; actually

the efficiency concept refers to the concept of production possibility frontier, which indicates the quantity of output which can be efficiently produced for a given input level. In other words, the greater the output for a given input or the lower the input for a given output, the more efficient is the activity. (EU, 2009b, p. 37)

More efficiency in local government could mean either a reduction of the cost of the whole system of local government (input efficiency) or an increase of the number and/or the quality of the services delivered (output efficiency). Citizens contribute to the functioning of the system of local government by funding it as taxpayers. A reduction of the cost of the whole system of local government could mean a lower taxation level, which could contribute to determine a value for the citizens as taxpayers.

Following the approach described by Mandl, Dierx, and Ilzkovitz (2008), the public spending allocated to the production of a given public service, like public spending on health, education or infrastructure, can be considered as a measure of input (p. 5). In general terms, such a measure is not the best one because the way public sector accounts are typically designed makes it difficult to obtain information on all input costs (Estache, Gonzalez, & Trujillo, 2007; Mandl, Dierx, & Ilzkovitz, 2008; Codagnone & Undheim, 2008). However, since the holistic point of view taken in this chapter does not require a disaggregated analysis of the costs, the total amount of local government expenditures gives a sufficiently adequate measure of the inputs the system of local government consumes to produce its outputs (services).

Figure 5, that reports the level of local government expenditures in Italy from 1995 to 2010, clearly shows that in the period considered the local government current expenses increased constantly. This is a relevant point to stress since more efficiency in local government should determine cost savings exactly at the level of the current expenses. Thus the data in Figure 5 allow concluding that from 1995 to 2010 there has not been any increase in input efficiency in the Italian system of local government. This includes also the period in which the projects funded under the NAP should have started spreading their benefits. Indeed, the local government expenditures increased sensibly in 2008 and continued to increase also in 2009 and 2010. Of course, this does not mean that the implementation of the NAP increased the local government expenditures. However, since the level of the expenditures has not decreased at more than 50 months distance from the conclusions of the projects funded under the first phase of the NAP, and at 30 months distance from the starting of the projects funded under the second phase of the NAP, it can be concluded that no positive effects of the NAP on the input efficiency of local government have emerged with evidence yet. This means that the implementation of the NAP did not contribute to reduce the costs of local government, which could have meant a possible lowering of the taxation level; from this point of view, no positive effects on the citizens as taxpayers have been derived yet from the implementation of the NAP.

Although it did not have a positive impact on the reduction of local government expenditures, the NAP could have contributed to reduce the costs citizens and enterprises incur for accessing the services delivered by local government, while maintaining or increasing the quality of the services, thus creating a value both for citizens as users/consumers and citizens as entrepreneurs.

Concerning citizens, there are no specific direct costs for them to access the services delivered by local government, besides the general cost they pay as taxpayers. Moreover, there are no complete and reliable data that can be used to measure the possible indirect costs citizens incur for accessing the services. Such data are available for the Italian small to medium enterprises (SME) instead, which allow measuring the administrative costs incurred by SMEs for their relationships with public administration. The implementation of the NAP could have determined a value for citizens

Figure 5. Local government expenditures in Italy 1995-2010 (source: ISTAT, 2011)

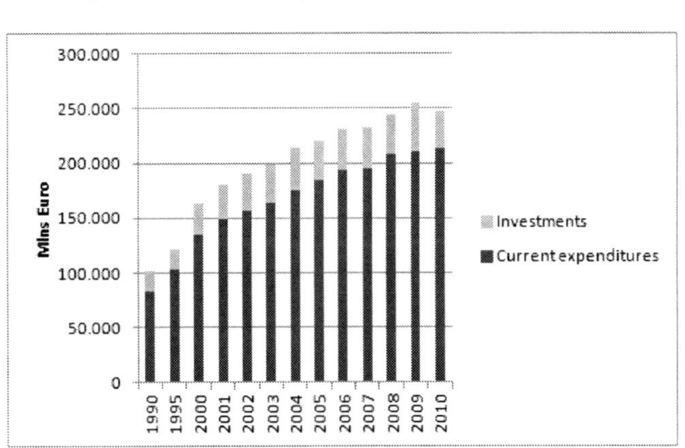

as entrepreneurs by contributing to reduce the administrative costs enterprises incur for their relationships with local government organizations.

Every year a survey is conducted in Italy to analyse the relationships between SMEs and public administration. Figure 6 shows some of the main results of the 2011 survey (based on a representative sample of 1.732 enterprises), as reported in (PromoPa, 2011).

As shown in the Figure 6, in 2011 the administrative costs for SME are lower than they were in 2009 and in 2010, although they are still sensibly higher than in 2008. This could mean that the online services for enterprises implemented under the NAP (even with some delay) are starting spreading some positive effect on the reduction of the administrative burden on SMEs. However, although the perceived quality of online services improved in the past two years, the data concerning both the degree of satisfaction toward the availability of online services and the overall degree of satisfaction towards local government in 2011 is sensibly lower than in 2007. From this point of view, it could be concluded that at more than 50 months distance from the conclusions of the first phase and at 30 months distance from the starting of the projects funded under the second phase, the NAP is still far from determining a positive effect on the quality of local government as perceived by the Italian SMEs. This confirms the difficulties the NAP encounters also in determining benefits in terms of value for citizens as entrepreneurs.

In the discussion above only external stakeholders have been considered; however, as observed, e-government can deliver a public value to internal stakeholders too. The training of the employees is a quite obvious condition for successful innovation; at the same time, investing in training and skills upgrading programmes is a way to increase

Figure 6. The relationships between SMEs and local government in Italy (source: PromoPA, 2011)

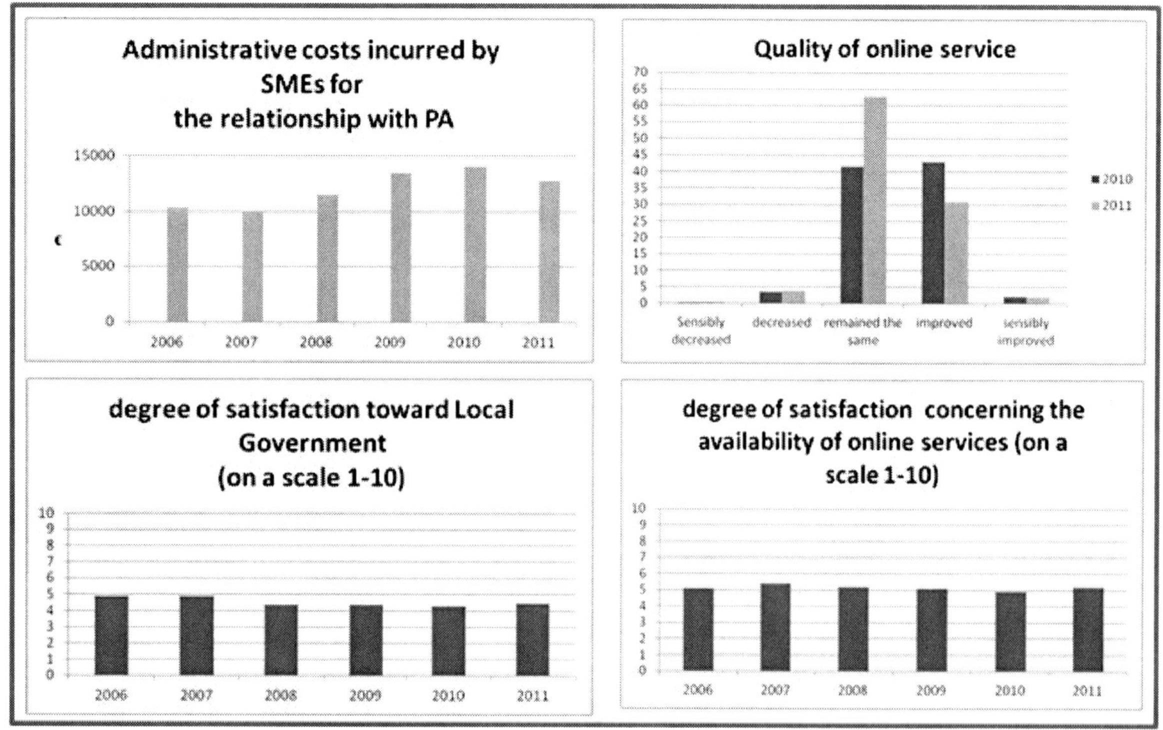

the organizational human capital, which is the knowledge, skills and capabilities of the employees that can improve the organization's performance.

At a first sight, the human capital of the employees could be considered as a form of private value since the employees themselves are the primary beneficiaries of it. However, as long as it impacts on the employees' working practices, the human capital of the public servants can also be considered as a public value. From this point of view, the capability of the NAP to deliver public value to citizens as public servants can be evaluated by considering whether it had a positive impact on the training programmes implemented by local government organizations.

There are no complete data available concerning all the training activities in all the 8902 Italian municipalities. However, data are available concerning the municipalities that delivered ICT courses to their employees (although the last survey available concerns courses delivered in 2008). According to the data collected by ISTAT, the percentage of the Italian municipalities that delivered ICT courses to their employees was 20% in 2005, 19,6% in 2007 and 17% in 2009 (ISTAT, 2006; 2008; 2010).

ISTAT does not report the incidence of the municipalities involved in projects funded under the NAP on the sample considered in the surveys; hence the data reported do not allow evaluating the direct impact of the NAP on the ICT training of the employees. However, the data clearly show a generalized reduction of the training activities in the years immediately following the conclusion of the projects funded under the NAP. Hence, it seems reasonable to conclude at least that the NAP did not determine, as an indirect effect, a rising of the Italian municipalities' awareness toward the need to implement ICT skills upgrading programmes as a way to foster innovation and increasing the quality of the services delivered (Arduini et al., 2010). From this point of view, it can be concluded that the NAP did not determine benefits visible at the country level in terms of an increase of the human capital of the employees.

Is there an "E-Government Paradox"?

The data discussed in the section above show that the policies for the diffusion of e-government at the local level implemented in Italy are still far from succeeding in delivering the expected value, at least with respect to the citizens' roles considered in this chapter (citizen as such, citizen as tax payer, citizen as entrepreneur, citizen as civil servant). In this section, it will be considered whether this unsatisfactory result can be explained simply in terms of unforeseen contingencies (like the global financial and economic crisis) and the particular learning curve that characterizes e-government applications, or it depends (mainly) on the principles the policies for the diffusion of e-government at the local level have been based on Italy.

From the data considered so far a sort of "e-government paradox" seems to arise (Bertot & Jaeger, 2008; Foley & Alfonso, 2009; Castelnovo, 2010), similar to the "productivity paradox" (Brynjolfsson, 1993; Brynjolfsson & Hitt, 1998; Bresnahan, Brynjolfsson, & Hitt, 2002) or the "performance paradox" discussed by Abhijit (2003). In its more simplified form the productivity paradox amounts to the observation that there is no relationship between ICT investments and productivity.

During the years, an extensive literature has been devoted to the productivity paradox, and some explanations of it have been suggested (see, for instance, Gunnarsson, Mellander, and Savvidou, (2004)). Although efficiency and productivity are different concepts (IDABC, 2005), some of the explanations of the paradox that have been suggested can also help explaining why the NAP did not succeed in increasing the capability of local government to deliver public value.

There are three main arguments from the literature on the productivity paradox that can be used in the present discussion; the first concerns the time investments in technology need to show productivity-enhancing effects; the second concerns some well known problems related to technology adoption whereas the third concerns the relation between ICT investments and organizational innovation.

Abhijit (2003) reports data that show that the relationship between IT investments and government performance in 50 State Governments in the U.S.A., that was found to be negative at the beginning, becomes more positive with time (Abhijit reports that the effect of IT investments on performance tend to change from negative to positive after two years). Along the same lines, in (CNIPA, 2008) it has been claimed that the investments made under the NAP would require 5 years (on the average) to fully deliver their benefits. According to CNIPA (2007), at May 2006 the earned value of the NAP (first phase) was 91%; this means that the benefits of the NAP should have already been apparent in 2011. Hence it is very unlikely that the limited results achieved so far can be explained by the learning curve alone.

A critical factor determining the rate of return on most public sector ICT investments is the number of users and/or frequency of use of the services (Foley & Alfonso, 2009; Codagnone & Undheim, 2008). As shown in Figure 1, the data concerning the percentage of Italian citizens that use online services is quite low, about a half of the average value of the EU27. Interestingly enough, the data concerning the use of online services by the Italian enterprises are completely different; indeed, Italian enterprises use online services more than enterprises do in the countries of the EU27. This could be explained by considering that the use of online services in many cases is mandatory for the Italian enterprises.

Making it mandatory obviously increases the use of online services; however, as shown by the data reported in Figure 6, the high rate of use of online services by enterprises did not determine a higher level of satisfaction toward local government. This lead to hypothesize that there are some inadequacies in the way the online services for enterprises have been implemented according to the principles stated by the NAP. Since both online services for enterprises and online services for citizens have been implemented based on the same principles, the analysis of the case of enterprises, for which data are available, could give some insight to understand also why the use of online services by citizens is so low.

On the one hand, the NAP (both in the first and in the second phase) did not provide any information and communication campaign to raise the level of awareness of both citizens and enterprises toward the online services delivered by government organizations. Indeed, the second phase of the NAP included a line specifically devoted to information and communication initiatives for promoting the use of online services by citizens and enterprises. Nevertheless, this line that was funded with € 9 Mln has never been implemented. A consequence of this choice is, for instance, the fact that still in 2011 only 27,6% of the Italian SMEs declared to know what the One Stop Shop for enterprises (that is the most typical e-government service for enterprises) is and how it works (PromoPa, 2011, p. 30).

On the other hand, to use the e-government services citizens and enterprises should perceive them as useful and important. As Figure 7 shows, although online services are considered as somewhat important by the Italian SMEs, they are not regarded as a priority. In all the surveys from 2006 to 2011 SMEs indicated other priorities for local government organizations, namely the simplification of the bureaucratic procedures, the competence of the personnel, the reduction of the delivery time and the cooperation among different offices.

Moreover, among the online services available to them, the Italian SMEs consider as more important (and hence more useful for them) the fiscal services (59,1%), the online release of authorizations and concessions (17,6%), the online registration and certification services (13,9%) and the online services for starting, transforming or closing a business (7,4%) (PromoPA, 2011). As these data clearly show, the online services de-

Figure 7. Priorities for local government as perceived by Italian SMEs (source: PromoPA, 2011)

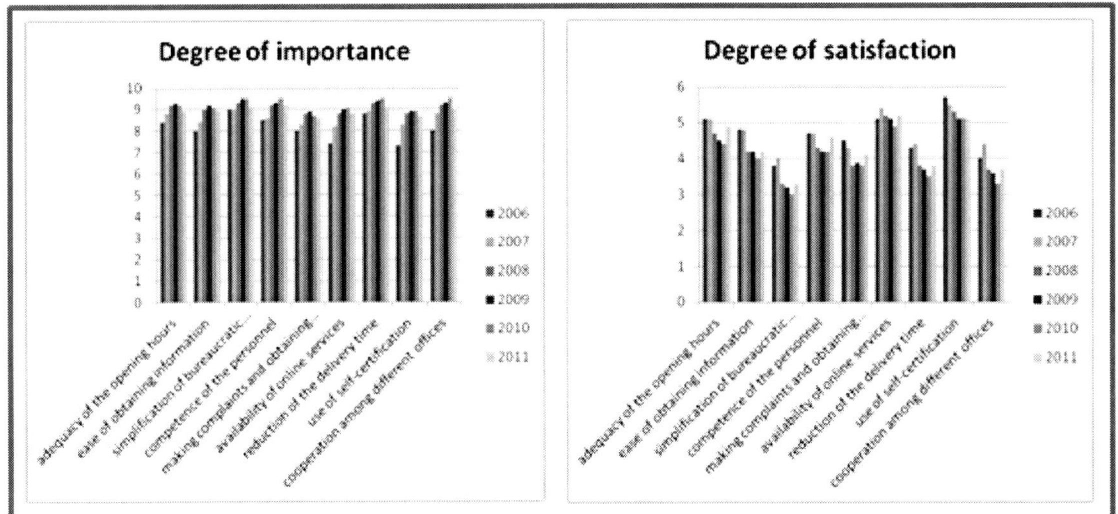

livered by local government (all those in the list above, but the fiscal services) are not considered to be really important (and consequently useful) for enterprises, although the use of some of them is mandatory (services for starting, transforming or closing a business).

From the observations above, it can be concluded that the low use of online services strictly depends on two main problems affecting the NAP:

- The lack of a widespread diffusion of information to the users concerning the services available and how to use them,
- An inadequate consideration of what services are really relevant for the users, that would have required a more structured approach to the development of new services (Angelopoulos et al., 2010), including a preliminary assessment of the impact of the planned services on the targeted users.

The more common explanation of the productivity paradox refers to the misalignment of technology and organization. As argued by Brynjolfsson and Hitt (1998, p. 3), "The greatest benefits of computers appear to be realized when computer investment is coupled with other complementary investments; new strategies, new business processes and new organizations all appear to be important in realizing the maximum benefit of IT." Similarly, Bresnahan, Brynjolfsson, and Hitt (2002) show that firms with high levels of both IT and human capital are the most productive. The same conclusion has been drawn by Foley and Alfonso (2009) that explicitly discuss the impact of different e-government projects on government, citizens and enterprises. In their analysis of 28 different e-government projects, Foley and Alfonso found that the highest net benefits for both government (in terms of direct cash benefits and efficiency savings) and users (in terms of monetary benefits and time-based non-monetary benefits) are achieved by projects that involve back-office reform or reorganization.

The funding announcement for the first phase of the NAP did not provide any organizational requirement to be satisfied by the recipients of the funding. This led to consider the funding provided by the NAP programme simply as a way to support technological innovation, as explicitly recognized also by CNIPA (2007). Indeed, as reported in Figure 3, as a consequence of the NAP since 2009 in the Italian municipalities there has been an adequate availability of ICT infrastructures and ICT equipment (both hardware and software). However, the NAP did not provide funds for process reengineering, back-office re-organization and training of the employees. These are exactly the elements that, according to the data reported in Figure 7, are perceived by SMEs as priorities for Local Government; thus it is not surprising that the degree of satisfaction concerning these elements did not increase during the period in which the benefits of the NAP should have become apparent. Not having included any organizational requirement in the funding announcement can be considered one of the main deficiencies of the NAP, one that helps explaining the still unsatisfactory results achieved so far.

FUTURE RESEARCH DIRECTIONS

The evaluation of the impact of the NAP on the capability of local government to deliver public value has been based on secondary data sources, including some international surveys (the E-Government and the Human Development Rankings of the United Nations, the Digital Economy Rankings of the Economist Intelligence Unit; the Global Competitiveness Rankings of the World Economic Forum and the Ease of Doing Business Rankings of the World Bank), the data delivered by both the Italian National Institute of Statistics (ISTAT) and the European Institute of Statistics (EUROSTAT) and the surveys that each year measure the degree of satisfaction of the Italian small to medium enterprises toward government.

The use of secondary data sources could represent a limitation of the approach described in the chapter. Indeed, the use of secondary data limits the analysis to those factors for which information is available. For instance, in the chapter the possible value created for some of the roles citizens can play in their relationships with public administration have not been considered because the selected data sources do not provide the relevant information. Hence, further research is needed to identify other secondary data sources that can be used in the evaluation of the country level impact of the policies for the diffusion of e-government.

The use of secondary data sources provides some advantages as well, such as easy reproducibility, ability to generalize the results arising from larger datasets, reliability of the data deriving from their having been compiled by trustworthy organizations, taking into account suitable procedures for ensuring reliability and validity (Srivastava & Teo, 2007). Moreover, all the data referred to in the chapter are available for other countries as well (at least for all the countries of the EU27). This makes it possible a cross-country comparison of different policies for the diffusion of e-government with respect to their capability of creating public value, measured as in the section above. Such a cross-country comparison can be the focus of further research, with the specific aim of identifying the elements that fostered or limited the success of the policies that have been implemented in different countries.

CONCLUSION

In the chapter a holistic approach to the evaluation of e-government has been described that considers whether the implementation of the policies for the diffusion of e-government determined benefits at the country level. This approach has been applied to the evaluation of the impact of the innovation projects funded under the Italian National Action Plan for e-government (NAP) on the capability of local government to deliver public value. The aim of the evaluation was to verify whether after the conclusion of the projects funded under the NAP benefits emerged for citizens as such (in terms of the country's global wellbeing), for citizens as taxpayers (in terms of the reduction of the global cost of local government), for citizens as public servants (in terms of the increase of their human capital) and for citizens as entrepreneurs (in terms of the reduction of the administrative burdens on enterprises).

The analysis showed that, after 50 months from the conclusion of the first phase of the NAP and 30 months from the beginning of the second phase, the benefits of the NAP are still far from being apparent. This unsatisfactory result has been discussed by considering some well known explanations of the so called "productivity paradox."

From this discussion it has been concluded that the scarce impact of the NAP depends on two principles that characterized it. On the one hand, the NAP has been focused mainly on the technological aspects of innovation, neglecting the role of the non technological aspects that are critical for the success of ICT-based innovation, including the necessity of adequately inform the potential users about the services made available; a more careful analysis of what services are really useful and important for the potential users; the need to support technological innovation with the training of the employees, the reengineering of the administrative processes and the reorganization of the back-office. On the other hand, the NAP adopted a two-step strategy for the diffusion of e-government at the local level: the first step was the funding of a limited number of selected projects whereas the second step was the inclusion of all the remaining municipalities through the re-use of the systems implemented in the first step. However, at 30 month distance from the launching of the second step, this result is still far from being achieved. The first aspect explains why the projects implemented under the NAP encountered difficulties in spreading their benefits; the second aspect explains why those benefits are not visible yet at the country level.

REFERENCES

Abhijit, J. (2003). Performance paradox: Information technology investments and administrative performance in the case of the 50 U.S. state governments. In *Proceedings of the Twenty Fourth International Conference on Information Systems* (pp. 389-400). Retrieved from http://aisel.aisnet.org/icis2003/33

Alalwan, J., & Thomas, M. A. (2011). A holistic framework to evaluate e-government systems. In *AMCIS 2011 Proceedings*. Retrieved from http://aisel.aisnet.org/amcis2011_submissions/67

Alford, J. (2002). Defining the client in the public sector: A social-exchange perspective. *Public Administration Review*, *62*(3), 337–346. doi:10.1111/1540-6210.00183.

Alford, J., & O'Flynn, J. (2009). Making sense of public value: Concepts, critiques and emergent meanings. *International Journal of Public Administration*, *32*(3,4), 171–191.

Alshawi, S., & Alalwany, H. (2009). E-government evaluation: Citizen's perspective in developing countries. *Information Technology for Development*, *15*(3), 193–208. doi:10.1002/itdj.20125.

Angelopoulos, S., Fotis, K. F., Naousa, G. N., & Papadopoulos, T. (2010). New service development in e-government: Identifying critical success factors. *Transforming Government: People. Process and Policy*, *4*(1), 95–118.

Arduini, D., Belotti, F., Denni, M., Giungato, G., & Zanfei, A. (2010). Technology adoption and innovation in public services the case of e-government in Italy. *Information Economics and Policy*, *22*(3), 257–275. doi:10.1016/j.infoecopol.2009.12.007.

Bannister, F. (2002). Citizen centricity: A model of IS value in public administration. *Electronic Journal of Information Systems Evaluation, 5*(2).

Benington, J. (2009). Creating the public in order to create public value? *International Journal of Public Administration, 32*(3), 232–249. doi:10.1080/01900690902749578.

Bertot, J. C., & Jaeger, P. T. (2008). The e-government paradox: Better customer service doesn't necessarily cost less. *Government Information Quarterly, 25*(2), 149–154. doi:10.1016/j.giq.2007.10.002.

Bresnahan, T. F., Brynjolfsson, E., & Hitt, L. M. (2002). Information technology, workplace organization, and the demand for skilled labor: Firm-level evidence. *The Quarterly Journal of Economics, 117*(1), 39–376. doi:10.1162/003355302753399526.

Brynjolfsson, E. (1993). The productivity paradox of information technology. *Communications of the ACM, 36*, 67–77. doi:10.1145/163298.163309.

Brynjolfsson, E., & Hitt, L. (1998). Beyond the productivity paradox: Computers are the catalyst for bigger changes. *Communications of the ACM, 41*, 49–55. doi:10.1145/280324.280332.

Castelnovo, W. (2010). Is there an e-government paradox? In D. O'Donnell (Ed.), *Proceedings of the 10th European Conference on eGovernment* (pp. 99-106). Academic Publishing Limited, Reading, UK.

Castelnovo, W., & Simonetta, M. (2007). The evaluation of e-government projects for small local government organisations. *The Electronic. Journal of E-Government, 5*(1), 21–28.

Castelnovo, W., & Simonetta, M. (2008). A public value evaluation of e-government policies. *Electronic Journal Information Systems Evaluation, 11*(2), 61–72.

CNIPA. (2007). *Monitoraggio dei progetti di E-Government - Fase 1. Rapporto finale*. Retrieved March 1, 2012, from http://archivio.cnipa.gov.it/site/_files/EG000_RP05_0007_V1_RapportoSintesiConclusivo_ExecSummary.pdf

CNIPA. (2008). *Analisi delle valutazioni di impatto di alcuni dei progetti della prima fase del piano di E-Government*. Retrieved March 1, 2012, from http://archivio.cnipa.gov.it/site/_files/EGMON_Analisi_ExecSummary.pdf

Codagnone, C., & Undheim, T.A. (2008). Benchmarking eGovernment: Tools, theory, and practice. *European Journal of ePractice*, 4, 4-18.

Digit, P. A. (2011). *2010 E-Gov Report Italy*. Roma: Edizioni Forum PA.

Digital Agenda Scoreboard, E. U. (2011). *Digital agenda scoreboard 2011 – Italy*. Retrieved March 1, 2012, from http://ec.europa.eu/information_society/digital-agenda/scoreboard

E-Gov 2012 Plan. (2012). Website. Retrieved March 1, 2012, from http://www.e2012.gov.it/

Estache, A., Gonzalez, M., & Trujillo, L. (2007). Government expenditures on education, health and infrastructure. A naïve look at levels, outcomes and efficiency. *World Bank Policy Research Working Paper*, 4219.

EU. (2009a). *Ministerial declaration on egovernment*. Retrieved March 1, 2012, from http://www.egov2009.se/wp-content/uploads/Ministerial-Declaration-on-eGovernment.pdf

EU. (2009b). *Making public support for innovation in the EU more effective: Lessons learned from a public consultation for action at Community level* – SEC (2009) 1197.

EU. (2009c). *i2010 eGovernment action plan progress study, Summary report, November 2009*. Retrieved March 1, 2012, from http://www.dti.dk/27666

Ferro, E., & Sorrentino, M. (2010). Can intermunicipal collaboration help the diffusion of E-Government in peripheral areas? Evidence from Italy. *Government Information Quarterly*, *27*(1), 17–25. doi:10.1016/j.giq.2009.07.005.

Foley, P., & Alfonso, X. (2009). eGovernment and the Transformation Agenda. *Public Administration*, *87*(2), 371–396. doi:10.1111/j.1467-9299.2008.01749.x.

Grimsley, M., & Meehan, A. (2008). Attaining social value from electronic government. *The Electronic Journal of E-Government*, *6*(1), 31–42.

Gunnarsson, G., Mellander, E., & Savvidou, E. (2004). *Human capital is the key to the IT productivity paradox*. Institute for Labour Market Policy Evaluation (IFAU). WORKING PAPER 13.

Harrison, T. M., Guerrero, S., Burke, G. B., Cook, M., Cresswell, A., Helbig, N., et al. (2011). *Open government and e-government: Democratic challenges from a public value perspective*. Paper presented at the 12th Annual International Conference on Digital Government Research. New York. Retrieved from http://www.ctg.albany.edu/publications/journals/dgo2011_opengov/dgo2011_opengov.pdf

IDABC. (2005). *The impact of e-government on competitiveness, growth and jobs*. IDABC eGovernment Observatory - Background Research Paper.

ISTAT. (2006). *Le tecnologie dell'informazione e della comunicazione nelle amministrazioni comunali - Anno 2005*. Retrieved March 1, 2012, from http://www3.istat.it/salastampa/comunicati/non_calendario/20060703_00/testointegrale.pdf

ISTAT. (2008). *L'ICT nelle amministrazioni locali - Anno 2007*. Retrieved March 1, 2012, from http://www3.istat.it/salastampa/comunicati/non_calendario/20080307_00/testointegrale.pdf

ISTAT. (2010). *Le tecnologie dell'informazione e della comunicazione nelle amministrazioni locali - Anno 2009*. Retrieved March 1, 2012, from http://www3.istat.it/salastampa/comunicati/non_calendario/20101103_00/testointegrale20101103.pdf

ISTAT. (2011). *Conti ed aggregati economici delle Amministrazioni pubbliche*. Retrieved March 1, 2012, from: http://www.istat.it/it/archivio/47334

Karunasena, K., & Deng, H. (2010). Exploring the public value of e-government: An empirical study from Sri Lanka. In *eTrust: Implications for the individual, enterprises and society; 23rd Bled eConference* (pp. 286-300). Bled, Slovenia.

Karunasena, K., & Deng, H. (2012). Critical factors for evaluating the public value of e-government in Sri Lanka. *Government Information Quarterly*, *29*(1), 76–84. doi:10.1016/j.giq.2011.04.005.

Kearns, I. (2004). *Public value and e-government*. Institute for Public Policy Research (ippr).

Kelly, G., Mulgan, G., & Muers, S. (2002). *Creating public value: An analytical framework for public service reform*. Discussion paper prepared by the Cabinet Office Strategy Unit, UK.

Mandl, U., Dierx, A., & Ilzkovitz, F. (2008). The effectiveness and efficiency of public spending. *Economic Papers*, 301. Retrieved March 1, 2012, from http://ec.europa.eu/economy_finance/publications/publication_summary11904_en.htm

Misuraca, G., Alfano, G., & Viscusi, G. (2011). A multi-level framework for ICT-enabled governance: Assessing the non-technical dimensions of 'Government Openness'. *Electronic Journal of E-Government*, *9*(2), 152–165.

OECD. (2003). *The e-Government Imperative: main findings*. OECD Policy Brief. Retrieved March 1, 2012, from www.oecd.org

OECD. (2009). *The impact of the crisis on ICTs and their role in the recovery*. Unclassified OECD document. Retrieved March 1, 2012, from http://www.oecd.org/dataoecd/33/20/43404360.pdf

PromoPa. (2011). *Imprese e Burocrazia - Come le micro e piccole imprese giudicano la Pubblica Amministrazione*. Fondazione PromoPa. Retrieved March 1, 2012, from http://www.unioncamere-lombardia.it/images/File/NE_Eventi%202011/UNIONCAMERE_copIMPRESA.pdf

Rowley, J. (2011). e-Government stakeholders - Who are they and what do they want? *International Journal of Information Management*, *31*, 53–62. doi:10.1016/j.ijinfomgt.2010.05.005.

Scholl, H. J. (2001). Applying stakeholder theory to e-government: Benefits and limits. In *Proceedings of the 1st IFIP Conference on E-Commerce, E-Business, and EGovernment*. Zurich, Switzerland.

Srivastava, S. C., & Teo, T. S. H. (2007). E-government payoffs: Evidence from cross-country data. *Journal of Global Information Management*, *15*(4), 20–40. doi:10.4018/jgim.2007100102.

Srivastava, S. C., & Teo, T. S. H. (2010). E-government, e-business, and national economic performance. *Communications of the Association for Information Systems*, *26*, 267–286.

Ubaldi, B. (2011). The impact of the Economic and Financial crisis on e-Government in OECD Member Countries. *European Journal of ePractice*, 11, 5-18.

Yu, C. C. (2008). Building a value centric e-government service framework based on a business model perspective. In M.A. Wimmer, H.J. Scholl, and E. Ferro (Eds.), *EGOV 2008, Lecture Notes in Computer Science* (LNCS) (vol. 5184, pp. 160–171). Berlin, Heidelberg: Springer-Verlag.

ADDITIONAL READING

Akman, I., Yazici, A., Mishra, A., & Arifoglu, A. (2005). E-government: A global view and an empirical evaluation of some attributes of citizens. *Government Information Quarterly*, *22*(2), 239–257. doi:10.1016/j.giq.2004.12.001.

Anthopoulos, L., Siozos, P., & Tsoukalas, I. A. (2007). Applying participatory design and collaboration in digital public services for discovering and re-designing e-government services. *Government Information Quarterly*, *24*(2), 353–376. doi:10.1016/j.giq.2006.07.018.

Bertot, J., Jaeger, P., & McClure, C. (2008). Citizen-centered e-Government services: Benefits, costs, and research needs. In *Proceedings of the 2008 International Conference on Digital Government Research* (pp. 137-142). Montreal: Canada.

Chircu, A. M. (2008). E-government evaluation: Towards a multi-dimensional framework. *Electronic Government: an International Journal*, *5*(4), 345–363. doi:10.1504/EG.2008.019521.

Flak, L. S., Dertz, W., Jansen, A., Krogstie, J., Spjelkavik, I., & Ølnes, S. (2009). What is the value of eGovernment and how can we actually realize it? *Transforming Government: People. Process and Policy*, *3*(3), 220–226.

Flak, L. S., & Rose, J. (2005). Stakeholder governance: Adapting stakeholder theory to the e-government field. *Communications of the Association for Information Systems*, *16*(31), 1–46.

Ghapanchi, A., Albadvi, A., & Zarei, B. (2008). A framework for e-government planning and implementation. *Electronic Government: An International Journal*, *5*(1), 71–90. doi:10.1504/EG.2008.016129.

Gil-García, J. R., & Pardo, T. A. (2005). E-Government success factors: Mapping practical tools to theoretical foundations. *Government Information Quarterly*, *22*(2), 187–216. doi:10.1016/j.giq.2005.02.001.

Heeks, R., & Bailur, S. (2007). Analyzing e-government research: Perspectives, philosophies, theories, methods, and practice. *Government Information Quarterly*, *24*(2), 243–265. doi:10.1016/j.giq.2006.06.005.

Helbig, N., & Gil-García, J. R. (2008). Understanding the complexity of electronic government: Implications from the digital divide literature. *Government Information Quarterly*, *26*(1), 89–97. doi:10.1016/j.giq.2008.05.004.

Jaeger, P. T., & Thomson, K. M. (2003). E-government around the world: Lessons, challenges, and future directions. *Government Information Quarterly*, *20*(4), 389–394. doi:10.1016/j.giq.2003.08.001.

Karunasena, K., & Deng, H. (2011). A revised framework for evaluating the public value of e-government. In *Proceedings of PACIS 2011*. Retrieved March 1, 2012, from: http://aisel.aisnet.org/pacis2011/91

Kunstelj, M., & Vintar, M. (2004). Evaluating the progress of e-government development: A critical analysis. *Information Polity*, *9*, 131–148.

Layne, K., & Lee, J. (2001). Developing fully functional e-government: A four stage model. *Government Information Quarterly*, *18*, 122–136. doi:10.1016/S0740-624X(01)00066-1.

Lee, H., Irani, Z., Osman, I., Balcı, A., Özkan, S., & Medeni, T. (2008). Research note: Toward a reference process model for citizen-oriented evaluation of e-government services. *Transforming Government: People, Process and Policy*, *2*(4), 297-310.

Millard, J. (2006). User attitudes to e-government citizen services in Europe. *International Journal of Electronic Government Research*, *2*(2), 49–58. doi:10.4018/jegr.2006040103.

Piaggesi, D., Sund, K. J., & Castelnovo, W. (Eds.). (2011). *Global strategy and practice of e-governance: Examples from around the world*. New York: IGI Global. doi:10.4018/978-1-60960-489-9.

Saha, P. (Ed.). (2012). *Enterprise architecture for connected e-government: Practices and innovations*. New York: IGI Global. doi:10.4018/978-1-4666-1824-4.

Srivastava, S. C. (2011). Is e-government providing the promised returns? A value framework for assessing e-government impact. *Transforming Government: People. Process and Policy*, *5*(2), 107–113.

Srivastava, S.C., & Teo, T.S.H. (2007). What facilitates e-government development? A cross-country analysis. *Electronic Government, an International Journal*, *4*(4), 365-378.

Van Velsen, L., van der Geest, T., ter Hedde, M., & Derks, W. (2009). Requirements engineering for e-Government services: A citizen-centric approach and case study. *Government Information Quarterly*, *26*(3), 477–486. doi:10.1016/j.giq.2009.02.007.

Verdegem, P., & Verleye, G. (2009). User-centered e-government in practice: A comprehensive model for measuring user satisfaction. *Government Information Quarterly*, *26*(3), 487–497. doi:10.1016/j.giq.2009.03.005.

Yildiz, M. (2007). E-government research: Reviewing the literature, limitations, and ways forward. *Government Information Quarterly*, *24*(3), 646–665. doi:10.1016/j.giq.2007.01.002.

KEY TERMS AND DEFINITIONS

E-Government: The government's use of ICT to achieve better policy outcomes, higher quality services and greater engagement with citizens.

E-Government Paradox: A form of the productivity paradox; in its more general form it amounts to the claim that there does not seem to be a direct positive relation between investments in e-government initiatives and the increase of the public value created by government organizations.

External Stakeholder: Citizens that receive a value from public administration as users/beneficiaries of services or as participants in democratic processes.

Holistic Evaluation: Evaluation that considers the global impact at the country level of the policies for the development of e-government.

Internal Stakeholder: Citizens directly involved in the execution of the processes through which public administration can create and deliver public value.

Public Value: Public value refers to the value created by government through services, laws, regulations and other actions. It includes outcomes, the means used to deliver them as well as trust and legitimacy. It also addresses issues such as equity, ethos and accountability.

SMEs: Enterprises with less than 250 employees; most of the Italian SMEs are microenterprises (94,6% of all the enterprises), that is enterprises with less than 10 employees.

Chapter 16
How do French Municipalities Communicate on Citizen Involvement?
The Success of Participatory Democracy in France

Christophe Premat
Centre Émile Durkheim (Sciences Po Bordeaux), France & Institut Français of Sweden, Sweden

ABSTRACT

The chapter updates a former study on digital communication at local level in France in 2006. The goal is to analyse the explanatory factors which influence the digital communication of municipalities on participatory democracy. Why are there municipalities which communicate more on these resources than others? It is important to compare the situation of these municipalities in 2006 and in 2012 because there was a power shift after the last municipal election in 2008. The focus will be on municipalities of more than 30.000 inhabitants as they have the possible resources to support a digital strategy. A quantitative method was used to select the variables which affect the communication on participatory tools. In other words, the article deals with the way politicians promote citizen engagement at local level through updated websites.

1. INTRODUCTION

With the advent of web 2.0 technologies (Barber, 1998), many politicians promoted a new citizen engagement based on a high level of information (Chung & Chatfield, 2011). In France, the political debate at the local level has been strongly affected by the necessity of a closer link between local representatives and electors. Some politicians promoted the idea of neighbourhood democracy (Behrer, 2003). French mayors used this repertoire by elaborating an image of local leaders acting closer to the electors (Premat, 2006-2007). Since 2001, mayors have been communicating on par-

DOI: 10.4018/978-1-4666-4173-0.ch016

Copyright © 2013, IGI Global. Copying or distributing in print or electronic forms without written permission of IGI Global is prohibited.

ticipatory democracy (Hatzfeld, 2005). The local e-governments included different interactive possibilities: chat, e-forums, internet conferences and social networks (Becker, 2001). Previous studies showed that mayors used electronic instruments to reinforce their legitimacy (Premat, 2008). A first quantitative study made in 2006 concluded that the creation of electronic participatory tools (Lascoumes & Le Galès, 2004) renewed the image of local elites and was not necessarily linked to a new generation of politicians (Dewoghélaëre & Premat, 2007). The age of mayors was not an explaining factor as many old mayors adapted themselves to the evolution of practices. The struggle for a better image is quite important for those who have the most positive impact in the public opinion. Factors such as the career of mayors, the age of mayors, the municipality size (Larsen, 2002) and the territorial configuration (Elias, 1991)[1] were taken into account to explain the use of electronic resources.

The set of data can be updated after the political shift of 2008 at municipal level to see if there is a significant evolution. Does the ideology of mayors have an influence on the way they communicate on participatory tools? The study deals with municipalities which have more than 30.000 inhabitants in France as they have an updated website with detailed information. France has around 36.700 municipal governments but 90% of them have less than 500 inhabitants (Hoffmann-Martinot & Wollmann, 2006). What does the digital strategy depend on? It is possible to infer from this study how local governments renewed their websites (Scott, 2005) in order to promote participatory instruments and citizen engagement.

2. STATE OF THE ART

There is a distinction between local e-government and e-democracy. The local e-government refers to the digital interface between local authorities and citizens. "E-government is not an end in itself. It is at the heart of the drive to modernise government. Modernising local government is about enhancing the quality of local services and the effectiveness of local democracy" (Raynsford & Beecham, 2002, p. 5). The need for an efficient e-government grew with the use of computers by local administrations (Jaeger, 2003). The first studies on the question were made in the U.S. with an analysis of the services provided through internet to citizens. In September 2001, 56% of U.S. households had computers; they were just 42% in December 1998 (Hauer et al., 2002). The promotion of e-government was all the easier as most of citizens were connected to internet. Different studies were made on e-government in Europe and in Asia at the beginning of the years 2000 (Howard, 2001; OECD, 2003; Holzer & Kim, 2004).

The relation between local democracy and local e-government has been examined since the beginning of 2000. The e-government was regarded as a way of enhancing the opportunities for citizens to debate with each other (Fishkin, 1995). As a matter of fact, there was a common point between democracy and efficient management (Pollitt & Bouckaert, 2004). E-government was introduced in the early 1990s as a way of modernising the public administration (Moon, 2002; Rose, 2005). According to Graafland-Essers and Ettedgui´s (2003), the e-government has three aspects: government to citizen, government to business (Backhouse, 2007) and government to public authorities. The third aspect will be dealt with in this article as local authorities have to include more and more citizens in order to act (Carrizales, 2008). E-democracy focuses on electronic votes or tools which allow citizens to express a political opinion (Altman, 2011). Some tools are really interactive (digital forums) whereas others are more informative (Wojcik, 2003). According to Lawrence K. Grossmann, e-democracy replaces the antique model of direct democracy as well as the modern representative regime (Grossmann, 1995). E-democracy reintroduces a potential conflict between representative democracy and direct democracy (Kaase, 2002). This case study aims at analysing how French mayors communicate on participatory democracy. As a matter of fact, all e-democracy tools will be not regarded here. Some participatory tools belong to e-democracy such as digital forums and interactive citizen conferences (Bützer, 2004) but most of them refer to concrete tools which exist outside the virtual sphere (Bogumil et al., 2006). Little is said about e-democracy in cities under 50.000 inhabitants (Scott, 2005) as most of studies focus on big cities and metropolitan areas. In France, the power of mayors has increased since the first Decentralization Act in 1982 (Rose L., 2005). Many studies focus on the role of mayors in local democracy but not much is said about the way mayors use new technologies (McLean, 1989) in order to preserve a special link with electors.

The main hypothesis here is that mayors are the key persons in the digital communication on participatory democracy. "In France, the commune possesses a very definite mark of originality: in its efforts to establish a perfectly interlocking network for the whole of its national territory, the state has made the commune an administrative constituency. The state, however, does not delegate any representative, preferring instead to make use of the mayor, who thus wears two hats: that of a local agent and that of an agent for the state [...] When the mayor draws up his electoral list, he thereby establishes his authority over the municipal council, rather than having to depend on the council to designate him. The fact that he is not elected by universal suffrage does not prevent him playing the leading role on the local political stage, easily keeping control – as party or majority coalition leader – over the local assembly" (Egner & Kerrouche, 2012, pp. 142-143). The mayor establishes his electoral list; he is not directly elected by citizens who only vote for the municipal list. The next step is the election of the mayor by the new local council which dates back to the law of 5th April 1884. If he is not directly elected by citizens, the mayor has a prevailing leadership because of his attributions (legal power) and because of the electoral system (he chooses the list of persons with whom he governs). This is why all public policies at local level depend on the mayoral agreement (Vetter & Hoffmann-Martinot, 2012). The sphere of communication (relation of the citizens to the local administration) is controlled by mayors who use it to renew their image (Le Bart, 1998). In France, as in many other countries, politicians began their career at the local level. At the end of the 1990s, around 90% of French parliamentarians hold one local office and all the mayors of cities of more than 80.000 inhabitants also held a national office in 1990 (Mény, 1998).

3. RESEARCH FRAMEWORK

In 2006, a first study was made on the way the municipalities above 5 000 inhabitants in France (1882 cases) communicated on participatory democracy. The information was extracted from the different websites and some data were collected from the website "Profession Politique." It was interesting to notice how French municipalities worked on a digital strategy. The small municipalities do not have resources to support such a strategy; this is why the analysis is more striking for the municipalities of more than 30.000 inhabitants. 455 communes of more than 5 000 inhabitants (out of 1882) did not have any website in 2006. 96% of these cases concerned municipalities which had between 5.000 and 30.000 inhabitants. The calls for participatory democracy (Hatzfeld, 2005), which were frequent in the sixties and seventies, re-emerged at the end of the nineties. A study was made in 2004 on European mayors (Egner & Kerrouche, 2012) of municipalities above 10.000 inhabitants. The number of French respondents was 188. French mayors relied on information collected by local councils but began to integrate new tools of communication (Kerrouche, 2005) such as panels, forums and surveys.

The municipalities have different strategies to highlight the ways citizens can take part in local life (Birkenmaier, 2004). Some of them just have informative websites. Other municipalities created a special option for participatory democracy where the citizens see information on participatory tools. The typical participatory tools which can be found are the following ones: senior local council, children local council, young local council, district council and citizen conferences. District councils have been obligatory for cities above 80.000 inhabitants since the Act of 27 February 2002. This is why those councils were not encoded as new tools in the empirical investigation. Nevertheless, some municipalities communicate more on the role of those council districts by explaining how they work. Different labels exist for those councils such as *conseil de secteurs* and *conseils de quartiers*. A municipality can have a website without offering any possibility to take part in political debates. The citizen has an open access to the local administration but there are no other means to take part in local political life.

3.1 The Digital Agenda in France

In 1980, a decentralization report pointed out that all local administrations of more than 100.000 inhabitants had computers whereas this was the case for only 44% of municipalities with a population between 5.000 and 10.000 inhabitants (Perrin, 1986). The big cities continued to invest in electronic resources to modernise local administrations. The problem of French administration was to be as transparent as possible. The Act of 17 July 1978 was a strong change as the law of secrecy included different exceptions. The citizens have the right to access to administrative documents under the control of the especially-created Commission for Access to Administrative Documents (Meininger, 1998). The laws of decentralization in 1982 had an impact on the role of mayors who had more and more power but more responsibility at the same time. The act of 2 March 1982 was the first step of decentralization. The authorities wanted to transfer responsibilities to local governments (Verpeaux, 2001). At the same time, some municipalities experienced different technological tools to involve citizens. The municipalities of Nantes, Marne-la-Vallée and Grenoble used cable networks with open forum discussions and the possibility to access to local council meetings (Vedel, 2003). Marne-la-Vallée had the Aspasie network in 2004 with multimedia poles opened to citizens[2]. Some cities experimented different electronic resources at that time as the demand for local democracy was strong in France during the seventies.

Since the act of 6 February 1992, the local councils have had an obligation to publish the details of decisions. Municipalities with less than 3.500 inhabitants can post on the door of the Town Hall the new by-laws; otherwise, all other local authorities are obliged to issue a collected bulletin of administrative decisions in which all by-laws and legal decrees are published (Bécet, 2001). When the municipalities created websites (Loiseau, 2003), they included information on new by-laws.

French mayors were scared by the evolution of digital means which could create local communities out of their control (Descolonges, 2002). They slowly began to accept the democratic potential of these tools. In an interview made on European mayors of cities above 10.000 inhabitants in 2004, 44.7% of the French mayors found those instruments efficient (but they were only 5.3% who thought that those electronic forums could be used as a communicative strategy)[3]. All the big cities in France have a digital strategy; the local governments took part in a real effort of modernisation.

A plan on "digital France in 2012" was launched a few years ago to modernise the administration. Since 2003, many municipalities have been improving their websites to offer modern public services to citizens. In 2008, the percentage of individuals using Internet at least once a week was around 63% (E-government in France, 2008); the percentage of households with internet connection was 62%. The people using Internet for interacting with public authorities wanted to obtain information (40.5%), download forms (29.9%) and return filled forms (59%). These figures illustrate that e-government practices increased in France (E-government in France, 2008). Internet was traditionally used in the business field. French citizens began to use more and more internet to take part in local life; this is also why many municipalities improved their websites. This is possible for the middle-sized cities and the bigger municipalities to invest in electronic forums whereas for other municipalities the website is merely informative. In October 2008, Éric Besson, the former Secretary of State to the French Prime Minister, presented the digital agenda for France. The plan highlighted four priorities: «to enable all citizens to access all digital networks and services; to develop the production and supply of digital contents; to increase and diversify the use of digital services by companies, public administrations and services; to modernise the governance of the Digital Economy» (E-government in France, 2010). The plan referred to the digital fracture between people who do not have the same resources and skills to access to internet and high-educated people who regularly use digital means. This is why the municipalities could provide some adequate services in order to reach all the social backgrounds. Some of these issues have been discussed among forums and conferences such as the Internet Rights Forum in May 2001 which gathered many actors of the Internet to discuss the rules and the uses of online activities. The forum provided information and regulations concerning the use of internet but closed its activities in 2010[4].

The websites of local governments have been introduced since 2000 and all the main local governments invested in the development of a strong e-communication based upon an interactive website, a regular newsletter and other interactive tools where citizens can take part in the elaboration of specific policies. In many municipalities, the communication officer has had a prevailing role. Albert Lévy noted that the average proportion of internet users was around 40% of the population in 2001 (Lévy, 2003). Some portals gather the information concerning the access to the websites of different municipalities such as Cit@enet[5]. Some companies proposed different models of websites to municipalities. A lot of municipalities have a website but it is interesting to analyse the websites of middle-sized and big municipalities as the websites are more detailed. Some of those websites are well-equipped with a simple access to administrative papers as well as efficient interactive platforms.

3.2 Methodology

A smaller database was chosen in 2012 in order to analyse the evolution of practices. The study was based upon the websites of the cities of more than 30.000 inhabitants (254 cases). Every city has its own website and communicates on political life (local life, participatory instruments). There is an electronic communication on participatory tools as the websites enhance the possibilities for citizens to take part in local life. There is also an attempt to harmonise the profile of the websites with a clear distinction between local political life ("vie municipale") and local administration ("administration communale"). Hence, all websites offer practical information on local life. Some municipalities propose a section named "citoyenneté" where all the existing participatory tools are presented. The identification of the participatory label is very strategic as there is a big difference between municipalities which have a minimalist approach of participatory democracy and the others which use several tools. The term of participatory democracy includes all the citizen-oriented tools. King presented a more detailed categorisation of citizen tools (King, 2006): anticipatory democracy (informed guiding of future decisions), deliberative democracy (debating and analysing potential policy), grassroots democracy (bottom-up initiatives), participatory democracy (consensus decision-making and resolving disagreement) and world democracy (informing world-wide movements) (Fishkin, 1991). The present study shows that participatory democracy is a plus in the repertoire of mayors, even though all the participatory tools do not necessarily influence local decisions. The difficulty was also to classify the occasional tools such as citizen enquiries. They were registered as participatory tools as they reflect the citizens´will to have a feed-back on local policies.

In France, the mayor has the executive power; he is the head of the local administration. He governs the local council (Svara, 1987), but he is the one who has a real political direction. This is why he takes important decisions at the local level. A new mayor can implement different local policies and a political style. The database was updated with the analysis of each website. Some municipalities clearly label a participatory section whereas others just refer to a specific tool.

4. POLITICAL PROFILE OF MUNICIPALITIES ABOVE 30.000 INHABITANTS (2006-2012)

In 2007, the Socialist candidate Ségolène Royal who challenged Nicolas Sarkozy for the presidential election used the participatory democracy as a new form of administrating relations between citizens and representatives (Premat, 2007). She failed but her ideas were taken into account by the Socialist Party which won the municipal elections of 2008. She defended different ideas such as citizen juries, consensus conferences as well as other participatory tools to involve the citizens (Sintomer, 2007). New local councils were elected and this is why it is important to see whether there is a shift in the electronic communication on participatory tools. When municipalities of more than 30 000 inhabitants are compared between 2006 and 2012, French mayors in 2012 are younger. The average age in 2012 is 56 years old whereas it was 58 years old in 2006 (Premat & Dewoghélaëre, 2006). Most of mayors are from left parties in 2012 whereas the majority of them came from Conservative parties in 2006. Considering the political affiliation, in 2006, 8 mayors did not have any political belonging, 107 were Conservatives (UMP), 75 were Socialists, 28 were Communists, 2 were from the Green party, 5 were from the Liberal Party, 1 was from the far-right party (Front National), 7 were from other right tendencies, 6 were from other left tendencies and 3 mayors came from local parties. The local election in 2008 was a success for the Socialists who won the majority of cities in France. There were 102 mayors from the Socialist Party (136 from left parties). There was a shift in the local governance but for municipalities above 30.000 inhabitants, the majority of mayors had a strong local experience. It shows a professionalization of those positions. The experience of mayors was almost the same in 2006 and in 2012 as the average mayor elected had been on duty for 11 years. The renewal is due to a political shift rather than the arrival of new mayors with a participatory ideology. At the same time, deliberative communities did not really emerge in France (De Cindio et al., 2007).

In 2006, most of French mayors were engaged in politics before 1986. The mayors who came to power in 2008 have been engaged in local politics since 1995. 69 politicians became new mayors in 2008. According to the database, nearly all of them had a digital strategy with a strong communication on participatory tools. Those mayors are professional politicians who know the rules and how to communicate on participatory democracy. They are high educated and they come from the middle and upper social classes. Michel Koebel showed in different works that 44% of the mayors of communes of more than 3.500 inhabitants come from the upper class (Koebel, 2006). This fact is reinforced for cities above 30.000 inhabitants.

5. THE EXPLAINING FACTORS OF THE EVOLUTION OF LOCAL DEMOCRACY

5.1 Dependent Variables

The communication on participatory democracy is here targeted. It is the dependent variable. The variable is progressive and is encoded in the following way:

- No communication on participatory democracy tools = 0
- Communication on one participatory democracy tool = 1
- Communication on two participatory democracy tools = 2
- Communication on n participatory democracy tools = n

A participatory instrument is a tool which gives the opportunity for citizens to take part in local political life outside elections. A "conseil des enfants" (youth local council) is regarded here as a participatory instrument. An "on-line forum" is also another instrument. Table 1 shows the proportion of municipalities which communicate on participatory tools in 2006 and in 2012.

There is an evolution between 2006 and 2012 considering the number of instruments. Municipalities which had several participatory tools could communicate on other tools. The average municipality above 30.000 inhabitants communicates on two participatory tools in 2012 whereas it was one instrument in 2006. There is a change as municipalities do not hesitate to elaborate a section on local citizenship with different possibilities of taking part in local life. It is interesting to note that the political shift in 2008 helped to implement those tools even though the political belonging is not crucial in the choice of communicating on participatory democracy. Table 2 shows the relation between the political belonging of the mayor and the communication on participatory instruments. Left-wing and right-wing may-

Table 1. Communication on participatory tools for municipalities of more than 30.000 inhabitants in France

Proportion of municipalities which communicate on participatory tools	2006	2012
Municipalities which do not communicate on participatory tools	18 (7%)	22 (8.7%)
Municipalities which communicate on one instrument	124 (48.5%)	107 (42.%)
Municipalities which communicate on two instruments	59 (23%)	58 (23%)
Municipalities which communicate on three instruments	26 (10.5%)	34 (13.2%)
Municipalities which communicate on four instruments	27 (11%)	28 (11.1%)
Municipalities which communicate on five instruments	0	5 (2%)
Total	254 (100%)	254 (100%)

Source: Analysis on the updated sample of municipalities above 30.000 inhabitants in 2012

ors adopted the participatory norm but left-wing mayors are more willing to communicate on several participatory tools. For instance, the municipality of Bobigny (located near Paris, between 30.000 and 50.000 inhabitants) developed a participatory trend. On the website of Bobigny, it is possible to find a complete presentation of participatory democracy. This presentation refers to the local referendum held on the right of non-European immigrants to vote in local elections. Different tools are described: the Consult´action, which is the local investigation on local public services[6], the "Observatoire des engagements," which is the regular confrontation between citizens and local representatives. Elected local representatives are more accountable (Newell & Bellour, 2002). There are also a children council, a "collectifs locaux d´initiatives citoyennes" (local groups of citizen initiatives) and a city plan network.

Participatory democracy is a real strategy which characterizes the action of those mayors. If those mayors communicate on participatory democracy, there is not a real innovation in e-democracy with online forums. Conservative mayors feel comfortable with internet innovations such as chat. For instance, the mayor of Rosny-sous-Bois (40.000 inhabitants) organizes once a month a chat with electors who can directly communicate with him[7]. There is a solid description on the net of how citizens should use the system. There is a screen capture so that the electors can easily access the communicative platform. In 2010, the municipality got the "Ville internet @@@@@" label which rewards the best digital communication of cities in France.

Table 2 shows that left-wing mayors communicate more on participatory tools, especially when there are several tools that citizens can use. Conservative mayors prefer to limit themselves to one instrument. The political affiliation has an impact on the way mayors communicate on participatory democracy. The communist mayors promote the participatory ideology: out of 31 mayors in the database, there are just 5 who do not communicate on participatory instruments (Sintomer, 2007). This is very interesting as the Communist Party is declining in France (Grésil, 1996). The participatory ideology is used to renew the image of a political party which can survive thanks to electoral alliances with other parties or thanks to the reputation of some mayors.

During a series of interviews made in participatory municipalities in France, it was easy to feel the positive image of mayors in France. A participatory municipality means a municipality which implemented a participatory tradition thanks to the use of several tools (Blondiaux, 2008).

Table 2. Belonging of the mayors and communication on participatory instruments in 2012

Pol. Belonging of mayors Number of instruments	Without any political affiliation	Centre and Right-wing mayors	Left wing mayors
0	0	8	13
1	3	57	47
2	0	21	38
3	1	8	25
4	2	7	19
5	0	1	4
	6	102	146

Source: Own research

"The mayor is the most appreciated representative among citizens. It is necessary to reshape the link between decision-makers and the population, the first step is thus the neighbourhood. The participatory method is inclusive, it does not contradict the representative system"[8]. Arcueil is an example of a municipality which had a Communist mayor during decades before adopting other participatory tools. The municipality belongs to the former red belt of Communist municipalities around Paris. The mayors of those municipalities adopted a participatory strategy to change their image.

5.2 Independent Variables

The profile of municipalities of more than 30 000 inhabitants was compared between 2006 and 2012. 254 communes were targeted: 131 have between 30.000 and 50.000 inhabitants, 86 between 50.000 and 100.000 inhabitants, 26 between 100.000 and 200.000 and 11 above 200.000 inhabitants. As years 2006 and 2012 are compared, the number of cases is 508. The age of mayors is important as well as if they were running for another term (Avellaneda, 2009).

The integration into an inter-municipal structure is the fact for most of municipalities: 47 municipalities (19%) are without any inter-municipal structure whereas 81% are a part of an inter-municipal body. 152 municipalities are a part of a *communauté d´agglomération* in 2012. The situation is similar in 2008 considering the inter-municipal integration of the municipalities.

Most of municipalities which belong to an inter-municipal body choose to communicate on participatory democracy. The territorial configuration is important but Table 3 does not take the situation of the municipality in the inter-municipal body into account. Some municipalities belong to the periphery of the inter-municipal body and are more willing to communicate on participatory democracy in order to affirm a local identity. They allocate more digital resources on those tools because they want to create a community link. Most municipalities, which are part of a *communauté d'agglomération*, build participatory platforms.

In 2006, there were only 25 municipalities where the mayor was a woman (less than 10%), 229 municipalities had a man as a mayor. The tendency is almost the same in 2012 with 222 men and 32 women. But if the municipality size and the gender are crossed, there are 8 male and 3 female mayors for the municipalities above 200.000 inhabitants. If the gender variable is crossed with the communication on participatory tools, then there are no specific differences (Premat, 2009b) certainly because the sample is too little (there are just 32 female mayors for mu-

Table 3. Digital strategy and situation of the municipality

Intermunicipal Structure Digital communication	Without any inter-municipal body	Communauté de communes	Communauté d´agglomération	Communauté Urbaine or Syndicat d´Agglomération Nouvelle	Total
No participatory tools	3	4	14	1	22
One instrument	18	11	66	12	106
Two instruments	8	5	34	11	58
Three instruments	9	0	22	3	34
Four instruments	7	0	15	5	28
Five instruments	2	2	1	1	6
Total	47	22	152	33	254

Source: Own research

nicipalities above 30.000 inhabitants). 40% of female mayors communicate on two participatory tools but the proportion is not that different from male mayors. The sample is too small to draw any conclusion regarding the attitude of female mayors vis-à-vis the repertoire of participatory democracy.

5.3 Empirical Results

The new mayors adapted themselves to the necessity of communicating on participatory democracy (Premat, 2009a). The websites of these communes are well built with a very clear presentation. The political affiliation can play a role as leftist mayors always promoted participatory democracy. Communist mayors near Paris built a strong participatory agenda with online forums, citizen focus groups or different planning cells. They try to reinforce a feeling of local identity and strongly promote participatory democracy. Table 4 presents 508 cases as the municipalities (254) were compared in 2006 and 2012.

The hypotheses are tested through a logistic regression with standard errors presented in Table 4. This model shows that the communication on citizen involvement mainly depends on the type of environment (rural or urban district) and on the age of the mayor. The higher the density of population is, the more the mayor communicates on participatory democracy. The younger the mayors are, the more they communicate on participatory tools. There is a generation factor which explains that some mayors are more willing to use those instruments (Vetter & Hoffmann-Martinot, 2012). The date of entrance in local politics is also a strong explanatory factor because it illustrates how experienced the mayors are (Guérin-Lavignotte & Kerrouche, 2006). The mayors coming to power in 2008 had a local mandate from 1995. In 2012, the portrait of the participatory mayor could be the following one: he was recently elected (2001 or 2008), he has had a local mandate since 1995 and his municipality is a part of a *communauté d'agglomération*. He has one other mandate but both the integration

Table 4. Factors explaining the digital communication on participatory tools in 2006 and in 2012

Digital communication on participatory democracy	**Coefficient**	**Sig.**
Size of the municipality	0.268	0.08*
Age of the mayor	-0.018	0.169
Sex of the mayor	-0,087	0.823
Integration in an inter-municipal structure	0.277	0.072*
Population density of the *département* where the municipality is located	0.0001	0.021**
Proximity with Paris	0.211	0.249
Date of first election as a mayor	0.058	0.001***
Date of entrance in local politics	-0.028	0.072*
Multiple mandates	-0.110	0.512

Number of observations = 508
Ordinal regression
Chi Square (significance) = 30.59
Prob > chi2 = 0.0003
Pseudo R2 – 0.1339
Significance: ***P<0.01, **P<0.05, *P<0.1

into an inter-municipal body and the multiple mandates are not determining factors explaining why some mayors communicate on participatory democracy. In 2006 and in 2012, 87% of mayors had another political mandate (deputy, senator or another local mandate). The multiple mandates is a French tradition (Dewoghélaëre et al., 2006) which is about to be reformed by the current political majority.

The size of the municipality is another explaining factor: the big municipalities promote participatory democracy in an efficient way. Robert A. Dahl pointed out the antagonistic relation between participation and size of units (Dahl, 1971). According to him, the higher the size increases, the higher the efficiency (Bönisch, Haug, Illy, & Schreier, 2011) is but the poorer the citizen participation gets. In this case, this hypothesis is confirmed as big cities invest more in digital communication on participatory democracy (Dahl & Tufte, 1974).

The territorial configuration does not have any implication in the use of participatory tools. The fact that a municipality is a peripheral part of a *communauté de communes* does not have any consequences on the promotion of participatory democracy. However, the personal factor (mayoral leadership) is all the more important as the mayor is a real link between the electors and the local system (Premat, 2005). The participatory ideology is now shared by a lot of local representatives in France even though they see those tools as merely consultative (Paoletti, 1997). Participatory tools can improve electronic governance in some cases where municipalities collect some information from citizens concerning local issues (Rui, 2004).

6. THE MAYORAL LEADERSHIP IN FRANCE

Mayors have played a significant role in local politics since the election of local councils in 1884. The different laws of decentralization in 1982 gave much power and responsibility to mayors. Citizens are really attached to the personality of mayors and this is why mayors use different tools to reinforce this link (Doig & Hargrove, 1990). The communication on participatory tools illustrates the modernisation of local leadership. As Thierry Vedel wrote, « in a way, the political applications of internet modernise representative democracy by giving it a more participatory trend without questioning its principle » (Vedel, 2001, p. 159). Mayors took participatory norms into account by informing and including more citizens to local debates. The sociologist Gabriel Tarde noted at the end of the nineteenth century that media built new arenas of power which replaced the former influence of the church (Tarde, 1989). Media have a strong impact on public opinion and social networks strengthen the personal leadership of politicians. Mayors of big cities understood that they had to use all these instruments to reinforce their leadership and show an image of both competency and openness (M'Rad, 2006).

Local politics in France is strongly linked to the leadership of mayors, this is why the municipalities implement participatory tools and communicate on them. All the mayors of big cities have either a blog or a twitter account and some municipalities introduced possibilities to call the mayor on some specific hours ("Allô, Monsieur le Maire"). For instance, the mayor of Saint-Germain-en-Laye (near Paris) can be reached on the phone twice a month during one hour (Ziller, 2000)[9]. In Melun, there is a municipal service called "Service Allô Monsieur le Maire" which is presented on the website of the municipality[10]. The mayors use simple means to reach them and communicate on those direct call numbers to reinforce the proximity with electors. Those mayors are not innovative, they just use the websites to communicate on those tools whereas other mayors feel comfortable with some e-participation platforms where it is possible to chat or communicate with electors. In Bordeaux, Alain Juppé used what he called "clavardage"[11]: it was possible to ask him questions about local policies in Bordeaux. He improved those instruments and even initiated other e-participation platforms where the citizens could express themselves (Premat, 2008). Some mayors are specialists of e-technologies such as André Santini in Issy-Les-Moulineaux who is very innovative in e-democracy and electronic referenda. The website of Issy-les-Moulineaux includes a section where citizens can comment the performances of the local administration[12]. The different advices of internet users are collected and it is then possible to vote for the best advice. The feed-back to the citizens is also followed up by the website. André Santini is well-known for the use of a very modern administration and is often quoted as an example of local e-democracy in France. He belongs to the category of entrepreneurial mayors who act for democracy with new technologies (Le Bart, 1994).

The mayors renewed their image by adapting themselves to those new technologies (Becker, 2001), but they also feared that some new actors would use those technologies to create other local communities (Premat, 2012). The local political system preserves its influence, mayors stay as close as possible to electors. They cannot resemble their electors (Alonso et al., 2011), but they do not leave away the control of participatory instruments. Even if the mayor is not very familiar with participatory tools, he communicates on them. Some tools are very specific such as the children council which is more a way of teaching young children how the political system works. The websites have a section for those children councils and communicate on their decisions and the different events organised by those councils. Those councils are registered as participatory tools but in fact they aim at implementing the current rules of the representative system. Lille developed an extended repertoire of participatory tools under the leadership of Martine Aubry with district councils, young councils, senior councils and councils of foreigners[13]. In France, every city tries to set an example of local democracy, but the next step in decentralization could be an opportunity to have a unique model of participatory chart which includes e-participation possibilities.

7. FOUR RECOMMENDATIONS ON CITIZEN INVOLVEMENT AT THE LOCAL LEVEL IN FRANCE

Four main recommendations for French municipalities above 30.000 inhabitants can be made to strengthen the electronic governance of participatory instruments. Electronic resources are essential to produce more participatory democracy but they are not sufficient to create local communities. They are complementary to other participatory tools otherwise they could be simply rejected by citizens.

1. It is important to gather the information on participatory tools in a unique section ("citizen participation"). The websites should use the same generic names in order to improve the communication between representatives and citizens (Mahrer, 2003).
2. Municipalities should systematically open a citizen room where citizens could be helped when using the net or taking part in e-participatory tools. This is very important in order to fight against the digital fracture. A lot of citizens are reluctant to get information on participatory democracy via internet. A network of municipal citizen officers should be created in all municipalities above 30.000 inhabitants. The example of Arcueil is interesting as the "pôle citoyenneté" proposed a real platform of citizen involvement. Before dealing with inclusive governance, it is important to enlarge as much as possible the targeted public (Webler, 1999).
3. The citizen feed-back of some participatory tools should be published somewhere and clearly analysed. How did participatory tools influence local decisions? The closure of decision-making processes should be highlighted. What were the ideas produced? By whom? And what were the ideas selected? This perspective is prevailing for tools like consensus conferences or citizen forums (Renn & Schweizer, 2003).

4. The e-participation is efficient if it produces concrete and physical interaction (Holtkamp et al., 2006). Each online forum on a specific local policy should be followed by a feed-back meeting where the different opinions could be discussed. The relation between digital communication and physical assemblies should be encouraged. Virtual communities should have some concrete connections. The example of Issy-Les Moulineaux is all the more interesting as virtual tools produce concrete connections. The connection between virtual and real spheres is important in the next development of e-government procedures. The goal is to recreate specific face-to-face relations (Fishkin, 1995) such as focus groups thanks to an efficient communication on participatory democracy.

These recommendations are all the more important as the websites do not communicate in the same way on participatory tools. Some instruments are well-known such as senior local councils but others are not perceived in the same way by local representatives (city urban plans, climate consensus conferences). A municipal forum on the use of participatory tools could be worth as innovations can be shared. Those forums do exist at the regional level in France but are fairly poor at the municipal level. The definition of the tools and their evaluation are important in order to improve the quality of relation between citizens and local representatives. Some controversial issues would be dealt with and the decision-making process would be strengthened (Von Schomberg, 1995).

CONCLUSION

The mayors who came recently to power in France have a participatory ideology, which means that they shared the participatory norm. Local governments in France do have a real digital strategy and the digital communication on participatory democracy is present in most of the websites. It is all the more important to communicate on participatory tools as citizen participation is something which is never questioned. The mayors perceive themselves as key-persons in local democracy (Guérin-Lavignotte & Kerrouche, 2006) and the use of participatory tools reinforces this tendency. The municipal election of 2008 was very important in the legitimacy of the participatory repertoire. Socialist mayors who came to power could not neglect this topic as they had been promoting it for many years. There is a generation shift and the socialization of mayors is crucial in the use of this repertoire (Vetter, 2003). In 2012, mayors of municipalities above 30.000 inhabitants are experimented and know how to tackle the digital strategy which is also a resource to make the municipality more attractive. At the same time, the inter-municipal structures have been generalized and the belonging to those structures is not an explanatory factor. The left mayors find it easy to communicate and invent some participatory tools whereas conservative mayors are more influenced by the neighbourhood ideology and the classical link between representatives and citizens. Conservative mayors can sometimes prefer online forums and electronic participatory tools in order to communicate with electors. The mayors control the local arena in France and used the websites to communicate with citizens in a more direct way (chat with the mayor, interactive conferences).

REFERENCES

Alonso, S., Keane, J., & Merkel, W. (2011). *The future of representative democracy*. Cambridge: Cambridge Press. doi:10.1017/CBO9780511770883.

Altman, D. (2011). *Direct democracy worldwide*. Cambridge: Cambridge Press.

Avellaneda, C. N. (2009). Mayoral quality and local public finance. *Public Administration Review*, (May/June): 469–486. doi:10.1111/j.1540-6210.2009.01993.x.

Backhouse, J. (2007). e-Democracy in Australia: The challenge of evolving a successful model. *The Electronic. Journal of E-Government*, *5*(2), 107–116.

Barber, B. R. (1998). Three scenarios for the future of technology and democracy. *Political Science Quarterly*, *113*, 573–589. doi:10.2307/2658245.

Bécet, J.-M. (2001). The structure and working of local government. In Local government in France (pp. 53-68). Paris: la Documentation Française.

Becker, T. (2001). Rating the impact of new technologies on democracy. *Communications of the ACM*, *44*, 49–51. doi:10.1145/357489.357503.

Behrer, L. (2003). *Une lecture institutionnaliste du phénomène participatif, La politique consultative de la Ville de Québec*. Bordeaux, PhD.

Birkenmaier, P. (2004). *E-democracy - Der Wandel der Demokratie durch das Internet*. Berlin: Rhombos Verlag.

Blondiaux, L. (2008). *Nouvel esprit de la démocratie: Actualité de la démocratie participative*. Paris: Seuil.

Bobigny.fr. (n.d.). Website. Retrieved April 21, 2012 from http://www.bobigny.fr/jsp/site/Portal.jsp?page_id=185

Bönisch, P., Haug, P., Illy, A., & Schreier, L. (2011). Municipality size and efficiency of local public services: Does size matter? *IWH-Diskussionspapiere,* n°18.

Bützer, M. (2005). Continuity or innovation? Citizen involvement and institutional reforms in Swiss cities. In K. Steyvers, J.B. Pilet, H. Reynaert, and P. Delwit (Eds.), Revolution or renovation? Reforming local politics in Europe (pp. 213-234). Brugge: Vanden Broele Publishers.

Carrizales, T. (2008). Critical factors in an electronic democracy: A study of municipal managers. *The Electronic. Journal of E-Government*, *6*(1), 23–30.

Chung, K. S. K., & Chatfield, A. T. (2011). An empirical analysis of online social network structure to understand citizen engagement in public policy and community building. *International Journal of Electronic Governance*, *4*(1/2), 85–103. doi:10.1504/IJEG.2011.041709.

Citaenet.com. (n.d.). Website. Retrieved April 23, 2012, from http://www.citaenet.com/

Corbineau.net. (n.d.). Website. Retrieved April 22, 2012, from http://www.corbineau.net/IMG/Acces_au_savoir.pdf

Dahl, R. A. (1971). The city in the future of democracy. In Cook, M. (Ed.), *Participatory democracy* (pp. 85–114). San Francisco: Canfield Press.

Dahl, R. A., & Tufte, E. A. (1974). *Size and democracy*. Stanford: Stanford University Press.

De Cindio, F., De Marco, A., & Grew, P. (2007). Deliberative community networks for local governance. *International Journal of Technology. Policy and Management*, *7*(2), 108–121.

Descolonges, M. (2002). *Vertiges technologiques*. Paris: La Dispute.

Dewoghélaëre, J., Magni-Berton, R., & Navarro, J. (2006). The *cumul des mandats* in contemporary French politics: An empirical study of the *XIIe Législature* of the *Assemblée Nationale*. *French Politics*, 312–332. doi:10.1057/palgrave.fp.8200104.

Dewoghélaëre, J., & Premat, C. (2007). La stratégie de communication numérique des élus locaux français. *Pyramides*, *13*, 155–171.

Dewoghélaëre, J., & Premat, C. (2008). Le profil des maires urbains en 2006. *Sens Public*, *25*(March), 1–8.

Doig, J. W., & Hargrove, E. C. (1990). *Leadership and innovation: Entrepreneurs in government*. Baltimore, MD: Johns Hopkins University.

E-government in France. (2010). *Invest in France*. Retrieved from http://www.invest-in-france.org/Medias/Publications/1171/ifa-e-government-in-france-july-2010.pdf

Egner, B., & Kerrouche, E. (2012). Local democracy – a comparison of mayoral perceptions. In O.W. Gabriel, S. I. Keil, and E. Kerrouche (Eds.), Political participation in France and Germany (pp. 137-160). Essex: EPCR Press studies.

Elias, N. (1991). *Qu'est-ce que la sociologie?* French translation of Yamin Hoffmann. La Tour d'Aigues: L'Aube.

Ensemble-simplifions.fr. (n.d.). Website. Retrieved April 21, 2012, from http://www.ensemble-simplifions.fr/

Fishkin, J. S. (1991). *Democracy and deliberation. Yale*. Yale University Press.

Foruminternet.org. (n.d.). Website. Retrieved April 21, 2012, from http://www.foruminternet.org/institution/espace-presse/communiques-de-presse/suite-a-sa-dissolution-le-forum-des-droits-sur-l-internet-partage-ses-contenus-3119.html

Fuchs, D., Roller, E., & Weßels, B. (Eds.). (2002). *Bürger und Demokratie in Ost und West, Studien zur Politischen Kultur und zum Politischen Prozess*. Wiesbaden: Westdeutscher Verlag.

Graafland-Essers, I., & Ettedgui, E. (2003). *Benchmarking e-government in Europe and the U.S.* Santa Monica, CA: RAND.

Grésil, R. (1996). *Main basse sur les banlieues rouges*. Paris: Picollec.

Grossmann, L. K. (1995). *The electronic republic. Reshaping democracy in the information age*. New York: Viking.

Guérin-Lavignotte, E., & Kerrouche, E. (2006). *Les élus locaux en Europe, un statut en mutation*. Paris: La Documentation Française.

Hatzfeld, H. (2005). *Faire de la politique autrement, les expériences inachevées des années 1970*. Rennes: Presses Universitaires de Rennes.

Hauer, J., Sandberg, J., Olson, K., Meyerhoff, C., & Moses, L. G. (2002). *Local e-government*. Minnesota: Office of the legislative auditor.

Hoffmann-Martinot, V., & Wollmann, H. (2006). *State and local reforms in France and Germany: Divergence and convergence*. Wiesbaden: VS Verlag für Sozialwissenschaften. doi:10.1007/978-3-531-90271-5.

Holtkamp, L., Bogumil, J., & Kißler, L. (2006). Kooperative Demokratie, Das politische Potenzial von Bürgerengagement. Frankfurt, New-York: Campus Verlag.

Holzer, M., & Kim, B. J. (Eds.). (2004). *Building good governance: Reforms in Seoul*. Newark, NJ: National Center for Public Productivity.

Howard, M. (2001). e-Government across the world: How will „E" change government? *Government Finance Review*, 6-9.

Jaeger, P. T. (2003). The endless wire: E-government as global phenomenon. *Government Information Quarterly*, *20*, 323–331. doi:10.1016/j.giq.2003.08.003.

Kerrouche, E. (2005). The powerful French mayor: Myth and reality. In Berg, R., & Rao, N. (Eds.), *Transforming local political leadership*. Basingstoke: Palgrave Macmillan.

Koebel, M. (2006). *Le pouvoir local ou la démocratie improbable*. Bellecombe-en-Bauges: éditions du Croquant.

Larsen, C. A. (2002). Municipal size and democracy: A critical analysis of the argument of proximity based on the case of Denmark. *Scandinavian Political Studies*, *25*(4), 317–332. doi:10.1111/1467-9477.00074.

Lascoumes, P., & Le Galès, P. (Eds.). (2004). *Gouverner par les instruments*. Paris: Presses de la Fondation Nationale des Sciences Politiques.

Le Bart, C. (1994). *La rhétorique du maire entrepreneur*. Paris: Pedone.

Le Bart, C. (1998). *Le discours politique*. Paris: PUF.

Lévy, A. (2003). La démocratie locale en France: Enjeux et obstacles. *Espaces et Sociétés (Paris, France)*, 112.

Loiseau, G. (2003). L'assujettissement des sites internet municipaux aux logiques sociétales. *Science and Society*, *60*, 107–125.

M'Rad, H. (2006). La démocratie d'opinion le dépassement de la démocratie représentative? In R. Ben Achour, J. Gicquel, and S. Milacic (dir.), La démocratie représentative devant un défi historique. Bruxelles: éditions Bruylant.

Mahrer, H. (2003). *SMP: A model for the transformation of political communication*. Vienna: Legend Research.

Mairie-lille.fr. (n.d.). Website. Retrieved April 21, 2012, from http://www.mairie-lille.fr/fr/Citoyennete_-_Concertation/conseil-lillois

McLean, I. (1989). *Democracy and the new technology*. Cambridge: Polity Press.

Meininger, M. C. (1998). Public service, the public's service. In Gallouédec-Genuys, F. (Ed.), *About French administration*. Paris: La Documentation Française.

Mény, Y. (1998). *The French political system*. Paris: La Documentation française.

Moon, M. J. (n.d.). The Evolution of E-Government among Municipalities: Rhetoric or Reality? *Public Administration Review, 62*(4), 424-433.

Newell, P., & Bellour, S. (2002). Mapping accountability: Origins, contexts and implications for development. *IDS Working Paper 168*. Brighton: Institute of Development Studies.

OECD. (2003). e-Government imperative. Organisation for economic co-operation and development: E-Government Studies. Paris: OECD Publication Service.

Paoletti, M. (1997). *La démocratie locale et le référendum: Analyse de la démocratie à travers la genèse institutionnelle du référendum*. Paris: L'Harmattan.

Perrin, B. (1986). *Décentralisation, le droit et le fait*. Moulins-lès-Metz: Est-Imprimerie.

Pollitt, C., & Bouckaert, G. (2004). *Public management reform, a comparative analysis*. Oxford: Oxford University Press.

Premat, C. (2005). The growing use of referenda in local politics: A comparison of France and Germany. In K. Steyvers, J.B. Pilet, H. Reynaert, & P. Delwit (Eds.), Revolution or renovation? Reforming local politics in Europe (pp. 185-212). Brugge: Vanden Broele Publishers.

Premat, C. (2006/2007). À la recherche d'une communauté perdue: Les usages de la proximité dans le discours participatif en France. *Argumentum, 5*, 59–78.

Premat, C. (2007). L'idée d'une 6e République dans la campagne des élections présidentielles. *Revista de Ştiinţe Politice, Revue des sciences politiques. Université de Craiova, 13*, 45–58.

Premat, C. (2008). La participation, métonymie de la communication? Les maires français et l'usage de la cyberdémocratie. *COMMposite, 11*(1), 87–99.

Premat, C. (2009a). The implementation of participatory democracy in French communes. *French Politics, 7*, 1–18. doi:10.1057/fp.2009.5.

Premat, C. (2009b). Genre et discours participatif dans les villes françaises. In Gubin, E., Piette, V., & Benvindo, B. (Eds.), *Masculinités, sextants* (pp. 257–272). Bruxelles: Presses de l'Université Libre de Bruxelles.

Premat, C. (2012). Initiatives and referendums. In O. W. Gabriel, S. I. Keil, & E. Kerrouche (Eds.), Political participation in France and Germany (pp. 161-188). Essex: EPCR Press studies.

Raynsford, N., & Beecham, S. J. (2002). *The national strategy for local e-government*. London: crown.

Renn, O., & Schweizer, P.-J. (2012). In O.W. Gabriel, S.I. Keil, & E. Kerrouche (Eds.), Political participation in France and Germany (pp. 273-295). Essex: EPCR Press studies.

Rose, L. (2005). Territorial and functional reforms: Old wine in new bottles- or a new vintage? In K. Steyvers, J.B. Pilet, H. Reynaert, & P. Delwit (Eds.), Revolution or renovation? Reforming local politics in Europe (pp. 397-419). Brugge: Vanden Broele Publishers.

Rose, R. (2005). A global diffusion model of e-governance. *Journal of Public Policy*, *25*(1), 5–27. doi:10.1017/S0143814X05000279.

Rosny93.fr. (n.d.). Website. Retrieved April 21, 2012, from http://www.rosny93.fr/spip.php?article1297

Rui, S. (2004). La démocratie en débat. Les citoyens face à l´action publique. Paris: éditions Colin.

Saintger.blogencommun.fr. (n.d.). Website. Retrieved from http://saintger.blogencommun.fr/2009-06-allo-monsieur-le-maire-demain-a-18h/

Scott, J. K. (2005). E-services: Assessing the quality of municipal government web sites. *State and Local Government Review*, *37*(2), 151–165. doi:10.1177/0160323X0503700206.

Sintomer, Y. (2007). *Le pouvoir au peuple: jurys citoyens, tirage au sort et démocratie participative*. Paris: La Découverte.

Svara, J. H. (1987). Mayoral leadership in council-manager cities: Preconditions versus preconceptions. *The Journal of Politics*, *49*(1), 207–227. doi:10.2307/2131141.

Tarde, G. (1989). *L´opinion et la foule*. Paris: éditions PUF.

Urbandive.com. (n.d.). Website. Retrieved April 21, 2012, from http://www.urbandive.com/lieu/stade/mairie-service-allo-monsieur-le-maire/4d6c2d0dfc692507839f0dd7#/0/M1/P1/F4d6c2d0dfc692507839f0dd7/Cmairies/N151.12061,6.11309,2.66049,48.5396/B2.66049,48.5396/Z10/

Vedel, T. (2001). La démocratie électronique. In F. Hamon & O. Passelecq (Eds.), Le Référendum en Europe, Bilan et perspectives. Paris: éditions L'Harmattan.

Vedel, T. (2003). *L'idée de démocratie électronique, origines, visions, questions*. La Tour d'Aigues: éditions de l'Aube.

Verpeaux, M. (2001). Decentralisation since 1982. In *Local government in France* (pp. 37–52). Paris: La Documentation Française.

Vetter, A. (2003). La fonction de socialisation de la politique locale en Europe. In V. Hoffmann-Martinot & C. Sorbets (Eds). Démocraties locales en changement (pp. 165-189). Paris: éditions Pedone.

Vetter, A., & Hoffmann-Martinot, V. (2012). In O.W. Gabriel, S.I. Keil, & E. Kerrouche (Eds.), Political participation in France and Germany (pp. 137-160). Essex: EPCR Press studies.

Von Schomberg, R. (1995). Erosion of the value spheres: The ways in which a society copes with scientific, moral and ethical uncertainty. In Von Schomberg, R. (Ed.), *Contested technology: Ethics, risk and public debate. Tillburg*. International Centre for Human Public Affairs.

Wojcik, S. (2003). Les forums électroniques municipaux. Espaces du débat démocratique? *Science and Society*, 60.

Ziller, J. (2000). Fragmentation/participation: Quelle bonne dimension? *Pouvoirs*, *95*, 19–31.

ADDITIONAL READING

Ackermann, B. (1998). *We the people, II Transformations. Harvard*. Harvard University Press.

Applbaum, A. I. (2002). Failure in the cybermarket of ideas. In E.C. Kamarck & J.S. Nye Jr. (Eds.), Governance.com – Democracy in the information age (pp. 17–31). Brookings, Washington, DC, USA.

Avellaneda, C. N. (2009). Municipal performance: Does mayoral quality matter? *Journal of Public Administration: Research and Theory*, *19*(2), 285–312. doi:10.1093/jopart/mun001.

Bellamy, C., & Taylor, J. A. (1998). *Governing in the information age*. Buckingham: Open University Press.

Blair, H. (2000). Participation and accountability at the periphery: Democratic local governance in six countries. *World Development*, *28*, 21–39. doi:10.1016/S0305-750X(99)00109-6.

Browning, G. (2002). *Electronic democracy: Using internet to transform American politics*. Medford: CyberAge Books.

Chadwick, A., & May, C. (2003). Interaction between states and citizens in the age of the internet: 'e-Government' in the United States, Britain, and the European Union. *Governance: An International Journal of Policy, Administration and Institutions*, *16*, 271–300. doi:10.1111/1468-0491.00216.

Coleman, S. (1999). Cutting out the middle man: From virtual representation to direct deliberation. In Hague, B. N., & Loader, B. D. (Eds.), *Digital democracy: Discourse and decision making in the information age* (pp. 195–210). London: Routledge.

Fishkin, J. (1995). *The voice of the people, public opinion and democracy*. New Haven: Yale University.

Gattiker, U. E. (2001). *The Internet as a diverse community: Cultural, organizational, and political issues*. Mahwah, NJ: Lawrence Erlbaum.

Genieys, W. (2005). The sociology of political elites in France: The end of an exception? *International Political Science Review*, *26*(4), 413–430. doi:10.1177/0192512105055808.

Heeks, R. (Ed.). (1999). *Re-inventing government in the information age: International practises in IT-enabled public sector reform*. London: Routledge. doi:10.4324/9780203204962.

Kamarck, E., & Nye, J. (Eds.). (2003). *Governance.com: Democracy in the Information age*. Washington, DC: Brookings Institution Press.

Latour, B. (2006). *Changer de société – Refaire de la sociologie*. Paris: La Découverte.

Layne, K., & Lee, J. (2001). Developing fully functional e-government: A four stage model. *Government Information Quarterly*, *18*, 122–136. doi:10.1016/S0740-624X(01)00066-1.

Levin, Y. (2002). Politics after the internet. *The Public Interest*, *149*, 80–94.

Loader, B. D. (Ed.). (1997). *The governance of cyberspace: Politics, technology and global restructuring*. London: Routledge. doi:10.4324/9780203360408.

Macintosh, A. (2003). *Using information and communication technologies to enhance citizen engagement in the policy process*. OECD Report: Promise and Problems of E-Democracy, Challenges of Online Citizen Engagement.

Mahrer, H., & Brandtweiner, R. (2004). Success factors for implementing e-government services. *International Journal of Information Technology and Management*, *3*, 235–245. doi:10.1504/IJITM.2004.005034.

Nugent, J. D. (2001). If e-democracy is the answer, what's the question? *National Civic Review*, *90*, 221–233. doi:10.1002/ncr.90303.

Okot-Uma, R. W. (2000). *Electronic governance: Re-inventing good governance*. London: Commonwealth Secretariat.

Premat, C. (2006). Castoriadis and the modern political imaginary – Oligarchy, representation, democracy. *Critical Horizons*, *7*(1), 251–275. doi:10.1163/156851606779308170.

Rose, J., & Sanford, C. (2007). Mapping eparticipation research: Four central challenges. *Communications of the Association for Information Systems*, *20*, 55.

Rose, R. (2008). Political communication in a European public space: Language, the Internet and understanding as soft power. *Journal of Common Market Studies*, *46*(2), 451–475. doi:10.1111/j.1468-5965.2007.00783.x.

Rux, J. (2008). *Direkte Demokratie in Deutschland: Rechtsgrundlagen und Rechtswirklichkeit der unmittelbaren Demokratie in der Bundesrepublik*. Baden-Baden: Nomos.

Saxena, K. B. C. (2005). Towards excellence in e-governance. *International Journal of Public Sector Management*, *18*(6), 498–513. doi:10.1108/09513550510616733.

Schlosberg, D., & Dryzek, J. S. (2002). Digital democracy: Authentic or virtual? *Organization & Environment*, *15*, 332–335. doi:10.1177/1086026602153011.

Webler, T. (1999). The craft and theory of public participation: A dialectical process. *Risk Research*, *2*(1), 55–71. doi:10.1080/136698799376989.

Westen, T. (2000). Can technology save democracy? *National Civic Review*, *87*(1), 47–56. doi:10.1002/ncr.87103.

Wilhelm, A. G. (2000). *Democracy in the digital age. Challenges to political life in cyberspace*. New York: Routledge.

Yildiz, M. (2007). E-government research: Reviewing the literature, limitations and ways forward. *Government Information Quarterly*, *24*, 646–665. doi:10.1016/j.giq.2007.01.002.

KEY TERMS AND DEFINITIONS

Digital Communication: Communication through websites. It is merely informative but can also include e-participatory tools.

Digital Fracture: Social and cultural discrimination between citizens who are familiar with social networks and websites and citizens who do not control those instruments.

Mayoral Leadership: Influence of mayors in politics. The mayoral leadership goes over the one of the local council.

Neighbourhood Ideology: Ideology which promotes a closer link between representatives and electors. This ideology differs from participatory ideology where citizens get involved in politics.

Participatory Ideology: Ideology which promotes interactive tools such as citizen forums, panels and district councils.

Participatory Tools: Instruments which allow citizens to take part in politics outside elections. These instruments include citizen forums, citizen conferences, panels, district councils, youth councils and so on. In France, the review *Territoires* established in 2007 a list of more than 180 participatory instruments used in French municipalities.

ENDNOTES

1. The territorial configuration describes the interaction between the municipality and

its environment (integration in an inter-municipal body).

2. See corineau.net (n.d.).
3. SSD 0822 database, « The European mayor – Political leaders in the changing context of local democracy », Henry Bäck, School of Public Administration, Göteborg University. The data were collected between 2002 and 2004.
4. See foruminternet.org (n.d.).
5. See citaenet.com (n.d.).
6. See bobigny.fr (n.d.).
7. See rosny93.fr (n.d.).
8. Interview made with Farid Benadou, responsible for the citizen pole of the municipality of Arcueil, 12 December 2003.
9. See saintger.blogencommun.fr (n.d.).
10. See urbandive.com (n.d.).
11. Clavardage is a neologism which refers to "gossip" (*bavardage*) and "keyboard" (*clavier*).
12. See ensemble-simplifions.fr (n.d.).
13. See mairie-lille.fr (n.d.).

Chapter 17
eParticipation in Europe: Current State and Practical Recommendations

Efthimios Tambouris
University of Macedonia, Greece

Simon Smith
The University of Leeds, UK

Ann Macintosh
The University of Leeds, UK

Eleni Panopoulou
University of Macedonia, Greece

Efpraxia Dalakiouridou
University of Macedonia, Greece

Konstantinos Tarabanis
University of Macedonia, Greece

Jeremy Millard
Danish Technological Institute, Denmark

ABSTRACT

During the past few years, information and communication technologies and especially the internet are increasingly used in a vast range of human activities, including citizens' interaction with government. In this context, advanced technologies are also being used to more actively engage citizens in democratic processes, which are termed as electronic participation (eParticipation). eParticipation has attracted considerable attention worldwide. In Europe, a large number of initiatives have been funded providing valuable lessons. The aim of this chapter is to map the current state of eParticipation in Europe and provide practical recommendations. More specifically, the authors first present the results of a review of policy documents in the European Union in order to understand how eParticipation fits into European policies. They then present an analytical framework to aid theoretical understanding of eParticipation, followed by the results of a European study on eParticipation initiatives. Based on all these, the authors propose a number of recommendations on eParticipation for policy makers, practitioners, evaluators and research funders.

DOI: 10.4018/978-1-4666-4173-0.ch017

Copyright © 2013, IGI Global. Copying or distributing in print or electronic forms without written permission of IGI Global is prohibited.

INTRODUCTION

Governmental processes are not limited to citizen-related top-down government services but also include citizen involvement in decision-making processes. In this context, it can be argued that electronic participation (eParticipation) is an integral part of electronic government (eGovernment). Today, European Institutions are sensing an increased demand by all sections of society for participation in EU level decisions as they realise that some citizens feel alienated from policy making and that the type and strength of citizen involvement in legislative processes is far from desirable. There are a number of specific Information and Communication Technologies (ICT) which can contribute to the inclusion of citizens in decision-making processes, in co-shaping the public services they receive or in public debate that prefigures formal decision making and service design. This is the context for the current interest in eParticipation.

The proliferation of eParticipation offerings during the past years as well the variety of forms in which eParticipation manifests itself, require a solid conceptual and empirical understanding to provide a foundation for future endeavours. eParticipation evolved by evangelising the reconnection of citizens to policy, claiming to reduce the complexity of decision making and legislative processes, contribute to better legislation, broaden citizen participation in decision making and advance transparency so as to reduce the perceived democratic deficit. A significant number of national and regional authorities of the EU Member States as well as civil society have undertaken actions in these areas. However, these are not being systematically mapped, and even those which are have not yet been analyzed for their potential impact at the European level, or for developing good practice and policy for wider dissemination. Although assumed, it has not yet been demonstrated how these activities could be used and operationalized for positive contributions to achieving the Digital Agenda 2020 goals and the renewed goals of the Europe 2020 strategy.

The overall objective of this chapter is to provide a synoptic but coherent overview of the current state of European eParticipation in order to produce recommendations which can assist policy-makers to harness the benefits of ICT for better legislation and better decision-making at all levels of government, and for enhanced public participation in such processes. More specific objectives include:

- To identify and study European Union eParticipation policies and conceptualize how eParticipation is perceived by European Institutions.
- To construct a framework for analysing eParticipation initiatives. The framework identifies the key variables of eParticipation and serves as a conceptual-analytical tool for understanding eParticipation offerings and settings.
- To survey European eParticipation initiatives in order to map the current state of play.
- To derive a set of recommendations on the use of eParticipation.

The chapter is organized as follows. We start by presenting a brief background of eParticipation and explaining the motivation for this study. Then we present the main contribution of the chapter which refers to eParticipation in Europe. More specifically, this includes the methods employed, an outline of relevant policy documents, the theoretical foundation of the study, the results of a survey on eParticipation initiatives and relevant guidelines and recommendations. Finally, future research directions are presented before concluding.

BACKGROUND

There is a widespread sense that the public has disengaged from formal political processes, such as voting, joining parties and following political news (Hay, 2007; Stoker, 2006). This growing apathy to formal politics not only does nothing to change current political policies but is also at risk of undermining our current model of representative democracy. When that representation is through representatives elected by a minority of the electorate, this brings into question the legitimacy of political decision-making. In a number of European countries where voting is not obligatory there has been a growing decline in the number of people willing to turn out and vote in European level elections. The European Parliament was directly elected for the first time in 1979 with ten member states and at each election since then (every five years) the overall voter turnout has fallen. The turnout in the 2009 elections, with 27 member states, was only 43%. Many experts (e.g. Dryzak, 2000; Fishkin, 1991) see active citizen participation as a vital part of a thriving democracy as well as being necessary for the successful transformation of modern societies.

Researchers have stressed the widespread potential of the internet and other digital technologies to broaden and deepen the democratic process, making it more transparent, inclusive and accessible (e.g. Dutton, 1992; Blumer & Gurevitch, 2001; Dahlgren, 2005). However, only relatively recently has there been sufficient application of ICT to support democracy so that this potential could be considered within a real-world context (Weber et al, 2003). ICT offers new channels and processes for participation, a potentially more inclusive involvement of citizens in the decision making process, and the ability to compensate for certain democratic deficits. It can also lead to better legislation, to changes in the way both Parliaments in EU Member States and the European Parliament in Brussels interact with European citizens, and can produce new tools for democratic participation. It is, perhaps, not surprising that the European Parliament and the European Commission are attempting to provide an effective channel between themselves and civil society using ICT to deliver a more open and transparent democratic decision-making process.

The generic term 'eDemocracy' (sometimes called digital democracy, cyberdemocracy and teledemocracy) captures both the intent to support democracy and studies of outcomes and context. Hacker and van Dijk (2000) describe the early emergence of the concept. eDemocracy is concerned with the use of ICT to engage citizens, support the democratic decision-making processes and strengthen representative democracy. Previous work (Macintosh, 2004) usefully considered two components to eDemocracy: addressing the electoral process, including e-voting, and addressing citizen eParticipation in democratic decision-making. This in turn provides a more detailed definition of eParticipation, as the use of ICT to support information provision and "top-down" engagement i.e. government-led initiatives, or "ground-up" efforts to empower citizens, civil society organizations and other democratically constituted groups to gain the support of their elected representatives. Effective information provision is often seen as a corollary of effective engagement and empowerment (Macintosh & Whyte, 2006). Other authors (e.g. Pratchett and Krimmer (2005)) provide similar definitions, although Coleman and Shane (2011) prefer the term 'online consultations' to refer to Internet-based discussion forums that represent top-down, government-run or at least government-endorsed solicitations of public input with regard to policy making.

For the purposes of this chapter, the working definition of eParticipation is:

- eParticipation is seen as participation using ICT, either as the only channel or alongside other non-ICT channels.
- Participation relates mainly to inputs to policy- and decision-making for political or public policy purposes, both within formal systems and through informal systems where these can have a real impact at any stage of the policy lifecycle.
- Participation is embedded in particular governance regimes.
- Participation should be seen in the context of different political cultures.
- Participation has direct impacts on, and relations to, other public policy goals and values like democracy, inclusion, accountability, better legislation, trust, cohesion, legitimacy, transparency and subsidiarity, but it should not be examined only for its impact on these other policies.

In the context of our specific study detailed in this chapter, there is no intention to impose or imply any normative views of participation. Nevertheless we make reference to the normative goals embedded in a European governance regime, some of which are made explicit in strategic programmes and statements of principle, notably the White Paper on European Governance (European Commission, 2001).

Even as the political currency of eParticipation has risen, it can still be characterized as 'experimental' and evaluation of the quality of eParticipation in the policy process is a huge challenge (Tambouris, Liotas, & Tarabanis, 2007; Coleman, Macintosh, & Schneeberger, 2008). In such circumstances it is not surprising that evidence about benefits is very thin and opinions vary wildly as to the advantages and disadvantages of eParticipation.

EPARTICIPATION IN EUROPE

Methods

The methods employed in this research include four inter-connected steps.

The first step involves reviewing eParticipation policies in the European Union. This has been performed using desktop research of primary and secondary legislation, as well as relevant policy documents.

The second step involves constructing an analytical framework to be used for understanding. This framework evolved through three iterations. The first two versions were essentially deductive, based on a literature review of previous attempts to evaluate eParticipation and public participation in policy-making, feedback from three external reviewers, and input from participants at workshops. Further refinement took account of empirical findings from the eParticipation survey described in step 3.

The third step involves performing a survey of European eParticipation initiatives. We have used three methods for identifying initiatives. First, we have searched through award schemes and online databases in the fields of eParticipation and in eGovernment (e.g. eEurope awards, ePractice.eu database, etc.). Second, we have performed desktop research, through relevant literature references and through Web surfing, using keywords such as "eParticipation," "consultation," "citizen forum," etc. Finally, we have exploited connections to key experts and project owners in the field for communicating our intention to gather eParticipation initiatives across Europe. To facilitate the survey, a template for recording the initiatives was also created at this step.

The fourth and final step involves interpreting our findings from step 3 in the context of our policy review (step 1) and our theoretical framework (step 2), and hence deriving practical guidelines and recommendations, addressed principally at the European Institutions themselves, but also relevant to other policy makers, practitioners, evaluators and research funders.

ePARTICIPATION POLICIES IN THE EUROPEAN UNION

ePartication policies in the European Union are extrapolated by investigating the legal arrangements pertaining to citizen participation, embedded in primary and secondary legislation, as well as by reviewing relevant policy documents. eParticipation is not therefore disentailed by the EU as a stand-alone policy, rather it is intertwined with values such as openness, transparency as well as the use of Internet facilities.

The legal basis for citizen engagement and democratic arrangements in the European Union is given by primary legislation, i.e. the Treaties of the European Union. The Treaty on the European Union (TEU, 1992), the Treaty of Amsterdam (1997) and the Treaty of Nice (2001) anchor representative democracy through political parties and the rights of European citizens to address petitions to the European Parliament. Article 11 of the TEU is the symbolic commitment to democracy and specifies that the "institutions shall maintain an open, transparent and regular dialogue with representative associations and civil society." The Treaty of Amsterdam introduces the basis of consultations, by stipulating that "the Commission should consult widely before proposing legislation." In 2004, the Treaty establishing a Constitution for Europe (2004) includes democratic equality, representative and participatory democracy as its basic principles. Nonetheless, participation mediated through parties remains the dominant mode (Dalakiouridou et al, 2012). Finally, the Treaty of Lisbon (2007, entered into force in 2009) envisages a more democratic, transparent and legitimate Europe with a strengthened role for national parliaments and a stronger voice for citizens through the novel concept of the Citizens Initiative (European Parliament, 211/2011).

Secondary legislation (regulations, directives, decisions, recommendations etc.) does little more to institutionalize citizen participation (Smith & Dalakiouridou, 2009), but some rhetorical and practical measures relevant to eParticipation have been introduced by European institutions since the turn of the century.

The White Paper on European Governance (European Commission, 2001) calls for openness, transparency and enhanced participation to restore public trust and legitimacy. Citizen participation is engendered by the establishment of minimum standards for consultation in a governance setting that emphasizes structures of functional representation and segmented publics. Notwithstanding arrangements that permitted public access to Community documents in the context of accountability and transparency, the first signs of ICT-enabled participatory processes originated in the White Paper on reforming the Commission (European Commission, 2000) and the Information and Communication policy of the EU (2001). These documents prepared the ground for new communication and interaction policies such as the Europa portal and the Europe Direct service. The emergence of consultations and the Interactive Policy Making online tool, (later migrated to the Debate Europe portal and now part of the Your Voice in Europe portal) were the primary building blocks for online citizen contributions to Community policy making (European Commission, 2002; Smith & Dalakiouridou, 2009).

The period around 2005 was marked by the defeated referenda on the proposed constitution and a "period of reflection" deriving from a constitutional crisis. In 2005, the Action Plan for Communicating Europe and the Plan D for Democracy, Dialogue and Debate (European Commission, 2005) launched a period of democratic "renewal" by means of the Europa portal, plans for more effective consultations and a website and other tools to stimulate debate on European issues; nonetheless most actions remained on Member State level. The 2006 White Paper on a European

Communication Policy and the European Transparency Initiative (European Commission, 2006) introduced further communication technologies, for instance virtual meeting places, audiovisual facilities and other channels of communication, whilst the Plan D programme (European Commission, 2006) formally acknowledged the internet as a means to stimulate dialogue and make European citizens heard.

In 2007, the adoption of two European communications (Europe in Partnership and Communicating about Europe via the Internet, see European Commission (2007)) marked a newer, more centralized internet strategy based on audiovisual networks, information networks and communication tools. These served the attempt to create a European Public Sphere[1] and adopt a new internet strategy focused on the Europa portal, as well as Web 2.0 functionalities and social networks (Dalakiouridou et al., 2009). Finally, in 2008, the Commission reinforced the use of audiovisual and other media (European Commission, 2008) to encourage the connectivity of public spheres. From 2008 onwards, no further relevant documents have been produced but a revamping of the Europa portal took place and the proliferation of previous initiatives (mostly fragmented) is now refocused on social networks, audiovisual media and consultations.

The growing presence of European Institutions on social networks reflect their perceived utility for governments to communicate with citizens and have increasingly involved attempts to identify key opinion-makers and issues of salience for European citizens in order to connect networks of strong and segmented publics. In parallel, the role of the media in pan-European programmes was reinforced in 2008 when print, audiovisual and electronic media were presented as means to encourage the formation of a European Public Sphere or prepare the ground for unleashing the participatory dynamics of European citizens in European politics.

To simplify the timeline, the evolution of eParticipation and citizen participation can be conceptualized as follows. Before 1992, the rationale was bestowing legal rights by delivering effective policies to citizens. From the TEU there was a shift of emphasis towards making the Union more transparent to its citizens through information provision. Transparency and accountability were promoted from 2000 onwards, while after 2005, linking institutions with citizens became a key concern (Dalakiouridou et al., 2012). Citizen empowerment was emphasized from around 2007, and the older concepts of accountability and proximity underwent a shift in meaning (Maiani, 2011; Dalakiouridou et al., 2009).

The main impetus for this evolution has been the perceived degree of disengagement of European citizens with regard to participation in European politics. The first legitimacy crisis was identified in 1992 at the time of the TEU. Subsequent Eurobarometer surveys (2006) indicated distrust towards a complex system to deliver effective policies. A recent Eurobarometer (European Commission, 2010) indicated that the personal concerns of Europeans are dominated primarily by economic issues (prices, unemployment, healthcare and pension systems) and not necessarily European-wide issues. This finding highlights the difficult position of the EU if "salient political rhetoric and increased opportunities to participate do not as a rule, generate more intensive public deliberation or greater public trust, identity and legitimacy, particularly where the issues are not highly salient" (Moravsic 2006; 2004).

Theoretical Understanding

In this section we present various dimensions that are essential for analyzing eParticipation initiatives. These include parameters generated by democracy and governance theory such as participation rationale and governance mode. They also include a multi-layered analytical framework that can be used for the analysis of eParticipation initiatives (Smith et al., 2011).

Our study took the view that any framework for analyzing or evaluating eParticipation needs to be calibrated against existing democratic institutional arrangements and normative ideals about political and social participation, as the intended benefits and possible democratic effects of participation will differ in different modes of governance. If what counts as political participation is not a constant (Schwarz 1984), it is crucial to identify the mode(s) of participation that any given eParticipation initiative aims to generate, and to assess how well or badly this corresponds to the relevant mode(s) of governance. As we have argued in more detail elsewhere (Smith & Dalakiouridou, 2009; Smith, 2009), the dominant mode of governance in the EU combines hierarchical elements, notably the European Parliament, with a more pronounced network modus operandi centred on the committees and expert groups used extensively in policy formulation by the European Commission, and in some instances (e.g. elections and referenda) it also appeals to a market mode of governance. For example, structures of functional representation – a type of 'segmented public' (Eriksen, 2007) – fulfil a crucial role in EU policy-making, and hence they are likely to be an important target for efforts to democratise representative democracy and bureaucratic decision-making in the EU. On the other hand, the idea of a single, coherent and permeable, European public sphere, while propagated by EU policy documents (e.g. the 2007 Communicating Europe in Partnership document, the 2006 White Paper on a European Communication Policy, or the 2005 Plan-D for Democracy), has little grounding in actors' social and political experience (Eriksen, 2007; Bader, 2008; Bärenreuter et al., 2008).

Based on such an analysis, the rationale for participation at the EU level is closely tied to problem-solving through strong and segmented publics such as the European Parliament, the committee system and the organized political, economic and social interests that engage directly with the EU administration. But it can also be argued that the longer-term health of the EU as a democratic regime depends on popular participation in problem-*framing* (i.e. in defining the European project itself), and hence on the capacity of the political system to tap into innovative ideas that may surface on the margins of the public sphere. This means that in addition to a problem-solving rationale, European eParticipation also fulfils a relegitimizing rationale (particularly in response to the 'democratic deficit' commonly imputed to the EU) as well as a decoupling rationale emphasising the intrinsic benefits of participation and the tendency of contemporary social movements to "uncoupl[e] themselves from the 'big' political problems in favour of a variety of 'small' projects of local involvement" (Bang & Dyrberg, 2003, p. 234). In another paper we used a typology of governance modes and participation rationales to assess the EU institutions' eParticipation policies (Dalakiouridou et al., 2012) and found that most of the documents analyzed have a legitimizing and problem-solving role while some network elements of governance began to frame vertical and horizontal accountability spaces.

Our analytical framework combines insights from earlier work in the eParticipation field (e.g. Macintosh & Whyte, 2008; Fagan et al., 2006) with logical models already used for policy analysis at the European level (e.g. Millard, 2008; European Commission, 2009) underpinned by a realist evaluation philosophy intended to uncover the theories embedded in policies, programs or projects in order to get at the assumptions about how an initiative is supposed to work and assess the extent to which the moderators of a program's success or failure can be manipulated (Pawson, 2006)[2]. The framework attempts to identify the key variables for studying eParticipation, distinguishing between factors which lie at least partly within the control of the stakeholders in an eParticipation initiative and factors which are largely external and differentiating aspects of eParticipation which are aligned with the goal-setting strategic rationality of a governance regime from those aspects of eParticipation which are relatively insulated from these power relations. It uses an impact assessment framework distinguishing between outputs, outcomes and impacts, and employs the notion of an intervention logic to specify the types of actions necessary to successfully initiate and manage the participation process. Its multi-layered character is intended to prompt policy makers to consider conceptual links to high-level policy goals, culturally-specific understandings of eParticipation and the chain of transformations which condition long-term impacts.

Figure 1 outlines the model's key components, showing how outputs are transformed into outcomes, and in turn into impacts, via a series of intervention logics, and how these transformations are co-determined by interaction with moderators, here termed external drivers and barriers.

The text embedded in Figure 1 is, in some cases, sufficient to explain the specific level or intervention, but for clarity more detail is provided here.

Considering external factors is important to understand the likely or potential impact of eParticipation processes. They include factors such as the structure of the governance regime, political culture, legal and policy environment, technological infrastructure, socio-economic and cultural environment.

The potential impacts or general objectives of eParticipation can be viewed from either a policy or a societal perspective. In many cases the objectives are not specific to eParticipation, but articulated as public policy goals and values to which the specific objectives can contribute. The intervention logic necessary to achieve wider impacts concerns structuration effects (interaction between an intervention and the broader institutions in which it is embedded) and strategic planning (actions such as foresight planning, policy and strategy development, financial allocation, leadership and commitment, legislation and research and evaluation). Both shape the opportunity structure for continued eParticipation.

Specific objectives refer primarily to usage of the tool and costs/benefits for different affected groups. In some cases the achievement of a set of eParticipation objectives for one group (e.g. citizens) may result in the non-achievement of a different set of eParticipation objectives for another

Figure 1. eParticipation analytical framework (from Millard et al, 2009)

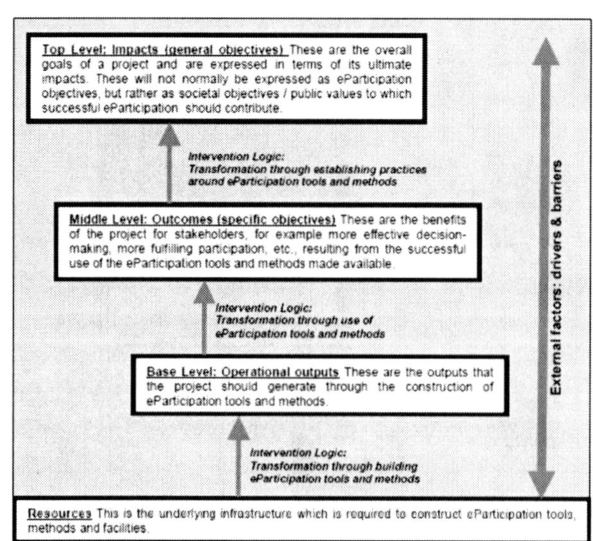

group (e.g. civil servants or organized interests). The intervention logic necessary to transform outputs into outcomes concerns the development of practices, use values and relationships.

Operational outputs comprise working and available hardware, software and applications, organizational outputs and eParticipation process outputs such as awareness raising campaigns or data from the eParticipation process. The intervention logic necessary to transform raw materials into outputs centers on the acquisition and mobilization of the materials and on process design, including decisions about what participation activities are intended.

Finally, raw materials for eParticipation projects can include ICT infrastructure, human and organizational resources, materials and facilities, finance and investments of time.

The three levels are offset from each other to emphasize that the achievement of objectives at one level does not necessarily translate into the achievement of objectives at the level above. Such translation depends on the successful implementation of the intervention logic, which does not necessarily take place. For example, the successful development of ICT tools may not result in successful usage of those tools if users do not have the appropriate skills or incentives.

Survey of eParticipation Initiatives

Our survey of eParticipation initiatives identified 255 initiatives originating from 22 different countries (detailed results in Panopoulou et al., 2009, and Millard et al., 2009). These initiatives have international[3], European, transnational, regional or local scope and are offered in 34 different languages. Table 1 presents a summary of the surveyed initiatives in terms of scope and participation area (participation areas are defined according to DEMO-net, 2006)[4]. Most initiatives focus on providing information, deliberation and consultation facilities on various subjects and target the local and national levels.

Most initiatives with a European scope either offer information or provide deliberation and consultation facilities on a number of significant European issues. The vast majority offer such facilities in more than one language with the most usual being English, French and German. However, most EU-driven initiatives are offered in all EU official languages; even though not all languages are used to the same degree (e.g. big differences in user visits and posts between languages have been observed).

Most international initiatives identified are launched by non-governmental organizations and civil society organizations. Therefore, it comes

Table 1. Initiatives per participation area and scope

Participation level	Campaigning	Community building	Consultation	Deliberation	Electioneering	Information Provision	Mediation	Polling	Voting	Total
European	6	10	8	24	0	33	1	4	0	48
International	3	1	0	3	0	9	0	0	0	11
Transnational	0	0	0	2	0	0	0	0	0	2
National	10	10	23	43	2	34	0	15	6	76
Regional	4	5	10	17	0	20	1	2	1	33
Local	6	5	36	54	0	51	4	9	6	85
Total	29	31	77	143	2	147	6	30	13	255

as no surprise that they mainly focus on information provision and campaigning, and less on deliberation and community building/collaborative activities.

The transnational level is the least frequent level of participation in Europe, potentially because EU-driven initiatives cover relevant cross-border, multi-national participation needs. Our survey identified two transnational eParticipation cases, both focusing on deliberation activities.

At the local, regional and national levels it is again observed that most initiatives focus on information provision, deliberation and consultation, while some participation areas, i.e. voting, electioneering and polling, are more usual at these narrower levels than in wider, i.e. European, ones.

SOLUTIONS AND RECOMMENDATIONS

Based on the analysis above, combined with an extensive engagement process with eParticipation researchers, practitioners and policy makers that included three workshops, an open online consultation and regular feedback from peer reviewers, the paper concludes by briefly outlining a number of recommendations of four main types (Millard et al., 2009):

1. **eParticipation policy framework:** It is important to initiate actions which can help mainstream eParticipation as part of a concerted "open engagement policy," fully embedded into all aspects of the overall policy architecture, whilst learning from other global players about what works and what does not and under which circumstances.
2. **eParticipation of citizens in public policy:** The most challenging issue is how to better engage citizens as individuals, communities, and through interest groups. Public authorities could meet this challenge by creating cross institutional, simple and effective eParticipation systems, so that users do not have to apply different tools and approaches dependent on the institution being addressed. For example, a coordinated horizontal "Service for Public Engagement" might be established at national or supra-national level, with appropriate political support to ensure its effectiveness and that citizen input is taken seriously, as well as seen to be so. Direct cooperation with public, private and civil actors and electronic listening to the public-domain internet "buzz" are also crucial to supporting citizen participation.
3. **eParticipation across national borders and by organized groups:** eParticipation could support the networks of organized groups in decision- and policy-making processes opening them up to new groups and interests. In Europe, for example, identifying and supporting existing cross-border communities and interest groups and providing incentives for European Parliamentarians and other professional communities to adopt eParticipation, could help move the European policy-building network to a more effective, open and transparent system.
4. **eParticipation implementation and research:** A cross-institutional eParticipation research and implementation agenda should be established to counter the current fragmentation which wastes resources and effort, and mitigates useful learning at all levels. It is also important to highlight and promote exceptional initiatives to ensure wider take-up and inspiration, as well as build comparable monitoring and evaluation into all funded initiatives. There should be greater focus on the use of social media, on inclusion as well as on data protection, privacy and security in order to improve trust in online systems. Close linking to relevant policy objectives is also critical.

FUTURE RESEARCH DIRECTIONS

Stemming from the analysis above, two trends can be extrapolated: on the one hand the increasing embedding of eParticipation in social networking tools and the potential this has for public sphere creation, and on the other hand the moderating effect of particular modes of governance.

Social networking sites have proliferated as eParticipation practitioners try to reach more people with minimum investments (Boyd, 2007). Social networks have started to attract considerable attention from policy makers in the context of eParticipation initiatives, as a tool to attract the wider public, especially younger groups. According to Eurostat (2010), eight in ten young internet users use social networking sites and this percentage is about 40% in 25-54 age group.

The potential of this new strand of research can be assessed against the convergence of public spheres and pronounced changes in social capital. For instance, Castells (2007) asserts that in new online communication spaces, communication networks tend to converge and consequently the public sphere shifts from institutional settings to an enabled communication space. In the light of evidence that personal networks, can foster social capital (offline or online) and encourage political engagement (Lake & Huckfeldt, 1998; Putnam, 2000; Bojović & Mrakjić, 2011), eParticipation promises to reach wider publics. But new methodologies and models are needed to elucidate the degree that eParticipation through social networks can spur citizen participation that can be effectively used in governance, as these tools have often been trivialized as spaces for distantiated and isolated self-expression.

The type of governance regime moderates the eParticipation process as it underlies preconditions, rationale, objectives and benefits, and indicates relevant stakeholders and beneficiaries of eParticipation. Network governance has gained prominence at the local/regional and the supranational scale in recent decades, partly in response to the challenges of an increasingly knowledge- and information-based society (Smith, 2009). Network governance, as distinct from hierarchies and markets, creates strong and segmented publics, targets experts and/or citizens and connects networks horizontally. In a network governance regime such as the European Union, eParticipation could deliver benefits for better governance in three broad directions: making the 'strong publics' of policy networks more accessible to new participants; encouraging and protecting independent or oppositional public enclaves where alternative discourses can emerge and develop; and improving the connectivity of the system as a whole (Smith, 2009). This does not provide a recipe for the selection or configuration of particular tools, but it affects the expectations of participants, the atmosphere within which use patterns develop and the outcomes that it would be most relevant to evaluate.

CONCLUSION

eParticipation initiatives are not immune from the challenges of citizen disengagement and considerations of efficiency, but a belief remains that ICT can enhance and broaden the democratic process, increase institutional transparency and dialogue with citizens and encourage new forms of participation.

This chapter has contributed towards a firmer conceptually- and empirically-grounded understanding of eParticipation concepts and processes by presenting the state of play of eParticipation in the European Union. Relevant policy considerations were explored to help understand how eParticipation is actually perceived under an institutional prism. The role of policy and legislation was to emphasize structures of functional representation, support dialogue, association and segmented publics and encourage an open communication policy on behalf of the institutions based on transparency, accountability, and openness. ICT-enhanced citizen participation emerged as a priority for citizen engagement in late 2006.

We also proposed a conceptual framework for analysing eParticipation initiatives. This framework broadens the scope of conventional impact assessment by incorporating typologies of governance mode and participation rationale. Current democratic and institutional arrangements have been taken into account to enable a concrete conceptualization of specific processes and output variables. The framework illustrates the transformation of outputs to outcomes and in turn into impacts through intervention logics to enable understanding of the temporal and contextual aspects of eParticipation.

In the EU, it has been argued, ''*the civic-institutional infrastructure is deficient*'' and the realm of European politics does not leave room for self-regulating citizens (Eriksen & Fossum, 2004, p. 19). In addition, there is no evidence whether the political rhetoric and increased opportunities to participate did in fact generate intensive and informed public deliberation (Dalakiouridou et al., 2011). Given only a weak commitment to citizen participation and the general failure of the EU to ensure meaningful empowerment for citizens (Flear, 2010), our findings are broadly in line with Smismans' earlier conclusion (2003) that European-level endeavours contribute to legitimacy but not active citizenship. Although important preconditions for participation such as openness, transparency and accountability exist, citizen participation is viewed through the prism of "legitimization" more than as an input to processes of government. Nevertheless, the "legitimacy-enhancing deliberation" rationale (Fung, 2006) that seems to be in place in the EU reveals the intention to rectify one of the important problems of democratic governance by creating forums that are more inclusive and communicative.

In terms of practice, our survey of 255 eParticipation initiatives throughout Europe revealed the prominence of an information-provision rationale in most cases. Although deliberation and consultation were also important considerations for many initiatives, we concluded that eParticipation potential had not been fully harnessed, as information availability, information exchanges, accountability and transparency are assessed as the main benefits.

Finally, we outlined several recommendations for strengthening the overall policy context for eParticipation, better engaging citizens and informal interest groups, supporting and widening the network of organized groups participating and focusing eParticipation research and implementation to maximise its effectiveness and impact.

ACKNOWLEDGMENT

Part of this study was financed by the European Union under the Study and supply of services on the development of eParticipation in the EU (European eParticipation Study).

REFERENCES

Bader, V. (2008). Eurospheres? Fragmented and stratified or integrated and fair? A conceptual and pre-theoretical mapping exercise. *Eurosphere working paper 9*. Retrieved from http://www.eurosphere.uib.no/knowledgebase/wpsdocs/Eurosphere_Working_Paper_9_Bader.pdf

Bang, H., & Dyrberg, T. (2003). Governing at close range: demo-elites and lay people. In Bang, H. (Ed.), *Governance as social and political communication* (pp. 222–240). Manchester: Manchester University Press.

Bärenreuter, C., Brüll, C., Mokre, M., & Wahl-Jorgensen, K. (2008). An overview of research on the European public sphere. *Eurosphere working paper 3*. Retrieved from http://eurospheres.org/files/2010/08/Eurosphere_Working_Paper_3_Barenreuter_etal.pdf

Blumler, J. G., & Gurevitch, M. (2001). The new media and our political communication discontents: Democratizing cyberspace. *Information Communication and Society*, *4*(1), 1–13.

Bojović, D., & Mrakjić, V. (2011). *The role of social networks in environmental eParticipation*. Paper presented at ESEE 2011 conference, Advancing Ecological economics, theory and practice. Retrieved from http://www.esee2011.org/registration/fullpapers/esee2011_3dd942_1_1304865599_6312_2236.pdf

Boyd, D. M., & Ellison, N. B. (2007). Social network sites: Definition, history, and scholarship. *Journal of Computer-Mediated Communication*, *13*(1), 16–31. doi:10.1111/j.1083-6101.2007.00393.x.

Castells, M. (2007). Communication, power and counter-power in the network society. *International Journal of Communication*, *1*, 238–266.

Coleman, S., & Shane, P. (Eds.). (2012). *Connecting democracy online consultation and the flow of political communication*. Cambridge, MA: MIT Press.

Dahlgren, P. (2005). The Internet, public spheres, and political communication: Dispersion and deliberation. *Political Communication*, *22*(2), 147–162. Retrieved from http://www.ingentaconnect.com/content/routledg/upcp;jsessionid=4kbt0wnfdtvhf.alice doi:10.1080/10584600590933160.

Dalakiouridou, E., Smith, S., Tambouris, E., & Tarabanis, K. (2012). eParticipation policies and initiatives in the European Union Institutions. *Social Science Computer Review*, *30*(3), 297–323. doi:10.1177/0894439311413436.

Dalakiouridou, E., Tambouris, E., & Tarabanis, K. (2009). Mapping the state of play in eParticipation in the EU. *European eParticipation study*, Deliverable D1.4.c. Retrieved from http://islab.uom.gr/eP/

Dryzek, J. S. (2000). *Deliberative democracy and beyond. Liberals, critics, contestations*. New York: Oxford University Press.

Dutton, W. H. (1992). Political science research on teledemocracy. *Social Science Computer Review*, *10*(4), 505–522. doi:10.1177/089443939201000405.

Eriksen, E. (2007). Conceptualising European public spheres. General, segmented and strong publics. In Fossum, J., & Schlesinger, P. (Eds.), *The European Union and the public sphere: a communicative space in the making?* (pp. 23–43). London: Routledge.

Eurobarometer. (2006). *EU communication and the citizens*. September/October. Retrieved from http://ec.europa.eu/public_opinion/flash/fl_189b_en.pdf and http://ec.europa.eu/public_opinion/flash/fl_189a_en.pdf

European Commision. (2010). Internet usage in 2010-households and individuals. *Eurostat*, data in focus, 50/2010. Retrieved from http://epp.eurostat.ec.europa.eu/cache/ITY_OFFPUB/KS-QA-10-050/EN/KS-QA-10-050-EN.PDF

European Commission. (2000). *Reforming the commission, a white paper – Part II*. COM(2000) 200, Brussels: CEC.

European Commission. (2001). *European governance. A white paper*. COM(2001) 428 final, Brussels: CEC.

European Commission. (2001). *A new framework for co-operation on activities concerning the information and communication policy of the European Union. COM(2001) 354*. Brussels: CEC.

European Commission. (2002). *General principles and minimum standards for consultation of interested parties by the Commission. COM(2002) 704*. Brussels: CEC.

European Commission. (2005). *Action plan to improve communicating Europe by the commission*. Retrieved from http://ec.europa.eu/dgs/communication/pdf/communication_com_en.pdf

European Commission. (2005). *The Commission's contribution to the period of reflection and beyond: Plan-D for democracy, dialogue and debate. COM(2005) 494*. Brussels: CEC.

European Commission. (2006). *White paper on a European communication policy*. COM(2006) 35, Brussels: CEC European Commission. (2006). *Green paper on the proposal of the European transparency initiative*. COM(2006) 194, Brussels: CEC.

European Commission. (2007). *Communicating Europe in partnership. COM(2007) 568*. Brussels: CEC.

European Commission. (2007). *Communicating about Europe via the Internet, engaging the citizens. SEC(2007) 1742*. Brussels: CEC.

European Commission. (2008). *Communicating Europe through audiovisual media. SEC(2008) 506/2*. Brussels: CEC.

European Commission. (2008). *Debate Europe – building on the experience of Plan D for democracy, dialogue and debate. COM(2008) 158/4*. Brussels: CEC.

European Commission. (2009). *Impact assessment guidelines. SEC(2009) 92*. Brussels: CEC.

European Parliament & Council of the European Union. (2011, February 16). Regulation No. 211/2100 of 16 February 2011 on the citizens' initiative. OJ L 65/1

Fagan, G. Honor, Newman, D., McCusker, P., & Murray, M. (2006). *E-consultation: Evaluating appropriate technologies and processes for citizens' participation in public policy*. Final Report for the HEA. Retrieved from http://www.nuim.ie/nirsa/econsult/

Fishkin, J. S. (1991). *Democracy and deliberation*. New Haven, CT: Yale University Press.

Flear, M., & Vakulenko, A. (2010). A human rights perspective on citizen participation in the EU's governance of new technologies. *Human Rights Law Review*, *10*(4), 661–688. doi:10.1093/hrlr/ngq039.

Hacker, & van Dijk. (2000). What is digital democracy? In K. L. Hacker and J. van Dijk. (Eds.), *Digital democracy issues of theory and practice*. London: Sage Publications.

Hay, C. (2007). *Why we hate politics*. Cambridge, UK: Polity Press.

Lake, R., & Huckfeldt, R. (1998). Social capital, social networks and political participation. *Political Psychology*, *19*(3), 567–583. doi:10.1111/0162-895X.00118.

Macintosh, A. (2004). Characterizing e-participation in policy-making. *Proceedings of the 37th Annual Hawaii International Conference on System Sciences (HICSS-37)*, USA (pp.117-12). ISBN: 0-7695-2056-1.

Macintosh, A., Coleman, S., & Schneeberger, A. (2009). eParticipation: The research gaps. In A. Macintosh & E. Tambouris (Eds.), *Electronic participation: Proceedings of First International Conference, ePart 2009, LNCS 5694* (pp.1-11). Germany: Springer-Verlag. ISSN 0302-9743.

Macintosh, A., & Whyte, A. (2008). Towards an evaluation framework for eparticipation. *Transforming Government: People. Process & Policy*, *2*(1), 16–30.

Maiani, F. (2011). Citizen participation and the Lisbon Treaty: A legal perspective. *Studies in Public policy, 484*, 1-24.

Millard, J. (2008). eGovernment measurement for policy makers. *European Journal of ePractice*, 4. Efficiency and Effectiveness. Retrieved from http://www.epractice.eu

Millard, J., Nielsen, M. M., Warren, R., Smith, S., Macintosh, A., Tarabanis, K., & Parisopoulos, K. (2009). European eparticipation summary report. Retrieved from http://islab.uom.gr/eP/index.php?option=com_docman&task=cat_view&gid=36&&Itemid=82

Moravsik, A. (2004). Is there a "Democratic Deficit" in world politics? A framework for analysis. *Government and Opposition*, *39*(2), 336–363. doi:10.1111/j.1477-7053.2004.00126.x.

Moravsik, A. (2006). What can we learn from the collapse of the European constitutional project? A symposium. *Politische Vierteljahresschrift*, *47*(2), 219–241. doi:10.1007/s11615-006-0037-7.

Panopoulou, E., Tambouris, E., & Tarabanis, K. (2009). eParticipation initiatives: How is Europe progressing? *European Journal of ePractice*, 7. Retrieved from http://www.epractice.eu/en/document/287931

Pawson, R. (2006). *Evidence-based policy: A realist perspective*. London: Sage.

Plan D-Wider and deeper Debate on Europe. (2006). SeC (2006)1553. Brussels: Information Note form Vice President Wallstom to the Commission

Pratchett, L., & Krimmer, R. (2005). The coming of e-democracy. *International Journal of Electronic Government Research*, *1*(3).

Putnam, R. (2000). *Bowling alone: The collapse and revival of american community*. New York: Simon & Schuster. doi:10.1145/358916.361990.

Schwartz, J. D. (1984). Participation and multisubjective understanding: An interpretivist approach to the study of political participation. *The Journal of Politics*, *46*, 1117–1141. doi:10.2307/2131245.

Smismans, S. (2003). European civil society: Shaped by discourses and institutional interests. *European Law Journal*, *482*(9), 499–503.

Smith, S. (2009). Main benefits of eParticipation developments in the EU – a contextualisation with reference to the EU governance regime and the European public sphere. *European eParticipation study*, Deliverable 1.3c. Retrieved from http://islab.uom.gr/eP/

Smith, S., & Dalakiouridou, E. (2009). Contextualising public (e)Participation in the governance of the European Union. *European Journal of ePractice*, 7. Retrieved from http://www.epractice.eu/en/document/287931

Smith, S., Macintosh, A., & Millard, J. (2011). A three-layered framework for evaluating eParticipation. *International Journal of Electronic Governance*, *4*(4), 304–321. doi:10.1504/IJEG.2011.046013.

Stoker, G. (2006). *Why politics matters: Making democracy work*. Basingstoke: Palgrave Macmillan.

Tambouris, E., Liotas, N., & Tarabanis, K. (2007). A framework for assessing eparticipation projects and tools. In *Proc. 40th Int. Conf. on System Sciences*, Hawaii, 2007, (pp.90a).

Treaty establishing a Constitution for Europe. (2004). *Official Journal of the European Union, 310.*

Treaty of Amsterdam. (1997). Official Journal of the European Union, 340..

Treaty of Lisbon (Treaty on the Functioning of the European Union). (2007). Official Journal of the European Union, 306..

Treaty of Nice. (2001). Official Journal of the European Union, 80..

Treaty on the European Union-TEU. (1992). Official Journal of the European Union, 224..

Weber, L., Loumakis, A., & Bergman, J. (2003). Who participates and why? An analysis of citizens on the internet and the mass public. *Social Science Computer Review*, *21*(1), 25–32. doi:10.1177/0894439302238969.

ADDITIONAL READING

Chadwick, A. (2009). Web 2.0: New challenges for the study of e-democracy in an era of informational exuberance. *A Journal of Law and Policy for the Information Society*, *5*(1), 9-41.

Chappelet, J.-L., Glassey, O., Janssen, M., Macintosh, A., Scholl, J., Tambouris, E., & Wimmer, M. A. (Eds.). (2010). *Electronic government and electronic participation: Joint Proceedings of Ongoing Research and Projects of IFIP EGOV and ePart 2010*. Linz, PA: Trauner Druck.

Heritier, A. (2003). New modes of governance in Europe: Increasing political capacity and policy effective-ness? In Borzel, T. A., & Cichowski, R. (Eds.), *The state of the European Union – Law, politics, and society* (pp. 105–126). Oxford: Oxford University Press.

Hirzalla, F., Van Zoonen, L., & De Ridder, J. (2010). Internet use and political participation: Reflections on the mobilization/normalization controversy. *The Information Society*, *27*(1), 1–15. doi:10.1080/01972243.2011.534360.

Janssen, M., Macintosh, A., Scholl, J., Tambouris, E., Wimmer, M. A., de Bruijn, H., & Tan, Y.-H. (Eds.). (2011). *Electronic government and electronic participation: Joint Proceedings of Ongoing Research and Projects of IFIP EGOV and ePart 2011*. Linz, PA: Trauner Druck.

Kies, R. (2010). *Promises and limits of web-deliberation*. Wiltshire: Palgrave Macmillan.

Macintosh, A., & Tambouris, E. (Eds.). (2009). *Electronic participation: First International Conference, ePart 2009, Lecture Notes in Computer Science, 5694*. PA: Springer.

Mandarino, L., Meenar, M., & Cristopher, S. (2010). Building social capital in the digital age of civic engagement. *Journal of Planning Literature*, *25*(2), 123–135. doi:10.1177/0885412210394102.

Tambouris, E., & Macintosh, A. (Eds.). (2009). *Electronic participation: Proceedings of Ongoing Research, General Development Issues and Projects of ePart 2009*. Linz, PA: Trauner Druck.

Tambouris, E., Macintosh, A., & de Bruijn, H. (Eds.). (2011). *Electronic participation: Third IFIP WG 8.5 International Conference, ePart 2011, Lecture Notes in Computer Science, 6847*. PA: Springer

Tambouris, E., Macintosh, A., & Glassey, O. (Eds.). (2010). *Electronic participation: Second IFIP WG 8.5 International Conference, ePart 2010, Lecture Notes in Computer Science, 6229*. PA: Springer

ENDNOTES

1. For more information on public spheres, see the Eurosphere project website: http://www.eurosphere.uib.no/ and the AIM project's EPS database: http://www.aim-project.net/index1e85.html?id=54.
2. This is described in more detail in Smith et al., 2011.
3. Including international initiatives may at first seem contradictory to the European scope of our survey. However, the number of these cases is limited and they were selected due to the high-profile of the organizations supporting them (e.g. Greenpeace, Aarhus Clearinghouse).

4. Campaigning: ICT in protest, lobbying, petitioning and other forms of collective action (except election campaigns, covered under electioneering area).
Community Building/Collaborative Environments: ICT to support individuals coming together to form communities, to progress shared agendas and to shape and empower such communities.
Consultation: ICT in official initiatives by public or private agencies to allow individuals and groups to contribute their opinion, either privately or publicly, on specific issues.
Deliberation: ICT to support virtual, small and large-group discussions, allowing reflection and consideration of issues. In our survey deliberation also includes discussion and consideration of issues in an unstructured and non-moderated manner.
Electioneering: ICT to support politicians, political parties and lobbyists in the context of election campaigns.
Information Provision: ICT to structure, represent and manage information in participation contexts.
Mediation: ICT to resolve disputes or conflicts in an online context.
Polling: ICT to measure public opinion and sentiment.
Voting: ICT in the context of public voting in elections, referenda or local plebiscites.

Compilation of References

Abdul Karim, M. R., & Mohd Khalid, N. (2003). E-government in Malaysia. Kuala Lumpur: Pelanduk Publications (M) Sdn. Bhd.

Abdul Karim, M. R. (1999). *Reengineering the public service leadership and change in an electronic age. Subang Jaya Selangor: Pelanduk Publications (M).* Sdn. Bhd.

Abdullah, H.Z., Kaliannan, M., Mohamed Ali, A.J., & Bakar, A.N. (2006). eGoverment in evolution an evaluation survey of government websites in Malaysia. *e-Gov,* 8-12.

Abhijit, J. (2003). Performance paradox: Information technology investments and administrative performance in the case of the 50 U.S. state governments. In *Proceedings of the Twenty Fourth International Conference on Information Systems* (pp. 389-400). Retrieved from http://aisel.aisnet.org/icis2003/33

Accenture. (2003). *eGovernment leadership report: The citizen's view.* Retrieved May 11, 2012, from http://www.accenture.com/us-en/Pages/insight-egovernment-2003-summary.aspx

Adams, N., Stubbs, V., & Woods, V. (2005). Psychological barriers to Internet usage among older adults in the U.K. *Medical Informatics and the Internet in Medicine, 30*(1), 3–17. doi:10.1080/14639230500066876 PMID:16036626.

AGIMO. (2009). *Engage. Getting on with Government 2.0.* Report of the Government 2.0 Taskforce. Australian Government Information Management Office. Retrieved September 15, 2010, from www.finance.gov.au

Ahmad, M. B. H. J. (2006). Implementation of electronic government in Malaysia: The status and potential for better service to the public. *Public Sector ICT Management Review, 1*(1), 1–9.

Ahmed, M. A. (2008). Developing parliamentary web portals for citizens, MPs and related groups — Challenges and proposed solutions. *IEEE International Symposium on Technology and Society,* 26-28 June 2008, 1-7, Fredericton, NB (Online Xplore).

Akkaya, C., Wolf, P., & Krcmar, H. (2012). Factors influencing citizen adoption of e-government services: A cross-cultural comparison. Research in progress presented at *the 45th Hawaii International Conference on System Sciences.*

Akman, I., Yazici, A., Mishra, A., & Arifoglu, A. (2005). E-Government: A global view and an empirical evaluation of some attributes of citizens. *Government Information Quarterly, 22*(2), 239–257. doi:10.1016/j.giq.2004.12.001.

Alalwan, J., & Thomas, M. A. (2011). A holistic framework to evaluate e-government systems. In *AMCIS 2011 Proceedings.* Retrieved from http://aisel.aisnet.org/amcis2011_submissions/67

Alford, J., & O'Flynn, J. (2009). Making sense of public value: Concepts, critiques and emergent meanings. International Journal of Public Administration, 32(3,4), 171–191.

Alford, J. (2002). Defining the client in the public sector: A social-exchange perspective. *Public Administration Review, 62*(3), 337–346. doi:10.1111/1540-6210.00183.

Alghamdi, I. A., Goodwin, R., & Rampersad, S. (2011). E-government readiness assessment for government organizations in developing countries. *Computer and Information Science, 4*(3), 3–17. doi:10.5539/cis.v4n3p3.

Al-Hadidi, A., & Rezgui, Y. (2009). *Critical success factors for the adoption and diffusion of m-government services: A literature review*. Paper presented at the 9th European Conference on e-Government.

Ali, A., & Bahroom, L. (2008). Integrated e-learning at Open University Malaysia. *Public Sector ICT Management Review*, *2*(2), 33–39.

Al-khamayseh, S., Lawrence, E., & Zmijewska, A. (2006). Towards understanding success factors in interactive mobile government. *ColleCTeR Europe*, *2006*, 129.

Alkhatib, S. (2012). IRAS says 78% of taxpayers have filed tax returns. Retrieved September 14, 2012, from http://www.channelnewsasia.com/stories/singaporelocalnews/view/1050329/1/.html

Al-Omari, A., & Al-Omari, H. (2006). E-Government readiness assessment model. *Journal of Computer Science*, *2*, 841–845. doi:10.3844/jcssp.2006.841.845.

Alonso, A. L. (2009). E-Participation and local governance: A case study. *Theoretical and Empirical Researches in Urban Management*, *3*(12), 1–14.

Alonso, S., Keane, J., & Merkel, W. (2011). *The future of representative democracy*. Cambridge: Cambridge Press. doi:10.1017/CBO9780511770883.

Alshawi, S., & Alalwany, H. (2009). E-government evaluation: Citizen's perspective in developing countries. *Information Technology for Development*, *15*(3), 193–208. doi:10.1002/itdj.20125.

Al-Sobhi, F., Weerakkody, V., & Al-Shafi, S. (2010). The role of intermediaries in facilitating egovernment diffusion in Saudi Arabia. *Proceedings of the European and Mediterranean Conference on Information Systems*, 1-17.

Al-Sobhi, F., Weerakkody, V., & El-Haddadeh, R. (2012). Building trust in e-government adoption through an intermediary channel. *International Journal of Electronic Government Research*, *8*(2), 91–106. doi:10.4018/jegr.2012040105.

Altameem, T., Zairi, M., & Alshawi, S. (2006). Critical success factors of e-government: A proposed model for e-government implementation. *Proc. Innovations in Information Technology Conference*. IEEE. Retrieved from http://ieeexplore.ieee.org/stamp/stamp.jsp?tp=&arnumber=4085489

Alter, S. (2002). *Information systems: The foundation of e-business* (4th ed.). New Jersey: Pearson Education, Inc..

Altman, D. (2002). Prospects for e-government in Latin America: Satisfaction with democracy, social accountability and direct democracy. *International Review of Public Administration*, *7*, 201–219.

Altman, D. (2011). *Direct democracy worldwide*. Cambridge: Cambridge Press.

Aman, A., & Kasimin, H. (2011). E-procurement implementation: A case of Malaysia government. *Transforming Government: People. Process and Policy*, *5*(4), 330–344.

American Library Association. (2010). *A perfect storm brewing: Budget cuts threaten public library services at time of increased demand.* Chicago, IL: American Library Association. Retrieved from http://www.ala.org/ala/research/initiatives/plftas/issuesbriefs/issuebrief_perfectstorm.pdf

Angeles, R., Corritore, C. L., Basu, S. C., & Nath, R. (2001). Success factors for domestic and international electronic data interchange (EDI) implementation for US firms. *International Journal of Information Management*, *21*, 329–347. doi:10.1016/S0268-4012(01)00028-7.

Angelopoulos, S., Fotis, K. F., Naousa, G. N., & Papadopoulos, T. (2010). New service development in e-government: Identifying critical success factors. *Transforming Government: People. Process and Policy*, *4*(1), 95–118.

Anselm, S., & Corbin, J. (1998). *Basics of qualitative research: Techniques and procedures for developing grounded theory*. Thousand Oaks, California: Sage Publication.

Arduini, D., Belotti, F., Denni, M., Giungato, G., & Zanfei, A. (2010). Technology adoption and innovation in public services the case of e-government in Italy. *Information Economics and Policy*, *22*(3), 257–275. doi:10.1016/j.infoecopol.2009.12.007.

Arpaci, I. (2010). E-government and technological innovation in Turkey: Case studies on governmental organizations. *Transforming Government: People. Process and Policy*, *4*(1), 37–53. doi: doi:10.1108/17506161011028795.

Asiimwe, E., & Lim, N. (2010). Usability of government websites in Uganda. *Electronic. Journal of E-Government*, *8*(1), 1–12.

Atkinson, J., Black, R., & Curtis, A. (2008). Exploring the digital divide in an Australian Regional City: A case study of Albury. *The Australian Geographer*, *39*(4), 479–493. doi:10.1080/00049180802419203.

Audunson, R., Essmat, S., & Aabo, S. (2011). Public libraries: A meeting place for immigrant women? *Library & Information Science Research*, *33*, 220–227. doi:10.1016/j.lisr.2011.01.003.

Aurigi, A. (2000). Digital city or urban simulator? In Ishida, T., & Isbister, K. (Eds.), *Digital cities: Technologies, experiences, and future perspectives* (pp. 33–44). Berlin: Springer. doi:10.1007/3-540-46422-0_4.

Aurigi, A. (2005). Competing urban visions and the shaping of the digital city. *Knowledge, Technology & Policy*, *18*(1), 12–26. doi:10.1007/s12130-005-1013-z.

Aurigi, A. (2005). *Making the digital city: The early shaping of urban internet space*. Aldershot, Hampshire: Ashgate Publishing Limited.

Aurigi, A. (2006). New technologies, same dilemmas: Policy and design issues for the augmented city. *Journal of Urban Technology*, *13*(3), 5–28. doi:10.1080/10630730601145989.

Austin, J. (Ed.). (1996). *Praise, protest greet telecom bill. 1996 CQ almanac* (*Vol. LII*, pp. 3–46). Washington, DC: CQ Inc..

Australian Bureau of Statistics. (2008). *8146.0 - Household Use of Information Technology, Australia, 2007-08*. Retrieved on March 12, 2012, from http://www.abs.gov.au/AUSSTATS/abs@.nsf/0/A6CCA61410C0B988CA25768D0021D429

Australian Bureau of Statistics. (2009). *8146.0 - Household Use of Information Technology, Australia, 2008-09*. Retrieved on March 12, 2012, from http://www.abs.gov.au/AUSSTATS/abs@.nsf/0/5B15663305C2B5DCCA25796600153023?opendocument

Australian Bureau of Statistics. (2010). *Regional population growth, Australia (No. 3218.0)*. Canberra, Australian Capital Territory: Australian Bureau of Statistics.

Australian Bureau of Statistics. (2012). *8153.0 - Internet Activity, Australia, Dec 2011*. Retrieved on March 12, 2012, from http://www.abs.gov.au/ausstats/abs@.nsf/Lookup/8153.0Chapter3Dec%202011

Australian Electoral Commission. (2010). *Fact sheet: Three levels of government*. Retrieved on March 14, 2012, from http://www.aec.gov.au/About_AEC/Publications/Fact_Sheets/three_lvls.htm

Australian Government Information Management Office (AGIMO). (2006). *Responsive government a new service agenda 2006 e-government strategy*. Retrieved on April 12, 2012, from http://www.finance.gov.au/publications/2006-e-government-strategy/docs/e-gov_strategy.pdf

Australian Government Information Management Office (AGIMO). (2011). *Interacting with Government: Australians' use and satisfaction with e-government services*. Retrieved on March 25, 2012, from http://www.finance.gov.au/publications/interacting-with-government-2011/docs/interacting-with-government-2011.pdf

Australian Government. (2012). *Local government national report 2008-2009*. Department of Regional Australia, Local Government, Arts and Sport. Retrieved on July 9, 2012, from http://www.regional.gov.au/local/publications/reports/2008_2009/LGNR_2008-09.pdf

Australian Government. (2012). *Local government (councils)*, Retrieved on July 9, 2012, from http://australia.gov.au/about-australia/our-government/local-government-councils

Auyang, S. Y. (1998). *Foundations of complex-system theories in economics, evolutionary biology, and statistical physics*. New York: Cambridge University Press.

Avellaneda, C. N. (2009). Mayoral quality and local public finance. *Public Administration Review*, (May/June): 469–486. doi:10.1111/j.1540-6210.2009.01993.x.

Ayanso, A. et al. (2011). E-government readiness index: A methodology and analysis. *Government Information Quarterly*, *28*, 522–532. doi:10.1016/j.giq.2011.02.004.

Azad, B., & Faraj, S. (2008). Making e-government workable: Exploring the evolution of frames. *The Journal of Strategic Information Systems*, *17*(1), 75–98. doi:10.1016/j.jsis.2007.12.001.

Azmi, A. C., & Bee, N. G. (2010). The acceptance of the e-filing system by Malaysian taxpayers: A simplified model. *Electronic. Journal of E-Government*, *8*(1), 13–22. Retrieved from http://www.ejeg.com.

Backhouse, J. (2007). e-Democracy in Australia: The challenge of evolving a successful model. *The Electronic. Journal of E-Government*, *5*(2), 107–116.

Bader, V. (2008). Eurospheres? Fragmented and stratified or integrated and fair? A conceptual and pre-theoretical mapping exercise. *Eurosphere working paper 9*. Retrieved from http://www.eurosphere.uib.no/knowledgebase/wps-docs/Eurosphere_Working_Paper_9_Bader.pdf

Bailey, C., & Singleton, R. (2010). *National survey of social media use in state government*. Lexington: NASCIO.

Bakry, S. H. (2004). Development of e-Government: A STOPE view. *International Journal of Network Management*, *14*(5), 339–350. doi:10.1002/nem.529.

Bang, H., & Dyrberg, T. (2003). Governing at close range: demo-elites and lay people. In Bang, H. (Ed.), *Governance as social and political communication* (pp. 222–240). Manchester: Manchester University Press.

Bannister, F. (2002). Citizen centricity: A model of IS value in public administration. *Electronic Journal of Information Systems Evaluation, 5*(2).

Bannister, F. (2003). Deep e-government. *EGPA 2004 Annual Conference*. Slovenia. Retrieved May 11, 2012, from http://scholar.google.com.hk/scholar_url?hl=zh-CN&q=http://citeseerx.ist.psu.edu/viewdoc/download%3Fdoi%3D10.1.1.118.1451%26rep%3Drep1%26type%3Dpdf&sa=X&scisig=AAGBfm1gZi5rQWXIc-O-ggj9xs_mikCFEg&oi=scholarr&ei=XpOtT_rFPK2tiQeMyK3sCA&ved=0CBwQgAMoATAA

Barber, B. R. (1984). *Strong democracy: Participatory politics for a new age*. Berkeley, California: University of California Press.

Barber, B. R. (1998). Three scenarios for the future of technology and democracy. *Political Science Quarterly*, *113*, 573–589. doi:10.2307/2658245.

Bärenreuter, C., Brüll, C., Mokre, M., & Wahl-Jorgensen, K. (2008). An overview of research on the European public sphere. *Eurosphere working paper 3*. Retrieved from http://eurospheres.org/files/2010/08/Eurosphere_Working_Paper_3_Barenreuter_etal.pdf

Barki, H., Rivard, S., & Talbot, J. (1993). Toward an assessment of software development risk. *Journal of Management Information Systems*, *10*(2), 203–223. Retrieved from http://dl.acm.org/citation.cfm?id=1189679.

Bar, M., Aminoff, E., Mason, M., & Fenske, M. (2007). The Units of tought. *Hippocampus*, *17*(6), 420–428. doi:10.1002/hipo.20287 PMID:17455334.

Baum, S., Yigitcanlar, T., Mahizhnan, A., & Andiappan1, N. (n.d.). ICTs and e-governance in Singapore. Retrieved March 14, 2012, from http://unpan1.un.org/intradoc/groups/public/documents/un-dpadm/unpan043267.pdf

Baum, S., Yigitcanlar, T., Mahizhnan, A., & Andiappan, N. (2006). Singapore government online: A consideration of e-government outcomes. *Journal of E-Government*, *3*(4), 65–84. doi:10.1300/J399v03n04_04.

BBVA Research. (2011). *Avanza el pago electrónico de programas sociales en América Latina y el Caribe*. México City: BBVA Research.

Becerra, M., & Gupta, A. K. (1999). Trust within the organization: Integrating the trust literature with agency theory and transaction costs economics. *Public Administration Quarterly*, *23*(2), 177–203.

Bécet, J.-M. (2001). The structure and working of local government. In Local government in France (pp. 53-68). Paris: la Documentation Française.

Becker, J., Niehaves, B., Algermissen, L., Delfmann, P., & Falk, T. (2004). e-Government Success Factors. EGOV Lecture Notes in Computer Science, 3183, 503–506. doi: doi:10.1007/978-3-540-30078-6_87.

Becker, T. (2001). Rating the impact of new technologies on democracy. *Communications of the ACM*, *44*, 49–51. doi:10.1145/357489.357503.

Behn, R. D. (2002). The psychological barriers to performance management: Or why isn't everyone jumping on the performance-management bandwagon? *Public Performance and Management Review*, *26*(1), 5–25. doi:10.2307/3381295.

Behrer, L. (2003). *Une lecture institutionnaliste du phénomène participatif, La politique consultative de la Ville de Québec*. Bordeaux, PhD.

Bekkers, V. (2003). E-government and the emergence of virtual organizations in the public sector. *Information Polity*, *8*, 89–101.

Belanger, A., & Carter, L. (2008). Trust and risk in e-government adoption. *The Journal of Strategic Information Systems*, *17*, 165–176. doi:10.1016/j.jsis.2007.12.002.

Benbasat, I., Goldstein, D. K., & Mead, M. (1987). The case study research strategy in studies of information systems. *Management Information Systems Quarterly*, *11*(3), 369–386. doi:10.2307/248684.

Benington, J. (2009). Creating the public in order to create public value? *International Journal of Public Administration*, *32*(3), 232–249. doi:10.1080/01900690902749578.

Berntzen, L., & Olsen, M. G. (2009). Benchmarking e-government: A comparative review of three international benchmarking studies. *Proceedings of the 2009 Third International Conference on Digital Society*, 77-82.

Berryman, J. (2004). *E government: Issues and implications for public libraries, a report on trends and themes in the literature*. Retrieved on March 20, 2012, from http://www.sl.nsw.gov.au/services/public_libraries/docs/egov_issues_implications_pln.pdf

Bertot, J. C., Lincoln, R., McDermott, A. M., Real, B., & Peterson, K. J. (2012). *Public libraries and the Internet 2012: Study results and findings*. Information Policy & Access Center, University of Maryland, College of Information Studies. Retrieved from http://www.plinternetsurvey.org

Bertot, J. C., & Jaeger, P. T. (2006). User-centered e-government: Challenges and benefits for government Web sites. *Government Information Quarterly*, *23*, 163–168. doi:10.1016/j.giq.2006.02.001.

Bertot, J. C., & Jaeger, P. T. (2008). The e-government paradox: Better customer service doesn't necessarily cost less. *Government Information Quarterly*, *25*, 149–154. doi:10.1016/j.giq.2007.10.002.

Bertot, J. C., & Jaeger, P. T. (2012). Implementing and managing public library networks, connectivity, and partnerships to promote e-government access and education. In Aikins, S. (Ed.), *Managing e-government projects: Concepts, issues and best practices* (pp. 183–199). Hershey, PA: IGI Global. doi:10.4018/978-1-4666-0086-7.ch007.

Bertot, J. C., Jaeger, P. T., & Grimes, J. M. (2012). Promoting transparency and accountability through ICTs, social media, and collaborative e-government. *Transforming Government: People. Process and Policy*, *6*(1), 78–91.

Bertot, J. C., Jaeger, P. T., & Hansen, D. (2012). The impact of polices on government social media usage: Issues, challenges, and recommendations. *Government Information Quarterly*, *29*(1), 30–40. doi:10.1016/j.giq.2011.04.004.

Bertot, J. C., Jaeger, P. T., Langa, L. A., & McClure, C. R. (2006). Public access computing and Internet access in public libraries: The role of public libraries in e-government and emergency situations. *First Monday*, *11*(9). Retrieved from http://www.firstmonday.org/issues/issue11_9/bertot/index.html.

Bertot, J. C., Jaeger, P. T., Langa, L. A., & McClure, C. R. (2006). Drafted: I want you to deliver e-government. *Library Journal*, *131*(13), 34–39.

Bertot, J. C., McClure, C. R., & Jaeger, P. T. (2008). The impacts of free public Internet access on public library patrons and communities. *The Library Quarterly*, *78*, 285–301. doi:10.1086/588445.

Beynon-Davies, P., & Martin, S. (2004). Electronic local government and the modernisation agenda: Progress and prospects for public service improvement. *Local Government Studies*, *30*(2), 214–229. doi:10.1080/0300303042000267245.

Bharadwaj, A. S. (2000). A resource-based perspective on information technology capability and firm performance: An empirical investigation. *Management Information Systems Quarterly*, *24*(1), 169–196. Retrieved from http://www.jstor.org/stable/3250983 doi:10.2307/3250983.

Bhatnagar, S. (2002). E-government: Lessons from implementation in developing countries. *Regional Development Dialogue*, 24, 1–9 (Autumn). Retrieved from http://www.iimahd.ernet.in/~subhash/pdfs/RDDAutumn2002.pdf

Bhuiyan, M. S. H. (2011). Public sector eservice development in Bangladesh: Status, prospects and challenges. *Electronic. Journal of E-Government*, *9*(1), 15–29.

Biasiotti, M. A., & Nannucci, R. (2004). Learning to become an e-citizen: The European and Italian policies. In M.A. Wimmer (Ed.), *Knowledge Management in Electronic Government, 5th IFIP International Working Conference, KMGov 2004* (pp. 269-280). Krems: Springer.

Biehl, M. (2007). Success factors for implmenting global information systems. *Communications of the ACM*, *50*(1), 53–58. doi:10.1145/1188913.1188917.

Birkenmaier, P. (2004). *E-democracy - Der Wandel der Demokratie durch das Internet*. Berlin: Rhombos Verlag.

Blondiaux, L. (2008). *Nouvel esprit de la démocratie: Actualité de la démocratie participative*. Paris: Seuil.

Blumler, J. G., & Gurevitch, M. (2001). The new media and our political communication discontents: Democratizing cyberspace. *Information Communication and Society*, *4*(1), 1–13.

Bobigny.fr. (n.d.). Website. Retrieved April 21, 2012 from http://www.bobigny.fr/jsp/site/Portal.jsp?page_id=185

Bocij, P., Chaffey, D., Greasley, A., & Hickie, S. (2006). *Business information systems: Technology, development & management for the e-business* (3rd ed.). Harlow: Prentice Hall.

Bojović, D., & Mrakjić, V. (2011). *The role of social networks in environmental eParticipation*. Paper presented at ESEE 2011 conference, Advancing Ecological economics, theory and practice. Retrieved from http://www.esee2011.org/registration/fullpapers/esee2011_3dd942_1_1304865599_6312_2236.pdf

Bonham, G., Seifert, J., & Thorson, S. (2001). *The transformational potential of e-government: At the role of political leadership*. Paper read at the 4th Pan European International Relations Conference, University of Kent.

Bönisch, P., Haug, P., Illy, A., & Schreier, L. (2011). Municipality size and efficiency of local public services: Does size matter? *IWH-Diskussionspapiere,* n°18.

Bonsón, E., Torres, L., Royo, S., & Flores, F. (2012). Local e-government 2.0: Social media and corporate transparency in municipalities. *Government Information Quarterly*, *29*, 123–132. doi:10.1016/j.giq.2011.10.001.

Boozallen.com. (2013). Website. Retrieved August 15, 2008, from http://www.boozallen.com/consulting

Borins, S. (2007). Introduction. In Borins, S. et al. (Eds.), *Digital state at the leading edge*. Toronto: University of Toronto Press.

Borman, M., & Janssen, M. (2012). *Critical success factors for shared services: Results from two case studies*. Paper presented at the HICSS2012.

Borman, M., & Janssen, M. (2012). Reconciling two approaches to critical success factors: The case of shared services in the public sector. *International Journal of Information Management*. doi: doi:10.1016/j.ijinfomgt.2012.1005.1012.

Borzel, T., & Risse, T. (2008). Public-private partnership: Effective and legitimate tools of transnational governance? In E. Grande & L.W. Pauly, L. W. (Eds.), Complex sovereignty: Reconstituting political authority in the twenty first century. Toronto: University of Toronto Press.

Bovee, C., & Thill, J. (2007). *Business communication essentials* (3rd ed.). New Jersey: Pearson Education, Inc..

Boyd, D. M., & Ellison, N. B. (2007). Social network sites: Definition, history, and scholarship. *Journal of Computer-Mediated Communication*, *13*(1), 16–31. doi:10.1111/j.1083-6101.2007.00393.x.

Boynton, A. C., & Zmud, R. W. (1984). An assessment of critical success factors. *Sloan Management Review*, *25*(4), 17–27.

Bresnahan, T. F., Brynjolfsson, E., & Hitt, L. M. (2002). Information technology, workplace organization, and the demand for skilled labor: Firm-level evidence. *The Quarterly Journal of Economics*, *117*(1), 39–376. doi:10.1162/003355302753399526.

Brown, J. S., & Duguid, P. (1998). Organizing knowledge. *California Management Review*, *40*(3), 90–111. doi:10.2307/41165945.

Brown, M. M. (2001). The benefits and costs of information technology innovations: An empirical assessment of a local government agency. *Pubic Performance and Management Review*, *24*(4), 351–366. doi:10.2307/3381224.

Brown, V. C., Dehayes, D. W., Hoffer, J. A., Martin, E. W., & Perkins, W. C. (2009). *Managing information technology* (6th ed.). New Jersey: Pearson, Inc..

Bruns, A. (2008). *Blogs, wikipedia, second life, and beyond: From production to produsage*. New York: Peter Lang Publishing, Inc..

Bryman, A. (2004). *Social research methods*. Oxford University Press.

Brynjolfsson, E. (1993). The productivity paradox of information technology. *Communications of the ACM*, *36*, 67–77. doi:10.1145/163298.163309.

Brynjolfsson, E., & Hitt, L. (1998). Beyond the productivity paradox: Computers are the catalyst for bigger changes. *Communications of the ACM*, *41*, 49–55. doi:10.1145/280324.280332.

Bullen, C. V., & Rockart, J. F. (1981). *A primer on critical success factors*. Sloan School of Management, Massachusetts Institute of Technology.

Bunduchi, R. (2005). Business relationships in internet-based electronic markets: The role of goodwill trust and transaction costs. *Information Systems Journal, 15*(4), 321. doi:10.1111/j.1365-2575.2005.00199.x.

Burbridge, L. (2002). Accountability and MIS. *Public Performance and Management Review, 25*(4), 421–423. doi:10.1177/15357602025004013.

Burke, S. K. (2008). Public library resources used by immigrant households. *Public Libraries, 47*(4), 32–41.

Burke, S. K. (2008). Use of public libraries by immigrants. *Reference and User Services Quarterly, 48*, 164–174.

Burnes, B., & Anastasiadis, A. (2003). Outsourcing: A public-private sector comparison. *Supply Chain Management: An International Journal, 8*(4), 355–366. doi:10.1108/13598540310490116.

Burns, D., Heywood, F., Taylor, M., Wilde, P., & Wilson, M. (2004). *Making community participation meaningful: A handbook for development and assessment*. Bristol: Policy Press.

Burt, R. S. (1992). *Structural holes: The social structure of competition*. Cambridge: Harvard Univ. Press.

Burt, S., & Sparks, L. (2003). E-commerce and the retail process: A review. *Journal of Retailing and Consumer Services, 10*(5), 275–286. doi:10.1016/S0969-6989(02)00062-0.

Bushell-Embling, D. (2008). *Dial-up fading, DSL still King*. IDG Communications. Retrieved on March 14, 2012, from http://www.pcworld.idg.com.au/article/261414/dial-up_fading_dsl_still_king/

Bützer, M. (2005). Continuity or innovation? Citizen involvement and institutional reforms in Swiss cities. In K. Steyvers, J.B. Pilet, H. Reynaert, and P. Delwit (Eds.), Revolution or renovation? Reforming local politics in Europe (pp. 213-234). Brugge: Vanden Broele Publishers.

Cabrera, J. (2007). Política social: cambio y resultados. In Cordera, R., & Cabrera, J. (Eds.), *La política social en México: tendencias y perspectivas* (pp. 67–94). Mexico City: UNAM.

Caidi, N., & Allard, D. (2005). Social inclusion of newcomers to Canada: An information problem? *Library & Information Science Research, 27*, 302–324. doi:10.1016/j.lisr.2005.04.003.

Calista, D. J., & Melitski, J. (2007). e-Government and e-Governance: Converging constructs of public sector information and communications technologies. *Public Administration Quarterly, 31*(1), 87–120.

Camarota, S. A. (2010). *Immigration and economic stagnation: An examination of trends, 2000 to 2010*. Washington, DC: Center for Immigration Studies. Retrieved from http://www.cis.org/articles/2010/highest-decade.pdf

Campbell, J. L. (2004). *Institutional change and globalization*. Princeton: Princeton University Press.

Canada, S. (2010). Enquête canadienne sur l'utilisation d'Internet 2010. Retrieved May 29, 2012, from www.statcan.gc.ca/daily-quotidien/110525/dq110525b-fra.htm

Carnesi, M. S., & Fiol, M. A. (2000). Queens Library's New Americans Program: 23 years of services to immigrants. In Guerena, S. (Ed.), *Library Services to Latinos: An Anthology* (pp. 133–142). Jefferson, NC: McFarland & Company, Inc., Publishers.

Carratta, T., Dadayan, L., & Ferro, E. (2006). ROI analysis in e-government assessment trials: The case of Sistema Piemonte. *5th International Conference, EGOV 2006, Poland. Computers & Society, 4084*, 501–505. doi: doi:10.1007/11823100_29.

Carrizales, T. (2008). Critical factors in an electronic democracy: A study of municipal managers. *The Electronic. Journal of E-Government, 6*(1), 23–30.

Carter, L., & Bélanger, F. (2005). The utilization of e-government services: Citizen trust, innovation and acceptance factors. *Information Systems Journal, 15*(1), 5–25. doi:10.1111/j.1365-2575.2005.00183.x.

Carter, L., & Weerakkody, V. (2008). E-government adoption: A cultural comparison. *Information Systems Frontiers, 10*(4), 473–482. doi:10.1007/s10796-008-9103-6.

Castells, M. (2007). Communication, power and counter-power in the network society. *International Journal of Communication, 1*, 238–266.

Castelnovo, W. (2010). Is there an e-government paradox? In D. O'Donnell (Ed.), *Proceedings of the 10th European Conference on eGovernment* (pp. 99-106). Academic Publishing Limited, Reading, UK.

Castelnovo, W., & Simonetta, M. (2007). The evaluation of e-government projects for small local government organisations. *The Electronic. Journal of E-Government, 5*(1), 21–28.

Castelnovo, W., & Simonetta, M. (2008). A public value evaluation of e-government policies. *Electronic Journal Information Systems Evaluation, 11*(2), 61–72.

Cattell, R. B. (1966). The Scree test for the number of factors. *Multivariate Behavioral Research, 1*(2), 245–276. doi:10.1207/s15327906mbr0102_10.

Cerrillo i Martínez, A. (2010). Web 2.0 y la participación ciudadana en la transparencia administrativa en la sociedad de la información. In Cotino, L. (Ed.), *Libertades de expresión e información en Internet y las redes sociales: ejercicio, amenazas y garantías*. Valencia: Publicacions de la Universitat de València.

CGAP. (2009). Banking the poor via G2P payments. *Focus Note*, 1-24.

Chadwick, A. (2011). Explaining the failure of an online citizen engagement initiative: The role of internal institutional variables. *Journal of Information Technology & Politics, 8*(1), 21–40. doi:10.1080/19331681.2010.507999.

Chadwick, A., & May, C. (2003). Interaction between states and citizens in the age of the internet: "e-Government" in the United States, Britain, and the European Union. *Governance: An International Journal of Policy, Administration and Institutions, 16*(2), 271–30. doi:10.1111/1468-0491.00216.

Chan, C. M. L., Lau, Y. M., & Pan, S. L. (2008). E-government implementation: A macro analysis of Singapore's e-government initiatives. *Government Information Quarterly, 25*(2), 239–255. doi:10.1016/j.giq.2006.04.011.

Chan, C. M. L., & Pan, S. L. (2008). User engagement in e-government systems implementation: A comparative case study of two Singaporean e-government initiatives. *The Journal of Strategic Information Systems, 17*(2), 124–139. doi:10.1016/j.jsis.2007.12.003.

Chen, Y., & Perry, T. (2003). Outsourcing for e-government: Managing for success. *Public Performance & Management Review, 26*(4).

Chen. (2005). Ten-thousand meter unit network--New mode of city management. *Urban and Rural Development, 10*, 10-13.

Chen. (2005). Developing a new approach of urban management on the basis of digital city technology. *Bulletin of Chinese Academy of Sciences, 20*(3), 220-222.

Chen. (2006). An analysis on digital urban management model. *Journal of Peking University, 1*, 142-148.

Cheng & Bai. (2008). Implications of ICT use and urban grid management. *Journal of Information, 27*(10), 56–59.

Cheng & Zhang. (2007). Urban city management: A new direction in modern city governance. *Science and Technology Association Forum, 5*.

Cheng. (2007). *Digital city management: A powerful engine for administrative operation*. Paper presented at China Construction Information, 2007(10X). Retrieved from http://www.cqvip.com/qk/83587x/200710x/25751982.0.html

Cheng. (2008). Rational thoughts on ways to refine mechanisms in urban city management- A case study in Shanghai. *Journal of Shanghai Polytechnic College of Urban Management, 17*(3), 2-5.

Chen, K., & Yen, D. C. (2004). Improving the quality of online presence through Interactivity. *Information & Management, 42*, 217–226. doi:10.1016/j.im.2004.01.005.

Chen, Y. C., & Knepper, R. (2005). Digital government development strategies. Lessons for policy makers from a comparative perspective. In Huang, W., Siau, K., & Kwok, K. W. (Eds.), *Electronic government strategies and implementation* (pp. 394–420). Hershey, PA: Idea Group Publishing.

Chen, Y., & Dimitrova, D. (2006). Electronic government and online engagement: Citizen interaction with government via Web portals. *International Journal of Electronic Government Research, 2*(1), 54–76. doi:10.4018/jegr.2006010104.

Chen, Y., & Dimitrova, D. V. (2008). Civic engagement via e-government portals: Information, transactions, and policy making. In Norris, D. (Ed.), *E-Government research: Policy and management* (pp. 205–209). Hershey, Pennsylvania: IGI Global.

Chen, Zhou, & Wang. (2007). Griddling management and its research progress. *Science and Technology Management Research*, *27*(5), 40–41.

Ching, Y. L. S. (2009). The impact of leadership and stakeholders on the success/failure of e-government service: Using the case study of e-stamping service in Hong Kong. *Government Information Quarterly*, *26*, 594–604. doi:10.1016/j.giq.2009.02.009.

Chi, Wang, & Chen. (2008). Thoughts on Shanghai municipal management model. *Technology Advancement and Strategy*, *25*(1), 40–43.

Chu, C. M. (1999). Literacy practices of linguistic minorities: Sociolingusitic issues and implications for literacy services. *The Library Quarterly*, *69*, 339–359. doi:10.1086/603093.

Chung, M. K. (2007). *Singapore e-government experience*. Paper presented at Asia e- Government Forum 2007, 20 September 2007, Seoul, Korea.

Chung, K. S. K., & Chatfield, A. T. (2011). An empirical analysis of online social network structure to understand citizen engagement in public policy and community building. *International Journal of Electronic Governance*, *4*(1/2), 85–103. doi:10.1504/IJEG.2011.041709.

Chun, S. A., Shulman, S., Sandoval, R., & Hovy, E. (2010). Government 2.0. Making connections between citizens, data and government. *Information Polity: The International Journal of Government & Democracy in the Information Age*, *15*, 1–9.

Chun, S. A., & Warner, J. (2010). Finding information in an era of abundance: Towards a collaborative tagging environment in government. *Information Polity. The International Journal of Government & Democracy in the Information Age*, *15*, 89–103.

Chuttur, M. Y. (2009). Overview of the technology acceptance model: Origins, developments, and future directions. *Working papers on Information Systems, 9*(37), 1-21.

Ciborra, C. (2005). Interpreting e-government and development: Efficiency, transparency or governance at a distance? *Information Technology & People*, *18*(3), 260–279. doi:10.1108/09593840510615879.

Citaenet.com. (n.d.). Website. Retrieved April 23, 2012, from http://www.citaenet.com/

City of Casey. (2009). *Council meeting agenda*. October 20, 2009, City of Casey, Victoria: City of Casey. Retrieved December 7, 2011, from http://www.casey.vic.gov.au/meetings/article.asp?Item=14187

City of Casey. (2012). *Casey connect: Connecting communities online*. Retrieved January 20, 2012, from http://www.caseyconnect.net.au

City of Casey. (2012). *Casey conversations*. Retrieved March 2, 2012, from http://caseyconversations.com.au

City of Casey. (2012). *City of Casey*. Retrieved February 8, 2012, from http://www.casey.vic.gov.au

Clift, S. (2002). *E-Governance to e-democracy: Progress in Australia and New Zealand toward information-age democracy*. Retrieved on March 14, 2012, from http://www.publicus.net/articles/aunzedem.html

CNIPA. (2007). *Monitoraggio dei progetti di E-Government - Fase 1. Rapporto finale*. Retrieved March 1, 2012, from http://archivio.cnipa.gov.it/site/_files/EG000_RP05_0007_V1_RapportoSintesiConclusivo_ExecSummary.pdf

CNIPA. (2008). *Analisi delle valutazioni di impatto di alcuni dei progetti della prima fase del piano di E-Government*. Retrieved March 1, 2012, from http://archivio.cnipa.gov.it/site/_files/EGMON_Analisi_ExecSummary.pdf

Codagnone, C., & Undheim, T.A. (2008). Benchmarking eGovernment: Tools, theory, and practice. *European Journal of ePractice*, 4, 4-18.

Cohen, D., & Prusak, L. (2001). *In good company: How social capital makes organizations work*. Boston: Harvard Business School Press. doi:10.1145/358974.358979.

Cohen, G., van Geenhuizen, M., & Nijkamp, P. (2005). ICT as a contributing factor to urban sustainable development: Policymaking in Dutch cities. In van Geenhuizen, M., Gibson, D. V., & Heitor, M. V. (Eds.), *Regional development and conditions for innovation in the network society* (pp. 99–117). West Lafayette, Indiana: Purdue University Press.

Coleman, S., & Shane, P. (Eds.). (2012). *Connecting democracy online consultation and the flow of political communication*. Cambridge, MA: MIT Press.

Colesca, S. E. (2009). Understanding trust in e-government. *Engineering Economics*, (3).

Commonwealth of Australia. (2009). *Australian citizenship: Our common bond*. Retrieved on March 15, 2012, from http://www.citizenship.gov.au/learn/cit_test/_pdf/australian-citizenship-nov2009.pdf

Commonwealth of Australia. (2010). *Our government*. Retrieved on March 15, 2012, from http://australia.gov.au/about-australia/our-Government

Compaine, B. (2001). Epilogue. In Compaine, B. (Ed.), *The digital divide: Facing a crisis or creating a myth?* (pp. 337–339). Cambridge, MA: MIT Press.

Comune de Bologna. (2012). *Iperbole: La rete vivica di Bologna*. Retrieved January 20, 2012, from http://www.comune.bologna.it/

Consulting, D. M. R. (2003). E-government benefits study (Commonwealth of Australia ed.). Canberra (Australia): National Office for the Information Economy.

Cook, M. E., LaVigne, M. F., Pagano, C. M., Dawes, S. S., & Pardo, T. A. (2002). *Making a case for local e-government*. Retrieved April 26, 2007, from http://www.ctg.albany.edu/ publications/guides/making_a_case/making_a_case.pdf

Corbineau.net. (n.d.). Website. Retrieved April 22, 2012, from http://www.corbineau.net/IMG/Acces_au_savoir.pdf

Cordera, R. (2007). Mercado y equidad: de la crisis del Estado a la política social. In Cordera, R., & Cabrera, J. (Eds.), *La política social en México: tendencias y perspectivas* (pp. 25–66). Mexico City: UNAM.

Couldry, N., & Langer, A. I. (2005). Media consumption and public connection: Towards a typology of the dispersed citizen. *Communication Review*, *8*(2), 237–257. doi:10.1080/10714420590953325.

Couldry, N., Livingstone, S., & Markham, T. (2007). *Media consumption and public engagement: Beyond the presumption of attention*. Basingstoke, Hampshire: Palgrave Macmillan. doi:10.1057/9780230800823.

Council for Excellence in Governance. (2001). *E-Government, the next American revolution*. Washington, DC: Council for Excellence in Governance.

Coursey, D., & Norris, D. (2008). Models of e-Government: Are they correct? An empirical assessment. *PAR*, *68*, 523–536.

Cox, R. H. (2001). The social construction of an imperative: Why welfare reform happened in Denmark and the Netherlands but not in Germany. *World Politics*, *53*(April). PMID:17595731.

Cremonini, L., & Valeri, L. (2003). *Benchmarking security and trust in Europe and the US*. Rand Monograph Report MR-1763, Europe.

Criado, J. I., & Rojas-Martin, F. (2012). *Strategies and realities of social media diffusion in the public sector. Evidence from the regional government in Spain*. Paper presented at the annual meeting of the European Group of Public Administration. Bergen, Norway.

Criado, J. I., Martín, Y., & Camacho, D. (2011). *Experiences using social networks in Spanish public administration*. Paper presented at the meeting of the 1st International Workshop on Social Data Mining for Human Behaviour Analysis. Songndal, Norway.

Criado, J. I. (2009). *Entre Sueños Utópicos y Visiones Pesimistas. Internet y las TIC en la Modernización de las Administraciones Públicas*. Madrid: Instituto Nacional de Administración Pública.

Cross, R., & Cummings, J. N. (2004). Tie and network correlates of individual performance in knowledge-intense work. *Academy of Management Journal*, *47*(6). doi:10.2307/20159632.

Cuban, S. (2007). *Serving new immigrant communities in the library*. Westport, CT: Greenwood.

Cunningham, I. (2002). Developing human and social capital in organizations. *Industrial and Commercial Training*, *34*(3), 89–94. doi:10.1108/00197850210424926.

Currie, W. L. (1996). Outsourcing in the private and public sectors: an unpredictable IT strategy. *European Journal of Information Systems*, *4*, 226–236. doi:10.1057/ejis.1996.4.

Dada, D. (2006). E-readiness for developing countries: Moving the focus from the environment to the users. *The Electronic Journal on Information System in Developing Countries*, *27*, 1–14.

Dahlgren, P. (2005). The Internet, public spheres, and political communication: Dispersion and deliberation. *Political Communication*, *22*(2), 147–162. Retrieved from http://www.ingentaconnect.com/content/routledg/upcp;jsessionid=4kbt0wnfdtvhf.alice doi:10.1080/10584600590933160.

Dahl, R. A. (1971). The city in the future of democracy. In Cook, M. (Ed.), *Participatory democracy* (pp. 85–114). San Francisco: Canfield Press.

Dahl, R. A., & Tufte, E. A. (1974). *Size and democracy*. Stanford: Stanford University Press.

Dalakiouridou, E., Tambouris, E., & Tarabanis, K. (2009). Mapping the state of play in eParticipation in the EU. *European eParticipation study*, Deliverable D1.4.c. Retrieved from http://islab.uom.gr/eP/

Dalakiouridou, E., Smith, S., Tambouris, E., & Tarabanis, K. (2012). eParticipation policies and initiatives in the European Union Institutions. *Social Science Computer Review*, *30*(3), 297–323. doi:10.1177/0894439311413436.

Damodaran, L., Olphert, W., & Balatsoukas, P. (2008). Democratizing local e-government: The role of virtual dialogue. In. T. Janowski & T.A. Pardo (Eds.), *Proceedings of the 2nd international conference on theory and practice of electronic governance (ICEGOV'08)* (pp. 388-393). New York: ACM.

Damodaran, L., Nicholls, J., Henney, A., Land, F., & Farbey, B. (2005). The contribution of sociotechnical systems thinking to the effective adoption of e-government and the enhancement of democracy. *The Electronic Journal of E-Government*, *3*(1), 1–12.

Damsgaard, J., & Lyytinen, K. (2001). The role of intermediating institutions in the diffusion of electronic data interchange (EDI): How industry associations intervened in Denmark, Finland, and Hong Kong. *The Information Society*, *17*(3), 195–210. doi:10.1080/01972240152493056.

Danziger, J. N., & Andersen, K. V. (2002). Impacts of information technology on public administration: An analysis of empirical research from the "Golden Age" of transformation. *International Journal of Public Administration*, *25*(5), 591–627. doi:10.1081/PAD-120003292.

Davenport, E., & Hall, H. (2002). Organizational knowledge and communities of practice. *Annual Review of Information Science & Technology*, *36*, 171–222.

Davenport, T. (1993). *Process innovation: Reengineering work through information technology*. Harvard Business School Press.

Davis, F. D. (1989). Perceived usefulness, perceived ease of use and user acceptance of information technology. *Management Information Systems Quarterly*, *13*, 319–330. Retrieved from http://www.jstor.org/stable/249008 doi:10.2307/249008.

Davis, F. D., Bagozzi, R. P., & Warshaw, P. R. (1989). User acceptance of computer technology: A comparison of two theoretical models. *Management Science*, *35*(8), 982–1002. doi:10.1287/mnsc.35.8.982.

Dawes, S. S. (1996). Interagency information sharing: Expected benefits, manageable risks. *Journal of Policy Analysis and Management*, *15*(3), 377–394. doi:10.1002/(SICI)1520-6688(199622)15:3<377::AID-PAM3>3.0.CO;2-F.

Dawes, S. S. (2008). The evolution and continuing challenges of e-governance. *Public Administration Review*, *68*, 86–102. doi:10.1111/j.1540-6210.2008.00981.x.

Dawes, S. S. (2009). Governance in the digital age: A research and action framework for an uncertain future. *Government Information Quarterly*, *26*, 257–264. doi:10.1016/j.giq.2008.12.003.

Dawes, S. S., & Nelson, M. R. (1995). Pool the risks, share the benefits: Partnerships in IT innovation. In Keyes, J. (Ed.), *Technology trendlines. Technology Success Stories from Today's Visionaries. New York7 Van Nostrand Reinhold.*

Dawes, S. S., & Pardo, T. (2002). Building collaborative digital government systems. In McIver, W. J., & Elmagarmid, A. K. (Eds.), *Advances in digital government. Technology, human factors, and policy*. Norwell, MA: Kluwer Academic Publishers. doi:10.1007/0-306-47374-7_16.

Dawson, P. (1994). *Organizational change: A processual approach*. London: Paul Chapman Publishing.

De Cindio, F., De Marco, A., & Grew, P. (2007). Deliberative community networks for local governance. *International Journal of Technology. Policy and Management*, *7*(2), 108–121.

DeLone, W., & Mclean, E. (1992). Information systems success: The quest for the dependent variable. *Information Systems Research*, *3*(1), 60–95. doi:10.1287/isre.3.1.60.

DeLone, W., & Mclean, E. (2003). The DeLone and McLean Model of information systems success: A ten year update. *Journal of Management Information Systems, 19*(4), 9–30.

Demand Media. (2010). *The Australian government structure: An outline of the 3 levels of government in Australia and their respective responsibilities*. Retrieved on March 15, 2012, from http://www.essortment.com/all/australiangover_rbpt.htm

Department of Broadband, Communications and the Digital Economy (DBCDE). (2012). *National broadband network: Empowering Australia*. Retrieved January 20, 2012, from http://www.nbn.gov.au/

Department of Broadband, Communications and the Digital Economy. (2011). *National digital economy strategy: Leveraging the national broadband network to drive Australia's digital productivity*. Canberra. Retrieved on July 12, 2012, from http://www.nbn.gov.au/files/2011/05/National_Digital_Economy_Strategy.pdf

Department of Economic and Social Affairs Division for Public Administration and Development Management. (2008). *United Nations e-government survey 2008: From e-Government to Connected Governance*. New York: United Nations.

Department of Justice, Civil Rights Division. (2012). Executive Order 13166. Retrieved from http://www.lep.gov/13166/eo13166.html

Dertz, W., Moe, C., & Hu, Q. (2003). Influential factors in IT sourcing decisions of Norwegian public sector: An exploratory study. Tampa: *Proceeding of Ninth Americas Conference on Information Systems.*

Descolonges, M. (2002). *Vertiges technologiques*. Paris: La Dispute.

Dewoghélaëre, J., Magni-Berton, R., & Navarro, J. (2006). The *cumul des mandats* in contemporary French politics: An empirical study of the *XIIe Législature* of the *Assemblée Nationale. French Politics*, 312–332. doi:10.1057/palgrave.fp.8200104.

Dewoghélaëre, J., & Premat, C. (2007). La stratégie de communication numérique des élus locaux français. *Pyramides, 13*, 155–171.

Dewoghélaëre, J., & Premat, C. (2008). Le profil des maires urbains en 2006. *Sens Public, 25*(March), 1–8.

Di Maria, E., & Rizzo, L. S. (2005). E-democracy: The participation of citizens and new forms of the decision-making process. In E. Di Maria & S. Micelli (Eds.), On line citizenship: Emerging technologies for European cities (pp. 71-106). New York: Springer Science+Business Media, Inc.

Dickard, N. (2003). Edtech 2002: Budget challenges, policy shifts and digital opportunity. In N. Dickard Benton (Ed.), *The sustainability challenge: Taking edtech to the next level.* The Foundation and the Education Development Center's for Children and Technology. Retrieved December 19, 2003, from http://www.benton.org/publibrary/sustainability/sus_challenge.html

Digital Agenda Scoreboard, E. U. (2011). *Digital agenda scoreboard 2011 – Italy*. Retrieved March 1, 2012, from http://ec.europa.eu/information_society/digital-agenda/scoreboard

Digit, P. A. (2011). *2010 E-Gov Report Italy*. Roma: Edizioni Forum PA.

Ding, F., Wang, Y., & Ye, X. (2008). E-government for the people: Learn from North America and European Union. *IEEE/WIC/ACM International Conference on Web Intelligence and Intelligent Agent Technology* (vol. 3, pp. 211-214). 9-12 Dec (Online Xplore).

Dingjun. (2008). Urban grid management in Chaoyang district, Beijing. *China Public Administration Review,* (S1), 108-110.

Diniz, E., Fingermann, N., & Best, N. (2011). *Banca Móvil y programas de transferencia monetarias condicionadas*. En Breve.

Dirks, K. T., & Ferrin, D. L. (2001). The role of trust in organizational settings. *Organization Science, 12*(4), 450–467. doi:10.1287/orsc.12.4.450.10640.

Dixon, B. E. (2010). Towards e-Government 2.0: An assessment of where e-government 2.0 is and where it is headed. *Public Administration & Management, 15*(2), 418–454.

DNP. (2011). *Evaluación de la gestión y la operación de la bancarización a través del programa Familias en Acción*. DNP.

Doig, J. W., & Hargrove, E. C. (1990). *Leadership and innovation: Entrepreneurs in government*. Baltimore, MD: Johns Hopkins University.

Dong & Liu. (2009). A research on the technological structure of urban grid management system. *Zhejiang Fabrics and Clothing Professional School Journal*, (3), 57-61.

Donker-Kuijer, M. W., Jong, M., & Lentz, L. (2010). Usable guidelines for usable websites: An analysis of five e-government heuristics. *Government Information Quarterly*, *27*, 254–263. doi:10.1016/j.giq.2010.02.006.

dotMobi. (2012). *Global mobile statistics 2012: All quality mobile marketing research, mobile Web stats, subscribers, ad revenue, usage, trends*. Retrieved on March, 25, 2012, from http://mobithinking.com/mobile-marketing-tools/latest-mobile-stats

Dryzek, J. S. (2000). *Deliberative democracy and beyond. Liberals, critics, contestations*. New York: Oxford University Press.

Duchessi, P., & Chengalur-Smith, I. (1998). Client/server benefits, problems, best practices. *Communications of the ACM*, *41*(5), 87–94. doi:10.1145/274946.274961.

Dugdale, A., Daly, P. A. F., & Maley, M. (2005). Accessing e-government: Challenges for citizens and organizations. *International Review of Administrative Sciences*, *71*(1), 109–118. doi:10.1177/0020852305051687.

Dunleavy, P., Margetts, H., Bastow, S., & Tinkler, J. (2006). *Digital era governance: IT corporations, the state, and e-government*. Oxford: Oxford University Press. doi:10.1093/acprof:oso/9780199296194.001.0001.

Dutta, S., & Mia, I. (2011). *Global information technology*. Geneva: World Economic Forum.

Dutton, W. H. (1992). Political science research on teledemocracy. *Social Science Computer Review*, *10*(4), 505–522. doi:10.1177/089443939201000405.

Ebbers, W. E., Pieterson, W. J., & Noordman, H. N. (2008). Electronic government: Rethinking channel management strategies. *Government Information Quarterly*, *25*, 181–201. doi:10.1016/j.giq.2006.11.003.

Ebbers, W. E., & van Dijk, J. A. G. M. (2007). Resistance and support to electronic government, building a model of innovation. *Government Information Quarterly*, *24*(3), 554–575. doi:10.1016/j.giq.2006.09.008.

Ebrahim, Z., & Irani, Z. (2005). E-government adoption: Architecture and barriers. *Business Management Process*, *11*(5), 589–611. doi:10.1108/14637150510619902.

ECLAC. (2007). Las transferencias condicionadas en América Latina: Luces y Sombras. In CEPAL, *Seminario Internacional*. In *Evolución y desafíos de los programas de transferencias condicionadas* (pp. 1–44). Brasilia: ECLAC.

ECLAC. (2011). *La Trayectoria de los programas de transferencias con corresponsabilidad (PTC) en América Latina y el Caribe*.

Economist Intelligence Unit. (2009). *E-readiness rankings 2009: The usage imperative*.

Economists Intelligence Unit. (2005). *The 2005 E-readiness rankings, a white paper from the economists intelligence unit*. Retrieved May 11, 2012, from http://graphics.eiu.com/files/ad_pdfs/2005Ereadiness_Ranking_WP.pdf

Edmiston, K. D. (2003). State and local e-government: Prospects and challenges. *American Review of Public Administration*, *33*(1), 20–45. doi:10.1177/0275074002250255.

Eggers, W. D. (2005). *Government 2.0: Using technology to improve education, cut red tape, reduce gridlock, and enhance democracy*. Lanham, Maryland: Rowman & Littlefield Publishers, Inc..

Egner, B., & Kerrouche, E. (2012). Local democracy – a comparison of mayoral perceptions. In O.W. Gabriel, S. I. Keil, and E. Kerrouche (Eds.), Political participation in France and Germany (pp. 137-160). Essex: EPCR Press studies.

E-Gov 2012 Plan. (2012). Website. Retrieved March 1, 2012, from http://www.e2012.gov.it/

E-government in France. (2010). *Invest in France*. Retrieved from http://www.invest-in-france.org/Medias/Publications/1171/ifa-e-government-in-france-july-2010.pdf

Eisenhardt, K., & Martin, J. A. (2000). Dynamic capabilities: What are they? *Strategic Management Journal, 21*, 1105–1121. doi:10.1002/1097-0266(200010/11)21:10/11<1105::AID-SMJ133>3.0.CO;2-E.

Ekdahl, C., Karlsson, D., Wigertz, O., & Forsum, U. (2000). A study of the usage of a decision-support system for infective endocarditis. *Medical Informatics and the Internet in Medicine, 25*(1), 1–18. doi:10.1080/146392300298229 PMID:10757478.

El Kiki, T., & Lawrence, E. (2006). Government as a mobile enterprise: Real-time, ubiquitous government. Information technology: New Generations, 2006. *ITNG 2006. Third International Conference* (pp.320-327). 10-12 April 2006. doi: 10.1109/ITNG.2006.68

Elgarah, W., Falaleeva, N., Saunders, C. S., Ilie, V., Shim, J. T., & Courtney, J. F. (2005). Data exchange in interorganizational relationships: Review through multiple conceptual lenses. *The Data Base for Advances in Information Systems, 36*(1). doi:10.1145/1047070.1047073.

Elias, N. (1991). *Qu'est-ce que la sociologie?* French translation of Yamin Hoffmann. La Tour d'Aigues: L'Aube.

Ensemble-simplifions.fr. (n.d.). Website. Retrieved April 21, 2012, from http://www.ensemble-simplifions.fr/

Enyon, R., & Dutton, W. H. (2007). Barriers to networked governments: Evidence from Europe. *Prometheus, 25*(3), 225–242. doi:10.1080/08109020701531361.

Eom, S. J. (2012). 'Institutional dimensions of e-government development: Implementing the business reference model in the United States and Korea. *Administration & Society*. doi:10.1177/0095399712445870.

Eriksen, E. (2007). Conceptualising European public spheres. General, segmented and strong publics. In Fossum, J., & Schlesinger, P. (Eds.), *The European Union and the public sphere: a communicative space in the making?* (pp. 23–43). London: Routledge.

Ernst, C., & Young (2004). Online availability of public services: How is Europe progressing? (Web-based Survey on Electronic Public Services: Report of the Fourth Measurement, October 2003). European Commission DG Information Society.

Erwin, G. J., & Taylor, W. J. (2004). Social appropriation of internet technology: A South African platform. *The Journal of Community Informatics, 1*(1), 21–29.

Eschenfelder, K. R., & Miller, C. (2005). *The openness of government websites: Toward a sociotechnical overnment website evaluation toolkit*. MacArthur Foundation/ALA Office of Information Technology Policy Internet Credibility and the User Symposium, Seattle, WA.

Esmark, A., & Triantafillou, P. (2007). Document analysis of network topography and network programmes. In Bogason, P., & Zølner, M. (Eds.), *Methods in democratic network governance* (pp. 99–124). Basingstoke, Hampshire: Palgrave Macmillan.

Estache, A., Gonzalez, M., & Trujillo, L. (2007). Government expenditures on education, health and infrastructure. A naïve look at levels, outcomes and efficiency. *World Bank Policy Research Working Paper*, 4219.

EU. (2009). *Ministerial declaration on egovernment*. Retrieved March 1, 2012, from http://www.egov2009.se/wp-content/uploads/Ministerial-Declaration-on-eGovernment.pdf

EU. (2009). *Making public support for innovation in the EU more effective: Lessons learned from a public consultation for action at Community level* – SEC (2009) 1197.

EU. (2009). *i2010 eGovernment action plan progress study, Summary report, November 2009*. Retrieved March 1, 2012, from http://www.dti.dk/27666

Eurobarometer. (2006). *EU communication and the citizens*. September/October. Retrieved from http://ec.europa.eu/public_opinion/flash/fl_189b_en.pdf and http://ec.europa.eu/public_opinion/flash/fl_189a_en.pdf

European Commision. (2010). Internet usage in 2010-households and individuals. *Eurostat*, data in focus, 50/2010. Retrieved from http://epp.eurostat.ec.europa.eu/cache/ITY_OFFPUB/KS-QA-10-050/EN/KS-QA-10-050-EN.PDF

European Commission. (2000). *Reforming the commission, a white paper – Part II*. COM(2000) 200, Brussels: CEC.

European Commission. (2001). *A new framework for co-operation on activities concerning the information and communication policy of the European Union. COM(2001) 354*. Brussels: CEC.

European Commission. (2001). *European governance. A white paper*. COM(2001) 428 final, Brussels: CEC.

European Commission. (2002). *General principles and minimum standards for consultation of interested parties by the Commission. COM(2002) 704*. Brussels: CEC.

European Commission. (2005). *Action plan to improve communicating Europe by the commission*. Retrieved from http://ec.europa.eu/dgs/communication/pdf/communication_com_en.pdf

European Commission. (2005). *The Commission's contribution to the period of reflection and beyond: Plan-D for democracy, dialogue and debate. COM(2005) 494*. Brussels: CEC.

European Commission. (2006). *White paper on a European communication policy*. COM(2006) 35, Brussels: CEC European Commission. (2006). *Green paper on the proposal of the European transparency initiative*. COM(2006) 194, Brussels: CEC.

European Commission. (2007). *Communicating about Europe via the Internet, engaging the citizens. SEC(2007) 1742*. Brussels: CEC.

European Commission. (2007). *Communicating Europe in partnership. COM(2007) 568*. Brussels: CEC.

European Commission. (2008). *Communicating Europe through audiovisual media. SEC(2008) 506/2*. Brussels: CEC.

European Commission. (2008). *Debate Europe – building on the experience of Plan D for democracy, dialogue and debate. COM(2008) 158/4*. Brussels: CEC.

European Commission. (2009). *Impact assessment guidelines. SEC(2009) 92*. Brussels: CEC.

European Parliament & Council of the European Union. (2011, February 16). Regulation No. 211/2100 of 16 February 2011 on the citizens' initiative. OJ L 65/1

Evans, D., & Yen, D. C. (2005). E-government: An analysis for implementation: Framework for understanding cultural and social impact. *Government Information Quarterly*, *22*(3), 354–373. doi:10.1016/j.giq.2005.05.007.

Evans, D., & Yen, D. C. (2006). E-government: Evolving relationship of citizens and government, domestic, and international development. *Government Information Quarterly*, *23*(2), 207–235. doi:10.1016/j.giq.2005.11.004.

Fagan, G. Honor, Newman, D., McCusker, P., & Murray, M. (2006). *E-consultation: Evaluating appropriate technologies and processes for citizens' participation in public policy*. Final Report for the HEA. Retrieved from http://www.nuim.ie/nirsa/econsult/

Fagan, M. H. (2006). Exploring city, county and state e-government initiatives: An East Texas perspective. *Business Process Management Journal*, *12*(1), 101–112. doi:10.1108/14637150610643797.

Fan. (2009). An investigation of new management models in modern city grid management. *Shangqiu Normal School Journal, 25*(12), 111-115.

Fang. (2006). Urban grid management is testing water in Jiangcheng. *Shanghai Informatization,* (5), 43-45.

Farbey, B., Land, F., & Targett, D. (1993). *How to assess your IT investment: A study of methods and practice*. Oxford: Butterworth-Heinemann Ltd..

Fcw.com. (2013). Website. Retrieved June 15, 2007, from http://fcw.com/Articles/2007/03/26/2007-Federal-100-winners--From-Q--Z.aspx?Page=7

Federal Communication Commission. (2010). *National broadband plan: Connecting America*. Retrieved April 11, 2011, from http://www.broadband.gov/

Federal Communications Commission. (2012). *National Broadband Plan*. Washington, DC: Federal Communications Commission. Retrieved from http://www.broadband.gov/plan/

Feldman, M. S., & Khademian, A. M. (2007). The role of the public manager in inclusion: Creating communities of participation. *Governance: An International Journal of Policy, Administration and Institutions*, *20*(2), 305–324. doi:10.1111/j.1468-0491.2007.00358.x.

Fenster, M. (2006). The opacity of transparency. *Iowa Law Review*, *91*, 885–949.

Ferro, E., & Sorrentino, M. (2010). Can intermunicipal collaboration help the diffusion of E-Government in peripheral areas? Evidence from Italy. *Government Information Quarterly*, *27*(1), 17–25. doi:10.1016/j.giq.2009.07.005.

Filgueiras, L., Aquino, P. Jr, Tokairim, V., Torres, C., & Barbarian, I. (2004). *Usability evaluation as quality assurance of e-government services* (*Vol. 146*, pp. 77–87). IFIP International Federation for Information Processing. doi:10.1007/1-4020-8155-3_5.

Fiore, A. M. (2008). The digital consumer: Valuable partner for product development and production. *Clothing & Textiles Research Journal*, *26*(2), 177–190. doi:10.1177/0887302X07306848.

Fisher, K. E., Becker, S., & Crandall, M. (2010). E-government service use and impact through public libraries: Preliminary findings from a national study of public access computing in public libraries. In *Proceedings of the 43rd Hawaii International Conference on System Sciences* (pp. 1-10).

Fishkin, J. S. (1991). *Democracy and deliberation*. New Haven, CT: Yale University Press.

Flamm, K., & Chaudhuri, A. et al. (2006). The internet, the government, and e-governance. In Hernon, P., Cullen, R., & Relyea, H. C. (Eds.), *Comparative perspectives on e-government: Serving today and building for tomorrow* (pp. 331–348). Lanham, Maryland: Scarecrow Press Inc..

Flear, M., & Vakulenko, A. (2010). A human rights perspective on citizen participation in the EU's governance of new technologies. *Human Rights Law Review*, *10*(4), 661–688. doi:10.1093/hrlr/ngq039.

Flowers, S., Tang, P., Molas-Gallart, J., & Davies, A. (2005). Contrasting approaches to the adoption of e-government: The UK and the Netherlands. *Journal of E-Government*, *2*(3), 51–83. doi:10.1300/J399v02n03_04.

Foley, P., & Alfonso, X. (2009). eGovernment and the Transformation Agenda. *Public Administration*, *87*(2), 371–396. doi:10.1111/j.1467-9299.2008.01749.x.

Foruminternet.org. (n.d.). Website. Retrieved April 21, 2012, from http://www.foruminternet.org/institution/espace-presse/communiques-de-presse/suite-a-sa-dissolution-le-forum-des-droits-sur-l-internet-partage-ses-contenus-3119.html

Fountain, J. E. (2003). *Information, institutions and governance: Advancing a basic social science research program for digital government*. Kennedy School of Government Faculty Research Working Paper, RWP03-004.

Fountain, J. E. (2004). *Prospects for the virtual state*. Center of Excellence Program on Invention of Policy Systems in Advanced Countries, Graduate School of Law and Politics, University of Tokyo. Working paper.

Fountain, J. E. (2011, June). Bringing institutions back in to strategic management: The politics of digitally mediated institutional change. Unpublished paper presented at the Public Management Research Conference. Syracuse, NY.

Fountain, J. E. (2001). *Building the virtual state: Information technology and institutional change*. Washington, DC: Brookings Institution Press.

Fountain, J. E. (2007). Challenges to organizational change: Multi-level integrated information structure. In Mayer-Schöenberger, V., & Lazer, D. (Eds.), *Governance and information technology: Form electronic government to information government*. Cambridge, MA: MIT Press.

Fox, J. (2007). El acceso a la rendición de cuentas: ¿voces individuales o colectivas? In *Documento presentado al Seminario Internacional sobre Candados y Derechos*. Protección de Programas Sociales y Construcción de Ciudadanía.

Frank, D., & Riedl, P. (2004). Theoretical foundations of contemporary qualitative market research Forum: An overview and an integrative perspective. *Qualitative Social Research*, *5*(2), 30. Retrieved from http://www.qualitative-research.net/index.php/fqs/article/view/596/1294

Freeman, J. (2011). *Local e-government: Politics and civic participation*. (Unpublished doctoral thesis). Monash University, Australia.

Freeman, J., & Hutchins, B. (2009). Balancing the digital democratic deficit? E-government. *Media International Australia*, *130*, 17–27.

Fuchs, D., Roller, E., & Weßels, B. (Eds.). (2002). *Bürger und Demokratie in Ost und West, Studien zur Politischen Kultur und zum Politischen Prozess*. Wiesbaden: Westdeutscher Verlag.

Gagnon, Y.-C. (2001). The behavior of public managers in adopting new technologies. *Pubic Performance and Management Review, 24*(4), 337–350. Retrieved from http://www.jstor.org/stable/3381223

Galperin, H. (2005). Wireless networks and rural development: Opportunities for Latin America. *Information Technologies and International Development*, *2*(3), 47–56. doi:10.1162/1544752054782420.

Gamm, L. D., Hutchinson, L. L., Dabney, B. J., & Dorsey, A. (Eds.). (2003). *Rural healthy people 2010: A companion document to healthy people 2010* (Vol. 1). College Station, TX: The Texas A & M University System Health Science Center, School of Rural Public Health, Southwest Rural Health Research Center. Retrieved February 19, 2003, from http://www.srph.tamhsc.edu/centers/rhp2010/publications.htm

Gant, J. P., & Gant, D. B. (2002). Web portal functionality and state government eservice. System Sciences, 2002. HICSS. *Proceedings of the 35th Annual Hawaii International Conference* (pp. 1627- 1636). doi: 10.1109/HICSS.2002.994073

Gao & Meng. (2011). The successful implementation and use of the third generation wireless video monitoring system in urban management. *City Management and Science and Technology*, *13*(2), 50–51.

Gao, Zhao, & Ma. (2007). The role of urban grid management in emergency response. *Cities and Disaster Relief,* (3), 2-4.

Gates Foundation. (2009). *Diconsa: financial services for the rural poor. Grantee profile.*

Gauld, R., Gray, A., & McComb, S. (2009). How responsive is e-government? Evidence from Australia and New Zealand. *Government Information Quarterly*, *26*(1), 69–74. doi:10.1016/j.giq.2008.02.002.

Gefen, D., Warkentin, M., Pavlou, P., & Rose, G. (2002). *E-government adoption*. Paper presented at the *Americas Conference on Information Systems (AMCIS)*. Paper 83 of the AIS Electronic Library (AISeL).

Gefen, D., Karahanna, E., & Straub, D. W. (2003). Trust and TAM in online shopping: An integrated model. *Management Information Systems Quarterly*, *27*(1), 51–90.

Gefen, D., Rose, G. M., Warkentin, M., & Pavlou, P. A. (2005). Cultural diversity and trust in IT adoption: A comparison of USA and South African e-voters. *Journal of Global Information Management*, *13*(1), 54–78. doi:10.4018/jgim.2005010103.

Generalitat de Cataluña. (2012). Guía de usos y estilo en las redes sociales de la Generalitat de Cataluña. Retrieved May 13, 2012, from http://www.gencat.cat/web/meugencat/documents

Gibney, J. (2011). Knowledge in a shared and interdependent world: Implications for a progressive leadership of cities and regions. *European Planning Studies*, *19*(4), 613–627. doi:10.1080/09654313.2011.548474.

Gibson, A. N., Bertot, J. C., & McClure, C. R. (2009). Emerging role of public librarians as E-government providers. In R. H. Sprague, Jr. (Ed.), *Proceedings of the 42nd Hawaii International Conference on System Sciences* (pp. 1-10). doi: 10.1109/HICSS.2009.183

Giddens, A. (1979). *New rules of sociological method.* London: Hutchinson.

Giddens, A. (1984). *The constitution of society*. Cambridge: Polity Press.

Giddens, A. (1989). In Held, D., & Thompson, J. B. (Eds.), *A reply to my critics' in Social theory of modern societies: Anthony Giddens and his critics* (pp. 249–305). Cambridge: Cambridge University Press. doi:10.1017/CBO9780511557699.013.

Gilbert, D., Balestrini, P., & Littleboy, D. (2004). Barriers and benefits in the adoption of e-government. *International Journal of Public Sector Management*, *17*(4), 286–301. doi:10.1108/09513550410539794.

Gil-Garcia, J. R. (2005). *Enacting state websites: A mixed method study exploring e-government success in multi-organizational settings*. (Unpublished Doctoral Dissertation). University at Albany, State University of New York, Albany, NY.

Gil-García, J. R. (2012). *Enacting electronic government success: An integrative study of government-wide websites, organizational capabilities, and institutions*. New York: Springer. doi:10.1007/978-1-4614-2015-6.

Gil-Garcia, J. R., Chengalur-Smith, I. N., & Duchessi, P. (2007). Collaborative e-government: Impediments and benefits of information sharing projects in the public sector. *European Journal of Information Systems*, *16*(2), 121–133. doi:10.1057/palgrave.ejis.3000673.

Gil-Garcia, J. R., & Martinez-Moyano, I. J. (2007). Understanding the evolution of e-government: The influence of systems of rules on public sector dynamics. *Government Information Quarterly*, *24*(2), 266–290. doi:10.1016/j.giq.2006.04.005.

Gil-Garcia, J. R., & Pardo, T. A. (2005). E-government success factors: Mapping practical tools to theoretical foundation. *Government Information Quarterly*, *22*, 187–216. doi:10.1016/j.giq.2005.02.001.

Glaser, B. G. (1992). *Emergence vs. forcing: Basics of grounded theory*. Mill Valley, CA: Sociology Press.

Glaser, B. G., & Strauss, A. L. (1967). *The discovery of grounded theory: Strategies for qualitative research*. Chicago: Aldine Publishing Company.

Glazer, A., Kanniainen, V., & Niskanen, E. (2002). Bequests, control rights, and cost–benefit analysis. *European Journal of Political Economy*, *19*(1), 71–82. doi:10.1016/S0176-2680(02)00130-1.

Gleason, J. P., & Lane, D. R. (2009). *Interactivity redefined: A first look at outcome interactivity theory*. Retrieved from http://people.eku.edu/gleasonj/Outcome_Interactivity_Theory.pdf

Gobierno Vasco. (2011). Guía de Usos y Estilos del Gobierno Vasco. Retrieved May15, 2001, from http://www.irekia.euskadi.net/assets/a_documents/

Goldfinch, S., Gauld, R., & Herbison, P. (2009). The participation divide? Political participation, trust in government, and e-government in Australia and New Zealand. *Australian Journal of Public Administration*, *68*(3), 333–350. doi:10.1111/j.1467-8500.2009.00643.x.

Goldstein, J., & Keohane, R. O. (1993). Ideas and foreign policy: An analytical framework. In Goldstein, J., & Keohane, R. O. (Eds.), *Ideas and foreign policy: Beliefs, institutions, and political change*. Ithaca, NY: Cornell University Press.

González de la Rocha, M. (2008). La vida después de Oportunidades: Impacto del Programa a diez años de su creación. In SEDESOL, Evaluación Externa del Programa Oportunidades 2008. A diez años de intervención en zonas rurales (1997-2007). SEDESOL.

Gordon, M. L., & Walsh, T. P. (1997). Outsourcing technology in government: Owned, controlled, or regulated institutions. *Journal of Government Information*, *24*(4), 267–283. doi:10.1016/S1352-0237(97)00026-9.

Gorsuch, R. L. (1983). *Factor analysis* (2nd ed.). Hillsdale, NJ: Lawrence Erlbaum.

Goulding, C. (1999). *Grounded theory: Some reflections on paradigm, procedures and misconceptions*. Working paper series, WP006/99, Wolverhampton: University of Wolverhampton

Government Accounting Office. (1996). *Rural development: Steps toward realizing the potential of telecommunications technologies (GAO/RCED-96-155)*. Washington, DC: U.S. Government Printing Office.

Government of Western Australia. (2012). *Local government directory*. Department of Local Government. Retrieved on July 16, 2012, from http://www.dlg.wa.gov.au/Content/Directory/Default.aspx

Government, N. S. W. (2012). *Local government directory - Local councils*. Division of Local Government - Department of Premier and Cabinet. Retrieved on July 16, 2012, from http://www.dlg.nsw.gov.au/dlg/dlghome/dlg_LocalGovDirectory.asp?index=1&mi=2&ml=2

Graafland-Essers, I., & Ettedgui, E. (2003). *Benchmarking e-government in Europe and the U.S.* Santa Monica, CA: RAND.

Graham, S., & Aurigi, A. (1997). Virtual cities, social polarization, and the crisis in urban public space. *Journal of Urban Technology*, *4*(1), 19–52. doi:10.1080/10630739708724546.

Grandison, T., & Sloman, M. (2000). A survey of trust in internet applications. *IEEE Communications Survey and Tutorials*, 3.

Green, L. (2008). Is it meaningless to talk about 'the internet'? *Australian Journal of Communication, 35*(3), 1–14.

Grésil, R. (1996). *Main basse sur les banlieues rouges*. Paris: Picollec.

Griffin, D., & Halpin, E. (2005). An exploratory evaluation of UK local e-government from an accountability perspective. *The Electronic Journal of E-Government, 3*(1), 13–28.

Grimsley, M., & Meehan, A. (2007). E-government information systems: Evaluation-led design for public value and client trust. *European Journal of Information Systems, 16*(2), 134–148. doi:10.1057/palgrave.ejis.3000674.

Grimsley, M., & Meehan, A. (2008). Attaining social value from electronic government. *The Electronic. Journal of E-Government, 6*(1), 31–42.

Grizzle, G.A., & Pettijohn, C. D. (2002). Implementing performance-based program budgeting: A system-dynamics perspective. *Public Administration Review*, January/February 2(X)2, *62*(1).

Grossmann, L. K. (1995). *The electronic republic. Reshaping democracy in the information age*. New York: Viking.

Guérin-Lavignotte, E., & Kerrouche, E. (2006). *Les élus locaux en Europe, un statut en mutation*. Paris: La Documentation Française.

Guerrini, A. W., & Aibar, E. (2007). Towards a network government? A critical of current assessment methods for e-Government. *EGOV*, 330-341.

Guidi, L. (2009). Participation at the municipal level in Italy: The case of Bologna. In *Organisation for Economic Co-operation and Development (OECD). Focus on citizens: Public engagement for better policy and services* (pp. 261–266). Paris: OECD Studies on Public Engagement.

Gulati, R. (1995). Social structure and alliance formation patterns: A Longitudinal analysis. *Administrative Science Quarterly, 40*, 619–653. doi:10.2307/2393756.

Gunnarsson, G., Mellander, E., & Savvidou, E. (2004). *Human capital is the key to the IT productivity paradox*. Institute for Labour Market Policy Evaluation (IFAU). WORKING PAPER 13.

Guo. (2011). Research on the use of grid management in irregular emergency response. *Commercial Culture,* (5).

Gupta, B., Dasgupta, S., & Guptac, A. (2008). Adoption of ICT in a government organization in a developing country: An empirical study. *The Journal of Strategic Information Systems, 17*(2), 140–154. doi:10.1016/j.jsis.2007.12.004.

Gupta, M. P., Debashish Jana. (2003). E-government evaluation: A framework and case study. *Government Information Quarterly, 20*(4), 365–387. doi:10.1016/j.giq.2003.08.002.

Ha, H. (2012). A new SWOT analysis of e-government systems in Singapore. In C-P., Rueckemann (Ed.), Integrated information and computing systems for natural, spatial, and social sciences (pp. 75-96). USA: IGI Global.

Hacker, & van Dijk. (2000). What is digital democracy? In K. L. Hacker and J. van Dijk. (Eds.), *Digital democracy issues of theory and practice*. London: Sage Publications.

Hadi, A. S., Jelas, Z. M., Mokhtar, M., & Abdul Aziz, Y. F. (2002). *Universiti Kebangsaan Malaysia, The national university with an international reach: Opportunities and challenges in the 21st century*. Paper presented at The 16th Australian International Education Conference. Hobart.

Ha, H. (2011). Security and privacy in e-consumer protection in Victoria, Australia. In Wakeman, I. et al. (Eds.), *IFIPTM 2011, IFIP AICT 358* (pp. 240–252). Berlin, Heidelberg: Springer-Verlag. doi:10.1007/978-3-642-22200-9_19.

Ha, H., & Coghill, K. (2006). E-government in Singapore: A SWOT and PEST analysis.[APSSR]. *Asia-Pacific Social Science Review, 6*(2), 103–130.

Ha, H., & Coghill, K. (2008). Online shoppers in Australia: Dealing with problems. *International Journal of Consumer Studies, 32*(1), 5–17.

Hale, M., Musso, J., & Weare, C. (1999). Developing digital democracy: Evidence from Californian municipal web pages. In Hague, B. N., & Loader, B. D. (Eds.), *Digital democracy: Discourse and decision making in the information age* (pp. 96–115). London: Routledge.

Hall, P. A. (1983). Policy innovation and the structure of the state: The politics-administrative nexus in France and Britain.[Implementing Government Change]. *The Annals of the American Academy of Political and Social Science*, 466.

Hall, P. A. (1989). Conclusion: The politics of Keynesian Ideas. In Hall, P. A. (Ed.), *The political power of economic ideas: Keynesianism across nations*. Princeton, NJ: Princeton University Press.

Hall, P. A. (1993). Policy paradigms, social learning, and the state: The case of economic policymaking in Britain. *Comparative Politics*. doi:10.2307/422246.

Han, H.-S., Lee, J.-N., & Seo, Y.-W. (2008). Analyzing the impact of a firm's capability on outsourcing success: A process perspective. *Information & Management*, *45*(1), 31–42. doi:10.1016/j.im.2007.09.004.

Hanseth, O., Ciborra, C., & Braa, K. (2001). The control devolution. ERP and the side effects of globalization. *The Data base for advances in information systems. Special issue: Critical Analysis of ERP systems, 32*(4), 34-46.

Hanseth, O., & Lyytinen, K. (2010). Design theory for adaptive complexity in information infrastructures. *Journal of Information Technology*, *25*(1), 1–19. doi:10.1057/jit.2009.19.

Hanseth, O., Monteiro, E., & Hatling, M. (1996). Developing information infrastructure: The tension between standardization and flexibility. *Science, Technology & Human Values*, *21*(4), 407–442. doi:10.1177/016224399602100402.

Hard, M. (1998). German regulation: The integration of modern technology into national culture. In Hard, M., & Jamison, A. (Eds.), *In Intellectual appropriation of technology, discourse on modernity* (pp. 33–68). M.I.T press.

Hargadon, A. B. (2002). Brokering knowledge: Linking learning and innovation. *Research in Organizational Behavior*, *24*, 41–85. doi:10.1016/S0191-3085(02)24003-4.

Harrison, T. M., Guerrero, S., Burke, G. B., Cook, M., Cresswell, A., Helbig, N., et al. (2011). *Open government and e-government: Democratic challenges from a public value perspective*. Paper presented at the 12th Annual International Conference on Digital Government Research. New York. Retrieved from http://www.ctg.albany.edu/publications/journals/dgo2011_opengov/dgo2011_opengov.pdf

Hart, P., & Saunders, C. (1997). Power and trust - Critical factors in the adoption and use of electronic data interchange. *Organization Science*, *8*(1), 23–42. doi:10.1287/orsc.8.1.23.

Hashim, J. (2008). Factors influencing the acceptance of web-based training in Malaysia: Applying the technology acceptance model. *International Journal of Training and Development*, *12*(4), 253–264. doi:10.1111/j.1468-2419.2008.00307.x.

Hatzfeld, H. (2005). *Faire de la politique autrement, les expériences inachevées des années 1970*. Rennes: Presses Universitaires de Rennes.

Hauer, J., Sandberg, J., Olson, K., Meyerhoff, C., & Moses, L. G. (2002). *Local e-government*. Minnesota: Office of the legislative auditor.

Hay, C. (2007). *Why we hate politics*. Cambridge, UK: Polity Press.

Head, R. (1982). *Federal information systems management: Issues and new directions. Staff Paper*. Washington, DC: Brookings Institution.

Heanue, A. (2001). In support of democracy: The library role in public access to government information. In Kranich, N. (Ed.), *Libraries & democracy: The cornerstones of liberty* (pp. 121–128). Chicago: American Library Association.

Heeks, R. (2003). *Most e-government for development projects fail: How can risks be reduced*? I-Government, Working Paper Series, Paper no. 14.

Heeks. (2006). *Implementing and managing e-government. An International Text*. London: Sage Publications.

Heeks, R. (2005). e-Government as a career of context. *Journal of Public Policy*, *25*, 51–74. doi:10.1017/S0143814X05000206.

Heeks, R., & Bailur, S. (2006). Analyzing e-government research. Perspectives, philosophies, theories, methods, and practice. *Government Information Quarterly*, *24*(2), 243–265. doi:10.1016/j.giq.2006.06.005.

Heidinger, C., Buchmann, E., & Böhn, K. (2010). Impact assessment in public policy: Towards a Web 2.0 application. *Information Polity: The International Journal of Government & Democracy in the Information Age*, *15*(1-2), 33–50.

Heimbur, Y.V., Wolf, P., & Krcmar, H. (2012). *E-government monitor 2012*. Report from TNS Infratest.

Heintze, T., & Bretschneider, S. (2000). Information technology and restructuring in public organizations: Does adoption of information technology affect organizational structures, communications, and decision making? *Journal of Public Administration: Research and Theory*, *10*(4), 801–830. Retrieved from http://jpart.oxfordjournals.org/citmgr?gca=jpart;10/4/801 doi:10.1093/oxfordjournals.jpart.a024292.

Hermana, B., & Sulfianti, W. (2011). Evaluating e-government implementation by local government: Digital divide in internet-based public services in Indonesia. *International Journal of Business and Social Sciences*, *2*(30), 156–163.

Hirschheim, R., & Adams, D. (1991). Organizational connectivity. *Journal of General Management*, *17*(2), 65–76.

Ho, A. T.-K. (2002). Reinventing local governments and the e-government initiative. *Public Administration Review*, *62*(4), 434–444. doi:10.1111/0033-3352.00197.

Hochheiser, H., & Shneiderman, B. (2000). Performance benefits of simultaneous over sequential menus as task complexity increases. *International Journal of Human-Computer Interaction*, *12*(2), 173–192. doi:10.1207/S15327590IJHC1202_2.

Hochstrasser, B. (1992). Justifying IT investment. *Proceedings of the Advanced Information Systems Conference; The New Technologies in Today's Business Environment*, (pp. 17–28). UK.

Hoffmann-Martinot, V., & Wollmann, H. (2006). *State and local reforms in France and Germany: Divergence and convergence*. Wiesbaden: VS Verlag für Sozialwissenschaften. doi:10.1007/978-3-531-90271-5.

Holden, S. H., Norris, D. F., & Fletcher, P. D. (2003). Electronic government at the local level: Progress to date and future issues. *Public Performance and Management Review*, *26*(4), 325–344. Retrieved from http://www.jstor.org/stable/3381110

Holtkamp, L., Bogumil, J., & Kißler, L. (2006). Kooperative Demokratie, Das politische Potenzial von Bürgerengagement. Frankfurt, New-York: Campus Verlag.

Holt, L. E., & Holt, G. E. (2010). *Public library services for the poor: Doing all we can*. Chicago: ALA Editions.

Holzer, M., & Kim, B. J. (Eds.). (2004). *Building good governance: Reforms in Seoul*. Newark, NJ: National Center for Public Productivity.

Homburg, V. (2008). *Understanding e-government: Information systems in public administration*. New York: Routledge.

Hood, C., & Margetts, H. (2007). *The tools of government in the digital age*. London: Palgrave.

Horst, H., & Miller, D. (2005). From kinship to link-up: The cell phone and social networking in Jamaica. *Current Anthropology*, *46*, 755–778. doi:10.1086/432650.

Horst, M., Kuttschreuter, M., & Gutteling, J. M. (2007). Perceived usefulness, personal experiences, risk perception and trust as determinants of adoption of e-government services. *Computers in Human Behavior*, *23*(4), 1838–1852. doi:10.1016/j.chb.2005.11.003.

House of Representatives Bill 2762. (2005). *Health Technology To Enhance Quality Act of 2005*. 109th U.S. Congress.

How many are there? (2012). *How many mobile phone users in the world*. Retrieved on March, 25, 2012, from http://www.howmanyarethere.org/how-many-mobile-phone-users-in-the-world/

Howard, M. (2001). e-Government across the world: How will „E" change government? *Government Finance Review*, 6-9.

Hrdinová, J., Helbig, N., & Peters, C. S. (2010). *Designing social media policy for government: Eight essential elements*. Albany: The Research foundation of State University of New York. Retrieved February 20, 2012, from http://www.ctg.albany.edu/publications

Huang, Z., & Brooks, L. (2011). Credibility and usability evaluation of e-governments: Heuristic evaluation approach. *Transforming Government Workshop*, 1-15.

Huang, Z. (2007). A comprehensive analysis of U.S. counties' e-Government portals: Development status and functionalities. *European Journal of Information Systems*, *16*(2), 149–164. doi:10.1057/palgrave.ejis.3000675.

Huang, Z., & Bwoma, P. O. (2003). An overview of critical issues of E-government. *Issues in Information Systems*, *4*(1), 164–170. Retrieved from http://iacis.org/iis/2003/HuangBwoma.pdf.

Hung, S.-Y., Chang, C.-M., & Yu, T. (2006). Determinants of user acceptance of the e-Government services: The case of online tax filing and payment system. *Government Information Quarterly*, *23*(1), 97–122. doi:10.1016/j.giq.2005.11.005.

Hung, S.-Y., Tang, K.-Z., Chang, C.-M., & Ke, C.-D. (2009). User acceptance of intergovernmental services: An example of electronic document management system. *Government Information Quarterly*, *26*(2), 387–397. doi:10.1016/j.giq.2008.07.003.

Hu, Qian, & Yang. (2010). The use of urban grid management model in city greenbelt. *Urban Governance and Technology*, *12*(2), 49–51.

i4d. (2005). *e-Governance in Africa*. Retrieved on March 20, 2012, from http://www.i4donline.net/dec05/knowledge.pdf

Iaconline.org. (2013). Website. Retrieved March 5, 2008, from http://www.iaconline.org/portal

IDABC. (2005). *The impact of e-government on competitiveness, growth and jobs*. IDABC eGovernment Observatory - Background Research Paper.

IDB. (2009). *Telefonía Móvil y Desarrollo Financiero en América Latina*. Barcelona: Editorial Ariel.

IICA. (2009). *Mujeres Ahorradoras en Acción. Una sistematización de la mirada de sus protagonistas*. Bogotá: IICA - Acción Social.

iN2015 Steering Committee. (2006). *Innovation. Integration. Internationalisation*. Singapore: Infocomm Development Authority of Singapore.

Infocomm Development Authority of Singapore. (2006). *Singapore: A world class e-government*. Singapore: Singapore Government.

Infocomm Development Authority of Singapore. (2010). *Realising the iN2015 vision. Singapore: An intelligent nation, a global city, powered by Infocomm*. Singapore: Singapore Government.

Infocomm Development Authority of Singapore. (2011). *Singapore eGov: Connecting people – enriching lives*. Singapore: Singapore Government.

Infocomm Development Authority of Singapore. (2012). *Accolades and awards*. Singapore: Singapore Government.

Infocomm Development Authority of Singapore. (2012). *Singapore Infocomm statistics at a glance*. Retrieved March 22, 2012, from http://www.ida.gov.sg/Publications/20061130175201.aspx

Infocomm Development Authority of Singapore. (2012). *Factsheet: Silver Infocomm Initiative*. Singapore: Infocomm Development Authority of Singapore.

Infocomm Development Authority of Singapore. (n.d.). *Singapore's e-Government journey*. Singapore: Singapore Government.

InfoDev. (2005). *e-Ready for what? E-Readiness for developing countries: Current status and prospects toward Millennium Development Goals*. Retrieved May 11, 2012, from http://www.infodev.org/en/Publication.3.html

Inland Revenue Authority of Singapore (IRAS). (2010). *Annual report 2009/10*. Singapore: Singapore Government.

Irani, Z., Love, P. E. D., Elliman, T., & Jones, S. (2008). Learning lessons from evaluating eGovernment: Reflective case experiences that support transformational government. *The Journal of Strategic Information Systems*, *17*(2), 155–164. doi:10.1016/j.jsis.2007.12.005.

ISTAT. (2006). *Le tecnologie dell'informazione e della comunicazione nelle amministrazioni comunali - Anno 2005*. Retrieved March 1, 2012, from http://www3.istat.it/salastampa/comunicati/non_calendario/20060703_00/testointegrale.pdf

ISTAT. (2008). *L'ICT nelle amministrazioni locali - Anno 2007*. Retrieved March 1, 2012, from http://www3.istat.it/salastampa/comunicati/non_calendario/20080307_00/testointegrale.pdf

ISTAT. (2010). *Le tecnologie dell'informazione e della comunicazione nelle amministrazioni locali - Anno 2009*. Retrieved March 1, 2012, from http://www3.istat.it/salastampa/comunicati/non_calendario/20101103_00/testointegrale20101103.pdf

ISTAT. (2011). *Conti ed aggregati economici delle Amministrazioni pubbliche*. Retrieved March 1, 2012, from: http://www.istat.it/it/archivio/47334

Jaeger, P. T. (2003). The endless wire: E-government as global phenomenon. *Government Information Quarterly*, *20*, 323–331. doi:10.1016/j.giq.2003.08.003.

Jaeger, P. T., & Bertot, J. C. (2009). E-government education in public libraries: New service roles and expanding social responsibilities. *Journal of Education for Library and Information Science*, *50*, 40–50.

Jaeger, P. T., & Bertot, J. C. (2010). Designing, implementing, and evaluating user-centered and citizen-centered e-government. *International Journal of Electronic Government Research*, *6*(2), 1–17. doi:10.4018/jegr.2010040101.

Jaeger, P. T., & Bertot, J. C. (2011). Responsibility rolls down: Public libraries and the social and policy obligations of ensuring access to e-government and government information. *Public Library Quarterly*, *30*(2), 1–25. doi: 10.1080/01616846.2011.575699.

Jaeger, P. T., Bertot, J. C., Shuler, J. A., & McGilvray, J. (in press). A new frontier for LIS programs: E-government education, library/government partnerships, and the preparation of future information professionals. *Education for Information*.

Jaeger, P. T., & Thompson, K. M. (2003). E-government around the world: Lessons, challenges, and future directions. *Government Information Quarterly*, *20*(4), 389–394. doi:10.1016/j.giq.2003.08.001.

Jaeger, P., & Bertot, J. (2010). Transparency and technological change: Ensuring equal and sustained public access to government information. *Government Information Quarterly*, *27*(4), 371–376. doi:10.1016/j.giq.2010.05.003.

Janssen, M., & Kuk, G. (2006, 5-7 January). *A complex adaptive system perspective of enterprise architecture in electronic government*. Paper presented at the Hawaii International Conference on System Sciences (HICSS-39).

Janssen, M., Chun, S. A., & Gil-Garcia, J. R. (2009). Building the next generation of digital government infrastructures. *Government Information Quarterly*, *26*(2), 233–237. doi:10.1016/j.giq.2008.12.006.

Janssen, M., Joha, A., & Weerakkody, V. (2007). Exploring relationships of shared service arrangements in local government. *Transforming Government: People, Process & Policy*, *1*(3), 271–284.

Janssen, M., Joha, A., & Zuurmond, A. (2009). Simulation and animation for adopting shared services: Evaluating and comparing alternative arrangements. *Government Information Quarterly*, *26*(1), 15–24. doi:10.1016/j.giq.2008.08.004.

Jarvenpaa, S. L., Knoll, K., & Leidner, D. E. (1998). Is anybody out there? Antecedents of trust in global virtual teams. *Journal of Management Information Systems*, *14*(4), 29.

Jarvenpaa, S. L., & Leidner, D. E. (1999). Communication and trust in global virtual teams. *Organization Science*, *10*(6), 791. doi:10.1287/orsc.10.6.791.

Jarvenpaa, S. L., Shaw, T. R., & Staples, D. S. (2004). Toward contextualized theories of trust: The role of trust in global virtual teams. *Information Systems Research*, *15*(3), 250–267. doi:10.1287/isre.1040.0028.

Jassen, A., Rotthier, S., & Snijkes, K. (2004). If you measure it they will score: An assessment of international eGovernment benchmarking. *Information Polity*, *9*, 121–130.

Jayakar, K., & Park, E. (2012). Funding public computing centers: Balancing broadband availability and expected demand. *Government Information Quarterly*, *29*(1), 50–59. doi:10.1016/j.giq.2011.02.005.

Jenkins, G. (2002). *Observations from the trenches of electronic government*. Retrieved on March, 25, 2012, from http://ubiquity.acm.org/article.cfm?id=504686

Jensen, M. J. (2009). Electronic democracy and citizen influence in government. In Reddick, C. G. (Ed.), *Handbook of research on strategies for local e-government adoption and implementation: Comparative studies* (pp. 288–305). Hershey, PA: Information Science Reference. doi:10.4018/978-1-60566-282-4.ch015.

Jiang & Liang. (2008). Emergency management employing urban grid management model. *Journal of Intelligence*, (6), 26-28.

Jiang & Ren. (2007). Grid management: New mode of modern urban management—Research on certain questions of urban grid management mode. *Shanghai Urban Planning Review*, (1), 9-11.

Jiang. (2007). The current status and trend in urban grid management projects. *China Information Times,* (11), 38-47.

Jiang. (2009). Shanghai: Practice of gradding urban management in the digital city. *Construction Science and Technology,* (21), 38-40.

Jimenez, B. S., Mossberger, K., & Wu, Y. (2012). Municipal government and the interactive web: Trends and issues for civic engagement. In Manoharan, A., & Holzer, M. (Eds.), *E-governance and civic engagement: Factors and determinants of e-democracy* (pp. 251–271). Hershey, PA: Information Science Reference. doi:10.4018/978-1-4666-1740-7.ch006.

Johnson-George, C., & Swap, W. (1982). Measurement of specific interpersonal trust: Construction and validation of a scale to assess trust in a specific other. *Journal of Personality and Social Psychology, 43*(6), 1307–1317. doi:10.1037/0022-3514.43.6.1306.

Jones, L. R. (1992). Public budget execution and management control. In Rabin, J. (Ed.), *Handbook of public budgeting* (pp. 147–164). New York: Marcel Dekker.

Jones, P. A. Jr. (1999). *Libraries, immigrants, and the American experience*. Westport, CT: Greenwood.

Joyce, P. G., Lee, R. D., & Johnson, R. W. (2004). *Public budgeting systems* (7th ed.). Jones and Bartlett Publishers.

Jung, Y. (1997). Administrative reorganization in the strong state: The case of the Kim Young-Sam Regime. In Cho, Y. H., & Frederickson, H. G. (Eds.), *The white house and the blue house: Government reform in the United States and Korea*. New York: University Press of America, Inc..

Kachwamba, M., & Hussien, A. (2009). Determinants of e-government maturity: Do organizational specific factors a atter? *Journal of US-China Public Administration, 6*(50).

Kaiser, H. F., Hunka, S., & Bianchini, J. C. (1971). Relating factors between studies based upon different individuals. *Multivariate Behavioral Research, 6*(4), 409–422. doi:10.1207/s15327906mbr0604_3.

Kaliannan, M., Raman, M., & Dorasamy, M. (2009). ICT in the context of public sector service delivery: A Malaysian perspective. *WSEAS TRANSACTIONS on SYSTES, 8*(4), 543–556.

Kamal, M. M. (2006). IT innovation adoption in the government sector: Identifying the critical success factors. *Journal of Enterprise Information Management, 19*(2), 192–222. doi:10.1108/17410390610645085.

Kano, Y. (2007). Selection of manifest variables. In *Handbook of latent variable and related models*. Oxford, UK: North-Holland.

Kantner, L., & Rosenbaum, S. (1997). Usability studies of WWW sites: Heuristic evaluation vs. laboratory testing. *Proceedings of the 15th Annual International Conference on Computer Documentation*, Salt Lake City, UT, 153-60.

Kaplan, A. M., & Haenlein, M. (2010). Users of the world, unite! The challenges and opportunities of social media. *Business Horizons, 53*(1), 59–68. doi:10.1016/j.bushor.2009.09.003.

Karner, J., & Onyeji, R. (2007). *Telecom private investment and economic growth: The case of African and Central & East European countries*. Jonkoping University.

Karunasena, K., & Deng, H. (2010). Exploring the public value of e-government: An empirical study from Sri Lanka. In eTrust: Implications for the individual, enterprises and society; 23rd Bled eConference (pp. 286-300). Bled, Slovenia.

Karunasena, K., & Deng, H. (2012). Critical factors for evaluating the public value of e-government in Sri Lanka. *Government Information Quarterly, 29*(1), 76–84. doi:10.1016/j.giq.2011.04.005.

Kašubienė, L., & Vanagas, P. (2007). Assumptions of e-government services quality evaluation. *The Engineering Economist, 55*(5), 68–74.

Katz, R. (2009). *El papel de las TIC en el desarrollo. Propuesta de América Latina a los retos económicos actuales*. Barcelona: Ariel.

Kaylor, C., Deshazo, R., & Eck, D. V. (2001). Gauging E-government: A report on implementing services among American cities. *Government Information Quarterly, 18*(4), 293. doi:10.1016/S0740-624X(01)00089-2.

Kearns, I. (2004). *Public value and e-government*. Institute for Public Policy Research (ippr).

Kelly, G., Mulgan, G., & Muers, S. (2002). Creating public value: An analytical framework for public service reform. Discussion paper prepared by the Cabinet Office Strategy Unit, UK.

Kennedy Information Inc. (2007). IT strategy and planning consulting marketplace 2006-2009: Key data, trends and forecasts. Peterborough, NH.

Kerrouche, E. (2005). The powerful French mayor: Myth and reality. In Berg, R., & Rao, N. (Eds.), *Transforming local political leadership*. Basingstoke: Palgrave Macmillan.

Kertesz, S. (2003). *Cost-benefit analysis of e-government investments*. Cambridge: Harvard University Press.

Ke, W., & Wei, K. K. (2004). Successful e-government in Singapore. *Communications of the ACM*, *47*(6), 95–99. doi:10.1145/990680.990687.

Ke, W., & Wei, K. K. (2006). Understanding e-government project management: A positivist case study of Singapore. *Journal of Global Information Technology Management*, *1*(2), 45–61.

Khalfan, A. M. (2004). Information security considerations in IS/IT outsourcing projects: A descriptive case study of two sectors. *International Journal of Information Management*, *24*, 29–42. doi:10.1016/j.ijinfomgt.2003.12.001.

Khalfan, A., & Gough, T. G. (2002). Comparative analysis between the public and private sectors on the IS/IT outsourcing practices in a developing country: A field study. *Logistics Information Management*, *15*(3), 212–222. doi:10.1108/09576050210426760.

Khalil, O. (2011). E-Government readiness: Does national culture matter? *Government Information Quarterly*, *28*, 522–532. doi:10.1016/j.giq.2010.06.011.

Khan, M. Y., & Jain, P. K. (2001). Capital budgeting: Principles and techniques. In *Financial Management* (pp. 171–273). New Delhi: Tata McGraw-Hill Publishing Company.

Kiousis, S. (2002). Interactivity: A concept explication. *New Media & Society*, *4*(3), 355–383.

Kit Siang, L. (2001). IT and governance in Malaysia. In Becker, J., & Hashim, R. (Eds.), *internet M@laysia* (pp. 159–169). Universiti Kebangsaan Malaysia, Malaysia: Department of Commmunication.

Kitaw, Y. (2006). *E-Government in @frica: Prospects, challenges and practices*. Retrieved on March 20, 2012, from http://people.itu.int/~kitaw/egov/paper/EGovernment_in_Africa.pdf

Klievink, B., & Janssen, M. (2009). Realizing joined-up government. Dynamic capabilities and stage models for transformation. *Government Information Quarterly*, *26*(2), 275–284. doi:10.1016/j.giq.2008.12.007.

Koebel, M. (2006). *Le pouvoir local ou la démocratie improbable*. Bellecombe-en-Bauges: éditions du Croquant.

Koh, C. E., Ryan, S., & Prybutok, V. R. (2005). Creating value through managing knowledge in an e-government to constituency (G2C) environment. *Journal of Computer Information Systems*, *45*, 32–41.

Kong, H., Ogata, H. C., Arnseth, C. K. K., Chan, T., Hirashima, F., & Klett, J. H. M. Yang. (Eds.). (n.d.). *Paper presented at the 17th International Conference on Computers in Education*, Hong Kong. Retrieved from http://www.apsce.net/ICCE2009/pdf/C6/proceedings784-791.pdf

Kong, Su, & Zhu. (2008). Framework of urban grid management systems. *Geospatial Information*, *6*(4), 28–31.

Koohang, A., & Ondracek, J. (2005). Users' views about the usability of digital libraries. *British Journal of Educational Technology*, *36*(3), 407–423. doi:10.1111/j.1467-8535.2005.00472.x.

Korean Institute of Public Administration (KIPA). (2007). *The impact of PMIS on the effectiveness of public organizations: Centering on 'ON-Nara' system*. KIPA Policy Report 2007-06. Seoul: Korean Institute of Public Administration.

Korteland, E., & Bekkers, V. (2007). Diffusion of E-government innovations in the Dutch public sector: The case of digital community policing. *Information Polity*, *12*(3), 139–150. Retrieved from http://iospress.metapress.com/content/7PH50Q3771845628

Kostova, T., & Roth, K. (2003). Social capital in multinational corporations and a micro-macro model of its formation. *Academy of Management Review*, *28*(2), 297–317.

Kumar, K., & Van Dissel, H. G. (1996). Sustainable collaboration: Managing conflict and cooperation in interorganizational systems. *Management Information Systems Quarterly*, *20*(3), 279–300. doi:10.2307/249657.

Kunstelj, M., & Vintar, M. (2004). Evaluating the progress of e-government development: A critical analysis. *Information Polity*, *9*(3/4), 131–148.

Lacity, M. C., & Willcocks, L. (2000). Survey of IT outsourcing experiences in US and UK organizations. *Journal of Global Information Management*. April-June.

Lake, R. L. D., & Huckfeldt, R. (1998). Social capital, social networks, and political participation. *Political Psychology*, *19*, 567–584. doi:10.1111/0162-895X.00118.

Landsbergen, D. J., & Wolken, G., Jr. (1998, October). *Eliminating legal and policy barriers to interoperable government systems*. Paper presented at the Annual Research Conference of the Association for Public Policy Analysis and Management. New York.

Langford, J., & Harrison, Y. (2001). Partnering for e-government: Challenges for public administrators. *Canadian Public Administration*, *44*(4). doi:10.1111/j.1754-7121.2001.tb00898.x.

Langford, J., & Roy, J. (2006). E-government and public-private partnerships in Canada: When failure is no longer an option. *International Journal of Electronic Business*, *4*(2).

Larkey, P. D. (1995). *Good budgetary decision processes*. (Unpublished manuscript). Carnegie Mellon University.

Larsen, C. A. (2002). Municipal size and democracy: A critical analysis of the argument of proximity based on the case of Denmark. *Scandinavian Political Studies*, *25*(4), 317–332. doi:10.1111/1467-9477.00074.

Larson, A. (1992). Network dyads on entrepreneurial settings: A study of the governance of relationships. *Administrative Science Quarterly*, *36*, 76–104. doi:10.2307/2393534.

Larson, K. C. (2001). The Saturday evening girls: A progressive era library club and the intellectual life of working class and immigrant girls in turn-of-the century Boston. *The Library Quarterly*, *71*, 195–230. doi:10.1086/603261.

Lascoumes, P., & Le Galès, P. (Eds.). (2004). *Gouverner par les instruments*. Paris: Presses de la Fondation Nationale des Sciences Politiques.

Latre, M. A., Lopez-Pellicer, F. J., Nogueras-Iso, J., B'ejar, R., & Muro-Medrano, P. R. (2010). Facilitating e-government services through SDIs, an Application for Water Abstractions Authorizations. In Andersen, K. N., Francesconi, E., Grönlund, A., & van Engers, T. M. (Eds.), *Electronic government and the information systems perspective. Verlag* (pp. 108–119). Berlin, Heidelberg: Springer. doi:10.1007/978-3-642-15172-9_11.

Laudon, K. C., & Laudon, J. P. (2010). *Management information systems: Managing the digital firm* (11th ed.). New Jersey: Pearson Education, Inc..

Lawrence, J. E., & Tar, U. A. (2010). Barriers to ecommerce in developing countries. *Information. Social Justice (San Francisco, Calif.)*, *3*(1), 23–35.

Layne, K., & Lee, J. (2001). Developing fully functional e- Government: A four stage model. *Government Information Quarterly*, *18*(2), 122–136. doi:10.1016/S0740-624X(01)00066-1.

Le Bart, C. (1994). *La rhétorique du maire entrepreneur*. Paris: Pedone.

Le Bart, C. (1998). *Le discours politique*. Paris: PUF.

Leach, S., & Pratchett, L. (2005). Local government: A new vision, rhetoric or reality? *Parliamentary Affairs*, *58*(2), 318–334. doi:10.1093/pa/gsi025.

Leaning, M. (2005). The modal nature of ICT: Challenging historical interpretation of the social understanding and appropriation of ICT. *The Journal of Community Informatics*, *2*(1), 35–42.

Lean, O., Zailani, S., Ramayah, T., & Fernando, Y. (2009). Factors influencing intention to use e-government services among citizens in Malaysia. *International Journal of Information Management*, *29*(6), 458–475. doi:10.1016/j.ijinfomgt.2009.03.012.

Lee, Y. N. (2010). *E-government application*. UN-APCICT. Retrieved March 10, 2012, from http://www.unapcict.org/academy

Lee, J., & Rao, H. R. (2007). Perceived risks, counter-beliefs, and intentions to use anti-counter-terrorism websites: An exploratory study of government–citizens online interactions in a turbulent environment. *Decision Support Systems, 43*, 1431–1449. doi:10.1016/j.dss.2006.04.008.

Levin, D. Z., & Cross, R. (2004). The strength of weak ties you can trust: The mediating role of trust in effective knowledge transfer. *Management Science, 50*(11), 1477–1490. doi:10.1287/mnsc.1030.0136.

Lévy, A. (2003). La démocratie locale en France: Enjeux et obstacles. *Espaces et Sociétés (Paris, France)*, 112.

Levy, S. (2006). *Progress against poverty. Sustaining the Progresa-Oportunidades program*. Washington, DC: Brookings Institution Press.

Levy, S. (2007). *Productividad, crecimiento y pobreza en México: ¿Qué sigue después de Progresa-Oportunidades?* Banco Interamericano de Desarrollo.

Li & Quan. (2009). Urban digitalization and data collection in urban grid management systems. *Surveying and Mapping Standardization, 25*(4), 11–14.

Li, et al. (2009). Discussion on the urban grid management. *Geomatics & Spatial Information Technology, 32*(6), 141–143.

Li, et al. (2007). The construction and application of Wuhan urban grid management and service system. *Bulletin of Surveying and Mapping,* (8), 1-4.

Li, Zhang, & Kui. (2006). Study about emergency and non-emergency unified pattern of griding management. *Urban Management Science and Technology,* (1), 18-22.

Li. (2007). Analysis of Shenzhen's digital city management model. *Journal of Fujian University of Technology, 5*(6), 581-585.

Li. (2011). The Chinese urban grid management and research. *Urban Studies, 18*(2), 114-118.

Li, L., & Zhao, X. (2006). Enhancing competitive edge through knowledge management in implementing ERP systems. *Systems Research and Behavioral Science, 23*(2), 129–140. doi:10.1002/sres.758.

Lim, L., & Koh, A. (2008). *The acceleration of SOA adoption in Singapore: Challenges and issues.* Paper read at The 19th Australasian Conference on Information Systems, 3-5 Dec 2008, Christchurch.

Lim, T. K. E., Tan, C-W., Cyr, D., Pan, S. L., & Xiao, B. (2011). Advancing public trust relationships in electronic government: The Singapore e-filing journey. *Information Systems Research,* Article in Advance, 1-21.

Lin, H., Fan, W., & Zhang, Z. (2009). A qualitative study of web-based knowledge communities: Examining success factors. *International Journal of e-Collaboration, 5*(3). Retrieved from http://find.galegroup.com/itx/infomark.do?&contentSet=IAC- Documents&type=retrieve&tabID=T002&prodId=AONE&docId=A203129230&source=gale&srcprod=AONE&userGroupName=adelaide&version=1.0

Lin, C., Pervan, G., & McDermid, D. (2007). Issues and recommendations in evaluating and managing the benefits of public sector IS/IT outsourcing. *Information Technology & People, 20*(2), 161–183. doi:10.1108/09593840710758068.

Lindert, K. (2007). *The nuts and bolts of Brazil's Bolsa Familia Program: Implementing conditional cash transfers in a descentralized context.* The World Bank.

Lindlof, T. R., & Taylor, B. C. (2002). *Qualitative communication research methods* (2nd ed.). Thousand Oaks, California: Sage.

Ling, R. (2008). *New tech, new ties: How mobile communication is reshaping social cohesion.* Cambridge: MIT Press.

Lin, H. F., & Lee, G. G. (2006). Determinants of success for online communities: An empirical study. *Behaviour & Information Technology, 25*(6), 479–488. doi:10.1080/01449290500330422.

Liu, et al. (2006). Implementation of urban grid management in Shenzhen. *China Construction Information,* (24), 25-28.

Liu. (2009). Components acquisition on the urban grid management. *Geomatics and Spatial Information Technology, 32*(1), 98-101.

Liu., et al. (2011). Mobile governance and city management in China. Electronic Government, (6), 2-12.

Local Government Association of South Australia. (2012). *Councils*. Retrieved on July 16, 2012, from http://www.lga.sa.gov.au/site/page.cfm?u=210

Loiseau, G. (2003). L'assujettissement des sites internet municipaux aux logiques sociétales. *Science and Society*, *60*, 107–125.

Loo, W. H., Yeow, P. H. P., & Chong, S. C. (2009). User acceptance of Malaysian government multipurpose smart-card applications. *Government Information Quarterly*, *26*, 358–367. doi:10.1016/j.giq.2008.07.004.

Lu & Zhang. (2008). The integration of GIS in urban grid management system. *Transportation Technology and Economy*, *10*(3), 68–69.

Lüder, K. G. (1992). A contingency model of governmental accounting innovations in the political-administrative environment. *Research in Governmental and Nonprofit Accounting*, *7*, 99–127.

Lukenbill, W. B. (2006). Helping youth at risk: An overview of reformist movements in public libraries to youth. *New Review of Children's Literature and Librarianship*, *12*, 197–213. doi:10.1080/13614540600982991.

Luk, S. C. Y. (2009). The impact of leadership and stakeholders on the success/failure of e-government service: Using the case study of e-stamping service in Hong Kong. *Government Information Quarterly*, *26*(4), 594–604. doi:10.1016/j.giq.2009.02.009.

Luna-Reyes, L. F., Gil-Garcia, J. R., & Celorio Mansi, J. A. (2011). Citizen-centric approaches to e-government and the back-office transformation. In *Proceedings of the 12th annual international conference on digital government research* (pp. 213-218). New York: ACM.

Luna-Reyes, L. F., Gil-Garcia, J. R., & Romero, G. (2012). Towards a multidimensional model for evaluating electronic government: Proposing a more comprehensive and integrative perspective. *Government Information Quarterly*, *29*(3), 324–334. doi:10.1016/j.giq.2012.03.001.

Luo. (2006). Talking about urban grid management model. *China Urban Economy*, (2), 74-75.

Lu, X.-H., Huang, L.-H., & Heng, M. (2006). Critical success factors of inter-organizational information systems - A case study of Cisco and Xiao Tong in China. *Information & Management*, *43*, 395–408. doi:10.1016/j.im.2005.06.007.

Lynn, L. E., Jr. (1998). *Requiring bureaucracies to perform: What have we learned from the U.S. Government Performance and Results Act (GPRA)?* Working paper no. 98-3, The Harris School, University of Chicago.

M'Rad, H. (2006). La démocratie d'opinion le dépassement de la démocratie représentative? In R. Ben Achour, J. Gicquel, and S. Milacic (dir.), La démocratie représentative devant un défi historique. Bruxelles: éditions Bruylant.

Ma. (2009). Rethinking about urban grid management system. *Informatization*, (7), 19-22.

Macintosh, A. (2004). Characterizing e-participation in policy-making. *Proceedings of the 37th Annual Hawaii International Conference on System Sciences (HICSS-37)*, USA (pp.117-12). ISBN: 0-7695-2056-1.

Macintosh, A., Coleman, S., & Schneeberger, A. (2009). eParticipation: The research gaps. In A. Macintosh & E. Tambouris (Eds.), *Electronic participation: Proceedings of First International Conference, ePart 2009, LNCS 5694* (pp.1-11). Germany: Springer-Verlag. ISSN 0302-9743.

Macintosh, A., & Whyte, A. (2008). Towards an evaluation framework for eparticipation. *Transforming Government: People. Process & Policy*, *2*(1), 16–30.

Madon, S. (2004). Evaluating E-governance projects in India: A focus on micro-level implementation. *Department of Information Systems Working Paper Series*. London School of Economics and Political Science.

Mahler, J., & Regan, P. M. (2002). Learning to govern online: Federal agency Internet use. *American Review of Public Administration*, *32*(3), 326–349. doi:10.1177/0275074002032003004.

Mahrer, H. (2003). *SMP: A model for the transformation of political communication*. Vienna: Legend Research.

Mahrer, H., & Brandtweiner, R. (2004). Success factors for implementing e-government services: The case of the Austrian e-government service portal. *International Journal of Information Technology and Management*, *3*(2-4), 235–245. doi:10.1504/IJITM.2004.005034.

Maiani, F. (2011). Citizen participation and the Lisbon Treaty: A legal perspective. *Studies in Public policy*, *484*, 1-24.

Mairie-lille.fr. (n.d.). Website. Retrieved April 21, 2012, from http://www.mairie-lille.fr/fr/Citoyennete_-_Concertation/conseil-lillois

Maldonado, J. (2011). *Los programas de transferencias condicionadas: ¿hacia la inclusión financiera de los pobres en América Latina?* Ottawa: International Development Research Centre.

Maldonado, J., & Tejerina, L. (2010). *Investing in large scale financial inclusion: The Case of Colombia*. Banco Interamericano de Desarrollo.

Malhotra, Y. (2001). *Enabling next generation e-business architectures: Balancing Integration and Flexibility for Managing Business Transformation*. Portland, Oregon: Intel Corporation.

Mandl, U., Dierx, A., & Ilzkovitz, F. (2008). The effectiveness and efficiency of public spending. *Economic Papers*, 301. Retrieved March 1, 2012, from http://ec.europa.eu/economy_finance/publications/publication_summary11904_en.htm

Margetts, H., & Dunleavy, P. (2002). Cultural barriers to e-government. In *Better public services through e-government: Academic article in support of better public services through e-government*. National Audit Office Report by the Comptroller and Auditor General, HC 704-III Session 2001-2002, 4 April.

Margetts, H. (1999). *Information technology in government: Britain and America*. London: Routledge. doi:10.4324/9780203267127.

Margolis, M., & Moreno-Riaño, G. (2009). The prospect of internet democracy. Farnham, Surrey: Ashgate Publishing Limited.

Markus, M. L., & Lee, A. L. (2000). Special issue on intensive research in information technology: Using qualitative, interpretative, and case methods to study information technology-Foreword. *Management Information Systems Quarterly*, *23*(1), 35–38.

Markus, M. L., & Robey, D. (1988). Information technology and organizational change: Causal structure in theory and research. *Management Science*, *34*(5), 583–598. doi:10.1287/mnsc.34.5.583.

Mayer, R. C., Davis, J. H., & Schoorman, F. D. (1995). An integrative model of organizational trust. *Academy of Management Review*, *20*, 709–734.

Mayer-Schönberger, V., & Lazer, D. (2007). From electronic government to information government. In Mayer-Schönberger, V., & Lazer, D. (Eds.), *Governance and information technology: From electronic government to information government* (pp. 1–14). Cambridge, Massachusetts: MIT Press.

McClure, C. R., & Bertot, C. J. (2002). *Public library internet services: Impact of the digital divide*. Retrieved March 12, 2003 from http://slis-two.lis.fsu.edu/~jcbertot/DDFinal03_01_02.pdf

McCook, K. D. P. (2011). *Introduction to public librarianship* (2nd ed.). New York: Neal Schuman.

McDaniel, E. M. (2003). Facilitating cross-boundary leadership in emerging e-government leaders. IS2003 Proceedings. *Informing Science*.

McDowell, K. (2010). Which truth, what fiction? Librarians' book recommendations for children, 1877-1890. In Nelson, A. R., & Rudolph, J. L. (Eds.), *Education and the culture of print in modern America* (pp. 15–35). Madison, WI: University of Wisconsin.

McDowell, K. (2011). Children's voices in librarians' words, 1890-1930. *Libraries & the Cultural Record*, *46*, 73–100. doi:10.1353/lac.2011.0005.

McKinsey México. (2009). *Creating change at scale through public-private partnerships. Lessons from an innovative financial inclusion partnership in Mexico. A case study prepared for the Clinton Global Initiative*. Working Paper.

McKnight, D. H., Choudhury, V., & Kacmar, C. (2002). Developing and validating trust measures for e-commerce: An integrative approach. *Information Systems Research*, *13*(3), 334–359. doi:10.1287/isre.13.3.334.81.

McLean, I. (1989). *Democracy and the new technology*. Cambridge: Polity Press.

McNamara, K. S. (2003). *Information and communication technologies, poverty and development: Learning from experience*. A Background Paper for the infoDev Annual Symposium December 9-10, 2003, Geneva, Switzerland. Washington, DC: The World Bank.

McNeal, R., & Schmeida, M. (2007). Electronic campaign finance reform in the American states. In Anttiroiko, A.-V., & Malkia, M. (Eds.), *The encyclopedia of digital government* (*Vol. III*, pp. 624–628). Idea Group Publishing.

McNeal, R., Tolbert, C., Mossberger, K., & Dotterweich, L. (2003). Innovating in digital government in the American states. *Social Science Quarterly*, *84*(1), 52–70. doi:10.1111/1540-6237.00140.

MDS. (2012). *Ministério do Desenvolvimento Social e Combate à Fome*. From www.mds.gov.br.

Measin, A., Mansor, M., Shafie, L. A., & Nayan, S. (2009). A study of collaborative learning among Malaysian undergraduates. *Asian Social Science*, *5*(7), 70–76.

Meijer, A., & Thaens, M. (2010). Alignment 2.0: Strategic use of new internet technologies in government. *Government Information Quarterly*, *27*(2), 113–121. doi:10.1016/j.giq.2009.12.001.

Meininger, M. C. (1998). Public service, the public's service. In Gallouédec-Genuys, F. (Ed.), *About French administration*. Paris: La Documentation Française.

Melkers, J.E., & Willoughby, K.G. (2001). Budgeters' view of state performance-budgeting systems: Distinctions across branches. *Public Administration Review*, January/February, *61*(1).

Mény, Y. (1998). *The French political system*. Paris: La Documentation française.

Meskell, D. (2003). High payoff in electronic government: Measuring the return on e-government investment. Washington, DC: Federation of Government Information Processing Councils.

Meyer, M. (2010). The rise of the knowledge broker. *Science Communication*, *32*(1), 118–127. doi:10.1177/1075547009359797.

Millard, J. (2008). eGovernment measurement for policy makers. *European Journal of ePractice*, 4. Efficiency and Effectiveness. Retrieved from http://www.epractice.eu

Millard, J., Nielsen, M. M., Warren, R., Smith, S., Macintosh, A., Tarabanis, K., & Parisopoulos, K. (2009). European eparticipation summary report. Retrieved from http://islab.uom.gr/eP/index.php?option=com_docman&task=cat_view&gid=36&&Itemid=82

Millham, R., & Eid, C. (2009). Digital cities: Nassau and Bologna – A study in contrasts. In *Proceedings of the IEEE Latin-American Conference on Communications, IEEE Communications Society* (pp. 1-6). Medllin, Colombia: LATINCOM. Retrieved January 20, 2012, from http://ieeexplore.ieee.org/xpls/abs_all.jsp?arnumber=5305144

Mina, L. (2011). *La efectividad de las redes de protección social: el rol de los sistemas integrados de información social en Colombia*. Banco Interamericano de Desarrollo.

Mir Cervantes, C. (2008). Evaluación operativa y de la calidad de los servicios que brinda Oportunidades. In SEDESOL, Evaluación Externa del Programa Oportunidades 2008. A diez años de intervención en zonas rurales (1997-2007). SEDESOL.

Miranda-Murillo, D. (2006). New immigrants centers at the Austin Public Library. *Texas Library Journal*, *82*(4), 144–147.

Mishra, A., & Mishra, D. (2011). E-government: Exploring the different dimensions of challenges, implementation, and success factors. *The Data Base for Advances in Information Systems*, *42*(4), 23–37. doi:10.1145/2096140.2096143.

Mistry, J. (2001). *Developing security policies for protecting corporate assets*. SANS Institute, Version 1.2d, Retrieved on July 13, 2012, from http://www.sans.org/reading_room/whitepapers/policyissues/developing-security-policies-protecting-corporate-assets_490

Misuraca, G., Alfano, G., & Viscusi, G. (2011). A multilevel framework for ICT-enabled governance: Assessing the non-technical dimensions of 'Government Openness'. *Electronic. Journal of E-Government*, *9*(2), 152–165.

Mitchell, J. I., Gagne, M., Beaudry, A., & Dyer, L. (2012). The role of perceived organizational support, distributive justice and motivation in reactions to new information technology. *Computers in Human Behavior*, *28*, 729–738. doi:10.1016/j.chb.2011.11.021.

MoGAHA. (2007). *Annual Report of e- Government 2006*. Seoul: MoGAHA.

MoGAHA. (2007). *Request for Proposal: On-Nara system*. Internal Document.

Mohamed, N., Hussin, H., & Hussein, R. (2009). Measuring users' satisfaction with Malaysia's electronic government systems. *Electronic. Journal of E-Government*, *7*(3), 283–294. Retrieved from http://www.ejeg.com.

Mohd Majzub, R. (2008). *The challenge of Research Universities: A SWOT Analysis*. Paper presented at the ASAIHL International Conference 2008. Nonthaburi, Thailand.

Mohd, H., & Syed Mohamad, S. M. (2005). Acceptance model of electronic medical record.[from http://www.health-informatics.kk.usm.my/pdf/JAIMS.pdf]. *Journal of Advancing Information and Management Studies*, *2*(1), 76–92. Retrieved August 15, 2010

Moon, J., Jung, G.-H., Chung, M., & Choe, Y. C. (2007). IT outsourcing for E-government: Lesson from IT outsourcing projects initiated by agricultural organizations of the Korean government. *Proceeding of the 40th Hawaii International Conference on System Sciences*, Hawaii, USA.

Moon, J. M., & Norris, D. F. (2005). Does managerial orientation matter? The adoption of reinventing government and e-government at the municipal level. *Information Systems Journal*, *15*(1), 43–60. doi:10.1111/j.1365-2575.2005.00185.x.

Moon, M. J. (2002). The evolution of e-government among municipalities: Rhetoric or reality? *Public Administration Review*, *62*(4), 424–433. doi:10.1111/0033-3352.00196.

Moore, A. (2005). Implementing e-government portals, technical and organizational issues: Montgomery county (USA) portal. *Proceedings of the E-Gov VC Series Under Joint Economic Research Program of the Government of Kazakhstan and the World Bank, World Bank Video Conference*.

Moravsik, A. (2004). Is there a "Democratic Deficit" in world politics? A framework for analysis. *Government and Opposition*, *39*(2), 336–363. doi:10.1111/j.1477-7053.2004.00126.x.

Moravsik, A. (2006). What can we learn from the collapse of the European constitutional project? A symposium. *Politische Vierteljahresschrift*, *47*(2), 219–241. doi:10.1007/s11615-006-0037-7.

Mossberger, K., Tolbert, C. J., & McNeal, R. S. (2008). *Digital citizenship: The internet, society and participation*. Cambridge, Massachusetts: MIT Press.

Mossberger, K., Tolbert, C., & McNeal, R. (2007). *Digital citizenship: The internet, society and participation*. Cambridge, MA: MIT Press.

Mossberger, K., Tolbert, C., & Stansbury, M. (2003). *Virtual inequality: Beyond the digital divide*. Washington, DC: Georgetown Press.

Mui, L., Mohtashemi, M., & Halberstadt, A. (2002). A computational model of trust and reputation. In *Proceedings of the35th Hawaii International Conference on System Sciences* (pp. 2431- 2439).

Myers, M. D. (1997). Qualitative research in information systems. *Management Information Systems Quarterly*, 241–242. doi:10.2307/249422.

Naficy, H. (2009). Centering essential immigrant help on the library Web site: The American Place (TAP) at Hartford Public Library. *Public Library Quarterly*, *28*(2), 162–175. doi:10.1080/01616840902892440.

Nahapiet, J., & Ghoshal, S. (1998). Social capital, intellectual capital, and the organizational advantage. *Academy of Management Review*, *23*(2), 242–266.

Nah, F. F., Lau, J., & Kuang, J. L. (2001). Critical factors for successful implementation of enterprise systems. *Business Process Management Journal*, *7*(3), 285–296. doi:10.1108/14637150110392782.

Nam, T., & Sayogo, D. S. (2011). Who uses e-government?: Examining the digital divide in e-government use. In E. Estevez & M. Jansen (Ed.), *Proceedings of the 5th International Conference on Theory and Practice of Electronic Governance*. Tallinn, Estonia.

Nam, T. (2012). Dual effects of the internet on political activism: Reinforcing and mobilizing. *Government Information Quarterly*, *29*(1), 90–97. doi:10.1016/j.giq.2011.08.010.

National Information Society Agency (NIA). (2003). *Policy Implications of the U.S. FEA. NCA Policy Report*. Seoul: NIA.

National Information Society Agency (NIA). (2003). *A Study of the Development and the Usage of BRM. NCA Policy Report*. Seoul: NIA.

National Information Society Agency (NIA). (2007). *20th Anniversary National Information Society Agency*. Seoul: NIA.

National Telecommunications and Information Administration. (2000). *Falling through the net: Toward digital inclusion. A report on Americans access to technology tools*. Retrieved October 14, 2005, from http://www.ntia.doc.gov/files/ntia/publications/fttn00.pdf

National Telecommunications and Information Administration. (2002). *A nation online: How Americans are expanding their use of the internet*. Retrieved October 14, 2005, from http://www.ntia.doc.gov/report/2002/nation-online-internet-use-america

National Telecommunications and Information Administration. (2011). *Digital nation: Expanding internet usage*. Retrieved March 15, 2012, from http://www.ntia.doc.gov/files/ntia/publications/ntia_internet_use_report_february_2011.pdf

Ndou, V. (2004). E-government for developing countries: Opportunities and challenges. *Electronic Journal of Information Systems in Developing Countries*, *18*, 1–24.

Nesti, G., & Valentini, C. (2010). E-democracy and Italian public administration: New media at the service of citizens. In Ardizzoni, M., & Ferrari, C. (Eds.), *Beyond monopoly: Globalization and contemporary Italian media* (pp. 151–170). Plymouth, UK: Lexington Books.

Neu, C., Anderson, R., & Bikson, T. (1999). *Sending your government a message: E-mail communication between citizens and government*. Santa Monica, CA: Rand Corp..

Newell, P., & Bellour, S. (2002). Mapping accountability: Origins, contexts and implications for development. *IDS Working Paper 168*. Brighton: Institute of Development Studies.

Ni, A. Y., & Bretschneider, S. (2007). *The decision to contract out: A study of contracting for e-government services in state governments. Public Administration Review*. May/June.

Nidumolu, S. R. (1989). The impact of interorganizational systems on the form and climate of seller-buyer relationships: A structural equations modelling approach. In *Proceedings of the 10th International Conference on Information Systems* (pp. 289-304).

Nielsen, J. (1994). Heuristic evaluation. In Nielsen, J., & Mack, R. L. (Eds.), *Usability inspection methods*. New York, NY: Wiley.

Ninghui, L., Mitchell, J. C., & Winsborough, W. H. (2005). Beyond proof-of-compliance: Security analysis in trust management. *Journal of the ACM*, *52*(3), 474–514. doi:10.1145/1066100.1066103.

Norris, D. F. (2005). E-government at the American grassroots: Future trajectory. In *Proceedings of the 38th Hawaii International Conference on System Sciences (HICSS'05)* (pp. 125-132). Washington: Computer Society Press.

Norris, D. F. (2010). E-government... not e-governance... not e-democracy: Not now! Not ever? In J. Davies & T. Janowski (Eds.), *Proceedings of the 4th international conference on theory and practice of electronic governance (ICEGOV'10)* (pp. 339-346). New York: ACM.

Norris, D. F. (2007). Electronic democracy at the American grassroots. In Norris, D. F. (Ed.), *Current issues and trends in e-government research* (pp. 164–179). Hershey, Pennsylvania: IGI Global. doi:10.4018/978-1-59904-283-1.ch008.

Norris, D. F., & Moon, M. J. (2005). Advancing e-government at the grassroots: Tortoise or hare? *Public Administration Review*, *65*(1), 64–75. doi:10.1111/j.1540-6210.2005.00431.x.

Norris, P. (2001). *Digital divide: Civic engagement, information poverty, and the internet worldwide*. New York: Cambridge University Press. doi:10.1017/CBO9781139164887.

Northern Territory Government. (2012). *Council information*. Department of Housing, Local Government and Regional Services. Retrieved on July 16, 2012, from http://www.localgovernment.nt.gov.au/council_information

O'Brien, J. (2002). *Management information systems: Managing information technology in the e-business enterprises* (5th ed.). Boston, MA: McGraw-Hill Irwin.

O'Looney, J. (1998). *Outsourcing the city: State and local government outsourcing*. New York: Quorum Books.

O'Toole, K. (2009). Australia local government and e-governance: From administration to citizen participation? In Khosrow-Pour, M. (Ed.), *E-government diffusion, policy, and impact: Advanced issues and practices* (pp. 174–184). Hershey, Pennsylvania: IGI Global.

O'Brien, J., & Marakas, G. (2011). *Management information systems* (10th ed.). New York: McGraw Hill.

OECD. (1997). *In search of results: Performance management practices*. Paris: PUMA/OECD.

OECD. (2003). e-Government imperative. Organisation for economic co-operation and development: E-Government Studies. Paris: OECD Publication Service.

OECD. (2003). *The e-Government Imperative: main findings*. OECD Policy Brief. Retrieved March 1, 2012, from www.oecd.org

OECD. (2007). *Performance Budgeting in OECD Countries*. Paris, France: Organisation for Economic Co-operation and Development.

OECD. (2009). *The impact of the crisis on ICTs and their role in the recovery*. Unclassified OECD document. Retrieved March 1, 2012, from http://www.oecd.org/dataoecd/33/20/43404360.pdf

Office of Citizenship, U.S. Citizenship and Immigration Services. (2010, September 15). *Library services for immigrants: A report on current practices*. Retrieved from http://www.uscis.gov/USCIS/Office%20of%20Citizenship/Citizenship%20Resource%20Center%20Site/Publications/PDFs/G-1112.pdf

Office of Management and Budget (OMB). (2002). *E-government strategy 2002*. Washington, DC: Author.

Office of Technology Assessment (OTA). (1981). Computer-based national information systems: Technology and public policy issues (Washington DC: OTA).

Ojo, A., Janowski, T., & Estevez, E. (2007). Determining progress towards e-Government – What are the core indicators? *United Nation University – International Institute for Software Technology Report*, No. 360.

Ojo, A., Janowski, T., Estevez, E., & Khan, I. K. (2007). *Human capacity development for e-government*. UNU-IIST Report No. 362 T. Yokyo: United Nations University, International Institute for Software Technology.

Olmedilla, D., Rana, O., Matthews, B., & Nejdl, W. (2005). Security and trust issues in semantic grids. In Proceedings of the Dagsthul Seminar, *Semantic Grid: The Convergence of Technologies*, volume 05271.

ONTSI. (2011). *Informe Anual de la Sociedad de la Información en España*. Industria y hábitos de consumo. Retrieved April 20, 2012, from http://www.ontsi.red.es/ontsi/es/estudios-informes/

Organization for Economic Co-operation and Development (OECD). (2003). *Checklist for e-Government leaders*. Paris: OECD.

Orlikowski, W. J., & Robey, D. (1991). Information technology and the structuring of organizations. *Information Systems Research*, *2*(2), 143–169. doi:10.1287/isre.2.2.143.

Othman, M., Ismail, S. N., & Md Raus, M. I. (2009). The development of the web-based Attendance Register System (ARS) for higher academic institution: From feasibility study to the design phase. *International Journal of Computer Science and Network Security*, *9*(10), 203–208.

O'Toole, K. (2007). E-Governance in Australian local government: Spinning a web around community? *International Journal of Electronic Government Research*, *3*(4), 58–75. doi:10.4018/jegr.2007100104.

O'Toole, L. J., & Meier, K. J. (1999). Modeling the impact of public management: Implications of structural context. *Journal of Public Administration: Research and Theory*, *9*(4), 505–526. doi:10.1093/oxfordjournals.jpart.a024421.

Pan. (2007). When it comes to urban grid management model. *Journal of the Party School of CPC Ningbo Municipal Committee, 29*(3), 41-46.

Panopoulou, E., Tambouris, E., & Tarabanis, K. (2009). eParticipation initiatives: How is Europe progressing? *European Journal of ePractice,* 7. Retrieved from http://www.epractice.eu/en/document/287931

Pantti, M., & van Zoonen, L. (2006). Do crying citizens make good citizens? *Social Semiotics*, *16*(2), 205–224. doi:10.1080/10350330600664797.

Paoletti, M. (1997). *La démocratie locale et le référendum: Analyse de la démocratie à travers la genèse institutionnelle du référendum*. Paris: L´Harmattan.

Parasuraman, A., Berry, L. L., & Zeithaml, V. A. (1985). A conceptual model of service quality and its implications for future research. *Journal of Marketing*, *49*(4), 41–50. doi:10.2307/1251430.

Parasuraman, A., Berry, L. L., & Zeithaml, V. A. (1988). SERVQUAL: A multiple-item scale for measuring consumer perceptions of service quality. *Journal of Retailing*, *64*(1), 12–40.

Parasuraman, A., Berry, L. L., & Zeithaml, V. A. (1991). Refinement and reassessment of the SERVQUAL scale. *Journal of Retailing*, *67*(4), 420–450.

Pardo, T. A., Cresswell, A. M., Dawes, S. S., & Burke, G. B. (2004). Modeling the social and technical processes of interorganizational information integration. Paper presented at *HICSS2004, 37th Hawaiian International Conference on System Sciences*.

Pardo, T. A., Cresswell, A. M., Thompson, F., & Zhang, J. (2006). Knowledge sharing in cross-boundary information systems development. *Journal of Information Technology Management*, *7*(4).

Park, R. (2008). Measuring factors that influence the success of e-government initiatives. *Proceedings of the 41st Hawaii International Conference on System Sciences – 2008* (pp. 218). doi: 10.1109/HICSS.2008.244

Parker, S., & Berham, J. (2008). Seguimiento de adultos jóvenes en hogares incorporados desde 1998 a Oportunidades: impactos en educación y pruebas de desempeño. In SEDESOL, Evaluación Externa del Programa Oportunidades 2008. A diez años de intervención en zonas rurales (1997-2007). SEDESOL.

Park, Y., Son, H., & Kim, C. (2012). Investigating the determinants of construction professionals' acceptance of web-based training: An extension of the technology acceptance model. *Automation in Construction*, *22*, 377–386. doi:10.1016/j.autcon.2011.09.016.

Parveen, F., & Sulaiman, A. (2008). Technology complexity, personal innovativeness and intention to use wireless internet using mobile devices in Malaysia. *International Reviews of Business Research Papers*, *4*(5), 1-10. Retrieved July 8, 2010, from http://www.bizresearchpapers.com/1[1].%20Ainin.pdf

Patricia, R. (1983). A structrationist accounts of political culture. *Administrative Science Quarterly*, *28*(3), 414–437. Retrieved from http://www.jstor.org/stable/2392250 doi:10.2307/2392250.

Patton, M. Q. (2002). *Qualitative research and evaluation methods*. Thousand Oaks, California: Sage Publications.

Pawlowski, S. D., & Robey, D. (2004). Bridging user organizations: Knowledge brokering and the work of information technology professionals. *Management Information Systems Quarterly*, *28*(4), 645–672.

Pawson, R. (2006). *Evidence-based policy: A realist perspective*. London: Sage.

PCGID. (2005). *E-government of participatory government*. Seoul: Author.

Peng, et al. (2008). Grid management and service system in city based on SIG. *Computer Engineering*, *34*(13), 245–257.

Perrin, B. (1986). *Décentralisation, le droit et le fait*. Moulins-lès-Metz: Est-Imprimerie.

Peters, B. G., & Pierre, J. (2000). *Governance, politics, and the state*. New York: St. Martin's Press.

Peterson, R. (2004). Crafting information technology governance. *Information Systems Management*, *21*(4), 7–22. doi:10.1201/1078/44705.21.4.20040901/84183.2.

Petter, S., DeLone, W., & McLean, E. (2008). Measuring information system success: Models, dimensions, measure, and relationships. *European Journal of Information Systems*, *17*, 236–263. doi:10.1057/ejis.2008.15.

Pew Internet & American Life Project. (2002). *Health information online. Daily tracking survey December 2002*. Retrieved February 20, 2012, from http://www.pewinternet.org

Pew Internet & American Life Project. (2004). *Health information online. Activity tracking survey November 2004.* Retrieved February 20, 2012, from http://www.pewinternet.org

Pew Internet & American Life Project. (2006). *Health information online. August 2006 daily tracking survey.* Retrieved February 20, 2012, from http://www.pewinternet.org

Pew Internet & American Life Project. (2007*). Information searches that solve problems.* Retrieved February 20, 2012, from http://www.pewinternet.org/reports/

Pew Internet & American Life Project. (2008). *Health information online. Fall tracking 2008.* Retrieved September 15, 2010, from http://www.pewinternet.org

Pew Internet & American Life Project. (2010). *Home broadband.* Retrieved February 20, 2012, from http://pewinternet.org/Reports/2010/Home-Broadband-2010.aspx

Pew Internet & American Life Project. (2010). *Health information online. August change assessment 2010.* Retrieved February 20, 2012, from http://www.pewinternet.org

Pew Internet & American Life Project. (2012). *Digital Differences.* Retrieved February 20, 2012, from http://pewinternet.org/Reports/2012/Digital-differences/Overview.aspx

Phang, M. (2002). *A study on policy network in the e-government building.* (Unpublished doctoral dissertation). Sungkyunkwan University, Korea.

Phang, R. (2010). Asian e-government in 2010. Retrieved on March 20, 2012, from http://www.futuregov.asia/articles/2010/jul/13/asian-e-government-2010/

Phang, C. W., Kankanalli, A., & Ang, C. (2008). Investigating organizational learning in egovernment projects: A multi-theoretic approach. *The Journal of Strategic Information Systems*, *17*(2), 99–123. doi:10.1016/j.jsis.2007.12.006.

Phang, C. W., Sutanto, J., Kankanhalli, A., Li, Y., Tan, B. C. Y., & Teo, H. H. (2006). Senior citizens' acceptance of information systems: A study in the context of e-government services. *IEEE Transactions on Engineering Management*, *53*(4), 555–569. doi:10.1109/TEM.2006.883710.

Pierre, J., & Peters, B. G. (2005). *Governing complex societies: Trajectories and scenarios.* New York: Palgrave Macmillan. doi:10.1057/9780230512641.

Pierson, P. (1994). *Dismantling the welfare state? Reagan, thatcher, and the politics of retrenchment.* Cambridge, UK: Cambridge University Press. doi:10.1017/CBO9780511805288.

Pierson, P. (2000). Increasing returns, path dependence, and the study of politics. *The American Political Science Review*, *94*(2), 251–267. doi:10.2307/2586011.

Pierson, P. (2004). *Politics in time: History, institutions, and political analysis.* Princeton: Princeton University Press.

Pingdom. (2012). *Pingdom tools - Full page test.* Retrieved on March 1, 2012, from http://tools.pingdom.com/

Plan D-Wider and deeper Debate on Europe. (2006). SeC (2006)1553. Brussels: Information Note form Vice President Wallstom to the Commission

Pollit, C., & Bouckaert, G. (2011). *Public management reform: A comparative analysis* (3rd ed.). Oxford: Oxford University Press.

Pollitt, C. (2001). Clarifying convergence: Striking similarities and durable differences in public management reform. *Public Management Review*, *3*(4), 471–492. doi:10.1080/14616670110071847.

Pollitt, C., & Bouckaert, G. (2004). *Public management reform, a comparative analysis.* Oxford: Oxford University Press.

Potnis, D., & Pardo, T. (2011). Mapping the evolution of e-Readiness Assessments. *Transforming Government: People. Process and Policy*, *5*(4), 345–363.

Powell, W. K., Koput, K. W., & Smith-Doerr, L. (1996). Interorganizational collaboration and the locus of innovation: Networks of learning in biotechnology. *Administrative Science Quarterly*, *41*, 116–145. doi:10.2307/2393988.

Prananto, A., & McKemmish, S. (2007). *Critical success factors for the establishment of e-government.* RISO Working Paper. Melbourne, Victoria: Faculty of Information and Communication Technologies, Swinburne University of Technology.

Pratchett, L. (1999). New technologies and the modernization of local government: An analysis of biases and constraints. *Public Administration*, *77*(4), 731–750. doi:10.1111/1467-9299.00177.

Pratchett, L., & Krimmer, R. (2005). The coming of e-democracy. *International Journal of Electronic Government Research*, *1*(3).

Preece, J. (2001). Sociability and usability in online communities: Determining and measuring success. *Behaviour & Information Technology*, *20*(5), 347–356. doi:10.1080/01449290110084683.

Premat, C. (2005). The growing use of referenda in local politics: A comparison of France and Germany. In K. Steyvers, J.B. Pilet, H. Reynaert, & P. Delwit (Eds.), Revolution or renovation? Reforming local politics in Europe (pp. 185-212). Brugge: Vanden Broele Publishers.

Premat, C. (2012). Initiatives and referendums. In O. W. Gabriel, S. I. Keil, & E. Kerrouche (Eds.), Political participation in France and Germany (pp. 161-188). Essex: EPCR Press studies.

Premat, C. (2006/2007). À la recherche d'une communauté perdue: Les usages de la proximité dans le discours participatif en France. *Argumentum*, *5*, 59–78.

Premat, C. (2007). L'idée d'une 6e République dans la campagne des élections présidentielles. *Revista de Ştiinţe Politice, Revue des sciences politiques. Université de Craiova*, *13*, 45–58.

Premat, C. (2008). La participation, métonymie de la communication? Les maires français et l'usage de la cyberdémocratie. *COMMposite*, *11*(1), 87–99.

Premat, C. (2009). The implementation of participatory democracy in French communes. *French Politics*, *7*, 1–18. doi:10.1057/fp.2009.5.

Premat, C. (2009). Genre et discours participatif dans les villes françaises. In Gubin, E., Piette, V., & Benvindo, B. (Eds.), *Masculinités, sextants* (pp. 257–272). Bruxelles: Presses de l'Université Libre de Bruxelles.

Previtali, P., & Bof, F. (2009). E-government adoption in small Italian municipalities. *International Journal of Public Sector Management*, *22*(4), 338–348. doi:10.1108/09513550910961619.

PromoPa. (2011). *Imprese e Burocrazia - Come le micro e piccole imprese giudicano la Pubblica Amministrazione.* Fondazione PromoPa. Retrieved March 1, 2012, from http://www.unioncamerelombardia.it/images/File/NE_Eventi%202011/UNIONCAMERE_copIMPRESA.pdf

Puron-Cid, G. (2010). *Extending structuration theory: A study of an IT-enabled budget reform in Mexico.* (Doctoral Thesis). University at Albany, State University of New York, Albany, New York.

Puron-Cid, G. (2012). Interdisciplinary application of structuration theory for e-government: A case study of an IT-enabled budget reform. Accepted for publication at *Government Information Quarterly*.

Putnam, R. (2000). *Bowling alone: The collapse and revival of American community*. New York, NY: Simon & Schuster. doi:10.1145/358916.361990.

Qi, et al. (2008). Urban gridization in modern city management. *China Public Administration Review,* (S1), 79-81.

Qiu & Zhang. (2008). Design of city-grid management system platform. *Journal of Xi'An University of Science and Technology*, *28*(1), 96–99.

Queensland Government. (2012). *Search the local government directory*. Department of Local Government. Retrieved on July 16, 2012, from http://www.dlgp.qld.gov.au/local-government-directory/search-the-local-government-directory.html

queenslibrary.org. (2013). Website. Retrieved from http://www.queenslibrary.org/services/citizenship-immigration

Rabaiah, A., & Vandijck, E. (2009). A strategic framework of e-government: Generic and best practice. *Electronic. Journal of E-Government*, *7*(3), 241–258.

Rahman, H. (2007). E-government readiness: From the design to table to the grass roots. *Proceedings of the 1st International Conferences on Theory and Practices of Electronic Governance* (pp. 225-232). ACM Press.

Rallet, A., & Rochelandet, F. (2004). La fracture numérique: Une faille sans fondement? *Réseaux*, 2004/5, *127*(128), 19-54.

Ramayah, T., & Mohd Suki, N. (2006). Intention to use mobile PC among MBA students: Implications for technology integration in the learning curriculum. *UNITAR E-Journal, 1*(2). Retrieved from http://ejournal.unirazak.edu.my

Ramlah, H., Norshidah, M., Ahlan, A. R., & Mahmud, M. (2010). E-government application: An integrated model on G2C adoption of online tax. *Transforming Government: People. Process and Policy*, *5*(3), 225–248.

Ramo'n Gil-Garcı'a, J., & Pardo, T. A. (2005). E-government success factors: Mapping practical tools to theoretical foundations. *Government Information Quarterly*, *22*(2), 187–216. doi:10.1016/j.giq.2005.02.001.

Ramón, F. (2010). La red social como ejemplo de participación: casos y cuestiones. In Cotino, L. (Ed.), *Libertades de expresión e información en Internet y las redes sociales: ejercicio, amenazas y garantías*. Valencia: Publicacions de la Universitat de València.

Randall, S. (2010, September 18). Why bricks and clicks don't always mix. *New York Times*. Retrieved on March 20, 2012, from http://www.nytimes.com/2010/09/19/business/19digi.html

Rashid, N., & Rahman, S. (2010). An investigation into critical determinants of e-government implementation in the context of a developing nation. In K. N. Andersen, Francesconi, E., Grönlund, A., & van Engers, T. M. (Eds.), Electronic government and the information systems perspective (pp. 9-21). Verlag, Berlin and Heidelberg: Springer.

Raynsford, N., & Beecham, S. J. (2002). *The national strategy for local e-government*. London: crown.

Recovery Accountability and Transparency Board. (2010). *Recovery funds satellite broadband to rural America*. Retrieved March 15, 2011, from http://www.Recovery.gov

Reddick, C. G. (2009). Factors that explain the perceived effectiveness of e-government: A survey of United States city government information technology directors. *International Publication of Electronic Government Research*, *5*(2), 1–15. doi:10.4018/jegr.2009040101.

Reddick, C. G., & Frank, H. A. (2007). The perceived impacts of E-Government on U.S.cities: A survey of Florida and Texas city managers. *Government Information Quarterly*, *24*(3), 576–594. doi:10.1016/j.giq.2006.09.004.

Reece, B. (2006). E-government literature review. *Journal of E-Government*, *3*(1), 69–110. doi:10.1300/J399v03n01_05.

Reed, M. I. (2001). Organization, trust and control: A realist analysis. *Organization Studies*, *22*(2), 201. doi:10.1177/0170840601222002.

Reffat, R. M. (2006) Developing a successful e-government. *Electronic Government, an International Journal*, 2(3), 247-276. Retrieved from http://www.imamu.edu.sa/Scientific_selections/files/DocLib/E16.pdf

Renn, O., & Schweizer, P.-J. (2012). In O.W. Gabriel, S.I. Keil, & E. Kerrouche (Eds.), Political participation in France and Germany (pp. 273-295). Essex: EPCR Press studies.

Riley, J. (2009). *The world now has 4 billion mobile phone users*. ITWire, Retrieved on March, 25, 2012, from http://www.itwire.com/it-industry-news/market/27107-the-world-now-has-4-billion-mobile-phone-users

Ring, P. S., & Van de Van, A. H. (1994). Developmental processes of cooperative interorganizational relationships. *Academy of Management Review*, *19*(1), 90–118.

Ritchie, J. (2003). The applications of qualitative methods to social research. In Ritchie, J., & Lewis, J. (Eds.), *Qualitative research practice: A guide for social science students and researchers* (pp. 24–46). London: Sage.

Rocheleau, B. (2006). *Public management information systems*. Hershey, PA: Idea Group Publishing.

Rockart, J. F. (1979). Chief executives define their own data needs. *Harvard Business Review*, (March-April): 81. PMID:10297607.

Rockart, J. F., & Scott Morton, M. S. (1984). Implications of changes in information technology for corporate strategy. *Interfaces*, *14*(1), 84–95. doi:10.1287/inte.14.1.84.

Rogers, E. M. (1995). *Diffusion of innovations* (4th ed.). New York, NY: The Free Press.

Rogers, E. M. (2003). *Diffusion of Innovations* (5th ed.). New York: The Free Press.

Rolfe, P. (2012, April 15). The case against Casey council. *Herald Sun*, (pp. 18-19).

Romero, S. (2008). *Evaluación de Consistencia y Resultados 2007. Programa de Desarrollo Humano Oportunidades*. CONEVAL.

Rorissa, A., Demissie, D., & Pardo, T. (2011). Benchmarking e-government: A comparison of frameworks for computing e-Government index and ranking. *Government Information Quarterly, 28*(3), 354–362. doi:10.1016/j.giq.2010.09.006.

Rose, J. (1998). *Evaluating the contribution of structuration theory to the information systems discipline*. Presented at 6th European Conference on Information Systems, Aix-en-Provence. Retrieved from http://folk.uio.no/patrickr/refdoc/ECIS1998-Rose.pdf

Rose, L. (2005). Territorial and functional reforms: Old wine in new bottles- or a new vintage? In K. Steyvers, J.B. Pilet, H. Reynaert, & P. Delwit (Eds.), Revolution or renovation? Reforming local politics in Europe (pp. 397-419). Brugge: Vanden Broele Publishers.

Rose, R. (2005). A global diffusion model of e-governance. *Journal of Public Policy, 25*(1), 5–27. doi:10.1017/S0143814X05000279.

Rose, W. R., & Grant, G. G. (2010). Critical issues pertaining to the planning and implementation of E-Government initiatives. *Government Information Quarterly, 27*(1), 26–33. doi:10.1016/j.giq.2009.06.002.

Rosny93.fr. (n.d.). Website. Retrieved April 21, 2012, from http://www.rosny93.fr/spip.php?article1297

Rotchanakitumnuai, S. (2008). Measuring e-government service value with the E-GOVSQUAL-RISK model. *Business Process Management Journal, 14*(5), 724–737. doi:10.1108/14637150810903075.

Rowley, J. (2011). e-Government stakeholders - Who are they and what do they want? *International Journal of Information Management, 31*, 53–62. doi:10.1016/j.ijinfomgt.2010.05.005.

Rueschemeyer, D. (2006). Why and how ideas matter. In Goodin, R. E., & Tilly, C. (Eds.), *The Oxford handbook of contextual political analysis*. Oxford: Oxford University Press. doi:10.1093/oxfordhb/9780199270439.003.0012.

Rui, S. (2004). La démocratie en débat. Les citoyens face à l´action publique. Paris: éditions Colin.

Sagheb-Tehrani, M. (2010). A model of successful factors towards e-government implementation. *Electronic Government, an International Journal, 7*(1), 60-74.

Saintger.blogencommun.fr. (n.d.). Website. Retrieved from http://saintger.blogencommun.fr/2009-06-allo-monsieur-le-maire-demain-a-18h/

Saint-Martin, D. (2004). *Building the new managerialist state* (2nd ed.). Oxford: Oxford University Press. doi:10.1093/acprof:oso/9780199269068.001.0001.

Saint-Martin, D. (2005). Management consultancy. In Ferlie, E., Lynn, L. E., & Pollitt, C. (Eds.), *The Oxford handbook of public management*. Oxford: Oxford University Press.

Sakowicz, M. (2004). How to evaluate e-government? Different methodlogies and methodes. In *NISPAcee occasional papers, V*(2), 18-26. Retrieved from http://unpan1.un.org/intradoc/groups/public/documents/NISPAcee/UNPAN009486.pdf

Salamon, L. (2002). The new governance and the tools of public action: An introduction. In Salamon, L. M. (Ed.), *The tools of government: A guide to the new governance*. New York: Oxford University Press.

Salman, A. (2009). ICT, the new media (internet) and development: Malaysian experience. *The Innovation Journal: The Public Sector Innovation Journal, 15*(1).

Sambamurthy, V., & Zmud, R. W. (1999). Arrangements for information technology governance: A theory of multiple contingencies. *Management Information Systems Quarterly, 23*(2), 261–290. doi:10.2307/249754.

Sandoval-Almazan, R., & Gil-Garcia, J. R. (2012). Are government internet portals evolving towards more interaction, participation, and collaboration? Revisiting the rhetoric of e-government among municipalities. *Government Information Quarterly, 29*(Supplement 1), S72–S81. doi:10.1016/j.giq.2011.09.004.

Sariego, J. (2008). Cobertura y operación del Programa Oportunidadesen regiones interculturales indígenas. In SEDESOL, Evaluación Externa del Programa Oportunidades 2008. A diez años de intervención en zonas rurales (1997-2007). SEDESOL.

Schick, A. (2008). Getting performance budgeting to perform. *Paper presented at the Conferencia Internacional de Presupuesto por Resultados, Mexico City.*

Schick, A. (1998). Why most developing countries should not try New Zealand reforms. *The World Bank Research Observer, 13*(1), 123. doi:10.1093/wbro/13.1.123.

Schmeida, M., McNeal, R., & Mossberger, K. (2007). Policy determinants affect telehealth implementation. *Journal of Telemedicine and e-Health, 13*(2), 101-108.

Schmeida, M. (2004). *Telehealth and state government policy. Book Chapter. Encyclopedia of Public Administration and Public Policy*. New York, NY: Marcel Dekker, Inc..

Schmeida, M. (2005). *Telehealth innovation in the American states*. Ann Arbor, MI: ProQuest.

Schmeida, M. (2006). *State government policy initiatives: Improving access for the medically underserved. Encyclopedia of Public Administration and Public Policy*. New York, NY: Marcel Dekker, Inc..

Schmeida, M., & McNeal, R. (2007). The telehealth divide: Disparities in searching public health information online. *Journal of Health Care for the Poor and Underserved, 18*, 637–647. doi:10.1353/hpu.2007.0068 PMID:17675719.

Schmeida, M., & McNeal, R. (2009). Demographic differences in telehealth policy outcomes. In Lazakidou, A., & Siassiakos, K. (Eds.), *Handbook of research on distributed medical informatics and e-health* (pp. 500–508). Hershey, PA: Medical Information Science Reference.

Scholl, H. J. (2001). Applying stakeholder theory to e-government: Benefits and limits. In *Proceedings of the 1st IFIP Conference on E-Commerce, E-Business, and EGovernment*. Zurich, Switzerland.

Scholl, H. J. (2009). Electronic government: A study domain past its infancy. In Scholl, H. J. (Ed.), *Electronic government: Information, technology and transformation*. M.E. Sharpe Armonk.

Schuppan, T. (2008). E-Government in developing countries: Experiences from sub-Saharan Africa. *Government Information Quarterly, 26*(1), 118–127. doi:10.1016/j.giq.2008.01.006.

Schuppert, G. F. (2011). Partnership. In Bevir, M. (Ed.), *The Sage handbook of governance*. London: Sage Publication Inc. doi:10.4135/9781446200964.n18.

Schwartz, J. D. (1984). Participation and multisubjective understanding: An interpretivist approach to the study of political participation. *The Journal of Politics, 46*, 1117–1141. doi:10.2307/2131245.

Schwester, R. W. (2009). Examining the barriers to e-government adoption. *Electronic. Journal of E-Government, 7*(1), 113–122.

Scott, J. K. (2005). E-services: Assessing the quality of municipal government web sites. *State and Local Government Review, 37*(2), 151–165. doi:10.1177/0160323X0503700206.

Seifert, J. W. (2006). E-government in the United States. In Hernon, P., Culleen, R., & Relyea, H. C. (Eds.), *Comparative perspectives on e-government: Serving today and building for tomorrow* (pp. 25–54). Lanham, Maryland: Scarecrow Press, Inc..

Seifert, J. W. (2006). *Federal enterprise architecture and e-government: Issues for information technology management. Congressional Research Service, Report for Congress*. Washington, DC: The Library of Congress.

Seira, E., Parker, S., Silva, P., Marcué, E., & Cárdenas, C. (2011). *Estudio para el H. Congreso de la Union en cumplimiento del artículo 55 BIS 2 de la Ley de Instituciones de Crédito. Banco del Ahorro Nacional y Servicios Financieros, Sociedad Nacional de Crédito, Institución de Banca de Desarrollo*. BANSEFI.

Seitz, N. E. (1989). *Capital budgeting and long term financing decision*. Hindsdale, IL: Dyden Press.

Selwyn, N. (2004). Reconsidering political and popular understandings of the digital divide. *New Media & Society, 6*(3), 341–362. doi:10.1177/1461444804042519.

Sen, A. (1999). *Development as freedom*. New York: Oxford University Press.

Senate Hearing 103-515. (1993). *Reinventing government: Using new technology to improve service and cut costs*. 103rd Congress.

Seo, S. (2004). *The prospect of e-government promotion in participatory government*. A presentation in the Korea IT Leaders Forum.

Serafeimidis, V., & Smithson, S. (2000). Information systems evaluation in practice: A case study of organizational change. *Journal of Information Technology*, *15*(2), 93–105. doi:10.1080/026839600344294.

Shackleton, P., Fisher, J., & Dawson, L. (2005). From dog licenses to democracy: Local government approaches to e-service delivery in Australia. In D. Bartmann, F. Rajola, J. Kallinikos, D. Avison, R. Winter, P. Ein-Dor, J. Becker, F. Bodendorf, & C. Weinhardt (Eds.), *Proceedings of the thirteenth European conference on information systems* (pp. 724-735). Regensburg, Germany: ECIS Standing Committee.

Shailendra, C., Palvia, J., & Sharma, S. S. (2007). E-government and e-governance: Definitions/domain framework and status around the world. In Agarwal, A., & Ramana, V. V. (Eds.), *Foundations of E-government* (pp. 1–12). India: Computer Society of India.

Shan, S., Wang, L., Wang, J., Hao, Y., & Hua, F. (2011). Research on e-Government evaluation model based on the principal component analysis. *Information Technology Management*, *12*(2), 173–185. doi:10.1007/s10799-011-0083-8.

Shapiro, S. P. (1987). The social control of impersonal trust. *American Journal of Sociology*, *93*(3), 623–658. doi:10.1086/228791.

Shareef, M., et al. (2008). A readiness assessment framework for e-Government Planning – Design and Application. *Proceedings of the 2nd International Conferences on Theory and Practices of Electronic Governance* (pp. 403-409). ACM Press.

Sharma, S., & Gupta, J. (2002). *Transforming to e-government: A framework*. Paper presented at the 2nd European Conference on E-Government, Public Sector Times (pp. 383-390). 1-2 Oct 2002, St. Catherine's College Oxford, United Kingdom.

Sharma, A., & Sheth, J. N. (2004). Web-based marketing: The coming revolution in marketing thought and strategy. *Journal of Business Research*, *57*(7), 696–702. doi:10.1016/S0148-2963(02)00350-8.

Sharma, S. (2007). Exploring best practices in public-private partnership (PPP) in e-government through select Asian case studies. *The International Information & Library Review*, 39.

Sheingate, A. D. (2003). Political entrepreneurship, institutional change, and american political development. *Studies in American Political Development*, *17*(2), 185–203. doi:10.1017/S0898588X03000129.

Shin, E. (2012). Attitudinal determinants of e-government technology use among U.S. local public managers. In *Proceedings of the 45th Hawaii Conference on System Science* (pp. 2613-2622). Washington: Computer Society Press.

Sigler, K. I., Jaeger, P. T., Bertot, J. C., DeCoster, E. J., McDermott, A. J., & Langa, L. A. (2012). Public libraries, the Internet, and economic uncertainty. In A. Woodsworth (Ed.), Advances in librarianship, vol. 34: Librarianship in times of crisis (pp. 19-35). London: Emerald.

Sikkink, K. (1991). *Ideas and institutions*. Ithaca, London: Cornell Univ. Press.

Silcock, R. (2001). What is e-government? *Parliamentary Affairs*, *54*(1), 88–101. doi:10.1093/pa/54.1.88.

Singapore Ministry of Finance and Infocomm Development Authority of Singapore. (2001). *E-government 2001: Accelerating, integrating, transforming public services*. Singapore: Singapore Government.

Singh, S. H. (2003). Government in the digital era and human factors in e-governance. Paper read the Regional Workshop on e-Government, 1-3 Dec 2003, Sana'a.

Singh, A. (2010). Role of information technology in enabling e-governance. *The IUP Journal of Systems Management*, *8*(1), 7–14.

Singh, G., Pathak, R. D., Naz, R., & Belwal, R. (2010). E-governance for improved public sector service delivery in India, Ethiopia and Fiji. *International Journal of Public Sector Management*, *23*(3), 254–275. doi:10.1108/09513551011032473.

Sintomer, Y. (2007). *Le pouvoir au peuple: jurys citoyens, tirage au sort et démocratie participative*. Paris: La Découverte.

Sipior, J., & Ward, B. (2005). Bridging the digital divide for e-Government inclusion: A United States Case Study. *The Electronic. Journal of E-Government, 3*(3), 137–146.

Skelcher, C. (2005). Public-private partnerships and hybridity. In Ferlie, E., Lynn, L. E., & Pollitt, C. (Eds.), *The Oxford handbook of public management*. Oxford: Oxford University Press.

Skocpol, T., & Rueschemeyer, D. (1996). Introduction. In Rueschemeyer, D., & Skocpol, T. (Eds.), *States, social knowledge, and the origins of modern social policies*. Princeton: Princeton University Press.

Smismans, S. (2003). European civil society: Shaped by discourses and institutional interests. *European Law Journal, 482*(9), 499–503.

Smith, S. (2009). Main benefits of eParticipation developments in the EU – a contextualisation with reference to the EU governance regime and the European public sphere. *European eParticipation study*, Deliverable 1.3c. Retrieved from http://islab.uom.gr/eP/

Smith, S., & Dalakiouridou, E. (2009). Contextualising public (e)Participation in the governance of the European Union. *European Journal of ePractice, 7*. Retrieved from http://www.epractice.eu/en/document/287931

Smith, K. G. et al. (1995). Intra- and Interorganizational Cooperation: Toward a Research Agenda. *Academy of Management Journal, 38*(1), 7–23. doi:10.2307/256726.

Smith, S., Macintosh, A., & Millard, J. (2011). A three-layered framework for evaluating eParticipation. *International Journal of Electronic Governance, 4*(4), 304–321. doi:10.1504/IJEG.2011.046013.

Snellen, I. (2005). E-government: A challenge for public management. In Ferlie, E., Lynn, J. L. E., & Pollitt, C. (Eds.), *The Oxford handbook of public management*. Oxford: Oxford University Press.

Sohail, M. S., & Shanmugham, B. (2003). E-banking and customer preferences in Malaysia: An empirical investigation. *Journal Information Sciences-Informatics and Computer Science, 150*(3-4), 207-217. Retrieved June 29, 2010, from http://www.sciencedirect.com/science/article/pii/S002002550200378X

Solimano, A. (2005). Hacia nuevas políticas sociales en América Latina: Crecimiento, clases medias y derechos sociales. *Revista de la CEPAL*, 45-60.

Somers, T. M., & Nelson, K. (2001, 3-6 January). *The impact of critical success factors across the stages of enterprise resource planning implementation*. Paper presented at the 34th Hawaii International Conference on Systems Sciences, Maui, Hawaii.

Song, H., & Tak, C. (2007). E-government in Korea: Performance and tasks. *Informatization Policy, 14*, 20–37.

Srivastava, S. C. (2011). Is e-government providing the promised returns? A value framework for assessing e-government impact. *Transforming Government: People. Process and Policy, 5*(2), 107–113. doi: doi:10.1108/17506161111131159.

Srivastava, S. C., & Teo, T. S. H. (2007). E-government payoffs: Evidence from cross-country data. *Journal of Global Information Management, 15*(4), 20–40. doi:10.4018/jgim.2007100102.

Srivastava, S. C., & Teo, T. S. H. (2010). E-government, e-business, and national economic performance. *Communications of the Association for Information Systems, 26*, 267–286.

Stair, R., & Reynolds, G. (2010). Principles of business information systems (9th ed.). Course Technology, CENGAGE Learning, USA.

Stair, R., Reynolds, G., & Chesney, T. (2008). *Principles of business information systems*. Cengage Learning, USA: Course Technology.

Stanley, L. (2003). Beyond access: Psychosocial barrier to computer literacy. *The Information Society, 19*(5), 407–416. doi:10.1080/715720560.

State Government of Victoria. (2012). *Find your local council*. Department of Planning and Community Development. Retrieved on July 16, 2012, from http://www.dpcd.vic.gov.au/localgovernment/find-your-local-council#councils

Steyaert, J. C. (2004). Measuring the performance of electronic government services. *Information & Management, 41*(3), 369–375. doi:10.1016/S0378-7206(03)00025-9.

Stoker, G. (2006). *Why politics matters: Making democracy work*. Basingstoke: Palgrave Macmillan.

Stone, R. W., Good, D. J., & Baker-Eveleth, L. (2007). The impact of information technology on individual and firm marketing performance. *Behaviour & Information Technology, 26*(6), 465–482. doi:10.1080/01449290600571610.

Stover, S. (1999). *Rural internet connectivity*. Rural Policy Research Institute. Retrieved June 21, 2000, from http://www.rupri.org

Stover, S., Chapman, G., & Waters, J. (2004). Beyond community networking and CTCs: Access, development, and public policy. *Telecommunications Policy, 28*(7-8), 465–485. doi:10.1016/j.telpol.2004.05.008.

Strauss, A., & Corbin, J. (1990). *Basics of qualitative research: Grounded theory procedures and techniques*. Newbury Park: Sage.

Streib, G., & Navarro, I. (2006). Citizen demand for interactive e-government: The case of Georgia consumer services. *American Review of Public Administration, 36*, 288–300. doi:10.1177/0275074005283371.

Streib, G., & Navarro, I. (2008). City managers and e-government development: Assessing technology literacy and leadership needs. *Journal of Electronic Government Research, 4*(4), 37–53. doi:10.4018/jegr.2008100103.

Stromer-Galley, J. (2000). Online interaction and why candidates avoid it. *The Journal of Communication, 50*(4), 111–132. doi:10.1111/j.1460-2466.2000.tb02865.x.

Stromer-Galley, J. (2004). Interactivity-as-product and interactivity-as-process. *The Information Society, 20*(5), 391–394. doi:10.1080/01972240490508081.

Suan, B. H. (2003). Making e-governance happen—a practitioner's perspective. In Yong, J. S. L. (Ed.), *Enabling public service innovation in the 21st century: e-Government in Asia* (pp. 366–391). Singapore: Times Editions.

Sulaiman, A., Ng, J., & Mohezar, S. (2008). E-ticketing as a new way of buying tickets: Malaysian perceptions. *Journal of the Social Sciences, 17*(2), 149–157.

Sundell, J. (2000). Library service to Hispanic immigrants of Forsyth County, North Carolina: A community collaboration. In Guerena, S. (Ed.), *Library Services to Latinos: An Anthology* (pp. 143–168). Jefferson, NC: McFarland & Company, Inc,Publishers.

Su, S. S., & Conaway, C. W. (1995). Information and a forgotten minority: Elderly Chinese immigrants. *Library & Information Science Research, 17*(1), 69–86. doi:10.1016/0740-8188(95)90006-3.

Susanto, T. D., & Goodwin, R. (2010). Factors influencing citizen adoption of SMS-based e-government services. *Electronic. Journal of E-Government, 8*(1), 55–71. Retrieved from http://www.ejeg.com.

Svara, J. H. (1987). Mayoral leadership in council-manager cities: Preconditions versus preconceptions. *The Journal of Politics, 49*(1), 207–227. doi:10.2307/2131141.

Swan, J., Newell, S., & Robertson, M. (1999). Central agencies in the diffusion & design of technology: A comparison of the UK & Sweden. *Organization Studies, 20*(6), 905–931. doi:10.1177/0170840699206001.

Swan, J., Newell, S., & Robertson, M. (2000). The diffusion, design & social shaping of production management information systems in Europe. *Information Technology & People, 13*(1), 27–46. doi:10.1108/09593840010312744.

Swar, B., Moon, J., Oh, J., & Rhee, C. (2012)... *Information Systems Frontiers, 14*, 457–475. doi:10.1007/s10796-010-9292-7.

Szulanski, G. (1996). Exploring internal stickiness: Impediments to the transfer of best practice within the firm. *Strategic Management Journal*, 17.

Talaga, J. (2009). Online payments in the new retail environment. *Healthcare Financial Management, 63*(3), 86–91. PMID:20669848.

Tambini, D. (1997). Civic networking and universal rights to connectivity: Bologna. In Tsagarousianou, R., Tambini, D., & Bryan, C. (Eds.), *Cyberdemocracy: Technology, cities and civic networks* (pp. 84–109). London: Routledge.

Tambouris, E., Liotas, N., & Tarabanis, K. (2007). A framework for assessing eparticipation projects and tools. In *Proc. 40th Int. Conf. on System Sciences*, Hawaii, 2007, (pp.90a).

Tan, B. C. C., Pan, S. L., & Cha, V. (2008). The evolution of Singapore's government Infocomm plans: Singapore's e-government journey from 1980 to 2007. Singapore: Singapore eGovernment Leadership Centre and School of Computing, National University of Singapore.

Tapscott, D. (2009). *Grown up digital: How the net generation is changing your world.* New York: McGraw-Hill.

Tarde, G. (1989*). L´opinion et la foule*. Paris: éditions PUF.

Tasmania Government. (2012). *Local government directory*. The Department of Premier and Cabinet. Retrieved on July 16, 2012, from http://www.dpac.tas.gov.au/divisions/lgd/local_government_directory

Tassabehji, R., Elliman, T., & Mellor, J. (2007). Generating citizen trust in e-government security: Challenging perceptions. *International Journal of Cases on Electronic Commerce*, *3*(3). doi:10.4018/jcec.2007070101.

Tate, M., Hynson, R., & Toland, J. (2007). The disconnect between the current orthodoxy of local government and the promise and practices of information technology management: An illustrative case study. *Electronic Government: An International Journal*, *4*(4), 509–526. doi:10.1504/EG.2007.015041.

Teicher, J., & Dow, N. (2002). E-government in Australia: Promise and progress. *Information Polity*, *7*(4), 231–246.

Teo, T. S. H., Srivastava, S. C., & Jiang, L. (2009). Trust and electronic government success: An empirical study. *Journal of Management Information Systems*, *25*(3), 99–131. doi:10.2753/MIS0742-1222250303.

Teow, P. L., & Zainab, A. N. (2003). Access to online database at private colleges and universities in Malaysia. *Malaysian Journal of Library & Information Science*, *8*(1), 91–101.

Terry Ma, H., & Zaphiris, P. (2003). *The usability and content accessibility of the e-government in the UK.* London: Centre forHuman-Computer Interaction Design, City University. Retrieved October, 2007, from http://www.soi.city.ac.uk/~zaphiri/Papers/HCII2003/HCII2003-Accessibility.pdf

Tetteh, B. (2011). Serving African immigrants in Colorado Public Libraries. *Colorado Libraries, 35*(4). Retrieved from http://coloradolibrariesjournal.org/?q=content/serving-african-immigrants-colorado-public-libraries

The Economist. (2010). *Online retailing in China: Clicks trumps bricks*. Retrieved on March 20, 2012, from http://www.economist.com/node/15955376

The Institute for Public-Private Partnerships. (2009). Public-private partnerships in e-government: Handbook. Washington, DC: infoDev/World Bank.

Thelen, K. (2004). *How institutions evolve: The political economy of skills in Germany, Britain, the United States and Japan.* New York: Cambridge University Press. doi:10.1017/CBO9780511790997.

Thomas, J., & Streib, G. (2003). The new face of government: Citizen-initiated contacts in the era of e-government. *Journal of Public Administration: Research and Theory*, *13*(1), 83–102. doi:10.1093/jpart/mug010.

Thompson, J. B. (2005). The new visibility. *Theory, Culture & Society*, *22*(6), 31–51. doi:10.1177/0263276405059413.

Thong, J. Y. L., Hong, W., & Tam, K. Y. (2004). What lead to user acceptance of digital libraries? *Communications of the ACM*, *47*(11), 79–83. doi:10.1145/1029496.1029498.

Tian. (2010). Research on emergency resource management based on urban grid management model. *Science and Technology Management Research.* Retrieved from http://d.wanfangdata.com.cn/Periodical_kjglyj201008046.aspx

Tong, R. (2007). Gender-based disparities east/west: rethinking the burden of care in the United States and Taiwan. *Bioethics*, *21*(9), 488–499. doi:10.1111/j.1467-8519.2007.00594.x PMID:17927625.

Torres, L., Pina, V., & Acerete, B. (2005). EGovernment developments on delivering public services among EU cities. *Government Information Quarterly*, *22*(2), 217–238. doi:10.1016/j.giq.2005.02.004.

Treaty establishing a Constitution for Europe. (2004). *Official Journal of the European Union, 310.*

Treaty of Amsterdam. (1997). Official Journal of the European Union, 340..

Treaty of Lisbon (Treaty on the Functioning of the European Union). (2007). Official Journal of the European Union, 306..

Treaty of Nice. (2001). Official Journal of the European Union, 80..

Treaty on the European Union-TEU. (1992). Official Journal of the European Union, 224..

Tu, Zhang, & Mei. (2005). *Urban grid management in Jianghan district in Wuhan city*. Retrieved from http://news.sina.com.cn/c/2005-10-21/06447225553s.shtml

Turban, E., McLean, E., & Wetherbe, J. (2004). *Information technology for management: Transforming organisations in the digital economy* (4th ed.). USA: John Wiley & Sons, Inc..

U.S. Government. (2002). The Business Reference Model Version 1.0. Washington, DC.

U.S. Government. (2003). The Business Reference Model Version 2.0. Washington, DC.

U.S. Government. (2005). Enabling citizen-centered electronic government 2005-2006: Federal enterprise architecture program management office action plan. Washington, DC.

Ubaldi, B. (2011). The impact of the Economic and Financial crisis on e-Government in OECD Member Countries. *European Journal of ePractice*, 11, 5-18.

Ullmann, C. (2006). *Les politiques regionales a l'epreuve du developpement numérique: Enjeux, strategie et impacts*. (Doctoral dissertation). In Institut de Géographie, Université Paris 1 Panthéon Sorbonne: Paris.

Un Jan, A., & Contreras, V. (2011). Technology acceptance model for the use of information technology in universities. *Computers in Human Behavior*, *27*, 845–851. doi:10.1016/j.chb.2010.11.009.

UNDESA. (2002). *Benchmarking e-government: A global perspective: Assessing the progress of the UN member States*. Retrieved May 11, 2012, from http://unpan1.un.org/intradoc/groups/public/documents/un/unpan021547.pdf

UNDESA. (2003). *UN global e-government survey: E-government at the crossroads*. Retrieved May 11, 2012, from http://www.unpan.org/egovkb/global_reports/08report.html

UNDESA. (2004). *Global e-government readiness report 2004: Towards access for opportunity*. Retrieved May 11, 2012, from http://www.unpan.org/egovkb/global_reports/08report.htm

UNDESA. (2005). *Global e-government readiness report: From e-Government to e-Inclusion*. Retrieved May 11, 2012, from http://www.unpan.org/egovkb/global_reports/08report.htm

UNDESA. (2008). *United Nations e-government survey: From e-government to connected governance*. Retrieved May 11, 2012, from http://www.unpan.org/egovkb/global_reports/08report.htm

UNDESA. (2010). *United Nations e-government survey: Leveraging e-government at a time of financial and economic crisis*. Retrieved May 11, 2012, from http://www.unpan.org/egovkb/global_reports/08report.htm

United Nations Department of Economic and Social Affairs. (2012). *United Nations e-government survey 2012: E-government for the people*. New York: United Nations.

United Nations Development Program. (2003). *Reporte de Desarrollo Humano 2003*. New York: Oxford University Press.

United Nations Educational, Scientific and Cultural Organisation. (2005). *Examples of e-governance*. Retrieved on March 25, 2012, from http://portal.unesco.org/ci/en/ev.php-URL_ID=6616&URL_DO=DO_TOPIC&URL_SECTION=201.html

United Nations Public Administration Network. (n.d.). United Nations e-government survey2010special awards. New York: United Nations.

United Nations. (2010). World e-government rankings. *United Nations E-Government Survey*. Retrieved on March 20, 2012, from http://unpan1.un.org/intradoc/groups/public/documents/un-dpadm/unpan038848.pdf

Urbandive.com. (n.d.). Website. Retrieved April 21, 2012, from http://www.urbandive.com/lieu/stade/mairie-service-allo-monsieur-le-maire/4d6c2d0dfc692507839f0dd7#/0/M1/P1/F4d6c2d0dfc692507839f0dd7/Cmairies/N151.12061,6.11309,2.66049,48.5396/B2.66049,48.5396/Z10/

Uscis.gov. (2013). Website. Retrieved from http://www.uscis.gov/portal/site/uscis

Valacich, J., & Schneider, C. (2010). *Information systems today: Managing in the digital world* (4th ed.). USA: Pearson Education, Inc.

Van de Ven, A. H., Polley, D., Garud, R., & Venkataraman, S. (1999). *The innovation journey*. New York: Oxford University Press.

Van Der Wal, Z., Huberts, L., Van Den Heuvel, H., & Kolthoff, E. (2006). Central values of government and business: Differences, similarities and conflicts. *Public Administration Quarterly*, *30*(3), 314–364.

Van Dijk, J., & Hacker, K. (2003). The digital divide as a complex and dynamic phenomenon. *The Information Society*, *19*(4), 315–326. doi:10.1080/01972240309487.

van Dijk, J., Peters, O., & Ebbers, W. (2008). Explaining the acceptance and use of government Internet services: A multivariate analysis of 2006 survey data in the Netherlands. *Government Information Quarterly*, *25*(3), 379–399. doi:10.1016/j.giq.2007.09.006.

Van Reeth, W. (2002). *The bearable lightness of budgeting. An explorative research on the uneven implementation of performance oriented budget reform*. (Doctoral Degree Thesis). Catholic University of Leuven, Leuven, Germany.

Varheim, A. (2010). Gracious space: Library programming strategies towards immigrants as tools in the creation of social capital. *Library & Information Science Research*, *33*, 12–18. doi:10.1016/j.lisr.2010.04.005.

Vedel, T. (2001). La démocratie électronique. In F. Hamon & O. Passelecq (Eds.), Le Référendum en Europe, Bilan et perspectives. Paris: éditions L'Harmattan.

Vedel, T. (2003). *L'idée de démocratie électronique, origines, visions, questions*. La Tour d'Aigues: éditions de l'Aube.

Veenstra, A. F. V., & Janssen, M. (2012). Policy implications of top-down and bottom-up patterns of e-government infrastructure development. In E. T.M. & D. C. Mehos (Eds.), Inverse infrastructures. Disrupting networks from below: Edward Elgar.

Velaga, N. R., Beecroft, M., Nelson, J. D., Corsar, D., & Edwards, P. (2012). Transport poverty meets the digital divide: Accessibility and connectivity in rural communities. *Journal of Transport Geography*, *21*, 102–112. doi:10.1016/j.jtrangeo.2011.12.005.

Venkatesh, V., Morris, G. M., Davis, G. B., & Davis, F. D. (2003). User acceptance of information technology: Toward a unified view. *Management Information Systems Quarterly*, *27*(3), 425–478.

Verpeaux, M. (2001). Decentralisation since 1982. In *Local government in France* (pp. 37–52). Paris: La Documentation Française.

Vetter, A. (2003). La fonction de socialisation de la politique locale en Europe. In V. Hoffmann-Martinot & C. Sorbets (Eds). Démocraties locales en changement (pp. 165-189). Paris: éditions Pedone.

Vetter, A., & Hoffmann-Martinot, V. (2012). In O.W. Gabriel, S.I. Keil, & E. Kerrouche (Eds.), Political participation in France and Germany (pp. 137-160). Essex: EPCR Press studies.

Vilvovsky, S. (2008). Difference between public and private IT outsourcing: common themes in the literature. The *Proceedings of the 9th Annual International Digital Government Research Conference* (289, pp. 337–346).

Vintar, M., Kunstelj, M., Decman, M., & Bercic, B. (2003). Development of e-government in Slovenia. *Information Polity*, *8*(3,4), 133–149. Retrieved from http://iospress.metapress.com/content/ARCQJ62E942M2PEY

Von Schomberg, R. (1995). Erosion of the value spheres: The ways in which a society copes with scientific, moral and ethical uncertainty. In Von Schomberg, R. (Ed.), *Contested technology: Ethics, risk and public debate. Tillburg*. International Centre for Human Public Affairs.

Walsh, L. (2007). *Darebin eForum Evaluation Report*. Report commissioned by Darebin City Council. Centre for Citizenship & Human Rights, Deakin University, Melbourne Australia. Retrieved on July 12, 2012, from http://www.darebin.vic.gov.au/Files/Darebin_eForum_Evaluation_090807.pdf

Wan Mohd Isa, W. A. R., Suhami, M. R., Safie, N. I., & Semsudin, S. S. (2011). Assessing the usability and accessibility of Malaysia e-government website. *American Journal of Economics and Business Administration*, *3*(1), 40–46. doi:10.3844/ajebasp.2011.40.46.

Wang, Bai, & Tian. (2010). Grid management of city emergencies. *Journal of Intelligence*, (4), 31-35.

Wang, L., Bretschneider, S., & Gant, J. (2005). Evaluating web-based e-government services with a citizen-centric approach. *Proceedings of the 38th Hawaii International Conference on System Sciences*. doi: 10.1109/HICSS.2005.252

Wang. (2007). Urban grid management: Innovation in urban community management model. *Planner*, (5), 46-49.

Wang. (2009). Urban grid management and safe community construction. *Safety*, *30*(10), 8-11.

Wang, Chen, & Weng. (2007). Technological implementation of city grid management of Shanghai. *Geomatics and Spatial Information Technology*, *30*(4), 71–77.

Wang, S. (2009). Research on urban grid management models. *Software and Educational Technology*, *8*(3), 115–116.

Wang, W., & Benbasat, I. (2005). Trust in and adoption of online recommendation agents. *Journal of the Association for Information Systems*, *6*(3), 72–101.

Wang, Y.-S., & Liao, Y.-W. (2008). Assessing eGovernment systems success: A validation of the DeLone and McLean model of information systems success. *Government Information Quarterly*, *25*(4), 717–733. doi:10.1016/j.giq.2007.06.002.

Wang, Yang, & Fan. (2006). Study on the key technologies and demonstrating application of urban griddization management system. *Science of Surveying and Mapping*, *31*(4), 117–119.

Warkentien, S., Clark, M., & Jacinto, B. (2009). *English literacy of foreign-born adults in the United States: 2003*. National Center for Education Statistics. Retrieved from http://nces.ed.gov/pubs2009/2009034.pdf

Warkentin, M., Gefen, D., Pavlou, P. A., & Rose, G. (2002). Encouraging citizen adoption of egovernment by building trust. *Electronic Markets*, *12*(3), 157–162. doi: 10.1080/101967802320245929.

Waverman, L., Meschi, M., & Fuss, M. (2005). The impact of telecoms on economic growth in developing countries. In Africa: The Impact of Mobile Phones: Moving the Debate Fordward. The Vodafone Policy paper series, No. 2.

Weber, L., Loumakis, A., & Bergman, J. (2003). Who participates and why? An analysis of citizens on the internet and the mass public. *Social Science Computer Review*, *21*(1), 25–32. doi:10.1177/0894439302238969.

Weill, P., Broadbent, M., & Butler, C. (1996). *Exploring how firms view IT infrastructure. Melbouren*. Melbourne Business School, the University of Melbourne.

Wenger, E. (1998). *Communities of practice: Learning, meaning and identity*. Cambridge: Cambridge University Press.

Wescott, D. (2004). E-government and the transformation of service delivery and citizen attitudes. *Public Administration Review*, *64*(1), 15–27. doi:10.1111/j.1540-6210.2004.00343.x.

West, D. M. (2003). *Global e-government 2003, Centre for Public Policy*. Brown University, Providence. Retrieved from http://www.InsidePolitics.org

West, D. M. (2005). *Global E-government*. Retrieved May 11, 2012, from http://www.insidepolitics.org/egovtdata.html

West, D. M. (2008). State and federal electronic government in the United States, 2008. Washington, DC: Brookings Institution. Retrieved from http://www.brookings.edu/~/media/Files/rc/reports/2008/0826_egovernment_west/0826_egovernment_west.pdf

West, J. P., & Berman, E. M. (2001). The impact of revitalized management practices on the adoption of information technology: A national survey of local governments. *Pubic Performance and Management Review, 24*(3), 233–253. Retrieved from http://www.jstor.org/stable/3381087

West, D. (2005). *Digital government: Technology and public sector performance*. Princeton, NJ: Princeton University Press.

West, D. M. (2004). Equity and accessibility in e-Government: A policy perspective. *Journal of E-Government*, *1*(2), 31–43. doi:10.1300/J399v01n02_03.

West, D., & Miller, E. (2006). The digital divide in public e-health: Barriers to accessibility and privacy in state health department Web sites. *Journal of Health Care for the Poor and Underserved*, *17*, 652–666. doi:10.1353/hpu.2006.0115 PMID:16960328.

White House. (2012). *Digital government: Building a 21st century platform to better serve the American people*. Washington, DC: The White House. Retrieved from http://www.whitehouse.gov/sites/default/files/omb/egov/digital-government/digital-government.html

Whitehouse.gov. (2013). Website. Retrieved March 12, 2008, from http://www.whitehouse.gov/omb/egov

Wiegand, W. A. (1986). *The politics of an emerging profession: The American Library Association, 1876-1917*. New York: Greenwood.

Wiegand, W. A. (1989). *An active instrument for propaganda: The American public library during World War I*. Westport, CT: Greenwood.

Williams, L. R. (1994). Understanding distribution channels: An interorganizational study of EDI adoption. *Journal of Business Logistics*, *15*(2), 173–203.

Winkel, J. (2007). Lessons on evaluating programs and collections for immigrant communities at the Queens Borough Public Library. *Colorado Libraries*, *33*(1), 43–46.

Wojcik, S. (2003). Les forums électroniques municipaux. Espaces du débat démocratique? *Science and Society*, 60.

Wong, S.L., & Teo, T. (2009). Determinants of the intention to use technology: Comparison between Malaysia and Singaporean female student teachers.

Wong, P., & Cha, V. (2009). *The evolution of government Infocomm plans: Singapore's e-government journey (1980 – 2007)*. Singapore: Institute of Systems Science, National University of Singapore.

Wong, W., & Welch, E. (2004). Does e-government promote accountability? A comparative analysis of website openness and government accountability. *Governance: An International Journal of Policy, Administration and Institutions*, *17*(2), 275–297. doi:10.1111/j.1468-0491.2004.00246.x.

Wood, F., Siegel, E., LaCroix, E., Lyon, B., Benson, D., Cid, V., & Fariss, S. (2003). A practical approach to e-government web evaluation. *IT Professional*, *5*(3), 22–28. doi:10.1109/MITP.2003.1202231.

World Bank and National Institute of Education (NIE). (2008). *Toward a better future: Education and training for economic development in Singapore since 1965*. Washington, DC: The International Bank for Reconstruction and Development/The World Bank.

World Bank. (2006). *Information and communications for development 2006: Global trends and policies*. Washington, DC: The World Bank.

World Bank. (2011). *Definition of e-government*. Retrieved September 14, 2012, from http://web.worldbank.org/WBSITE/EXTERNAL/TOPICS/EXTINFORMATIONANDCOMMUNICATIONANDTECHNOLOGIES/EXTEGOVERNMENT/0,contentMDK:20507153~menuPK:702592~pagePK:148956~piPK:216618~theSitePK:702586,00.html

Wu, Chen, & Sun. (2007). Study on development and construction of grid management platform of municipal professional. *Management Forum, 29*(4), 140-143.

Wu. (2005). Urban Grid management in Dongcheng district in Beijing. *Informatization Construction*, (8), 24-26.

www.lep.gov. (2013). Website. Retrieved from www.lep.gov

Xie & Ren. (2007). Urban management system based on urban grids. *Geospatial Information*, *5*(3), 28–29.

Xu. (2007). Mobile applications are serving the needs of modern city management. *System Simulation and Technology,* (2), 121-123.

Yan. (2006). The nature and implication of urban grid management. *City Issues,* (2), 76-79.

Yang. (2008). City emergency management employing grids. *Journal of Kaili University, 26*(6), 62-64.

Yang, H. D., & Yoo, Y. (2003). It's all about attitude: Revisiting the technology acceptance model. *Decision Support Systems*, *38*(1), 19–31. doi:10.1016/S0167-9236(03)00062-9.

Yang, T.-M., & Maxwell, T. A. (2011). Information-sharing in public organizations: A literature review of interpersonal, intra-organizational and inter-organizational success factors. *Government Information Quarterly*, *28*(2), 164–175. doi:10.1016/j.giq.2010.06.008.

Yaniv, O. (2005, Oct. 19). Immigrants warned on green card cons. *New York Daily News*. Retrieved from http://articles.nydailynews.com/2005-10-19/local/18313877_1_immigrants-application-eligible-countries

Yeo, V. (2011). *Asia speeds up e-government efforts*. Retrieved on March 20, 2012, from http://www.zdnetasia.com/asia-speeds-up-e-government-efforts-62300717.htm

Yi. (2006). Interpreting digital city. *The Urban Construction Archive Magazine,* (5), 5-8.

Yildiz, M. (2004). *Peeking into the black-box of e-government: Evidence from Turkey.* (Unpublished doctoral dissertation). Indiana University, Indiana.

Yildiz, M. (2007). E-government research. Reviewing the literature, limitations, and ways forward. *Government Information Quarterly, 24*(3), 646–665. doi:10.1016/j.giq.2007.01.002.

Yin, R. (1981). The case study crisis: Some answers. *Administrative Science Quarterly, 26,* 58–65. doi:10.2307/2392599.

Yong, J. S. L. (2003). *Enabling public service innovation in the 21st century: e-Government in Asia.* Singapore: Times Editions.

Yoo, H., & Yoon, S. (2005, Winter). *A study of the conflict between the MoGAHA and the MIC in the course of e-government building.* Paper presented at the Annual Conference of the Korean Association of Public Administration. Seoul, Korea.

Yu, C. C. (2008). Building a value centric e-government service framework based on a business model perspective. In M.A. Wimmer, H.J. Scholl, and E. Ferro (Eds.), EGOV 2008, Lecture Notes in Computer Science (LNCS) (vol. 5184, pp. 160–171). Berlin, Heidelberg: Springer-Verlag.

Yuan. (2007). Reflection on urban ten-thousand-meter basic grid management—Discussion be combined with construction of Chengdu digital urban management system. *Urban Management Science and Technology, 9*(4), 45-48.

Zaheer, A., McEvily, B., & Perrone, V. (1998). Does trust matter? Exploring the effects of interorganizational and interpersonal trust on performance. *Organization Science, 9,* 141–158. doi:10.1287/orsc.9.2.141.

Zeng, Hong, & Zhou. (2009). Key technology and system composition of urban grid management. *Railway Investigation and Surveying, 35*(5), 39–42.

Zhang, Feixu, & Xia. (2008). The new urban management model based on ten thousand meter unit grid. *CD Technology,* (2), 20-22.

Zhang. (2006). Urban grid management: A project serving the people digitally. *Community,* (17), 12-13.

Zhang. (2006). Innovation on urban grid management- A case study in Jianghan district in Wuhan city. *Theory and Reform,* (5), 56-57.

Zhang. (2008). Innovation in city management based on urban grids. *Administrative Forum,* (3), 83-86.

Zhang, X. (2001). The practice and politics of public library services to Asian immigrants. In Lueveno-Molina, S. (Ed.), *Immigrant politics and the public library* (pp. 141–150). Westport, CT: Greenwood Press.

Zheng, D., Chen, J., Huang, L., & Zhang, C. (2012). E-government adoption in public administration organizations: Integrating institutional theory perspective and resource-based view. *European Journal of Information Systems* (Advance online publication 19 June 2012).

Zhou. (2011). Investigations of urban grid management innovation in Pudong district in Shanghai. *Management and Technology in SME,* (22), 184.

Zhu & Yuan. (2011). Public crisis and emergency preparation mechanisms based on urban grids. *China Public Administration Review,* (10), 102-105.

Zhu. (2009). Urban management technology and methods research. *Science and Technology Innovation Herald,* (30), 4-5.

Zhuang. (2011). Exploration of urban grid management development in small cities—A case study in Jinjiang. *China State Economy,* (9), 40-41.

Ziller, J. (2000). Fragmentation/participation: Quelle bonne dimension? *Pouvoirs, 95,* 19–31.

Zucker, L.-G. (1986). Production of trust: Institutional sources of economic structure, 1840–1920. *Research in Organizational Behavior, 8,* 53–111.

伊凡 (2006). 解读数字城市. 城建档案, 2006(5), 5-8. Retrieved from http://d.g.wanfangdata.com.cn/Periodical_cjda200605002.aspx

刘文清, 廖齐梅, 黄明钢, 杜夏雨, 秦斌 (2006). 深圳: 数字化城市管理建设?实. 中国建设信息, 2006(24), 25-28. Retrieved from http://10.55.100.201/kns50/detail.aspx?QueryID=51&CurRec=1

刘淑华,詹华,袁千里,武明戈(2011).移动政务与中国城市治理.电子政务 2011(6),2-12. Retrieved from http://www.cqvip.com/qk/94368c/201106/38203077.html

刘静(2009).浅谈城市网格化管理中的部件采集.测绘与空间地理信息, 32(1), 98-101. Retrieved from http://d.g.wanfangdata.com.cn/Periodical_dbch200901030.aspx

卢廷玉, 张忠岩 (2008). 地理信息系统在城市网格化管理中的应用. 交通科技与经? 10(3), 68-69. Retrieved from http://d.wanfangdata.com.cn/Periodical_jtkjyjj200803028.aspx

吴倚天(2005).网格下的城市——北京市东城区依托信息技术探索城市管理新模式.信息化建设, 2005(8), 24-26. Retrieved from http://d.g.wanfangdata.com.cn/Periodical_xxhjs200508008.aspx

吴海涛, 陈亚萍, 孙海浩 (2007). 市政专业网格化管理平台开?建设研究. 管理论坛 29(4), 140-143. Retrieved from http://d.wanfangdata.com.cn/Periodical_szjs201104044.aspx

周莉 (2011). 上海浦东新区城市网格化管理的建设探析. 中小企业管理与科技(上旬刊), 2011(22), 184. Retrieved from http://d.g.wanfangdata.com.cn/Periodical_xzqykj201122167.aspx

姜爱林, 任志儒 (2007). 网格化:现代城市管理新模式——网格化城市管理模式若干问?初探. 上海城市规划 2007(1), 9-11. Retrieved from http://d.wanfangdata.com.cn/Periodical_shcsgh200701003.aspx

姜金贵, 梁静国 (2008). 基于网格化管理的突发事件应急管理机制研究. 情报?志2008(6), 26-28. Retrieved from http://www.cqvip.com/qk/90226x/20086/27608083.0.html

孔凡敏,苏科华,朱欣焰(2008).城市网格化管理系统框架研究.地理空间信息,6(4),28-31.Retrieved from http://d.g.wanfangdata.com.cn/Periodical_dlkjxx200804010.aspx

庄毅 (2011). 中小城市网格化管理的有益探索—以晋江市为例. 中国集体经济, 2011(9), 40-41. Retrieved from http://d.g.wanfangdata.com.cn/Periodical_zgjtjj201119022.aspx

张冲, 徐飞, 夏建磊 (2008). 基于万米单元网格管理法的数字城管新模式. 光盘技术 2008(2), 20-22. Retrieved from http://d.wanfangdata.com.cn/Periodical_gpjs200802006.aspx

张勇进(2008).基于网格空间的城市管理创新.行政论坛 2008(3), 83-86. Retrieved from http://d.wanfangdata.com.cn/Periodical_xingzlt200803020.aspx

张大维(2006).城市网格化管理"数字化为民"工程.社区,2006(17),12-13. Retrieved from http://10.55.100.201/kns50/detail.aspx?QueryID=238&CurRec=1

张大维 (2006). 城市网格化管理模式的创新研究——以武汉市江汉区为例. 理论与改革, 2006(5), 56-57. Retrieved from http://10.55.100.201/kns50/detail.aspx?QueryID=284&CurRec=1

张超, 吴丹, 范况生 (2006). 城市网格化管理. 城建档案 2006(7), 8-12. Retrieved from http://d.wanfangdata.com.cn/Periodical_cjda200607003.aspx

彭程, 李京, 廖通逵, 刘纯波, 蔡洪春 (2008). 基于SIG的城市网格化管理与服务系统. 计算机工程 34(13), 245-247. Retrieved from http://d.wanfangdata.com.cn/Periodical_jsjgc200813088.aspx

徐波 (2007). 移动?用服务现代城市管理. 系统?真技术 2007(2), 121-123. Retrieved from http://www.cqvip.com/qk/88720x/200702/1000960150.html

承建文 (2008). 城市网格化管理机制完善的理性思考——以上海为例. 上海城市管理职业技术?院学? 17(3), 2-5. Retrieved from http://d.wanfangdata.com.cn/Periodical_shcsglzyjsxyxb200803019.aspx

方家平 (2006). "网格化管理"试水江城. 上海信息化, 2006(5), 43-45. Retrieved from http://d.g.wanfangdata.com.cn/Periodical_shxxh200605008.aspx

曾绍炳, 洪中华, 周世健 (2009). 城市网格化管理关键技术与系统构成.铁道勘察35(5),39-42. Retrieved from http://d.wanfangdata.com.cn/Periodical_tlhc200905014.aspx

朱彤 (2009). 网格化城市管理技术与方法研究. 科技创新导? 2009(30), 4-5. http://d.wanfangdata.com.cn/Periodical_kjzxdb200930003.aspx

李国明, 孟现? 徐志强, 王长春 (2009). 浅谈城市网格化管理. 测绘与空间地理信息, 32(6), 141-143. Retrieved from http://d.g.wanfangdata.com.cn/Periodical_dbch200906045.aspx

李平, 全斌 (2009). "网格化"城市管理系统中城市部件数字化采集方法的探讨. 测绘标准化, 25(4), 11-14. Retrieved from http://10.55.100.201/kns50/detail.aspx?QueryID=3&CurRec=1

李德仁, 李宗华, 彭明军, 邵振峰 (2007). 武汉市城市网格化管理与服务系统建设与应用. 测绘通报, 2007(8), 1-4. http://d.g.wanfangdata.com.cn/Periodical_chtb200708001.aspx

李林 (2007). 深圳市数字化城市管理模型探析. 福建工程学院学报, 5(6) 581-585. Retrieved from http://d.g.wanfangdata.com.cn/Periodical_fjgcxyxb200706006.aspx

李立明, 张骥, 傀乔 (2006). 网格化城市管理应急与非应急统一模式研究. 城市管理与科技, 2007(1), 18-22. Retrieved from http://d.g.wanfangdata.com.cn/Periodical_csglykj200701005.aspx

李鹏 (2011). 我国城市网格化管理研究的拓展. 城市发展研究, 18(2), 114-118. Retrieved from http://d.g.wanfangdata.com.cn/Periodical_csfzyj201102018.aspx

杨宏波 (2008). 网格化的城市危机管理研究. 凯里学院学? 26(6), 62-64. Retrieved from http://d.g.wanfangdata.com.cn/Periodical_qdnmzsfgdzkxxxb200806022.aspx

江绵康 (2009). 上海市:网格化在数字城管中的实践. 建设科技, 2009(21), 38-40. Retrieved from http://d.wanfangdata.com.cn/Periodical_jskj200921012.aspx

池忠仁, 王浣尘, 陈云 (2008). 上海城市网格化管理模式探讨. 科技进步与对策, 25(1), 40-43. Retrieved from http://d.g.wanfangdata.com.cn/Periodical_kjjbydc200801011.aspx

汪云峰, 白庆? 田欣 (2010). 城市突发公共事件管理的网格化:控制结构的功能障碍及其突破. 情报?志 2010(4), 31-35. Retrieved from http://www.cqvip.com/qk/90226x/201004/33504785.html

涂亚卓, 张新, 梅智云 (2005). 武汉?点城市网格化管理江汉区建成投入试?行. http://news.sina.com.cn/c/2005-10-21/06447225553s.shtml

潘兴? (2007). 浅谈网格化城市管理模式. 中共宁波市委党校学报, 29(3), 41-46. Retrieved from http://d.g.wanfangdata.com.cn/Periodical_zgnbswdxxb200703008.aspx

王保森 (2007). 网格化管理:城市社区管理模式的创新. 规划师, 2007(5), 46-49.

王喜, 杨华, 范况生 (2006). 城市网格化管理系统的关?技术及示范应用研究. 测绘科学 31(4), 117-119. Retrieved from http://d.wanfangdata.com.cn/Periodical_chkx200604041.aspx

王爽 (2009). 城市网格化管理模式研究. 软件导刊 8(3), 115-116. Retrieved from http://10.55.100.201/kns50/detail.aspx?QueryID=188&CurRec=2

王立(2009). 城市网格化管理与安全社区建设. 安全 30(10), 8-11. Retrieved from http://d.wanfangdata.com.cn/Periodical_aq200910003.aspx

王金诚, 陈晓岚, 翁裔 (2007). 上海市城市网格化管理的技术实现. 测绘与空间地理信息, 30(4), 71-77. Retrieved from http://d.g.wanfangdata.com.cn/Periodical_dbch200704019.aspx

田依林 (2010). 基于网格化管理的突发事件应急资源管理研究. 科技管理研究 30(8), 135-137. Retrieved from http://d.wanfangdata.com.cn/Periodical_kjglyj201008046.aspx

皮定均 (2008). 朝阳区利用网格化管理的实践与创新. 中国行政管理, 2008(S1), 108-110. Retrieved from http://10.55.100.201/kns50/detail.aspx?QueryID=97&CurRec=1

祝小宁, 袁何俊 (2011). 基于网格化管理的突发公共事件预警机制探析. 中国行政管理 2006(10), 102-105. Retrieved from http://www.cqvip.com/qk/81961x/200610/22945833.html

程方升, 张敏娜 (2007). 网格化管理:数字时代城市治理的新取向——城市网格化管理模式问?的探究. 科协?坛(下半月), 2007(5). Retrieved from http://d.g.wanfangdata.com.cn/Periodical_kxlt-x200705031.aspx

程艳秋 (2007). 数字化城管:提升行政执行力的有力推手. 中国建设信息, 2007(10X), 10-12. Retrieved from http://www.cqvip.com/qk/83587x/200710x/25751982.0.html

程述, 白庆?(2008). 网格技术?示及网格化城市管理机制研究. 情报?志, 27(10), 56-59. Retrieved from http://d.g.wanfangdata.com.cn/Periodical_qbzz200810018.aspx

罗建宾(2006). 谈谈数字化城市管理模式. 中国城市经济, 2006(2), 74-75. Retrieved from http://d.g.wanfangdata.com.cn/Periodical_zgcsjj200602026.aspx

胡春凌, 钱杰, 杨学军 (2010). 城镇?地网格化管理模式探讨. 城市管理与科技12(2), 49-51. Retrieved from http://d.wanfangdata.com.cn/periodical_csglykj201002014.aspx

范况生(2009). 现代城市网格化管理新模式探讨. 商丘师范学院学报, 25(12), 111-115. Retrieved from http://www.cqvip.com/qk/97536b/200912/32713566.html

董云铮, 刘瑜 (2009) 城市网格化管理系统技术框研究. 浙江纺织服装?业技术?院学?, 2009(3), 57-61. DOI: 10.3969/j.issn. 1674-2346.2009.03.014

蒋荣(2007). 数字化城市管理项目现?与趋? 中国信息界 2007(11), 38-47. Retrieved from http://d.wanfangdata.com.cn/Periodical_zgxxj200711011.aspx

袁翱(2007). 城市万米网格化管理的思考——结合成都市数字化城市管理建设的探讨. 城市管理与科技 9(4), 45-48. Retrieved from http://d.wanfangdata.com.cn/Periodical_csglykj200704012.aspx

谢伟文, 任福(2007). 基于空间基本网格的城市公共管理体系. 地理空间信息, 5(3), 28-29. Retrieved from http://d.g.wanfangdata.com.cn/Periodical_dlkjxx200703010.aspx

邱春霞, 张亚南 (2008). 城市网格化管理系统平台初步?计. 西安科技大学学报 28(1), 96-99, 127. Retrieved from http://d.wanfangdata.com.cn/Periodical_xakyxyxb200801021.aspx

郭苗苗(2011). 非常规突发事件网格化管理研究. 商业文化 2011(5). Retrieved from http://www.cnki.com.cn/Article/CJFDTOTAL-SYWH201105054.htm

阎耀军(2006). 城市网格化管理的特点及启示. 城市问题 2006(2), 76-79. Retrieved from http://d.wanfangdata.com.cn/Periodical_cswt200602017.aspx

陈云, 周曦民, 王浣尘 (2007). 政府网格化管理的现状与展望. 科技管理研究, 27(5), 40-41. Retrieved from http://d.g.wanfangdata.com.cn/Periodical_kjglyj200705013.aspx

陈平 (2005). 解读万米单元网格城市管理新模式. 城乡建设, 2005(10), 10-13. Retrieved from http://d.g.wanfangdata.com.cn/Periodical_cxjs200510004.aspx

陈平 (2005). 依托数字城市技术, 创建城市管理新模式. 中国科学院院刊, 20(3), 220-222. Retrieved from http://d.g.wanfangdata.com.cn/Periodical_zgkxyyk200503011.aspx

陈平 (2006). 数字化城市管理模式探析. 北京大学学报(哲学社会科学版), 2006(1), 142-148. Retrieved from http://www.cqvip.com/qk/81274x/2006001/21149564.html

马龙(2009). 对数字化城市管理系统的再思考. 信息化建设 2009(7), 19-22. Retrieved from http://d.wanfangdata.com.cn/Periodical_xxhjs200907007.aspx

高淑华, 孟庆海 (2011). 3G无线?频?控系统在城市管理领域的成功应用. 城市管理与科技 13(2), 50-51. Retrieved from http://www.cqvip.com/qk/93666a/201102/37764886.html

高琦, 赵铁汉, 马玉梅 (2007). 城市管理新模式在应对突发公共事件中的作用. 城市与减? 2007(3), 2-4. Retrieved from http://www.cqvip.com/qk/91118a/200703/24525133.html

齐国生, 李立明, 曹杰峰, 朱光宇 (2008). 城市管理的"网格化"——从政务网格到行业网格再到公务网格. 中国行政管理 2008(S1), 79-81. Retrieved from http://10.55.100.201/kns50/detail.aspx?QueryID=142&CurRec=1

About the Contributors

J. Ramon Gil-Garcia is an Associate Professor in the Department of Public Administration and the Director of the Data Center for Applied Research in Social Sciences at *Centro de Investigación y Docencia Económicas (CIDE)* in Mexico City. Dr. Gil-Garcia is a member of the National System of Researchers as Researcher Level II. In 2009, he was considered the most prolific author in the field of digital government research worldwide. Currently, he is a Research Fellow at the Center for Technology in Government, University at Albany, State University of New York (SUNY) and a Faculty Affiliate at the National Center for Digital Government, University of Massachusetts Amherst. Dr. Gil-Garcia is the author or co-author of articles in numerous prestigious academic journals. Some of his publications are among the most cited in the field of digital government research worldwide. His research interests include collaborative electronic government, inter-organizational information integration, smart cities and smart governments, adoption and implementation of emergent technologies, information technologies and organizations, digital divide policies, new public management, public policy evaluation, and multi-method research approaches.

* * *

John Carlo Bertot is Professor and co-director of the Information Policy & Access Center in the College of Information Studies at the University of Maryland. He is President of the Digital Government Society of North America and serves as chair of the International Standards Organization's Library Performance Indicator (ISO 11620) working group. John is Editor of *Government Information Quarterly* and co-Editor of *The Library Quarterly*. Over the years, John has received funding for his research from the National Science Foundation, the Bill & Melinda Gates Foundation, the Government Accountability Office, the American Library Association, and the Institute of Museum and Library Services.

Mark Borman worked for a number of years in senior consulting and executive roles in the UK, USA, and Australia prior to joining the University of Sydney. His principal research interests relate to understanding the role of information systems in inter-firm collaborations and the requirements for successfully managing the change associated with their introduction. Mark has a Ph.D. in Management Science from the University of Strathclyde in Glasgow. He has published more than 30 papers in leading journals and conferences including JIT, JORS, System Dynamics Review, Electronic Markets, IJIM, ECIS and HICSS.

Walter Castelnovo, Ph.D., is Assistant Professor of Information Systems at the University of Insubria (Italy). His research interests concern technological and organizational innovation in Public Administration and Interorganizational Information Systems. He is one of the founders of the Research Center for "Knowledge and Service Management for Business Applications" of the University of Insubria and he is member of the Scientific Committee of the "Interdepartmental Center for Organizational Innovation in Public Administration" of the University of Milan. He served as member of the committee for many international conferences on E-Government and ICT evaluation. He was the General Chair of The 5th European Conference on Information Management and Evaluation (ECIME 2011) and he is the General Chair of The 13rd European Conference on eGovernment (ECEG 2013). He is co-founder with Danilo Piaggesi and Edson Luiz Riccio of the "ICT for Development International School" (ICT4DEVIS) and is the Director of the first edition of the School in 2012.

Anne Chartier is Associate Professor and Head of Département systèmes d'information organisationnels at Université Laval, Québec, Canada. She is interested in organizational and social transformation resulting from the design, the deployment or the use of information systems. Her main research topics are about ethics and IT and online social networks in the workplace.

Ritesh Chugh lectures in the Faculty of Arts, Business, Informatics and Education at Central Queensland University Melbourne, Australia. He teaches to both postgraduate and undergraduate students in the fields of Information Systems (IS) Management and Development, IS Project Management, and Electronic Commerce. Ritesh has been awarded many teaching awards, over the past few years, recognising his teaching excellence and commitment to improved student outcomes. His range of interests includes project management, knowledge management, electronic commerce and developing varied teaching and learning practices on a formal note and philately and numismatics on a more casual note. Ritesh is a member of the Australian Computer Society, IEEE, and IEEE's Computer Society too.

J. Ignacio Criado is an assistant professor at Universidad Autónoma de Madrid, Spain. He has been visiting researcher in different international institutions (Monash University, University of Manchester, London School of Economics, or European Institute of Public Administration), visiting fellow at Oxford Internet Institute, University of Oxford, and postdoctoral scholar at Center for Technology in Government, State University of New York (SUNY at Albany). He has published two award-winning books about e-Government. He is also the author or co-author of articles published (or to be published) in *Government Information Quarterly, Social Science Computer Review, Information Polity, International Journal of Electronic Governance, Internacional Journal of Public Sector Management, Gestión y Política Pública, Reforma y Democracia*, among others. His research interests include Web 2.0, social media and open government interoperability, inter-organizational collaboration, Europeanisation of e-Government, leadership and Internet in the public sector, Latin American public administration, regional and local government adoption and utilization of ICTs, citizens perception and evaluation of public services, quality management in public administration, or information society policy.

Efpraxia Dalakiouridou is a Researcher and ICT Consultant at the Laboratory of Information Systems (ISLAB) in the University of Macedonia. She has graduated from the Department of International and European Economic and Political Studies of the University of Macedonia and has acquired a postgraduate degree in European Economy and Internal Market from the Free University of Brussels. She currently attends the external program of London School of Economics and Political science in Information Systems and Management. Her professional background includes working for the European Commission (DG Enterprise and Industry), and consultancy firms. She has worked on several eParticipation projects and published relevant articles on the field, covering both theoretical and empirical aspects.

Seok-Jin Eom is an assistant professor of Graduate School of Public Administration at Seoul National University, Korea. He received his Ph.D. in Public Administration from Seoul National University, Korea and has published several papers on e-government including "Institutional Dimensions of e-Government Development: Implementing the Business Reference Model in the United States and Korea." His current research interests include the relationship between information technology, institutions, and organizations as well as public governance in the era of economic development in Korea.

Jane E. Fountain is Professor of Political Science and Public Policy at the University of Massachusetts Amherst. She is the founder and director of the National Center for Digital Government. Fountain is the author of numerous scholarly articles, papers and reports and author of *Building the Virtual State: Information Technology and Institutional Change* (Brookings Institution Press, 2001). She has been a member of the World Economic Forum Global Agenda Council on the Future of Government since 2007. She was chair of the Council in 2010-11 and vice chair in 2011-12 and coauthored the Forum report, *The Future of Government: Lessons Learned from around the World*. She is an elected Fellow of the National Academy of Public Administration.

Julie Freeman is a postdoctoral research fellow in communication and media studies at the University of Canberra, Australia. Julie received her PhD from Monash University in 2011, where she taught in the communications and media studies program and received a Dean's Award for excellence in teaching. Julie is currently the chief investigator on a funded projected that examines citizens' perspectives on public participation and the role of information and communication technologies. Her research focuses on local e-government, citizen engagement, political representation, digital democracy, and the policy contexts of e-government.

Ursula Gorham is a doctoral student in the College of Information Studies at the University of Maryland and currently works as a Graduate Research Associate at the Information Policy & Access Center. She holds a law degree, as well as graduate degrees in library science and public policy, from the University of Maryland. She is admitted to practice in Maryland, and she has served as a law clerk in the Maryland Court of Special Appeals and the U.S. Bankruptcy Court for the District of Maryland. Her research interests include e-government applications in the judiciary.

Srimannarayana Grandhi joined the Faculty of Arts, Business, Informatics and Education as a lecturer at CQUniversity, Australia in 2001. Over the past decade he has fulfilled several academic and administrative roles in different campuses of CQUniversity. The wide experience has given him an exposure to a multi-cultural environment, which he applies in everyday teaching and learning activities. He currently teaches courses in the area of Database Development and Management, Digital Forensics, Enterprise Systems, Electronic Commerce, and Project Management. Srimannarayana is a member of the Australian Computer Society. His main interests are business process reengineering, system implementation, web services, and in-memory computing.

Natalie Greene Taylor is a doctoral student at the University of Maryland's College of Information Studies. She is a Graduate Research Associate at the Information Policy& Access Center in Maryland's iSchool, where she is working on an Institute of Museum and Library Services (IMLS) grant studying partnerships between public libraries and government agencies. She received her Masters of Library Science at the University of Maryland-College Park, specializing in e-government and school library media, for which she is certified in the state of Maryland.

Huong Ha is currently lecturing at University of Newcastle, Singapore. She was Dean of Business School, and Director of R&D, TMC Academy. She has been the Vice President (Member Service) of HRDGateway, an international non-profit organisation. She holds a PhD from Monash University, Australia and a Master Degree from National University of Singapore. She has several years of working and teaching experience. She has been a member of the Cyberlaws 2010, 2011 and 2012 conference committees, the International Advisory Board of South Asia Association in Criminology & Victimology, the Chinese American Scholars Association Board and many others. She is a reviewer of many academic journals, e.g. *Thunderbird International Business Review*, Academy of Management (conference), *International Journal of Environment and Sustainable Development*, etc. She served as the Chief Editor of *TMC Academic Journal*, a peer-reviewed journal listed on Ulrichs global serials directory, Directory of Open Access Journals and the Australian ERA list.

Paul T. Jaeger, Ph.D., J.D., is Associate Professor and Co-Director of the Information Policy and Access Center and in the College of Information Studies at the University of Maryland. His research focuses on the ways in which law and public policy shape information behavior. He is the author of more than one hundred and twenty journal articles and book chapters, along with seven books. His most recent book is *Disability and the Internet: Confronting a Digital Divide* (Lynne Reiner, 2011). Dr. Jaeger is Co-Editor of *Library Quarterly* and Co-Editor of the *Information Policy Book Series* from MIT Press.

Marijn Janssen is the director of the interdisciplinary Systems Engineering, Policy Analyses and Management (SEPAM) Master programme and Associate Professor within the Information and Communication Technology section of the Technology, Policy and Management Faculty of Delft University of Technology. His research interests are in the field of ICT and governance in particular e-government, compliance orchestration, (shared) services, intermediaries, open data and infrastructures for coordinating public-private service networks. He serves on several editorial boards, is associate editor of Government Information Quarterly and the International Journal of E-Government Research and is involved in the organization of a number of conferences, including IFIP EGOV. He published over 220 refereed publications. More information: www.tbm.tudelft.nl/marijnj.

Shuhua Monica Liu brings in expertise in the field of Government Operation and Public Innovation. She is specifically interested in interactions between innovative mechanisms (technologies, tools, new business models and decision-making /planning strategies) and government operations. Her research focuses on understanding institutional setup, laws, policies and regulations, processes and factors shaping public agencies in daily operations and in the case of emergencies. Dr. Liu is currently an Assistant Professor and the Deputy Director of the Research Center of Emergency Response and Crisis Management at Fudan University. Her work appears in various books and journals. Graduated with a Ph.D. in Information Science from the University of Washington, Dr. Liu also holds a Masters degree in Management and a dual-Bachelor degree in Economics and Information Science from Nankai University. Before joining Fudan, Dr. Liu worked as a journalist with Xinhua News Agency and a Senior Assistant to the Director of Production in Bridgestone China.

Ann Macintosh is Emeritus Professor of Digital Governance at the University of Leeds. Ann joined the University in 2007 to establish and co-direct the Centre for Digital Citizenship in the Institute of Communications Studies. In 1999, she founded the International Teledemocracy Centre (ITC) at Edinburgh Napier University. Her internationally funded research, focusing on the use of digital technologies to facilitate political communication, has influenced research and policy-making in the UK, Europe and elsewhere. She has been an advisor to a number of national and regional governments, including the German Bundestag, the Canadian government, the state legislature of Queensland and the Scottish Government. She has also acted as a specialist advisor for the OECD, the Council for Europe and the Commonwealth Secretariat. In 2009, she was awarded an Honorary Doctorate from Örebro University, Sweden for recognition of her work in eParticipation, in particular the interplay between humans, technology and governance.

Judith Mariscal (Ph.D. LBJ School of Public Affairs at UT in Austin), is full Professor at the Centro de Investigación y Docencia Economica (CIDE) where she is Director of the Telecommunications Research Program, Telecom-CIDE. She is a member of the Steering Committee for DIRSI, a research network on ICT policy for development in Latin America as well as Social Witness for Transparency International Chapter Mexico Her research focuses on ICT regulatory and public policies and has published in leading journals such as *Telecommunications Policy*, *Latin American Studies* and *Information Technologies and International Development*. She has authored two books: *Unfinished Business: Telecommunications Reform in Mexico*, published by Praeger Press in 2000, and *Digital Poverty: Latin American and Caribbean Perspectives*, published by ITDG in 2007, coauthored with Hernan Galperin.

Ramona McNeal, Ph.D. is an assistant professor in the Department of Political Science at the University of Northern Iowa. Her chief research interest is the impact of technology on participation, including its relationship to voting, elections, public opinion, and interest group activities. She also studies e-government, telehealth, campaign finance reform and telecommunications policy. She has published work in a number of journals including *Journal of Information Technology & Politics, Social Science Quarterly, Political Research Quarterly, State Politics & Policy Quarterly*, and *Public Administration Review*. She is a coauthor of *Digital Citizenship*: *The Internet, Society and Participation* (MIT Press, 2007) with Karen Mossberger and Caroline Tolbert.

Sehl Mellouli is an associate professor at the Management Information Systems Department, Faculty of Business Administration, Laval University, Quebec, Canada. He received his Ph.D in Computer Science from Laval University. His main research interests are related to e-governement, smart cities, intelligent systems, and knowledge management. Professor Mellouli has several publications in well known journals and conferences. He acts as a reviewer for different journals. He also acted for program committees and organization committees of different conferences. Professor Mellouli is a member of the board of the digital government society. He is a former member of the North American Digital Government Group. He is currently a member of the eGovPolinet research consortium funded by the European Union.

Jeremy Millard has been Chief Policy Advisor at the Danish Technological Institute since 1999, after working with Tele Danmark for 13 years and moving from the UK where he worked in academia and government. He provides global consultancy concerning new technology and society for clients including the European Commission, the UN and the OECD, as well as individual governments, regions and private companies. Recent European Commission assignments include a study on new business and financial models for ICT and Ageing, leading an impact assessment of the European eGovernment 2010 Action Plan, leading a large Europe-wide survey and analysis of eParticipation, and developing the eGovernment 2020 Study on Future Public Service Delivery. He is also currently working as an expert for the UN on the global eGovernment development survey, working with the OECD on user-centred eGovernment strategies, and supporting Swedish local government in developing eParticipation strategies.

Bjoern Niehaves is Professor for E-Governance and Innovation at the Hertie School of Governance. He is also Schumpeter Fellow of the Volkswagen Foundation and a Visiting Professor at the Aalto School of Economics, Helsinki. He received a PhD in Information Systems and a PhD in Political Science from Muenster University. Niehaves held visiting positions at Harvard University (Cambridge, MA), London School of Economics and Political Science, Waseda University (Tokyo), and the Royal Institute of Technology (Stockholm). He has published more than 150 articles in international journals and conference proceedings.

Eleni Panopoulou is a Researcher and ICT Consultant at the Information Systems Laboratory at the University of Macedonia. She holds a diploma on Electrical and Computer Engineering from Aristotle University in Thessaloniki, Greece and a Masters in Business Administration (M.B.A.) from Surrey University, UK. Her previous work experience includes working for Siemens SA in Munich, Germany and for Spirit SA in Athens, Greece. She has been employed at a full time basis at eGovernment and eParticipation research projects for the last six years undertaking tasks related both to research and management. Eleni has relevant publications in refereed journals and conference proceedings in the fields of eGovernment and eParticipation; her current research interests focus on eParticipation evaluation and success.

Diane Poulin is Full Professor of Management at Université Laval (Canada). She is a member of the Research Centre on Enterprise Networks, Logistics and Transportation (CIRRELT) and of the For@c Research Consortium. She was the director of the Institute for Information Technologies and Societies (IITS). She has taught in American and European universities as a visiting professor. Her areas of research and consulting are mainly in strategy and networking.

Christophe Premat is associate researcher at the Centre Emile Durkheim (Sciences Po Bordeaux) and head of the language and education unit at the Institut français of Sweden. He co-edited in 2011 a book entitled *Destins exilés: trois philosophes grecs à Paris (Kostas Axelos, Cornelius Castoriadis, Kostas Papaïoannou*, éditions Manuscrit). He published different articles on participatory democracy such as *The implementation of participatory democracy in French communes, French Politics, 2009* (n°7, 1-18), *Autonomy as a balance of freedom and equality, International Social Science Journal,* n°190, 2008 (681-695) and *Castoriadis and the modern political imaginary – Oligarchy, representation, democracy, Critical Horizons* (volume 7, n°1, December 2006, 251-275).

Gabriel Puron-Cid obtained his Ph.D. in Public Administration from the Rockefeller College, University at Albany, New York. His areas of interest are technology applications in government, open government and open data, different uses of data, technology, and analytical methods for policy analysis, performance management and evaluation, public budget management, and government accounting. His publications discuss the joint adoption of management, budgeting and technology in contexts of collaboration. He has a solid formation and experience in the U.S. and Mexico. Today he is collaborating in several research projects with colleagues in Mexico and international teams: the North American Digital Government Working Group (NADGWG), the International Information Sharing Research Network (IISRN), the Interdisciplinary Project, and the Regional Studies Project. These projects are funded by the Center for Technology in Government in the U.S. and the CIDE, INEGI, y CONACYT in Mexico.

César Rentería (MSc Public Policy in Centro de Investigación y Docencia Económica), is associated professor at the Centro de Investigación y Docencia Económica (CIDE) and Researcher at the Telecommunications Research Program, Telecom-CIDE. He has collaborated in several studies conducted at CIDE and in some publications of United Nations Development Program. His area of research is ICT for development and public policies.

Francisco Rojas-Martín is currently a PhD candidate at Science Politics and International Relations Department at the Universidad Autónoma de Madrid (UAM) and Visiting Researcher at the School of Management Technology and Information Management, Royal Holloway University of London (RHUL). He completed a MA in Democracy and Government (UAM) and a MA in Public Management and Administration at the School of Public Management (AFI-Madrid). Professionally Francisco has led the development of the communications strategy at the Ideas Foundation (Spain), a global leading policy think tank. During his career as Director of Communications at Ideas, Francisco has contributed to position this organisation as a world leader in the use of politics 2.0 tools. He is also experienced in innovation, strategic planning, reengineering process and quality management in the public sector. His research interests are focused on e-Government, social media management in the public sector and political communication 2.0.

Marie-Christine Roy is a professor of information systems at Laval University. She received her Ph.D. from Carnegie Mellon University in 1991. Her primary research interests focus on the behavioral aspects of information systems and knowledge management. Professor Roy has published several articles in journals such as Small Group Research, Information Systems Research and the Journal of knowledge management practice. She also serves regularly as a consultant in the private and public sectors on issues such as interface design, evaluation, knowledge management, and IS strategy.

Mohd Azul Mohamad Salleh is a Lecturer at School of Media and Communication Studies, Faculty of Socail Sciences and Humanities, The National University of Malaysia (UKM). His education backgrounds are Bachelor in Information Technology (Computer Science), Master in Computer Science, and Master in Corporate Communication. His research interests include information and communication technology (ICT), new media, online communication satisfaction and network society. He has published numerous book chapters in the area of ICT, teaching and learning, and new media in organization. He is currently undertaking a PhD study in media and e-governance at The University of Adelaide, Australia.

Mary Schmeida, Ph.D. is an expert in public health policy and has served in several key research positions in the U.S. including the Cleveland Clinic. Her main research interests are social and welfare policy and include e-government and e-commerce, telehealth, Medicare & Medicaid, and mental-health policy. She also studies campaign finance reform, and interest group behavior. She has published work in numerous journals including *Administration and Policy in Mental Health and Mental Health Services Research, Journal of Telemedicine and e-Health, Journal of Health Care for the Poor and Underserved, and Social Science Quarterly.* Her research has been presented nationally and internationally.

Simon Smith is a Research Fellow at the Leeds Institute of Health Sciences and a visiting researcher at the Centre for Digital Citizenship, Institute of Communications Studies, University of Leeds. He obtained his PhD from the University of Bradford in 1998 for a thesis on spaces of independent cultural production in communist Czechoslovakia. Since then he has conducted research on a variety of topics including interest representation in post-communist societies, community studies, partnership and public involvement in local and regional strategic planning, digital inclusion, eParticipation and organisational knowledge creation. He is currently investigating issues connected with online cultural production, professional identities and collaborative research networks.

Efthimios Tambouris is an Assistant Professor of Information Systems at the Department of Technology and Management at the University of Macedonia, Thessaloniki, Greece. Before that, he served as a Researcher Grade D at Research Center CERTH/ITI and at Research Center NCSR 'Demokritos'. He was also founder and manager of the eGovernment Unit at Archetypon S.A., an international IT company. Dr. Tambouris holds a Diploma in Electrical Engineering from the National Technical University of Athens (NTUA), Greece, and an MSc and PhD from Brunel University, UK. During the last years he has initiated and managed several international research projects. He has also participated in numerous research projects, service contracts and standardisation activities at CEN. He is currently chair of the International Conference on eParticipation (ePart). He has more than 120 publications in eGovernment, eParticipation, eLearning and eHealth.

Konstantinos A. Tarabanis is Professor of Information Systems at the Department of Business Administration at the University of Macedonia, Greece, and Director of the Information Systems Laboratory at the same University. He received his Engineering diploma from the National Technical University of Athens (1983), M.Sc. degrees in both Mechanical Engineering and Computer Science (1984 and 1988 respectively) and a Ph.D. degree in Computer Science (1991) at Columbia University, New York. He was Research Staff Member at the IBM T.J. Watson Research Center. His current research interests include conceptual modeling of information systems, service models and architectures, as well as the domains of e-government, e-participation and e-business. He has authored several research publications in the areas of software modeling and development for the domains of e-government, e-business, e-learning and e-manufacturing.

Qianli Yuan's research interest lies in the area of Metropolitan Affair Management. He focuses specifically on interactions between public and private sectors shaping urban policies, regulations, and government performance in daily operations and emergency management. His study aims to understand different roles played by different stakeholders in urban affair management and their impact on policy and operation in different political systems and cultures. Mr. Yuan is currently a graduate student in Department of Public Administration, Fudan University. He worked with Dr. Shuhua Monica Liu as a research assistant and co-authored in several journal papers.

Lei Zheng is Assistant Professor at the Department of Public Administration and Director of the Digital and Mobile Governance Lab at Fudan University, Shanghai, China. He holds a Ph.D. in Public Administration and Policy from the Rockefeller College of Public Affairs and Policy, University at Albany, State University of New York. From 2006 through 2009, he worked as a graduate assistant at the Center for Technology in Government at University at Albany. Lei Zheng serves as the Deputy Chief Editor of Fudan Public Administration Review and also serves on Editorial Board of China E-Government Journal and the Advisory Committee for Informatization of China National Forestry Bureau. His research interests include e-governance, cross-boundary Information sharing and integration, government use of social media, E-government performance evaluation, transnational and comparative E-government Research.

Index

J

K

L

M

N

O

P

Q

R

S

T

U

V

W

Y

CPSIA information can be obtained at www.ICGtesting.com
Printed in the USA
BVOW041648180413

318454BV00007B/69/P

9 781466 641730